ASIA

IN THE MAKING OF EUROPE

ASIA

IN THE MAKING OF EUROPE

DONALD F. LACH and EDWIN J. VAN KLEY

VOLUME

III

A
Century of
Advance

BOOK TWO: SOUTH ASIA

THE UNIVERSITY OF CHICAGO PRESS

CHICAGO AND LONDON

Donald F. Lach is the Bernadotte E. Schmitt Professor of
Modern History, Emeritus, at the University of Chicago.

Edwin J. Van Kley is Professor of History at Calvin College.

The University of Chicago Press, Chicago 60637
The University of Chicago Press, Ltd., London

© 1993 by The University of Chicago
All rights reserved. Published 1993
Printed in the United States of America
98 97 96 95 94 93   5 4 3 2 1

Library of Congress Cataloging-in-Publication Data
(Revised for volume 3)

Lach, Donald F. (Donald Frederick), 1917–
   Asia in the making of Europe.

   Vol. 3–   by Donald F. Lach and Edwin J. Van Kley.
   Includes bibliographies and indexes.
   Contents: v. 1. The century of discovery.   2 v.—
v. 2. A century of wonder.   Book 1. The visual arts.
Book 2. The literary arts.   Book 3. The scholarly dis-
ciplines.   3 v. — v. 3. A century of advance. Book 1.
Trade, missions, literature. Book 2. South Asia.
Book 3. Southeast Asia. Book 4. East Asia. 4 v.
   1. Europe—Civilization—Oriental influences.
2. Asia—History.   3. Asia—Discovery and exploration.
I. Van Kley, Edwin J.   II. Title.
CB203.L32   303.48'2405'0903   64-19848
ISBN 0-226-46753-8 (v. 3. bk. 1)
ISBN 0-226-46754-6 (v. 3. bk. 2)
ISBN 0-226-46755-4 (v. 3. bk. 3)
ISBN 0-226-46756-2 (v. 3. bk. 4)
ISBN 0-226-46757-0 (v. 3 : set)

This publication has been supported by a grant
from the National Endowment for the Humanities,
an independent federal agency.

This book is printed on acid-free paper.

Endpaper: The ten avatars of Vishnu. From Abraham Roger,
Le théâtre de l'idolatrie, ou la porte ouverte (Amsterdam, 1670).

Contents

Contents

Contents

(Contents of other books in Volume III)

BOOK ONE

PART I

The Continuing Expansion in the East

PART II

The Printed Word

Contents

Contents

Contents

Abbreviations

AHSI	*Archivum Historicum Societatis Iesu*
Annales. *E.S.C.*	*Annales: Economies, sociétés, civilisations; revue trimestrielle*
Asia	Earlier volumes of this work: D. Lach, *Asia in the Making of Europe,* Vols. I and II (Chicago, 1965–77)
BR	Blair, Emma H., and Robertson, James A. (eds.), *The Philippine Islands, 1493–1898* (55 vols., Cleveland, 1903–9)
BTLV	*Bijdragen tot de taal-, land- en volkenkunde van Nederlandsch-Indië*
BV	[Commelin, Isaac (ed.)], *Begin ende voortgangh van de Vereenighde Nederlantsche Geoctroyeerde Oost-Indische Compagnie . . .* ([Amsterdam], 1646). (First edition published 1645. Facsimile edition published in Amsterdam, 1969. The facsimile edition has volumes numbered I, II, III, and IV, corresponding to vols. Ia, Ib, IIa, and IIb of the 1646 edition.)
CV	[Churchill, Awnsham and John (eds.)], *A Collection of Voyages and Travels, Some Now First Printed from Original Manuscripts . . .* (4 vols.; London, 1704)
"HS"	"Works Issued by the Hakluyt Society"
JRAS	*Journal of the Royal Asiatic Society*

Abbreviations

NR   L'Honoré Naber, Samuel Pierre (ed.), *Reisebeschreibungen von deutschen Beamten und Kriegsleuten im Dienst der Niederländischen West- und Ost-Indischen Kompagnien, 1602–1797* (The Hague, 1930–32)

NZM   *Neue Zeitschrift für Missionswissenschaft*

PP   Purchas, Samuel, *Hakluytus Posthumus, or Purchas His Pilgrimes:* . . . (20 vols.; Glasgow, 1905–7. Originally published 1625.)

SCPFMR   *Sacrae Congregationis de Propaganda Fide Memoria Rerum* (Freiburg, 1971)

Streit   R. Streit, *Bibliotheca Missionum* (30 vols.; Münster and Aachen, 1916–75)

Ternaux-   H. Ternaux-Compans, *Bibliothèque asiatique et africaine*
Compans   (Amsterdam, 1968; reprint of Paris, 1841–42 ed.)

TR   Thévenot, Melchisédech, *Relations de divers voyages curieux qui n'ont point esté publiées, ou qui ont esté traduites d'Hacluyt, de Purchas & d'autres voyageurs anglois, hollandois, portugais, allemands, espagnols; et de quelques Persans, Arabes, et autres auteurs orientaux* (4 vols.; Paris, 1663–96)

"WLV"   "Werken uitgegeven door de Linschoten Vereeniging"

ZMR   *Zeitschrift für Missionswissenschaft und Religionswissenschaft*

A Note to the Illustrations

Study of the illustrations of Asia published in seventeenth-century Europe shows that the artists and illustrators tried in most cases to depict reality when they had the sources, such as sketches from the men in the field or the portable objects brought to Europe—plants, animals, costumes, paintings, porcelains, and so on. Many of the engravings based on sketches and paintings are convincing in their reality, such as the depiction of the Potala palace in Lhasa (pl. 384), the portrait of the "Old Viceroy" of Kwangtung (pl. 323), and the drawings of Siamese and Chinese boats. A number of Asian objects—Chinese scroll paintings, a Buddhist prayer wheel, and small animals—appeared in European engravings and paintings for the first time. Asians, like the Siamese emissaries to France, were sketched from life in Europe and their portraits engraved.

When sources were lacking, the illustrators and artists filled in the gaps in their knowledge by following literary texts, or by producing imaginary depictions, including maps. The illustrations of Japan, for example, are far more fantastic than those depicting other places, perhaps because Japan so stringently limited intercourse over much of the century. Printing-house engravers frequently "borrowed" illustrations from earlier editions and often "improved" upon them by adding their own touches which had the effect of Europeanizing them.

Illustrations were "translated" along with texts in various ways. If the publisher of a translation had close relations with the original publisher or printer he might borrow the original copperplate engravings or have the original publisher pull prints from the original plates to be bound with the translated pages. Engraved captions could be rubbed out of the plate and redone in the new language, although many printers did not bother to do so. Lacking the cooperation of the original printers, new engravings could still be made from a print. The simplest method was to place the print face down on the varnished and waxed copper plate to be engraved and then to rub the back of the print causing the ink from the print to adhere to the waxed surface of the plate. The resulting image was then used to engrave, or etch with nitric acid, the new plate, and being reversed it would print exactly as the original version printed. If the engraver wanted to avoid damaging the print, however, which he might well need to finish the engraving, he would use a thin sheet of paper dusted with black lead or black chalk to transfer the image from the print to the new copper plate. He might further protect the print by putting oiled paper on top of it while he traced the picture. This procedure worked whether the print was face down or face up against the plate. In fact it was easier to trace the picture if the print were face up, in which case the new plate would be etched in reverse of the original plate. For a seventeenth-century description of the ways in which new plates could be etched from prints see William Faithorne, *The Art of Graving and Etching* (New York, 1970), pp. 41–44 (first edition, London, 1662). See also Coolie Verner, "Copperplate Printing," in David Woodward (ed.), *Five Centuries of Map Printing* (Chicago, 1975), p. 53. We have included a number of illustrations that were "borrowed" by one printer from another: see, for example, plates 113 and 114; 117, 118, 121; 174; 312 and 313; 412 and 413; 419–21.

Most of the following illustrations were taken from seventeenth-century books held in the Department of Special Collections in the Regenstein Library at the University of Chicago. Others have been obtained from libraries and archives in Europe and the United States, which have kindly granted us permission to reproduce them. Wherever possible, efforts are made in the captions to analyze the illustrations and to provide relevant collateral information whenever such was available.

Almost all of the four hundred or so illustrations were reproduced from the photographs taken (or retaken) by Alma Lach, an inveterate photographer and cookbook author. We were also aided and abetted by the personnel of the Special Collections department—especially the late Robert Rosenthal, Daniel Meyer, and Kim Coventry—in locating the illustrations and in preparing them for photography. Father Harrie A. Vanderstappen, professor emeritus of Far Eastern art at the University of Chicago and a man endowed with marvelous sight and insight, helped us to analyze the illustrations relating to East Asia. C. M. Naim of the Department of South Asian Languages at the University of Chicago likewise contributed generously of his skills, particularly with reference to the Mughul seals (pls. 117, 118, and 121) here depicted. The China illustrations have benefited from the contributions of Ma Tai-loi and Tai Wen-pai of the East Asian Collection of the Regenstein Library and of Zhijia Shen who generously gave freely of her time and knowledge. The captions for the Japan illustrations have been improved by the gracious efforts of Yoko Kuki of the East Asian Collection of the Regenstein Library. Tetsuo Najita of Chicago's History Department lent a hand in the preparation of the caption for pl. 432. Ann Adams and Francis Dowley of Chicago's Art Department helped us to analyze some of the engravings, especially those prepared by Dutch illustrators.

To all of these generous scholars we express our sincere gratitude for their contributions to the illustration program.

Illustrations

[xvii]

Illustrations

BOOK THREE

FOLLOWING PAGE 1380

BOOK FOUR

FOLLOWING PAGE 1730

Illustrations

Illustrations

Maps

[xxix]

PART

III

The European Images of Asia

Introduction

The images of Asia that had evolved in the sixteenth century became, during the seventeenth century, more numerous, sharper, and much richer in detail. In particular, the Portuguese profile of India inherited from the previous century was filled in by missionaries and merchants who penetrated almost every sector of the subcontinent from the Himalayas to Cape Comorin. Much that was "discovered" in the sixteenth century, such as Hinduism, was rediscovered and studied by the Jesuits and the Protestant pastors of the seventeenth century. The Mughul state, which governed north India, admitted and employed Europeans, and its subjects traded with them through the port of Surat and in Bengal. The Jesuits were even encouraged by the Mughuls to investigate Tibet and the overland route to China. In politically divided south India, the Portuguese and Dutch established commercial enclaves in which their merchants lived on a semi-permanent basis and from which their missionaries and merchants were able to push into the hinterlands and the archipelagos of South Asia. In Coromandel the Europeans witnessed the demise of the Hindu empire of Vijayanagar and of the Muslim state of Golconda. Across the Bay of Bengal the traders and missionaries advanced into the remotest reaches of insular and continental Southeast Asia. From the Dutch, Europe learned in detail about Indonesia, from the Dutch and the French, especially, about Siam and its satellites, from the French about Vietnam, and from the Spanish about the Philippines and the Marianas. A rosy image of China was delineated by the Jesuits who penetrated into its court, into many of its interior cities, and even into its periphery. The Jesuits studied and translated Confucian texts to deepen their understanding of China's ancient civilization. Because China possessed a

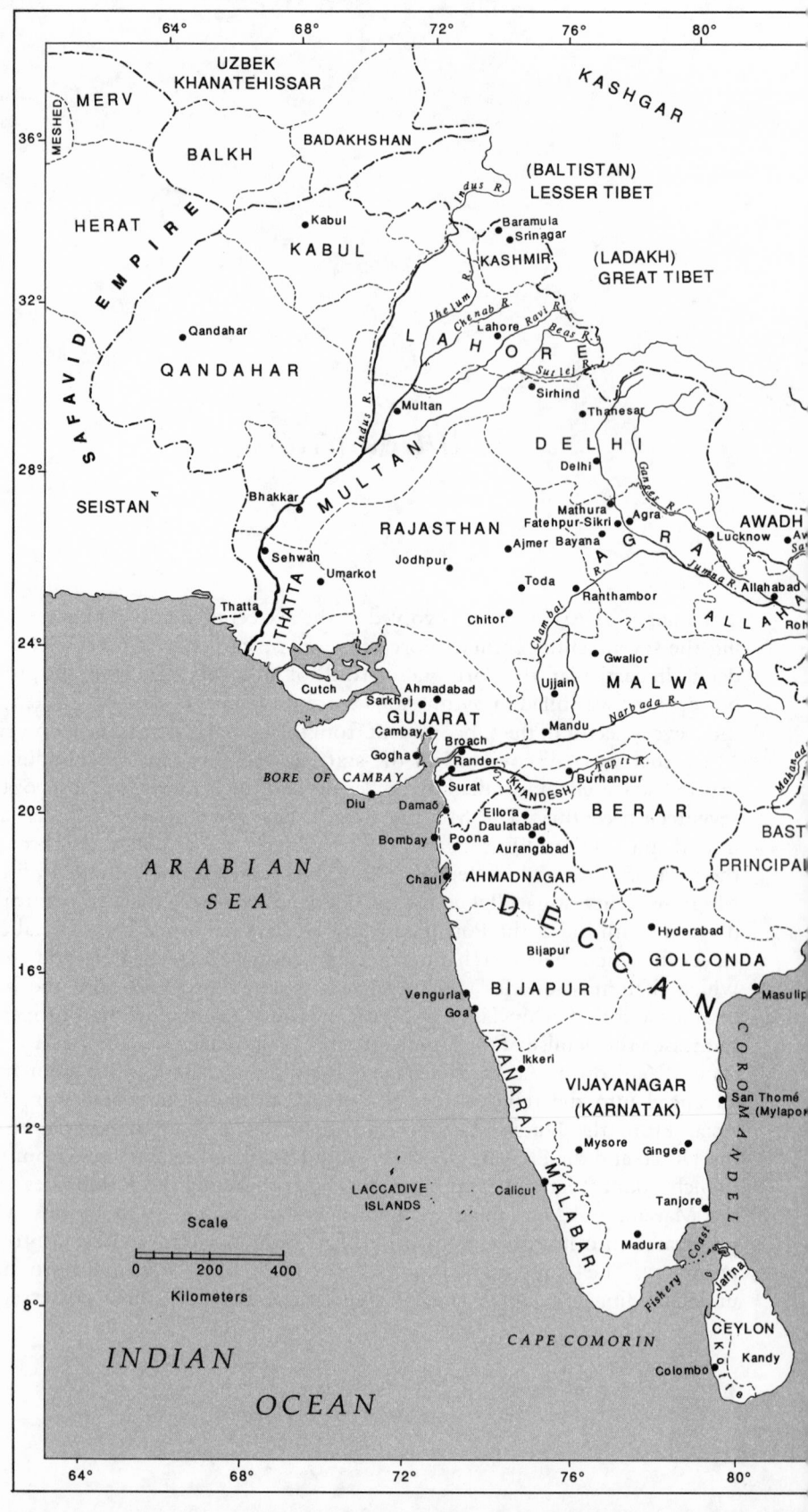

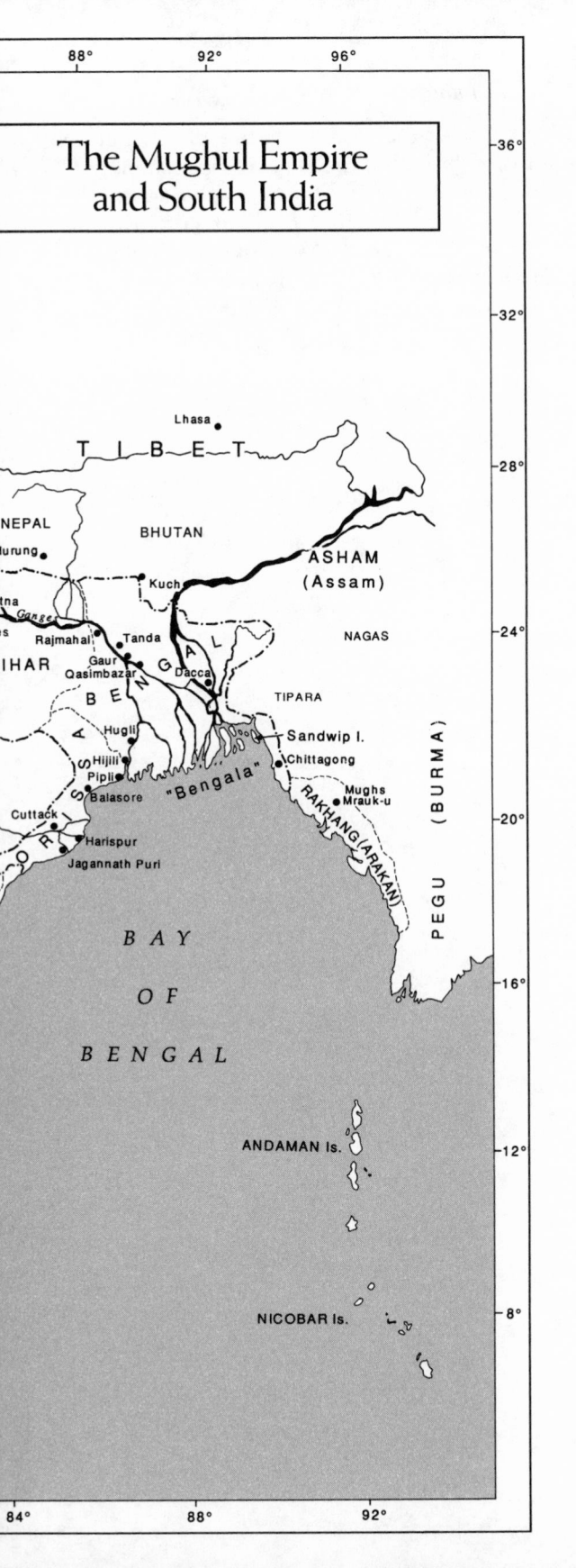

The Mughul Empire
and South India

single culture and a unified state, what they learned in one place could in many instances be applied universally within the empire. Japan alone was closed after 1640 to all the Europeans except the Dutch. So it was from the Dutch that the Europeans had to learn what they could about Japan and Korea. By century's end every continental state in Asia east of the Indus was known to the Europeans. Of all the important islands only Australia, the "empty continent," remained little more than an outline on the map.

The Mughul Empire before Aurangzib

The geographical profile of the Indian subcontinent had first been traced out in the Portuguese secular writings of the sixteenth century. Details about trade and life in Gujarat and eastern Bengal had then been gradually etched into this coastal outline, primarily by the sketches of Humayun's disastrous wars of the 1530's. Beginning in 1545 the Jesuit letter-writers had gradually shaded new lines into this rough likeness by their reports of the Fishery Coast and the Serra of the St. Thomas Christians. The Italian, English, and Dutch commercial travelers and commentators of the latter half of the century had added touches and contours of their own, particularly on interior routes, marts, products, and military activities. Three Jesuit missions from Goa to the court of Akbar in 1580–83, 1591, and 1595–1605 had as by-products new European reports and books highlighting the hopes of the Christians for the conversion of the Mughul ruler. As the new century dawned, the prospects in India seemed bright for both the Portuguese and the missionaries. In Europe their optimism was reflected in the publications of the Jesuits, especially Peruschi (1597), Rebello (1598), and Guzman (1601), and in those of secular authors, especially Balbi (1590), Linschoten (1595–96), and Fitch (1599). The map of India, now far more than a profile, would soon be filled in, it was confidently expected, to the satisfaction and profit of the Europeans.[1]

At the beginning of the new century the Portuguese and the Jesuits were the only Europeans to enjoy relations with the Mughul Empire. In England the desire for an all-sea route to India had risen swiftly during the last decade of the sixteenth century. In the buoyant mood following the victory over

[1] See *Asia,* I, chap. vi, particularly the map facing p. 356.

the Spanish Armada, the lure of India became ever more powerful in London as the Dutch rivals of England began to send their pre-Company voyages to the East. Envious of the Dutch direct penetration of the spice trade, the London merchants began to petition the crown for the formal right to send their own voyages to the East. After the formation of the chartered English East India Company in 1600, two reconnaissance voyages were sent to the Indies. In 1603 John Mildenhall was dispatched overland to Agra to establish relations with Akbar and the mainland of India. The presence of an English Protestant intruder at the imperial court immediately aroused the opposition of the Jesuits at Agra and of the Portuguese at Goa. Although Mildenhall failed to obtain a *farman* (a written order) permitting the English to trade in India, the Company nonetheless sent its third fleet to Surat in 1607 with Ambassador William Hawkins on board.

Despite the opposition of local authorities, Hawkins finally made his way to the emperor Jahangir's court at Agra early in 1609. Able to speak directly to the emperor in Turkish, Hawkins soon won assurances that the English would be permitted to trade legally at Surat. Again, however, the Jesuits and Portuguese working through courtiers friendly to them convinced the emperor that the English were potentially a danger to his ports and trade. While Hawkins negotiated at Agra, the Company sent another fleet to Surat with orders to establish a factory and obtain a privilege exempting their trade from duty. This fleet, under Captain Thomas Best, in 1612 defeated a Goa armada off Surat, thus opening India's west coast to the English. The Mughuls, impressed by this decisive English action, began to see the English as a counterweight to the Portuguese. Thomas Kerridge, the English factor, was therefore informally permitted to establish a factory at Surat. Three years later Sir Thomas Roe arrived at Jahangir's court, where he worked for three years in a vain effort to secure a formal treaty of commerce. While Roe obtained nothing more than orders allowing the continuance of trade, the English were hereafter treated with greater respect as they gradually replaced the Portuguese as the paramount power in the foreign trade of the Mughul Empire.[2]

I

THE ENGLISH AND DUTCH PROFILE: FIRST GENERATION

Many of the earliest English adventurers wrote journals and narrative accounts of their Indian experiences. For example, Robert Coverte, who was shipwrecked off Surat, spent most of 1610–11 traveling about in northern

[2] See above, pp. 561–65. For greater detail on these early British activities see H. G. Rawlinson, *British Beginnings in Western India, 1579–1657* (Oxford, 1920), chaps. iii–iv.

India; on his return home he published in 1612 a report of his "hard and paineful Pilgrimage."[3] The journals of many other English sailors, merchants, chaplains, and emissaries were published as a whole or in part by Samuel Purchas in his massive *Pilgrimes* (London, 1625).[4] In this collection were issued the accounts of John Mildenhall (II, 297–304), William Hawkins (III, 1–51), William Finch (IV, 1–77), Nicholas Downton (IV, 214–51), Richard Steele (IV, 266–80), Sir Thomas Roe (IV, 310–468), Edward Terry (IX, 1–54), Thomas Best (IV, 119–47), Nicholas Withington (IV, 162–75), and Thomas Coryate (IV, 469–94). Finch (in India 1608–11), Withington (1612–16), Best (1612), and Steele (1615) were sailors and merchants; Mildenhall (1603–5), Hawkins (1608–13), and Roe (1615–19) were royal emissaries to the court; Terry (1616–19) was chaplain to Roe's embassy; and Coryate (1615–16) was an adventurer who wrote five letters home to his friends and relatives about his experiences and observations in India which were published separately (1616, 1618) in London before appearing in Purchas' compendium.[5] The most comprehensive of these accounts are those by Finch, Roe, and Terry. Purchas published only a truncated version of Roe's journal, about one-third or less, in fact, along with excerpts from several of his letters.[6] Terry's narrative was amplified substantially by the author and republished at London in revised form in 1655.[7]

Many of these English authors, in contrast to the more experienced Jesuit and Portuguese writers, were intent upon relaying to their insular readers general information on the extent, geography, peoples, products, and politics of the Mughul Empire. Roe and Terry, in particular, provide an account of the political divisions of the empire. Shortly after his return to England in 1619, Roe had William Baffin, a surveyor and mapmaker who had been a master-mate on Roe's ship, prepare a map of the Mughul Empire. This

[3] See B. Penrose (ed.), *The Travels of Captain Robert Coverte* (Philadelphia, 1931). Between 1612 and 1631 this little book was reissued three times. It was not published again until 1931.

[4] For bibliographical detail see above, pp. 556–68. The references which follow are to the reprint in twenty volumes published at Glasgow in 1905–7 by James MacLehose and Sons as *Hakluytus Posthumus, or Purchas His Pilgrimes* (cited as *PP*).

[5] According to Roe and Terry, Coryate died at Agra in December, 1617. Purchas reprinted a substantial portion of his letter of 1615 and the "notes made in India" relayed to Purchas by Roe. For a study of Coryate's letters see R. C. Prasad, *Early English Travellers in India* (Delhi, 1965), pp. 170–209, and especially Michael Strachan, *The Life and Adventures of Thomas Coryate* (London, 1962), chaps. xiv–xvi.

[6] See W. Foster (ed.), *The Embassy of Sir Thomas Roe to the Great Mogul, 1615–1619, As Narrated in His Journal and Correspondence*, in "HS," 2d ser., I and II (2 vols. in 1; 1967 reprint of the original edition of 1899; Nendeln, Liechtenstein), pp. lxii–lxiv; and W. Foster (ed.), *The Embassy of Sir Thomas Roe to India, 1615–19* (new and rev. ed.; London, 1926), p. lxxvii, where Foster notes that Purchas, despite the deficiencies of his edition, preserved "extracts from nearly a full year of Roe's Journal (1617–18), for which no manuscript account is now available."

[7] *A Voyage to East-India* (London, 1655). This new edition of 545 pages is about seven times longer than the version in Purchas' *Pilgrimes*. Many of the additions are disquisitions on moral and religious subjects which add little to his descriptions of India. See Prasad, *op. cit.* (n. 5), pp. 281–83. In the amplified book Terry occasionally makes references to Indian sources not cited in the Purchas version. He also derives many of his additions from Roe's account.

map, now in the British Library (K115[22]), was re-engraved and reduced in size for inclusion in the *Pilgrimes*. In 1655 it appeared as a frontispiece to Terry's independent book. For unexplained reasons the map and the literary descriptions of Roe and Terry do not always agree. Still, despite all its inaccuracies, Baffin's map delineates the territories of the Mughul Empire, particularly its interior places, more clearly and with greater precision than any other contemporary European maps. In fact, it remained the base for most later maps of the Mughul Empire.[8]

As Terry described it, the Mughul Empire is bounded on the east by "the Kingdome of Maug" (the Mughs),[9] on the west by Persia, on the north by the mountains of Caucasus and Tartary, and on the south by the Deccan and "the Gulfe of Bengala." The Deccan, "lying in the skirts [borders] of Asia," is divided among three Muslim rulers as well as some other "Indian Rhajaes."[10] This spacious monarchy, called "Indostan" (Hindustan) by its inhabitants, is divided into thirty-seven provinces "which anciently were particular Kingdomes." Terry follows this with a list of the "provinces," their geographical positions, and their chief cities, all of "which we there had out of the Mogol's own records." His catalog of the "provinces" proceeds from Qandahar in the northwest to the mouths of the Ganges and the Bay of Bengal at the empire's eastern extremity. In listing the chief cities of the "provinces," Terry adds bits of information about the rivers on which they lie, their distances from one another, and the most notable sights to be observed in some of them.[11]

This vast empire is fertile, abundant, and self-sufficient "in all necessaries for the use of man." Its land produces wheat, rice, barley, and various other grains. Their wheat "growes like ours, but the Graine [head] of it is somewhat bigger and more white." From it they make a "bread that is better than bread" as they do in Liège. The ordinary people shape their bread into cakes (*chapati*) which they bake on small iron hearths. With their bread they eat butter and cheese made from the milk of "Kine, Sheepe, and Goats." Meat is abundant and cheap, for they have buffaloes, cattle, sheep, venison, hares, and a wide variety of fish and poultry. Their beef cows differ in that they have "a great Bunch of grisselly flesh" between their front shoulders; their sheep "exceed ours in great bob-tayles, which cut off are very pon-

[8] See pls. 107–10. For a history and analysis of this map see Foster (ed.), *op. cit.* (n. 6), 1926 ed., pp. 497–501. *Cf.* map OA in I. Habib, *An Atlas of the Mughal Empire* (Delhi, 1982).

[9] The Mughs inhabited the northern part of Arakan.

[10] The three Muslim sultans of Ahmadnagar, Bijapur, and Golconda and the Hindu rajas of Rajputana.

[11] Roe, *PP*, IV, 430–34; Terry, IX, 13–16, and expanded 1655 edition (see n. 7), pp. 78–89. For an analysis of this listing see Foster (ed.), *op. cit.* (n. 6), 1926 ed., pp. 489–96. William Hawkins, who was in Agra a few years earlier, reports that the empire is divided into "five great Kingdomes"; "Pengab [Punjab], whereof Lahor is the chiefe Seate," Bengal and its capital of "Sonargham" (Sonargaon), Malwa and its chief city called "Ugam" (Ujjain), Deccan and its main town of "Bramport" (Burhanpur), and Gujarat with its capital at "Amadavar" (Ahmadabad). See *PP*, III, 30–31. *Cf.* Bernier on the provinces, below, pp. 728–39.

derous [heavy]." ¹² Salt and sugar "to season this good provision" are both abundant and cheap. The country is full of fruits: muskmelons, watermelons, pomegranates, "Pome-citrons" (pomelos?), lemons, oranges, dates, figs, grapes, plantains or bananas, mangoes, pineapples, apples, and pears. They have root crops, especially good carrots and potatoes, as well as onions, garlic, and herbs for salads. In the south, ginger grows everywhere. Terry calls "Taddy" (Hindi, *tāṛī,* or English, toddy) "a pleasant cheere liquor . . . as pleasing to the taste as any white Wine." ¹³

In northwestern India, it "never raines but one season of the yeere," during the summer monsoon of May to September. These "violent Raines" commence and end with "Fearefull tempests of Thunder and Lightning . . . yet seldome doe harme." Once this hot, rainy season ends, "the Skie is so cleere, as that scarecely one cloud is seene in their Hemisphere, the nine months after." The monsoon blows constantly, six months from the south and six months from the north. In the dry season these heavy winds sometimes raise "thick clouds of dust and sand" which "annoy the people when they fall among them." ¹⁴

Without rain for almost nine months the land "lookes like to barren sand" at winter's end. One week or so "after the Raine begins to fall, it puts on a greene Coate." In May and at the beginning of June, the farmers plant their plots tilled "with Oxen, and foot-Ploughs." They harvest in November and December the grain "which came up as thicke as the land could well beare it." Their fields are not enclosed unless they lay close to the numerous villages and towns which "stand very thicke" in the countryside. They do not mow their grass to make hay but cut it, green or dry, only when they wish to use it. While they raise much tobacco, their curing methods do not please Terry.¹⁵ Many woodlots lend beauty to the landscape, but the trees are all different from those of England. One tree, obviously the banyan, has branches "which grow little sprigs downward till they take root." The flowers of India are colorful and a delight to the eye, but very few of them except roses "are any whit fragrant." They are so plentiful "they seeme never to fade." ¹⁶

¹²Here Terry is referring to the Indian humped cattle and the broad-tailed sheep often remarked on by European travelers.

¹³ *PP,* IX, 17–19.

¹⁴The Tropic of Cancer passes through the middle of India. Its southern half unquestionably therefore has a tropical climate and, like the north, has a rainy season. During the period from mid-September to about mid-May, its northern half is warmer and the temperature more constant than other areas of similar latitude, such as the United States. The cold polar air which penetrates the United States is effectively prevented from entering India by the mountain barriers of the north. The result is that northern India is mildly warm or mildly cool most every day during the winter. The wind blows from the Indian Ocean over the land during the summer, rainy season, and in the reverse direction during the winter. See G. Singh, *A Geography of India* (2d ed.; Delhi, 1976); chap. i.

¹⁵In his revised edition of 1655 (*op. cit.* [n. 7], pp. 101–2), Terry explains how they smoke it in a water-pipe.

¹⁶ *PP,* IX, 19–20, 24–25.

The large animals, except for horses and mules, are likewise very different from those of England. Native horses, as well as "many of the Persian, Tartarian, and Arabian breede," are "kept daintly" by being rubbed down two or three times a week with butter. They are fed a boiled grain called "Donna" (Hindi, *dāna*) which when cold they mix with coarse sugar. Many camels and dromedaries are used for transport. Occasionally a rhinoceros may be seen, whose "skins lye platted, or as it were in wrinkles upon their backs." Elephants are numerous, the royal beasts alone numbering fourteen thousand. After telling several familiar stories about the tractable and rational elephants, Terry reports that Jahangir delights in putting on elephant fights. Many of the imperial elephants are trained for military service. They are taught to carry an iron gun and a gunner. Other elephants are trained to participate in state occasions and royal processions. Although many nobles try to keep elephants of their own, these beasts are inordinately expensive to maintain, and the males are dangerous when in rut. Each of the imperial males is allocated four females as "wives." Among the harmful beasts are lions, tigers, wolves, and jackals, as well as crocodiles, snakes, stinging scorpions, annoying and numerous flies, mosquitoes, and "bigge hungrie Rats." [17]

Besides having many rivers, northern India is dotted with wells fed by springs "upon which in many places they bestow great cost in stone-worke." In addition, "they have many ponds" which they call "Tankes," [18] some "more then [than] a mile or two in compasse, made round or square." These tanks are generally surrounded by stone walls and usually have stone steps which lead down into the water. In these tanks water is stored during the rainy season for use during the dry months. The Indians commonly drink water rather than any other beverage since "in these hot countries, [it] agreeth better with mens bodies, then any other Liquor." They also drink, though not commonly, a small quantity of "Rache" (arrack) and "Cohha [Arabic, *ḳahwa*, or coffee], a black seed boyled in water, which doth little alter the taste of the water." [19] Coffee "is very good to helpe digestion," as is "an herbe called Beetle [betel] or Paune [Hindi, *pān*, the betel leaf]." Its leaf looks like ivy and they chew it with "a hard nut [areca nut]" and a bit of "pure white Lime among the leaves." [20]

Ordinary dwellings are generally poor, except in the cities where there are "many faire Piles." Better houses "are built high and flat on the toppe," the roof being used as a veranda in the cool of the day. Since they use

---

[17] *Ibid.*, pp. 24–29.

[18] Reservoirs. On the debate regarding the etymology of the word "tank" see H. Yule and A. C. Burnell, *Hobson-Jobson* (new edition of W. Crooke; London, 1968), pp. 898–900.

[19] *PP*, IX, 21. In his edition of 1655 (*op. cit.* [n. 7], p. 106) Terry uses the word "coffee," thus clearly indicating that this beverage and its English name had by then become familiar to him and his readers. Indeed, in 1652, three years before the publication of his book, London had its first coffee house. On beverage drinking in north India, see P. N. Ojha, *North Indian Social Life during the Mughal Period* (Delhi, 1975), pp. 11–13.

[20] *PP*, IX, 20–21.

heat only for cooking, their houses have no chimneys. Their upper rooms have many windows without glass as well as doorways to let in the air. In "Amadavar" (Ahmadabad), for example, the buildings are well-constructed of brick and stone. This "most spacious and rich Citie" is surrounded by a stone wall pierced by "twelve faire Gates." Around their houses, whether in town or country, they plant many trees for shade. The trees are planted so thickly "that if a man behold a Citie or Towne from some conspicuous place, it will seeme a Wood rather than a Citie."

The main export products of the Mughul Empire are cotton, cotton goods, and indigo. Cotton seeds are planted which grow into shrubs that produce yellow blossoms. When the blossom falls off, a "cod [pod] remains about the bigness of a man's thumb," in the interior of which there is a moist, yellow material. As this capsule ripens it swells and finally breaks "and so in short time becomes white as Snow, and then they gather it." These plants bear for three or four years before being replaced.[21] From the cotton wool they make a "pure white cloth, some of which I have seene as fine, if not purer than our best Laune [lawn]."[22] The coarser cotton cloth they dye in various colors "or else in it steyn [stain] varietie of curious [intricate] Figures."[23] Indigo or "Nill" (*nīl*, the common name for indigo in India is derived from Sanskrit, *nīla* meaning "blue") is a shrub not more than one yard high, and with a stalk about the diameter of a man's thumb. It produces a pod about one inch long, which holds a seed that becomes ripe for gathering and planting in November. Shrubs used to make blue dye are pulled up at the end of the rainy season and soaked in water. After the shrubs rot, they press out the juice and put the pasty substance on a cloth to dry in the sun. Once it is somewhat hard, they roll it by hand into little balls which are put on sand to dry. When dry, these balls become the indigo of commerce.[24] The empire also produces a "good store of Silke, which they weave curiously [skillfully], sometimes mingled with Silver or Gold [threads]." They also make a hard wax from "gum-lac" (shellac).[25] The earth yields lead, iron, copper, and brass (?) "and they say Silver, which, if true, they neede not open, being so enriched by other Nations."[26]

---

[21] This is the *Gossypium neglectum* which was extensively cultivated in India as a field crop.

[22] Lawn was at this time a linen fabric. It probably got this name from Laon, a weaving town in northern France.

[23] *PP*, IV, 21–22.

[24] This description of the wet plant process is from William Finch in *PP*, IV, 45–46. In some places indigo grows as a wild shrub. Finch, however, is clearly talking about the plant as cultivated in northern India. In his edition of 1655 (*op. cit.* [n. 7], pp. 113–14) Terry reports that they dry and soak the leaves only; he is here adverting to the dry leaf process. *Cf.* Tavernier's account in V. Ball and W. Crooke (trans. and eds.), *Travels in India by Jean-Baptiste Tavernier* (2d ed.; 2 vols.; London, 1925), II, 8–9, and below, p. 618. For the wet plant process see G. Watt, *A Dictionary of the Economic Products of India* (10 vols.; reprint; Delhi, 1972), IV, 428–34.

[25] For a contemporary description of the manufacture of hard or Spanish wax in Goa, see Yule and Burnell, *op. cit.* (n. 18), p. 500.

[26] *PP*, IX, 24. Actually India had no silver mines of consequence.

Silver streams into the empire from all over the world in exchange for Indian commodities. The huge pilgrim ships plying annually between Surat and the Red Sea usually return with great supplies of precious metals. Silver remains in the empire, for it is "a Crime not lesse than Capitall, to carry any great summe thence." Bullion imports are melted, refined, and made into coins "and then the Mogols stampe (which is his Name and Title in Persian Letters) put upon it." Their silver coins are the purest known "without any allay [alloy], so that in the Spanish Rial [the purest money of Europe] there is some losse [in exchange]." Silver "Roopees" (*rūpaya* or rupees), the basic coins of the realm, are minted in several denominations, and are "either round or square, but so thicke" that they never break or wear out. In Gujarat there is a coin of inferior value called "Mamoodies" (*maḥmūdīs*). For petty payments they use "brass" (actually copper) coins called "Pices" (Hindi, *paisa*) which are large and heavy.[27]

The people of Hindustan are "called in general Hindoos" but ever since Tamerlane subdued them they "have been mixed with Mahometans." The population also includes many Persians, Tartars, Ethiopians, and Armenians, as well as a few of almost "every people of Asia, if not of Europe." While some Jews live there, the "very name is a . . . word of reproch." The Indians are tawny or olive in color with straight black hair and erect posture. They do not admire white or fair-skinned people because they look like lepers to them.[28] Most Muslim males, except for "Moolaes" (mullahs) and the aged, shave their chins "but suffer the haire on their upper lip to grow as long as Nature will feed it." They shave their head bare except for a lock on the crown which Muhammed will use "to pull them into Heaven." People of all persuasions wash their bodies often and anoint themselves with sweet-smelling oils.

Men and women dress in similar fashion in white cotton gowns which fall below the knee. Underneath they wear tight pants from the waist to the ankles which are wrapped "like the boots on the smal of their legs." On their bare feet, they wear slippers, which they remove indoors. Floors are covered with carpets ("made in that Kingdom, good as any in Turkie or Persia") or something similar, upon which they sit like tailors to visit, to conduct business, or simply to eat. The men wrap a long, thin band of cloth, either white or colored, around their heads which they call a *"Shash"* (Arabic, *shāsh*, turban cloth). When saluting superiors they do not bare their heads but bow and put the right hand to the top of the head; equals exchange greetings by grasping the chin or the beard of each other. To wish a friend well they use many expressions such as "Greeb-a Nemoas" (Hindi,

---

[27] *Ibid.*, p. 23. For the coins and their circulation in the Mughul Empire see T. Raychaudhuri and I. Habib (eds.), *The Cambridge Economic History of India* (2 vols.; Cambridge, 1982), I, 260–66. The basic silver rupee "weighed 178 grains troy in which the alloy was never allowed to rise above 4 percent" (*ibid.*, p. 360).

[28] On the Mughul preference for light-skinned people see below, p. 724.

gharib nawaz), or "I wish [for you] the Prayers of the Poore."[29] Muslim women of quality, who rarely are seen outdoors, cover their heads with veils, tie silks in the long hair that hangs down their backs, bedeck their necks and wrists with jewelry, and wear ornaments in their ears and in one nostril. Women of all classes have an easy time in childbirth.[30]

When traveling, men and women of the lower classes usually ride on oxen, horses, mules, camels, or dromedaries. They are sometimes borne in two-wheeled coaches covered on the top and back, with the front and sides open. Drawn by oxen, these coaches will easily carry two riders and a coachman. The oxen are guided by lines which are run through their nostrils, between their horns, and into the coachman's hands. These conveyances can traverse twenty miles in a day at a good speed. More important travelers ride elephants or are carried in covered palanquins. Inns are found only in large towns and cities. These hostels called "Sarray" (Persian, *sarāy*) are open and free to travelers. The individual is required only to supply his own bedding and food. Where there are no inns, travelers pitch the tents they usually carry in their baggage.[31]

Among the Englishmen of the early years of the century, one of the most experienced in India travel was William Finch, the indigo merchant based in Surat from 1608 to 1611. He gives in detail the names of the towns through which the trade routes ran from Surat to Agra (via Burhanpur), from Agra to Ahmadabad, and from Lahore to Kabul.[32] His other itineraries as well are, in Purchas' somewhat extravagant words, "supplied in substance, with more accurate observations of Men, Beasts, Plants, Cities, Deserts, Castles, Buildings, Regions, Religions, than almost any other, as also of Waires, Wares, Warres."[33] Finch left Surat in January, 1610, for Agra. Besides giving a description of the port of Surat itself, he notes the towns in its immediate vicinity and observes that in "Ranele" (Rander) live the "Naites" (Konkani (?), *Nawāyit*), a seafaring people who speak another language.[34] Of the cities on the road, he describes in some detail the "beastly" city and fortress of Burhanpur, the ruined city of Mandu, and the "pleasant" city and adjacent fortress of Gwalior. Arrived in Agra on April 4, Finch describes the devastating fires which swept the city in May and part of June. During July, news reaches the capital of the setbacks suffered by Jahangir's armies in the Deccan. Finch reports on the arrival of Father Manuel Pinheiro in Agra

---

[29] In his 1655 edition (*op. cit.* [n. 7], pp. 213–14) Terry gives additional examples of salutations.
[30] *PP*, IX, 29–31.
[31] *Ibid.*, p. 33.
[32] For a convenient listing of the towns on each of these routes see M. A. Ansari, *European Travellers under the Mughals (1580–1627)* (Delhi, 1975), p. 32.
[33] *PP*, IV, 1.
[34] Muslim seafarers, probably Arabs, who had intermarried with the local women of India's west coast. Etymology of the word "Naites" is uncertain. See Yule and Burnell, *op. cit.* (n. 18), p. 620; and for further discussion see V. S. D'Souza, *The Navayats of Kanara* (Dharwar, 1955), pp. 12–20.

and the christening of three nephews of the emperor, the sons of his dead brother Danyl. Leaving Agra on November 1 for Bayana, Finch notes that the road to Ajmer is lined with stone pillars marking each "coss."[35] Akbar's unfinished city of Fatehpur-Sikri is totally devastated and depopulated, with "much of the ground now being converted to Gardens." All that remains standing are the city's stone walls with their four gates. Its tanks, like those of Agra, are covered with "Hermodactyle," a weed that produces a soft and tender fruit, "white and of a mealish taste, much eaten in India."[36] The city of Bayana where Finch went to purchase indigo is also in ruins except for two inns and a bazaar.[37]

After returning to Agra, Finch was again quickly on the road, this time to Lahore. At Delhi he describes Humayun's tomb and asserts that in the successive cities of Delhi "the Kings of India are crowned." He digresses on the rebellion of Salim and notes that Akbar had mulberry trees planted on both sides of the six-hundred-mile highway from Agra to Kabul to commemorate the defeat of the prince.[38] Lahore, "now to be inclosed with a strong wall," is one of the greatest cities of the East. It was first made into an imperial center by Humayun. Lahore's fortress and royal abode is situated on the Ravi, a river that empties into the Indus. Ships transport goods down this river system to Thatta in Sind, passing by Multan and Bhakkar on their way southward. Within a retiring room of the imperial residence are mural portraits of Jahangir and other Mughul notables. In a small sitting room overlooking the river there are murals of Akbar and Prince Salim as well as other portraits. The women of the court, to the number of two hundred, are lodged in a new palace whose end walls are covered with portraits "of the King in state sitting amongst his women." In the emperor's own, sumptuous apartment are paintings of his ancestors from Babur onward. On the east side of the palace-fortress outside the wall is a beautiful garden and on the west a ferry which connects with the highway to Kabul. On May 17, 1611, news arrives in Lahore of the sack of Kabul by Pathan rebels from the surrounding mountains. Finch follows this with a list of the routes into the Mughul Empire through the mountain passes of the north.[39]

From his friend Nicholas Uphet, Finch learned of another route from Agra to Surat via Ajmer and Gujarat. The city of Ajmer is famous for the sepulchre of "Hoghee Mundee" (Khwaja Muinuddin), a "saint much re-

[35] *Cos,* the common measure of distance in India, the exact length of which varies considerably from region to region.

[36] A reference to the caltrop (Hindi, *singhārā*) or the water chestnut.

[37] *PP,* IV, 29–45.

[38] On the rebellion see below, pp. 631–32. They are ash trees that are planted, in later reports; see below, p. 792.

[39] His descriptions of the trade routes to Central Asia, probably obtained from merchants at Lahore, are remarkably clear and accurate. See Aurel Stein, "Note on the Routes from the Panjab to Turkestan and China Recorded by William Finch (1611)," *Journal of the Panjab Historical Society,* Vol. VI, No. 2 (1917), pp. 144–48.

spected by the Mogols," to whose tomb Akbar made a pilgrimage on foot from Agra. At Jalor there stands a great mountain-top fortress, which Finch describes in some detail, that is called the Gate to Gujarat.[40] After crossing "a deepe sandy Desart [in Rajasthan]," the traveler arrives at Ahmadabad, a city whose buildings are "comparable to any citie in Asia or Africa." Within this walled city the streets are wide and well paved, its merchants rich, and its artisans "excellent for Carvings, Paintings, Inlayd Workes, imbroydery with Gold and Silver." Since the emperor's authority in Gujarat is constantly being threatened, persons entering or leaving Ahmadabad are required to obtain passes.[41] South of Ahmadabad is Cambay, the mart of Gujarat and the haunt of the Portuguese merchants. On the road to Surat there is a great agate mine at Broach, a city also renowned for its rich "Baffatas" (Persian, *bafta,* woven), or white cotton textiles.[42]

From Agra eastward the route leads into the Ganges valley. Thirty rivers flow into the Ganges making it normally three-quarters of a mile in width. When rains are heavy it floods the whole valley before falling into the Bay of Bengal. On one of its eighteen distributaries stands Lucknow, an important linen center. At Awadh, an ancient city and once an important Pathan center, are ruins in which Brahmans live who record the names of all Hindus who bathe in its river. Pilgrims from all parts of India come here and carry away with them tokens of remembrance in the form of grains of black rice. The route then goes to Jaunpur, a commercial town on a small river (the Gumti) "over which is a bridge with Houses like London Bridge, but nothing so good."[43]

A second route from Agra to Jaunpur runs through a continual forest to Allahabad. This Ganges city, anciently called "Praye" (Prayaga), is one of the wonders of the East.[44] The construction of its fort was begun by Akbar forty years ago at the point where the Jumna river flows into the Ganges. For many years, twenty thousand persons were assigned to its construction, and it is still unfinished. Its walls, like the fort at Agra, are of red, square stone. Prince Salim (later Jahangir) stayed here after he rebelled against Akbar and before he became emperor. In its first courtyard stands a tall stone pillar which is sunk so deeply into the ground "that no end can be found." It seems to have been erected "by Alexander or some other great Conqueror,

[40] Both Jalor and Ajmer had famous fortresses. Ajmer was annexed by Akbar in 1556.

[41] On the economic importance of Ahmadabad see B. G. Gokhale, "Ahmadabad in the Seventeenth Century," *Journal of the Economic and Social History of the Orient* (Leyden), XII (1969), 187–97.

[42] *PP,* IV, 47–65.

[43] This bridge, begun around 1564, was one of the great construction works of the Mughuls. It was designed and built by workmen from Hazara in Afghanistan. For a modern photograph of it see H. H. Dodwell (ed.), *The Cambridge History of India* (6 vols.; Cambridge, 1922–53), Vol. IV, pl. 14.

[44] *Prayāg,* or "place of sacrifice," is the Hindu name for this old and holy city. Akbar named it Allahabad or *Ilāhabād* after he began construction of the fort.

who could not pass further for Ganges." [45] In an inner courtyard the emperor sits on an elevation to hold court or to watch animal fights. Immediately beneath this dais is a vault which contains idols representing "Baba Adam and Mama Havah (as they call them) and of their Progenie, with Pictures of Noah and his Descent." The Hindus believe, as these idols indicate, that the first humans lived here. Thousands of pilgrims come here to bathe in the Ganges and to revere these relics. [46] In another richly paved court the emperor holds his "Derbar" (*durbar*) or court. Beyond it is another in which there is an entry into the great "Moholl" (*mahal,* palace). The palace has forty-eight richly decorated living and sleeping rooms for the emperor and sixteen of his wives as well as their attendants and slaves. The palace has also within its confines a "curious Tanke" and tree known as the "Tree of Life." This tree, which defied all efforts of previous Muslim rulers to kill it, is now protected by Jahangir, and it continues to enjoy "no small esteeme with the Indians." [47] On the river side of the palace there are several large "Devoncans" (from Arabic, *dīwān,* and Persian, *khāna,* audience hall, and referring in this case to balconies), where the emperor and his women can take their ease while watching the Jumna river "pay tribute to the Ganges." Between the palace and the river is a pleasant garden which includes a "faire Banquetting House, with privie staires to take Boate." [48]

Finch follows his tour of the Ganges valley with a catalog of the towns and principalities of the north, stretching eastward from Lahore to Arakan. Among the most important of these places are "Serenegar" (Srinagar) in cold and snowy Kashmir and "Camow" (Kumaun), a source of musk and small horses called "Gunts" (Hindi, *ghūnṭ,* hill pony), renowned for their ability to climb hills. To the east the authority of the Mughuls ends at the land of Mugh (Arakan), an unstable frontier in Bengal north of the Ganges where Jahangir maintains an army. Further south, Mughul rule extends to the mouth of the Ganges where "the Portugall Out-laws hold a small Fort, and doe much mischiefe." [49]

Akbar, who was forced to abandon Fatehpur-Sikri by the lack of fresh, unsalty water in its vicinity more than fifty years ago, turned his attention to Agra, a village before his time. [50] Built in crescent shape and facing the

---

[45] The famous pillar (*lāt*) of Asoka of the third century B.C. On it are inscribed the edicts of Asoka.

[46] Finch appears to be confused about the beliefs of the Hindu pilgrims. Prayag is a holy site because they believe that it was here that Brahma, the creator, performed the horse sacrifice in memory of his recovery of the four Vedas.

[47] The "curious Tanke" is a deep octagonal well at the entry to an underground passage which leads to the *Akshai Vata,* or undying banyan, still revered by Hindus.

[48] *PP,* IV, 65–69.

[49] *PP,* IV, 69–71.

[50] *Ibid.,* p. 43. This reason for Akbar's desertion of Fatehpur-Sikri, while common in the seventeenth century, is now questioned. Its decline began in 1585, when Akbar left to defend the northwest frontier. Its real destruction began with the rise of the Jats around 1680. See S. A. A. Rizvi, *Fatehpur Sikri* (New Delhi, 1972), pp. 9–11.

Jumna river, Agra is now so heavily populated that people can hardly pass one another in its narrow, dirty streets. The city and suburbs are seven miles long and three wide. The houses of nobles and merchants are built of brick and stone with flat roofs; the houses of commoners are simple mud walls covered with thatch "which cause often and terrible fires." Most of the nobles' houses are on the riverside.[51] The Jumna itself is "broader than the Thames at London." On the banks of the river stands its fort-palace, "one of the fairest and admirable buildings of the East, some three or foure miles in compasse." It is surrounded by a strong wall of "squared stone" and a moat crossed by drawbridges. The fort has four gates. The north gate leads to the "Rampire" (rampart). The west gate near the bazaar is called the "Cichery" (*Kacheri* or court gate), within which is situated the *Kacheri* of Rolls, where the emperor's chief minister every morning for three hours handles "all matters of Rents, Grants, Lands, Firmans, Debts etc." The south gate, which leads to the emperor's durbar (council chamber), is always chained; it is called "Arabar Drswage" (*Akbar Darwaza*), and within it is the compound (*chawk*) where hundreds of whores constantly await a call from the palace. The east gate, on the river side, is called the "Dersane" (*Darshani*), in the court of which the emperor every morning receives "Tessilam" (*taslim,* a ceremonial salutation) from his nobles. Every noon he watches animal fights in this courtyard; on Tuesdays he also witnesses executions of condemned persons here.

Behind the third, or south, gate is a spacious court with "Atescanna's [Persian, *ātishkhāna,* artillery park] round about like shops or open stalls, wherein his Captaines according to their degrees, keep their seventh day Chockeis [Hindi, *chaukī,* guard duty]." Still further inward is a railed court where none may enter on pain of whipping except the imperial "Addees" (*ahādīs,* gentlemen troopers). Following this there is another small railed court covered with rich "Semianes" (*shāmiānah,* or awnings) to keep the sun off. Above, in a gallery, the emperor sits in his chair of state in the company of his children, chief minister, and fan bearers. On the wall behind the emperor hang pictures of Christ and the Virgin Mary. Nobody under the rank of "foure hundred horse" may come within these rails. On the opposite side of this court hang the golden bells of justice. If anyone is unable to obtain justice from the imperial officials, he may ring these bells when the emperor is holding court and be heard. Usually court is held between three and four o'clock each afternoon. Later in the evening, two hours after the durbar ends, the emperor comes to the small inner court near the palace to socialize with a select company of nobles who are admitted by ticket only.

Not far from Agra at Sikandra on the road to Lahore is Akbar's tomb, still unfinished "after tenne yeares worke." It stands in the middle "of a large Garden enclosed with brick walls neere two miles in circuit." Only one of

[51] See below, pp. 620–21.

the four gates planned for this wall is in place. Nearby is a spacious palace which houses Akbar's wives, "each enjoying [the revenues from] the lands they before had." The square tomb itself, "about three quarters of a mile in compasse," is approached by way of a small terraced garden, "four-squared" and enclosed by a railing. This is the lowest of five planned terraces. On each corner of the cut-stone mausoleum rises a small marbled "turret," with identical "turrets" exactly in between the corner "turrets." In a great hall with spacious galleries on each side, the body of Akbar lies in a "faire round coffin of Gold." By his head stands "his Sword and Target [shield], and on a small pillow his Turbant, and thereby two or three faire gilded bookes." At his feet stand his shoes as well as "a rich Bason [basin] and Ewre [pitcher]." The coffin, at Finch's departure, is covered only with a tent and awning. Around three thousand workers are still employed in completing this great memorial. The stone brought from a quarry near Fatehpur they "cut in length and forme, as Timber with sawes, and Plankes and seelings [wainscoting] are made thereof." Muslims and Hindus alike worship at this tomb, for both consider Akbar to be a saint.[52]

Roe had warned London in 1618 that the Dutch "maggots" were well entrenched in Surat and enjoyed almost as good a position there as the English. Two years later Pieter van den Broecke (1585–1640) became Director of the Dutch factory and supervisor of trade for the VOC in its "Western Quarter." He retained these offices until 1629. In the meantime Francisco Pelsaert (d. 1630) of Antwerp acted as Dutch factor at Agra from 1620 to 1627. Near the end of his stay in Agra, Pelsaert wrote a "Remonstrantie" (1626), or a commercial report, for the Dutch Company. He also collected materials, presumably from Persian chronicles, for a history of Hindustan. These two documents were forwarded to Van den Broecke, who sent them on to Amsterdam. While the name of Van den Broecke is associated with the chronicle, it appears to be primarily the product of Pelsaert's efforts. The "Remonstrantie" and what came to be called Van den Broecke's "Fragment of Indian History" were entrusted by the VOC to Joannes de Laet (1593–1649), a Flemish geographer and naturalist. Using these and other published and unpublished materials on the Mughul Empire, De Laet compiled and issued his *De imperio magni mogolis sive India vera commentarius e varijs auctoribus congestus* (Leyden) in 1631. This book, written in Latin for more general distribution, constitutes the first effort to provide a systematic description and history of the Mughul Empire for European readers.[53]

---

[52] *PP*, IV, 72–77. For a modern description of Akbar's tomb see *The Cambridge History of India* (see n. 43), IV, 549–51. On the working of the red sandstone of Fatehpur see *ibid.*, p. 539.

[53] For an English translation of Pelsaert's entire "Remonstrantie" see W. H. Moreland and P. Geyl (trans. and eds.), *Jahangir's India: The Remonstrantie of Francisco Pelsaert* (Cambridge, 1925); for an English translation of Pelsaert's chronicle see B. Narain and S. R. Sharma (trans. and eds.), *A Contemporary Dutch Chronicle of Mughul India* (Calcutta, 1957); for an English translation of De Laet's compilation see J. S. Hoyland and S. N. Banerjee (trans. and eds.), *The*

Part I of De Laet's compilation details the geography and administration of the Mughul Empire. This description is pieced together from the *Coloquios* (1563) of Garcia da Orta,[54] the history of Persia (1610) by Pedro Teixeira (not Texeira as in De Laet),[55] the appropriate writings in Purchas' *Pilgrimes* (1625), and the "Remonstrantie" (1626) of Pelsaert. De Laet's topography of the empire, its boundaries, and the list of its provinces are taken directly from Terry and Roe. His itineraries and his remarks on towns and monuments owe much to Finch, Withington, and Hawkins. He also refers to the Jesuit letters, many collections of which circulated in the Low Countries while he was preparing his compendium. Most of what is new in Part I of De Laet's work derives from the "Remonstrantie" of Pelsaert and whatever else he was able to extract from unpublished letters and reports in the archives of the VOC.[56]

De Laet is, of course, best on northwestern India. He provides a clear description of the boundaries of Gujarat, notes that its territory used to stretch much further to the east and south, and lists thirteen of its chief ports. Ships of a moderate size can ascend the Tapti river as far as Surat, a medium-sized port protected by an adjacent fort and by earthen ramparts and a dry moat. Close to the town there is a large and elegant tank cut out of the living rock, called *Gopi Talao,* or tank of Gopi.[57] Gujarat's port of Cambay, a place greatly frequented by the Portuguese, is twice as big as Surat and is enclosed within "a triple wall of brick." Its inhabitants, mostly Banyans, operate three large markets in the middle of the town. Robbers prey on trade and travelers on the roads leading out of town. The gates of Cambay are locked each night, presumably to prevent raids on the town itself.

Ahmadabad, the capital of Gujarat, is almost as large as London, is situated on a plain, and is surrounded by a strong wall. Every ten to twenty days its Banyan merchants send two hundred carts to Cambay loaded "with every description of merchandise." Its gates are strongly guarded, and passes from

---

Empire of the Great Mogol: A Translation of De Laet's "Description of India and Fragment of Indian History" (Bombay, 1928).

[54] De Laet extracts from this varied work a list of Indian kings. See Hoyland and Banerjee, *op. cit.* (n. 53), pp. 119–22. On Orta see *Asia,* I, 192–94.

[55] Teixeira, a Portuguese Jew, traveled overland from Ormuz to Antwerp in 1604–5. On the urging of friends in Antwerp he prepared in Spanish, rather than in his native Portuguese, the *Relaciones . . . d'el origen, decendencia y succession de los Reyes de Persia, y de Hormuz, y de un viage hecho . . . desde la India Oriental hasta Italia por tierra* (Antwerp, 1610). De Laet uses Teixeira, (*ibid.,* pp. 91–92) in his descriptions of Cutch and Kabul, territories formerly in Persian hands. He also uses his description of Gujarat (*ibid.,* pp. 93–98) and extracts from Teixeira's text the names of the Indian rulers descended from Tamerlane.

[56] Much of what De Laet takes from the Dutch archives is to be found in the *Gujarat Report,* a manuscript relating to the various Gujarati markets in the years before 1630. It is No. 28 of the W. Geleynssen de Jongh Collection at The Hague. See W. H. Moreland, *From Akbar to Aurangzeb. A Study in Indian Economic History* (London, 1923), p. 201, n. 1.

[57] On the Gopi tank see B. G. Gokhale, *Surat in the Seventeenth Century* (Copenhagen, 1979), pp. 18–20. This reference is missing from the list of such allusions compiled in M. S. Commissariat, *Studies in the History of Gujarat* (Bombay, 1935), p. 97, n. 1.

the governor are required to leave or enter the city. No duties are paid on goods leaving or entering. Six thousand horsemen are maintained to insure the city's safety from the brigand "Badur" (Bahadur), whose stronghold lies east of the capital. This robber chieftain has successfully stood off the Mughul forces, and even had the temerity to plunder Cambay.[58] Other insurgents called "Collees" (*Koli*) "live in solitary places" in the mountains between Ahmadabad and "Trape" (Traj); periodically they make raids upon roads and settlements.[59] Another raja, a vassal of "Gydney Caun" (Ghazin Khan of Jalor), lives further to the east in "an impregnable fortress situated on a deserted plain." He can raise ten thousand horsemen and frequently refuses to pay tribute to his overlord.[60]

Ahmadabad is headquarters for thirty-five large rural districts which together contain 2,995 villages. Revenues from the villages are funneled to the capital by local collection offices; practically all public funds come from agriculture, for no duties are charged on internal trade. Governor "Chan-Szan" (Khan Jahan Lodi), the most powerful of Jahangir's vassals, commands in 1621 an unusually large contingent of fifteen thousand horsemen, more than twice the number ordinarily maintained in the city. North of Ahmadabad is the large village of "Sarques or Sirhesa" (Sarkhej), where the former kings of Gujarat are buried.[61] Indians come from all directions to visit these tombs as well as a nearby palace and garden constructed by "Chou-Chin-Nauw" (*Khān-khānān,* the title of Mirza Abdurrahim), the Mughul general who defeated the last king of Gujarat at this place and established Mughul control in Gujarat.[62] Sarkhej produces much indigo, "great mountains" of which are exported to Europe even though it is inferior to that originating in Bayana.[63]

The Gujarati city next in importance to the capital is "Barocke or Brochia" (Broach), located between Surat and Cambay. This city is built on a high hill; it is surrounded by a high wall and overlooks a beautiful river (the Narbada). At the foot of the hill is a town, almost as large as the city itself, which is inhabited by artisans and sailors. In the fertile surrounding region on the road to Surat is the place where agates are dug. To a certain town between Ahmadabad and Broach pilgrims come from all over India to visit the tomb of a Muslim saint called "Polle Medonii" (Pir Ali Madani). Some of the pil-

[58] Bahadur (d. 1615), son of the last Gujarati king, headed the anti-Mughul forces in Gujarat. In 1606 he held Cambay for two weeks.

[59] A tribal people, the *Koli* operated mainly in the well-wooded country between Ahmadabad and Cambay.

[60] Hoyland and Banerjee (trans. and eds.), *op. cit.* (n. 53), pp. 19–21.

[61] Father Manuel Pinheiro had earlier commented on these fifteenth-century tombs. See *Asia,* I, 461.

[62] *Khān-khānān* or Khanan Khan (the honorific title means Khan of Khans) defeated Muzaffar III in January, 1584, and thereafter converted the battlefield into this magnificent garden.

[63] Sarkhej indigo, known to European merchants as "flat," was prepared in the form of cakes; the indigo of Bayana, prepared as balls, was called "round" in the trade. On the Bayana type see above p. 609.

grims wear chains on their legs or muzzles on their faces which they believe will be struck off after they have offered their prayers to the saint.[64] South of Broach is the beautiful inland town of "Brodera" (Baroda) built on a sandy plain near a small river called the "Wassah" (Vishva-mitri). It is surrounded on all sides by a wall and its people are mainly "Banians." In the 210 surrounding villages lac is collected, indigo produced, and textiles woven.

The fortress of "Jelour" (Jalor) stands on the boundary between Rajasthan and Gujarat. It is built on a high mountain to whose peak runs a broad road paved with stone interrupted by guarded gates. Within the gates of the fortress there is a beautiful mosque, the governor's palace, and a temple built by the Hindu forefathers of Ghazin Khan. Here is also the tomb of "King Hassuard" (Husain Khangsawar) "who was respected . . . during his lifetime for his warlike courage and after his death for his supposed saintliness." Between Ajmer and Ahmadabad are the impassable mountains of "Maroa" (Mewar). On one of their rocky ridges stands the great fortress of "Gur-Chitto" (Garh-Chittor), the stronghold of a ruler who has successfully maintained his independence against both Pathans and Mughuls. All the entrances to his mountain fastness are protected by strong fortifications. The Hindus "have from ancient times" revered this ruler as the "Roman Catholics venerate the Pope of Rome."[65]

East of Gujarat is the province of "Chandies" (Khandesh) directly upriver from Surat through territories infested by brigands. Its first large town is "Nacanpore" (Narainpur), the seat of a local princeling named "Pectosphavus" (Pratap Sah) who holds control over the surrounding country. Two of his most important towns and citadels are "Saleri" (Salher) and "Mulere" (Mulher). In Mulher the Gujarati coins called "Mamudies" (*mahmūdis*) are minted. Akbar spent seven years besieging these strongholds and ended by agreeing to let Pratap Sah remain in power as a tributary ruler providing he would refrain from molesting trade and travelers.[66] "Barampore or Bramport" (Burhanpur), the capital of the province, is a very large but poorly built city with a well-fortified citadel. In the Tapti River at Burhanpur stands a rock elephant which the common people worship. A road shaded on either side by trees leads from the city to the enclosed park (*Lal Bagh*) of Khanan Khan, the great Mughul noble and general. Other worthwhile sights in Khandesh are the fortresses of Asirgarh and the ancient city of

---

[64] This is probably a reference to the village of Pirana ten miles southeast of Ahmadabad. Imam Shah from Medina, the founder of its monastery, is said to have converted many Hindus in the sixteenth century by a display of his miraculous powers. See M. R. Majumdar, *Cultural History of Gujarat* (Bombay, 1965), pp. 254–55.

[65] For the Portuguese view of the Rajput fortress of Chitor see *Asia*, I, 422. The above materials on Gujarat extracted from De Laet's account in Hoyland and Banerjee (trans. and eds.), *op. cit.* (n. 53), pp. 16–27.

[66] A reference to Rana Pratap of Mewar who held out against Akbar's forces until his death in 1597. His successor, Rana Amar Singh (d. 1620), became a tributary of Delhi in 1615 and was required to send his eldest son as a hostage to the Mughul court. See B. S. and J. S. Mehta, *Pratap the Patriot* (Udaipur, 1971), p. 65.

"Mandoa" (Mandu). The mountain fortress of Mandu is entirely in ruins "with the exception of a few tombs and temples." The new city of Mandu, while far smaller than the ancient citadel, "has many fine buildings cut out of the living rock," as well as "lofty gateways" of a unique type. It boasts a splendid mosque and tower near which stands a magnificent palace housing the tombs of four kings.[67]

North of mountainous Khandesh is the fertile province of Malwa, a great producer of opium, grain, and wine made from the "Meira" (Hindi, *Mahwa;* Latin, *Bassia latifolia*). East of Malwa is the province of "Gualiar" (Gwalior) with a capital city of the same name which was at one time a frontier outpost between the kingdoms of Mandu and Delhi. It is famous for its hilltop fortress which stands to the west and above the city proper. A stone pathway protected by four successive and strongly guarded gates leads uphill to the citadel. In front of the final gateway, which is made of green and blue marble, there stands a stone elephant.[68] The governor dwells in an adjacent palace which also serves as a prison for erring nobles. The Mughuls have three such prisons, the other two are at "Rantipore" (Ranthambor) in Jaipur and at "Rotas" (Rohtas) in Bengal. Those condemned to death are imprisoned at Ranthambor for two months. On the day of execution they are given a drink of "milk" (*i.e., posto*, poppy juice, which gradually renders them insensible) and then cast down on the rocks from a wall above. Those sentenced to confinement at the remote and desolate fortress of Rohtas are prisoners for life.[69]

De Laet's description of the province of Agra derives mainly from the English authors and from Pelsaert, who spent most of seven years there. This province is separated from Gwalior by the river "Cambere" (Chambal). Akbar, who reportedly made Agra his capital in 1566, had five gateways constructed "for its defense and adornment."[70] De Laet lists the names and ranks (in number of horse cavalry) of the noble owners of the great residences which line the river bank. From these data it is possible to identify most of the nobles listed.[71] The Agra fort, which is also the imperial abode, "stands on rising ground . . . and is most beautiful to look at . . . especially from the river bank." The imperial "Gussal-can" (*ghusl-khana*), or audience chamber, "is a magnificent building, square in shape, and constructed of alabaster covered with gold plates." Beneath it are the quarters (called the *ma-*

---

[67] Hoyland and Banerjee (trans. and eds.), *op. cit.* (n. 53), pp. 28–33. The mosque of Mandu, the Jami Masjid, was completed around 1454; it is a fine specimen of Afghan architecture. The tombs are those of the Khalijis of Malwa, the rulers of Mandu during most of the fifteenth and the early years of the sixteenth century.

[68] This is the *Hathiya Paur*, or Elephant Gate built by Man Singh in the sixteenth century. It forms part of the palace.

[69] Hoyland and Banerjee (trans. and eds.), *op. cit.* (n. 53), pp. 33–36.

[70] Pelsaert gives their names; four of them survive in modern street names. See *ibid.*, p. 37, n. 49.

[71] *Ibid.*, pp. 37–39, n. 50.

hal) belonging to "Nourzian Begem" (Nur Jahan Begam), Jahangir's favorite wife.[72] Of the other buildings in the fort the most important are those which house the rest of the women. Three of these palaces are reserved for the imperial concubines. They are called "Lethevar" (Sunday), "Mongrel" (Tuesday), and "Zenisser" (Saturday), "for on these days the king is wont to visit the said palaces." Another palace called "Bengaly Mahal" houses the emperor's foreign concubines. Outside the fort are the palaces of many leading nobles. And on the opposite side of the river is the "finely built city" of "Secundra" (Sikandra) which is mainly inhabited by "Banians" who import products from eastern India. Sikandra also boasts magnificent palaces, such as that of Prince Parviz, as well as lovely pleasure-grounds. The impressive tomb of "Etham Doulat" (Itimad-ud-daula, d. 1618) is now being built there at a very high cost in rupees.

In this same province, twelve *cos* (twenty-three miles) from Agra, is Fatehpur-Sikri, the splendid city built by Akbar. To the name of the original village of Sikri, Akbar had added the word "Fetipore, i.e. the wish fulfilled" after the birth of Salim, his son and heir.[73] Now it is deserted and it is dangerous to walk through the city's ruins at night. Within its "north gate" (Agra gate to the northeast), a stone-paved market place still stands, at the end of which a palace and mosque are to be seen. Through a gateway one ascends twenty-five or thirty steps to "the most glorious mosque in the whole East." Near the gate in the courtyard of the mosque is the splendid tomb of a "Mahometan saint" who "is said to have built this mosque at his own expense."[74] Outside the city's walls towards the northwest is a great swamp replete with fish and birds. The marsh is covered by plants which produce "Hermodactylus" (water chestnuts) and "Camolochacheri" (Hindi, *kanwal kakri,* or lotus root). The latter produces a fruit "shaped like a small ladle, and contains inside six or eight kernels, which are joined together by a white membrane."

Further to the southwest of Agra is the indigo-producing region centering on Cannova and Bayana. The road from Agra to Ajmer which passes through this region is lined with stone columns marking each *cos*. At every eight-*cos* post, Akbar had a hostel erected able to accommodate sixteen ladies and their servants. The one near Cannova is a square building with the imperial bedroom at the center surrounded by the sixteen bedrooms of

---

[72] In 1622 she was given the title of Badshah Begam (the first lady of the realm), hence Palsaert's use of "Begem." See C. Pant, *Nur Jahan and Her Family* (Allahabad, 1978), p. 46. Also see pl. 116.

[73] This is incorrect. It was given the joint name after Akbar's conquest of Gujarat in 1573. The word "Fatehpur" means "victory town." See Hoyland and Banerjee (trans. and eds.), *op. cit.* (n. 53), n. 56.

[74] The mausoleum of Shaikh Salim Chishti to whom the mosque was dedicated by Akbar. *Ibid.,* p. 43, n. 56. This holy man (*pir*) was of the *Chisti* order introduced into India at Ajmer. He was revered by Akbar for prophesying the birth of Salim and his other sons. Salim was named for the holy man. For a color photograph of his tomb see Rizvi, *op. cit.* (n. 50), pl. ix.

the concubines. The building also includes spacious audience halls. Bayana, a ruined town, and Cannova, a village, are collection centers for the indigo produced in their vicinities, as well as headquarters of local taxing units. Northwest and south of Bayana are sites of impressive ruins, particularly those of "Seanderbad" (Sikandarabad). On the craggy summit of a mountain near Sikandarabad stands the ruins of a royal palace, once the residence of "a most powerful Pathan King." [75] Now that the Mughuls rule Sikandarabad, it is inhabited only by shepherds called "Goagers" (*gujars*).[76]

From Agra to Lahore the route passes through the famous old "kingdom of Dely, or Delhi." On the way to the present city are the ruins of the ancient city of Delhi; it is said that it once had nine fortresses and fifty-two gates.[77] Not far from here a stone bridge across the Jumna runs into a broad shaded avenue which leads to Humayun's tomb. Delhi itself is a great city, but many of its walls and houses are in ruins. Outside its walls stand about twenty well-built tombs of the Pathan kings. A bit further out is a hunting palace which, it is said, was built by "Sultan Berusa" (Firoz Shah, r. 1351–88). In that place is also seen "a very lofty obelisk" with an inscription on it said by some to be in Greek.[78] Similar obelisks reportedly exist in other places in India, one such having been discovered recently buried in the earth near Fatehpur. While being conveyed to Agra, it was carelessly broken and presumably destroyed.

The route from Delhi to Lahore, capital of the Punjab, runs through a fertile country which is a haunt of robbers who prey on travelers. At "Siryna" (Sirhind) there is a beautiful tank in the middle of which "is a temple approached by a stone bridge of 15 arches." Close by is a huge park square in shape and enclosed by a brick wall. In the middle of the park stands a royal palace surrounded by an impressive colonnade.[79] Along the road, "every 5 or 7 *cos*," there is a "saray" where travelers may find lodgings for themselves and stables for their animals. These inns, "built by the king or some noble," provide spaces for the traveler from which he may not be evicted once he has occupied them. Upon arriving in Lahore, the traveler is within "by far the largest city in the East." Most of what De Laet reports about Lahore is derived directly from Finch and other English writers published in Purchas' collection.[80] Most of what he has to say of Kabul, Kashmir, and other northern places is extracted from the English authors and the itinerary of Brother Bento de Goes. There are also bits of new material on what De

---

[75] A reference to Sultan Sikandar Ghazi (1489–1517), the second ruler of the Lodi dynasty.
[76] Hoyland and Banerjee (trans. and eds.), *op. cit.* (n. 53), pp. 41–47.
[77] Probably a reference to the ruins of Tughlakabad, five miles east of the Qutb, built by Ghiyassuddin Tughluq Shah (r. 1321–25). *Ibid.*, p. 47, n. 62.
[78] This is a *lāt* erected by Asoka; it is not by Alexander as a number of European commentators surmised. The inscriptions are in Brahmi and not in Greek. *Ibid.*, p. 48, n. 64.
[79] Probably a reference to the garden of Hafiz Rakhnah, a noble of Humayun's court. See *ibid.*, p. 49, n. 65.
[80] *Ibid.*, pp. 51–55; see above, p. 612.

Laet calls the province of "Purropia" (*purab,* meaning east) which begins at Allahabad and continues down the Ganges.

Somewhat more original, but also very limited, is De Laet's description of Bengal, which "has only recently been conquered by the Mogols and brought under their control." [81] Watered by the Ganges from the northwest, Bengal produces "quantities of rice, wheat, sugar, ginger, pepper, cotton, and silk." Its chief cities are "Gowro" (Gaur) and "Bengala," both of which are rich, well-built places. [82] Other Ganges towns are Tanda, a "famous center of trade"; "Banaras" (Benares), "whose inhabitants are . . . hardened idol-aters"; "Patanow" (Patna), whose houses are built of sod, and very poor; and "Chatigan" (Chittagong), a fine town served by the ports of "Ugeli" (Hugli) and "Angeli" (Hijili) in Orissa. "Orixa" (Orissa) belongs to Bengal province, though it was formerly an independent kingdom before being subdued by the Pathans and again by the Mughuls. [83] The natives of Orissa are subtle and depraved; in religion they are Muslims. [84] Clearly the northern Europeans knew very little about Bengal at the end of the first generation of the seventeenth century. [85]

In his chapter on the character and customs of the Indians, De Laet sum-marises Terry's account and includes additions from Pelsaert's and Teixeira's descriptions of their manner of life. Indians hunt game with trained dogs and leopards. [86] In catching water fowl they are ingenious. They stuff the skin of a bird of the kind they wish to catch and immerse themselves up to the neck and cover their heads with the sham bird. So disguised they mingle with the wild birds whom they catch by seizing their feet beneath the water. [87] Their archers make bows of buffalo horn and arrows of dried, light reeds. At home they play chess and card games, but with cards "very differ-ent from ours." [88] They enjoy the shows put on by snake-charmers and revel in the antics of apes and monkeys.

In most large towns and cities, markets are held each day before sunrise and again before sunset. During the heat of the day the rich Indians sit at

[81] Akbar's forces ended the Afghan dominion over Bengal in 1576.

[82] Gaur, much better known to the Portuguese in the sixteenth century than to the northern Europeans of the early seventeenth century, was already in decline when De Laet wrote. See *Asia,* I, 414–15. "Bengala" is a designation commonly used by European writers for the Ganges city or cities most frequented by traders, perhaps Chittagong or Sonargaon at this time. Also see below, pp. 712–13.

[83] Man Singh crushed Orissa in 1590 and brought it under Mughul authority.

[84] Orissa was fundamentally a Hindu kingdom with a few influential Muslims. See *Asia,* I, 411. *Cf.* below, pp. 673–78.

[85] Hoyland and Banerjee (trans. and eds.), *op. cit.* (n. 53), pp. 71–73, 77–78.

[86] On how they hunted with leopards (cheetahs) see M. A. Ansari, *Social Life of the Mughal Emperors (1526–1707)* (Allahabad, 1974), p. 121.

[87] For a similar idea see the engraving of Philippe Galle after Stradanus entitled "Hunting for Wild Ducks in China" in *Asia,* II, Bk. 1, pl. 47. Also see below, pp. 819–20.

[88] Muslims as well as Hindus commonly played a form of chess. Playing cards (*ganjfah*) seem to have been introduced into India by the Mughuls. Humayun, Akbar, and Jahangir were all cardplayers. See Ansari, *op. cit.* (n. 86), pp. 177–78.

home while servants fan them with "large leather fly-flops" or massage "their arms and other members." The common diseases of India are dysentery, fevers, and venereal complaints. Praise is owed by travelers to those low-paid Hindus and Muslims who guide and protect them on their journeys everywhere. Indians show great devotion to their parents, "preferring to die of famine rather than that their parents should suffer hunger." Certain Hindus and Muslims exhibit remarkable boldness and courage, notably the "Baloches or Boloohes" (Baluchs) of "Haiaca" (Hajikhan or Chachgan) on the Persian frontier and the Pathans of Bengal. Only one of the Hindu groups, the "Rasboots" (Rajputs), are infamous for brigandage and for preying upon and murdering travelers. The other Indians are "cowardly, and love quarreling rather than fighting."

The language of the common people is easy to pronounce and is written from left to right. The educated use Persian or Arabic. They have but few books and manuscripts in these languages, although they know several of the lesser works of Aristotle (whom they call "*Aplis*") in Arabic and are acquainted with the teachings of Avicenna.[89] They cultivate astronomy, and everyone, including the emperor, believes in auspicious and inauspicious days. While they like music and have both string and wind instruments, "they are ignorant of true harmony." They also compose verses and annals. Their huge ships which annually carry the Muslim pilgrims to the Red Sea are carelessly built and inadequately armed. They worship cows as the recipients of the best souls and great sums are expended, especially by the Jains, in caring for sick animals.

In Gujarat, according to Teixeira,[90] the Hindu sects are almost infinite in number, the three most important being the "Lonkah" (Lonka, a Jain *gaccha,* or subsect), the "Mexery" (Maheshri), and the "Baman" (Brahmans). The Maheshri worship idols while the Lonka do not, but they intermarry and eat together.[91]

The Brahmans of Gujarat, who sacrifice to the idols and perform marriage and other rites, are centered at "Bysantager" (Visalnagar), around which thirty thousand of them live in villages. Throughout their lives these Brahmans take but one wife. Formerly they were poverty-stricken, but are now rich from agriculture and the rearing of animals. The "Rasboots" (Rajputs) are Hindus who arm themselves with a javelin, a sword, and "a small shield made in the fashion of a beehive, so that they can carry in it drink for their camels and grain for their horses." Their strong and agile horses, which they learn to ride at a tender age, are never shod. The Hindus who

---

[89] Aristotle is usually called "Arastu." This may be a reference to him as "the philosopher," *al failsuf.* Avicenna (Abu Allah Ibn Sina), the genius of Bukhara who lived A.D. 980–1037, composed works in medicine, law, and philosophy.

[90] *Op. cit.* (n. 55), pp. 93–98.

[91] On the Lonka sect and its aversion to religious images see H. von Glasenapp, *Der Jainismus* (Berlin, 1925), pp. 69–70.

live to the north of Ajmer are unorthodox, for they eat both fish and meat. They remain naked to pray, and eat their food in a circle within which others may not enter. Their women wear rings of gold, brass, and iron, and armbands of ivory.[92]

In India the condition of the common people is miserable. Its numerous and poorly paid artisans rarely rise in social status. They teach their handicrafts to their children. No entire piece of work is done by the same worker but by several different ones. The whole family eats from the same vessel. The most usual dish is called "Kitsery" (*kichrī,* or kedgeree in Anglo-Indian). It is made of peas (*dāl,* split peas) and rice boiled in water. Generally it is eaten hot with a little melted butter poured over it. In their low mud and thatch huts they have very little furniture. Aside from a few earthen vessels, they have a bed for the husband and another for his wife. Their scanty and thin bedding is inadequate in cold weather. They try to keep warm by building a fire of dried cow dung in front of the house. Since they never light a fire indoors, their towns and villages are polluted by the smoke and smell from the many outdoor fires.

Servants and slaves are very numerous, and persons of substance usually keep several. They are well trained, attentive to their own tasks, and unwilling to touch the job of another servant. Each type of servant has a distinctive name and set of duties. "Seluidares" (*salotri*) work only with horses; the "Billewani" (*bahlīwāni*) take care of the carts and carriages for travel; the "Frassi" (*farrāsh*) attend to tents and curtains; the "Serriwani" (*sārbān*) look after camels; the "Mahauti" (*mahāuti*) tend the elephants; and the "Zantelis" (*jalabdars*?) are runners. Imperial officials are often lazy because they have so many low-paid servants at their beck and call. The servants usually increase their income by demanding a little for themselves when they make purchases for the master. While the masters are well aware of this petty graft, they seem not to realize that "they themselves have to pay more" as a consequence. As a class, merchants are better off than most other nonnobles, but they must always keep their wealth hidden to avoid being squeezed unmercifully by the officials.

Nobles live extravagantly and dedicate themselves to pleasure. Most have three or four wives at a time, who live magnificently in the women's quarters or *mahal.* Within the *mahal* each wife lives separately in her own apartment with her personal servants. She receives a monthly allowance from her husband for her personal and domestic expenses; such stipends vary according to the wealth of the husband and may be adjusted as his favor changes. While their houses are large and roomy, they are generally of one story with a flat roof. Houses are often built around a courtyard where they have a tank and trees to help keep them cool. Because these people use no lime in constructing walls, their buildings readily fall into disrepair. Sometimes they

[92] Hoyland and Banerjee (trans. and eds.), *op. cit.* (n. 53), pp. 82–88.

wash the walls with lime and cover them with a plaster which they polish "till the walls shine like a mirror." While furnishings are generally sparse, gold and silver vessels are often numerous in the *mahal*. Persian carpets are spread on the floors in the men's sitting room called "Diwan-Gana" (*diwan-khana*) where they receive visitors. Inferiors greet superiors by bowing low with the right hand on the head; equals simply bow. Visitors are seated on either side of the host "in order of precedence." In conversation they are modest and polite, never talking loudly or gesticulating. Ordinary callers leave once they have accomplished what they came for; relatives and good friends remain until the host rises "or goes to a meal." At a meal, guests sit on a carpet and the "zattersu" (*sharbatdār* or butler) places before each one a round dish of food. Napkins are not used and the food is eaten with the right fingers. To use the left hand or to lick the fingers is considered bad manners. Nothing is drunk until they finish dining.[93]

De Laet in chapter iv gives a summary description of political and civil government based on Roe, Terry, and Paelsaert. He emphasizes that there are no written laws, the will of the absolute emperor being the law. The emperor is also the supreme judge in both civil and criminal cases, though provincial governors are granted *farmans* by which they share his judicial powers. The chief ministers of the court and empire are the treasurer, the chief eunuch (who is also master of the court), the secretary, the master of the elephants, and the guardians of the tents, the wardrobe, and the jewels. A "Cutwall" (*kotwal*) governs the palace and similar officers superintend the chief cities and towns. The "Cadeae" (*kazi*) imprison debtors and govern the prisons. All affairs of state are discussed in public and well-placed bribes and gifts will open the mouth of any official. To obtain an audience with the emperor requires a gift. The ruler gives and takes away at will. Even the common folk live insecurely on their land never knowing when they will be required to move. Peasants are required to tell the royal official what and how much land they intend to sow and where they will pasture their animals. Very little or nothing is paid for the use of pasture land. About three-quarters of the peasant's harvest is taken by the state. As a result "the whole country is carelessly cultivated."[94]

The emperor alone bestows all titles and promotions. Ranks and income of officials and dignitaries are reckoned in terms of the number of horses each commands. The imperial sons and the four highest nobles are ranked at a level of twelve thousand horses. Below this number there are many grades down to the level of twenty. It is not necessary for the individual actually to keep the number of horses of his rank. His title merely indicates that he has

---

[93] *Ibid.*, pp. 88–92. *Cf.* the descriptions of upper-class Muslim and Hindu eating customs in Ojha, *op. cit.* (n. 19), pp. 5–9.

[94] Hoyland and Banerjee (trans. and eds.), *op. cit.* (n. 53), pp. 93–95. On the oppressive land taxes of the seventeenth century see I. Habib, *The Agrarian System of Mughal India (1556–1707)* (Bombay, 1963), pp. 240–42, and *The Cambridge Economic History of India* (see n. 27), I, 172–73.

been assigned properties large enough to support the requisite number of horses.[95] When a noble dies, the grants from the emperor as well as his own acquisitions revert to the emperor. The heirs usually receive only "the horses and furniture" of the deceased along with a "title of dignity."

De Laet proceeds, in what amounts to a *tour de force,* to estimate the wealth of the "Great Mogul" who controls an empire "larger than that of Persia and equal to, if not greater than, that of Turkey," who owns everything in it, and who regularly receives gifts from abroad. Starting from the inventory made of Akbar's treasure at the time of his death, De Laet adds to it the estimate made by William Hawkins of Jahangir's hoard. To this figure he adds the tribute paid by provincial governors and cities. Finally, he notes that while the empire has no silver and gold mines of its own, imports of gold, and especially of silver, are vast and reexport is prohibited. While De Laet gives precise figures for Akbar's and Jahangir's treasure troves, this is at best an impressionistic estimate of the wealth of the Mughul rulers. Nonetheless it is still cited by recent scholars, who even accept De Laet's precise figures, as a prime example of the wasteful hoarding of the Mughul ruling class.[96] And it let European readers of the time know in quantitative terms that the real wealth of India might genuinely be as great as it was fabled to be.[97] At a more practical level De Laet provides a brief but accurate set of remarks on the coins and weights of the Mughul Empire which was of use to European traders. And from the works of Pelsaert and Hawkins he compiled a list of the empire's military forces during Jahangir's early reign which gives the number of officers holding *mansab* as well as a census of the *ahadī,* or gentlemen volunteers. He also emphasizes that the Mughuls are "almost powerless on the sea" and that the Portuguese compel them to purchase passes to leave their own ports.[98]

Part II of De Laet's book reproduces "A Fragment of the History of India, Gathered from Dutch Sources," probably the work of Pelsaert.[99] This is a chronicle of the Mughul rule from the reign of Humayun (d. 1556) to the accession of Shah Jahan in 1628. The period to the death of Akbar in 1605 is based exclusively on certain chronicles in Persian which Pelsaert consulted

[95] Stated as a military rank (*mansab*) in terms of horses commanded.

[96] See T. Raychaudhuri in *The Cambridge Economic History of India* (see n. 27), I, 183.

[97] *Cf.* the discussion of contemporary European ideas on the wealth of India in W. H. Moreland, *India at the Death of Akbar: An Economic Study* (London, 1920), pp. 282–86.

[98] Hoyland and Banerjee (trans. and eds.), *op. cit.* (n. 53), pp. 104–18. The materials on Akbar's treasures and military strength were taken from an unpublished *Hindu Chronicle* in the Dutch archives. See Narain and Sharma (trans. and eds.), *op. cit.* (n. 53), pp. 33–35. These materials in turn were extracted from the imperial account books and registers by Pelsaert or his associates. On the *ahadī* see A. Aziz, *The Mansabdari System and the Mughul Army* (Delhi, 1972), pp. 200–201. For lack of other sources, most modern students of the military forces of Mughul India must continue to rely on the materials in De Laet and Hawkins for the early years of Jahangir's reign. De Laet is also used as a respectable source for naval history. See A. C. Roy, *A History of Mughal Navy and Naval Warfares* (Calcutta, 1972), pp. 52–55, *passim.*

[99] See the preface to Narain and Sharma (trans. and eds.), *op. cit.* (n. 53).

or had translated for his own use. Most of this earlier section deals with the conquests of Akbar, but it is flawed by many omissions and inaccuracies. The account of Jahangir's reign is more authoritative in that it is a compilation of events by contemporary European observers as well as a chronicle based on local records. To Europe the chronicle published by De Laet presented for the first time a systematic treatment of recent and contemporary Indian history.

In what follows we shall summarize the final part of "A Fragment" which complements and continues the historical accounts of the English writers, for the period from 1612 to 1628.[100]

Especially novel are the materials on the revolts in Bengal from 1612 to 1620 and the efforts of the Mughuls to suppress them. Contemporaneously Jahangir dispatched an embassy (1613–29) to Persia under "Chan Azem" (Azam Khan) to negotiate frontier questions. The chronicle describes the campaign in the Deccan from 1617 to 1622, during part of which time Ambassador Roe was attached to the imperial entourage.[101] It tells of the surrender of Qandahar to Persia in 1622 after a brief war and siege. In connection with this loss and because of political divisions in the court, Shah Jahan tried in 1623 "to seize the reins of government whilst his father was still alive." While this revolt was being quelled by those loyal to the emperor, the supporters of Shah Jahan in Gujarat undertook a revolt which quickly proved to be abortive. Defeated in both the north and west, Shah Jahan fled to the south and east and finally wound up in Bengal. After a series of debilitating campaigns in the east, Shah Jahan returned to the region of Burhanpur, headquarters of the imperial Deccan army under Prince Parwiz. In 1626 Parwiz died at Burhanpur, and in the next year the emperor became ill and died while in Kashmir. Although efforts were made to abrogate Shah Jahan's claim, certain leading officers of the army turned their backs on his enemies and called for the prince to assume the throne. Throughout this stark outline of events, the reader is overwhelmed by the names of numerous persons and places, most of which were certainly unknown to contemporaries in Europe. Modern students of Indian history, however, have but few problems in identifying the actors who crowd this drama of Jahangir's last years.

In his conclusions De Laet summarizes the impressions conveyed to him by his sources regarding conditions in the Mughul Empire. It is most evident, from all recent reports, that the Mughul Empire is "exceedingly large," and its rulers wealthy and militarily powerful. A closer inspection "of the affairs of each province" reveals, however, that it suffers widely from internal unrest and disorder as well as external pressures and assaults. Within the imperial family itself, as well as within the nobility, there exists a "spirit eager and ripe for insurrection and revolution." This spirit of revolt which

---

[100] Hoyland and Banerjee (trans. and eds.), *op. cit.* (n. 53), pp. 189–241.
[101] See below, pp. 636–44.

exists in all social classes is inflamed by an absolutism approaching tyranny, by a wide diversity in religious beliefs, and by the ability of petty princes to defy imperial authority from their mountain strongholds and forest retreats. Even those Hindu princelings who pay formal tribute to the Mughuls will revolt at the first opportunity and raze those regions closest to their fortresses. "Radias" (rajas) prey upon travelers, generally incite unrest, and tenaciously uphold Hindu traditions despite Mughul pressure. It is disunity, inefficiency, and debilitating luxury which produce the instability and weakness of the empire.

To protect and extend their empire, the Mughuls are required to employ foreign mercenaries. The greatest external threats come from Persia and "the Tatars and Usbeks" on the northern frontier. No threat exists from the east or from the Deccan in the south. But most frustrating is the empire's inability to conquer and annex the independent kingdoms of the Deccan. The Portuguese and the northern Europeans are not direct threats to the empire's integrity, but are constant reminders of Mughul weakness on the seas. Since opening some ports to the English and Dutch, the Mughuls no longer are at the mercy of the Portuguese for European trade. Already the Portuguese have suffered setbacks and could be permanently excluded from the empire if the Mughuls would determinedly carry forward a program of expulsion. It is the avarice and venality of the emperor and his nobles which permit the Portuguese to retain their privileged position in foreign trade and to control their coastal outposts by the ready and constant payment of petty bribes called "gifts." The Mughul Empire for all its obvious wealth and power remains essentially unstable and weak. The "probable explanation is to be found in the sloth, cowardice, and weakness of the last emperor Selim [Jahangir], and in the domestic discords of his family." [102]

2

THE MUGHUL COURT TO 1618

Two great Jesuit compilations of the early seventeenth century focused Europe's attention upon the Mughul Empire and its court. Fernão Guerreiro's *Relaçam annual,* a compendium and summary in Portuguese of Jesuit contemporary reports on the Eastern mission for the years 1600 to 1608, was published in five volumes (or parts) between 1603 and 1611.[103] Much more widely circulated, probably because it was written in French and in a livelier

---

[102] Hoyland and Banerjee (trans. and eds.), *op. cit.* (n. 53), pp. 241–46. On the character of Jahangir see I. Prasad, *The Mughal Empire* (Allahabad, 1974), pp. 454–60.

[103] See above, pp. 315–18, for complete data on this work. The references which follow are to the modern reprint prepared by Artur Viegas and published in three volumes at Coimbra (1930–31) and Lisbon (1941).

style, was the retrospective *magnum opus* of Pierre Du Jarric called *Histoire des choses plus memorable advenues tant ez Indes Orientales* (3 vols. [parts], Bordeaux, 1608, 1610, 1614).[104] Most of the materials on northern India in these two compilations have appeared in modern English translations and have been incorporated into recent special and general studies.[105] Consequently, in what follows, we shall cite wherever possible the translations and summaries rather than the original editions of Guerreiro and Du Jarric.

At the beginning of the seventeenth century Akbar is pictured as being master of most of Hindustan between the Indus and the Ganges and as determined to extend his authority southward over the Deccan states, Goa, Malabar, and Vijayanagar. After an initial setback, he takes over control of Ahmadnagar and "Breampur" (Burhanpur). On his approach to Burhanpur its "Miram" (*Miran,* or Bahadur Khan of Khandesh) abandons the city and flees to the nearby fortress of "Syr" (Asirgarh), his chief stronghold. Unable to take by siege or assault this virtually impregnable mountain fortress, Akbar requests Father Jerome Xavier and Brother Bento Goes "who were in his camp" to write to the Portuguese at Chaul asking for artillery and munitions. When they refuse this appeal as requiring an action contrary to their Christian faith, the Jesuits temporarily fall out of favor. Akbar then "bombards" the fortress with gold and silver to corrupt and undermine its defenders. In January, 1601, Asirgarh finally falls to Akbar and as a result he controls both Khandesh and Ahmadnagar.[106]

Before leaving the Deccan, Akbar receives Father Manuel "Pignero" (Pinheiro) at the camp. The Jesuit came from his post in Lahore to complain about the ill treatment he and his converts were experiencing there. Among the many gifts the Jesuits bring to Akbar there is a picture of "our Lady of Lorete, painted on gilded calaim."[107] In the meantime Akbar determines to

[104] For complete bibliographical detail see above, p. 396.

[105] Father H. Hosten, S.J., inaugurated the process of translating into English the Jesuit reports on northern India. For a listing of his numerous writings published between 1906 and 1927 see Sir Edward Maclagan, *The Jesuits and the Great Mogul* (London, 1932), pp. 391–94. C. H. Payne (trans. and ed.), *Akbar and the Jesuits* (London, 1926), puts into English the matter on the "Great Mogul" from Du Jarric (II, 429–93; III, 27–97) which the French Jesuit derived from Peruschi, Guzman, the Annual Letters, and Guerreiro. Payne has also published, in his *Jahangir and the Jesuits* (New York, 1930), the materials in Guerreiro (Viegas [ed.], *op. cit.* [n. 103], I, 310–14; II, 366–86; III, 6–30) on the Mughul Empire from 1605 to 1609, the overland journey to China of Bento Goes, and the Portuguese advent in Pegu. Maclagan's thorough general study of the Jesuits in the Mughul Empire to 1734 has been amplified by Arnulf Camps, O.F.M., in his *Jerome Xavier, S.J., and the Muslims of the Mogul Empire: Controversial Works and Missionary Activity* (Schöneck-Beckenried, 1957). Camps supplements the old Jesuit compilations and histories with unpublished materials from the Roman Archives of the Society and from other European libraries and archives.

[106] Payne (trans. and ed.), *Akbar* (n. 105), pp. 102–9; and Maclagan, *op. cit.* (n. 105), pp. 57–58. For the eyewitness account of Father J. Xavier see H. Heras, "The Siege and Conquest of the Fort of Asirgarh by the Emperor Akbar," *Indian Antiquary,* LIII (1924), 33–41. Also see Appendix A in I. Prasad, *op. cit.* (n. 102), pp. 286–88. Prasad was evidently unacquainted with the Xavier letter earlier translated and edited by Heras.

[107] Guerreiro explains in Payne (trans. and ed.), *Akbar* (n. 105), p. iii: "Calaim is a metal which

send an embassy to Goa, which he orders Brother Goes to accompany. The emperor's letter of accreditation requests a political alliance, the dispatch of skilled craftsmen, and facilities for the acquisition of precious stones and other rare objects.[108] Because he always has conquest of the Estado da India in view, the emperor frequently sends his agents to Goa when the ships from Europe arrive to determine the military strength of the Portuguese and to find out what new and exotic merchandise is available. This embassy reaches Goa in May, 1601, where its Gujarati ambassador and his retinue are received "with great magnificence" and treated significantly to "a terrific salute of artillery." While in Goa, Goes receives orders from his superiors to undertake an overland journey to Cathay (China).

Unsatisfactory conditions in his own realm brought on by the misconduct of Prince Salim forces Akbar to return to Agra in May before completing the conquest of the Deccan. Leaving certain of his captains behind to carry on the war against Bijapur, the "Great Mogul" retires to Agra accompanied by Xavier and Pinheiro "who usually traveled in his suite." In the following year (1602) the Jesuits are joined in Agra by Goes and Father Antonio Machado (1561–1627), a Portuguese Jesuit. The four Jesuits again complain to Akbar about the mistreatment of the Christians in Lahore and request from him a *farman* granting a general permission to his subjects to become Christians. While the ruler had previously granted liberty of worship orally, the Jesuits want a new royal command in writing to let all his subjects know that they are free to become Christians "without any person being able to hinder them." The Muslim officers at the court, especially "Agiscoa" (Aziz Koka) the first minister, and at Lahore try to obstruct the issuance of these letters patent as being prejudicial and offensive to their faith and its believers. Akbar nonetheless insists on their proclamation in 1602.[109] With Akbar's permission Pinheiro then leaves for Lahore to rejoin Francisco Corsi (1573–1635) who had been carrying on the mission there alone.[110] And with Akbar's financial and moral support Brother Goes sets off at the beginning of 1603 on his memorable overland journey that will take him from Lahore to Su-chou in northwestern China.[111]

Throughout most of 1602 Akbar continues to have serious problems with Prince Salim, his impatient heir apparent. While Akbar was busy in the Deccan, Salim had begun "to assume the name and to exercise the pre-

---

comes from China. Though it resembles tin, it is a different metal, and contains a large proportion of copper. Nevertheless it is white, and in India they make it into money. It can also be gilded, like silver." On the confusion in Europe over this metal see *Asia,* II, Bk. 3, pp. 426–27.

[108] For the text of this letter of March 20, 1601, as reproduced by Guerreiro, see Viegas (ed.), *op. cit.* (n. 103), I, 11; and Payne (trans. and ed.), *Akbar* (n. 105), pp. 115–17.

[109] For the text of the *farman* as relayed to Rome by Pinheiro in Portuguese translation see Camps, *op. cit.* (n. 105), p. 201.

[110] Payne (trans. and ed.), *Akbar* (n. 105), pp. 152–59.

[111] Payne (trans. and ed.), *Jahangir* (n. 105), Pt. II, for the travels of Goes as told by Du Jarric and Guerreiro.

rogatives of a king." On the sovereign's return to Agra, Salim repeatedly refuses his father's summons to appear at court and instead raises a large army to support his rebellion. While civil war appears to be in the offing, the father and son are finally reconciled peacefully "though they continued to live apart, and to hold separate courts." At his court in "Alahabech" (Allahabad) Salim favors the Jesuits and their religion even more than his father does at Agra. Still the Jesuits and their converts continue to be persecuted at Lahore, and even in Agra, by officials bold enough to defy the imperial edict granting freedom to the Christians. While Akbar lies dying in October, 1605, a minor succession crisis ensues, from which Salim emerges the victor. On his promising to defend Islam the court nobility and "groups of the common people" uphold Salim's right to succeed his father.

Akbar died in October, 1605, attended only by a few of his retainers and without acknowledging either the Muslim or the Christian God. In the eyes of the Jesuits he had been

a prince beloved of all, firm with the great, kind to those of low estate, and just to all men, high and low, neighbor or stranger, Christian, Saracen [Muslim], or Gentile; so that every man believed that the King was on his side.[112]

Although he could neither read nor write,[113] Akbar was informed by regular monthly reports from "his captains" about everything that occurred. They were read to him "after he had finished his other business, or before he retired to sleep." During the half century of his reign, Akbar, "one of the most fortunate monarchs of his time," extended the territories inherited from his father by his conquests of Kashmir, Sind, Gujarat, Khandesh, Bengal, and a great part of the Deccan. But in spite of all his achievements in this world, the Jesuits report that Akbar was "unable to escape everlasting torment," for he died without knowledge of the "true God and His only Son Jesus Christ."[114]

Eight days after Akbar's death, the new ruler takes formal possession of his realm. Gifts are showered upon him, and the people shout "Pad Iausalamat!" (Persian, *Pādshāh salāmat*), or "Hail, King!" as he enters the fortress of Agra. Anxious to build his new regime on Muslim support, Salim takes the name "Nurdim mohamad Iahanuir" (Persian, *Nur-ud-din Muhammad Jahangir*) which means "The Splendour of the Law of Mafamede, Conqueror of the World." He orders the mosques to be cleaned and restores in the royal palace the Islamic fasts and prayers discountenanced by his father. While Jahangir does not deprive the Jesuits of their privileges, they report that "of

---

[112] *Ibid.*, p. 205.

[113] On the debate over Akbar's alleged illiteracy see Ojha, *op. cit.* (n. 19), pp. 101–5.

[114] Payne (trans. and ed.), *Akbar* (n. 105), pp. 207–8. Akbar was buried at Sikandra about five miles from the fortress of Agra. For the differing viewpoints of contemporary Europeans about the faith in which he died see Maclagan, *op. cit.* (n. 105), pp. 64–65. For a portrait of Akbar see pl. 112.

the Fathers he took no more notice than if he had never seen them before" even though he had earlier been considered "almost a Christian." [115]

That the new "Mogul" needed a loyal following is best illustrated by the revolt of his son and heir, Prince Khusru. On the night of Saturday, April 15, 1606, Khusru "left the fortress with a number of his friends and adherents" allegedly "to visit the tomb of his grandfather." Once outside the royal confines, Khusru's friends begin to call him "Soltam Ia," or "King Soltam" and to recruit an army. As he flees toward Lahore, Khusru manages to garner money and support from certain apparently disaffected "Captains." With these monies he is able to raise "a considerable force." He besieges Lahore for eight days but fails to take the city. On hearing that his father's army is in hot pursuit and closing in, he gives up the siege and "turns to encounter his pursuers, hoping to prevent them from crossing the river [the Beas]." After a violent battle, Khusru flees northward towards Kabul and is captured en route by a royal governor. Chained hand and foot, the rebellious prince is led into his father's presence at Lahore along with his two chief supporters, both of whom are important imperial officials. After brutal public punishment, one of the officials is beheaded and the head sent to Agra where it is displayed on the city's gate. The other official, after diverse punishments and the payment of a huge fine, is set free and restored to his office. Two hundred of the lesser followers of the prince are impaled or hanged on either side of the route by which Jahangir enters Lahore. Khusru is deprived of his titles and his claim to the throne is given to Jahangir's second son. The hapless prince is kept in chains, and constantly shown off to the public. One of those who supported Khusru is a highly venerated person "whom the Gentiles call Goru [guru], a title equivalent to that of Pope amongst the Christians." When Jahangir learns that the "Goru" had dignified his son's rebellion with approbation, he imprisons the holy man and releases him only after a heavy fine is paid by one of his followers. [116]

Once this uprising is quelled, Jahangir turns his attention to administration. He eliminates many internal transit tolls illegally imposed by local authorities. He restores to certain noble heirs the properties which Akbar had confiscated for the state on the death of the owner. [117] To placate the Muslims he seeks to force some of his officials and their families in Lahore to acknowledge Islam. The Jesuits, constantly on the defensive in "this Moor-ridden land," continue to work quietly in 1606 to regain Jahangir's support.

[115] Payne (trans. and ed.), *Jahangir* (n. 105), p. 3.

[116] *Ibid.*, pp. 4–12. One of the "Captains" supporting Khusru was Husain Beg Badakshi, an official in charge of Kabul; the other was Abdur Rahim, diwan of Lahore. See *ibid.*, p. 90. The "Goru" was Guru Arjun, the fifth of the Sikh *gurus*. See *ibid.*, p. 93.

[117] Men were not born nobles, but chose state service as a career. Hence, on the death of a noble, most of his accumulated property reverted to the state. This law of escheat, most stringently enforced by Akbar, was liberalized by Jahangir and later rulers. See *The Cambridge History of India* (see n. 43), IV, 472.

They translate Christian works into Persian and present them to him. When Jahangir leaves for Kabul in 1607, they remain in Lahore celebrating with the other Christians the "times and feasts of the Church," often with "many kinds of fireworks, which they make very well in this country." As Jahangir solidifies his power, he begins "to show himself much less of a Moor than at first" and "to follow in his father's footsteps." In short, the Jesuits conclude he "continued to show himself worthy of the name 'The Just King,' which he had taken at the commencement of his reign."[118]

After a stay of several months in Kabul, Jahangir returns to Lahore in December, 1607. He is met at the outskirts of the capital by his four Jesuit admirers. Back in Lahore, Jahangir decides to send an embassy to Goa. He appoints as his emissary "an officer of very high authority."[119] Father Manuel Pinheiro is chosen to accompany the embassy, which leaves just before Christmas. The object of the embassy is to cement friendly relations with the Portuguese and to acquire "rare and curious objects" designed to tickle Jahangir's fancy. After Christmas, Jahangir decides to return to Agra and requests that two of the Jesuits follow him there. Machado remains in Lahore while Xavier and Corsi accompany Jahangir. The ruler and his army make a leisurely progress toward Agra as Jahangir hunts on the way. When the procession reaches the site of the battle between Jahangir and Khusru, the ruler orders his son, still in chains, and a rebellious official to be blinded as punishment for their disobedience.[120]

Returned to Agra and their small flock early in March, 1608, Xavier and Corsi take the first opportunity offered "to dispute with the Moors before the King." Jahangir, who is fascinated by the "colored pictures of sacred subjects" which the Jesuits present to him, asks the priests to explain their meaning. The interpretations of the Jesuits and Jahangir's questions provoke a debate with the Muslims of the court. The king's reader, a learned Muslim well versed in history and a man held in high esteem by both Akbar and Jahangir for being "of the lineage of the Prophet," is the Jesuits' chief rival. Called "Nagibusco" (Naqib Khan, the title of Ghiyas-ud-din Ali), the reader denounces the Christian scriptures as corrupt and denies the divinity of Christ. In their turn the priests denominate Mohammad a false prophet and the Koran a collection of nonsense. Jahangir, who apparently delighted in these acrimonious disputes, enjoys taunting the Muslims by speaking "strongly in favor of the use of pictures, which, amongst the Moors, are regarded with abhorrence." Himself a connoisseur of paintings, Jahangir has his palaces in Agra adorned with pictures, many of them illustrating Christian subjects. The Jesuits even supply him with portraits "of the Pope,

[118]Payne (trans. and ed.), *Jahangir* (n. 105), pp. 13–36, *passim*. Jahangir was called *adil padsha;* the Arabic word *adil* meaning "just" is in common use with Indian Muslims. *Ibid.,* p. 98.

[119]Muqarrib Khan of Panipat, at one time Jahangir's personal physician and at this period governor of Cambay. See Maclagan, *op. cit.* (n. 105), p. 177.

[120]Payne (trans. and ed.), *Jahangir* (n. 105), pp. 43–48.

the [Holy Roman] Emperor, King Philip, and the Duke of Savoy." While Jahangir prides himself on his knowledge of Christianity and Europe, he is held back in the Jesuits' view from accepting the Christian faith "because it forbids a man to take more than one wife." [121]

The embassy to Goa dispatched from Lahore arrives at Cambay in April, 1608. Its leader, the governor of Cambay named "Mocarebecam" (Muqarrib Khan), decides to wait in Cambay until news reaches there of the new viceroy's arrival in Goa. Pinheiro takes advantage of this break in the journey to carry on Christian work. But the Jesuit is soon recalled to Goa to report on the arrival at Surat and Agra in 1608 of the Englishman William Hawkins, who "styled himself the ambassador of his King." Hawkins had brought with him a letter from King James I written in Spanish, and he "conversed with the King [Jahangir] in Turki [Turkish], for he could speak and understand this language." Jahangir had immediately assented to Hawkins' request for permission to trade at his ports. As an additional mark of his favor, the emperor took Hawkins into his own service, which bound the Englishman "so that he could not return to his own country without permission." While Hawkins was still basking in the imperial favor at Agra, other Englishmen were shipwrecked on a sandbank at Surat.

When news of the advent and successes of the English reached Goa, its viceroy held that the peace between Goa and Agra had been breached and let the Mughul ambassador in Cambay know that he would not be welcome in Goa. The Portuguese viceroy also issued orders "prohibiting all persons from entering Cambaya," an action which produced discontent among merchants of all nationalities and resulted in seizures of goods at Damão. To bring an immediate end to these warlike conditions, Goa sent Pinheiro as its envoy to Cambay to inform the Mughuls that peace depended on exclusion of the English from the empire. Jahangir, urged on by Muqarrib Khan, agreed to the Portuguese proposal and revoked the permission earlier given to the English to establish a factory at Surat. Hawkins thereafter fell out of favor at court and was sent to Bengal "where he had not opportunity of communicating with his countrymen." [122] Pinheiro returned to Goa as the official emissary of Jahangir and as the bearer of peaceful tidings. [123]

Like the Jesuit letter-writers, Sir Thomas Roe was preoccupied with the Mughul court, its personalities, and intrigues. As the first fully accredited English ambassador to Jahangir's court, Roe was regularly in the company of the emperor and his entourage from January, 1616, to August, 1618. The abridged version of the *Journal* published by Purchas in 1625 preserves most of Roe's reactions and reflections on the emperor and his court while dis-

---

[121] *Ibid.*, pp. 49–67, *passim.*

[122] Not true. Hawkins left Agra for Cambay in 1611. He died on the return voyage to England in 1613.

[123] Payne (trans. and ed.), *Jahangir* (n. 105), pp. 77–87, *passim.* On Hawkins' mission see above, p. 604.

carding his complaints about the governor of Surat and his tedious negotiations with various Mughul officials and the English merchants in India. Because of his preoccupation with diplomacy and court politics, Roe's comments on Indian social and religious customs are at best casual and perfunctory. His travels, like that of the court during Roe's years in India, were limited to the region between Surat and Ajmer, or to Gujarat, Khandesh, Malwa, and Ajmer provinces.[124] He evidently acquired a smattering of the Persian spoken at court, but was generally dependent upon interpreters. Consequently, even though Roe was learned and perspicacious in his own right, he was never able fully to appreciate the learning and sophistication of the milieu in which he was working. His observations, sometimes impartial and sometimes bigoted, tend to be more Europocentric than those of the less-educated English commentators. In part, this can be explained by Roe's dedication to his assignment of winning equality of treatment for his countrymen; and in part it can be attributed to a personal unwillingness to admit the validity of ideas, premises, and practices differing from his own. Roe's *Journal* is nonetheless an important source for the study of Jahangir and Mughul court life, and a subject of consuming interest to Purchas' readers in Stuart England where king and court were being closely watched (see pl. 113).

On his way to "Adsmeere" (Ajmer), where Jahangir was holding court, Roe stopped over at "Brampore" (Burhanpur), the headquarters of the Mughul army of the Deccan.[125] Here he was met by the "Cuttwall" (*kotwal,* or general superintendent of the city), who escorted him to the local public inn. The official nominally in command of the Deccan army is "Sultan Pervies" (Parwiz), Jahangir's second son; the real commander is "Channa Channa" (*Khān-khānān,* an honorific title meaning Khan of Khans), "the greatest subject of the Mogall, Generall of his Armies."[126] After a few days' rest, Roe is received at the prince's court. Unacquainted with Mughul court etiquette, Roe makes demands for privileges of the sort granted to ambassadors in European courts. Here, as in his earlier negotiations with the governor of Surat, Roe shows himself to be a determined representative of his king and country. His perseverance finally pays off, and he receives a *farman* from the prince granting the English the right to establish a factory in Burhanpur.

On January 10, 1616, Roe made his first appearance at Jahangir's durbar in the palace of Ajmer. By this time he had learned something of the emperor's

[124] See the map of his routes in Foster (ed.), *op. cit.* (n. 6; 1926 ed.), facing p. 66. Also see Michael Strachan, *Sir Thomas Roe: A Life* (Salisbury, 1989), p. 83.

[125] On Burhanpur as an example of the medium-sized Indian city of the period see B. G. Gokhale, "Burhanpur. Notes on the History of an Indian City in the XVIIth Century," *Journal of the Economic and Social History of the Orient* (Leyden), XV (1972), 316–23.

[126] Mirza Abdurrahim, who was given this title for his role in reconquering Gujarat and subjugating Sind. See Foster (ed.), *op. cit.* (n. 6; 1926 ed.), p. 69, n. 2.

daily routine. After rising in the morning, Jahangir shows himself to his subjects by appearing in a window called the *"jarruco"* (*jharokha,* or interview window). At noon he returns to this window and "setts some howers" watching animal fights. Every Tuesday he sits there in his role as judge of complaints. Then "he retires to sleepe among his woemen." At 4:00 P.M. he convenes his durbar at which he greets strangers, receives petitions and presents, and issues commands. After supper, or at about 8:00 P.M., he appears in the *"guzelcan"* (*ghusl-khana,* or privy chamber) where he and a select company of courtiers review "all matters with much affabilitie."[127] Important affairs of state are discussed and often resolved at the durbar or in these evening sessions. This daily schedule is "unchangeable, except sicknesse or drink prevent it, which must be knowne: for as all his Subjects are slaves, so is hee in a kind of reciprocall bondage." Should he fail to follow this daily routine and no explanation for the lapse be given, his subjects would mutiny.

In his first appearance before the durbar, Roe is permitted to follow whatever courtly etiquette he knows. On approaching the imperial dais he makes three reverences in the English style. After Jahangir's welcome, Roe presents to the emperor a translation of King James' letter, his own commission, and the expected gifts. After receiving the presents graciously, the emperor asks Roe a few questions and offers him the services of his physicians. Pleased by this cordial reception, Roe quickly asks for an appointment with "Prince Sultan Coronne" (Khurram), Jahangir's favorite son (see pl. 113) and the recently appointed governor of Surat whose favor the ambassador especially needs if he is to work out a commercial treaty. On January 22 he is received cordially by the prince and is assured that conditions at Surat for Englishmen will improve and that a *farman* in their favor will be forthcoming. Two days later Roe returns to the durbar to ask justice of the emperor. He complains about the treatment of the English merchants stationed at Ahmadabad and about the new internal transit taxes being laid "at every Towne" on goods "passing to the Port." After expressing his regrets, Jahangir issues orders to the governor of Ahmadabad to treat the English fairly and to cease demanding internal customs payments.[128]

These business matters resolved, Roe turns his attention to unofficial activities. On March 1 he visits Jahangir's house of pleasure outside of Ajmer "given him by Asaph Chan [Asaf Khan, the title of Mirza Abu'l Hasan, an important courtier and the father-in-law of Prince Khurram]." Located between "two mighty rockes," this elegant house cut into the rock is in a little garden graced by fine fountains and two large tanks.[129] On his return to Ajmer, Roe witnesses the beginning of the "norose" (*Naw-roz,* or New

---

[127] *Cf.* Terry, *op. cit.* (n. 7), p. 389; and above, p. 615.
[128] *PP,* IV, 323–31.
[129] This spot was one of Jahangir's favorite resorts. It is known as the fountain of Hafiz Jamal.

[Year's] Day), "a custom of solemnizing the new yeare" which was instituted "in imitation of the Persian feast, and signifies in that language nine
days." But now the celebration is doubled in length.[130] In the "Durbar
Court" (*Diwan-i-Am*) a great rectangular tent is erected which is covered all
around with rich canopies and laid underneath with large Persian carpets.
Under this canopy the courtiers assemble before the emperor's elevated
throne at the back of the hall. Included among the displays are portraits of
the King and Queen of England, of several English notables, and of "a Citizens wife of London." At the left side of the throne Prince Khurram has his
own pavilion, the supports of which are covered with silver. Before the
throne the principal courtiers have tents of their own in which they show off
their rich possessions. In earlier times the emperor visited these tents himself and took whatever pleased him. Now he sits at the usual hour of his
durbar to receive the New Year's gifts they offer him. In return he bestows
titles and promotions.

Roe himself participates in the festivities by offering Jahangir a present
which is received with "extraordinary consent." Among those attending
this same durbar is "the son of Ranna, his new tributary."[131] On March 13,
Roe attends the *ghusl-khana* "where is best opportunitie to doe businesse."
Here, despite the wily machinations of Asaf Khan and his faction, Roe complains directly to the emperor about the procrastination he is experiencing in
working out a permanent treaty and about the continuing bad treatment of
his countrymen in India. Although repeatedly given *farmans* authorizing
trade, Roe is unwilling to accept additional permits of this sort since they are
"temporary commands, and respected accordingly." Ordered by Jahangir
to submit a draft treaty for his consideration, Roe is confronted by a conspiracy to thwart his mission. Prince Khurram, Asaf Khan (the prince's father-in-law), and "Zulpheckarcon" (Zulfakar Khan, the title of Muhammad
Beg, the prince's favorite and the former governor of Surat) head a faction
which argues against Roe's treaty and advocates better relations with the
Portuguese. Jahangir, ever on the lookout for expensive and novel gifts,
wearies of Roe's inability to accompany his requests with appropriate presents and is highly pleased with the rich gifts of the Portuguese. Discouraged
by this turn of events, Roe notes that the Portuguese have wealth, influence,
and power, in contrast to the English who "for our trade or any thing . . .
[are] not at all respected."[132]

Conditions at court begin to change in June, 1616, as a result of the failure
of Prince Parwiz to wind up the Deccan war. Jahangir determines to replace
Parwiz with Khurram despite the objections of the generals in the field.

---

[130] This vernal festival was instituted by Akbar and was celebrated by Jahangir for nineteen
days. Roe is incorrect in translating *Naw-roz* as "nine days." See R. C. Prasad, *op. cit.* (n. 5),
p. 152, n. 59.
[131] Karan, eldest son of Amar Singh, Rana of Udaipur.
[132] *PP*, IV, 331–39.

Roe, who trusts Khurram more than his minions, seeks unsuccessfully to persuade the prince before his departure of the importance of trade with the English. The emperor continues cordial in his relations to Roe and boasts to him about the skills of Mughul painters. Jahangir has one of his painters copy a Western painting; it is done so skillfully that Roe is not able to tell the difference between the original and the imitations. As a sign of his favor, the emperor presents Roe with "a Picture of himselfe set in Gold, hanging at a Wire Gold Chaine with one pendant foule Pearle" (*cf.* pl. 113). When the courtiers demand that Roe should follow custom and perform "Size-da" (*sijdah,* or prostration) as a sign of thanks, Jahangir himself excuses the proud Englishman from making such an obeisance. Even though Roe's gift from Jahangir is small, it is "five times as good" as the portrait medallions which the emperor awards to his own servitors.

While Roe dances attendance to the emperor in the summer of 1616, he seeks also to establish good relations with men of influence at the court. Among those whom he seeks to cultivate is "Abdala Hassan" (Khwaja Abul Hasan), commander of the imperial bodyguard and paymaster-general of the armies. He corresponds with "Mahobet Chan" (Mahabat Khan, the title of Zamana Beg), an enemy of Prince Khurram who is effectively in charge at Burhanpur. From him Roe receives a *farman* granting the English the right to trade freely and securely at "Barooch" (Broach). The English ambassador also strikes up a friendship with "Gemal-din-ussin" (Mir Jamal-ud-din Husain), the seventy-year-old "Vizeroy of Patan and lord of four cittyes in Bengala." [133] A cosmopolitan and hospitable gentleman, Jamal informs Roe about court personalities, customs, laws, and the history of the empire. He shows Roe his private journal and outlines for him the financial administration of the empire. Annually, he explains, each province pays an assessment to the crown. Anything in excess of this tribute belongs to the governor. He entertains Roe at the imperial pleasure house of Hafiz Jamal, and explicitly advises Roe to find an English interpreter "which the King would grant mee if I could fynd any." Jamal suggests quite seriously that he would like, if it is permissible, to send a "Gentleman" to England with Roe "to see the Country." Shortly after being made the new governor of Sind, Jamal is entertained at a banquet prepared by a Muslim cook in Roe's house. The guests refuse to touch meat prepared in the English style, but Jamal asks that dishes of these strange baked meats be sent to his house and says "that he would dine on them in private." [134]

On August 20 at the end of the rainy season Roe experiences the "Oliphant" (Portuguese, *elephante,* a translation of Hindi, *hathiya*), a storm so violent that his house is almost flooded out. "Thus," he writes, "were we in

---

[133] He was at this time *sūbadār* (governor) of Patna or Bidar. Shortly hereafter he was appointed governor of Malwa, and later of Sind.

[134] *PP,* IV, 340–50.

every way afflicted; fires, smokes, floods, stormes, heats, dust, flyes, and no temperate or quiet season." Even worse, the emperor is considering moving the court southward to Mandu to be at hand to supervise the replacement of Parwiz by Khurram as commander of the Deccan armies. To avoid a war between the two princely brothers, Parwis with his entourage is ordered to Bengal. Jahangir goes to Mandu personally to support Khurram against the generals who resist his elevation. As for Roe, he worries that if he follows the court to Mandu, "a castell neer Bramport [Burhanpur] wher is no town," he will have to build a new residence at "extreme trouble and cost."

On September 2, Jahangir returns to Ajmer to celebrate his birthday. On this occasion the emperor is "weighed against some Jewels, Gold, Silver, stuffes of Gold, Silver, Silke, Butter, Rice, Fruit, and many other things of every sort a little, which is given to the Bramini." While Roe accidentally misses the weighing ceremony, he is witness to a parade of the richly ca-parisoned imperial elephants and of their bows before the emperor. That night, after Roe is in bed, Jahangir sends a message asking the ambassador to bring him the picture which "hee heard I had . . . [but] which I had not shewed him." Roe takes two portraits to the emperor, one being a picture of a woman and the other a French oil painting.[135] The emperor, while sitting cross-legged on a little throne, examines the pictures and requests the woman's portrait as a gift. Once Roe finally agrees to present it to him, Jahangir re-lents and states that he will be happy with a copy. Then he asks Roe to par-ticipate in a drinking bout to celebrate his birthday. The emperor presents Roe with a golden drinking cup studded with gems. Despite Jahangir's gen-erosity and affability, Roe continues to be vexed by those "faithless people" whose promises relating to the treaty seem never to be kept. Finally, after much delay, he receives an acceptable *farman* from Khurram ordering pay-ment for goods purchased from the English merchants of Surat.[136]

The power struggle for command of the Deccan army continues to dis-rupt the court. Abdullah Khan, general and governor of Gujarat and oppo-nent of Khurram, is summoned to appear at court on October 10, 1616. Accused of insolently defying the imperial authority, Abdullah Khan ap-pears before the emperor in bare, chained feet. After making his reverence, the general is forgiven and restored to favor. Prince Khurram, whose ap-pointment had been even more staunchly opposed by Khanan Khan, now decides to replace Khanan Khan with Abdullah Khan as field commander of the Deccan army. Khanan Khan, who has secretly been in league with Bi-japur, arranges for the dispatch of a peace mission to Ajmer. Jahangir, who is well aware of Khurram's ambitions, lets him decide whether or not to accept this peace overture. The imperial father, knowing well the rivalry which exists between Khurram and his eldest brother "Corsoronne"

---

[135] The portrait of the woman was possibly that of Roe's wife. See Foster (ed.), *op. cit.* (n. 6; 1926 ed.), pp. 223–24, n. 1.

[136] *PP*, IV, 352–58.

(Khusru), nourishes "division and emulation betweene the brethren." Jahangir favors Khurram for the moment but does not intend to let him inherit the throne. Khusru, who, blind and imprisoned, is as much loved by the courtiers as Khurram is hated, is not favored at the moment by the emperor, who thinks that "his liberty would diminish his [the emperor's] owne glory." Roe believes that when Jahangir "shall pay the debt to Nature" the country will be destroyed by civil war.

A history of the Mughul Empire would be worth writing, Roe observes, if it were not so remote and if its people were not thought to be so barbarous. Even if few will believe it, there is much to learn from Mughul history about "rare and cunning passages of State, subtill evasions, policies, and adages." For example, a conspiracy to kill Khusru is planned by Khurram with the aid of "Normahall" (Nur Mahal, or Nur Jahan, who is the empress and aunt to Khurram's wife), Asaf Khan (Khurram's father-in-law and brother to the empress), and "Etiman Dowlett [Itimad-ud-Daula], father to them both." One night, while the emperor slept in a drunken stupor, an effort is made by this cabal to dupe "Anna Rah" (Anup Ray), Khusru's faithful Rajput bodyguard, to release the prince into his brother's custody. On the following day Anup Ray informs the emperor of what has transpired and they both agree to preserve discreet silence and watch the conspirators work. Khurram, who fears that his brother will take advantage of his absence in the Deccan to win over the emperor, finally persuades Jahangir to dismiss Anup Ray; Khusru is placed in the custody of Asaf Khan as part of an effort to reassure the Deccan generals of the emperor's unqualified support of Khurram. While it is rumored that Khusru's days are numbered, the prince is restored from time to time to the favor of his father. Thus, he escapes death at the hands of the faction, at least for as long as Roe remains in India.[137]

On October 19, 1616, the Persian ambassador "Mahomet Rosa Beag" (Muhammad Riza Beg) arrives at court with "about fiftie Horse well fitted in coats of cloth of Gold . . . and some two hundred ordinary Peons, and attenders on baggage." Roe's secretary, sent by the ambassador to observe the Persian's reception, notes that the newcomer submissively prostrates himself and knocks his head on the ground in a reverence Roe had refused to perform. The Persian, in Roe's estimation, is under orders to be obsequious and generous in his gifts because he is seeking Jahangir's support for Persia in its war against the Turk. Roe is embarrassed by the Persian's gifts, far richer than those he had presented, but contents himself with the observation that his own reception was more cordial and respectful. At a durbar Roe meets his Persian colleague who, in presenting his gifts to Jahangir, appears

---

[137] Khusru died in 1622, possibly at the hands of this faction. Four years later Parwiz followed him in death. See Foster (ed.), *op. cit.* (n. 6; 1926 ed.), p. 247, n. 1. In 1627 Khurram became emperor as Shah Jahan, with the support of the army and Asaf Khan.

to be "rather a Jester or Jugler, then a person of any gravity." Nonetheless the emperor awards expense money to the Persian envoy; he then promptly recovers it by fining his nobles for drunkenness. To obtain the dispatch of his business in this hectic and greedy court, Roe is finally forced to present Khurram with a gift of "two Pluriaes [?] and two Birds of Paradice." [138]

On November 1, Khurram finally makes his departure for the south. His entourage includes six hundred richly caparisoned elephants and an estimated ten thousand horsemen. After being embraced by his father, Khurram himself departs in a coach made in imitation of the English coach presented by Roe to Jahangir. On the following day Jahangir and the court begin their stately progress towards the Deccan. After receiving the accolades of his subjects, the bejeweled emperor enters his own coach (a modified version of Roe's English coach), its four horses being driven by an English coachman. Nur Jahan, the empress, rides behind in the original English coach "new covered and trimmed rich." [139] She is followed by the emperor's younger sons, who ride in an Indian cart, by his nobles on foot, and by his wives perched like parakeets on the backs of their elephants. This procession moves three miles southward to a "Leskar" (Persian, *lashkar*, an army camp), a city of tents already set up. The prince and his retinue lodge in a similar tent city nearby. [140] Here they wait for about two weeks to allow time for the people of Ajmer to follow. On November 16, Jahangir orders his artillery to bombard Ajmer "to compell the people to follow." The English and Persian ambassadors, as well as other foreigners, are likewise forced to leave the desolate city and to follow the imperial entourage. [141]

Roe, after winding up his affairs at Ajmer, finally finds enough transport to follow the emperor on December 1. Five days later he catches up with Jahangir at the walled town of "Todah, in the best country I saw since my landing." [142] The town itself had been the seat of a "Raza Rasboote" (Raja Rajput) until it was conquered by Akbar. In this well-built town, "a banished Englishman might have beene content to dwell" were it not for the Mughul law of escheat. Nobody maintains or repairs properties, since everything reverts to the crown. Thus "ruine and distruction eates up all." Still Roe finds admirable the efficiency displayed by the Mughuls in setting up orderly tent cities within four hours' time. In his "atasckanha" (*yatash-khana*, or audience chamber) in this military camp the emperor is closely guarded. He appears in public only in the morning, the durbar being omitted. All business is concluded in the *ghusl-khana* during the evening. Despite camp conditions, court intrigues continue over the fate of Khusru, and

[138] *PP*, IV, 358–72.

[139] On the English coach and the imitations see Terry, *op. cit.* (n. 7), p. 385.

[140] This first halting place was at Dorai, the locale of Aurangzib's victory in 1659. See Foster (ed.), *op. cit.* (n. 6; 1926 ed.), p. 286, n. 1.

[141] The Jesuit then in residence was Father Corsi. See above, p. 634.

[142] Toda is sixty-five miles southeast of Ajmer in Jaipur state (Rajasthan).

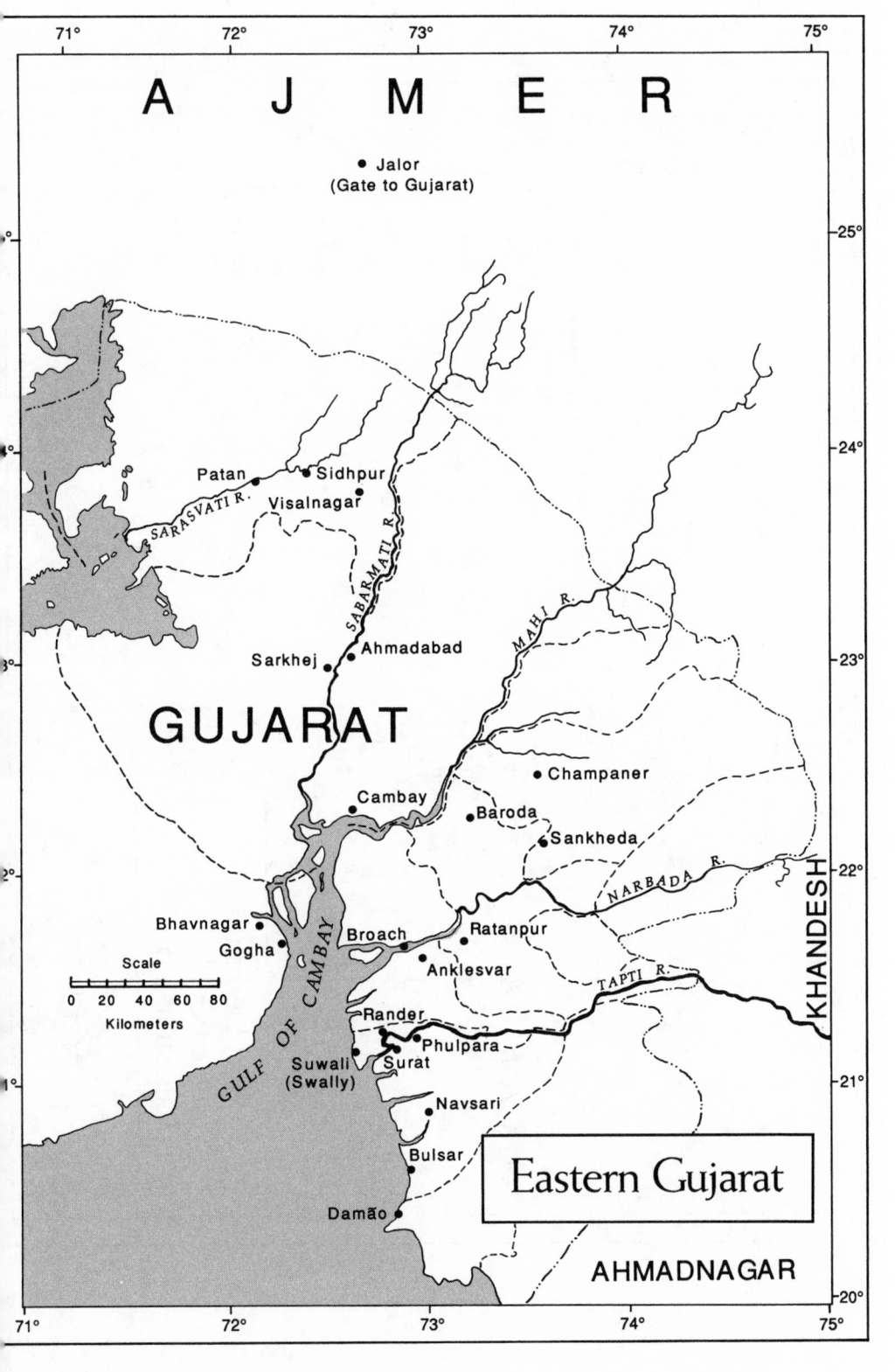

Eastern Gujarat

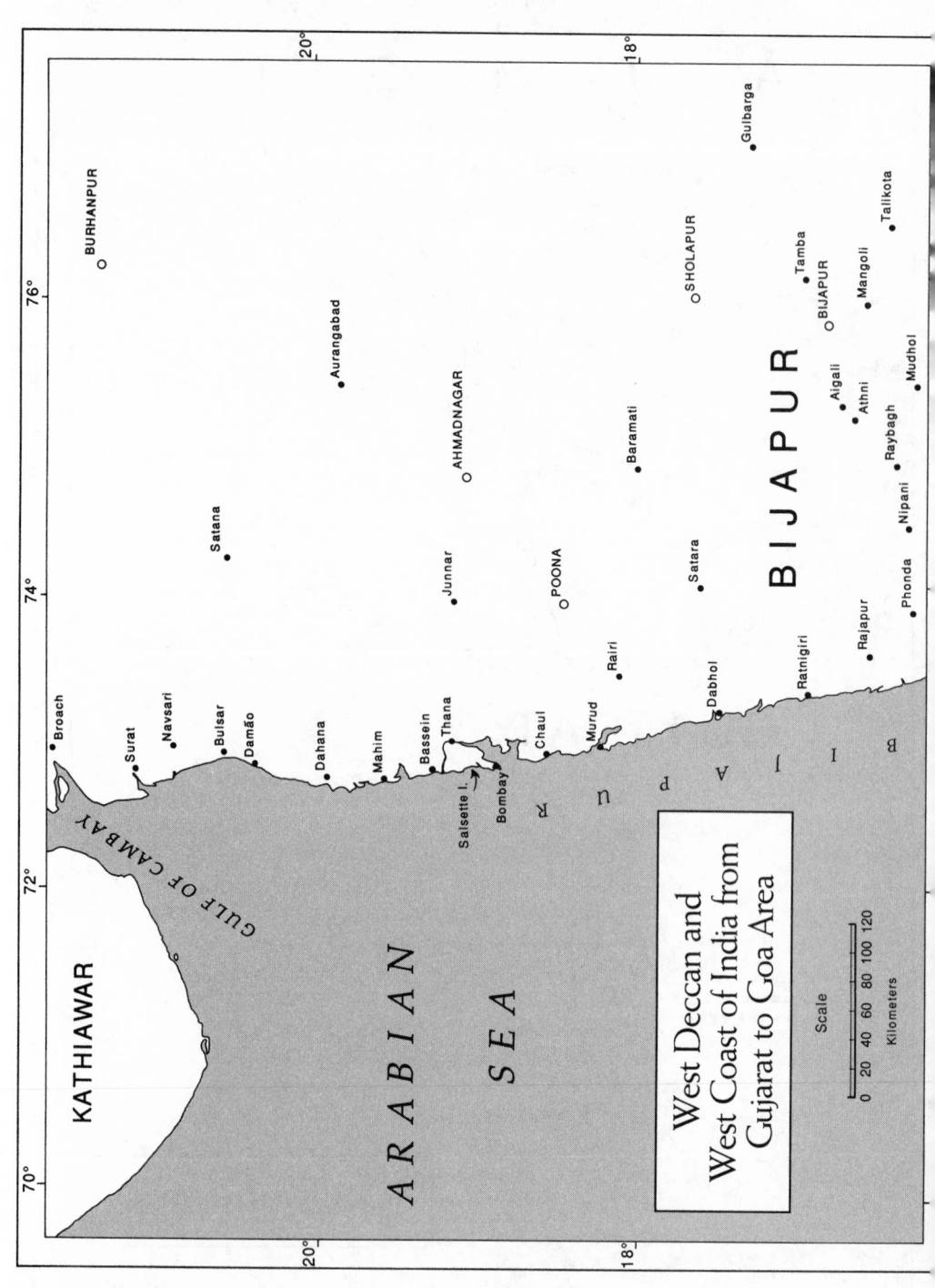

KATHIAWAR

GULF OF CAMBAY

ARABIAN

SEA

West Deccan and
West Coast of India from
Gujarat to Goa Area

Scale

0 20 40 60 80 100 120
Kilometers

20°

72°

74°

76°

18°

BURHANPUR ○

Aurangabad ●

Satana ●

AHMADNAGAR ○

Junnar ●

POONA ○

Baramati ●

Satara ●

SHOLAPUR ○

Gulbarga ●

Tamba ●
BIJAPUR ○
Mangoli ●
Talikota ●

Aigali ●
Athni ●
Mudhol ●

Raybagh ●

Nipani ●

Phonda ●

Rajapur ●

Ratnigiri ●

BIJAPUR

Dabhol ●

Rairi ●

Murud ●
Chaul ●

Bombay ●
Salsette I.
Thana ●
Bassein ●
Mahim ●
Dahana ●
Damão ●
Bulsar ●
Navsari ●
Surat ●
Broach ●

P U R A N D A R
B H I L

20°

18°

rumor alleges that Khurram and the empress have more in common than their conspiracy. The emperor meanwhile receives solace from the charity he shows to holy men and ascetics.

After leaving Toda, orderly marches and stable camp life degenerate into disruption followed by starvation and desertions. News arrives on January 24, 1617, that the "Decans," despite the prognostications of Asaf Khan and the empress, have not abandoned the battle field. They have rather reinforced their armies and are resolved to fight. Prince Khurram has advanced no further than "Mandoa" (Mandu) out of fear of the enemy and of Khanan Khan, Jahangir's obdurate field general and the prince's enemy. Disdaining advice to give up his plan, the emperor begins dispatching reinforcements to Khurram raised from his own troops and from local levies. The imperial entourage meanwhile moves on to "Calleada" (Kaliyada) in the vicinity of "Ugen" (Ujjain), the chief city of Malwa. Roe, still in conflict with Khurram over the Mughuls' treatment of the English, continues to complain to the emperor about his problems and to express irritation about the constant demand for better gifts being made upon him, especially English horses and dogs. Early in March Jahangir arrives in Mandu, a hill town where water and provisions are insufficient to meet the needs of the newcomers from the north.

Even while on the road, Roe receives communications from British merchants and seamen from places as widely separated as Masulipatam and Surat. British activities off India's west coast, especially at Dabhol, stir suspicions among the Mughuls that the English are planning the conquest of Surat. On March 30 the Persian ambassador, unable to receive satisfaction from Jahangir to his requests, suddenly flees the camp for Bijapur. Jahangir, rapacious and suspicious as ever, even seizes and opens goods sent to the Jesuits from Cambay, an act which Roe sees as a "warning to all that deale in this Kingdome, to be wary of what they write or send," for the emperor "will seize and see all, lest any Toy [trifle] should escape his appetite." Hardships bring an end, at least temporarily, to the factional divisions in the court, and the release of Khusru is expected. On September 1 the emperor again celebrates his birthday; this time Roe attends the weighing ceremony which he describes at length.[143] Eight days later the emperor on his way to the river of "Darbadath" (Narbada) passes by Roe's lodging. In honor of his appearance the ruler on such occasions is presented with a gift. The present is ceremonially called "mombareck" (Arabic, *mubārak*), a word meaning "good Newes or good Successe." Being bereft of rich gifts, Roe presents Jahangir with the latest edition of Mercator's atlas saying that he thereby is offering the world. Several weeks later Jahangir returns the atlas saying that neither the mullahs nor anyone else can read or understand it.

Jahangir's campaign in the Deccan continues to falter in the autumn of

[143] Terry was also present on this occasion. See his description in Terry, *op. cit.* (n. 7), p. 395.

1617. In the hills not far from the camp a local lord scornfully defies the ruler's authority. On October 2, Khurram joins the emperor at Mandu, leaving Burhanpur completely to Khanan Khan. Roe, ill most of the time at this period, continues to have trouble working out business relations between the Mughul authorities and the English merchants. He goes from prince to emperor to Asaf Khan in his determination to regularize sales and payments. He engages in intrigues and offers bribes to obtain a *farman* permitting the English to sell their goods at Surat.

At the end of October the emperor, followed by Roe, moves on to Ahmadabad. The weary Roe there urges his own countrymen to adapt their sales and practices to local conditions and to desist from all efforts "to alter the constant received customes of Kingdomes, where some drinke only rainewater, some of a holy river, some none but what is fetched by their owne cost." Many ideas about penetrating India sound fine in London "but in practice and execution are found difficult and ayrie." He denounces those servants of the East India Company who engage in private trade and urges stricter control over their activities in India. And he threatens the Mughuls that he will leave his post and the country if the prince persists in granting privileges one day and in countermanding them the next. Worn out by his efforts, Roe complains "my toyle with barbarous unjust people is beyond patience." When the emperor decides in August, 1618, that he will return to Agra, Roe determines to leave the court. For his gargantuan effort the tired ambassador receives a letter for King James and a general *farman* permitting the English to do business in the Mughul Empire. While he failed to receive the formal treaty he sought, Roe was successful in obtaining terms which in practice enabled the English to maintain their factory at Surat and to continue the process already falteringly begun of opening branches in the interior. As for Roe himself, he left India on February 17, 1619, never to return again.

3

GUJARAT UNVEILED

In the generation between 1630 and 1663 a series of books appeared in Europe which concentrated on the religions, cities, and trade of Gujarat. Much incidental information on commerce and travel in this province had already appeared in the sixteenth century and in the Purchas and De Laet collections published earlier.[144] In 1633 Christopher Farewell, an English factor who had gone to Surat in 1614, published at London a retrospective review of his experiences in Gujarat. This whimsical little book entitled *An East-India co-*

[144] See *Asia*, I, 392–406, for the sixteenth-century depictions; and for the major references in the Purchas collection see above, pp. 601–16.

lation might well be called "John Englishman Beholds India." An "India Collation homely drest" sparkles with reactions still evocative to Westerners who can recall a first visit to India. Multitudes of people crowd streets "humming like Bees in swarmes." Between the cities are pleasant country-sides replete with orchards, tanks, tombs, gardens, and temples around which naked penitents congregate "staring and stalking to and fro." On the highways run "Coaches and Carriages drawn by two faire fat oxen a peece," and in the country roundabout "whole fields [are] alive and the Trees covered with overgrowne Apes and Monkies."[145]

The senior English merchant at Surat was Thomas Kerridge, a native of Exeter. He had arrived in India in 1612 with the fleet of Thomas Best and stayed on at Surat as chief merchant for the next ten years. While on leave in England during 1622–24, Kerridge recruited Henry Lord (b. 1563), a native of Oxfordshire and an experienced curate, to act as chaplain in Surat. Lord returned to Surat with Kerridge and served there with him for the next four years.[146] Kerridge, who evidently felt a need to understand the beliefs and religious customs of his Indian trading associates, urged Lord to undertake a systematic study of the subject and introduced the cleric to local informants. After their return to England, Lord published in 1630 a book called *A display of two forraigne sects in the East Indies viz, the sect of the Banians the ancient natives of India and the sect of the Persees the ancient inhabitants of Persia together with the religion and maners of each sect. Collected into two books by Henry Lord* (London).[147]

In the introduction to this two-part work, Lord admits that personal wonder about the local people who are "so strangely notable, and notably strange" bred in him "the importunity of a Questioner." To his queries the reply came that they are "Banians," a people whose religion and customs are not Christian and are not understood by the Christian world.[148] To learn about the "Banians," or Hindus, Lord consulted Brahmans, probably Nagar Brahmans, and had materials translated from a book "called the Shaster [Sanskrit, *sāstra*] which is to theme as their Bible."[149] From these materials

---

[145] Full title is *An East-India colation; or a Discourse of travels; set forth in sundry observations, briefe and delightfull. Collected by the author in a voyage he made unto the East India of almost foure yeares continuance.*

[146] On Kerridge's tenure in Surat see Gokhale, *op. cit.* (n. 57), p. 148.

[147] For bibliographical detail see above, pp. 569–70. Lord's book was republished in the eighteenth-century collections of Picart and Churchill and in John Pinkerton (ed.), *A General Collection of the Best and Most Interesting Voyages and Travels* (London, 1808–14), VIII, 523–72. For general commentary see R. C. Prasad, *op. cit.* (n. 5), pp. 323–57, and Stephen Neill, *A History of Christianity in India. The Beginnings to A.D. 1707* (Cambridge, 1984), pp. 375–76.

[148] The word "Banians" derives from *Vāṇiya* or merchant. Great numbers of the traders of western India claim to be of the Vaisya (merchant) caste and devotees of Jainism; indeed, Vaisnavism and Jainism are intermixed in this region. Lord, like other early European observers, does not distinguish between the Vaisya who are Jains and those who are not. Most Jain merchants still call themselves Hindus. See Yule and Burnell, *op. cit.* (n. 18), pp. 63–64, and R. C. Prasad, *op. cit.* (n. 5), pp. 324–25, n. 7.

[149] A *sāstra* is a compilation similar to a manual which treats particular religious or philosophi-

the Anglican chaplain assembled a digest of the "best Essence and ground of this Sect" while "leaving out for the most part such prodigious Fictions as seeme independent on sense and reason."

Lord's *Discoverie of the Banian Religion,* or Part I of his *Display of two forraigne sects,* is the first printed summary of Hindu doctrines and practices to appear in Europe.[150] It is polemical in intent and tone, and comparative in method. Organizationally Lord follows at first a Biblical arrangement beginning with the creation of the world and humankind, the universal deluge, and the repeopling of the earth. The "great God (say the Banians), being alone" consulted with himself as to how best to make manifest his excellency, power, and great virtue. What better means could there be to achieve this end than to create a world and to place creatures within it? Therefore God created four elements—earth, air, fire, and water. Initially mingled and confused, the elements were separated and assigned to their respective permanent functions. Compounded of four elements, the world was given four directions, was to endure for four ages, and was to be peopled by four castes of men, descendants of the first parents' four sons, who were to be married to four designated women.[151]

Once God made the world and its creatures, He lastly created man as "a creature more worthy then the rest." The first man, named "Pourous" (Purush), emerged from the bowels of the earth and God breathed life into him. Since he was by nature a sociable being, God endowed Purush with a woman called "Parcoutee" (Prakriti). They lived together as man and wife "feeding on the fruits of the earth, without the destruction of any living creature."[152] This couple produced four sons: "Brammon" (Brahman), "Cuttery" (Kshatriya), "Shuddery" (Sudra), and "Wyse" (Vaisya). Each brother was endowed by the elements with a different nature: Brahman was earthly and melancholy; Kshatriya "was of a fiery constitution"; Sudra was phlegmatic and peaceable; and Vaisya was "of an ayery temper, and therefore full of contrivements and inventions." God endowed Brahman with

---

cal subjects systematically. The philosophy of the Jains is contained in four *āgamas,* twenty-four *puranas,* and sixty-four *sāstras,* according to the Abbé Du Bois in H. K. Beauchamp (ed.), *Hindu Manners, Customs, and Ceremonies* (3d ed., Oxford, 1959), p. 694.

[150] For a critical review of this part of Lord's book see H. N. Randle, "Henry Lord and His Discoverie of the Banians," in S. K. Belvalkar *et al.* (eds.), *Jha Commemoration Volume. Essays on Oriental Subjects,* "Poona Oriental Series," XXXIX (Poona, 1937), pp. 277–96.

[151] Here Lord, basing himself on native informants, exhibits only a vague and confused notion of the idea of *Brahman* or cosmic unity. This is hardly surprising, because Hindu stories of creation, when they are not based on the Hindu scriptures themselves, are a melange of popular myths and beliefs. See R. C. Prasad, *op. cit.* (n. 5), p. 331. Lord's account resembles in some of its aspects the Puranic stories of creation. For example, see Thomas Hopkins, *The Hindu Religious Tradition* (Encino, Cal., 1971), pp. 100–101.

[152] In the Vedic tradition Purush is the cosmic Man or primal Person and Prakriti is Nature, a female who continuously produces offspring. See Hopkins, *op. cit.* (n. 151), pp. 22, 66. The notion that they live without killing any living creature probably reflects the Jainism of Lord's informants.

knowledge, appointed him to teach the divine precepts and the laws to others, and presented him with the sacred scripture; He gave Kshatriya the power to rule and maintain public order; He made Sudra into a merchant "to inrich the Commonwealth by Trafficke"; and because Vaisya was inventive He assigned to him the role of artisan.[153] Purush and Prakriti were given no daughters because God wanted no incest in His first family. Instead He created four women independently and placed one of them at each of the four main points of the compass. Thus divided they provided "a better meanes for the spreading of their generations over the face of the earth."[154]

Lord lavishly devotes four chapters, or twenty-two pages, of his brief book to romantic and fanciful descriptions of how the four brothers met their wives. Once each of the four quarters of the world was inhabited by their progeny, the brothers returned to their original home to teach one another about their assigned caste occupations. For a time all went well, but then wickedness and sin inevitably raised their ugly heads. Disputes over religion and law angered God and He caused a flood to cover the world. The bodies of men thus "had their judgement, but the Soules were lodged in the bosome of the Almighty" and so ended the first age (*yuga*) of the world.[155] The second age of the world is a work assigned to persons of greater perfection: to "Bremaw" (Brahma), "Vistury" (Vishnu), and "Ruddery" (Rudra or Siva). God, "descending from heaven to a great Mountain," called "Meropurbatee" (*Meru-parvatu*), created these three as his deputies. To Brahma he gave the power of creation and production, to Vishnu the strength to preserve Brahma's creatures, and to Rudra the execution of God's justice and the lordship of death.[156] Each of these deputies was allotted a designated period of time on earth. Since the creation is to be completed in the second age, Brahma will return to the Almighty at its conclusion. Vishnu is to stay on earth for twice as long, and Rudra "because the world should end in destruction," for three times as long. In this second creation man and woman were born from Brahma's body "in full growth and perfect stature." The man was named "Manow" (Manu) and the woman "Ceteroopa" (*Satar-ūpā,*

---

[153] This confusion about the roles of the Sudra and Vaisya orders is an error which Lord persists in making throughout his book. The Vaisya, the third *varna* (social subdivision) in order, are farmers and merchants. The Sudra, the fourth of the castes of Manu, the Lawgiver, were not merchants but the servile class. Randle (*loc. cit.* [n. 150], p. 283) contends that Lord makes the "Wyse" into "the representative of the 'Mechanicke or handy-crafts man,' because he was not thinking of the *Vaisya-varna* at all, but of the *Vaish* or carpenter subcaste of Gujarat; which figures also in the accounts of Arab travellers to western India." Also see below, p. 1031.

[154] R. C. Prasad, *op. cit.* (n. 5), p. 332, waxes indignant over the reason Lord gives for God's refusal to provide daughters to the first family. Perhaps Lord was only here exhibiting his own concern over the failure of the Hebrew tradition to explain how Cain and Abel were able to continue peopling the earth! Certainly there is no basis for Lord's story in Hindu literature.

[155] In his vague Christian way, Lord appears to be referring to a *kalpa* (age), or the period between creation and destruction. See Hopkins, *op. cit.* (n. 151), p. 101.

[156] According to R. C. Prasad, *op. cit.* (n. 5), p. 336: "The duties assigned [here] to the three supreme gods . . . are exactly the same as every Hindu believes them to be."

also called *Sāvitri*), and from their three sons and three daughters, whose names Lord gives, the world was repeopled.[157]

God, having learned by hard experience about the sinful nature of man, again descended to Mount Meru to give Brahma a book called the "Shaster, or the book of their written Word." It consists of three tracts, one containing moral precepts, the second on ceremonies, and the third on social divisions or castes.[158] Lord summarizes the first tract by propounding, following the Biblical tradition, a series of eight commandments. Two of the commandments are most religiously followed by each of the four orders, but all owe a general observance to each of the eight commandments. Most difficult for Lord to understand are the commandments prohibiting the killing of living creatures, the drinking of wine, and the eating of meat. He therefore launches into a scholarly analysis of these subjects based on what he knows about them from Western classical learning and other religions. His preoccupaton with the eating of flesh leads Lord to denounce their belief in the equality of all souls and in transmigration or metempsychosis as "a vaine imagination."

The second tract given to Brahma enjoins ceremonial bathing, markings, tree worship, temple prayers in which they repeat the names of the gods, offerings to their idols, processions, pilgrimages, invoking of particular gods for happiness, health, victory in war, and so forth, devotion to the sun and moon, cow worship, child-naming rites, and child marriages. His account of death and funeral practices is obviously based on close inquiry and on acute observations of caste differences. Men who are sick beyond hope utter the name of "Narraune" (Narayana) while others pour water into the outstretched hand. Once dead, the body is washed and then they take it to the riverside, place it on the ground, and pray over it. Then Lord describes in some detail the burning ceremony and quotes certain of the prayers directed to the four elements. The mourning period lasts for ten days. Widow immolation along with the husband "to this day is observed in some places, and for some persons of great worth, though the examples be more rare now than in former times." Lord then goes on to give the reasons for suttee as propounded by Propertius and Strabo.[159]

The third tract delivered to Brahma concerned castes, a system "commodious for the government of the world." Brahmans are of two kinds, common and special. The common Brahmans are of eighty-two kinds differentiated by their places of residence. These Brahmans pray with the people or read "the Law" to them. They also instruct and discipline the

---

[157] For their names see Randle, *loc. cit.* (n. 150), p. 286.

[158] This divine book, according to R. C. Prasad, *op. cit.* (n. 5), p. 338, was "one of the *Smṛtis*," and not a *śāstra*. *Smṛti* is a term which refers to the whole corpus of sacred lore remembered and handed down by tradition.

[159] On foreign references and commentaries on suttee see Edward Thompson, *Suttee. A Historical and Philosophical Enquiry into the Hindu Rite of Widow-Burning* (Boston and New York, 1928), chap. ii.

youths between seven and fourteen years of age. The special Brahmans called the "Vertea" (Jains) are of the merchant caste, wear white woolen garments, and pluck out the hair of their chins and heads, except for a tuft on the crown.[160] There are five subsects of the "Vertea," and Lord gives their names and differing practices.[161] Every month these Brahmans hold a festival called "Putcheson" (*Pajjosana,* or rain-retreat), which lasts for five days.[162] Special Brahmans follow more austerities than common Brahmans in being celibate, more abstemious, and more cautious about the preservation of life. They are also different in that they own all things in common and place no faith in ritual bathing.[163]

The Kshatriya, or the order of soldiers and rulers, flourished in Gujarat under its early rajas. These Hindu rajas came exclusively from thirty-six noble families so that "no man of obscure birth might presse to dignity."[164] They ruled with the aid of soothsaying Brahmans, a "Pardon" (*Pradhān* or minister), a "Moldar" (?), or royal chamberlain, and a "Disnache" (?), or military commander. The decline of the Gujarati state began with the death of "Ravisaldee" (Ra Visaladeva, r. 1243–61). His son called "Syderaysaldee" (Sarangdeva, r. 1274–94) erected a costly commemorative monument to his father at a place named "Sythepolalpore" (Sidhpur). A famous Brahman prophesized that "Sultan Alaudin" (Ala-ud-din Khalji, r. 1296–1315), the Pathan ruler of Delhi, would deface the monument while warring in Gujarat. To forestall such a travesty "Syderaysaldee" sent the Brahman and the "Pardon" to Delhi to bribe "Alaudin" to spare his father's tomb. When the emissaries were unable to locate "Alaudin" in Delhi, they approached the son of a poor woodcutter who bore that name. After due persuasion, the youth took their money and gave his written promise to spare the tomb and temple.[165] In accord with the prophecy, "Alaudin" became ruler of Delhi and invaded Gujarat with his Muslim forces. He dismantled the temple in part but, tiring of Gujarat, he retired to Delhi, leaving the completion of his conquests to "Futtercon" (Fatah Khan), his cupbearer. The Delhi forces occupied the country but failed to eliminate all of its Hindu rajas. In the interior of Gujarat the Rajputs, descendants of these early Hindu rulers, still

---

[160] A reference to the Jain ascetics or monks of the *Svetāmbara* or white-clad sect. For this identification of the "Vertea" and the Jesuit references to them see *Asia,* I, 459–60.

[161] The only readily identifiable one of his subsects (*gacchas*) is the "Tuppaes" (*Tapās*). For a scholarly modern list see S. B. Deo, *History of Jaina Monachism from Inscriptions and Literature* (Poona, 1956), pp. 519–45.

[162] See *ibid.,* pp. 383–84.

[163] A non-monastic class of Jain Brahmans exists, but they are not members of a caste as the Vedic Brahmans are. See P. S. Jaini, *The Jaina Path of Purification* (Berkeley, 1979), p. 291.

[164] Lord, *op. cit.* (text at n. 147), p. 77, gives the names of five of these families. Lord is correct in noting that there were thirty-six prominent and traditional Kshatriya families. See Majumdar, *op. cit.* (n. 64), p. 45.

[165] This is a reference to the twelfth-century temple of Siva at Sidhpur on the Sarasvati river in northern Gujarat. While it lies in ruins today, its beauty is fulsomely extolled in Gujarati ballads and popular tales. See Percy Brown, *Indian Architecture (Buddhist and Hindu Periods)* (5th ed.; Bombay, 1965), p. 122; also Majumdar, *op. cit.* (n. 64), pp. 99, 105–6.

prey on caravans and on the outskirts of towns. Of the Rajput princes who remain unconquered, Lord names five.[166]

According to Lord's summary of Hindu teaching, the world again became evil in its second age. So its people, except for a few preserved by Vishnu, were destroyed by Rudra (Siva). From the remnant saved, the Almighty inaugurated a third age. His instrument was "Ram" (Rama), a god who became so revered by the people that "whenever they meete and salute one another, they cry 'Ram, Ram,' as a word importing the wishes of all good." [167] But again men became evil and in due course the third age was brought to an end. The fourth and final age of the world was inaugurated by "Kystney" (Krishna), a famous and pious ruler. Since this is the final and longest age, Vishnu is no longer needed as a Preserver and is recalled to heaven. These ages are named "Curtain" (*Kṛta*), "Duauper" (*Dvapara*), "Tetraioo" (*Tretā*), and "Kolee" (*Kali*).[168] The final age will end in an all-consuming fire, and all that will remain are the principles of the four elements from which everything began and the souls of all mankind. To Lord these Hindu beliefs are "a composed Fiction" based upon the number four: *i.e.,* there are four principles (elements), points of the compass, ages, and castes; four men are matched to four women; and all will be demolished by four different destructions.

Part II of Lord's *Display* relates to the history and religion of the "Persees" (Parsis), the Persian followers of Zoroaster who had arrived in India during the eighth century. A Parsi employed in the English factory of Surat acted as interpreter for Lord in his conversations with a "Darod" (dastur), one of their chief priests. From this priest the Englishman learned something about the history and beliefs of the Parsis as well as the scripture called the "Zundavastaw" (Zend-Avesta). His eight chapters on the Parsis are briefer and less confused than his lengthier discussion of Hindu beliefs and practices. The introductory chapter, perhaps more important for historical purposes than any of the other seven, relates to the early history of the Parsis. It is a sketchy but authentic account based on the oral tradition of the origins of their movement in Persia and of their migration to India.[169] The second

---

[166] The overthrow of the Solanki dynasty in 1297 brought Gujarat under the control of the Muslims of the Delhi sultanate. Gujarat was finally subdued by Ulugh Khan, brother of Ala-ud-din Khalji. For almost one century following, the sultans of Delhi ruled the open country of south Gujarat by governors. Many Hindu princes of Gujarat and Rajasthan continued to resist Muslim control and periodically revolted against the appointees of Delhi. In 1609 Baroda and Surat were invaded by Malik Ambar, a noble of Nizam Shah's court (Ahmadnagar), thus illustrating how shaky Mughul power still was in Gujarat when the Dutch and English became active at Surat. See Majumdar, *op. cit.* (n. 64), pp. 106–12.

[167] The name Rama is one of the basic mantras or prayers. "Ram" is sometimes considered the basic sound, the causal word from which all language is issued. See A. Daniélou, *Hindu Polytheism* (New York, 1964), p. 174.

[168] These are the four *yugas*, or ages of the world. Lord interchanges the second and third ages. He is also wrong in asserting that the final age is the longest; it is actually conceived to be the shortest. See *ibid.,* p. 249.

[169] His history of the early Parsis is based on oral traditions handed down over nine centuries.

chapter is an abridgment of their beliefs about creation and their relation to Persian historical legends. In the next three chapters, Lord gives a somewhat garbled biography of Zoroaster, his meditations on wickedness, his meeting with the Angel, and his struggle with the devil. In the final three chapters, Lord lists what he calls the "three several Tracts" of the Zend-Avesta and gives a digest of each in brief. From these scriptures he culled twenty-nine commandments in which he attempts to summarize the moral and religious precepts of the Parsis. Like many European Christians since, Lord was most impressed by the Parsis' veneration of fire and by the custom of exposing their dead on "Towers of Silence" to be devoured by divinely dispatched birds.[170]

The other mid-century commentators focus their attention on the cities, trade, and secular life of Gujarat. The "Indian letters" of Pietro della Valle (1586–1652) were first published in 1663 by four of his sons under the short title *Viaggi*.[171] "Il Pellegrino," as Della Valle styled himself, was in Gujarat from February 10 to March 22, 1623. Although he was an independent "pilgrim" unassociated with chartered companies or the Catholic church, Della Valle moved about readily, since he spoke Turkish, Persian, and Arabic, important languages of commerce and government in Gujarat. To an educated Roman humanist the seaport Portuguese spoken in western India was also no mystery: he repeatedly cites Portuguese authors, including João de Barros and Garcia da Orta. As a man of experience and education, the Italian was most hospitably received and entertained by the chief English and Dutch factors at Surat. His letters from India, unlike his Turkish and Persian letters, probably were published in their pristine form as received by his Neapolitan friend Mario Schipano. To judge from the context and their diary style, the Indian letters were left untouched by the author himself and by all the others associated with their publication.[172] The delay of forty years between their composition and their publication appears not to have lessened their attraction to contemporaries, for they immediately went through several subsequent editions in Italian and were quickly translated into French, English, Dutch, and German.[173]

During his forty days in Gujarat, Della Valle traveled from his base at Surat to Broach, Cambay, and Ahmadabad. In these travels he was aided by

---

These traditions were first summarized in writing in 1599 by a Parsi priest of Surat in a Persian poem entitled *Kisseh-i-Sanjan*. See M. S. Commissariat, *A History of Gujarat* (2 vols.; Bombay, 1957), II, 344–45.

[170] For further commentary see R. C. Prasad, *op. cit.* (n. 5), pp. 344–54.

[171] For bibliographical details see above, p. 380. What follows is based on the English translation of 1665 as edited by Edward Grey, in *The Travels of Pietro della Valle in India* (2 vols.; "HS," o.s., LXXXIV–V; London, 1892). Also see Peter K. Bietenholz, *Pietro Della Valla (1586–1652)* (Basel and Stuttgart, 1962), pp. 105–12, 197; and Commissariat, *op. cit.* (n. 169), II, 326–39.

[172] Grey (ed.), *op. cit.* (n. 171), I, xli.

[173] See above, p. 380.

the English and Dutch factors who permitted him to accompany their trading caravans and arranged for his lodging; indeed they vied with one another to help out the Italian and to make his stay comfortable. They freed thus from attending to his daily needs, Della Valle was able to make good use of his brief time. He was informed by the factors and their Indian associates about local history, customs, and important sites. They kept him abreast of events reported and rumored about the civil war then raging between Jahangir and his rebellious son Shah Jahan. Because he was an experienced Oriental traveler, Della Valle himself was prepared in terms of languages and his understanding of Islam to make the most of this opportunity. In India he was particularly interested, partly because of what he had learned in Persia, to observe non-Islamic monuments, customs, and beliefs. In Gujarat, as also later in Kanara, his major concern was to observe and understand the vestiges of pre-European civilization in India—*i.e.*, Hinduism.[174] To this end he had read widely about India in European classical and contemporary literature. His intellectual concern, as a humanist, was to determine what doctrines and traditions lay behind religious practices so utterly foreign to both Christianity and Islam. His visit in Gujarat, perhaps because it was so brief, raised for him more questions than answers about Hinduism.

Already in Surat he was impressed by the religious freedom and equality of treatment accorded by the Mughul authorities to all the diverse groups in the city. Its Hindu majority, although ruled by Muslim Mughuls, lives peaceably and freely with all the other groups in this mixed society, and many of its members are admitted to high government and military posts.[175] As part of his study of Hinduism, Della Valle observes and describes the weddings, funerals, and religious ceremonies of what he calls "Gentile Idolaters." He writes in particular about the worship in Surat of an idol engraved on the trunk of a huge "Nir" (*Bar*) or banyan tree dedicated to "Parveti" (*Parvati*), the wife of "Mahadeù" (*Maha-deva*, or Siva).[176] He finds most remarkable the "very large Cistern, or Artificial Pool" called "Gopi Telau" (*Gopi Talao*), or tank of Gopi. This huge tank was constructed by a former Hindu governor of Surat named Malik Gopi for the enjoyment of the public.[177] Other public tanks, even larger and more magnificent, exist elsewhere in India to help the public conserve water and escape from the oppressive heat. Always captivated by the strange flora and fauna of India, Della Valle visits gardens and parks to study and describe trees and flowers

[174] On his trip to Hindu-governed Ikkeri in Kanara see below, pp. 863–69.

[175] Grey (ed.), *op. cit.* (n. 171), I, 30, 35. *Cf.* Commissariat, *op. cit.* (n. 169), II, 329.

[176] Grey (ed.), *op. cit.* (n. 171), I, 35–38. On tree-worship see Majumdar, *op. cit.* (n. 64), pp. 244–45. See also our pl. 127.

[177] Grey (ed.), *op. cit.* (n. 171), I, 32–35. The *Gopi Talao* no longer functions as a reservoir, and few traces of it remain. On Malik Gopi see Commissariat, *op. cit.* (n. 57), pp. 99–100. Also see above, p. 617, for De Laet's reference.

unknown to Dioscorides, Pliny, or later botanists. He concludes "that to write fully of them would require express [special] volumes."[178]

Life in Surat is made easy and pleasant for Europeans, as well as for Indians of means, by the great number of available servants and slaves. Wherever they are, servants are always armed with "Sword, Buckler, Bows, and Arrows." Public personages and private individuals "of whatever Country or Religion" are free to live "with as much grandeur and equipage . . . as the King himself." Because servants and slaves are plentiful and inexpensive, even a person "of mean fortune keeps a great family." All classes wear white cotton clothes of various qualities "for the most part very fine in comparisons of those of our Countries." Della Valle was "taken with this Indian dress" because of its cleanliness and comfort, "and for the goodly show me thought it had on horseback." He therefore had one made for himself "complete in every point," to take back to Italy as a showpiece.[179]

Muslim women, especially Mughuls, also dress in white cottons or in certain textiles decorated with gold flowers (*kimkhbāb*, or gold brocade). They wear a short upper garment above their drawers; generally these are plain red or white in color but sometimes they dress in striped silks of various hues. Frequently they wear turbans like the men or, at other times, matching headbands. When they walk or ride in the city, the Muslim women cover their faces with a white veil. Hindu women generally dress in red or variegated cottons "which thay call cit [chintz]." Their "close wastecoat" (*choli*) has sleeves only to the middle of the arm, the rest of it being bedecked with bracelets. From the waist to the foot they wear a long skirt. When out-of-doors, they generally cover themselves with a red or variegated cloak. Those who can afford it wear jewelry, especially large ear-pendants. Although Hindu women do not cover their faces, they are nonetheless modest and respectable. Muslim women are more likely to be "publick Courtisans" than are their Hindu sisters.[180]

On February 23, Della Valle left Surat for his visit to Cambay, a city he had learned about in Persia. It is reputed to be "one of the ancientest of India" in which live numerous Hindus who are "above measure observers of their Rites." Proceeding due north, the five coaches in whose company he traveled are ferried across the Narbada River to "Barocci or Behrug" (Broach). This medium-sized city "built high upon a rising hill" is enclosed by a wall. Its substantial population produces vast amounts of cotton cloths for export to Asia and Europe. The Dutch and English maintain permanent factories there to purchase these textiles which are packed for shipping "in very great

[178] Grey (ed.), *op. cit.* (n. 171), I, 40. On the special volumes actually published in Europe during the late seventeenth century on flora, see below, pp. 925–27.
[179] *Ibid.*, pp. 41–44. After his return to Rome in 1626, Della Valle's collection of curiosities was visited regularly by interested people.
[180] *Ibid.*, pp. 44–46.

bales, each as big as a Roman Coach." The agates and chalcedonies (milky quartz) mined near Broach are marketed at Cambay, where some are also turned into jewelry and diverse ornaments. On the road the next day, Della Valle meets noble Mughul refugees from the civil war just before his arrival at "Giambaser" (Jambusar). Here he and his companions join a "great *Cafila* [*kafila*], or *Caravan*" for the last leg of the journey to Cambay. On nearing that town, Della Valle crosses the broad mouth of the "Mehi" (Mahi) river at the innermost part of the Gulf of Cambay. Here "the flux and reflux of the Sea is more impetuous and violent . . . than perhaps in any other part of the world." At low tide they traverse the lowland ordinarily under water and ford those deep streams still remaining. Arrived in Cambay, Della Valle and his group are lodged in the house of the Dutch merchants.

Cambay is "seated on the Seashore, in a plain almost in the utmost recess of that great Gulph whereunto it gives its name." It is of moderate size with most of its people living in suburbs outside the walls. Since most of its inhabitants are strict "Gentiles" (*i.e.*, Jains), Della Valle eagerly seeks out their most unique and characteristic institutions. He visits the bird (*parabdis*) and animal (*panjrapols*) hospitals of the Jains, whose attendants "are maintained by the publick alms." In one of these places the compassionate Jains, much to Della Valle's surprise, care for a Muslim thief whose hands had been cut off. Outside one of the city gates he sees herds of cows and goats put out to pasture after being cured of their ills. Among them are goats redeemed by Jain money payments to be saved from slaughter. Cows, calves, and oxen may not be slaughtered by anyone, since the Jains pay the governor of Cambay to enforce this prohibition.[181]

Thereafter Della Valle busily sets out to visit the Hindu and Jain temples of Cambay. He is particularly puzzled by their idols and other aspects of Hindu iconography. While disgusted by the "ridiculous stories" he hears from "foolish and ignorant Indians" about their gods, he is convinced that "these so monstrous figures have secretly some more rational significations." To investigate these matters further, he talks through an interpreter with an old Brahman who shows him certain Sanskrit books known only to the priestly caste. Dissatisfied by what he is able to learn from personal observations and his European merchant friends, Della Valle decides to defer his efforts to understand Hindu theology. Once in Goa he hopes to consult in Portuguese with a Brahman "perhaps turned Christian" and to read the books of "Father Francesco Negrone, or Negraone" relating to the trials and tribulations of the Franciscans in dealing with the Hindus.[182]

---

[181] Della Valle ascribes these charities to their belief in the transmigration of souls. These practices are actually related to the Jain doctrine of *ahimsa* (nonviolence). Bird and animal hospitals are still maintained in Gujarat by the Jains.

[182] *Ibid.*, pp. 109–11. Francisco Negrão, a Luso-Indian Franciscan, was the chronicler of the Province of St. Thomas. He spent about ten years gathering information on Hinduism in Vi-

Thwarted in his attempt to understand the authentic traditions of Hinduism, Della Valle is forced to content himself, as others generally were, with externals, such as temples, idols, ceremonies, and customs. He notices that the Muslims of Gujarat have adopted certain Hindu practices and attitudes.[183] The color red is for some reason favored by the Indians for interior decoration and personal costume. Hindus are divided into many social classes, "'Tis reckoned that they are in all eighty-four."[184] Each has its own name, employment, or function; social status is inherited and unalterable. Caste intermarriage is not practiced among the four principal groups: "the Brahmans, the Souldiers, the Merchants, and the Artificers." Religiously they are all in substantial agreement and regard "all other Nations and Religions besides themselves unclean." Brahmans, who "resemble the Levites of the Jews," are of several kinds, the most highly esteemed being the "Boti" (*Bhāt*) who act as temple priests.[185] Other Brahmans function as astrologers, physicians, court secretaries, and scholars. All of them fear being polluted by eating with others or being touched by others. In case of pollution, they purify themselves "by washing and other arrogant Ceremonies." The lower castes studiously avoid contact with members of the higher castes. To avoid defilement by drinking from the same cup, they have learned how to pour water into the mouth without placing the lips on the containing vessel. Intrigued by this technique of "drinking in the Air," Della Valle learned to do it himself as a social convenience.

Hindus of the same caste adhere to the same moral code. They denounce as sinful all fornication outside of marriage, especially adultery. Sodomy is particularly reprehensible, and they detest those Muslims addicted to it. Ordinarily they take but one wife and never divorce except for adultery. Sometimes, usually because they are rich or because the wife remains barren, they will take other wives. While polygamy is legal to all, it is not a highly regarded practice except in the case of princes. Should the wife die, the husband may remarry; widows are not able to remarry and consequently some of them secretly have liaisons with men of other nations or religions. Some widows voluntarily are burnt with the bodies of their husbands. While self-immolation is unusual, "she who does it acquires in the Nation a glorious

---

jayanagar, Ceylon, and other centers while preparing a book on the religious system of the Brahmans. In 1619 he was sent to Europe and on the way met Della Valle at Ispahan. Negrão was evidently unsuccessful in both Rome and Portugal in finding a publisher. In 1622 he returned to India. Both his "Chronicle" and his work on Hinduism went unprinted. When Della Valle later conversed with him in Goa, the Roman decided that Negrão was "very little vers'd in matters of ancient History and Geography," an irreparable deficiency when writing about "the Customs of the Indians, of which also he hath no other information but by interpreters." *Cf.* the work of the Jesuit Fenicio in Calicut, below, pp. 874–76.

[183] *Ibid.,* p. 69.

[184] This number "eighty-four," or a number close to it, appears regularly in the European works when caste is discussed. See below, pp. 807–8, for a possible explanation.

[185] The *Bhāt* were especially highly regarded in Rajputana and Gujarat.

name of Honour and Holiness." [186] The wives of persons of high station are usually burnt with the husband. Some women are reportedly burnt against their will by force or by familial and social pressure; this is firmly denied by the Hindus. In regions governed by the Mughuls, no widow may be burnt alive without the permission of the governor. He first determines if she desires suttee. If the answer is in the affirmative, he issues a license for which a sum of money is paid. [187] In Portuguese-controlled territories suttee and other Hindu religious practices are strictly prohibited. To the Hindus the greatest sin in the world is the spilling of blood and the eating of flesh, especially of humans and cows. All Hindus wash frequently both for the sake of cleanliness and as a ceremonial rite of purification.

The Brahmans and a few highly regarded members of the lower castes wear a "fillet of three braids, which they put next the flesh like a Neckchain, passing from the left shoulder under the right arm, and so round." [188] This fillet or thread, which the Portuguese call *linha,* occasioned a dispute in India between the Jesuits and the other Christian orders which was quickly carried to Rome. The debate revolved about whether or not this thread was "a badge of religion" and whether Christian converts might be permitted to retain it. While in Persia, Della Valle had learned that the Jesuits considered the thread to be "only an ensign of piety" and a simple mark of civil distinction awarded to Muslims as well as to Hindus. Consequently they would permit the converts to wear it but abolish the award ceremonies, which they considered to be religious in nature. They would also Christianize its symbolism by identifying the three threads with the Trinity, "or in some such manner turning it to a pious and lawful use." [189]

On the road going northeast to Ahmadabad, Della Valle observes great "Trees of Tamarinds, which the Indians call Hambele," mango trees, and small, white squirrels "leaping amongst the trees everywhere." [190] Many armed ruffians pretending to be beggars prey upon lone travelers on these roads. The highway into Ahmadabad, while dusty and dirty, is lined on both sides with tall hedges of cactus, "a plant always green and unfruitful, not known in Europe." Once at their destination, Della Valle and his companions live in a rented house in the quarter for foreigners called "Terzi Carvanserai" (*Darzi caravanserai*) or "Tayler's Inn." At night these streets are locked

[186] *Satī,* or "a woman who is pure."
[187] This is a correct statement of Mughul policy towards suttee. See Commissariat, *op. cit.* (n. 169), p. 335.
[188] This is the sacred thread (Sanskrit, *upavita*) ordained by the Vedas to be worn by members of the three highest castes. It is composed of three cords, each of which contains nine threads.
[189] Grey (ed.), *op. cit.* (n. 171), I, 77–91.
[190] Tamarind (Arabic, *tamr,* or fruit; hence fruit of India) trees (Gujarati, *ambli*) are almost as useful as the coco palm of India (see pl. 170). Practically all parts of this tree, which often grows to a huge size in south India, is used as food and medicine, or as sizing and creaming agents in industry. See J. S. Pruthi, *Spices and Condiments* (New Delhi, 1976), pp. 217–19. Light-colored squirrels with stripes on the back (*Funambulus pennanti*) are common from the Himalayas southward. See S. H. Prater, *The Book of Indian Animals* (2d rev. ed.; Bombay, 1965), p. 200.

up for the security of the wayfarer and his belongings. The straight streets of the city, like the country roads, are badly paved and unpleasantly dusty.[191]

Ahmadabad's principal business street is called "Bezari Kelan" (*Bazaar-i-Kalān*), or "Great Merkat." Three arches span its middle, and further on stands "a great well, round about which is built a square Piazzetta [an arched gallery]." At the end of the market street is a "Great Gate" which faces the three arches and opens into "a small Castle which they call by the Persian word Cut [*khat*]."[192] Near this gate, in an open area, stand two stone "pulpits" from which the imperial commands are proclaimed to the public. To the right at some distance is the imperial palace, for Ahmadabad "is one of the four cities . . . where the *Grand Moghul* by particular privilege hath a Palace and a Court."[193] This palace stands in a great square courtyard enclosed by white, polished walls, in the middle of which there is a "high Post to shoot at with arrows, as is usual in the *Piazzas* of Persia." On the left side of the yard is the imperial residence. Beneath its windows is a raised platform enclosed by a window railing where the "*Mansubdàr*" (*mansabdārs*, or officers) assemble to attend the emperor. Officers of higher ranks, such as the "Chans" (*Khāns*), take their places on nearby balconies while the common soldiers line up in the courtyard itself. At the front of the courtyard is the lodging of the palace guard; other plainer buildings here and there house the various bureaus of government.[194]

In his rambles about Ahmadabad and elsewhere, Della Valle is much impressed by the omnipresent "Gioghi" (yogis), whom he identifies as "the ancient Gymnosophists so famous in the world" of classical antiquity. Within a renowed temple dedicated to "Mahedeu" (*Maha-deva,* or Siva), stand many nearly naked yogis with disheveled hair and red, yellow, and other markings on their foreheads. They differ from other yogis in that their bodies are not smeared with colors and ashes but are "clean and smooth." Some of the younger yogis sell flowers to the temple's many worshippers who offer them to the idols. Other yogis "of more austere lives" congregate in the sun on the bank of the "little river called Sabermeti [Sabarmati]." They are of the type who sprinkle their bodies with ashes and paint themselves with white powder. Their hair and beards are long and untrimmed, and some style their hair to look like horns. Ordinarily they sit in a circle around a leader whom they religiously obey. Another yogi sits alone crosslegged in a little chapel meditating under cramped conditions.[195]

[191] Jahangir reputedly called it "Gardabad" or "city of dust." See John Murray (publ.), *A Handbook for Travellers in India, Pakistan, Burma, and Ceylon* (18th ed.; London, 1959), p. 160.
[192] Here he refers to the Triple Gateways (*Tin Darwaza*) which still stand above this main street, and to the east entrance of the Bhadar castle built in 1411. See *ibid.,* p. 162.
[193] The other cities were Agra, Mandu, and Lahore.
[194] This description of the old imperial palace is unique in travel literature. See Commissariat, *op. cit.* (n. 169), p. 337, n. 20. The present palace was built later in the seventeenth century by Azam Khan, viceroy from 1635 to 1642.
[195] Grey (ed.), *op. cit.* (n. 171), I, 99–101.

After one week in Ahmadabad, Della Valle leaves for Cambay on the return trip with the caravan in which he had come. Just outside the city he and his companions make a quick visit to a "great Artificial Lake . . . made of stone, with stairs at several angles about it." Estimating its diameter at "about half a mile," he notes that there is a little island garden in its middle that is attached to the shore "by a handsome Bridge of many Arches." [196] Shortly after arriving in Cambay, Della Valle goes to the tower of a tomb to observe "the coming in of the Tide" of the new moon which is much faster and greater than the usual tides. [197] Always on the watch for yogis, Della Valle visits a suburb of Cambay called "Causari" (Kaira?) to visit a temple of the "Vertia" (Jains), [198] an unusual group of Indians who shave their heads. At another nearby temple he sees yogis sitting in a circle around their leader like those observed earlier on the river bank at Ahmadabad. Men become yogis not "by Descent but by Choice, as our Religious Orders are." They live on alms and despise clothes and all worldly things. They profess chastity, but often engage in debaucheries. They have no settled residence but live "in society under the obedience of their Superiors." They wander about and congregate at places they consider holy. They practice spiritual exercises and follow a sacred book which in Persian is entitled "*Damerdbigiaska*" (*Svetāśvatara?*), a work that Della Valle intends to take back to Italy to translate. [199] According to this book, they hope by means of spiritual exercises to receive "Revelations." Forty "Immortal, Spiritual, Invisible Women," whom they worship as deities, foretell the future and have "carnal commerce" with them. [200] The yogis follow a method "of Divining by the breathing of a Man . . . which I upon tryal have found true." [201] While Della Valle denounces all of these exercises and beliefs as delusions inspired by the devil, he is nonetheless acutely interested in observing and studying them himself.

Two miles outside of Cambay, Della Valle visits the ancient town of "Nagra" (Nagara) to see a Hindu temple famous for being dedicated to Brahma and for its three-faced statue of him. [202] On the way back to Cambay he sees some of the low-caste people called "Der" (*Dher*) who eat every-

---

[196] This is Kankariya Lake, or Pebble Lake, constructed in 1451; it was surrounded by many tiers of cutstone steps. The island in the middle has a garden called *Nagina,* or "the Gem." See Murray, *op. cit.* (n. 191), p. 165.

[197] This is called the "Bore" of Cambay, a sudden influx of the tide which rises and falls in the spring by as much as thirty-three feet. While Della Valle seems to think of this as unique to the Gulf of Cambay, similar phenomena occur in many estuaries. The word "bore" is derived from Icelandic *bāra* meaning wave.

[198] Grey (ed.), *op. cit.* (n. 171), I, p. 104, n. 2, identifies, possibly wrongly, this sect as the worshippers of Vishnu. On the "Vertea" as Jains see above, p. 649.

[199] No record exists, so far as we know, of such a translation.

[200] A reference to the *apsaras* (essences); their numbers are large, far larger than forty.

[201] They produce ecstasy or fantasies by holding the breath as long as possible or by inhaling and exhaling through different nostrils. *Cf.* Du Bois' report in Beauchamp (ed.), *op. cit.* (n. 149), pp. 531–32.

[202] Very few Hindu temples are dedicated to Brahma. On Nagara see Commissariat, *op. cit.* (n. 169), p. 338.

thing including rats. Other groups will neither converse with nor touch them.[203] On the following day he again tours the gardens to observe the flowers unknown in Europe. One of those which he collected is a "very odiferous" flower called "Ciompa" (*champa*).[204] His time running short, he makes hurried visits to the seashore to see the salt-pans and the Hindu burning ground. Early the next morning, he and his companions return to observe "the Funeral of one Woman from the beginning to the end."[205] Shortly before leaving Cambay, they are entertained at "the Dutch house" by an Indian musician from the court of Bijapur. His instrument is "made of two round Gourds, dy'd black and varnish'd, with a hole bor'd in one of them to reverberate the sound." Della Valle then gives more details of its construction and describes how to play what was probably the seven-stringed *vina*.[206]

On March 7, 1623, Della Valle leaves Cambay with a caravan that crosses the delta of the Mahi River and on the following day arrives at Broach. On its outskirts he observes "a handsome structure standing upon a famous Sepulchre of I know not well whom." It seems to be the tomb of a famous person, for it is held sacred and worshipped by the Muslims. This mausoleum, pleasantly situated among the trees near a small lake, houses many "other Sepulchres of white Marble, of an oblong form." Around this central structure are a number of other graves; this seems to indicate that Muslims are buried there "out of devotion to the place."[207] On March 10 the Italian and his companions return to Surat, where he remains for thirteen days preparing for his voyage to Goa. Among other matters, he worries about problems with the customs authorities "upon the account of the Moorish books which I had with me." He is also a witness to the spring festival of "the Indian-Gentiles" which they riotously celebrate with dancing in the street, throwing of colored waters and powders on one another, and "other festivities of Songs and Mummeries."[208] He also attends a wedding of a Dutch merchant and the daughter of a Syrian or Armenian merchant, which he sees as an example of the Dutch policy of encouraging their

---

[203] *Dher* or *Dhēd* is the name of an exterior caste of field laborers and private servants of western India. In April, 1931, a social confrontation occurred at Kaira when *Dhēd*s took their seats with other Hindu boys in the municipal school. See J. H. Hutton, *Caste in India* (4th ed.; Bombay, 1963), p. 201. In Mughul Persian they are called *halalkhor*, or people who regard all things as being lawful to eat.

[204] A kind of magnolia, the flower of *Michelia champaca* (Linn.). The name *champaca* derives from the kingdom of Champa in Indochina where the tree also grows. The flower is pale yellow in color and is a favorite in India.

[205] He gives a very detailed description of the whole ceremony. Grey (ed.), *op. cit.* (n. 171), I, 114–16.

[206] *Ibid.*, p. 117, n. 4. On the *vina* or "Indian lyre" see C. R. Day, *The Music and Musical Instruments of Southern India and the Deccan* (Delhi, 1974 reprint of 1891 edition), pp. 109–10.

[207] This is a description of the *rauza* (mausoleum) of Imad-ul-Mulk who lived during the last days of the Gujarat sultanate. It was built in his honor by his son, Changiz Khan. See Commissariat, *op. cit.* (n. 169), pp. 338–39.

[208] Grey (ed.), *op. cit.* (n. 171), I, 122–23. This is the Holi festival held fifteen days before the vernal equinox in honor of Krishna and the approaching spring season.

nationals in the East to marry wives "of any kind" as part of its program for peopling "New Batavia" in Java. On March 23 Della Valle sets sail in a small shallop (*almadia*) for Damão, the first stopover on his way to Goa.[209]

Four and one-half years after Della Valle's departure from Surat, Thomas Herbert arrived at its port. The young Englishman was attached to the suite of Sir Dadmore Cotton, the English ambassador accredited to the court of Shah Abbas then on his way to Persia. After a brief stopover in Surat, Herbert and the embassy continued their voyage to Persia. Herbert came to Surat again late in 1628 on his way back to England. He returned to London in 1630 and four years later published there *A Description of the Persian Monarchy* in which he also recounts his experiences in India. In 1638 he published a revised and enlarged edition of this work under the title *Some yeares travels into divers parts of Asia and Afrique.* In his first edition Herbert freely included materials garnered from the writings of others; in his second edition he increased the size of his work by four-fifths through additions of more secondhand materials. His summaries of the religions of the "Bannyan" (1638 ed., pp. 40–48) and the "Perses" (pp. 48–54) are taken straight from Lord's work. Much of "The History of the great Mogull" (pp. 54–108) derives from Purchas' collection and especially from De Laet's Latin work. Herbert's chronicle carries the history of the Mughuls from Tamerlane to the 1630's and is the first systematic history of the Mughuls to appear in the English language. Herbert's "Third Book" (pp. 295–364), which deals with eastern India, the further East, and America, is derived exclusively from the works of others. His vocabularies and maps are likewise not original. His work on India is original only with respect to the descriptions of the west coast, especially Surat.[210]

Herbert was in Surat at the end of 1627 for almost three weeks; on the return he was there for more than three months from December, 1628, to March, 1629. From his ship anchored in "Swally Road" (Suwali) Herbert sees the ruined town of Gogha "beyond the sands."[211] After disembarking on December 1, he rides to Surat in an oxcart "with some Pe-unes (or olive-colored Indian foot-boys who very prettily prattle English)." On the way he passes through Suwali town and the villages of "Bathy [Batha], famous for good toddy," and "Damkee" (Damka). Surat itself is "the third-best town" in Gujarat and is surpassed only by Ahmadabad and Cambay. Its prominence as a mart goes back "scarce 100 years ago" when the Portuguese

[209] For the Della Valle materials on the trip from Ahmadabad to Surat see *ibid.*, I, 101–25; for his descriptions of Goa and the south, see below, pp. 845, 863–68.

[210] For an abridged version, based on the author's final revision and enlargement of 1677, see William Foster (ed.), *Thomas Herbert, Travels in Persia, 1627–1629* (Freeport, N.Y., 1972 reprint of edition of 1929). For further bibliographical details on Herbert's later editions see above, pp. 571–72.

[211] Formerly a seaport of importance, the town of Gogha (or Goga) was ruthlessly sacked and pillaged by the Portuguese on several occasions during the sixteenth century. See Yule and Burnell, *op. cit.* (n. 18), pp. 382–83.

burned down the original town. Now it is under a "quiet government" and is much more populous and richer than before.[212] Its houses are "indifferent beautiful: some (as to the outside) are of carved wood, others of bricks dried in the sun." Surat has no monuments or mosques worth noting.[213] Outside the town there is an English garden, and "adjoining Navsāri gate" is a very large tank capable of holding rainwater enough "to quench the flagrant thirst of these sun-burnt Indians."[214]

Herbert vividly describes the animation of the port of Suwali when the ships arrive there between September and March each year; these remarks are probably based on observations made in 1629 when he left that port in March. As the ships arrive, the "Banians" pitch tents and erect booths and straw huts in great numbers all along the coast. At the market so created they sell "calicoes, China satin, porcelains, scrutores [writing desks] or cabinets of mother of pearl, ebony, ivory, agates, turquoises, heliotropes, cornelians; as also rice, sugar, plantains, arrack etc." Many little boys work here for a pittance running errands, doing odd jobs, or acting as interpreters. The crafty merchants "make many simple men lose themselves" by "the sugared words" they use in trading. They are quick at numbers and well versed in the various currencies in common use. The tawny "Banians" are lean of body with long hair. Their heads they wrap in white turbans, and their bodies are generally covered with long, white coats. Footware is unique to each man and "various in color and fashions." The women, who are lighter than the men, rouge their faces and load themselves with bracelets and "fetters of brass, gold, and ivory." Over their long and disheveled hair they throw a piece of "fine white lawn, through whose transparency it seems more lovely."[215]

The Parsis, "another sort of Gentiles in Surat," are distinguished for Herbert by their funerals. They neither burn nor bury their dead. The corpse is first placed in a "winding-sheet" and carried in procession accompanied by relatives who quietly beat their breasts. Fifty paces or so from the resting place they are met by "the Herbood" (Persian, *hirbad,* a Parsi priest) who usually wears a yellow scarf and a thin turban. "Necesselars" (*nasāsālārs,* or bearers) carry the corpse on an iron bier, "for wood is forbidden in that it is dedicated to fire," to a little shed where the last rites are performed. Then they hoist the corpse to the top of a round building "some of which are twelve foot high and eighty in circuit." Through its entrance, generally on the northeast side, they take the corpse into the monument, "good men into

---

[212] Surat was burned in 1530 by Antonio da Silveira; the new town was taken by Akbar in 1573. See *ibid.,* pp. 874–75. On Akbar's relations with the Portuguese at Surat see *Asia,* I, 457.

[213] A strange remark from one who had never visited India before. Two important mosques constructed in 1530 and 1540 still stand there. See Murray, *op. cit.* (n. 191), p. 155.

[214] Again a reference to the *Gopi Talao. Cf.* above, pp. 617, 652. For Herbert's general comments on Surat see Foster (ed.), *op. cit.* (n. 210), pp. 32–34.

[215] *Ibid.,* pp. 34–36.

one, bad into another." Its flat roof is open to the air and is "plastered with white loam." In its center there is a hole "to let in the putrefactions from the melted bodies." The corpses are laid naked in two rows "exposed to the sun's rage and [to the] appetite of ravening birds." The stench from these unburied bodies, "in some places 300," is loathsome. Herbert admits that the Parsis expressed their displeasure "at my taking a view of this golgotha."[216]

Six or seven years after Herbert's arrival in Surat, the Dutch merchant Johan van Twist took up work in Gujarat for several years. In 1635 he became chief of the VOC factories at Ahmadabad, Cambay, and Broach. After being recalled to Batavia in 1636, he was sent in the following year to Bijapur as leader of the Dutch mission to the 'Adil Shah.[217] Successful in this mission, Van Twist in 1639 was elevated to be an extraordinary member of the Council of the Indies. While in Batavia he was probably engaged in writing his "Generale beschrijvinge van Indien ende in 't besonder van 't coninckrijck van Guseratten." This work was first published at Amsterdam in 1646 in Isaac Commelin's collection known as the *Begin ende Voortgangh*.[218] In 1640 Van Twist was given command of the siege of Malacca and after its capture became the first governor. He died at Batavia in 1643, several years before his book was printed.[219]

Van Twist's "General Description of India" is avowedly a work of compilation interspersed with personal observations, especially with reference to Gujarat and Bijapur. Its general matter, as well as many of its more specific data, is taken in large measure from De Laet's Latin compilation, Linschoten, the Jesuits, Teixeira, the Purchas collection, the "Remonstrantie" of Pelsaert, the then-unpublished Gujarat report (1629) of the Dutch factor Wollebrandt Geleynssen de Jongh (1594–1674), and other unnamed Dutch writers.[220] The new materials of interest to European contemporaries include those taken from the Gujarat report, the unidentified Dutch authors, and the eyewitness accounts by Van Twist himself.

Gujarat, the most fruitful part of India, traditionally is self-sufficient and even exports provisions to other places. Throughout its history Gujarat has carried on a flourishing trade with its neighbors and even distant countries. Representatives of all the Asian nations except China and Japan congregate there to carry on trade. But "God blazed up against the sins and abominations of these various nations and peoples" and punished them in 1630 with

[216] *Ibid.*, pp. 37–38. While brief and superficial, this is a generally correct description of this ceremony. For a modern description see S. K. H. Katrak, *Who Are the Parsees?* (Karachi, 1965), pp. 222–32. For a thorough discussion of Parsi funeral ceremonies see J. J. Modi, *The Religious Ceremonies and Customs of the Parsees* (2d ed.; Bombay, 1937), chap. iii.

[217] See below, pp. 857–58.

[218] Abbreviated *BV;* for bibliographical details see above, pp. 472–73.

[219] See W. Wijnaendts van Resandt, *De Gezaghebbers der Oost-Indische Compagnie op hare buiten-comptoiren in Azië* (Amsterdam, 1944), pp. 200–201.

[220] For further details on his sources and the use he made of them see W. H. Moreland, "Johan van Twist's Description of India," *Journal of Indian History*, XVI (1937), 63–65. For the Gujarat report see W. Caland (ed.), *De Remonstrantie van W. Geleynssen de Jongh* (Amsterdam, 1929).

a terrible drought followed in 1631 with tremendous rains and floods. As a result, a horrible famine swept the land, attended by disease, suicides, voluntary enslavement, sale of children, cannibalism, and plagues of locusts, rats, and other vermin. Even the rich suffered hunger and often died of one or the other of the rampant diseases. In the years following this great disaster, recovery was so slow that the "abundance of provisions are not to be compared to former times." [221]

In connection with his discussion of Ahmadabad, Van Twist tells a story which is almost identical to one later recounted by Mandelslo. [222] Since neither Van Twist nor Mandelslo was likely to have known the written work of the other, and since both were in Ahmadabad at roughly the same time, the probability is that this story was then current and that each learned of it independently of the other. Both mention the tomb of a wealthy Muslim merchant named "Hajom Mojom," which, according to Mandelslo, is in "Zirkees" (Sarkhej) near the *Jitbag,* or Garden of Victory (Jitbag in modern Jetalpur). The tomb in Mandelslo's transcription is called "Betti-Chuit" (*Beṭī-chod*), which is as much as to say "the daughter's shame discovered." [223] Both tell the story of the merchant, Hajom Mojom, who had a beautiful daughter and who was "inflamed with an improper passion for her." To achieve his wicked purpose the father went to a kazi (judge) and put a hypothetical question to him: "If there is an exceedingly productive field, should not the owner be able to enjoy the produce freely, and have it for himself?" On receiving an affirmative answer in writing, the father ravished his daughter while supposing himself to be fully protected by the unsuspecting kazi's note. The daughter revealed this vile attack to her mother. Eventually Sultan Muhammad Begarha (d. 1511) heard of it and had the offender beheaded. He now lies in this tomb along with his wife and daughter who died after him. Whether or not this is more than a story told to inquisitive and ignorant travelers is something no one has yet ascertained. [224] That Van Twist was genuinely interested in Islamic culture, and not just in sordid stories about Muslims, is attested by his notice of the mosque at Patan built "in the midst of the city . . . in former times by the heathen [Hindus] being a beautiful and costly work supported on 1050 pillars of marble and other stone." [225]

---

[221] *BV,* IIb, 7–9; also Moreland, *loc. cit.* (n. 220), pp. 66–68.

[222] *BV,* IIb, 14–15; cf. John Davies (trans.), *The Voyages and Travels of J. Albert de Mandelslo . . . into the East Indies* (London, 1662), p. 32, for Mandelslo's version. M. S. Commissariat, in *Mandelslo's Travels in Western India (A.D. 1638–39)* (London, 1931), untypically omits all mention of this story from his summation of Mandelslo's observations in Gujarat.

[223] Van Twist writes "Bety-chuit as a memorial of such a horrible deed." Translation in Moreland, *loc. cit.* (n. 220), p. 69.

[224] Moreland (*ibid.*) simply states: "I have no idea what Hajom Mojom represents." Apparently Commissariat, judging from his silence, is equally uninformed. On the moral breakdown in the upper strata of Muslim society see M. Yasin, *A Social History of Islamic India, 1605–1748* (2d rev. ed.; New Delhi, 1974), pp. 85–97.

[225] *BV,* IIb, 16. Also see J. Burgess, *The Architectural Antiquities of Northern Gujarat* (London, 1903), p. 53.

While Van Twist borrows most of his discussion of the Mughuls and their court from De Laet, he provides information on the state of Shah Jahan's army as of 1629–30, possibly derived from an official statement.[226] He also adds to De Laet's descriptions of court festivals his own account of the Muharram, the month-long festival with which the Muslim year begins.[227] In explaining the background to this festival, Van Twist again relates an unusual story. In his version "Janze" (Hasan) and "Jauwzee" (Husain) meet their end at the hands of Hindus on the Coromandel Coast rather than at Arbela in Persia.[228] His descriptions of the bloody clashes between Shiites and Sunnis and between Muslims and Hindus on these occasions generally conform to what other observers of the time note. The seventeenth-century notices on the Muharram celebration show that these festivities did not differ much from what is done today.[229]

On Gujarat itself, Van Twist depends heavily on Geleynssen de Jongh's report, with additions from De Laet and Linschoten. He describes Akbar's conquest, notes that the Mughul viceroys are frequently changed to insure their loyalty, and attempts to determine what income the Mughuls receive from Gujarat. While justice is harsh, punishments can be mitigated by appropriate gifts to officials. "Benjanen" (Banyans), or merchants, were formerly all Hindus, but now many Muslims are included among them. The Hindus are sharp traders and are often employed as scribes by the Muslims. There are twenty-seven occupational subcastes of Banyans in which sons follow the father's trade and always marry within the same group.[230] A man may take more than one wife if the first fails to bear children, but the first wife must give her consent, and she remains head of the household. Van Twist gives a description of a marriage ceremony, and an eyewitness account of a suttee he observed in Baroda. He asserts that suttee is illegal in Muslim-controlled territories; consequently in this case the family must bribe the governor to obtain the requisite permission.[231]

On the basis of the Gujarat report Van Twist attempts to describe religious groupings. The "Benjanen" (Banyans), according to him, include both Jains and Hindus. Like Lord he does not distinguish clearly the differ-

[226] *BV*, IIb, 19–20; also Moreland, *loc. cit.* (n. 220), pp. 69–70. There is no reference to this rather confused but useful document in R. J. Phul, *Armies of the Great Mughals (1526–1707)* (New Delhi, 1978), or in Aziz, *op. cit.* (n. 98).

[227] It is celebrated as an anniversary of the martyrdom of Husain at Karbala in Iraq, and is primarily a Shiite event in India. On its celebration at Golconda see below, pp. 1075–76. Mandelslo describes the Muharram as he saw it in Agra (Davies [trans.], *op. cit.* [n. 222], p. 45). For a general appraisal of its celebration in Hindustan at this period see Yasin, *op. cit.* (n. 224), pp. 49–51. See also our pl. 132.

[228] *BV*, IIb, 23. Apparently a story of this sort was current in India, for Pelsaert claims that the two brothers were killed in a battle against a Hindu raja. See Moreland, *loc. cit.* (n. 220), p. 71.

[229] Yasin, *op. cit.* (n. 224), p. 50.

[230] *Cf.* Gokhale, *op. cit.* (n. 57), p. 42.

[231] Moreland (*loc. cit.* [n. 220], p. 72) wonders if Shah Jahan early in his reign had outlawed suttee completely. Generally, the Mughuls granted permission for suttee once the governor became convinced that pressure was not involved.

ences separating Jains from Hindus, but sees both as native religions of great antiquity. Traditionally it is said that the natives are divided into eighty-three sects of which there are four main ones. The first of the major sects is called "Curawaek" (*Srāvaka,* or Jain laymen). Its members are exceedingly careful not to take life of any kind. To keep from inhaling bugs they wear a cloth over the mouth. They will not dine or go outdoors after nightfall. Anyone can belong to this sect by wearing the proper clothes and following its rules. They burn their dead, except for children under three years of age, whom they bury. This sect is despised by all other Banyans. The members of the "Samareth" (*Smārta*), Van Twist's second major sect, are generally employed in the trades and worship four main idols, the most important being "Permiseer" (Paramesvara, or Siva).[232] Suttee is often performed by women of this sect; the sect also includes a large subcaste of Rajputs. The third of the chief divisions is called "Bisnouw" (Vishnu).[233] Its members fast in August, and on holy days they sing hymns to their god "Ramram" (Rama). Most individuals in this group are employed as merchants, realtors, and interpreters. Early each morning they all bathe in the river.[234] The "d'Goegy" (Yogis) have no occupation, habitation, or temple of their own. They wear nothing but a loincloth and often sleep in the temples of the "Samareth." They are chaste and speak to no one. Their god is "Brun" (Brahma), and their lawgiver is "Mesis" (Maheśa or Siva). "Brun" is the creator; he is invisible and hence never depicted. After death the individual becomes one with "Brun." Yogis observe many long fasts, practice harsh austerities, and believe in omens of many sorts. Very few females belong to this sect. All Yogis enjoy great respect.[235]

The "Persias" (*Pārsīs*) are Persians who left their own country in 624 A.D. They believe in one god who has seven consorts and twenty-six minor servants.[236] They have no public churches or regular weekly day of worship. Their holy days are the first, twentieth, and last days of the month, as well as the first day of each new year. They live together in a special quarter of the city in dark houses where a fire burns constantly. They have great respect for fire and their god is like fire. They marry young and their widows may remarry. Among them there is more sexual misbehavior than among Muslims or "Banians," even though it is punishable by death. They are lighter-skinned than the true Indians. They are greedy and sharp traders like

[232] Certain groups of Hinduized Jains also worship idols. See Jaini, *op. cit.* (n. 163), p. 194.

[233] For a modern evaluation of this sect see N. A. Thoothi, *The Vaishṇavas of Gujarat* (Calcutta, 1935).

[234] Certain Jain groups also adopted Hindu deities and cultural heros while continuing to reject the authority of the Vedas. See *ibid.,* pp. 304–6.

[235] *BV*, IIb, 30–41. On the Jain yogis or mendicants see Jaini, *op. cit.* (n. 163), chap. viii.

[236] Their supreme god is Ahura Mazda or Ormazad. His "seven consorts" is a reference to the heptad of the Amesha Spentas or "holy immortal ones." The twenty-six servants are the *yazatas,* or angels. See Caland (ed.), *op. cit.* (n. 220), p. 110, n. 1. Van Twist gives the names and attributes of the *yazatas.*

the Chinese and "Banians," but they are not thieves and whoremongers like the Muslims. Many differences in custom exist between the Persians and the Parsis of Gujarat.[237]

About Islamic beliefs and practices Van Twist writes much but adds very little to what had been noted by earlier authors. Like most Christian observers, he adopts a critical stance with respect to polygamy and the treatment of women. Life for the poor Muslim is wretched, while the lustful rich live riotous lives and behave pompously in public. The leading three nations of Muslims are the Pathans (Afghans), the Mughuls, and the Hindustani natives of Gujarat. Pathans surpass the others in bravery, the Mughuls are clever and sharp, and the Gujaratis are more avaricious and demanding than the others. Within these nations are many sects, the most prominent of which are the "Saysedt" (Sayyids), "Seegh" (Shaikhs), and "Leet" (?).[238] The Muslims know Aristotle and Avicenna, but have no printed books. Muslims and Hindus follow different calendars, the Islamic year beginning between January 1 and January 10, and the Hindu on March 18. In Gujarat there is a caste of whores called "Bagowaro" (?), who are common to all.[239]

After describing in some detail the products of Gujarat, Van Twist gives correctly the main facts about its weights, measures, and coins.[240] He is particularly good on its maritime trade, a subject on which Geleynssen de Jongh and his other Dutch sources were especially well informed. Annually the Muslims sail from Surat to Mocha on large but badly built ships which have difficulty defending themselves. Each of such ships may carry one thousand passengers, most of whom are on pilgrimage. The pilgrim ships carry on a limited exchange of Gujarati products for red coral, amber, dyes, and coffee; "the rest of their returns consist of silver and gold ducats." Smaller ships sail annually from the ports of Gujarat to the Persian Gulf to buy textiles, pearls, and exotic fruits and nuts. Other Gujarati vessels sail annually to Acheh in Sumatra and Kedah in the Malay Peninsula after the Portuguese patrol vessels have been laid up for winter. In this way they avoid the Portuguese system of middlemen by carrying pepper and the fine spices directly from the East Indian ports to Gujarati harbors and warehouses. Many Gujarati coastal vessels trade with the Portuguese outposts in western India to supply them with foodstuffs and to buy salt, old nets useful

---

[237]*BV*, IIb, 41–45. Van Twist's account of the Parsis is a summary of Geleynssen De Jongh's authoritative description. See Caland (ed.), *op. cit.* (n. 220), pp. 104–250. While some of this discussion is only partially correct, it compares favorably to what Lord and other seventeenth-century commentators write about the Parsis. For a thorough study of their rites and customs see Modi, *op. cit.* (n. 216). Europeans generally found the Parsis congenial since they were in trade, not bothered by the problem of pollution, and not "Moors."

[238]Sayyids may be either Sunni or Shiite. They do not marry outside their group. The Mughuls are mainly of Persian and the Pathans of Afghan origin; both are Sunnis. Shaiks usually are Arabic in origin or are converts. See P. G. Shah, *Ethnic History of Gujarat* (Bombay, 1968), pp. 96–97.

[239]*BV*, IIb, 48–57.

[240]For an English translation and commentary see Moreland, *loc. cit.* (n. 220), pp. 72–74.

to paper makers, and soda. Ships from Malabar arrive in Gujarat during December with south Indian products and return in mid-April with "much opium, saffron, red coral," as well as coarse textiles and cotton thread. The Portuguese, who previously had a monopoly of the sea trade of Gujarat and Hindustan, saw it infringed upon with the arrival of the Dutch and English traders "20 or 30 years ago." Because they fear the superior vessels of the northern Europeans, the Portuguese come to Cambay and Surat only once each year to exchange the goods of south India for the textiles of Gujarat.[241]

Johann Albrecht von Mandelslo (1616–44), a German envoy, appeared at Surat near the end of April, 1638. Like Herbert, Mandelslo stopped at Surat in connection with travels to Persia. Also like Herbert, he was a young attaché of a commercial mission to the Persian court. Mandelslo accompanied a legation of 1635 sent out by the Duke of Holstein to Muscovy and Persia. The duke, in compliance with young Mandelslo's request, had agreed that he might leave the mission for an independent trip to India. After three years in Persia, Mandelslo left the mission in Ispahan for his personal expedition to India. In this enterprise he was encouraged and aided by the English factors whom he met in Persia. Taking an English ship at the Persian Gulf, he sailed for Surat. Once arrived there he was warmly greeted by William Methwold, the president of the English commercial organization in India. Methwold, who had a good command of Dutch, was able to communicate easily with the German youth and encouraged him to make friends with the Dutch merchants there. In this kind of situation, Methwold told him, "all Christians are obliged to assist one another."

With Methwold's aid Mandelslo spent a happy eight months (April, 1638, to January, 1639) in India. He passed the whole of the rainy season (April to October) in Surat. In October he journeyed through Gujarat to Ahmadabad and then went southward to Cambay. Returning to Ahmadabad, he joined at the end of the month a caravan going northward to Agra. After a brief stay in Agra, he went off to Lahore. He was soon recalled by Methwold to hasten back to Surat in order to catch the next sailing for Europe. On January 5, 1639, he and Methwold took ship for Goa and the long trip back to England. Back in Holstein in 1640, Mandelslo conferred with Adam Olearius (d. 1671) about editing his itinerary. Olearius, who had been secretary to the Persian embassy of Holstein, was the librarian of the ducal court and a learned person. He advised Mandelslo to rewrite and reorganize before publishing. Not heeding this advice, Mandelslo took employment in France as a soldier. In 1644 he died at Paris, one of the victims of a smallpox epidemic.

After his death, the manuscript of Mandelslo's itinerary was found among his effects. Eventually Olearius edited it and added materials to it as he pre-

---

[241] *BV*, IIb, 66–68; also Moreland, *loc. cit.* (n. 220), pp. 94–99. Also see S. Goysal, "Gujarati Shipping in the Seventeenth Century," *Indian Economic and Social History Review*, VIII (1971), 31–40.

pared it for publication. Certain writings by Mandelslo began to appear as early as 1645 as supplements to the report of Olearius on the embassy to Muscovy and Persia. In 1658 a greatly expanded version of this work was printed in Schleswig which includes at its end Mandelslo's augmented narrative with a separate title page. Dutch, French, and English translations quickly appeared. Like Olearius, the French translator Abraham de Wicquefort unhesitatingly added descriptive material from other writers, often without acknowledging fully the debt so incurred.[242] With the passage of time scholars began uncritically to quote Mandelslo as an authority on India and many other parts of Asia. Upon closer examination of his *Voyages,* it has been determined that Mandelslo's firsthand accounts of importance are limited to his descriptions of western India, especially those of Gujarat, Bijapur, and Goa.[243]

Upon his arrival at Suwali on April 28, 1638, Mandelslo notes that there are three seasons in this region: extreme heat from February to May, continual rain from June to September, and cold clear weather from October to Janaury. The customs officials of Surat, notably strict in their examinations, inspect Mandelslo's clothes and pockets. On the arrival of the foreigners the "Sulchan" (*shahbandar*) himself comes to the customs house looking for "gifts"; from Mandelslo he takes a bracelet of yellow amber which he promises to return when the German pays him a visit. Methwold at once takes Mandelslo under his wing and involves him in the activities of the English factory during his five-month stay in Surat. At meetings of the merchants, Mandelslo reports, "we took onely The [tea], which is commonly used all over India," as coffee is in Persia. He hears reports of the great drought and famine of 1630–31 and notes that Gujarat has totally recovered from its effects even though scars remain everywhere. News arrives in May, 1638, of the revolt of the Khan of Qandahar against Persia and the return of control over that province to the Mughuls. Methwold has twenty to twenty-four merchants and officials who assist him. It is presumably from these men that Mandelslo learns that customs on imports and exports are fixed at 3½ percent, except for gold and silver imports, which are charged only 2 percent.[244]

Even though it is the rainy season, Mandelslo and his friends regularly visit the English garden outside the city and occasionally make excursions to its suburbs. On the other side of the Tapti River he visits the old and ruined town of Rander which is inhabited by "Naites" (*Nawāyits,* or newcomers), Muslim traders and mariners well known on India's west coast.[245]

[242] For additional bibliographical detail see above, pp. 522–23.

[243] See Vincent A. Smith, "The Credit Due to the Book Entitled 'The Voyages and Travels of J. Albert de Mandelslo into the East Indies,'" *JRAS,* 1915, pp. 245–54; and Commissariat, *op. cit.* (n. 222). On his activities in Bijapur and Goa see below, pp. 846–48.

[244] Davies (trans.), *op. cit.* (n. 222), pp. 16–24, *passim;* also see Commissariat, *op. cit.* (n. 222), pp. 1–5.

[245] In 1530 Rander was sacked along with Surat by the Portuguese. Unlike Surat, it never

In the Surat region the Muslims enjoy greater respect than Hindus or Jains, since the Mughul ruler is a Muslim and he permits them to bear arms. In the village of Damri, Mandelslo drinks the famous local toddy in cups made of leaves and describes the method of extracting the liquid from the palm trees. After exclaiming that "the places about this city are the most delightful of any in the world," he comments on the Gopi tank and informs us that in its center stands the mausoleum of its founder. Three gates lead out of Surat, the first to Cambay, the second to Burhanpur, and the third to Navsari.[246]

On the last day of September Mandelslo leaves through the Cambay or northern gate for Broach, his ultimate destination being Ahmadabad. He travels for safety's sake in an English caravan consisting of thirty wagons loaded with quicksilver, spices, dye-roots, and money. Broach, a walled city standing on top of a high hill, has eighty-four villages within its jurisdiction and maintains a Mughul garrison in its fortress for protection and for collection of port taxes. Timbers in great quantities come down the Narbada River to be marketed in Broach. The majority of its inhabitants are weavers who produce *baftas*, textiles "finer than any made [elsewhere] in the province of Gujarat." Arrived at Baroda on October 7, Mandelslo becomes the center of attention for Hindu dancing girls, who are fascinated by his exotic European clothes. Most of the Europeans "who are settled in the Indies," he avers, dress in local costume for safety's sake.[247] Baroda, at this time, holds jurisdiction over 210 villages. At the prosperous village of "Sindickera" (Sankheda) lac is produced in quantity. On the road from Baroda to Ahmadabad the English caravan passes by the fort of Vasad, whose Mughul garrison tries illegally and unsuccessfully to collect a transit tax from its leaders. Finally, after no further untoward incidents, the caravan on October 12 arrives at Ahmadabad "the metropolis of all Guzurutta."[248]

Here Mandelslo is lodged at the English factory, a spacious structure in the heart of the city. His first visit is to the "Maidan Shah, or the king's market," a bazaar which occupies several tree-lined streets. The city boasts four other bazaars "where are sold all kinds of merchandise." Next he visits the Bhadar citadel, inside whose enclosure stands the royal palace built of brick. Over the palace gate is a balcony where musicians play four times each day, following a practice common to Muslim courts. After inspecting the interior of the palace, Mandelslo visits the "principal mosque of the Binjans" [Banyans], an edifice that is new, "for the Founder, who was a rich Binjan merchant, named Shantidas, was living in my time."[249] This noble

---

recovered from this attack. The *Nawāyits* are no longer of importance at Rander. See Commissariat, *op. cit.* (n. 222), pp. 7–8, nn. 2–3, and above, p. 611.

[246]Davies (trans.), *op. cit.* (n. 222), pp. 23–25.

[247]Commissariat (*op. cit.* [n. 222], p. 16) remarks: "it is not a generally accepted fact that . . . [the Europeans] who settled in Gujarat adopted the ordinary dress of the country."

[248]Davies (trans.), *op. cit.* (n. 222), pp. 25–28.

[249]Ahmadabad was once the stronghold of the northern Jains. This Jain temple was built only

structure graces a city that is a fantastic commercial emporium and a center of silk and cotton weaving. In making their silk fabrics they ordinarily "use that of China, which is very fine, mingling it with that of Bengala, which is not quite so fine . . . and much cheaper."²⁵⁰ They weave great numbers of gold and silver brocades, but they put too much thin lace in them. Now they are making new textiles "of Silk and Cotton with flowers of Gold." Local persons are forbidden to wear these new fabrics, for they are reserved to the emperor for his special use. Foreigners may buy them but only for export from the empire.²⁵¹ Other products commonly sold are sugar products, honey, cumin, lac, opium, borax, ginger, myrabolans, saltpeter, sal ammoniac, indigo, musk, and ambergris. Merchants readily obtain bills of exchange at Ahmadabad from its Banyan money-changers who have their correspondents in commercial centers as far distant as Constantinople. While duties on trade are not regularly levied, "gifts" to officials make things easier for the foreigners, especially when seeking licenses to export prohibited commodities such as gunpowder, lead, and saltpeter.²⁵²

Ahmadabad holds jurisdiction over twenty-five great towns and about three thousand villages. The revenues collected from these places go to the governor, "who hath the quality of 'Radia' or prince," for support of his armed force of twelve thousand cavalry. Civil government is in the hands of the *Kotwal* who shares with the *Kasi* (kazi) in the administration of justice. The entire city, dusty though it is, is surrounded by gardens connected to the center by straight highways lined with trees. He visits the village of Sarkhej and its famous tomb, the "Schackbag" (*Shahi Bag,* or *Jitbag*) gardens in the suburb of Begumpur, and the mountains of "Marva" (Malwa) where the Rajputs live. On these excursions he observes the large apes which still delight the foreign visitor to Ahmadabad and its environs. He is also intrigued by parrots who nest in the city and are a pest to vendors of rice and fruits. Around the river crocodiles and cormorants abound and through the air at nightfall fly "batts as big as crowes."²⁵³

During his stay in Ahmadabad the young German is privileged to have two interviews with "Arab-Chan" (Azam Khan), a famous Mughul gover-

a few years before Mandelslo's visit by Shantidas Jhaveri, a wealthy Jain jeweler and a favorite of Shah Jahan. Mandelslo's description, a rather lengthy one for him, is the earliest and most complete account known of this famous monument. Just seven years after the German's visit, it was forcibly converted into a mosque by Prince Aurangzib, then the viceroy of Gujarat. For a summary of Mandelslo's description and for a further commentary on the temple of Chintamani in Saraspur at Ahmadabad see Commissariat, *op. cit.* (n. 222), pp. 23–25, 101–2.

²⁵⁰ Probably the silk textiles called *patolas*. See J. Irwin, "Indian Textile Trade in the Seventeenth Century," *Journal of Indian Textile History,* I (1955), 21.

²⁵¹ Most of the so-called silks exported from western India to Europe were mixed fabrics of cotton and silk. See *ibid*.

²⁵² Davies (trans.), *op. cit.* (n. 222), pp. 31–32.

²⁵³ A reference to the famous "Indian flying fox," a bat which often has a wingspan of four feet. For a photograph of a specimen see Prater, *op. cit.* (n. 190), facing p. 161. Also see pl. 270.

nor who ruled Gujarat from 1636 to 1642. Escorted by the English factor, Mandelslo visits the governor on October 18, 1638. A man of sixty years of age, Azam Khan politely inquires about Mandelslo's background. Like many other Indians, the governor is intrigued by Mandelslo's European garments but gently mentions that other foreigners wear local costumes to avoid unfortunate incidents. After one hour's conversation, primarily about the German's experiences in Persia, Azam Khan invites his European visitors to stay and dine with him. Two days later Mandelso and his English friend return to make a farewell call on the governor; Mandelslo dresses this time according to the mode of the country. After observing the governor perform his official duties, the Europeans are hospitably offered opium and bhang (*Cannabis indica*). Since the governor first helps himself, the Europeans feel obliged to take a little of both though neither has before indulged in these narcotics. In the animated conversation following, the governor inquires whether or not Mandelslo had learned the Turkish language while in Persia. The German responds that he had spent much of his spare time studying Turkish, a language as widely used there as Persian itself. The governor lets Mandelslo know that in his opinion the shahs of Persia are cruel tyrants and not at all comparable to the Mughul rulers in wealth or military strength. Mandelslo agrees with this estimate and describes Azam Khan himself as "a judicious, understanding man, but hasty and so rigorous that his government inclined somewhat to cruelty."[254]

On October 21, after nine days or so at Ahmadabad, Mandelslo departs for a brief side-trip to Cambay. Three days later he is lodging with a Muslim merchant there. Most of Cambay's inhabitants are Hindu merchants who carry on an extensive foreign trade in textiles, which they exchange for gold and silver. Like Ahmadabad, the walled city of Cambay is surrounded by public gardens. Two of the English merchants resident there take Mandelslo to see a widow burn herself. This Rajput lady had long desired to follow her husband in death, but her wish for suttee had been delayed by the Mughul governor. Finally, as she persisted in her determination, he was required under Mughul law to accord her the desired permission to follow this ancient custom of her religion. Mandelslo piteously describes the young widow's immolation which he denounces as a "heathenish and barbarous custom." From his happy experiences with the merchants of Cambay, the German concludes that "there is more civility to be found among the Indians than there is among those [Christians] who pretend to the sole possession of it." On his return trip to Ahmadabad, Mandelslo visits the famous garden at Fateh Wadi on the Sabarmati River near Sarkhej. This lovely garden called "Tzietbagh" (*Jitbag*) or "Garden of Victory," stands on the battlefield where the Mughuls defeated the last king of Gujarat. Mandelslo's

---

[254] Davies (trans.), *op. cit.* (n. 222), pp. 29–39, for Mandelslo's description of Ahmadabad. On his opinion of Azam Khan *cf.* Commissariat, *op. cit.* (n. 222), p. 31, n. 1; p. 40, n. 1.

description provides one of the fullest available depictions of this garden which was constructed at the end of the sixteenth century to commemorate Abdurrahim Khan's victory of 1583–84 over the last of the independent sultans of Gujarat.[255]

On his return to Ahmadabad, Mandelslo quickly prepares to depart with a caravan headed for Agra. After a brief stay in Agra, he departs for Lahore via the tree-lined "alley" that connects the two Mughul capitals. Once in the Muslim city of Lahore, he explores its public bath houses (*hamams*) and treats himself to a Turkish bath and a massage with a "haircloth." His stay cut short by letters calling for his return to Surat, Mandelslo sourly concludes: "I found not anything remarkable about Lahore." In his rapid trip southward he comments on the remarkable speed and endurance of the oxen who pulled the carts in which he rode.[256] At his stopover in Ahmadabad, Mandelslo observes the lighted lamps and fireworks, including pinwheels, of Divali, the Hindu festival of illumination. On the road to Surat his caravan is attacked near Broach by Rajputs who are successfully turned back by the firearms of the Europeans. Back in Surat, Mandelslo attends ceremonies celebrating Methwold's retirement and the advent of his successor as president of the East India Company's hierarchy in India. On January 5, 1639, he and Methwold depart for Goa on their way back to Europe.[257]

4

SHAH JAHAN (R. 1627–58) AND HIS EMPIRE

The unveiling of Gujarat was accompanied in the 1630's and 1640's by the dissemination in Europe of new information on other parts of Mughul India. The Portuguese, who had dominated the sea traffic of eastern India during the sixteenth century, were forced on the defensive early in the seventeenth century by the appearance of Dutch and English ships in the delta of the Ganges. By 1630 several unsuccessful attempts to open trade were made by the northern Europeans while the Portugese continued to hold their trading base of Hugli. The Dutch and English sent ships out from their Coromandel factories in hopes of breaking into the delta trade. In 1632 Shah Jahan reversed the tolerant policies of his predecessors and drove the encroaching Portuguese from Hugli and ordained that it should become the imperial port of Bengal. The following year the Portuguese were permitted to return to Hugli under conditions—very favorable—prescribed by the

[255]Davies (trans.), *op. cit.* (n. 222), pp. 39–44; also see Commissariat, *op. cit.* (n. 222), p. 47.
[256]On the extraordinary speed of the white oxen of Gujarat see Commissariat, *op. cit.* (n. 222), p. 20, n. 2.
[257]Davies (trans.), *op. cit.* (n. 222), pp. 44–45, 54–60. On Mandelslo at Goa see below, pp. 846–48.

Mughuls. It was not long thereafter that the English and Dutch also began to secure important trading privileges in the region. One of the major advantages of the Bengali ports over Surat was the direct river transportation which they offered to Agra and other important cities of upper India.[258]

Very little substantial information on current conditions in the Ganges delta or Bengal was available in Europe before the Mughul descent on Hugli. The Portuguese settlements at Hugli and elsewhere were not governed as part of the Estado da India but existed simply as Christian merchant groups living in Mughul territory and subject to local law. Consequently little official information about them was available in Goa or Lisbon. While a few Jesuits and Augustinians worked in these settlements, the reports emanating from Bengal came mainly from traveling merchants. A number of these occasional reports were included in the commercial itineraries and Jesuit letterbooks published in Europe.[259] On the basis of such scattered references De Laet managed to produce a sketch of Bengal's delta region and Orissa in which its major ports are identified and their official subservience to the Mughuls noted.[260]

One of the first English missions to attempt the establishment of official trading relations with the Mughuls in eastern India was sent to Orissa from Masulipatam in 1633. William Bruton, a seaman who accompanied this mission, was in Orissa from May to November of that year on a side-trip he undertook as part of a seven-year voyage in the service of the East India Company. While he committed to writing many of the observations made during his lengthy voyage, he realized on his return to England that most of his personal discoveries had already been anticipated in the publications of others. So he decided to publish only those of his own observations which could contribute something fresh to the information on India being accumulated in England. His experiences in Orissa, then juridically a part of the Mughul Empire and commercially related to the delta region, he had printed at London in 1638 under the title *Newes from the East Indies; or, A Voyage to Bengalla, one of the greatest kingdomes under the high and mighty Prince Pedesha Shassallem; usually called the Great Mogul. . . .*[261] This small book of thirty-five pages was not printed again during the seventeenth century.[262]

---

[258] See A. C. Roy, *History of Bengal, Mughul Period, 1526–1765 A.D.* (Calcutta, 1968), chap. vi; and O. Prakash, "The Dutch East India Company in Bengal; Trade Privileges and Problems, 1633–1712," *Indian Economic and Social History Review,* Vol. IX, Pt. 3 (1972), 258–87.

[259] The best of the early reports is by François Pyrard of Laval. He describes conditions in Bengal as of 1607 after a brief stay there. See A. Gray and H. C. P. Bell (eds.), *The Voyage of François Pyrard of Laval to the East Indies, the Maldives, the Moluccas and Brazil* (2 vols.; "HS," LXXVI–VII; Cambridge, 1890; reprint ed. of Burt Franklin, N.Y., n.d.), I, 326–36.

[260] See above, p. 623.

[261] The title continues: *With the state and magnificence of the court of Malcandy, kept by the Nabob Viceroy, or Vice-King, under the aforesayd Monarch: also their detestable religion, mad and foppish rites, and ceremonies, and wicked sacrifices and impious customs used in those parts.*

[262] It was reissued by Thomas Osborne in 1745 and was reprinted in Osborne's enlarged *Col-*

Bruton and his companions anchor on April 21 (Easter Day), 1633, in the bay of "Harssapoore" (Harispur), a town at the mouth of the Patua River in Orissa. After misadventures here with a Portuguese vessel, Bruton and two of his companions set out for Cuttack, the major city of the region. Their first stopover is at "Balkhada" (Balikuda), a populous town wherein many weavers work.[263] Received courteously here they leave in the cool of the evening for "Harharrapoore" (Hariharpur) where they are welcomed in front of its sumptuous temple by "Mersymomeine" (Mirza Momein), an imperial noble delegated to receive and entertain them.[264] On May Day the English arrive at the residence of Mirza Momein in Cuttack, a city "several miles in compass" and one mile from "Malcandy" [*Māṇikhaṇḍī*] where the court is kept."[265]

Commanded to appear at the court of "Malcandy," the Englishmen go from the residence of Mirza Momein across a long, narrow, stone causeway at the end of which stands a great gate. After passing through the gate, they traverse a bazaar until they arrive at a second gate, guarded by fifty armed men. On the other side of this gate they pass through a "fair and spacious street" paved with stone where merchants on each side sell "rich and costly" domestic and foreign wares.[266] At a third gate, guarded by one hundred men, they approach a temple which joins "the southernmost part of the king's house." Beyond the "king's house" is a high double-storied gate supported by "mighty pillars of grey marble" and guarded by one hundred and fifty men. Between this gate and the court is "a great broad place, or street much of the breadth of the street between Charing-cross and White-hall" in London. Here one thousand horses stand "in readiness for the king's use; for he hath always three thousand at an hour's warning."

The palace itself is "a very great house of timber, whose chambers are made with galleries." Every morning at four o'clock, men begin to play loud instruments in these galleries. To the north of "the king's gate" stands a small tower "built with two hollow arches" which hold two stone images. Great iron pipes in the breasts of the images, regulated by devices in the tower, spout forth fire and water on days of festival. On the other side of this gate stands a great elephant of grey marble. The entrance to the palace is paved with "rough-hewn marble and in the interior are pillars of grey

---

[263] In this region muslins are woven.

[264] Hariharpur is the old name of modern Jagatisinghpur in the Cuttack district. See Acharya (ed.), *loc. cit.* (n. 262), p. 32, n. 29.

[265] No trace exists today of the *Māṇikhaṇḍī* palace. For this identification see *ibid.*, pp. 26–27.

[266] For trading wares the English merchants themselves had brought gold, silver, cloth, and "spices (of which spices those parts of India are wanting), and they almost are as dear there as in England" (*ibid.*, p. 32). He is certainly referring here to the fine spices of the Moluccas.

marble, carved three stories one above the other." On the south side of the palace are the houses of the "king's" artisans. In its north end are "two stately tombs" founded by "Backarcaune" (Baqir Khan), the immediate predecessor of the nabob now governing.[267] At the east end of the palace is a "faire Place" paved with grey marble and enclosed with railings. Here there is also a tank of grey marble, in the middle of which stands a pipe "whose water descends between two walls, with the forms of fishes of different kinds carved in [the] stone . . . as if they had been swimming . . . up the wall against the stream." At another gate near the east end of the palace they keep the time of day by observing measures of water. Into a pot holding three gallons of water they put a smaller pot holding a bit more than one-half pint with a hole in its bottom. When the smaller pot fills with water, a gong is struck to indicate the passage of a measure of time called a "gree" (Oriya, *ghaḍi*). Eight such "grees" equal one "par" (Oriya, *pahara*), or about three hours. Their day begins at six in the morning and ends at six in the evening: hence the day is divided into four "par" and the night likewise.[268]

The Englishmen, led by chief-merchant Richard Cartwright, finally make their way through another palace before arriving in the third and final palace where the durbar is located. Like a number of other places in the palace grounds, the durbar is adorned with trees and flowers irrigated by water from the aforementioned tank. Left to their own devices for about two hours, the Englishmen and the courtiers mutely stare at one another. After the arrival of the nabob and his entourage, Mirza Momein presents Cartwright to the ruler. The Englishman, after two refusals, finally kisses the nabob's foot as a gesture of respect. With the council seated cross-legged on the floor, Cartwright presents to the nabob the official gifts.[269] These amenities complete, Cartwright announces that the purpose of his visit is to ask for freedom to trade in Orissa without payment of customs and without interference from the natives. He also requests a license to coin in Orissa the monies commonly used by the merchants of the region. Since the deliberations over these matters continue until after nightfall, the durbar is lighted with as many as 130 silver lanterns. After further discussion, the durbar is adjourned, and the English merchants return to Momein's house without an answer to their petition for trade.

On their second day at court the English are confronted by a Portuguese

[267] Baqir Khan was recalled in 1632 and replaced by Mu'tazid Khan, alias Mirza Maki. When Bruton was in Cuttack, Orissa was being governed temporarily by Na'ib Nazim, the nabob with whom the English dealt. See R. D. Banerji, *History of Orissa from the Earliest Times to the British Period* (2 vols.; Delhi, 1980), II, 39, 62.

[268] On the principles of time measurement in traditional India see A. J. Qaisar, *The Indian Response to European Technology and Culture, A.D. 1498–1707* (Delhi, 1982), pp. 67–68. *Cf.* below, pp. 991–92.

[269] These included: twenty pounds each of cloves, mace, and nutmegs, two bolts of damask, fourteen yards of flannel, one gilt-framed mirror, one fowling piece, and one double pistol.

pilot who raises for the nabob the whole question as to which European nation has the right to issue passes to trading vessels plying the Bay of Bengal. When Cartwright's contention fails to win the nabob's immediate approval, the Englishman stomps out of the durbar in great anger and without the nabob's leave. On the following day Cartwright is summoned to the court; the nabob politely asks why he left in such a rage on the previous day. To this query Cartwright boldly replies that the nabob has done an injustice to the English Company by refusing to recognize the right of its servants to take as prizes those ships not possessing passes from the English, Danes, or Dutch; in this case the issue revolved about a Portuguese vessel which the English had taken because its pilot held only Portuguese passes. After being assured by his Persian advisers that the English were strong enough in the Bay of Bengal to blockade the ports of Orissa, the nabob "said but little." Finally he grants Cartwright's request for free trade, the establishment of a permanent factory, and the right to build and repair shipping in Orissa's harbors, on condition that the English should not interfere with Orissa's shipping and should agree to aid its ships when in distress or otherwise in need of help. To this decree the nabob later adds a stipulation permitting the English to coin money in his territories.[270]

While celebrating at Cuttack the success of these negotiations, the English merchants learn that the nabob has been ordered by Shah Jahan to wage war against Golconda. To this end an army of thirty thousand, ten cavalry and twenty infantry, is being mobilized at Cuttack. It is armed for the most part only with bows, arrows, javelins, swords, and scimitars.[271] On the night of May 9 the English leave for Hariharpur to make preparations for building a factory there. This populous town boasts three thousand weavers and is frequented by many merchants. On being hampered in their construction efforts by great rains, the English merchants undertake a reconnaissance of the neighboring towns. Cartwright and two associates go northward to "Ballazary" (Balasore) and eventually make their way to Pipli near the Ganges delta. Bruton himself is sent southward on November 5 on Company business to the "great city of Jaggarnat" (Jagannath Puri, or simply Puri).

On his way Bruton lodges his first night in a temple at "Madew" (Madhab). During the next day he meets at "Amudpoore" (Ahmudpur) a huge band of "Fackeires" (Hindi, *fakīr*, or mendicants) who are supposedly holy men but are really rogues like the gypsies of England. On November 7 he

---

[270] For the text of this "*Parwan*" (*farman*) of Na'ib Nazim signed on May 5, 1633, see Acharya (ed.), *loc. cit.* (n. 262), pp. 40–41; for the subsequent history of this English venture in Orissa see Banerji, *op. cit.* (n. 267), II, 62–63.

[271] This army was designed to help carry forward Shah Jahan's Deccan campaign. For Orissa's contributions to this campaign see H. K. Sherwani, *History of the Qutb Shāhī Dynasty* (New Delhi, 1974), pp. 434–35. Orissa's involvement in these wars may help to explain in part why its governor so easily capitulated to the demands of the English. It should also not be forgotten that the English factors at Masulipatam had close relations with Golconda. See below, p. 1019.

arrives at Puri where he lodges in a Brahman's house.[272] The following day he visits the city's great temple of Jagannath (or Juggernaut in Anglo-Indian) at which nine thousand Brahmans daily offer sacrifices to their great god for whom the city is named.[273] Sacrifices of children are made to this "ungodly god." Its image is "like a serpent with seven hoods, and on the cheeks of each head it hath the form of wing upon each cheek, which wings open and shut, and flap" when it is carried in a car (*rath*). For festivals they build a car with sixteen wheels on each side "and every wheel is five feet in height and the chariot itself is about thirty feet high."[274] When the idol is drawn in a nighttime procession it is attended by thousands of persons, many of whom carry lights. Everyone is eager to pull the ropes or simply to put a hand on them. Some throw themselves beneath its wheels and are injured or killed.[275] Another smaller twelve-wheel car carries an idol of inferior rank, which is put on display only at the pleasure of the Brahmans.[276] The temple itself stands by the sea in a square enclosure surrounded by a stone wall twenty-two feet high. Its four gates directly face the four directions with the south and west gates remaining barred except at festival times. The north gate is the place of entry most commonly used, for it opens onto the main street of the city.[277]

Bruton concludes his remarks on Orissa and Bengal by asserting that the people of this region worship "other creatures for their gods": planets, mountains, valleys, forests, seas, rivers, fountains as well as various animals, plants, and flowers. Most natives "have no learning, but do all things by memory." In some places their edicts and laws are written down. Elsewhere laws and contracts are unwritten. They even lend money without witnesses or promissory notes. For the most part the natives are black and of large stature. They dress in various ways and take many wives "which they purchase" from the parents. Orissa has more wild beasts of different

[272] Non-Hindus are not permitted today to enter Hindu temples and it would be most unusual for a Brahman to house a Christian. From this account, as well as those of other Europeans of the time, it appears that the Hindus of the seventeenth century were more inclined to open their temples and homes to non-Hindus than their descendants are. See Acharya (ed.), *loc. cit.* (n. 262), p. 46n.

[273] Today about six thousand male adults act as priests in the temple at Puri; the staff and attendants dependent on Jagannath number around twenty thousand persons. Jagannath is the Sanskrit word for "Lord of the Universe"; it is actually a name of Krishna worshipped as Vishnu. See Murray, *op. cit.* (n. 191), p. 332.

[274] Today the car of Jagannath "is forty-five feet high and thirty-five feet square, and is supported on sixteen wheels seven feet in diameter with prancing horses in front" (*ibid.*). It is destroyed and rebuilt each year.

[275] Today precautions are taken to prevent accidents and to keep votaries from throwing themselves beneath its wheels. See *ibid.*

[276] Balbhadra and Subhadra, respectively brother and sister of Jagannath, to this day have smaller cars of their own. See *ibid.*

[277] "The sacred enclosure is nearly a square, 652 ft. long and 630 ft. broad, within a stone wall about 20 ft. high, with a gateway in the centre of each side. . . ." Rather more than a mile to the north of the temple is the famous Garden House (*Candicha Mandir*) to which the "car of Jagannath is brought and stays for eight days during the [June] festival . . ." (*ibid.*, pp. 332–34).

sorts than any other place in the Indies and the people there delight in hunting them. The local craftsmen are ingenious and are able to copy or imitate
anything put before them. They hate idlers and every day check on their
children's accomplishments. They severely punish perjurers, blasphemers,
and drunkards and ever after brand perjurers as liars who are beyond
rehabilitation.[278]

About four years before Bruton's visit in Orissa, the Augustinian friar
Sebastião Manrique (d. 1669) spent a few months at the Portuguese settlement of Hugli in Bengal, probably during the summer of 1629. After a
lengthy tour of duty at Arakan and in eastern Asia, Manrique returned to
eastern India in 1640 and for the next fifteen months traveled in the Mughul
Empire before departing for Europe near the end of 1641. Finally he got
back to Rome via the overland route in July, 1643. Here he prepared for
publication his *Itinerario* (1649), which recounts in atrocious Spanish his experiences and observations during almost fifteen years (1629–43) of travel in
the East. In general, this book follows a chronological sequence and appears
to be based on notes made during his wanderings. Back in Rome he amplified his notes by unacknowledged borrowings from the works of De Laet,
Mendes Pinto, and probably others. Almost all of Manrique's Indian vernacular terms and names—and there are many of them—are given in their
Hindustani form, an indication that he was probably better acquainted with
that language than with any other tongue current in the subcontinent.[279]

Originally attached to the Augustinian residence at Cochin, Manrique
was sent in 1629 to his order's mission in Bengal along with several companions. The ship carrying the Augustinians, after a rather dull voyage, founders on the shoals of Chandkhan and finally washes ashore near Hijili in
Orissa. Here they are rescued by ships belonging to the "Musundulum"
(Masnad-i-Ali), the title of a local lord who is a vassal of the nabob of
Dacca. This chieftain, not wishing to violate the maritime arrangement of
his overlord and the Portuguese, finally agrees after haggling over ownership of the cargo in the wrecked ship to grant the Portuguese sanctuary in
Hijili. The Augustinians are lodged at the local residence of their order
while awaiting permission to depart for Hugli. Three days later they are
summoned along with the ship's captain and the superior of the Augustinian
residence to appear before the "Musundulum." They assemble in the "Droua"
(*dargāh,* or audience hall) along with certain "Mirzas [Persian, *mīrzas,* nobles]
who form the aristocracy of that country." While awaiting the "Musundulum," the nobles play chess to while away the time. Then a "baticha"
(Portuguese, *batega,* or gong) sounds, announcing the arrival of the ruler.

---

[278] Acharya (ed.), *loc. cit.* (n. 262), pp. 45–50.
[279] For further bibliographical detail see above, pp. 349–50. For a critical edition, English
translation, and scholarly introduction to the *Itinerario* see C. E. Luard and H. Hosten (trans.
and eds.), *Travels of Fray Sebastian Manrique 1629–43* (2 vols.; "HS," 2d ser., LIX, LI; Oxford,
1926, 1927).

After inquiring about conditions in Portuguese India, the "Musundulum" turns the negotiations over the ship's cargo to two "Mapatras" (Sanskrit, *mahāpatras*, or great officials) of his court. While these accounts are being settled, a "Gelviār" (Persian, *jalabdar,* messenger) arrives from the nabob of Dacca demanding a share of the cargo. That night the friars, fearing the intervention of the nabob, under cover of darkness steal away on a river boat which takes them to "Ugulim" (Hugli). Once in the Portuguese settlement, they feast on mangoes and other dainties before retiring to the monastery of St. Nicholas of Tolentino.[280]

The town of Hugli, Manrique reports, is situated on the banks of the Ganges "sixty leagues inland from the sea." It was founded in Akbar's time (that is, before 1605) by Portuguese traders. At first the merchants built bamboo storehouses for their wares and stayed at Hugli only for the five or six months of the rainy season. As time wore on, they began to stay for longer periods. Neither the Hindu natives nor the Muslim "Siguidar" (Arabic, *shiqdar,* or tax collector) objected to their presence; the officials even encouraged them to stay permanently and to bring their priests. Most of the goods imported by the Portuguese came from the south, including cowries from the Maldives, chanks from the Fishery Coast, pepper from Malabar, and cinnamon from Ceylon. Pepper and cinnamon, private trade in which was forbidden by the Portuguese crown, were shipped into Bengal surreptitiously by these merchants. They also began bringing in brocades, porcelains, lacquerworks, and curios from China. From the East Indies they carried into Bengal the sandalwoods of Solor and Timor, the fine spices of the Moluccas, and the precious camphor of Borneo. "Sodagores" (Persian, *saudagars,* merchants) then took these wares and European products to the court of Agra and to the emperor. Akbar soon ordered the nabob of Dacca to send representatives of the Portuguese merchants to Agra. Eventually a Captain Pero Tavares of Goa and three other Portuguese were taken to Agra. There they were given a *farman* permitting them to build a city in the Ganges delta with materials furnished by the nabob. Tavares also carried orders permitting the Augustinians to build churches and monasteries and to baptize "all the heathen [Hindus] who desired to follow" the Christian faith. By the first ship to leave the delta Tavares sent word to the viceroy at Goa and the bishop of Cochin about these events.[281]

The Augustinian superiors in Portuguese India were quick to take advantage of the opportunity offered. Four friars were soon dispatched to Bengal with Father Bernardo de Jesus, the superior of the mission. On hearing the news, Portuguese and native renegades also began to flock to Hugli. Others

[280] *Ibid.,* I, 3–26. This section includes (pp. 25–26) a detailed description of the mango and how to eat it.

[281] *Ibid.,* pp. 27–39. Hugli became of importance as a port around 1537. Tavares probably arrived at Akbar's court in 1577. While this account is clearly based on local tradition, other sources confirm its essential veracity.

who came to work as soldiers were especially attracted by the high monthly wages paid for service in that dangerous frontier area. Seven more Augustinians were shortly sent to minister to the Christians and to make converts. In the vicinity of Hijili they erected two new churches, and some of the friars penetrated southward into Orissa to build a church and residence at the port of Pipli. Others went northward to Dacca, "the chief city in Bengala" and its viceregal capital. In the suburbs of this metropolis the friars were able to build a small monastery and a "good Church." Manrique reports that Dacca, a city of more than two hundred thousand permanent residents, is wealthy beyond belief, especially its "Cataris" (Hindi, *khatris*, tradesmen). What adds materially to the wealth of Dacca is its proximity to several "fertile and pleasant principalities." In Dacca the friars meet great opposition from the Muslim "Moulas" (mullahs) and "Dravizes" (Persian, *darwesh*, religious mendicants also called fakirs). The latter, who live in retirement and are esteemed as saints, conspired with the nabob's senior wife to have the friars driven out. In this effort they failed, since the friars enjoyed the support of the emperor and consequently that of the nabob. Both Akbar and Jahangir tried to give the friars gifts of land and money in hopes that their presence in Bengal would attract more foreign merchants to its ports. The Augustinians, fearing the possible adverse consequences of accepting such gifts, politely rejected the Mughul overtures and continued to subsist on alms and on grants from the Portuguese crown. The friars, unlike the Jesuits, refused to engage in trade for fear of scandalizing and losing credit with both Christians and infidels.[282]

According to Manrique, Bengal includes twelve provinces which were formerly subject to their own emperor, a ruler who was equal in power to the independent monarchs of Gujarat and Vijayanagar.[283] Formerly the sultan lived in "Gauro" (Gaur), from which city he ruled with the aid of the twelve provincial governors commonly known as "the twelve Boiones [Bengali, *bhuyas*, landlords] of Bengal." After the Mughul takeover, the "grand Mogol" appointed "Nabobs" (*nawābs*) to be viceroys of these provinces. In their turn the nabobs appoint governors or "Siguidares" (tax collectors) of their own. To keep the people "more subject and impotent" these officials demand payments of taxes "four or six months . . . in advance." Ordinarily these officers, who serve entirely at the pleasure of the Mughul emperor, are in office for only short periods before being promoted, transferred, or fired. Consequently they demand tax advances and often employ

---

[282] *Ibid.*, pp. 40–51. Manrique does not mention the Jesuits by name, but he certainly had these chief rivals in mind when he reprimanded those missionaries who engage in commerce for forgetting "that such acts stand on a foundation of clay."

[283] *Ibid.*, p. 52. The twelve provinces may be identified as Bengal, Hijili, Orissa, Jessore, Chandkhan, Medinipur (Midnapur), Katrabuh, Bakla, Sulaimanabad, Bhalua, Dhaka (Dacca), and Rajmahal. The independent sultans of Bengal ruled from 1338 to 1576 when the Mughuls took over.

force to make their collections. Those debtors absolutely unable to pay are sold along with their families into slavery "as they are heathens." Despite these cruelties, the Bengalis consider it an act of cowardice to pay before "they have first been severely beaten." [284]

The climate and waters of Bengal are healthy and excellent. Food is abundant and cheap. The local rice, especially the scented varieties, is fine, delicate, and generally "far superior to that of Europe." [285] Since wine from grapes is not made in Bengal, a liquor is fermented from rice and a more "viscous liquor" is distilled from a kind of sugar that they call "jagra" (jaggery). In "Midinimpur" (Medinipur) they manufacture scented oils, which are exported to other parts of the Orient for use as bath oils. Bengal produces muslins so rich and fine that merchants, for security reasons, secrete them in hollow bamboos to carry them abroad. Many bamboos, especially those called male bamboos, are sometimes "as thick as a man's leg" and are in great demand as palanquin poles. They also cultivate a plant called "Anfion" (Arabic, *abyūn,* opium) which resembles "our hemp, though the seed is rather finer and it is sown afresh every year." From this plant and its fruit they obtain "a very bitter black extract," which the Orientals use to increase their sexual powers. If taken in large quantities, opium is very injurious. Those who became addicted to it may even die if they "fail to obtain it for three or four days, or, at most, six days." Opium, as well as "Posto" (from Persian, *post,* poppy seed) and "Bangue" (bhang), often produces unconsciousness and destroys intellectual powers. [286] For their delectation the rich often mix these drugs with fine spices, camphor, ambergris, and "almiscre" (Arabic, *al-misk,* musk). [287]

The natives of Bengal are generally medium dark in color, though many are as black as Sinhalese. Both sexes are well formed and of moderate height. Everyone wears cotton cloths "unshaped and unsewn." Common men wear a cloth from the waist down and a turban on the head; above the waist they are naked, and they wear no shoes. Males of higher station throw a cloth around their shoulders to cover the upper half of the body. Women cover the entire body with a long cloth of cotton for everyday wear. They decorate their arms with armlets and bracelets and wear large rings in their ears, necklaces on their necks, and a nose ornament in the left nostril. On their fingers and toes they wear rings and on their insteps often a foot orna-

---

[284] *Ibid.,* pp. 52–53. Enslavement of non-Muslim debtors was then a common practice in a number of Muslim countries.

[285] In India it is said that some varieties of rice have an aroma resembling that of the flavor of the flower of the *Bassia longifolia,* a tree whose flowers are roasted and eaten. On aroma in rice see D. H. Grist, *Rice* (3d ed.; London, 1959), pp. 70–71. Also see H. Drury, *The Useful Plants of India* (2d rev. ed.; London, 1873), p. 71.

[286] *Posto* (Urdu) is a decoction made from the poppy seed. *Bhāng* is a narcotic derived from various varieties of *Cannabis indica,* a hemp-like plant. It is usually smoked but is sometimes mixed in sweetmeats and eaten.

[287] Luard and Hosten (trans. and eds.), *op. cit.* (n. 279), I, 52–60.

ment. Their jewelry and ornaments are made of gold, silver, bell-metal (Sanskrit, *kansa,* or white copper), shells, ivory, and "Calaim, a metal resembling tin."[288] On festive occasions the women dress in silks of various colors and in cottons or silks embroidered with gold or silver threads. On special occasions men of substance wear trousers and a "cabaya" (tunic of muslin) in the Mughul style; the tunics of Muslims open on the right and those of the Hindus on the left. The common people merely wear very clean white clothes on such days.

As a people the Bengalis are characterized by meanness of spirit, cowardice, and servility. They willingly serve a harsh master, as is illustrated by their common saying: "He who chastizes is Lord, but who does not is a cur."[289] Ordinary Bengalis live in low mud huts thatched with straw or palm leaves. They daily scour walls and floors with cow dung. They sleep on straw mats and use cotton quilts as bed covers. They have several pots in which they cook rice and a few simple stews. Often their daily meal consists of nothing but rice to which a little salt is added. When they have it, they add "xaga" (Hindi, *sāga,* gram, an edible vegetable). Those of greater means add *ghī* (ghee, clarified butter) and other milk products. Some of them will eat fish, goat, wild boar, and wild birds; nobody will eat domesticated animals or eggs. Stricter pagans (Hindus) have many more food taboos; they will not even eat red vegetables or any other products having the color of blood. They usually restrict their diet to "kachari" (Hindi, *khichri,* kedgeree), a dish made of two parts rice to one of lentils (*dāl*) or of "Muhngo" (Hindi, *mung,* green-gram, or mung beans). To this mixture they add a large amount of "*ghī* so as to give it body." At feasts they prepare a "Gujarati kachari," a fancy dish which also includes nuts, raisins, and spices. They also make many types of sweetmeats in the preparation of which *ghī* plays an important role. Before meals the Hindus bathe and, if possible, anoint their bodies with oil. As a rule they have but one wife. Women serve the meal and then eat afterwards. The men, unlike the women, are not "much addicted to sexual intercourse," and are often secretly given aphrodisiacs by their wives. Their women, being "naturally impetuous," sometimes commit suicide by poisoning or drowning themselves. But as a rule these women are "humane, kindly, and easy to influence, and so more easily accept our true Catholic Faith than the men."[290]

Originally all the people of Bengal were heathens. Since becoming subject to the Mughuls, some have accepted the easier road to hell by embracing Islam. The majority, however, remain Hindus who follow the teachings of their Brahmans. While there are numerous Hindu sects, they all agree in

---

[288] On "Calaim" see above, p. 630, n. 107.
[289] This is indeed a common proverb. In Hindi it is rendered: "*Māre, Thākur; na māre, kukkur.*" On *Thākur* as a term of respect see Yule and Burnell, *op. cit.* (n. 18), p. 915.
[290] Luard and Hosten (trans. and eds.), *op. cit.* (n. 279), pp. 61–66.

worshipping the sun, the Ganges, and the cow. Whoever bathes in the Ganges, they believe, "is at once absolved from all the pains and penalties of sin." Those who live on the banks of this holy river bathe themselves each morning immediately after rising. Entry into the water is carried out ceremoniously; Brahmans, before entering the Ganges, take "some rice-straws in the right hand" and a small copper "spoon-like vessel" in the left.[291] While taking a prescribed number of strides to the river, the Brahman at every few paces throws one of the "straws" aside while uttering certain "laudatory and supplicatory phrases." Once he enters the river, he several times fills the "spoon" with water which he throws towards heaven. Then he makes a series of obeisances to the river and is purified. On returning home he kisses "the nastiest part of a Cow" and throws powdered cow dung over his head. Bengalis who live away from the Ganges perform similar ablutions in tanks built at village expense or by the charitable donations of rich and pious people.

The Hindus worship their idols in many temples, some of which are "fine, majestic structures, containing many riches." Most important is the temple of "Jagarnate" (*Jagannātha*; Anglo-Indian, Juggernaut, or Lord of the Universe) which stands on the seashore in Orissa.[292] This noted place of pilgrimage takes its name from the huge stone statue housed in its temple. Covered with "rich and valuable jewels and gold ornaments," this idol has one leg broken.[293] According to the books of the Brahmans the "Jagarnate" was cook to the Lord in heaven. One day he prepared such an atrocious meal that he was hurled from heaven to earth, his leg being broken by the fall. His statue now sits on a throne covered with gold cloth which is surrounded by a guard of giants called "Raiquos" (*Rākshas*) or demons. Most celebrated of the ceremonies dedicated to the idol are the sumptuous processions which attract vast throngs of pilgrims, especially yogis. In the month of June public processions are held in honor of "Druga" (*Durgā*, consort of Siva), who is described in their books as a prostitute to the gods. Accompanied by dancing girls and musicians, the idol's feast climaxes in a lascivious celebration. At its end the idol itself is hurled into a river or tank while its followers jeer, curse, and pelt it with stones.[294]

Far more authoritative is Manrique's description of the island of "Sagor"

[291] Manrique's "rice straws" are probably the pieces of *kusa* grass held by a Brahman when reciting the *Gayatri* (solar hymn). His "spoon-like vessel" is the *argha* used in making oblations. See *ibid.*, p. 68.

[292] *Cf.* above, pp. 676–77.

[293] The temple at Puti actually houses three wooden icons without arms or legs. The represent Jagannath, his sister Subhadra, and his brother Balbhadra. For photographs of them see K. Mahapatra (comp.), *The Jagannatha Temples in Eastern India* (Bhubaneswar, 1977), frontispiece. The likelihood is that Manrique's description is based on hearsay.

[294] Luard and Hosten (trans. and eds.), *op. cit.* (n. 279), I, 67–72. Most of what Manrique reports on Durga appears to be based on a misunderstanding of that goddess' role in the Hindu hierarchy of deities.

(Ganga Sagar), a place of pilgrimage which he personally visited.[295] This perfectly flat island at the mouth of the Hugli River was formerly a great Hindu center with many temples served by large numbers of Brahmans. Its importance as a religious place began to decline with the arrival of the Portuguese in Bengal and it was totally uninhabited at the time of Manrique's visit in 1629. Still, he says, pilgrims come to visit its ruined shrines in spite of the raids periodically carried out by the Portuguese and the Mughs of Arakan. The island is dotted with reservoirs whose banks are shaded and adorned by green areca palms. When male pilgrims arrive in these sacred precincts, they first have their heads and beards shaved, and then anoint themselves with oil before bathing in the reservoirs. Once both men and women have completed their ablutions they enter the temple to prostrate themselves before the idols. In their ecstasy certain devotees sacrifice themselves by walking into the surrounding waters to be devoured by the bloodthirsty sharks lurking there. Pilgrims and sailors on the Portuguese ships transport sacred waters to sell to devout Hindus in distant places. Christian ecclesiastical authorities, in the interest of religious peace, officially prohibit those subject to their jurisdiction from selling these waters.[296] Whenever possible, dying persons are taken to the Ganges to have its sacred waters poured into their mouths. Sometimes they even choke to death on the excess water and mud in their throats. Once dead they are cremated and their ashes thrown into the Ganges. The wives of married men, stupified by bhang and bereft of their senses, are burned on the pyre with their husbands.[297]

Manrique left Bengal for Arakan on September 11, 1629. More than ten years later, on his way back from the Far East, he journeyed through India from August 1640 to November 1641 on his way to Europe. He first arrived at Harispur in Orissa in the company of John Yard, a servant of the English East India Company stationed in that port.[298] Here Manrique, in consultation with Yard, decides to abandon all ideas of returning to Europe by sea and to take the land route instead. For safety's sake he decides to "adopt Mogor [Mughul] costume," the better to disguise himself as "a Dodagor [*saudagār*] or merchant." Attended by several native footmen, he leaves Harispur on horseback on August 4, 1640. At the end of àn eight-day journey, he arrives at Balasore "exhausted by the constant crossing and recross-

---

[295] *Sāgar* means "the sea." The island is situated at a place where once the holy waters of the Ganges entered the Bay of Bengal. Thousands of pilgrims still congregate there annually. See *Imperial Gazeteer of India, Provincial Series, Bengal*, p. 204.

[296] Manrique credits Meneses with promulgating this decree at the Synod of Diamper (1599). This commerce was actually first prohibited by the acts of the Third Provincial Council of Goa (1585).

[297] Luard and Hosten (trans. and eds.), *op. cit.* (n. 279), I, 73–79. In his substantial description of suttee Manrique does not even consider the possibility that it might be a voluntary rite.

[298] On John Yard's career see *ibid.*, II, 95, n. 1; on the English advent in Orissa see above, pp. 673–78.

ing of the rivers we met." Here he and his group acquire felt rain cloaks "to protect us from the waters of heaven." They then proceed to "Jalasor" (Jaleshwar), a trading center, where they stay at an excellent "Caravossora" (caravanserai, or rest-house) of thirty-three rooms.

Most such inns, Manrique reports, are located on the main travel routes and are provided by the neighboring villages or by the charity of rich and powerful men "in order to keep their memory green." Usually these edifices are built in a square form and are divided into chambers served by male and female attendants called respectively "Metres" (*mihtar*) and "Meteranis" (*mihtrānī*). These servants clean the rooms and provide cots; the bedding, usually carried by the traveler himself, includes a "Godorim" (Hindi, *gudrī*, quilt) or light cotton mattress which is placed on the webbing of the cot. The servants buy and prepare the food for both the travelers and his animals and provide for their other needs. In every regard Bengali innkeepers and stablemen are more obliging and less expensive than their counterparts in Europe.[299]

On the road to "Narangor" (Narayangadh) the Christian friar and his Muslim companions engage in a brief skirmish with local Hindus who are outraged when the travelers kill a brace of peacocks. Once they reach the town, Manrique and his companions are temporarily imprisoned by the authorities for violating customs and beliefs which the Mughuls had promised to respect and observe in the Hindu areas of Bengal. The friar is released after showing his passport, but one of his Muslim footmen is whipped to pay for the offense. From here, Manrique proceeds to the Ganges town of "Baligata" (Balaghat) through "flat, highly populated fertile country." After clearing the local customs and paying off his Muslim servants, Manrique makes his way to Dacca where he visits fellow Augustinians who are working there. Here he is detained for a period; the town's officials are too preoccupied to issue him a new passport, since the town is expecting an attack from a strong Mugh fleet. Finally he obtains the necessary papers from a lieutenant of the governor then residing at "Rajamol" (Rajmahal). At this juncture the nabob in charge is the second son of Emperor Shah Jahan.[300]

After twenty-seven days in Dacca fighting fever and officialdom, Manrique hires a boat and servitors to take him and his convert-companion up the Ganges. Progress is slow against the violent currents of the flooding river and the hostility of the Hindu pilgrims worshipping on its banks. He is astonished by the size and number of the crocodiles in the river and admires the intensive cultivation of its fertile banks. He and his servants land near the ruins of the city of "Gouro" (Gaur), in "former days the Capital and most famous of all cities in the Gangetic Empire." Warmly received by an official

[299] *Ibid.*, pp. 95–104.
[300] *Ibid.*, pp. 105–19. The second son of the emperor became governor of Bengal in 1639 and held that office until 1659 when he was deposed by his brother Aurangzib.

charged with examining the ruins for treasure, Manrique is given a guided tour of the ancient capital. The friar comments in some detail on its walls, gateways, and hewn stone reservoirs. He is particularly impressed by the excellent quality of the bricks used to construct the city's great wall, "a fact which accounted for its being still intact, save for a turret here and there." [301]

Proceeding upriver, Manrique anchors at Rajmahal, the city where the nabob is then holding court. With great difficulty the friar's boat enters its harbor through the more than "two thousand rowing vessels at anchor" there. The presence of the nabob has brought into existence a floating city of boats lined up in regular streets on which people live and offer for sale "every kind of merchandise which is met with in Cities on land." The friar is detained for nine days in Rajmahal while he copes with six customs and registry offices to obtain permission to continue on his journey. Between Rajmahal and Patna they halt at about eighteen more customs posts. Situated on the south bank of the Ganges, the commercial city of Patna is built on a flat plain. One of the most populous cities of the Mughul Empire, it boasts over two hundred thousand inhabitants and vast numbers of foreign traders. Its trade being so great, more than six hundred of its inhabitants work as brokers and middlemen.

Patna is the capital of the principality of the same name. [302] At this time the nabob is a son of "Assofo Kan" (Asaf Khan, the minister of Shah Jahan), named "Sexto Kan" (Shaista Khan), an official of great honor and high reputation. About him is told a story which Manrique relates at length and with many judgments about the moral conditions at the Mughul court. He asserts that it is customary for the emperor to enjoy the favors of the wives of his courtiers and officials, one day each week being set aside for such meetings. The wife of "Sexto Kan," a beautiful and chaste woman, for a long while successfully avoided this obligatory act. Other women of the court, who had themselves succumbed to the ruler's desires, plot to force "Sexto Kan's" wife to do likewise. Shah Jahan, the lascivious emperor, listens to the conspirators and sends "Sexto Kan" off to Patna with a strong force of cavalry to shortcircuit a plot against Mughul authority which is presumably being planned there. On leaving the court the prince entrusts his wife to his father's keeping. Shah Jahan, working with his daughter, manages to trick the innocent woman into a private meeting. On hearing of the violation of his wife, "Sexto Kan" refuses to pardon her and divorces her "on the spot." According to Manrique, "Sexto Kan," a "barbarian" exhibits by this act the strength the great Caesar displayed in divorcing Pompeia. [303]

[301] Gaur was entirely depopulated when an epidemic ravaged it in 1575. For a detailed account of its ruins see J. H. Ravenshaw, *Gaur* (London, 1878).

[302] Modern Patna, the capital of Bihar province, has a population of close to three hundred thousand.

[303] This same story is related by N. Manucci in his *Storia do Mogor* (2 vols.; London, 1907), I, 192; II, 125.

After this moralistic digression, Manrique again picks up the thread of his story. While in Patna, he learns that it is better to go overland to Agra even though it requires twenty-five days of hard travel. Consequently he hires a covered oxcart in which to continue his trip. Because of the summer heat he travels, as is customary in this part of the world, from "three hours before dawn until eleven o'clock" in the morning. After four days he arrives at "Benaros" (Benares) "the Rome and head of the Pagan religion in these parts." Pilgrims congregate, especially in the summer, in this city which reputedly has over four hundred "temples of their false gods." Here is produced a very fine cotton cloth on seven thousand looms which work constantly. Rich turbans made here are worn in countries as far away as Turkey.

Near Benares is the rich Hindu city of "Sansaram" (Sasaram), the site of a magnificent mausoleum or "Mochoroba" (from Arabic *maqbara*, a mausoleum). It was erected by a "very ancient Heathen King . . . as the future resting-place for his own body." [304] Manrique correctly notes that it is built in the center of a deep reservoir, is surmounted by a lofty, circular dome, and is entered through four great spherical arches. He reports, "according to their histories," that the interior of the dome was originally covered "from the base to the very top with heavy plates of gold, which can still be seen in some cavities." In the center of the hall under the dome four bronze bulls previously held on the points of their horns a "huge golden urn" containing the ashes of the "king." Sacred water from the Ganges which lay at "a distance of over four days' journey" was, at great expense, diverted into the tomb by "aqueducts and secret pipes." By Manrique's time the gold in the mausoleum had been carried off by "a whirlwind of human cupidity."

On leaving Benares he abandons the Ganges and strikes across country on narrow roads crowded by pilgrims on their way to the holy city. At the sides of the roads he sees the dead bodies of thieves hanging in trees, as well as columns of stone and lime "in which the skulls of malfactors are enclosed as a warning of what was done in the name of justice." The skulls of "unjust and corrupt judges" are placed in even loftier columns on which is inscribed the name of the culprit and the crime for which he was punished. After six days of travel Manrique again sees the Ganges when he registers and pays customs at the city of "Ilabas" (Allahabad). [305]

Manrique arrives in Agra on December 25, 1640. His description of the imperial capital, probably based in part on the accounts of Finch and De Laet, includes many references to places and events not previously described fully or at all. [306] The population of this crescent-shaped city on the Jumna numbers 660,000, and in addition, it hosts a great number of foreigners,

[304] This is actually the mausoleum of Sher Shah, the Afghan and Muslim emperor who ruled at Delhi from 1540 to 1545.
[305] Luard and Hosten (trans. and eds.), *op. cit.* (n. 279), II, 120–50.
[306] For the descriptions of Fitch and De Laet see above, pp. 614–15, 620–21.

who continually fill its ninety inns and its private houses. Its resident Jesuits, whose chapel is at that time in their house, receive the friar warmly and offer him the house usually occupied by a fellow Augustinian who is then languishing in prison.[307] After a brief journey to Bayana, Manrique returns to Agra to make arrangements for a trip to Lahore in the company of a high official ordered to report to the emperor there. Given an additional period of leisure in Agra, he examines the state of the court and is especially awed by the enormous treasure the emperor has stockpiled in various places. He is also impressed by the wealth and credit of the local merchants called "Katari" (Hindi, *khatris*) and by the quantities of "food-stuffs and dainties" available in the numerous bazaars. Entire streets are given over to makers of sweetmeats "which would stimulate the most jaded appetite to gluttony."

The fortress of Agra, "a small city in itself," is surrounded by a high wall of red stone. Because the stones are so well fitted and set, it requires a close inspection "to detect the joints between the blocks." Spherical towers which house cannons rise from the wall at regular intervals. Four lofty gates with drawbridges form the entryways to the fortress. The north gate is protected "by very large pieces of ordnance and the west gate, known as the 'Chicheri' [*Kachahri,* or court gate]," opens into a public square and marketplace. Two marble elephants stand just inside this west gate, on which ride effigies of the great Deccan nobles captured by Akbar.[308] Near this gate stands the kazi's tribunal where complaints are heard. Facing the tribunal is the palace of the principal nabob from which imperial edicts, decrees, and privileges are promulgated. The west gate is separated from the south gate, or the "Drouuage Achabar" (Akbar's gateway), by a square surrounded on all sides by tombs and mosques. Entrance through the south gate is barred by chains to all except the emperor and his sons. Near this gate is a "Maumetan [Muhammadan] College for whores" whose four hundred prostitutes are maintained at the emperor's expense "to answer his demands or those of his sons and concubines." The fourth gate, or "Dersane" (Hindi, *Darshan,* or sighting), looks out to the river over a handsome square.

Manrique, who repeatedly inveighs against Akbar, deigns nonetheless to describe the great emperor's tomb. The mausoleum at Sikandra, near Agra, was unfinished when Finch earlier wrote about it.[309] Manrique, who possibly learned about the tomb from hearsay, calls it a "magnificent building" which provides a striking sight for those who enter the imperial city from the Lahore road. The mausoleum stands in a square courtyard lined on each side by huts for pilgrims and dominated by a marble gateway to the tomb.

[307] The two Jesuits in Agra were Fathers Antonio de Olivera and Matheo de la Cruz. Neither is mentioned in standard reference works. The Augustinian was Father Antonio de Christo who had been prior in Hugli. He was captured along with several other priests and four thousand native Christians when the Mughuls invaded Hugli in 1632–33.

[308] This is a reference to the Khandesh nobles taken as hostages by Akbar after the fall of the Asirgarh in 1601. See above, p. 630.

[309] See above, pp. 615–16.

The interior of the mausoleum is covered from base to dome with paintings and its floor "is laid with glittering white marble." A marble-paved path leads to the tomb, which stands on a square plinth from the center of which a round tower emerges that terminates in a cupola. This central building is surrounded by similar but smaller edifices "all with long, wide corridors formed of parallel arches." Above the corridors stand splendid galleries which are divided into apartments for members of the imperial family when they visit there. Rooms below, used by those who hold ceremonies at the tomb, are ornamented "from roof to floor with gilded and painted leaves and flowers." In the center of the principal building stands Akbar's tomb, covered with a white sheet overlaid with a cloth of gold brocade. The entire mauseoleum is surrounded by pleasant gardens enclosed in a high wall. Water from the Jumna is piped into the gardens to keep them fresh and flourishing.

At the opposite end of Agra stands another mausoleum which is in process of being built. This still unfinished structure was initiated by the "Emperor Corrombo" (Khurram, Shah Jahan's name before he became emperor) in honor of his chief and favorite wife "Begoma" (Arjumand Bano Begam, Mumtaz Mahal).[310] The greater part of this mausoleum remains to be built but in 1641 Manrique sees being finished a tall square wall of "hewn stone of reddish hue" crowned with strong spikes. At its corners stand "four Palaces, built of great handsome blocks of white marble" brought from a long distance on carts drawn by teams of twenty or thirty oxen or buffaloes.[311] Inside the enclosure there rises "a vast lofty, circular structure" of white marble. A thousand workers are engaged in completing these buildings, in laying out gardens, in constructing roads, and in digging tanks. The architect of the Taj Mahal, according to Manrique, was a Venetian named "Geronimo Veroneo" who died at Lahore while Manrique was on his way there. Shah Jahan was pleased with the models and designs he made but wished the mausoleum to be richer and more costly than the Venetian had planned.[312]

After spending twenty-seven days in Agra, Manrique decides to depart immediately for the court at Lahore, where he wishes to solicit help from Asaf Khan in winning the release of the imprisoned Augustinian prior.[313]

[310] This is the famous Taj Mahal which was started in 1631, the year after Arjumand's death, and completed in 1648.

[311] The white Makrana marble was brought from Jaipur, about two hundred miles from Agra, and the red sandstone from the neighborhood of nearby Fatehpur-Sikri. See K. C. Mazumdar, *Imperial Agra of the Moghuls* (2d ed.; Agra, 1939), p. 168.

[312] For a discussion of the much-debated issue of Veroneo's role, if any, in the planning of the Taj Mahal see Luard and Hosten's special appendix in *op. cit.* (n. 279), II, 173–77. Mazumdar, *op. cit.* (n. 311), p. 167, brands as a myth the assertion that Veroneo was the architect of this mausoleum. He asserts that its chief architect was Muhammad Isa Afandi of Turkey who was assisted by Muhammad Sharif of Samarkand.

[313] Asaf Khan, *Vazīr* or chief minister to Shah Jahan, was the most influential person in the empire and the "channel through which at that time, the mercies, gifts, and favours of the Mogol Monarch flowed in a broad stream." See Luard and Hosten (trans. and eds.), *op. cit.* (n. 279), II, 178–79.

After a six-day journey by cart, he reaches the ancient city of "Deli" (Delhi), the "original home and source of the Mogol Monarchy." He visits the tombs of Sikandar Ghazi (r. 1489–1517) and other Pathan rulers as well as the palace built by Humayun.[314] He proceeds to "Tanassar" (Thanesar) where there is a fort and a famous tank surrounded by temples to which Hindus make pilgrimages. Near the temples is a deep pit from which sal ammoniac is extracted. At the next stage, called "Sirynam" (Sirhind), there is a substantial market in cotton textiles and a magnificent tank from the middle of which a circular tower rises which is dedicated to the five "Nimasas" (*nimāz*) or the times of prayer fixed for Muslims. This "Maumetan Oratory" is reached by a fine stone bridge supported by fifteen large arches. Manrique also visits the nearby imperial garden of the Mughuls, which is square in shape and entered through four gateways. The garden is divided into four equal sections by cypress-lined roadways which form a cross. In one section a number of fruit trees are cultivated, in another every kind of flower, and in the third every edible plant; in the last section stands a great palace.[315]

Twenty-one days after his departure from Agra, Manrique arrives at the outskirts of Lahore. On the advice of his guides, he and his group camp for the night near the tent city which has sprung up in the adjoining countryside to house and feed the thousands who have followed the emperor to Lahore. In the evening he explores the tent city, in particular its bazaars, which are brightly illuminated by "artificial lights." On the lookout for food, he visits the cook-shops where they sell roast poultry and meats "including horse-flesh, which is much used in place of pork." In other booths they purvey "rich and aromatic Mogol Bringes [Persian, *birinj,* rice dishes] and Persian pilaos [*pilāo,* rice with meat]," which differ mainly in name. Simple Hindu vegetarian dishes are also available, especially the dry rice preparations preferred by the Gujaratis. Flat cake-like breads are sold under three different names: "Apas" (Tamil, *appu,* a south Indian name for a *chapatī*), "Curuchas" (Hindi, *khjūrā,* a sweetened bread), and "Raqunis" (Hindi, *roghani,* an oily bread). The first is unleavened and is made entirely of flour baked on "iron plates or clay dishes"; it is the bread eaten ordinarily by the poor and by those traveling in caravans. The second is a "white, good bread" usually reserved to the upper classes. The third, because it is made from wheat flour and an abundance of *ghī,* is a delicate, flaky bread. The friar is impressed by the abundance, variety, and cheapness of the foods on sale in this makeshift city, as well as its organization, cleanliness, and "peace and quiet."[316]

[314] Manrique is here mistaken. This palace was built by Sher Khan and used by Humayun.
[315] This palace and its gardens were probably destroyed in 1709 when Sirhind was plundered by the Sikhs. Finch had also described this imperial garden. For its history and for other references to it see Ansari, *op. cit.* (n. 86), pp. 56–57.
[316] Luard and Hosten (trans. and eds.), *op. cit.* (n. 279), II, 185–89.

The next morning he enters Lahore at an early hour while the streets are still empty. While looking for the inn of the "Franquis" (Franks, or Europeans) he fortunately meets Giuseppe di Castro (1577–1646), an Italian Jesuit resident in Lahore. Since the emperor is in Lahore for the feast of "Nourous" (*Naw-roz,* or New [Year's] Day), Manrique describes in great detail the decorations adorning the city and the imperial palace. At this time all classes dress in their best clothes, and visit one another to exchange wishes for a happy feast. Commoners ornament the doors of their houses with green branches or with white plaster daubed with red coloring. Banners of green silk fly everywhere, for green is the favorite color of the Muslims. Within the confines of the imperial palace is a great square lined with four thousand gaily bedecked horsemen drawn up in two columns. Behind this avenue of cavalry stand six hundred armored elephants and their riders also lined up in two rows. Behind this phalanx of warrior elephants is the imperial bodyguard of picked men and beasts who guard the entry to the throne hall. In its interior gather the leading nobles of the empire, both civil and military, who are escorted to their places by eunuch ushers. The throne hall is permanently decorated from floor to roof with "inlay work of intertwined flowering branches and grotesques in the finest gold . . . traced out in agate in relief." In the center of the hall stands a superb throne or "tacto" (Persian, *takht,* throne) which contains "within its spherical circumference four separate stages [levels] each with six gold and silver steps." Eight golden columns hold up a golden cupola or canopy over a golden seat, the whole being decorated with diamonds, rubies, emeralds, sapphires, and pearls.[317]

Manrique also describes the celebration of Shah Jahan's birthday on July 8, 1641, in the city of his birth. After watching spectacles in the imperial palace for most of the day, the emperor goes to pay his respects to his mother and to receive her felicitations.[318] While he is at his mother's palace, the courtiers present him with "rich, sumptuous gifts." He then returns to the imperial palace, where he presides over a copious feast served by the palace eunuchs. At the end of this banquet he retires to a private chamber in which hangs a golden scales decorated with precious stones. Dressed in a white satin robe covered with jewels, the emperor squats in one of the balance's pans. At once the nobles fill the other pan with bags of silver rupees until the balance is in equilibrium. When the rupees are removed, they fill the same pan with bags of gold and precious stones. In a third weighing they balance the emperor's weight against rich textiles and in a fourth against foods and common cloths. The articles from the final weighing are distributed secretly to

[317] This account of the palace and throne is probably based on hearsay rather than on direct observation. See *ibid.,* II, 190–99. On the remains of this imperial palace, or *Diwan-i-Am,* built in the reigns of Jahangir and Shah Jahan, see Murray, *op. cit.* (n. 191), pp. 489–91.

[318] His mother was Balmati Begam, a Hindu woman of the royal house of Jodhpur.

poor Brahmans and "Baneanes" (Banyans). The riches from the first three weighings are converted into cash, which is regularly given out as alms over the ensuing year. This ceremony ended, the emperor returns to his throne and distributes "artificial and imitation fruits, in silver," to his courtiers. Persons of lesser rank receive newly minted rupees as gifts from the emperor. Compared to what he receives as presents, the avaricious emperor's gifts to others are pitifully small.[319]

Once the traditional holidays end, Manrique, with the help of Father di Castro and a eunuch friend, obtains permission to present his case for the liberation of his fellow Augustinian to Asaf Khan. Accompanied by four "sipais" (Persian, *sipāhī*, sepoys, or cavalrymen), he rides to the entrance of Asaf Khan's palace where he is met by Father di Castro. He is then taken to a gatehouse to change from his Mughul clothes into his clerical vestments; the Mughul prince, it was thought, could be expected to respect him more and treat him better if he appeared forthrightly as a European rather than as a counterfeit Mughul merchant. He carries with him the usual "adia" (Arabic, *hadīya*, or gift), as well as rarities from China. On entering the palace gate he walks on paths strewn with flowers through several courtyards and a lovely park dotted with "attractive bathing-places . . . enclosed in gilded and painted houses." The principal one of these Muslim baths contains murals depicting John the Baptist and Noah's Ark. In an audience hall in the center of this garden he is presented to Asaf Khan; the prince, being ill, remains in bed to receive him. When the usual polite inquiries and ceremonies are finished, Manrique importunes the prince for the release of Antonio de Cristo, the Augustinian prior who had by then been nine years in the imperial prison. After agreeing to investigate the matter and to see about the release of the prisoner, Asaf Khan compliments Manrique on his command of court etiquette and orders the attendants to grant the missionary free entry to his palace. Ultimately Manrique effects the release of the prior and obtains permission for him to return to Bengal. Taking further advantage of the prince's friendship, Manrique also obtains an imperial *farman* granting permission for the reconstruction in Sind of the Augustinian churches and residences which Shah Jahan himself had ordered destroyed a few years earlier. Manrique, for his part, agrees to make a detour to Sind to carry the *farman* and to undertake for Asaf Khan the negotiation of certain business matters with the Portuguese factors there.

Manrique delays for two days his departure from Lahore. He wishes to take advantage of an opportunity offered to observe a magnificent banquet given by Asaf Khan for Shah Jahan. Secreted in a gallery above the banquet hall, he and a companion, presumably Father di Castro, illicitly observe an occasion at which secluded ladies are present whom they are forbidden to

---

[319] See Luard and Hosten (trans. and eds.), *op. cit.* (n. 279), II, 200–204. *Cf.* above, p. 640, for a summary of Roe's description of the weighing of Jahangir.

see. Magnificent serving vessels stand on five-tiered buffets placed in the four corners of the room. Incense burns in braziers scattered around the hall. At its entrance stands a silver fountain with seven spouts from which perfumed waters fall into a silver trough in which the guests wash their feet. In the center of the rug-filled hall there is spread a "destercherana" (Persian, *dastār-khwān,* a tablecloth) of fine white muslin embroidered with flowers in gold and silver thread. At his entry the emperor is preceded by a bevy of beautiful women and accompanied by his mother-in-law and daughter.[320] Behind the emperor comes "Prince Sultan Dara Sucur" with his grandfather Asaf Khan on his right.[321]

The imperial entry is accompanied by music and followed by a series of ceremonial obeisances and prostrations as the company seats itself. While chants are sung celebrating the emperor's many victories, a hand-washing ceremony is performed. Four lovely and very white girls, relations of Asaf Khan and other courtiers, carry the "implements used in this ablution of the hands of that Imperial Majesty." One girl lays out a white satin cloth before him, the next places a rich golden vessel on it, the third pours water over the imperial hands from a golden ewer, and the last gives him a towel. As these girls retire, twelve others enter and perform a similar ceremony for the remaining members of the imperial party. Then the dishes arrive from another entrance, accompanied by the "deafening sound of instruments such as Atables [Arabic, *tabl,* a huge drum], Bergondas [?], and Vacas [?], instruments not unlike our trumpets."

The dinner is served in golden dishes by eunuchs richly dressed in white coats and in trousers of different colored silks. Four of the principal eunuchs station themselves next to the emperor. They pass dishes brought to them by other eunuchs to two lovely girls who kneel on either side of the ruler to offer him dishes and to remove those not wanted. Among the numerous dishes are European-type pastries, cakes, and sweetmeats "made by some slaves who had been with the Portuguese" at Hugli. After four hours of feasting and a multitude of ceremonial acts, the hall is cleared of food. For dessert twelve dancing girls appear whose suggestive dress and behavior appeal "to Maumetan sensuality and wickedness." Thereafter three other girls bring as a gift to the emperor three golden vessels filled with precious stones. While the greedy emperor runs the jewels through his fingers, the two European *voyeurs* are escorted safely out of the palace through subterranean passages.[322]

After a ten days' journey southward from Lahore, Manrique reaches

---

[320] The emperor's mother-in-law was the wife of Asaf Khan; the daughter, Jahanara Begam, was the granddaughter of Asaf Khan.

[321] Dara Shikoh, the heir apparent, was the eldest and favorite son of Shah Jahan. Born in 1618, this prince was murdered in 1659 on Aurangzib's orders. See Luard and Hosten (trans. and eds.), *op. cit.* (n. 279), II, 216, n. 12.

[322] *Ibid.,* pp. 205–20.

Multan, a wealthy city of moderate size, a halting place for the caravans from Persia and a gateway to the northwestern frontier region. On presenting his credentials to the local governor, Manrique is turned over to "Trucidas Babara" (Tulsi Das Bhabra), a merchant who "carried on most of the business in Sinde [Sind]." With this merchant's help, Manrique hires a large, flat-bottomed boat and a body of armed guards to conduct him and his goods down the Ravi river to the Indus. In the course of these negotiations the Augustinian friar learns how much respect the Westerners enjoy among the Indians for their superior firearms and their skills in medicine. After an uneventful eight-day voyage, he arrives at the city of "Bacher" (Bhakkar), from which this region takes its name.[323] The nabob has his headquarters here and many merchants frequent this city, from which annual caravans depart for Persia. Four days later he arrives at the beginning of the province of "Seivan" (Sehwan) at a narrow stretch of the Indus. South of this point, where the river widens and where much of the surrounding territory is uninhabited, Manrique's boat is attacked by pirates. After the marauders are driven off, he proceeds downriver to the city of Sehwan and four days later arrives at "Tata" (Thatta), the metropolitan city of Sind.

After seeing "Trucidas" get his goods safely through the customs, Manrique proceeds downstream to the "Bandel" (the harbor at Diul or Laribandar at the mouth of the Indus). Here he meets with Father Jorge de la Natividad, superior of the mission, to tell him about the *farman* in his possession. The two Augustinians return to Thatta to arrange with its governor for the implementation of the *farman*. Advised by local travelers to take the land route back to Lahore, Manrique rents two camels. Since it is the end of the rainy season, he is obliged to wait for about a month at Thatta before embarking on the return journey. He takes advantage of this enforced respite to examine the city of Thatta and its products. Besides wheat and rice, much cotton is marketed in Thatta. Two thousand of its looms weave rich cotton textiles for export to many parts of Asia and to Portugal. Thatta also produces "a species of silk" from which fine taffetas and "tafeciras" (Persian, *tafcilak*?)[324] could have been woven "had there been good handicraftsmen." Since cattle and buffalo abound in this region, Thatta exports hides in vast quantities. In the city they also manufacture fine Sind leather "ornamented with back-stitch work . . . and finished off with fringes of silk at the ends." Sind leathers are used in India as table covers, room hangings, bed coverings, and trappings for horses. In addition, they manufacture back-stitched quilts and excellent mattresses. In this rich port city with its many foreigners, depravity reigns supreme. Men and boys dressed as women roam its streets "solicitating others as abandoned as themselves." Women who profess to despise the world and live in retirement claim to possess the

[323] By the "Kingdom of Bacher" Manrique means Sind, or the region of the Indus.

[324] Probably a reference to the cheap striped cloth of mixed silk and cotton also known as "tapseels" in the English factory records. See Irwin, *op. cit.* (n. 250), p. 30.

privilege of satisfying their wicked desires with any man at hand. The men so preyed upon consider it a sin not to succumb to these wanton, hypocritical women.

Seven days after leaving Thatta, Manrique arrives at "Marum" (Umarkot) in the state of Jodhpur. Here he and his companions acquire leather buckets and long ropes to draw water from the deep wells in the "wild, dry, sandy deserts" through which they must pass. After seven days of desert hardships, they arrive at the settled and cultivated land belonging to "the Kingdom of Jeselmeere." At its capital city of the same name is the residence of its pagan ruler, a vassal of the Mughuls.[325] The women here pay taxes for a license to dress splendidly and to work as dancers and prostitutes. From this town Manrique proceeds to Multan, where he had visited earlier, only to hear of the death of his benefactor, Asaf Khan.[326] On learning this sad news, Manrique decides not to return to Lahore but to take the road to Persia directly.[327]

While Manrique prepares for his journey westward, the Mughul authorities at Multan make life difficult for him. As a protégé of Asaf Khan, the Augustinian must be cleared of all suspicion that he is carrying to Persia secret treasures amassed by the prince. Before being granted a passport, he is closely examined and even thrown into prison for a few days. Once he receives the necessary travel documents, Manrique leaves Multan for Qandahar with a Mughul noble who is leading a cavalry force of eight hundred men to the frontier. Constantly on the lookout for marauding Afghans, Manrique's group crosses "lofty and rugged mountains, all covered with snow," stopping only at Mughul frontier fortresses along the way. After eighteen days of hard travel, he arrives at Qandahar, a city mainly populated by Muslims. As a rule the Mughuls maintain here a permanent force of fifteen thousand cavalry to ward off the Afghans in the surrounding mountains and to guard against any attempt by Persia to recover this region which a few years earlier had been treacherously surrendered to the Mughuls by its Persian governor.[328] While numerous and well equipped, the Mughul cavalry "is in fact not very formidable most of it being merely good for show." Before ending his account of the Mughul Empire, Manrique concludes with several general chapters describing its extent, armed forces, provinces, and treasure, all drawn from De Laet and other earlier European authors.[329]

---

[325] This small Rajput state was then ruled by Maharawal Manchardas.

[326] He died on November 21, 1641, and was buried at Lahore. His properties were seized immediately by Shah Jahan following normal Mughul practice.

[327] Luard and Hosten (trans. and eds.), *op. cit.* (n. 279), II, 221–43.

[328] In 1637 Qandahar was turned over to Shah Jahan for a price. The Persians took it back in 1648.

[329] Luard and Hosten (trans. and eds.), *op. cit.* (n. 279), II, 245–98. Occasionally he adds a few remarks based on his own experiences and observations. But generally these additions repeat what he had earlier reported in his itinerary.

5

SHAH JAHAN AND HIS SONS

While Manrique toured the Mughul Empire, the French jewel merchant Jean Baptiste Tavernier (1605–1689?) was making his first trip (1640–42) in India. In conjunction with his trading activities Tavernier made four additional excursions in the subcontinent during 1645–48, 1652–54, 1659–61, and 1665–67. His experiences, mostly in the Mughul Empire and Golconda, relate to the last eighteen years of Shah Jahan's reign and to the first nine years of Aurangzib's lengthy era (1658–1707).[330] After his return to Paris in 1668, Tavernier began to assemble and organize his notes and his memories of India. With the help of others he produced the travelogues in which he recounts his six voyages to the East, five of which took him to India; they were published at Paris in 1676–77.[331]

Tavernier was naturally most interested and best informed on matters relating to trade. While he probably knew a smattering of Persian, he generally was obliged to do business through an interpreter. Most of what he relates he saw with his own eyes or heard about from other merchants. Unhappily, he ordinarily does not bother to distinguish in his narratives between what he knew from personal experience and what he learned from hearsay. He is perhaps at his best on trade routes, on the production and exchange of commodities, and on currencies and business practices.[332] Since he brought exotic European products, he was well received by the Mughul courtiers who were always on the lookout for splendid and unusual gifts to offer to the emperor. Thus he is able to provide insights into court life and the administration of commerce and justice based upon personal experience. While he understands very little about India's customs or beliefs, he describes accurately and painstakingly the monuments he saw, some of which have since disappeared or exist only in ruins. His accounts of political history and contemporary politics, based mainly on court or mercantile gossip, are generally impartial but are not well informed or trustworthy.[333] His "his-

---

[330] For his travels in Golconda see below, pp. 1077–79.

[331] On the preparation of *Les six voyages* and for its bibliographical history see above, pp. 416–18. The first edition is divided into two parts published separately in two volumes; the second part deals with India and the neighboring Indies. The citations which follow are from the 1889 English translation of V. Ball, as further edited by W. Crooke, *op. cit.* (n. 24).

[332] For example, Part II of Tavernier's first edition includes a series of crude engravings of the coins then circulating in India and of the numerous precious stones available in its markets. These illustrations are not included in the English versions.

[333] In writing about the accounts of Tavernier and his contemporaries as historical sources, Sir Jadunath Sarkar observes: "Their works are of undoubted value as throwing light on the condition of the people, the state of trade and industry, and the history of the Christian churches in India. Moreover, the criticism of Indian manners and institutions by foreign observers has a freshness and weight all its own. But of the political history of India, apart from the few events in which they took part or which they personally witnessed, their reports merely reproduced

torical and political description" of the Mughul Empire derives in large measure from Bernier's account.[334] His other observations, when tested by comparison with native records and modern scholarship, are generally more accurate than many of his detractors have supposed them to be.[335]

On his last trip to India, Tavernier met François Bernier (1620–88) at Delhi in December, 1665. A physician and a disciple of the philosopher Pierre Gassendi (1592–1655), Bernier had arrived at Surat on an Indian vessel around the end of 1658 or early in 1659. Like other European physicians of the time, he was quickly recruited by the Mughuls for their service. For a period of eight years he worked at the imperial court as a physician. Here he was placed under the protection of "Danechmend-Kan" (*Danishmand Khan*, or Learned Knight), "the most learned man of Asia" and one of the most powerful and distinguished lords of the empire.[336] Bernier soon learned Persian and discussed religion and philosophy with his patron and other courtiers. As a court attendant he had opportunities for travel which permitted him to traverse the empire from Bengal to Kashmir. Since he arrived on the scene during Aurangzib's ascent to power, he was in a position to observe and participate in certain of its events. Most of what he wrote about the civil war is based on the reports of others, but it should be recalled that the public memory of these wars, while probably confused and inaccurate, was still fresh when Bernier began to sample it. In 1667 he left India and took the overland route to Europe. Two years later he was back in Paris arranging for the publication of his *Histoire de la dernière révolution des États du Grand Mogul* (1670–71).[337]

In laying the background to the succession wars of 1655 to 1661, Bernier begins by discussing the family of Shah Jahan and the ambitions of his four sons: Dara Shikoh (1615–59), Shujah (1616–61?), Aurangzib (1619–1707), and Murad Bakhsh (1624–61). Dara, the eldest, is perceived as being bright, courteous, arrogant, irascible, and quick to anger. Although a Muslim by birth, Dara tolerantly consults with both the Hindu pundits and the Christian missionaries; indeed, he is accused of heresy by orthodox Muslims. Shujah, while sharing many of Dara's traits, is more discreet, better at in-

---

the bazaar rumours and the stories current among the populace, and cannot be set against the evidence of contemporary histories and letters in Persian" (*A Short History of Aurangzib, 1618–1707* [3d ed.; Calcutta, 1962], pp. 6–7).

[334] Ball and Crooke (trans. and eds.), *op. cit.* (n. 24), I, 257, n. 2.

[335] For a criticism of his trade routes by a contemporary, see the remarks of Daniel Havart as summarized below, p. 1086.

[336] This is the title of Muhammad Shah, the Persian merchant who brought Bernier from Ahmadabad to Agra. Shah Jahan took the Persian into the imperial service as paymaster of the army. Soon he began to take charge of foreign affairs for the emperor. Later he became governor of Shahjahanabad, or Delhi, where he died in 1670.

[337] For bibliographical details see above, p. 414. The citations which follow are from A. Constable (ed.), *Travels in the Mogul Empire, A.D. 1656–1668 by François Bernier: A Revised and Improved Edition Based upon Irving Brock's Translation* (2d ed.; Delhi, 1968). Constable's edition was first published in 1891.

trigue, and more of "a slave to his pleasures" than his elder brother. While his father and brothers follow the religion of the Turks, Shujah professes the Persian form of Islam, presumably to secure and retain the support of the many important Persian officials at the court. Aurangzib, the third brother, is "reserved, subtle, and a complete master of the art of dissimulation"; while devoid of urbanity, Aurangzib possesses sounder judgment than Dara in his selection of advisers and servants. Murad, the youngest, is "inferior to his three brothers in judgment and address," indulges too much in "the pleasures of the table," and trusts excessively in the strength of his arm and in the quickness of his sword. Begam-Saheb (1614–81), Shah Jahan's eldest daughter, who was also known as Jahanara Begam, is the emperor's favorite, and she exerts great influence over him. The affairs of Dara prosper because she supports him as the successor to her aged and ailing father.[338]

As the brothers age, each organizes his own party and sets up his claims to the succession. Fearful for his personal safety, the emperor appoints each of them as rulers over distant provinces: Shujah to Bengal, Aurangzib to the Deccan, Murad to Gujarat, and Dara to Kabul and Multan.[339] Dara, however, remains at court as heir apparent and rules his province from the capital. The other three immediately depart for their assigned provinces and begin to act "in every respect as independent sovereigns." In the absence of his brothers, Dara's star rises so swiftly "that two kings seemed to reign with equal power." While Shah Jahan publicly favors Dara, he secretly lives in dread of his eldest son and allegedly carries on a secret correspondence with Aurangzib "whose talents for government" he respects.

In the Deccan, meanwhile, Aurangzib is befriended by "Emir Jumla" (*Mīr Jumlā*), a famous Persian general in the service of Golconda.[340] Because the sultan of Golconda is planning to have him killed, the *Mīr Jumlā* devises a ruse by which Aurangzib is able to obtain a peaceful entry into Bhagnagar (Hyderabad), the capital of Golconda. While the deception succeeds and leads to the spoliation of Bhagnagar, the trapped sultan manages to escape to the nearby fortress of Golconda.[341] After an unsuccessful two months' siege of the fortress, Shah Jahan commands Aurangzib to retire westward, presumably because Dara and his party fear the overthrow of Golconda will make Aurangzib too powerful.[342] Before obeying the emperor's order, Au-

---

[338] *Ibid.*, pp. 4–12. Shah Jahan had more than four sons, but those mentioned here were all by the same mother. Long before he fell ill in 1657, the emperor had been grooming Dara as his successor. See Sarkar, *op. cit.* (n. 333), pp. 42–45.

[339] Tavernier (Ball and Crooke, *op. cit.* [n. 24], I, 261) asserts that Dara was assigned the province of Sind. In fact he was viceroy of the Punjab.

[340] *Mīr Jumlā* is the name of the office of first minister in Golconda. Muhammad Sa'id, who became inordinately wealthy and powerful as the *Mīr Jumlā*, aroused the hostility of Abdu'llah Qutb Shah, the sultan of Golconda. In 1656, fearful of his life, the *Mīr Jumlā* threw himself for protection on the Mughuls. In Hindustan he was generally called Mir Jumla as if it were his personal name. For Tavernier's relations with him in Golconda see below, pp. 1077–79.

[341] *Cf.* below, pp. 1073–74.

[342] On the influence of court politics on the Deccan programs of the Mughuls see Y. M. Khan, *The Deccan Policy of the Mughuls* (Lahore, 1971), pp. 196–97.

rangzib obtains an indemnity from the sultan, marries his son to the sultan's daughter, demands the fortress of "Ramgayre" (Ramagiri) for the princess' dowry, exacts a promise that his son will be named heir apparent of Golconda,[343] requires that the silver coins of Golconda be imprinted with the arms of Shah Jahan, and stipulates that Mir Jumla be granted permission to leave Golconda freely with his family, possessions, and troops. In short, Aurangzib requires Golconda to acknowledge the suzerainty of Shah Jahan.[344]

On their way to the Deccan, Aurangzib and Mir Jumla besiege and capture "Bider" (Bidar), one of the strongest fortresses of Bijapur. Back in Daulatabad, the successful conspirators plan great joint enterprises which will eventually make Aurangzib the emperor. Mir Jumla then goes to the court of Agra, where he presents to Shah Jahan a huge uncut diamond "generally deemed unparalleled in size and beauty."[345] He also convinces the emperor to concentrate his armies on the conquest of the Deccan and the south rather than wasting them in the north; the precious stones of Golconda, he asserts, are of much greater value than the rude rocks of Qandahar. It is rumored that the emperor, constantly becoming more fearful of the insolence of Dara, is glad to have a pretext for raising an army. Dara, impatient of any threat to his growing power, is charged with responsibility for the murder of "Sadullah-Kan" (Sa'dullah Khan), a Muslim noble whom the emperor esteemed most highly.[346] So, despite Dara's fervent objections, Mir Jumla is sent to the Mughul Deccan "at the head of a fine army." Shortly after his arrival there, Mir Jumla goes on to Bijapur and besieges its fortress of "Kaliane" (Kaliani).[347]

Shah Jahan falls seriously ill in 1657, thus producing a crisis which fills "the whole extent of his dominions with agitation and alarm." His sons immediately prepare for war as rumors circulate that the emperor is dying. Shujah in Bengal is the first to take the field. Pretending to believe that his father is actually dead and the throne vacant, Shujah announces his intentions to overthrow Dara, the alleged poisoner of his father, and take over the empire himself. Aurangzib also sets his forces in motion but is too weak to win by arms alone. Pretending to prefer a religious life to the responsibilities of ruling, Aurangzib resorts to trickery to make dupes of his brothers. In a letter to Murad in Gujarat, he declares that Dara and Shujah are unworthy to govern and pledges to support Murad, who alone possesses "the

---

[343] This provision was kept secret by Aurangzib and was not shown to the emperor. When Shah Jahan came to know of it, this clause was removed from the treaty. See *ibid.*, p. 221.

[344] Constable (ed.), *op. cit.* (n. 337), pp. 16–22. This is substantively a quite accurate account of the defection and of the peace arrangements concluded in 1656. *Cf.* Sherwani, *op. cit.* (n. 271), pp. 441–44. Also *cf.* below, pp. 1090–91.

[345] Dr. V. Ball, a geologist and the translator of Tavernier, identified this diamond as the famous Koh-i-Nur. See Ball and Crooke (trans. and eds.), *op. cit.* (n. 24), I, xxx; II, 331–48.

[346] This nobleman, an ardent supporter of Aurangzib, probably died of natural causes. Aurangzib saw Mir Jumla as his replacement at court. See Khan, *op. cit.* (n. 342), p. 222.

[347] Constable (ed.), *op. cit.* (n. 337), pp. 22–24. The death of Muhammad 'Adil Shah in 1656 diverted the Mughuls from Golconda to Bijapur. See Khan, *op. cit.* (n. 342), p. 227.

qualifications for ruling a mighty empire." Volunteering to put his armed forces and his fortune at Murad's disposal, Aurangzib urges his younger brother to capture Surat immediately, for "the vast treasure of the State" is deposited there. Delighted by Aurangzib's proffered support, Murad assumes "all the consequence and authority of a king" and in 1657 dispatches a small force of three thousand men to besiege Surat. The flower of his army Murad sends to Daulatabad to join Aurangzib and the army of the Deccan.

Although Surat puts up an unexpectedly stiff resistance, Murad finally succeeds in forcing the capitulation of its fortress by mining and blowing up its walls, a technique taught him by Dutch engineers. The sack of Surat fails to yield the treasure expected, but it wins a great name for Murad as an innovative military leader.[348] He then joins Aurangzib personally with the remainder of his army to plan a combined attack upon Dara and the army of Agra. Threatened by the Bengal and Deccan armies of his sons, the ailing emperor is left with no choice. He reluctantly agrees to support Dara's forces. Since the danger from the Bengal army is the most immediate, he sends the imperial army to halt its progress. While this battle goes on, the combined armies of Aurangzib and Murad move rapidly and steadily on Agra. An imperial army, under the joint command of "Kasem-Kan" (Kasim Khan Jawini), a first-rate soldier, and "Raja Jessomseingue" (Raja Jaswant Singh), an influential Rajput leader, is quickly put into the field to meet the growing threat from the south. In an initial engagement at the Narbada River, "Kasem-Kan," never a firm supporter of Dara, "ingloriously flees from the field" leaving "Jessomseingue" in terrible peril. The brave Rajput's life is saved by the valor of his devoted followers, and he and a remnant retire to his own territory rather than to Agra. Here he receives a "disdainful reception" from his wife for fleeing from the field of battle.[349]

The victorious forces of Aurangzib and Murad advance slowly and cautiously on Agra as they prepare for a decisive battle with Dara. With the reluctant acquiescence of the emperor, Dara assembles a fine army of at least "one hundred thousand horse, more than twenty thousand foot, and eighty pieces of cannon."[350] Aurangzib's army of not more than forty thousand fatigued troopers appears too weak to confront Dara's superior numbers. While still in unchallenged command of the emperor's person, treasures, and armies, Dara decides to strike quickly and decisively to eliminate Aurangzib and Murad from the contest for power. He first stations and for-

[348] *Cf.* Gokhale, *op. cit.* (n. 57), pp. 52–53.

[349] Constable (ed.), *op. cit.* (n. 337), pp. 24–41. Bernier digresses at this point on the Rajputs and their devotion to warfare.

[350] Dara's army "looked formidable in appearance only, being 60,000 troops in number . . . not properly coordinated nor trained in concerted action" (Sarkar, *op. cit.* [n. 333], p. 61). Bernier himself questions the numbers given by his contemporaries when they write of the vast size of the Mughul armies. The French physician suspects that they include in their estimates the "incredible number of camp-followers" who accompany these armies. See Constable (ed.), *op. cit.* (n. 337), p. 43.

tifies his forces at the river "Tehembel" (Chambal, a tributary of the Jumna) to await the arrival of his brothers' army. Aurangzib, well informed of Dara's movements, crosses the river at an unprotected ford and outflanks Dara's position. Once across the Chambal, Aurangzib takes up a position at "Samonguer" (Samugarh) east of Agra near the Jumna river. To protect the capital Dara quickly abandons his fortifications at the Chambal and interposes his forces between Aurangzib and Agra.

Dara lines up all his cannon in front of his camel corps, musketeers, and cavalry. This army comprises three divisions of Mughuls and Rajputs under separate commanders at least two of whom are not unqualifiedly loyal to Dara. Aurangzib and Murad make a similar disposition of their forces, except that they conceal some pieces of artillery among the cavalry. Once these preparations are complete, the artillery on both sides fires, their "invariable mode of commencing an engagement." As the cannonade ends, Dara, "seated on a beautiful elephant of Ceylon," boldly leads a cavalry charge against the enemies' artillery. In a second charge Dara forces an entry into the enemy camp and puts to rout the camel corps and infantry. A cavalry battle ensues in which Dara's superior numbers force a confused retreat of Aurangzib's remaining troopers. With both Aurangzib and Murad almost within his grasp, Dara's right wing of thirty thousand Mughuls under the command of "Calil-ullah-Kan" (Khalilullah Khan) treacherously keeps "aloof from the engagement" on the pretext that this division is "designed for a corps of reserve." Even worse, the disloyal Khalilullah misleads Dara about the course of battle and convinces him to dismount his elephant. Once Dara disappears from view, his troops, believing him to be dead or injured, are seized by panic. Aurangzib, still mounted on his elephant, rallies his forces and pounces on the disorganized enemy to win the day.[351]

Dara flees to Delhi in hopes of continuing his resistance from there; several of his supporters retire or are deported to other places far from Agra. In the meantime, the two victorious brothers present themselves to their aged father in Agra, imprison him in its fort, and require the nobles to take pledges of allegiance to Murad. While pretending fealty to Murad himself, Aurangzib secretly seeks to build up a following among the nobles. A few of the nobles remain loyal to Shah Jahan, but most hope to preserve their pensions by cooperating with Murad and Aurangzib. Reassured by the courtiers' acquiescence, the two brothers set out for Delhi to hunt down Dara. While stopping over at "Maturas" (Mathura), Aurangzib and his friends imprison Murad. From here they carry the betrayed prince to Delhi

---

[351] Constable (ed.), *op. cit.* (n. 337), pp. 42–55. *Cf.* the account of the battle of Samugarh (May 29, 1658) in Sarkar, *op. cit.* (n. 333), pp. 62–67, especially p. 66n. Bernier concludes his version by comparing unfavorably the disorderly and undisciplined Mughul armies to the highly organized and disciplined armies of France. He is generous, however, when acknowledging the valor of the princes.

for incarceration in the ancient citadel of "Selim-guer" (Salim-ghar).[352] With the exception of a few soldiers, Murad's army quickly submits to this new order and continues to pursue Dara. Once Aurangzib realizes that Dara has fled to Sind, he sends a detachment after him and retraces his own steps to Agra to check on conditions there. In Sind, meanwhile, Dara puts together a new army buttressed by numerous European artillerymen. With this force he proceeds into Gujarat and makes himself master of Ahmadabad with the connivance of its governor.

While perturbed by Dara's activities, Aurangzib sees the more immediate danger as coming from the east. Shujah, having recovered from his earlier defeat, has raised another powerful army in Bengal and is proceeding up the Ganges. The armies of Aurangzib and Shujah meet on a "spacious plain" between the Ganges and the Jumna. Shujah, who was initially successful in driving back the forces of Aurangzib, makes a mistake reminiscent of that committed by Dara at the battle of Samugarh. In his eagerness to follow his retreating foe, Shujah dismounts his elephant and takes to horseback. Again, as on the previous occasion, the leader's disappearance from view produces panic in the ranks.[353] His forces disperse and Shujah is obliged to retreat. Fearful of what might be happening in Agra, Aurangzib hurries back to the capital instead of following the defeated Shujah. Reassembling his forces and recruiting others, Shujah establishes a base at "Elabas" (Ilahbas or Allahabad), the city known as "the key of Bengale" where the Jumna joins the Ganges.

Back in Agra, Aurangzib decides to entrust "Sultan Mahmoud," his eldest son, and "Emir-Jemla" (Mir Jumla) with the campaign against Shujah. Aurangzib, in the clear knowledge that both men are potential sources of danger to his supremacy, promises Mir Jumla the governorship of Bengal after Shujah's defeat. On learning of these developments, Shujah retreats to Lower Bengal to prepare against a new onslaught; he is also forced to keep a watchful eye on the Hindu rajas of the Ganges delta, who resent his exactions and are on the brink of revolt. At "Rage-Mehalle" (Rajmahal) he makes a brief stand against the pursuing forces. During this new retreat, the rainy season begins, a period in which the roads become so difficult "that no army can act offensively during their prevalence." As a consequence Aurangzib's army is forced to remain at Rajmahal while Shujah seeks reinforcements and a new base.[354]

A serious disagreement now arises between Mir Jumla and "Sultan Mahmoud." Aurangzib's son, who "aspires to the absolute and undivided com-

---

[352] Murad was thereafter transferred to the state prison at Gwalior where he was beheaded on Aurangzib's orders in December, 1661. See Sarkar, *op. cit.* (n. 333), p. 71.

[353] Sarkar (*ibid.*, p. 86n.) indicates that this story is not supported in other contemporary sources and is probably based on "bazaar gossip."

[354] Constable (ed.), *op. cit.* (n. 337), pp. 55–82. According to Bernier, Shujah received support from the "eight or nine thousand" Europeans resident in the delta.

mand of the army," contemptuously insults Mir Jumla and openly boasts about the debt Aurangzib owes him for the crown. Learning of Aurangzib's anger, "Sultan Mahmoud" flees and seeks service with Shujah. Fearful that he might be falling into another of Aurangzib's famous traps, Shujah places no confidence in "Sultan Mahmoud" or his promises and keeps him where he can be watched. After several months of such indifferent treatment, "Sultan Mahmoud" returns in despair to Rajmahal hoping to receive a pardon for his betrayal. Instead he is seized and thrown into the prison of Gwalior "in which fortress he will probably end his days." [355] Aurangzib then warns "Sultan Mazum" (Mu'azzam) "not to imitate the lofty and unyielding spirit of his brother." On this score Aurangzib has no reason for suspicion or fear since his second son could not be "more tractable or obsequious." [356] Aurangzib himself, now moved from Agra to Delhi, there openly exercises "all the prerogatives of a legitimate King." [357]

With Shujah on the run in Bengal, Aurangzib turns his attention to the task of defeating Dara. In the hope of gaining Rajput support, Dara leaves Ahmadabad in Gujarat for "Asmire" (Ajmer) with his entire army. But the Rajputs, fearful of Aurangzib's vengeance, decide not to join with him in the hope of obtaining the government of neighboring Gujarat after Dara's defeat. In the meantime, Aurangzib "at the head of a fresh and numerous army" is moving on Ajmer. Isolated and unable to fall back on Ahmadabad, Dara decides to make a stand even though the contest is clearly unequal. Betrayed on all sides, Dara is routed and forced to flee towards Ahmadabad through territories belonging to unfriendly Rajputs. [358] Accompanied by "two thousand men at most," Dara is followed and harassed day and night by "Koullys" (*Koli*, or English, cooly), the peasant-robbers of Gujarat. Despite these attacks, he arrives within a day's journey of Ahmadabad, only to learn that its governor has turned against him. It is during this flight that Bernier meets Dara on the road and is compelled to serve as his physician while the prince's fortunes daily become more unbearable. In desperation Dara and his few remaining men set out for Sind leaving Bernier behind. [359]

With Dara in flight and Shujah still on the defensive in distant Bengal, Aurangzib turns his attention to "Soliman-Chekouh" (Sulaiman Shukoh), Dara's eldest son. On hearing of his father's defeat at Samugarh, Sulaiman had taken refuge with the raja of Srinagar in the Garhwal hills north of

[355] He died there on December 5, 1676, and was taken to Delhi for burial.

[356] Indeed he lived long enough to succeed his father in 1707.

[357] After his detention of Murad on July 5, 1658, Aurangzib proceeded to Delhi, where he crowned himself emperor on July 31.

[358] Cf. Sarkar, *op. cit.* (n. 333), pp. 73–75 on the battle of Deorai (March 12–13, 1659).

[359] The French physician saved his own life by tending the *Kolis* for seven or eight days. He was then taken to the vicinity of Ahmadabad to make his way to that city. There he met the Persian noble who took him safely to Agra and thereafter became his patron. Constable (ed.), *op. cit.* (n. 337), pp. 91–92. Also see Tavernier's remarks in Ball and Crooke (trans. and eds.), *op. cit.* (n. 24), I, 279.

Delhi. Now it is feared that he and the raja are about to descend from the hills upon the capital. To forestall such an eventuality, Aurangzib unsuccessfully tries by cajolery, promises, and military pressure to win over the raja and to convince him that the wisest course is to turn Sulaiman over to Delhi. In the meantime Dara is turned away from the fortress of Thatta in Sind and considers fleeing to Persia. Dissuaded by his wife from throwing himself on the mercy of the Persian monarch, Dara appeals for troops and succor to "Gion-kan" (Javan Khan), an Afghan whose life he had saved on two occasions. Instead of assisting Dara, the ungrateful Afghan kills his retainers and carries the prince off to Delhi. Here the captive is paraded through the streets in disgrace, he and his second son sitting on the back of a small and miserable elephant. Bernier, who witnessed this procession, wonders how the government has "the hardihood to commit all these indignities upon a Prince confessedly popular among the lower orders," particularly since the people generally view with horror and disgust the other excesses committed by Aurangzib during his rise to power.

On learning of this unfavorable popular reaction, Aurangzib and the majority of his advisers resolve to have Dara murdered immediately, alleging that he deserves death for his disavowal of Islam. Slaves decapitate Dara and present his head to Aurangzib, who orders that it be buried in Humayun's tomb. Of Dara's family only Sulaiman remains alive and a threat to Aurangzib. The raja of Srinagar is finally persuaded by the promises and threats of Aurangzib to bring Sulaiman to Delhi. Here he is shown off to the courtiers with his hands in chains. Condemned to the prison of Gwalior, Sulaiman requests an immediate death rather than slow death by the "poust" (poppy). While Sulaiman is forced to meet death by the "poust," Murad is decapitated at Gwalior on the demand of a "Sayed" (Sayyid) family of Ahmadabad who seek justice for their father whom Murad had earlier murdered for his wealth.[360]

Sultan Shujah is the only member of Aurangzib's family who remains alive and in a position to challenge the emperor's authority. Left alone, Shujah is gradually surrounded by the heavily reinforced army of Mir Jumla. Finally he is driven to "Daké" (Dacca) on the coast, "the last town in Bengale." Being without sailors or ships, the prince appeals for sanctuary to "the King of Racan [Arakan] or Mog [Mugh], a Gentile or idolater" who rules the land on the eastern side of the Bay of Bengal. The ruler of Arakan grants his request for temporary asylum and sends Portuguese ships to bring Shujah and his family to Arakan. While Shujah is well received and sustained, his requests to hire ships for a voyage to Mecca are ignored. Frustrated by these conditions and angered by the king's demand for one of his

[360]Constable (ed.), *op. cit.* (n. 337), pp. 83–108. Murad was beheaded on December 4, 1661; Sulaiman died in May, 1662. As descendants of the Prophet, the Sayyids formed a powerful clique at the Mughul court.

daughters in marriage, the desperate Shujah conspires with local Europeans and Muslims to plan a *coup d'état*. When the plot is discovered, the Mughul prince tries to escape overland to Pegu but is soon overtaken.[361] Whether or not Shujah died at this juncture is not known. Although Bernier believes that he was killed in his attempt to escape, persistent rumors of his whereabouts and movements continue to trouble Aurangzib. Determined to eliminate all opposition, the emperor orders the extermination of all the members of Shujah's family now in his hands. With this final brutal act, Aurangzib is left in 1661 "the undisputed master of this mighty Empire."[362]

[361] This event occurred in the reign of King Sandathudamma (r. 1652–84) of Arakan. See G. P. Harvey, *Outline of Burmese History* (Bombay, 1947), pp. 95–96.

[362] Constable (ed.), *op. cit.* (n. 337), p. 115. John Dryden's tragic drama, called *Auring-Zebe*, written in 1675, is laid in Agra, 1660, and is based on the English translation (1671–72) of Bernier's work. See *ibid.*, Appendix I. On the war in Bengal see Sarkar, *op. cit.* (n. 333), pp. 87–93.

CHAPTER X

The Empire of Aurangzib

The latter half of the seventeenth century is noteworthy for its lengthy, absolutist regimes: Leopold I in the Holy Roman Empire, Louis XIV in France, the K'ang-hsi emperor in China, and Aurangzib in India. The reign (1658–1707) of Aurangzib is perhaps the most important epoch in the annals of India, and it certainly marks the apogee of Mughul history. The largest single state ever to emerge in India to this time, the Mughul Empire reached its greatest territorial extent and its highest degree of political unity under Aurangzib. Its armies and its provinces were directly ruled by servants of the emperor and only occasionally by semi-independent princelings governing as vassals of a distant overlord. While religious pluralism continued, non-Muslims were placed under disabilities which steadily became more severe and onerous. Islam itself made its last great advances in India during this reign, for the emperor himself, unlike several of his predecessors, was a zealous, puritanical, and uncompromising Muslim. Still, the seeds of future decline were being sown during this glorious epoch. Agriculture was badly neglected, the Deccan wars drained away treasure and people, and non-Muslim warrior nationalities—Rajputs, Mahratta, and Sikhs—emerged in the borderlands who would long and successfully defy Aurangzib and his Mughul successors.

The Europeans, who had existed on sufferance at Surat and Hugli, began to make advances of their own during the second half of the seventeenth century. English traders and ships became bolder and more active on both coasts. In 1687 the English crown colony of Bombay became a presidency of the East India Company, and in 1690 Calcutta was founded, as Aurangzib gradually recognized his inability to keep the sea-lanes open for international trade and pilgrim traffic without the cooperation of the English. In

Europe, and particularly in England, a substantial amount of public attention was focused on the Mughuls. An "India Craze" developed in the last generation of the century, set in motion by a fad for cotton textiles. Revulsion emerged during the Mughul-British hostilities of the late 1680's, which culminated in riots by English textile workers put out of their jobs by the Indian imports. In England, as elsewhere in Europe, the public was furnished with substantial reading matter on Aurangzib's realm written by first-hand, acute, and well-informed observers. Many books and articles were written by English voyagers to India which quickly appeared in print. Most of those written in other European languages were quickly translated into English.

Particularly influential in Europe were the works of Tavernier and Bernier, already discussed.[1] Jean de Thévenot (1633–67), a young French traveler, visited Gujarat, the Deccan, and Golconda for slightly more than one year in 1666–67. He died in Persia on his return trip to Europe. The manuscript journals of his various travels were prepared for the press in Paris by two of his friends. They were published in successive installments between 1664 and 1684, the *Relation de l'Industan* appearing last in 1684.[2] John Ovington (1653–1731), a young chaplain and graduate of Trinity College, Dublin, was employed in 1689 to minister to the servants of the East India Company in Bombay and Surat. After a stay of over two years in India, he returned home and three years later published his travel experiences.[3] Dr. John Fryer (*ca.* 1650–1733), a young physician and graduate of Cambridge, was first employed by the East India Company to attend its servants in the East. While in India he was stationed at Bombay (1673, 1675) and at Surat (September, 1674, to April, 1675; December, 1676, to January, 1677; and January, 1679, to January, 1682); he also made a few side-trips to the Deccan, North Kanara, Goa, and other nearby places. His book contains eight long letters describing his experiences in India and Persia from 1672 to 1681.[4]

At Paris in 1699 there appeared the Abbe Carré's two-volume *Voyage des Indes Orientales, mêlé de plusieurs histoires curieuses*. Much of this work relates to his first experiences in India between 1668 and 1671. On this occasion he

[1] See above, pp. 414–18. V. Ball and W. Crooke (trans. and eds.), *Travels in India by Jean-Baptiste Tavernier* (2d ed.; 2 vols.; London, 1925); and A. Constable (ed.), *Travels in the Mogul Empire, A.D. 1656–1658 by François Bernier* (2d ed.; Delhi, 1968).

[2] The English translation of Thévenot (London, 1687) is reprinted, introduced, and edited in S. Sen (ed.), *The Indian Travels of Thevenot and Careri* (New Delhi, 1949). The introductory essay includes an excellent analysis of Thévenot's sources. For additional bibliographical detail on Thévenot's work, see above, p. 411.

[3] *A Voyage to Suratt, in the Year, 1689* (London, 1696). The modern critical edition is H. G. Rawlinson (ed.), *A Voyage to Surat in the Year 1689* (London, 1929). For additional bibliographical detail see above, pp. 579–80.

[4] *A New Account of East-India and Persia, in Eight Letters, Being Nine Years Travels, Begun 1672 and Finished 1681* (London, 1698). The Hakluyt Society published the modern critical edition of William Crooke ("HS," 2d ser., XIX, XX, XXXIX; London, 1909–15). For additional bibliographical analyses and detail see above, pp. 580–82.

was sent to the East by Colbert to accompany Caron and to work with the Dutch director of the French East India Company in establishing French factories in India and Persia. He kept a journal of his activities, on the basis of which he wrote reports for Colbert. After his return to France in 1671, he made a trip to India from 1672 to 1674. His journal for this second journey was not published until 1947–48.[5] The volumes published in 1699 include thumbnail sketches of Surat and Chaul, two biographical essays on Sivaji, and several "curious stories" about renegade Frenchmen and Portuguese slaves in India. It is not always clear in these volumes whether he is referring exclusively to his experiences of the first voyage or whether he is summarizing his journals and recollections from both trips. Certainly in his accounts of Chaul and Sivaji he is drawing upon both of his journals for his presentations. While much in this work repeats what had earlier been published, the biography of Sivaji is unrivaled among contemporary European works for its general chronological accuracy and its wealth of detail.[6]

At the very end of the century the Italian world-traveler Giovanni Francesco Gemelli Careri (1651–1725) published his *Giro del mondo* (Naples, 1699–1700) in six volumes.[7] His travels took him to India for the first few months of 1695. A lawyer by profession, he was apparently able to pay his own way. As a consequence he was warmly received wherever he went, particularly by the Portuguese Catholics in India. He was acquainted with the writings of Bernier, Tavernier, and Thévenot, and refers to them occasionally. Careri's account is chiefly based, however, on his diary, which he apparently kept faithfully even when conditions were trying.[8] What follows is based on the works of Tavernier, Bernier, Thévenot, Ovington, Fryer, Carré, and Careri, with additions from Manoel Godinho (1632–1712), a Portuguese Jesuit, and François L'Estra (1650–97), a French merchant.[9] As far as possible this account of Aurangzib's realm will be based only on what these observers themselves saw or learned about from others in India.

[5] Sir Charles and Lady Fawcett and Sir Richard Burn (trans. and eds.), *The Travels of the Abbe Carré in India and the Near East, 1672 to 1674* (3 vols.; "HS," 2d ser., XCV, XCVI, XCVII; London, 1947–48).

[6] The general estimate of S. N. Sen (trans. and ed.), *Foreign Biographies of Shivaji* (2d rev. ed.; Calcutta, 1977), pp. 7–8. Sen translates into English the "History of Sivaji" (*Voyage*, I, 49–100) and the "Sequel to the History of Sivaji" (*ibid.*, II, 1–85).

[7] In 1704 it was translated in English and included in Churchill's *Collection of Voyages*, Pt. III (1700); the volume on Hindustan in Churchill's English translation is reprinted and edited in Sen (ed.), *op. cit.* (n. 2). For additional bibliographical details see above, pp. 386–88.

[8] Careri's book is divided basically into two sections: the diary and general background information on the country under discussion. It is mainly for the extensive background descriptions that he uses the works of others. For an analysis of his sources on India see Alberto Magnaghi, *Il viaggiatore Gemelli Careri (secólo XVII) e il suo "Giro del Mondo"* (Bergamo, 1900), pp. 34–36, 47–48.

[9] The excellent *Storia do Mogor* of Niccolao Manucci (1653–1708) and some other pertinent materials are not included because they were not published in the seventeenth century. For a comparison of Manucci's *Storia* with the accounts of his contemporaries see G. L. Devra, "Manucci's Comments on Indian Social Customs and Traditions," in U. Marazzi (ed.), *La conoscenza dell'Asia . . . in Italia nei secoli XVIII e XIX* (2 vols.; Naples, 1984), I, 351–71.

THE COURT, THE NOBILITY, AND THE ARMY

Aurangzib crowned himself at Delhi, informally in 1658 and formally in 1659, before the wars of succession had ended. During the next two years he imprisoned his father, Shah Jahan, and wiped out the last elements of resistance to his authority. As a descendant of Tamerlane he is called "the Great Mogul" or "Burrow Mogul Podeshar" (Hindi/Urdu, *Bara Mughal Padishah*). Embassies quickly appear in Delhi from foreign Muslim powers and from the Dutch to offer congratulations to the new emperor.[10] The first to arrive are the emissaries of the Tartar Khans of Uzbek from north of the Oxus River. Clearly recognizing Aurangzib's overlordship, the Uzbeks proffer their services and solemnly express their wishes for a long and auspicious reign. After making the "Salam" at a distance, they advance and present their letters to an "Omrah" (*umar*, court noble) who opens them and hands them to the emperor. After studying the letters, Aurangzib commands that each ambassador be given a "Serapah" (Persian, *Sar-o-pā*, or robe of honor) which includes "a vest of brocade, a turban, and a sash or girdle, of embroidered silk." This ceremony is followed by a presentation of the gifts sent by the Khans: boxes of lapis lazuli "or the choicest Azure," some long-haired camels, several beautiful Tartar horses, and many camel-loads of fresh and dried fruits. Once he thanks the emissaries, the emperor asks two or three questions about the "College at Samarcande" before dismissing them.[11]

During their four months' stay in Delhi, Bernier attends certain of the sick Tartars and questions them on three occasions about their country. He finds them to be ignorant even of their own frontiers and personally narrow-minded, sordid, and unclean. He dines with them on horsemeat, learns that they do not converse while eating, and observes that they are totally unacquainted with the spoon. They boast about the physical strength of the Uzbeks and their prowess with bow and arrow. They relate endless tales of the strength and valor of their country's women "in comparison with whom the Amazons were soft and timorous."[12]

While the Tartars are still in Delhi, Aurangzib is "seized with a dangerous illness." Rumors immediately circulate that he is dying or dead. Conspiracies quickly spring up at court in anticipation of a new succession crisis. On the fifth day of his illness Aurangzib has himself carried into an assembly

---

[10] See G. Z. Refai, "Foreign Embassies to Aurengzeb's Court at Delhi," in R. E. Frykenberg (ed.), *Delhi through the Ages: Essays in Urban History, Culture, and Society* (Delhi, 1986), pp. 192–204.

[11] A reference in all probability to the *Ulug-beg* of Samarkand, a college renowned for its school of mathematics and astronomy. See Bernier in Constable (ed.), *op. cit.* (n. 1), pp. 116–19.

[12] On the Uzbek Khanatis in decline see Gavin Hambly *et al.*, *Central Asia* (New York, 1969), chap. xiii.

of the nobles to prevent "a public tumult, or any accident by which Shah-Jahan might effect his escape." He reappears repeatedly in public and regularly calls important nobles to his bedside to verify that he is still alive and in charge. During his convalescence Aurangzib tries unsuccessfully to arrange a marriage between his brother Dara's daughter and his own third son "Sultan Ekbar" (Akbar) whom "he intends for his successor." Aurangzib prefers this son over his elder brothers since his mother is a Muslim whereas the other two were born of Rajput (Hindu) princesses. The Mughuls, Bernier observes, "do not scruple to marry into heathen families" when it is advantageous to do so.

The emperor in 1662 receives "Monsieur Adrican," chief of the Dutch factory at Surat.[13] After performing the court ceremonies required, the Dutch ambassador is courteously received, even though the emperor pretends that as a strict Muslim he is an inveterate hater of "Franks or Christians." Once the Dutchman and some of his party receive their robes of honor, the ambassador produces his presents: fine scarlet and green broadcloths, "some large looking glasses," and several articles from China and Japan, including "a paleky [palanquin] and a Tack-ravan [*Takht-i-rawan*], or traveling throne, of exquisite beauty, and much admired." The objective of the Dutch mission is to win the emperor's favor, inform him about their nation, and impress him with the importance of Dutch trade to the economic health of his empire. The Dutch also hope to convince the local authorities with whom they deal that they possess the ability to gain direct access to the emperor for redress of grievances. While these negotiations proceed too slowly for the taste of the Dutch, Aurangzib finally permits them to depart with a rich robe of honor for the governor-general of Batavia and with "a very gracious letter."[14]

In 1664 five ambassadors arrive in Delhi at about the same time from Mecca, the Yemen, Bassora, and Ethiopia. The first three representatives are accorded little respect by the court, since it is "suspected they came merely for the sake of obtaining money in return for their presents" and in the hope of selling horses and other merchandise free of duty. With the monies so obtained, they seek to purchase local goods which they hope in turn to export without paying the imposts regularly charged. The two ambassadors from Ethiopia, Bernier caustically remarks, command just slightly

---

[13] Dirk van Adrichem was director at Surat from 1662 to 1665. His embassy to Aurangzib was undertaken between May 22 and December 15. For his career in the East see W. Wijnaendts van Resandt, *De gezaghebbers der Oost-Indische Compagnie op hare buiten-comptoiren in Azië* (Amsterdam, 1944), p. 280. For more details on this embassy see A. J. Bernet Kempers (ed.), *Journaal van Dircq van Adrichem's hofreis naar den Groot-Mogol Aurangzeb, 1662* ("WLV," XLV; The Hague, 1941). As Bernet Kempers points out (p. 232), Bernier was the first to inform Europe in a publication about this mission. Tavernier, possibly on the basis of Bernier's account, also mentions it. See Ball and Crooke (trans. and eds.), *op. cit.* (n. 1), I, 297.

[14] Bernier in Constable (ed.), *op. cit.* (n. 1), pp. 123–29. The "gracious letter" may have included the *farman* of October 29, 1662, which granted the Dutch important concessions in Bengal and Orissa.

more attention and respect. One is a Muslim merchant who wishes to sell slaves and the other an Armenian Christian trader; Bernier had met both men at Mocha several years before. Their presents were to include twenty-five "choice slaves," fifteen horses, a zebra skin, two huge elephant tusks, and an oxhorn filled with civet. But the ambassadors claim to have lost most of these gifts and their personal possessions in Surat when "Seva-Gi" (Sivaji) sacked that city.[15] Although the Armenian carried a letter to Bernier from Van Adrichem, the Frenchman finds it difficult to aid him since the empty-handed Ethiopian emissaries are so lowly regarded by the courtiers. Eventually Aurangzib is induced by Bernier's patron to receive the ambassadors in audience. The emperor makes them a cash present on condition that some of it be used to repair a famous mosque in Ethiopia earlier sacked by the Portuguese. Both Bernier and his patron ask the emissaries many questions about Ethiopia and the source of the Nile. Aurangzib likewise questions them on two occasions, since he wishes particularly to know about the condition of Islam in their country.[16]

News reaches Delhi that an embassy from Persia has arrived at the frontier, an event which produces great excitement among the Persians at court. On his appearance the ambassador is "received with every demonstration of respect." At his first audience with Aurangzib the Persian does not follow Mughul court custom but performs the salaam in the Persian manner. The emperor himself takes the letters of credence directly from the ambassador's hand and raises them to his head as a gesture of special respect. After reading the letters, Aurangzib orders that the ambassador be clothed in his presence in the traditional robes of honor. The Persian, following custom, then displays his presents: twenty-five beautiful horses "with housings of embroidered brocade," twenty large camels, numerous cases of bottled rosewater and a distilled drink called "Beidmichk" (*bedmushk*, a cordial), five or six carpets, a few flowered brocades, four bejeweled cutlasses, four similarly decorated poniards, and finally five or six sets of horse trappings ornamented with embroidery, small pearls, and turquoises. Assigned to a place among the principal nobles of the court, the ambassador lives sumptuously in Delhi at Aurangzib's expense. Court gossip circulates to the effect that the Persian king's letters reproach Aurangzib for the death of Dara and the imprisonment of Shah Jahan as acts unworthy of a brother, a son, and a faithful Muslim. While Bernier doubts the accuracy of these stories, he is convinced that either the letters or the haughty language and manner of the ambassador angered the emperor.[17]

[15] On Sivaji's attack on Surat in January, 1664, see B. G. Gokhale, *Surat in the Seventeenth Century* (London, 1979), pp. 24–25, and below, pp. 765–66.

[16] Constable (ed.), *op. cit.* (n. 1), pp. 133–44. This is the only non-Muslim embassy mentioned by Mughul historians. See Refai, *loc. cit.* (n. 10), p. 194.

[17] Constable (ed.), *op. cit.* (n. 1), pp. 146–54. This is a description of the Persian embassy of 1661. On Aurangzib's strained relations with Persia see J. Sarkar, *A Short History of Aurangzib* (3d ed.; Calcutta, 1962), pp. 106–8.

Aurangzib is not particularly reverent of his elders. He upbraids "Mullah Salé" (Mulla Shah), his former tutor, for failing to teach him properly about the importance of other nations, especially those of Europe, and of neglecting to instruct him in the language and customs of India's neighbors. The tutor is charged with filling the young prince's head with useless Arabic grammar and confusing philosophical jargon while failing to train him in subjects essential to kingship, such as war. Shah Jahan, although imprisoned in the fortress of Agra, is treated with "indulgence and respect." In his confinement the deposed ruler becomes a "wonderously devout" Muslim and amuses himself with animals. Aurangzib loads him with presents, treats him with consideration, and consults and debates with him on state matters. Eventually the aged father fondly grants a pardon to his rebellious son.[18]

The emperor, fearful of Mir Jumla's ambitions, makes him governor of distant Bengal following the defeat of Shujah. After elevating him to be "Mir-ul-omrah" (*Amir-ul-Umarā*, or principal noble), Aurangzib soon asks Mir Jumla to head an expedition against the rich and powerful raja of "Acham" (Assam) whose territories lie north of Dacca.[19] Mir Jumla acquiesces and begins preparing an army at Dacca. From here his forces go upriver, quickly overcome the fortress of "Azo" (Hajo), and advance on "Chamdara" (Samdhara). Here Mir Jumla defeats the raja and forces him to flee for refuge "to the mountains . . . of Lassa [Lhasa or Tibet]." After pillaging the capital city of "Guergnon" (Garhgaon), Mir Jumla's army is bogged down in Assam by heavy rains and harassed constantly by the raja's forces. Once the dry season arrives Mir Jumla abandons the campaign and returns with his loot and his battered men to Bengal. Shortly thereafter he falls ill and dies of dysentery. His death relieves Aurangzib of the persistent fear of rivalry from an overly powerful subject. The emperor for the first time really rules as "king of Bengale." Out of a mixture of gratitude and relief, the emperor declares the deceased's son Mahmet (Muhammad Amin Khan) "sole heir to his father's property" and does not seize it as he is legally entitled to do.[20]

Aurangzib's uncle, "Chan-hestkan" (Shaista Khan), succeeds Mir Jumla as *Amir-ul-Umarā* and as governor of Bengal. Instead of continuing the war against Assam, the new governor determines to undertake a campaign against Arakan to punish its ruler for his mistreatment of Shujah and his family and to halt the Arakan-Portuguese raids in the delta. The Europeans,

---

[18]Constable (ed.), *op. cit.* (n. 1), pp. 154–66.

[19]On the economy of Assam and its seventeenth-century wars with the Mughuls *cf.* the appendix by Amalendu Guha, in T. Raychaudhuri and I. Habib (eds.), *The Cambridge Economic History of India* (2 vols.; Cambridge, 1982), I, 478–86. Also see Tavernier in Ball and Crooke (trans. and eds.), *op. cit.* (n. 1), II, 216–24.

[20]Bernier in Constable (ed.), *op. cit.* (n. 1), pp. 169–73. Mir Jumla in 1657 had made Dacca the capital of Bengal. This expedition against Assam started from there in 1661. Mir Jumla died on March 31, 1663, in Kuch Bihar.

most of whom are fugitives from the Portuguese settlements in the East, center their activities at the port of "Chatigon" (Chittagong), where they live under Arakan's protection. From here these renegades pursue "no other trade than that of rapine and piracy." They descend upon Ganges towns and villages and carry off their inhabitants. These captives are sold either to the Portuguese at Hugli or at an international slave mart "in the vicinity of the island of Galles near Cape das Palmas [Palmyras Point on the Orissa coast]." Now the Portuguese occupy the island of "Sondiva" (Sundiap or Sandwip) at the mouth of the Ganges where an Augustinian friar rules as "a petty Sovereign." To help him wage a naval war against Arakan and these pirates, Shaista Khan negotiates an arrangement with the Dutch. Before the Dutch vessels have time to arrive, the Mughul governor lets the Europeans of Chittagong know that they will be received kindly in Bengal on submitting themselves peacefully to the authority of Aurangzib. On hearing of this offer, shiploads of Portuguese desert Chittagong for Bengal. But after using them to aid in the recovery of Sandwip Island, the governor treats the Portuguese badly since he no longer needs their services.[21]

One of the important courtiers and officials of Aurangzib's administration is Sultan "Mazum" (Mu'azzam), his second son. He is in charge of the Deccan but has only a very limited authority. "Mohabet-khan" (Mahabat Khan), the former governor of Kabul, is restored to the imperial favor and is now the governor of Gujarat (r. 1662–68). Danishmand Khan, Bernier's patron, is appointed governor of Delhi but also retains special duties in the imperial bureau of foreign affairs. Dianet Khan has become governor of Kashmir, a terrestrial paradise. The Rajput lords are embroiled with "Seva-Gi" (Sivaji), a Hindu of Bijapur, who has become an enemy of the sultan of Bijapur and a nuisance in the Deccan. For three days (in 1664) he plunders Surat, perhaps with the connivance of the Rajputs. Aurangzib finally prevails upon "Jesseingue" (Jai Singh I), the Rajput raja, to take command of the imperial Deccan forces and to curb Sivaji's activities. The Rajput attacks Sivaji's principal fortress and negotiates its peaceful surrender on the condition that Sivaji join the imperial cause and wage a joint war on Bijapur. Aurangzib even proclaims him a raja and awards a pension to his son. Shortly thereafter Sivaji visits the court on Aurangzib's invitation. While in the capital Sivaji learns of a conspiracy against him. In fear of his life, he flees from the court in disguise and under cover of night. Under these tense conditions Jai Singh gives up his command of the Deccan army and hastens to defend his own territories against reprisals. Shortly afterwards he dies a natural death at Burhanpur.[22]

---

[21] *Ibid.*, pp. 174–82.

[22] *Ibid.*, pp. 182–91. On Sivaji's negotiations of 1665 with Jai Singh and on his visit to Aurangzib in 1666 see J. Sarkar, *House of Shivaji* (3d ed.; Calcutta, 1955), chaps. ix–x. For further material on Sivaji see below, pp. 764–76. Jai Singh died in 1666.

In a letter of July 1, 1663, sent from Delhi to François de La Mothe Le Vayer (1588–1672), Bernier describes Delhi and Agra for his friend.[23] He starts by explaining that the architecture of these two capitals, while different from that of Paris, is appropriate to the hot climate of India and possesses its own kind of beauty. Around forty years ago (actually 1638) Shah Jahan to immortalize his name began erecting a new city on the ruins of old Delhi. Today this new capital is known as Shahjahanabad throughout the Indies.[24] This entirely new city, which Bernier continues to call "Delhi," is located on flat land on the west bank of the Jumna River. In the shape "of a crescent," Delhi with its fortress is encompassed by brick walls, except on the side which faces the river. It is linked to the country across the river by a single bridge of boats; outside its walls are the remains of the earlier city and several small suburbs. Its "semicircular" fortress, which includes the royal apartments and the harem, is separated from the river by a large sandy area where the animal fights and the parades of the nobles take place.[25] The walls of the citadel are of bricks and red stone and are protected on the sides away from the river by "a deep ditch" faced with hewn stone, filled with water, and stocked with fish.[26] Next to the moat is a large flower garden beyond which is a great square in which the two main streets of the city terminate.[27]

In the imperial square the Hindu rajas pitch their tents when it is their "weekly turn . . . to mount guard"; inside the fortress the guards are Mughul nobles. At daybreak they exercise and examine the royal horses; Turki horses are branded on the thigh with the imperial insignia and the mark of the "Omrah" to whose service they belong.[28] A daily market, which reminds Bernier of the *Pont-neuf* at Paris, attracts mountebanks, jugglers, and bazaar astrologers to the square. They come down the two principal streets which are from twenty-five to thirty paces in width and run in "a straight line nearly as far as the eye can reach." On either side these streets are lined with arcades "as in our *Place Royale*." During the day in its open shops the artisans work, the bankers exchange money, and merchants display their wares. At night they store their merchandise in warehouses at the back of the arcades. Over the warehouses many have their living quarters;

[23] La Mothe Le Vayer was a writer of many works on ethnographical, geographical, and historical topics. His interests in the civilizations of Asia were wide-ranging. Bernier wrote at a time when Delhi was at the height of its splendor. Its decline is usually dated as beginning with the death of Shah Jahan in 1666. See Gavin Hambly, *Cities of Mughul India* (New York, 1968), p. 122.

[24] In the twentieth century this city is known simply as "Delhi" or "Old Delhi." Shahjahanabad is the central section of present-day "Old Delhi." The modern New Delhi was constructed under the British rule and formally inaugurated in 1931.

[25] The fortress is actually an octagonal structure.

[26] The *Lāl-gil'a*, or the Red Fort as it is known to foreigners, was built by Shah Jahan between 1638 and 1648.

[27] This is a reference to the *Hayāt-Bakhsh-Bāgh* or "Life-Giving Garden." See Y. D. Sharma, *Delhi and Its Neighbourhood* (New Delhi, 1944), p. 127.

[28] On branding see William Irvine, *The Army of the Indian Moghuls* (London, 1903), pp. 49–51.

the roofs of their shops serve as terraces to these houses. Rich merchants live away from their businesses.

Delhi boasts five other main business streets and innumerable others which crisscross one another and are not as long and straight as the major thoroughfares. Here are the residences of the nobles, judges, and rich merchants. Most of their houses have a "tolerable appearance," even though they are little more than clay walls over which bamboos support a thatched roof. Scattered among these better houses with their courts and gardens are the mud huts of the common troopers, servants, and camp-followers. The thatched roofs of these houses and huts constitute a regular fire hazard; in the summer of 1662 alone three great fires consumed "more than sixty thousand roofs." Because of "these mud and thatch houses," Delhi appears as "a collection of many villages, or as a military encampment." The dwellings of the "Omrahs," while scattered everywhere, are mainly along the riverbank or in the suburbs.[29]

In this hot climate, a house is considered desirable and beautiful only when it is roomy and airy. Better houses have courtyards, trees, fountains, and subterranean rooms in which to escape the afternoon heat of summer. Instead of cellars, some prefer to build "Kas-kanays," or small houses "made of straw or odoriferous roots," placed close to a water supply that is used to dampen the outside.[30] The Indians admire most those houses situated in the middle of a large flower garden, elevated "the height of a man from the ground, and exposed to the four winds." Every "handsome dwelling" has sleeping terraces which join the bedrooms so that the bedstead can be moved outside if the weather permits. In a fine house the floor is overlaid with a light cotton mattress which is covered in summer with a white cloth and in winter by a silk carpet. Cushions with beautiful coverings are scattered about the room for its occupants to lean on. The walls are full of niches in which to display flowerpots and porcelains. While the ceiling is often gilded and painted, no portraits of animals or humans appear since such representations are forbidden by Islam.

The shops of Delhi are disappointing in their failure to display their fine merchandise. Most of their expensive items are kept in warehouses and brought out only on request. Ordinary food stalls by far outnumber the shops selling fine textiles. "There is, indeed, a fruit market that makes some show." In summer its many shops sell dried fruit from central Asia: nuts, raisins, prunes, and apricots; in winter they display from these same countries fresh black and white grapes wrapped in cotton, pears and apples of several sorts, and Persian melons. While these imported fruits are expensive,

---

[29] Bernier in Constable (ed.), *op. cit.* (n. 1), pp. 239–47. *Cf.* H. K. Naqui, "Shajahanabad, the Mughal Delhi, 1638–1803," in Frykenberg (ed.), *op. cit.* (no. 10), pp. 143–51.

[30] "Kas" derives from *khaskhas*, the root of *Andropogon muricatum* (Retz), or cuscus grass. Its roots are worked into bamboo frames or woven into mats. "Kanays" (*khanas*, or homes) are sometimes made of these mats. This grass is also used for fans, thatching bungalows, and covering palanquins. See H. Drury, *The Useful Plants of India* (2d ed.; London, 1873), p. 42.

the local products are cheap and inferior. "Ambas" (Hindi, *ambra*s or mangoes) from Bengal, Golconda, and Goa are plentiful and cheap during two months in summer. "Pateques" (Indo-Portuguese, *pateca,* derived from Arabic *al-battikh*), or watermelons, are available the year round. Since the local fruits are generally inferior, some nobles import seeds and try to grow their own. Confectionery and bakery shops are numerous but sweetmeats, and especially breads, are inferior to those of Paris. While meats, fresh and prepared, are sold throughout the city, mutton is often substituted for kid, the best meat they have. Poultry is readily available, "tolerably good and cheap." On occasion good fish can be bought. In general it is better to buy fresh products since "no food can be considered wholesome which is not dressed [prepared] at home."

No person wanting a good time, Bernier warns, should ever leave Paris for Delhi. While the rich enjoy every comfort, the rest of the people live miserably; "there is no middle state."[31] Wine, being prohibited by Islamic law, is not made in India and imports are so hard to find and so dear that "the taste is destroyed by the cost." Arrack, the local liquor, is distilled from unrefined sugar and is as "harsh and burning as that made from corn [grain] in Poland." The best things to drink are pure water and lemonade "which cost little and may be drunk without injury." Many ailments common to Europe are nearly unknown here because of the hot climate and the sobriety of the general public.[32] Despite their general good health, the Indians show less vigor of body and mind than Europeans because of the terrible heat.[33]

Delhi has very few workshops of skilled artisans according to Thévenot. Even though they lack the proper tools and training, some individuals are able to produce handsome pieces of their own as well as excellent imitations of European products. Their muskets and "fowling pieces," as well as gold ornaments, are as good as any made in Europe. Their paintings and miniatures are admirable for their "beauty, softness, and delicacy." While most Indian paintings are "dull pieces," those of Agra show figures in "Lacivious Postures." The artisans of Agra inlay agates, crystals, and other "brittle matters [materials]" with gold decorations.[34] The painters of Delhi are more respectable than those of Agra and depict princes and historical events such as battles. These paintings show skill in organization, a certain sense of propriety, and beautiful colors. Their miniatures are moderately good, but

[31] Recent research seems to indicate that this assertion is too categorical and that "whatever its relative position, in absolute terms there was a sizeable middle income group—lower ranks of the bureaucracy, professionals, holders of rent free tenures." See T. Raychaudhuri in *The Cambridge Economic History of India* (see n. 19), I, 264.

[32] Rarely do the Indians have the gout, the stone, kidney complaints, catarrhs, or "quartan agues" (recurrent attacks of fever), according to the French doctor.

[33] Bernier in Constable (ed.), *op. cit.* (n. 1), pp. 247–54.

[34] Thévenot describes in detail this engraving and inlaying process. Sen (ed.), *op. cit.* (n. 2), p. 55.

their depiction of faces leaves much to be desired.[35] The rajas living at the court of Delhi are rich in family hoards of precious stones which they part with only reluctantly. Although the artisans of Delhi display many skills, they "cannot make a Screw as our Locksmiths do." They are satisfied to fasten things together with wires "turned Screw-wise" and soldered to the objects.[36] In India the children have many of the same toys and games that European children enjoy: trumpets, tops, "Giggs" (whipping-tops), and "Bull-flies [?] in the season."[37] Lahore, a former capital, is no longer used by the emperor, and as a consequence its houses and palaces are in ruins and its arts languishing.[38]

The Mughul Empire lacks superior artistic productions not because of a dearth of individual talent but because the arts are not encouraged. Artists and craftsmen are treated badly and not paid adequately. Many poor artisans are forced to labor for whatever an employer is willing to pay. Consequently they have no incentive to produce artistically superior products but are satisfied merely to finish the assigned task and to collect enough to pay for something to eat. Only those few who work exclusively for the emperor or a powerful and rich noble achieve eminence in their art or craft.[39]

The fortress of Delhi stands as a testimonial to the talents of the imperial artists and craftsmen.[40] On either side of its principal gate stands a life-sized elephant with a statue seated on its back. The figures are those of "Jemel" (Jaimal) and "Polta" (Patta), the Hindu rajas of Chitor who won immortal fame in India by the bravery they exhibited in defending their territories against Akbar.[41] Beyond this gate is a long, wide street through the middle of which runs a canal.[42] On either side of the street are elevated passageways, "five or six feet high and four broad," where the collectors of market taxes stand above the throng to perform their duties. At night mounted guards patrol atop this raised passage. The water from the canal runs into the harem, "divides and intersects [its] every part," and then falls into the moat

[35] Practically all Mughul portraits are drawn in profile.

[36] Thévenot in Sen (ed.), *op. cit.* (n. 2), pp. 65–66. On the screw in India *cf.* A. J. Qaisar, *The Indian Response to European Technology and Culture (A.D. 1498–1707)* (Delhi, 1982), p. 144.

[37] Sen (ed.), *op. cit.* (n. 2), p. 72.

[38] *Ibid.*, p. 85.

[39] *Cf. The Cambridge Economic History of India* (see n. 19), I, 284–86, for confirmation of Bernier's assessment.

[40] Two architects, Ustad Hamid and Ustad Ahmad, supervised the construction of the Red Fort, aided by other imperial officials. See R. Nath, *Monuments of Delhi. Historical Study* (New Delhi, 1978), p. 11. For a plan of the Red Fort as of 1857 see John Murray (publ.), *A Handbook to India, Pakistan, and Burma and Ceylon* (18th ed.; London, 1959), p. 233.

[41] The statues stood at the Delhi gate until Aurangzib had them removed. In 1863 they were discovered buried in some rubbish in the fort. The two figures are now in the museum of Delhi, and one of the elephants stands in its public garden. The other elephant has evidently disappeared. In 1903 Lord Curzon had two new stone elephants erected as replacements.

[42] The *Chandni Chowk* or "Silver Street," was the city's marketplace. It is opposite the Red Fort and behind the Jami Masjid (means principal mosque) built by Shah Jahan.

around the fortress. This supply of water from the Jumna is brought into Delhi by a canal "cut with great labour through fields and rocky ground."[43]

The other principal gate opens onto a similar street and a bazaar which is covered "by a high and long roof."[44] The outer fortress also includes many smaller streets. Some lead to the splendid quarters where the "Omrahs" stay while on guard duty, and others to the "divans and tents" where public business is conducted. In other places the artisans within the fort busily work in large halls called "Kar-kanays" (*karkhanas*) under the supervision of masters of their crafts: embroiderers, goldsmiths, painters, varnishers, joiners, tailors, shoemakers, and fine textile workers. Each morning the artisan appears in the palace workshop and spends the day quietly following the trade to which he was born. No one aspires to anything more than to marry one of his same trade and to bring up sons to follow it. According to Bernier, Muslims adhere to these customs almost as rigidly as the Hindus, who are bound by caste regulations. As a consequence many women remain unmarried, since their parents will not marry them to men of lesser status.[45]

Near the imperial workshops is the "Ām-Kas" (*Am-Khas*),[46] a large square court of arcades similar to the *Place Royale* in Paris but without "buildings [apartments] over them." Above its "grand gate" is a large chamber which opens onto the court and is called the "Nagar-Kanay" (*Naqqar-Khana,* or Drum Room). Here the drums, cymbals, and "hautboys" (oboes) are stored "which are played in concert at certain hours of the day and night."[47] While initially unpleasant to the European ear, this music is heard after a while with pleasure, since it is played by musicians "instructed from infancy in the rules of melody." On the opposite side of the court stands a large pillared hall "open on the three sides that look into the court."[48] In the center of its rear wall is an opening or large window[49] "higher from the floor than a man can reach" where the emperor sits upon his throne when holding a public audience. Immediately beneath the throne is an enclosure encompassed by silver rails in which the nobles and ambassadors stand during audiences. While the audience proceeds "a certain number" of the imperial horses and elephants pass in review followed by other animals kept at the court. The

---

[43] The canal which links the river above Delhi to the fort was built under the supervision of Ali Mardan Khan (d. 1657), a Persian, and it bears his name. For more details see Hambly, *op. cit.* (n. 23), p. 103.

[44] This is "the covered market" behind the Lahore gate called *Chhattā Lahouri Darwaza*. See Nath, *op. cit.* (n. 40), p. 12.

[45] Indeed there was very little occupational mobility except for the transfer of rural producers to local centers of production.

[46] Probably an abbreviation of *Dīwān-i-'Ām* (Hall of Public Audience) and *Dīwān-i-Khās* (Hall of Special Audience).

[47] Actually they were played five times daily at propitious hours. The "oboe" is the *shahnāi,* a long double-reeded instrument used mainly out of doors. See S. Krishnaswami, *Musical Instruments of India* (Delhi, 1965), pp. 63–64.

[48] This is the *Dīwān-i-'Ām* or Hall of Public Audience. For a modern description see Sharma, *op. cit.* (n. 27), pp. 123–24.

[49] The *Jharokah*.

emperor reviews the cavalry of his bodyguard with particular attention and "since the war" makes a studied effort to know about each of his troopers personally. "All the petitions held up in the crowd" are read to the ruler who examines the complaint personally and often makes a judgment on the spot.[50] Flattery of the ruler is a vice natural to all ranks at these audiences. The court sycophants faithfully follow the Persian proverb:

> Should the King say that it is night at noon,
> Be sure to cry, Behold, I see the moon.

Off the grand hall is a smaller assembly court called the "Gosel-Kané" (*ghusl khana*), which is elevated and looks like a large platform. Here the emperor, seated in a chair, "grants more private audiences to his officers, receives their reports, and deliberates on important matters of state." Every "Omrah" must attend and all are fined equally for non-attendance at this evening meeting. While the animal parades of the public audience are omitted in these more restricted meetings, the *mansabdārs* (officers) on guard duty and the mace-bearers salute the emperor by passing before him with the "Kours" (*kur,* imperial insignia; see pl. 123).

Next to the great audience hall the seraglio stands, a building whose interior is off limits. As a physician, Bernier was sometimes allowed to enter its outer precincts to call on patients, but only with a shawl thrown over his head. From certain of the harem eunuchs he learns that it "contains beautiful apartments, separated, and more or less spacious and splendid, according to the rank and income of the females." Before nearly every apartment door there is a reservoir of running water and on every side are shady gardens and cool retreats. A small interior tower which faces the river is covered with plates of gold, and its apartments are decorated with rich and "exquisite paintings and magnificent mirrors."[51]

At the end of the civil war Aurangzib celebrates his victory with a magnificent display of overweening wealth and grandeur in the great public audience hall. He displays himself in "the most magnificent attire" seated on the rich peacock throne built for his father. On the pillars of the hall hang golden brocades, and above the imperial assemblage are raised canopies of flowered satins "fastened with red silken cords from which are suspended large tassels of silk and gold." Silk carpets of immense size completely cover the floor. The courtyard itself is half-covered by a huge red tent surrounded by a great silver-plated balustrade and supported by pillars emblazoned with silver. The interior of the tent is lined with elegant chintzes of Masulipatam made expressly for this occasion. Every "Omrah" is required to decorate an arcade of the audience hall at his own expense with brocades and car-

---

[50] *Cf.* earlier descriptions of durbars above, pp. 636–39, 641–42.

[51] Constable (ed.), *op. cit.* (n. 1), pp. 254–68. The *Khās Mahal* (private palace) was the residence of the chief ladies of the harem. For more detailed descriptions see Sharma, *op. cit.* (n. 27), p. 125, and Nath, *op. cit.* (n. 40), pp. 13–14.

pets. From the prominence of textiles in this exhibition, it is thought that Aurangzib sought by sponsoring this occasion to help the textile merchants dispose of their stocks not sold during the civil war. As at anniversary celebrations, the emperor is weighed in the scales and receives handsome personal gifts from the "Omrahs." [52]

During such festivities "a whimsical kind of fair" is sometimes held in the seraglio. [53] On these occasions the wives and daughters of the "Omrahs" and chief *mansabdārs* exhibit and sell rich textiles and other rare articles to the emperor and his ladies. The emperor amusedly disputes and whimsically haggles with the lady seller over the price. Eventually a price is agreed upon "and the whole ends amidst witty jests and good-humour." Shah Jahan, who was particularly fond of these fairs, began the practice of admitting "Kenchens" (*kanchani,* or dancing and singing girls) to them. Aurangzib, who is more puritanical than his father, forbids the "Kenchens" to enter the seraglio, although he permits them to make their obeisances at the Wednesday general audiences.

Mughul festivals in Delhi generally conclude with an elephant fight on the sandy flat by the river. The two selected beasts, each with two riders, meet face to face on opposite sides of an earthen wall. When the elephants attack, "the shock is tremendous." Eventually the wall is completely knocked apart and the victor pursues the vanquished and obstinately "fastens upon him." They can only be pulled apart by frightening them with "cherkys" (*charkhi,* pinwheel fireworks). In these fights the riders are often killed or badly wounded. The victorious riders win a raise in pay and a small cash bonus "at the moment they alight from the elephant." Spectators and their horses are often trampled or injured by the marauding elephants. [54]

Besides the fortress, Delhi boasts two other prominent edifices. From the distance one can see its principal mosque, on top of a great rock and a high platform in the center of the city. Around the rock is a spacious courtyard or square "where four fine long streets terminate." Three sets of stone steps lead from the marble-paved courtyard up to the three marbled gates of the mosque. The great doors of these magnificent gates are covered with "finely wrought plates of copper." From the principal gate rise several small white marble cupolas. Three large domes of marble grace "the back part" of the mosque, the center one being much larger and higher than the other two. Between the principal gate and the three domes there is no roof; only the end of the mosque is under cover. The covered mosque itself derives its red color from the local stone slabs of which it is constructed. While this structure does not follow European architectural ideals, every part is tasteful and

---

[52] On the weighing ceremony see above, pp. 691–92. The gifts called *Pesh-kash* were expected to correspond in value to the rank and pay of the "Omrah."

[53] The *Khush Ruz* or *Mina Bazar.* See M. A. Ansari, *Social Life of the Mughal Emperors* (Allahabad, 1974), pp. 85–86.

[54] Bernier in Constable (ed.), *op. cit.* (n. 1), pp. 268–78.

"appears well contrived, properly executed, and correctly proportioned."
Every Friday Aurangzib and his retainers parade to this mosque to worship.[55]

Another noteworthy sight in Delhi is the "Karvansara" (caravanserai)
founded by Jahanara Begam, Shah Jahan's eldest daughter, with the financial
help of certain nobles. The inn itself is built in arcades around a large open
square. Behind its arched galleries there are two stories of sleeping rooms.
Foreign merchants, especially rich Persian and Uzbek traders, are housed in
these chambers "in which they remain in perfect security," since the gate to
the square is locked at night. Bernier then advocates building in Paris "a
score of similar structures, distributed in different parts of the city" to provide safe and inexpensive lodgings for visitors.[56]

The population of Delhi "cannot be greatly less" than that of Paris.[57] Its
people are not well dressed, for only two or three out of ten "wear decent
apparel." Nonetheless one continually meets "persons neat and elegant in
their dress, finely formed, well mounted, and properly attended." The environs of Delhi are extremely fertile and produce an abundance of grain,
sugar, indigo, rice, millet, and three or four kinds of pulse eaten by the
common people. Not far from Delhi on the Agra road is a very old edifice
called "Koia Kotub-eddine" (*Khwāja-Kutub-ud-din*) by the Muslims, which
was formerly a Hindu temple. It contains inscriptions written in characters
so ancient and different that they are illegible.[58] The emperor's country residence is also close to Delhi, but in another direction; it is called "Chah-
limar" (Shalimar), a noble building but not to be compared to the great
chateaux in the environs of Paris.[59] Private country houses are almost non-
existent since "no subject can hold landed property in his own right."
About the only sight worth seeing on the road from Delhi to Agra is the
magnificent Hindu temple at Mathura (Muttra).[60]

Unlike Delhi, Agra gives the appearance of a country town when viewed
from a distant elevation. In extent it surpasses Delhi, boasts more and better

[55] The *Jami Masjid*, the largest mosque in India, was built by Shah Jahan between 1650 and
1658. It is situated about one thousand yards west of the Red Fort and it still functions. The
"mosque under cover" is the sanctuary or prayer-hall. For additional details see Nath, *op. cit.*
(n. 40), pp. 57–59.

[56] Built in 1650, this structure no longer exists. All that remains is the *Begum-ka-Bagh*, a garden near the *Chandni Chowk*. See *ibid.*, p. 59. Bernier is not always so favorably impressed by
the inns of India.

[57] The population of Paris around 1650 is usually estimated at about three hundred thousand.

[58] Built around A.D. 1200, this mosque apparently was raised on the remains of a Hindu
temple. The walls have Arabic inscriptions in a wide range of calligraphic styles. Also some of
the stones have earlier Hindu inscriptions.

[59] Shah Jahan began to build the Shalimar gardens, just six miles north of Delhi, in 1632. It
was here that Aurangzib held his first coronation in 1658.

[60] Bernier in Constable, *op. cit.* (n. 1), pp. 278–84. This temple was destroyed in 1669–70
when Aurangzib ordered the demolition of all infidel temples. See H. H. Dodwell (ed.), *The
Cambridge History of India* (6 vols.; Cambridge 1922–53), IV, 241–42. A mosque was built on
its site and the name of the town changed to Islamabad. On the Mathura temple as a place of
Hindu pilgrimage see the lengthy description by Tavernier in Ball and Crooke (trans. and eds.),
op. cit. (n. 1), II, 186–89. Also see Sarkar, *op. cit.* (n. 17), pp. 147–48.

residences, and provides more numerous and convenient inns. It lacks the planned character of Delhi, the uniform and wide streets and the surrounding walls. It has four or five main business streets, but the others are "short, narrow, and irregular." Less crowded in its better sections, Agra boasts more gardens and trees than Delhi.

In Agra the Jesuits now have a church and a college in which they instruct the children of the city's twenty-five or thirty Christian families. Under Shah Jahan the Jesuits had lost the annual imperial pension granted them by Akbar and had witnessed the demolition of their church. Despite setbacks of this sort, the missionaries continue their good and necessary work among the Hindus. Conversions of Muslims in any numbers are not to be expected. The Christians of Europe nevertheless should support and encourage the missions to counteract the "baneful progress" of Islam.

The Dutch maintain a factory at Agra manned usually by four or five merchants. But in recent years their trade has declined, perhaps because of competition from the Armenians or because of the long distance and bad roads between Agra and Surat. Despite these difficulties the Dutch will probably not abandon Agra as the English did. They are still able to sell their spices at a considerable profit here and they "find it useful" to keep representatives near the court to speak for their factories in Bengal, Patna, Surat, and Ahmadabad.[61]

Bernier concludes his letter to La Mothe Le Vayer with a description of the Taj Mahal as of 1663, about fifteen years after its completion.[62] Going east of Agra, one walks up a "gentle ascent" to the "magnificent gate of a spacious and square pavilion, forming the entrance into the garden, between two reservoirs, faced with hewn stone." The building itself is of stone "resembling red marble" and consists "wholly of arches upon arches, and galleries upon galleries, disposed and contrived in a hundred different ways." Once one enters the pavilion, he is under a "lofty cupola, surrounded above with galleries." Opposite the street entrance is an arch which opens into a raised walk "that divides nearly the whole of the garden into two equal parts"; it is paved with large, square stones. Its whole length is divided by a canal "faced with hewn stone and ornamented with fountains placed at certain intervals." From this walk one sees a large dome "in which is the sepulchre, and to the right and left of that dome" are several garden pathways. One also sees pavilions on either side of the dome "which are raised over each other in the form of balconies and terraces." Between the end of the principal walk and the dome is a "water parterre," so called because the stones in its walk are "cut and figured in various forms" to resemble rippling water.

---

[61] On the VOC in India see above, pp. 48, 51–54, 57–59.

[62] Tavernier, who probably visited it in the company of Bernier, claims to have witnessed its "commencement and accomplishment," a work on which "twenty-two years" were spent. See Ball and Crooke (trans. and eds.), *op. cit.* (n. 1), I, 91. Actually it was built between 1631 and 1648.

The building that contains the tomb is a vast dome of white marble encircled by white marble turrets; the whole "is supported by four great arches, three of which are quite open." The tomb itself is in a small chamber under the dome; it is opened once each year and only the faithful are admitted to it. Bernier avers that the Taj Mahal "deserves a place in our books on architecture" and that it is "much more to be numbered among the wonders of the world than the pyramids of Egypt . . . which are nothing more on the outside than heaps of large stones."[63]

The empire of Aurangzib includes numerous entities over which he is not complete master. Many are ruled by local chieftains who obey and pay him tribute "only by compulsion." The petty states between Persia and India seldom pay tribute to either of their great neighbors. In this same region the mountain peoples are equally independent and sometimes even extract "alms" from the Mughuls. The Pathans of these mountains, who had once ruled Delhi, mortally hate the Mughuls for dispossessing their forefathers and refuse to pay tribute. Bijapur engages in perpetual war with Aurangzib and is supported in its resistance by Golconda. More than one hundred Hindu rajas, "dispersed over the whole empire," likewise refuse to pay tribute. Fifteen or sixteen of these rajas have considerable wealth and excellent cavalry at their disposal.

Aurangzib's power is also limited by facts of religion and history. He is a Sunni Muslim while the majority of his courtiers are Persian Shiites. A descendant of Tamerlane the Tartar, he rules over a country that is basically hostile, sometimes openly, to Mughul dominion. Because there are hundreds of Hindus to every Muslim in the country, he must maintain numerous armies even in times of internal peace. These armies are composed of Rajput and Pathan levies and of genuine Mughuls as well as those who are called Mughuls because they are white, foreigners, or simply Muslims. Aurangzib's court likewise is a medley of genuine Mughuls and so-called Mughuls: Uzbeks, Persians, Arabs, and Turks or descendants of these peoples.

The native army which Aurangzib maintains is composed mainly of mercenary Rajputs to whose rajas he pays large sums to have twenty thousand troopers always ready and at his disposal. Fryer reports that the Rajputs fight valiantly with sword, pike, and buckler, and smear their faces with saffron to show their resolve to conquer or die. They frequently eat great quantities of opium to bolster their courage. Before fighting they embrace one another "as if parting for another World." Death is preferred to capture, for their women contemptuously reject them if they "once turn their Back upon their Enemies."[64] Their rajas hold a rank equal to foreign and Muslim nobles and are generally subject to the same regulations. Unlike the other

---

[63] Constable (ed.), *op. cit.* (n. 1), pp. 284–99.
[64] Fryer in Crooke (ed.), *op. cit.* (n. 4), II, 106–7. Preceding paragraphs, Bernier in Constable (ed.), *op. cit.* (n. 1), pp. 205–10.

nobles, these rajas usually live and work in their own tents outside the fortresses. They act as a check upon the other rajas not in Mughul pay and are willing and ready to war against the Pathans or rebellious Mughul nobles or governors. They are preferred over Mughuls in the Deccan and Persian wars because the latter are mostly Shiites and of the same faith as the sultan of Golconda and the shah of Persia. Aurangzib employs Pathans in his armies for the same reasons that he uses Rajputs.[65]

The principal armed forces are composed of Mughuls, so-called Mughuls, and foreigners. One army always acts as an imperial bodyguard and is with the emperor wherever he goes; the others are "dispersed in the several provinces." The cavalry of the emperor's bodyguard is headed by "Omrahs."[66] These nobles are not members of ancient families or necessarily the descendants of "Omrahs," since no line can for long "maintain its distinction" under the Mughul system of escheat. Ordinarily the emperor bestows only a small pension on the widow and family of a deceased noble. Nobles who serve for long periods are sometimes influential enough in their lifetimes to obtain imperial favors for children, "particularly if their persons be well formed, and their complexions sufficiently fair to enable them to pass for genuine Mogols."[67] Nobles are granted new titles with each advancement in rank. For example, Ovington says the governor of Surat was named "Muk Teer Chan" (*Mukhtār Khān*), a title meaning "Lord after my own Heart."[68] Advancement is a slow and uncertain process. Consequently most of the "Omrahs" are recruited from foreign adventurers and persons of low descent and little education "who entice one another to the court." Such "Omrahs" are regularly elevated or reduced in status at the emperor's "own pleasure and caprice."[69]

According to Bernier the "Omrahs" have titles ("Hazary" or *hazāri*) which indicate their level in the official hierarchy.[70] These ranks are based on the number of horses, ranging from one thousand to twelve thousand, which

---

[65] Bernier in Constable (ed.), *op. cit.* (n. 1), pp. 210–11. On the Rajput princes as imperial officers see R. C. Hallissey, *The Rajput Rebellion against Aurangzeb* (Columbia, Mo., 1977), chap. iii.

[66] This term in Mughul times "was applied to all officers holding the *mansabs* (ranks) of 1,000 and above, i.e. to all higher strata of the official class" (M. Athar Ali, *The Mughal Nobility under Aurangzeb* [Bombay, 1966], p. 2).

[67] Cf. *ibid.*, pp. 18, 63–65. Bernier asserts repeatedly (Constable [ed.], *op. cit.* [n. 1], pp. 3, 212, 404) that a foreigner will be considered a Mughul if he has a white face and professes Islam. Also see Fryer's similar assertion in Crooke (ed.), *op. cit.* (n. 4), II, 110.

[68] It really means "Independent Lord." See Ovington in Rawlinson (ed.), *op. cit.* (n. 3), p. 110. Rest of paragraph from Bernier in Constable (ed.), *op. cit.* (n. 1), pp. 211–12.

[69] Bernier's assertion that most of the "Omrahs" are of foreign origin needs qualification. In the period 1658–78, it appears that slightly fewer than one-half were foreigners. See Athar Ali, *op. cit.* (n. 66), p. 17.

[70] The Mughul aristocracy was essentially a military peerage, as Bernier (Constable [ed.], *op. cit.* [n. 1], p. 212) indicates when he uses the term *hazāri* as the title for the commander of one thousand horses. The *mansabdār* system included "the army, the peerage, and the civil administration rolled into one." See Abdul Aziz, *The Mansabdārī System and the Mughul Army* (Delhi, 1972), p. 1.

a noble is said to command. Payment to the nobles "is proportionate, not to the number of men, but to the number of horses."[71] Since two horses are provided to each trooper, it may be concluded that the number of horses provided by a noble is double the number of men.[72] But it must not be imagined, Bernier observes, that "a lord of ten thousand horse" is expected to maintain or the emperor to pay for that large a number of horses or men; these are merely high-sounding titles, intended to impress "the credulous and deceive Foreigners." The emperor himself decides how many effectives and nominals each "Omrah" is to maintain and pays certain sums for both.[73] To augment their incomes the "Omrahs" hold back 5 percent from each man's pay and inflate the number of horses actually being maintained. By these means their incomes get to be considerable, especially when they receive "Jah-ghirs" (*jagirs* or assigned rent-free lands) in lieu of cash. Those who have no *jagirs*, like Bernier's patron, are "Nagdy" (*naqdi*) and receive their income in cash alone.[74]

Fryer tells us that although they enjoy substantial incomes, very few "Omrahs" are wealthy; most are deeply in debt because of the numerous costly presents they must give to the emperor as well as the expenses they incur for their grandiose personal establishments. The number of "Omrahs" is great in the provinces, in the armies, and at court; they occupy all the highest posts in the state. The emperor keeps them strictly away from their *jagirs* to prevent them from using these lands as bases for revolt. For the same reason he keeps their wives and children as hostages at court while they are away at war or on administrative assignments in the provinces or distant cities.[75] Calling themselves the "Pillars of the Empire," the "Omrahs" maintain "the splendour of the court" by their ostentatious public parades. At court every "Omrah" is obliged to attend the emperor twice daily, at ten or eleven in the morning and at six o'clock in the evening. Each court noble must also, in rotation, stand guard in the fortress once each week for twenty-four hours. They must all accompany the emperor on his excursions, marches, travels, and hunting expeditions.[76]

Petty nobles are of two types, Bernier reports. "Mansebdars" (*mansab-dārs*) are horsemen who receive "Manseb" (*mansab*) pay, "which is a peculiar pay, both honourable and considerable," smaller than that of the "Omrahs" but higher than "the common pay."[77] A man of this rank acknowledges only the authority of the emperor and performs duties similar to those re-

---

[71] A reference to the pay of the *suwār* rank, according to Aziz, *op. cit.* (n. 70), p. 151, n. 2.
[72] See *ibid.*, p. 100.
[73] For an explanation of this somewhat confusing remark see *ibid.*, p. 152, n. 1.
[74] Bernier in Constable (ed.), *op. cit.* (n. 1), pp. 212–13. See also Aziz, *op. cit.* (n. 70), p. 152, n. 2.
[75] Fryer in Crooke (ed.), *op. cit.* (n. 4), II, 110.
[76] Bernier in Constable (ed.), *op. cit.* (n. 1), pp. 213–14.
[77] On the very complicated system of pay for the various ranks see Athar Ali, *op. cit.* (n. 66), pp. 43–53.

quired of the "Omrahs." While their numbers are not fixed, they are more numerous than the "Omrahs"; from two to three hundred serve at the court alone.[78] The second class of nobles are "Rouzindars" (*rozindārs*, or men with a daily salary), horsemen whose pay is sometimes higher than that of many of the *mansabdārs*. While not so much esteemed, they are also not subject as the *mansabdārs* are to the "Agenas" (Arabic, *ajnas*, plural of *jin* meaning goods); that is, they are not required to buy goods from the imperial palaces at stipulated, and often inflated, prices. Great in number, they serve as clerks. Some affix the emperor's seal to "Barattes" (*barāts*), the orders of payment for state work service. These civil servants will not hesitate to accept bribes for the prompt issuance of these pay orders.

The military is paid in part by the imperial treasury and in part by revenues derived from lands set aside for that purpose. Common cavalrymen of two classes serve under the "Omrahs," called two-horse and one-horse men. While the former receive higher pay than the latter, the income for both classes often depends on the whim of the "Omrah." There is, however, a minimum wage which is used in calculating the payments to be made by the emperor for each soldier. Infantrymen receive the smallest pay and are generally a sorry lot. Artillerymen can demand high pay, particularly the Europeans; however, they are not recruited or paid as much as formerly, since the Mughuls are now better able to manage their own artillery.

The Mughuls employ both heavy and light artillery, the latter being called "artillery of the stirrup" because it is supposed to be mobile enough to follow the emperor wherever he goes.[79] Aurangzib's heavy artillery consists of seventy cannons, mostly brass, and of small field pieces "the size of a double musket" mounted on the backs of camels "much in the same manner as swivels are fixed in our barks."[80] His "artillery of the stirrup" is made up of fifty to sixty small brass field pieces; each is mounted in a small painted carriage between two ammunition chests. The carriage itself is drawn by two horses and guided by a driver. When the imperial entourage camps, these gun carriages are lined up in front of the emperor's tent.

The provincial armies are identical in composition to the imperial bodyguard but exceed it in numbers. In the Deccan alone the cavalry runs between twenty and thirty thousand, in Kabul it is "not less" than twelve to fifteen thousand, in Kashmir there are more than four thousand in the cavalry, and in war-torn Bengal its numbers are far greater than elsewhere. The effective cavalry of the imperial bodyguard "including that of the Rajas and Patans," numbers thirty-five to forty thousand, thus bringing the cavalry's

---

[78] In Aurangzib's time the *mansabdārs* probably numbered no more than eight thousand. See *ibid.*, p. 7.

[79] *Topkhāna-i-rikāb*, or "artillery of the stirrup."

[80] The small field pieces were called *shutarnāls*. An offensive weapon called the *zamburak* was fired with the camel kneeling. See R. R. Puhl, *Armies of the Great Mughals* (New Delhi, 1978), p. 93.

grand total to more than two hundred thousand.[81] By way of contrast, the infantry in the imperial guard numbers fifteen thousand, much less than one-half the number of cavalry. If these proportions are applied to the armed forces as a whole, it is possible thus to make an estimate of the total number of effectives.[82] Most previous appraisals are swollen greatly by including under the infantry figures the huge numbers of camp-followers. There are so many of these because in times of peace the people in the capital cities derive their income almost exclusively from serving the armed forces. Thus when the emperor embarks on an extended campaign, the population of these camp-like cities "is reduced to the necessity of following" his army.[83]

With all his great riches, the emperor is still burdened by heavy and regular expenses. An incredible number of persons, especially soldiers and their families, are completely dependent upon the imperial purse. Consequently Aurangzib must pay them regularly to keep them loyal and active in his service. He maintains in Delhi and Agra alone two to three thousand horses, eight or nine hundred elephants, and large numbers of baggage horses and mules as well as porters, runners, and water-carriers. Add to these ongoing expenses the cost of maintaining a lavish seraglio and court. Although Bernier thinks his revenues probably exceed the joint incomes "of the Grand Seignior [of Turkey] and of the King of Persia, he cannot possess the vast surplus of wealth that most people seem to imagine." That the tales of his great pecuniary wealth are exaggerations is indicated by his inability to pay and supply his armies after the five years of civil war by which he came to power. Shah Jahan, who had reigned in relative peace for more than forty years, did not leave Aurangzib with a hoard of currency but only rich articles which he would have great difficulty selling for cash were he to try.[84]

The offensive weapons of the Mughul warriors for short-range fighting are the sword and various kinds of daggers (*katārs*). Their swords are "four Fingers broad, very thick, and by consequence heavy." They are slightly curved and sharp only on the convex side. The guard is a very plain handle of iron supported by a crossbar underneath its flat hilt. Their swords "are very brittle" so the English sell them others of better metal. Soldiers wear waist belts in which they hang two swords with points upward. Civilians carry their swords either in their hands or on "their shoulders like a Musket." Customarily the Mughul soldiers carry a dagger at their side, the blade "being near a foot long, and above four Fingers broad at the Handle." It has

---

[81] For the general accuracy of this figure *cf.* Aziz, *op. cit.* (n. 70), p. 23

[82] By using this device, the total number of Aurangzib's effectives early in his reign may be placed in the neighborhood of three hundred thousand. *Cf.* the table showing the army and equipment used in the siege of Qandahar (1649–53) in *ibid.,* pp. 234–35. For a somewhat higher estimate as of 1647 see *The Cambridge History of India* (see n. 60), IV, 316.

[83] In Akbar's time the camp-followers were all classed as infantry. See Bernier in Constable (ed.), *op. cit.* (n. 1), pp. 215–21.

[84] *Ibid.,* pp. 224–25.

"an odd kind of Guard" made of two square iron bars about one finger wide and one foot long. The bars are parallel to each other and about four inches apart. They are joined at the upper end of the blade by two smaller iron rods set two inches from each other. Officers of higher rank have similar daggers with decorations added.

Offensive arms for long-range fighting are the bow and arrow, the javelin or "Zugaye" (*sainthī*?, a type of spear), and sometimes the pistol.[85] Infantry soldiers carry either a musket or a pike twelve feet in length. A cavalier carries a poniard on his right side in his girdle, a broad-bladed sword on his left side in a hilt, a bow in one hand, and a lance in the other. His arrows are in a quiver attached to the saddle and his shield hangs across his shoulders. Cavalrymen are led by "Hazory" (*hazārī*, lord of one thousand horse) drawn from the chief nobles of the realm.[86] A foot soldier is armed with a matchlock gun, or a great lance and shield, or sometimes a sword.[87] Round Mughul shields made of heavy leather are about two feet in diameter. They are varnished black and held together by nails which protrude from the face by more than one inch. The soldiers wear various pieces of armor: the coat of mail and cuirass as body armor, a helmet to protect the head, and a "Vambrace" attached to the sword.[88] The last is an iron sleeve lined with velvet to protect the hand and sword. While the Mughuls manufacture cannons, they are generally "good for nothing." They make the mistake of mixing together metals melted in different furnaces which are necessarily of differing qualities.[89]

2

THE PROVINCES

Sir Thomas Roe had included in his journal a topographical list of the thirty-seven political divisions of the Mughul Empire in Jahangir's time.[90] In Aurangzib's era, according to Bernier, the empire comprised twenty "Soubahs" (Arabic, *subāh*s, provinces), divided into "Pragnas" (*pargana*s), or chief cities and subdivisions where imperial rents are collected, and "Serkars"

---

[85] *Ibid.*, pp. 217–19. The pistol, first used in Aurangzib's reign, was called a *tamanchah* or a *tapanchah*. See Puhl, *op. cit.* (n. 80), chap. x. On the pistol's introduction to India see Qaisar, *op. cit.* (n. 36), p. 54.

[86] On the great importance attached to the cavalry, see Puhl, *op. cit.* (n. 80), pp. 57–64.

[87] Fryer in Crooke (ed.), *op. cit.* (n. 4), II, 112–14.

[88] The "Vambrace," from French, *avant-bras*, is armor for the forearm.

[89] Thévenot in Sen (ed.), *op. cit.* (n. 2), pp. 61–62.

[90] See above, pp. 605–6. For a summary of the scholarship and learned debate on Roe's list see P. Saran, *The Provincial Government of the Mughals, 1526–1658* (2d ed.; New York, 1973), pp. 71–101.

The Provinces

(*sarkārs*), revenue districts within the *parganas*.[91] Early in Aurangzib's reign, the imperial treasury (*khazāna*) annually received 235,935,000 rupees from the provinces.[92] Delhi, the first province, includes sixteen *sarkārs*, and two hundred and thirty *parganas*. Agra, the second, comprises fourteen *sarkārs* and two hundred and sixteen *parganas*. Lahore, the third, has fourteen *sarkārs* and three hundred and fourteen *parganas*. The smaller frontier provinces, such as Kabul and Qandahar, appear to have no *sarkārs* and only a few *parganas*. Bengal, then occupied by Shujah, yields very little revenue even though it is the richest province of the empire.[93]

In a series of nine letters written from India in 1664–65, Bernier describes a journey from Delhi to Lahore and Srinagar and reports on his personal experiences during three months in Kashmir.[94] On this excursion he is attached to the entourage accompanying Aurangzib to Kashmir where the emperor hoped to recover from his long illness in the cool, clear air of the mountains.[95] Bernier was invited on this trip to accompany Danishmand Khan, his faithful patron at the court and his intellectual companion. According to Bernier, Danishmand Khan "can no more dispense with his philosophical studies in the afternoon than avoid devoting the morning to his weighty duties as Secretary of State for Foreign Affairs and Grand Master of the Horse." Astronomy, geography, and anatomy are his favorite pursuits, and he "reads with avidity the works of Gassendy and Descartes." The French physician was particularly honored to be included on the trip, be-

[91] The province was ruled by a *nazim*, or more commonly a *shahbandar*, whose administration was an exact replica in miniature of the central administration. Most of its officials worked in the provincial capitals. See J. Sarkar, *Mughal Administration* (3d ed.; Calcutta, 1972), p. 37. The *pargana* was a collection of villages and lands headed by a *chaudhuri* who was responsible for collecting imperial revenues. See *The Cambridge Economic History of India* (see n. 19), I, 58. For a general discussion of these provincial subdivisions see Saran, *op. cit.* (n. 90), chap. vi.

[92] These are land revenues only, and Bernier himself doubts their accuracy and reliability. He does not indicate his source. His figures were taken seriously by Edward Thomas in his *The Revenue Resources of the Mughal Empire in India from A.D. 1593 to A.D. 1707* (London, 1871). More scepticism is expressed about their reliability by W. H. Moreland, *From Akbar to Aurangzeb, A Study in Indian Economic History* (London, 1923), pp. 327–28. Around 1690 Aurangzib had land revenues on paper of 334,500,000 rupees. See *The Cambridge Economic History of India* (see n. 19), IV, 316. I. Habib, *The Agrarian System of Mughal India (1556–1707)* (Bombay, 1963), Appendix D, includes Bernier's data in his *Jama* and *Hasil* statistics.

[93] Bernier in Constable (ed.), *op. cit.* (n. 1), pp. 455–60. Thévenot's description of Hindustan (the Mughul Empire) is organized according to provinces. He lists twenty-two, or two more than Bernier. I. Habib, *An Atlas of the Mughal Empire* (Delhi, 1982), Map. OA gives twenty-two as of 1601. Since Thévenot traveled only in Gujarat, the Deccan, and Golconda, much of what he reports about the other provinces is from hearsay.

[94] Constable (ed.), *op. cit.* (n. 1), pp. 400–431. These letters are directed to a "Monsieur de Merveilles." The details of the journey itself are well summarized in J. P. Ferguson, *Kashmir. An Historical Introduction* (London, 1961), pp. 150–56. Bernier (and Ferguson also) dates Aurangzib's only visit to Kashmir at 1665. J. N. Sarkar, in his biography of Aurangzib, places it in 1663 (*History of Aurangzib, Mainly Based on Persian Sources* [2d rev. ed.; Calcutta, 1921], III, 14; V, 339). Since we are citing Bernier's report, we will use his date.

[95] On his illness see above, pp. 709–10.

cause Aurangzib strictly limited the numbers taken to Kashmir to keep from imposing too heavy a strain upon its feeble economy.

Arrived at Srinagar at the end of March, 1665, Bernier spends the next three months in what he calls "the Terrestrial Paradise of the Indies." His ninth and last letter, written from there, provides "an accurate description of the Kingdom of Kachemire." According to the histories of its "ancient Kings," the countryside of Kashmir was originally covered by a vast lake. The land emerged when an outlet for its waters was opened by a cut in the mountain of "Baramoulé" (Baramula) made by an aged saint named "Kacheb." [96] This story is told in the abridgment of the chronicles of the ancient Hindu kings made at Jahangir's command, which Bernier is "now translating from the Persian." [97] No longer a lake, Kashmir is a "beautiful country, diversified by a great many low hills." Situated to the north of Lahore, it is enclosed by mountains which belong to the neighboring rulers of "Great Tibet" (Ladakh) and of "Little Tibet" (Baltistan) and to the "Raja Gamon" (Raja of Jummoo). The lower mountains which surround its meadows are covered with trees and pasture lands. While small game is plentiful, there exist here few or no "serpents, tigers, bears, or lions." Very unusual are the vast numbers of bees which, with the cows, make this a veritable land of milk and honey. The distant mountains, whose summits are always crowned with snow, "gush forth innumerable springs and streams" which are channeled into the valley to irrigate its rice fields. After wandering through the tablelands, thousands of these rivulets join to form a beautiful river (the Jhelum) "navigable for vessels as large as are borne on our Seine." After gently winding around Kashmir, it passes between "two steep rocks" at Baramula. Thereafter it is joined by several smaller mountain streams and flows in the direction of "Atek" (Attock) to become part of the Indus. [98]

The whole "kingdom" looks as green as "a fertile and highly cultivated garden" with its luxuriant fields of rice, wheat, hemp, saffron, and many vegetables. Its tablelands are dotted with hillocks, intersected by trenches, rivulets, and canals, and brightened by several small lakes. In the private gardens of villages and hamlets grow most of the flowers, fruits, and vege-

[96] This is a Hindu tradition. "Kacheb" is the Persian form of Kasyupa, the *rishi* or sage who reputedly opened the passage or cascade at Baramula.

[97] This Sanskrit historical record written in verse is called *Rajatarangini* or "River of Kings." It was composed in A.D. 1148–50 by Kalhana, whose father, Chanpaka, was a minister to King Harsha (r. 1089–1101). It was gradually translated into Persian after the beginning of Muslim rule in 1339. At Jahangir's command, a Persian version in eight books was epitomized and continued in 1617–20 by Haidar Malik, son of a noble Kashmiri family. This abridged and extended version covers Kashmir's history from its beginnings until the conquest by Akbar. Bernier, according to his Address to the Reader, promised to undertake a translation of Haidar Malik's work. An English translation of Kalhana's *Rajatarangini* was published at London in 1900 by Aurel Stein. Another English translation by R. S. Pandit was published at New Delhi in 1935.

[98] Actually the Jhelum is first joined by the Chenab and the Ravi before falling into the Indus south of Multan. See map 2.

tables common to Europe, as well as others native to India. Their fruits, while good, are inferior to those of Europe "for they do not understand the culture and grafting of trees as we do in France."

The capital city of Kashmir "bears the same name as the kingdom."[99] An unwalled city, the capital is built on a freshwater lake (Dal Lake) in the midst of a plain ("Happy Valley") behind which stands a semicircle of mountains. The lake is linked by a canal to the river (Jhelum) coursing through the center of the city. Two wooden bridges cross the river to connect the two parts of this city of well-built and several-storied wooden houses. Most of the houses along the river boast gardens, while other houses have their own canals on which "the owner keeps a pleasure-boat." An "isolated hill" called "Harajperbet" (*Hari Parbat*), or what Bernier calls the "Verdant Mountain," rises "at the end of the town," on the sides of which stand handsome houses; near its tree-crowned summit stand a "Mosque and Hermitage."[100] Opposite this mountain rises another on which there is a small mosque and an ancient "temple for idols" named "Tact-Souliman" (*Takht-i-Suliman*) or the Throne of Solomon.[101] The lake is crowded with cultivated islands "covered with fruit trees, and laid out with regular trellised walks" which are surrounded by tall and stately large-leafed aspens planted at two-foot intervals.[102] The slopes bordering the lake are replete with houses and flower-gardens.

Of all the gardens of Kashmir the most beautiful is the imperial garden of "Chah-limar" (Shalimar, or the "Abode of Love"). From the lake it is entered by a "spacious canal, bordered with green turf, and running between two rows of poplars." It leads to a large summer house surrounded by a garden. Another canal paved with stone blocks runs to a second summer house at the end of the garden. In the center of the canal is a long row of regularly spaced fountains and from nearby circular reservoirs arise "other fountains formed into a variety of shapes and figures." The summer houses themselves are situated between the canals and are flanked by poplar trees. They are domed and "encircled by a gallery into which four doors open"; two of these lead to bridges which connect the buildings to the opposite

[99] Srinagar was its Hindu name. During Muslim times it was dropped and the city was called simply Kashmir. When the Sikhs captured it in 1819, they restored the Hindu name which is still in use.

[100] *Hari Parbat*, "Mountain of Lord Hari" (5,671 ft.), north of the city, is surrounded by a wall built by Akbar at the end of the sixteenth century. See Murray (publ.), *op. cit.* (n. 40), p. 522. The fortress now on the hill's summit was built in the eighteenth century. See Ferguson, *op. cit.* (n. 94), p. 38.

[101] A stone Hindu temple was erected here in the eighth century by the sage Shankar Acharya. Part of it was converted into a mosque by the invading Muslims in the early eleventh century. According to Bernier the Muslims believed that it was the creation of King Solomon when he visited Kashmir, a tradition which the learned French physician doubts. Today it is called Shankar Acharya Hill. See Murray (publ.), *op. cit.* (n. 40), p. 522.

[102] The famous "floating gardens" lie among certain of these islands in the Dal Kotwal. By "aspens" it is probable Bernier here refers to the *chenār* or the oriental plane tree.

banks. These valuable doors are made of stone, each being supported by two beautiful pillars. Each house consists of a large center room with small apartments at each corner. The interiors are "painted and gilt" and Persian inscriptions decorate the walls of all the chambers.[103]

Kashmiris are generally adjudged to be wittier and more ingenious than other Indians, and the equal of the Persians in poetry and the sciences. They are active, industrious, and intelligent, and their manufactures "are in use in every part of the Indies." They are great workers in wood and masters in the arts of varnishing and inlaying. Their unique and valuable textile industry produces a "prodigious quantity of shawls" for export. The weaving of these large, soft shawls "gives occupation even to the little children." In India they are worn in winter as head coverings and mantles by both sexes. These shawls are made of both local wool and "touz" (*tūs,* or shawl goat), the hair-like wool of a wild goat native to Tibet. Shawls of this softer Tibetan wool are more expensive and require more care than those woven from Kashmir wool. Imitation shawls produced elsewhere in India are never equal in "delicate texture and softness" to the shawls of Kashmir.

Admittedly charmed by the vale of Kashmir, Bernier admires equally the beauty of its women. The Mughul courtiers recruit their wives and concubines from Kashmir so that the "children may be whiter than the Indians and pass for genuine Mughuls." These cherished brunette women with "their fine and slender shapes" are kept as "hidden treasures." To obtain a glimpse of them Bernier resorts to various strategems. On the advice of a Persian friend, he poses as a Persian looking for a wife. Following his co-conspirator about, he goes from house to house distributing sweetmeats to the women and children to indulge his curiosity about the female faces of Kashmir.[104]

At the request of his patron, Bernier makes three short excursions into other parts of the valley to report on alleged "wonders." Accompanied by a native and escorted by a trooper, he pays a visit to "a certain fountain" to investigate the wondrous ebb and flow of its waters. At the side of its reservoir the Hindus have a small temple called "Send-brary" (*Sunda-Brari*), or water of Brari, to which pilgrims come to bathe.[105] After deciding that the ebb and flow is produced by the periodic melting of the snows on the mountain, Bernier visits nearby "Achiavel" (Achabal), where the rulers of Kashmir have maintained a country estate since antiquity. Built to enclose a spring, this house is surrounded by canals fed by its gushing waters.[106] He

---

[103] Built by Jahangir, Shalimar Bagh fell into ruin; Bernier's description of 1665 preserves for us a memory of its former glory. *Cf.* Ferguson, *op. cit.* (n. 94), pp. 120–22. It was restored and is still maintained by the government of India, though of course not in the Mughul style.

[104] *Cf. ibid.*, pp. 156–57.

[105] This is a spring in the eastern end of the valley. *Ibid.*, p. 157.

[106] *Cf. ibid.*, pp. 126–27. See S. C. Koul, *Srinigar and Its Environs* (3d ed.; Srinagar, 1962), pp. 53–55, for a detailed description of the modern Achabal garden.

then proceeds to another similar and nearby imperial garden renowned for its tame fish reputedly placed there by Nur Mahal, the wife of Jahangir.[107]

After returning to Srinagar, Bernier is sent on an expedition to Baramula to observe a "genuine miracle." There he is supposed to investigate the miraculous cures effected at a mosque by a dead dervish whose tomb reposes in its interior. This Muslim saint is renowned for using his powers to enable eleven men to lift a heavy stone with the tips of their fingers. Bernier proves to his personal satisfaction that this miracle is but another pious fraud and that the pilgrims are attracted to Baramula more by the free food handed out there than by the much vaunted miracles of its saint.[108] Leaving Baramula in a hurry, Bernier visits the gorge through which the Jhelum leaves the valley. He then leaves the high road to see a large lake that is "well stocked with fish, particularly eels, and covered with ducks, wild geese, and many other water birds." In its center stands a hermitage which allegedly floats on the water. Through the middle of this lake runs the river which disgorges at Baramula.[109] From here he climbs the adjacent mountain to see a large lake in which the winds pile up so much ice that it never completely melts.[110] At this point Bernier is recalled to Srinagar by his patron.

While traveling, Bernier continues to gather information from merchants about Kashmir's mountainous dependencies and its neighboring states. He learns that the valley peoples pay their taxes in leather and wool and that those who live in distant inaccessible regions refuse to pay any taxes at all. He is told stories about the polyandry prevailing in some of these remote valleys.[111] A few years before, when a succession crisis occurred in "Little Tibet" (Baltistan), the governor of Kashmir interfered on behalf of one of the parties. The successful claimant was thereafter required to pay to the Mughul Empire a tribute of crystals, musk, and wool. This puppet raja of Baltistan visits Srinagar to offer his respects to Aurangzib. Invited to dinner by Bernier's patron, the raja explains that his land is bounded on the east by "Great Tibet" (Ladakh), that it is basically a poor country without gold, and that he and most of his subjects are Shiites. He refers also to the attempt of Shah Jahan of "seventeen or eighteen years ago, to conquer Great Tibet, a country frequently invaded by the Kings of Kachemire."[112] Fearful that Au-

---

[107] The garden of Vernag or Nila Nag was built by Jahangir in 1620 around one of the largest springs in India. Close by is the source of the Jhelum River. For its history and present condition see Ferguson, *op. cit.* (n. 94), pp. 128–29, and Koul, *op. cit.* (n. 106), pp. 58–59.

[108] *Cf.* Ferguson, *op. cit.* (n. 94), pp. 157–58.

[109] This is the Wular Lake through which the Jhelum flows. For a modern description see Koul, *op. cit.* (n. 106), pp. 45–46.

[110] Probably one of the Gungabal lakes which were originally formed by the surrounding glaciers.

[111] In this form of polyandry the brothers of a family have one wife in common. *Cf.* P. N. Chopra, *Ladakh* (New Delhi, 1980), p. 48. For a study of modern Tibetan fraternal polyandry see Nancy E. Levine, *The Dynamics of Polyandry* (Chicago, 1988).

[112] Probably a reference to the attack of 1638 on Ladakh when Ali Mardan Khan was governor of Kashmir.

rangzib's presence in Kashmir might herald the onset of new invasions, a Tibetan embassy is sent from Lhasa to Srinagar in 1665 to investigate the situation. As gifts it presents crystals, musk, yaks' tails, and a large piece of highly valued green jade. The ambassador's retinue includes "three or four cavaliers, and ten or twelve tall men, dried-up looking and lean, with very scanty beards like the Chinese, and common red caps, such as our seamen wear." [113] By treaty the emissary promises Aurangzib that a mosque will be built in Lhasa, that Tibetan coins will be imprinted on one side with the emperor's portrait, and that annual tribute will be paid to Delhi. No one doubts, however, that this treaty will be swiftly abrogated or simply ignored once Aurangzib leaves Kashmir.

One member of the ambassador's suite is a physician of the Lama "tribe" of Lhasa. These Lamas form a spiritual caste similar to the Brahmans of India; they differ in that they respect a supreme pontiff while the Brahmans do not. Their Grand Lama is honored and revered as a "divine personage" throughout Tibet and "all Tartary." When he is on the point of death, the Grand Lama tells his council that his soul will pass to the body of a recently born infant. When the child reaches six or seven years of age, he establishes his legitimacy as Grand Lama by identifying his own belongings from a melange of furniture and clothes placed before him. The Tibetan physician has with him "a book of receipts," which he will not be induced to sell, that is written in a script "something like ours." On request he agrees to write down the alphabet, but his efforts fail to meet muster since "his writing is so wretchedly bad in comparison with that in his book." Although Bernier learns from the Tibetan that "Great Tibet" is covered with snow five months of the year and that it is frequently at war with the Tartars, he decides that the man is an ignoramus with whom he has wasted his time and energies. [114]

Until about 1640 caravans regularly made annual trips from Kashmir to China which took about three months each way. [115] The "extremely difficult road" which they followed across the mountains of "Great Tibet" and "Tartary" is rendered doubly perilous by "impetuous torrents that can be crossed only by means of cords extended from rock to rock." [116] Ordinarily these caravans returned with musk, China-wood or root, rhubarb, and "mamiron" (*mamiran-i-Chini*), a small root "in great repute for the cure of bad eyes." [117] From Tibet they brought musk, crystals, jade, and fine wool of

[113] Members of the Red Cap sect of the Tibetan Buddhists called *Dukpa* or *Shammar*.

[114] For the Tibetan embassy see Constable (ed.), *op. cit.* (n. 1), pp. 421–25. From 1643 to 1716 central Tibet was a dependency of Mongolia. The fifth Dalai Lama contested with the Mughuls to bring Ladakh and Baltistan within their respective spheres of influence. See Chopra, *op. cit.* (n. 111), pp. 26–27. Also see below on Tibet, pp. 1773–83.

[115] Cf. C. Wessels, S.J., *Early Jesuit Travellers in Central Asia 1603–1721* (The Hague, 1924), p. 13.

[116] Rope suspension bridges called *jholas* are common in the high mountains of Kashmir and Tibet.

[117] Still sold in the markets of the Punjab and Kashmir, *mamiran* is ground up and mixed with rose water before being applied to the eyes.

two kinds: ordinary sheep's wool and "touz" (*tūs*). But ever since Shah Jahan's invasion (*ca.* 1640) of "Great Tibet" (Ladakh), the merchants and caravans of Kashmir are interdicted from entering Ladakh. Consequently the trade between China and the Mughul Empire is now carried on by caravans which avoid Ladakh and proceed directly from Patna on the Ganges to Lhasa.[118]

From merchants of "Kacheguer" (Kashgar) who were in Srinagar, Bernier learns about the route to Kashgar which avoids Ladakh. It runs northeastward via "Gourtche" (Gurez), the last town of Kashmir, to "Eskerdou" (Skardu), the capital of "Little Tibet" (Baltistan), to the small town of "Cheker" (Shigar) on a river "celebrated for its medicinal waters," and ultimately to the town of Kashgar, the former capital of the rajas of Kashgar who now reside at "Jourkind" (Yarkand).[119] Caravans run annually from Kashgar to China "not more than a two months' voyage." On returning from China these caravans proceed to Persia via Uzbek.[120]

Bernier continues his discourse with responses to a set of inquiries directed to him from Paris by Melchisédech Thévenot, the celebrated French collector and publisher of travel literature. The first asks whether it is true that Jews have long resided in Kashmir. Bernier responds in the negative, adding that there seems to be "ground for believing that some of them were formerly settled in these countries": similar facial features and manners, prevalence of the name of "Mousa" (Moses), the tradition that Moses died in Srinagar, and the common belief that Solomon had visited Kashmir. Bernier reinforces this surmise by reference to the existence of Jews in surrounding places: China, Persia, Ethiopia, and Cochin.

After asking for Bernier's observations on the monsoon and the ocean currents of India, Thévenot asks whether Bengal is really "as fertile, rich, and beautiful as is commonly reported." Bernier, who had made two visits to Bengal, is "inclined to believe that the pre-eminence ascribed to Egypt is rather due to Bengal."[121] In this "finest and most fruitful country in the world," rice and sugar are produced in such abundance that they are both exported to neighboring places and to places as far away as Ceylon and Arabia. The Portuguese in Bengal prepare sweetmeats and preserved fruits which are also exported. While wheat is not exported, enough is raised locally to satisfy domestic needs. Poultry, fish, goats, and sheep are abundant and cheap, while pork is so plentiful that the Portuguese resident in Bengal live "almost entirely" on it. The Europeans provision their ships

---

[118] This route ran from Patna through Nepal, to Shigatse, and into Lhasa.

[119] Actually this route ran almost directly northward from Srinagar.

[120] *Cf.* the excellent general map of Central Asian trade routes appended to Wessels, *op. cit.* (n. 115).

[121] The date of his first visit is not known. His second tour came in 1665 after his return from Kashmir while on his way to Golconda. For the responses of Bernier on Bengal see Constable (ed.), *op. cit.* (n. 1), pp. 437–46.

with salt pork and the "excellent and cheap sea-biscuits" made locally. It is because of this abundance that the Europeans and Luso-Asians who have been driven "from their different settlements by the Dutch" seek asylum in Bengal. The Jesuits and Augustinians, "who have large churches and are permitted the free and unmolested exercise of their religion," claim eight to nine thousand Christians in Hugli alone and over twenty-five thousand in other parts of Bengal.

In no other part of the world is the foreign merchant able to find such a variety of "valuable commodities." In addition to sugar and confections, vast quantities of silk and cloths of every sort are available. While the silk textiles are not as fine or as delicate as those of Persia and the Levant, they are much lower in price. The Dutch alone sometimes employ as many as "seven or eight hundred natives in their silk factory at 'Kassem-Bazar' [Qasimbazar]," and the English and other merchants "a proportionate number." [122] Saltpeter sent down the Ganges from Patna is readily purchased in Bengal for export. Also available in its markets are the best lac, opium, wax, civet, long pepper, various drugs, and ghee. [123] While the English and Dutch at first had very high mortality rates in Bengal, they now live with greater caution and their health has improved. Masters do their best to keep their subordinates away from the local women and from dealers in arrack and tobacco; they especially try to limit their workers' consumption of "Bouleponge," a drink made of arrack mixed with lemon juice, water, and nutmeg, which is particularly "hurtful to body and health." [124]

Bernier expatiates on the beauty and complexity of the Ganges delta from Rajmahal to the Bay of Bengal. This land is divided by an infinite number of channels through which the sacred waters of the Ganges run into the sea. On both sides, these channels are lined with Hindu towns and villages in whose surrounding fields grow rice, sugar, grain, vegetables, mustard, sesame for oil, and small mulberry trees on whose leaves the silkworms feed. Innumerable islands fill "the vast space between the two banks of the Ganges," all extremely fertile, on which fruit trees and pineapples thrive. Certain of the islands closest to the sea have been abandoned because of the

---

[122] Tavernier was in Qasimbazar in February, 1666. He lodged there with Arnold van Wachtendonck, provisional director of Dutch operations in Bengal, whose headquarters was in Hugli.

[123] The European ships carried ghee from Bengal mainly to other Indian ports. It was transported in dried skins called *kuppah*.

[124] "Bouleponge" is a curious combination of the name of the beverage and the vessel in which it is brewed. *Bowle* is still the German word for punch. English "punch" possibly derives from Persian *panj*, or Hindu *pānch*, both words meaning "five" because this drink, despite Bernier's recipe, usually is made of five ingredients: arrack, sugar, lime juice, spice, and water. See H. Yule and A. C. Burnell, *Hobson-Jobson* (London, 1886; new ed., edited by W. Crooke, London, 1903, reprinted New Delhi, 1968), pp. 737–39. But the *Oxford English Dictionary* (under "punch") pronounces as uncertain the origin of this word. Its editors, like the French traveler De La Boullaye le Gouz (*ca.* 1653), claim that "Bouleponge" was originally an English word. The *OED* sees it as "an imperfect echo of the English 'bowl o' punch', a phrase already common in the seventeenth century."

attacks of the Arakan pirates. Most are now desolate and left to the animals, the most ferocious of which are the tigers "which sometimes swim from one island to the other." Bernier makes a nine-day voyage through these islands and channels up the delta from Pipli to Hugli in a seven-oared "scallop." [125] On the way he is particularly enthralled to see a "lunar rainbow" on several successive nights. On a quiet, suffocating night he observes that "the bushes around us are so full of glow-worms that they seem ignited." [126]

Gujarat, the province best known to the Europeans, includes nine *sarkārs* and one hundred and ninety *parganas*. [127] Ahmadabad is its capital and the headquarters of its provincial governor. Ordinarily the governor is a son of the emperor, but at present a great noble called "Muhabtat Can" (Mahabat Khan) holds that office. The city is situated on a lovely plain and is watered by a shallow river called the "Sabremetly" (Sabarmati), which floods in the rainy season. In its southeastern suburbs Ahmadabad boasts many large gardens enclosed in brick walls, as well as clusters of houses and tombs. A large reservoir stands here, in the middle of which there is a garden. One approaches the garden over a bridge "four hundred paces long." [128] The city itself is enclosed by brick and stone walls pierced by twelve gates and surmounted by great round towers. Its wall and garrison are well maintained to ward off the incursions of neighboring rajas, especially the raja of "Badur" (Bhadwar) whose residence is in the province of "Candich" (Khandesh). [129]

The lesser towns of Gujarat are about thirty in number, the largest being located near the sea. "Broudra" (Baroda), situated between Broach and Cambay, is a big, modern town in the center of a fertile but sandy country near "Rageapour" (Rajapur). [130] It has more than two hundred towns and villages within its jurisdiction, one of which is "Sindiguera" (Sindkheda). Baroda produces lac and the finest silks made in Gujarat. Between Baroda and Ahmadabad are the medium-sized towns of "Nariad" (Nadiad) and "Mamadebad" (Mahmudabad). Both make textiles, and the latter is famous for the cotton thread it exports. On the east side of the gulf is "Goga" (Gogha), a town peopled mainly by Banyans and sailors. Further to the south on this coast is Patan, a center of trade and silk production which boasts a beautiful Hindu temple that has been converted into a mosque. Offshore is the island and town of Diu, which commands the entry to the gulf. This strategic island, long battled over by the Portuguese, Egyptians, Turks,

---

[125] Pipli was then the most important port on the Orissa coast. Because of changes in the course of the river, it has since disappeared utterly.

[126] Constable (ed.), *op. cit.* (n. 1), pp. 429–31, 437–46.

[127] *Ibid.*, p. 456.

[128] This is a reference to the polygonal Hauz-i-Qutb or Kankariya tank, one of the largest in India; its area is seventy-two acres. It is said to have been completed in 1451. Murray (publ.), *op. cit.* (n. 40), p. 165.

[129] Thévenot in Sen (ed.), *op. cit.* (n. 2), pp. 11–12.

[130] As Thévenot indicates, modern Baroda was built on or near the site of the ancient city of Rajapur.

and Gujaratis, now has three fortresses and is governed by the Portuguese. It is also a center for the production of the cobra stone (snakestone).[131]

In Dr. Fryer's time the province of Gujarat is governed by "Mahmud Emier Caun" (Muhammad Amin Khan), the son of the Mir Jumla who put Aurangzib on the throne.[132] Although he has vast wealth and armed forces, the viceroy at Ahmadabad is not able to keep the "Coolies" (*Kolis*) from stealing and robbing, Sivaji from plundering, or the outlaw Rajputs from descending from their mountains to despoil whenever they please. As a consequence soldiers must be hired to convoy caravans through Gujarat. If these problems could be firmly handled, Surat would readily become the greatest emporium in the world. Nature has provided it with a central position on land and sea routes and its inhabitants have no equals in business acumen. The abundant resources of India's interior provide Surat with exports which enable it to enjoy constantly a favorable balance of payments. The emperor, depending as he does on the wealth of his own country, is content to leave control of the seas to others. He can consequently enjoy the fruits of international trade without spending vast sums to maintain a navy.[133]

The provinces in the vicinity of Gujarat receive small mention in the European accounts. Thévenot reports that Aurangabad, capital of "Balgate" (Balaghat),[134] is a wall-less town. Its governor, usually a prince, maintains a residence there. During the reign of Shah Jahan, Aurangzib acted as governor and had his headquarters there. His first wife died in Aurangabad and in her memory the emperor erected a "lovely mosque" of white, polished stone.[135] The city boasts other mosques, caravanserais, baths, and numerous public buildings. These low stone buildings stand on streets lined with trees, or in the midst of pleasant gardens.[136] "Telenga" (Telingana), a territory which had previously belonged to Bijapur, has "Beder" (Bidar) as its capital.[137] Encompassed by brick walls, battlements, and towers, Bidar is protected by an important frontier "Garrison of Three thousand Men, half Horse and half Foot, with Seven hundred Gunners." Its governor resides in

---

[131] Sen (ed.), *op. cit.* (n. 2), pp. 44–46.

[132] As thirty-sixth viceroy of Gujarat, Muhammad Amin Khan ruled from 1672 to 1682.

[133] Fryer in Crooke (ed.), *op. cit.* (n. 4), I, 300–303. Actually the Mughuls began under Aurangzib to build a west-coast navy. *Cf.* A. D. Roy, *A History of Mughal Navy and Naval Warfares* (Calcutta, 1972), chap. vii.

[134] The Balaghat, as used here, refers to the hilly country in the western part of the present state of Hyderabad. In Thévenot's day, it was at the center of Mughul-Bijapur hostilities in the Deccan. See Y. M. Khan, *The Deccan Policy of the Mughuls* (Lahore, 1971), p. 263.

[135] From 1636 to 1644, and again from 1652 to 1658, Aurangzib was viceroy of the Deccan with his seat at Aurangabad. Dilras Banu Begam, his first wife, died here on October 8, 1657. Her tomb was apparently built in 1660.

[136] Thévenot in Sen (ed.), *op. cit.* (n. 2), p. 103.

[137] Telingana was one of the four provinces of the Mughul Deccan. These provinces were created for the better administration of this hotly contested region during Aurangzib's first period as viceroy. See Y. M. Khan, *op. cit.* (n. 134), pp. 187–88.

a castle outside the town and enjoys "a rich Government."[138] The province of Sind, "which some call Tatta" after its chief town, is famous for its palanquins and two-wheeled carts.[139] Ponda (Phonda), northeast of Goa, is another frontier province of the southward-expanding empire. Situated in the mountains, it is ruled by a *shahbandar* (or *sūbahdār*) who receives revenues from the more than seven hundred villages within his jurisdiction.[140]

3

SURAT

Administration and justice at Surat are in the hands of a number of local officials appointed by the emperor. Exempt from all but imperial jurisdiction, Surat derives its revenues from thirty-six villages in its vicinity.[141] A "Mufty" (Arabic, *mufti*) supervises the Muslims in religious affairs and a "Cady" (*kazi*) acts as a judge of their suits.[142] An official called "Vaca-Nevis" (*wagi'a-navis,* or news recorder), who is responsible to the emperor alone, informs the court about everything that occurs within his assigned jurisdiction. At Surat there are two independent governors (*nawabs*) who report only to the emperor, one commanding the fortress and the other the town. The city's governor is in charge of civil justice and usually renders his decisions quickly. If one person sues another for a debt, the plaintiff must produce a contract, or two witnesses, or take an oath. Christians are required to swear on the Bible, Muslims on the Koran, and Hindus on the cow. Most Hindus would rather lose a case than to swear upon a cow. Those who plead before the governor first give him out of respect a gift of money, "everyone according to his Quality."

Criminal matters are attended to by a "Cotoual" (*kotwal*), the chief of police and jailer.[143] This "Governor of the Night" patrols the city on horseback accompanied by an armed retinue on foot; they make three rounds each

---

[138] Thévenot in Sen (ed.), *op. cit.* (n. 2), pp. 113–14. The governor's residence was built by Ahmad Shah-al-Wali between 1428 and 1432. On the fortifications of Bidar see S. Toy, *The Strongholds of India* (London, 1957), chap. viii. . Also see G. Yazdani, *Bidar: Its History and Monuments* (Oxford, 1947).

[139] Thévenot in Sen (ed.), *op. cit.* (n. 2), pp. 75–76. See pl. 128.

[140] Careri in *ibid.*, p. 211. By 1691 the Mughuls had advanced southward to Tanjore and Trichinopoly.

[141] Seaports were constituted as independent units of government within the Mughul administration. Surat, its most important port at this time, was designated as a *sarkār,* or revenue district, which included the city itself and the surrounding territory. See Saran, *op. cit.* (n. 90), pp. 198–200. It was subdivided into *mahāls* (subdistricts). See Gokhale, *op. cit.* (n. 15), p. 51.

[142] See Thévenot in Sen (ed.), *op. cit.* (n. 2), pp. 26–27. The *mufti* expounds Islamic law and supplies the *kazi* with the legal grounds for his decisions in criminal suits involving Muslims.

[143] *Ibid.,* pp. 27–28. Technically this official was in charge of internal defense, health, sanitation, and all other municipal functions. See Saran, *op. cit.* (n. 90), p. 158.

night looking for fires, debtors, thieves, and prostitutes. Persons found illegally in the streets at night are thrown in jail and are seldom released without first being whipped. The *kotwal* dispenses punishments in summary fashion, many offenders being whipped in his presence, in the street, or on the spot of the crime. While justice is rapid and severe, neither the *kotwal* nor the governor may put anyone to death. The *kotwal* is held responsible by the emperor for preventing thefts and for capturing criminals. If a robbery is committed, all members of the suspect's household are taken into custody and beaten severely. No examination is made of the accused's household or effects, but the beatings are continued until a confession is obtained, innocence determined, or the lost goods returned. In the territory outside of the city the public peace is maintained by a subordinate official called the "Foursdar" (*faujdar*).[144] Land taxes are collected locally by the "Desie" (Mahratti, *desāī*, headman of a district), who squeezes the cultivator as much as the governor does the city-dweller. He distributes seed to each cultivator, the amount being based on the size of the plot. At harvest three-quarters of the crop is taken for taxes. The rest of Surat's revenues comes from customs and tolls.[145]

If the custodians of justice call out "Doa-padecha" (*Duhai-Padshah*, or roughly, "Here is the emperor"), a suspect must heed this invocation on pain of being brought before the magistrate as a criminal. Still, despite the harshness of Mughul justice, few penalties are actually imposed in Surat so "the People live there with freedome enough."[146] Despite his great police powers, the governor of Surat is unable to control the fakirs who terrorize the public and take whatever they want. He and his minions are best at suppressing the poor, impressing craftsmen into service, and extorting money from merchants and artisans. It is only occasionally that exemplary punishments are meted out to lawbreakers and tyrannical officials, just frequently enough to make a show of justice.[147]

While the *kotwal*'s office is one of great trust, it is not as honorable or profitable as that of the "Shawbundar" (*shahbandar*, or *sūbahdār*), who is "King of the Port, or Chief Customer." The revenues of this official have recently fallen, since the emperor in a burst of "Religious Vanity" excused Muslims from paying duties.[148] At certain specified times the *shahbandar* marks goods being exported and clears those being brought in. Persons suspected of smuggling are whipped until a confession is obtained. Smugglers are subjected to bodily punishment but not to confiscation of their goods. The customhouse itself is crowded with porters and other attendants who

[144] On the *faujdar-i-gard* see Saran, *op. cit.* (n. 90), p. 164.
[145] Cf. Gokhale, *op. cit.* (n. 15), pp. 67–68.
[146] Thévenot in Sen (ed.), *op. cit.* (n. 2), pp. 28–29.
[147] Fryer in Crooke (ed.), *op. cit.* (n. 4), I, 241–46.
[148] Custom duties for Muslims were abolished in 1667.

delay deliveries of merchandise until a deal has been struck between the *shahbandar* and the merchants. Across from the customhouse stands the mint, behind whose "stately Entrance" there is a "large Town of Officers." Shroffs and bankers come to these offices to have their silver assayed which, like their gold, "is the most refined, and purest from Ollay [alloy], in the World." Between the mint and the customhouse is a crowded bazaar with stalls on either side where textiles are bought and sold.[149]

Father Manoel Godinho, a Portuguese Jesuit, visited Surat just before its first sack by Sivaji. Godinho, who had been in India since 1655, was dispatched by the governor of Goa from Bassein to Lisbon in 1662. He was in Surat from December 20, 1662, to February 5, 1663, before beginning his overland trip to Europe. Two years later he published at Lisbon his *Relação* in which he tells the story of his embassy.[150] Surat, previously a poor town and an unfrequented port, had become by Godhino's time "the major emporium of India" thanks to the Dutch and English. This "rather narrow" city "surpasses our Evora in grandeur" and in numbers of people "which I reckon to be more than 100,000."[151] People from all over the world reside there "or frequent that port on business." While most of its houses are humble dwellings with thatched roofs, the "chief lords" of the city live in "noble and stately houses." The exteriors of the better Moorish houses are purposely left unimposing, while their interiors are "like paradise" since they are built "as apartments for their women." The Banyans, on the contrary, pay greater attention to the exterior "than to the comforts within." The bottom stories of their houses are built of stone and lime, above which "there is nothing else but works carved in relief on teak, interspersed with enamels and lacquers of variegated hues."[152] The city has many mosques, the chief one of which is a "majestic structure" which stands outside the gates. In an imposing house adjoining its minaret lives the "Sheriff" (Arabic, *sharif*, eminence) who is "universally respected and venerated."[153] Surat also boasts two caravanserais and a publicly maintained bathhouse staffed by servants paid by the city. The city has no proper wall "but has a low en-

[149] Crooke (ed.), *op. cit.* (n. 4), I, 246–48. *Cf.* M. S. Commissariat, *A History of Gujarat* (2 vols.; Bombay, 1938, 1957), II, 375–76.

[150] The latest edition (Lisbon, 1944) of the *Relação do novo caminho que fez por terra e mar, vindo da India para Portugal, no ano de 1663* . . . has an introduction by A. R. Machado. For an English translation of the chapter on Surat see G. M. Moraes (trans.), "Surat in 1663 as Described by Manoel Godinho," *JRAS, Bombay Branch*, XXVI (1952), 121–33. Father John Correia-Afonso, S.J., has in preparation an English-language edition of the entire text. For further bibliographical detail see above, p. 354.

[151] *Cf.* on Surat's population Gokhale, *op. cit.* (n. 15), pp. 10–11. Gokhale does not cite Godinho. Also see below, p. 744.

[152] For a contrasting view of the Banyan houses as "simple structures" see *ibid.*, pp. 15, 41. Since Gokhale's observation stems from the comments of Thévenot and other later writers, it possibly reflects the devastation effected by Sivaji's sack of the city in 1664.

[153] Probably the Saiyad Idrur mosque built in 1639.

closure pierced by four gateways." [154] The guards at these gates escort all entrants to one of the city's two customhouses which "are close to the river and face each other." Maritime goods go through customs at the larger of these buildings and inland merchandise at the smaller. Exports are checked at a special bureau in the customhouses and no one may leave the city without showing a receipt from the assessor of customs. According to Godinho, duties are normally 5 percent, but the Dutch since 1661 receive a rebate of 1 percent given "by the present Emperor [Aurangzib] in consideration of a rich exquisite present . . . made to him in the name of the Company [VOC]." [155]

The defense of the city is left to the fortress on the river. It has three bulwarks and twenty pieces of iron and bronze artillery, mostly in bad condition. The moat of the fortress is very deep but narrow. Its garrison numbers two hundred "native soldiers" under a Mughul captain who reports only to the emperor and is independent of the governor. The captain is also in charge of the funds deposited in the fortress: "the revenues of the province, the customs dues and most of the coins that are struck in the city continuously." These coins, the finest in India, are minted from the European and Persian coins which are melted down and refined here. Drums are beaten at the fortress at sunrise and sunset. There are no houses around the fortress to "stand in the way of the artillery." Rather it is surrounded by a "beautiful open square in which a fair is held every evening."

Goods arrive at Surat by land and sea. The English and Dutch bring merchandise from Europe, the ships of the Red Sea carry the products of Africa, and the native (Indian) merchants import the merchandise of Asia Minor. The Indian merchants of Surat are rich and they have "fifty ships of their own going out to all the countries." Goods from inland production centers are carried into Surat by caravans, bullocks, and camels "which enter its gates every hour." The country around Surat produces wheat, pulses, and rice, as well as the date palm, from which a wine is produced by the Parsis. These white-skinned refugees from Persia worship the sun, the moon, and fire. If a house is on fire, they will not put the fire out "because that would amount to killing God." [156]

Outside the city to the west are the tombs of the Muslims which are "separated from one another by stones at the head of each grave." A bit further out are the English and Dutch cemeteries where the fine mausoleums of the chiefs

---

[154] Twenty-five years earlier Mandelslo had reported that the city had but three gates. See above, p. 669. The earlier walls had possibly been destroyed by Murad's invasion in 1657. See Tavernier in Ball and Crooke (trans. and eds.), *op. cit.* (n. 1), I, 262–64.

[155] Mandelslo reported in 1638 that duties on merchandise were 3½ percent and on gold and silver 2 percent. See above, p. 668. Others claim that the general duty on merchandise was 2½ percent. See below, p. 754.

[156] This is a common tale repeated by many European writers of the seventeenth century. The sacred writings of the Parsis advise believers to extinguish fire with water in cases of necessity.

of their factories stand.[157] There is a separate graveyard for Catholics, in which crosses are planted on the graves. Also outside the city are two wells which supply drinking water.[158] The gentry of Surat, both Muslim and Hindu, ride beautiful Arab horses but without the "solar hats" worn as "the royal headgear" in the Mughul Empire.[159] Some travel about in luxuriously appointed carriages drawn "by stately and swift-footed bullocks of beautiful colours."

At Surat "the Dutch Commodores and the English Presidents fly their national flags from masts . . . higher than . . . all the towers in the city." The Dutch, since their victories in south India, no longer send as many ships to Surat as formerly. But the English, since they have no usable port in India except for Madras on the inhospitable Coromandel Coast, continue to center their commerce at Surat. The European factors purchase cargoes for the expected ships in the local market or in the other ports to which they send coasting vessels. Formerly there was a Jesuit house in Surat whose fathers ministered to its Christians and carried on a mission. It was abandoned because its priests were too often taken as hostages by the emperor when an issue arose with the Portuguese viceroy at Goa. The Jesuits since have been replaced by "two bearded French Capuchins" sent by the Propaganda who have a chapel inside their house.

At the time of Godinho's visit in 1663, the governor of Surat is a highly regarded Persian "much given to hunting leopards." When the emperor hears of his addiction to the chase he is removed from office and replaced.[160] The emperor learned of this governor's neglect of duty through a Muslim agent he maintains at Surat to keep him informed in the minutest detail about the nabob and his aides.[161] These nabobs, who are treated with great deference, appear in public only in the company of a grand entourage. Whenever an imperial dispatch is expected, the governor goes outside the city to meet the messenger. On accepting the letter brought by the messenger, the nabob respectfully touches it to his head and returns with it unopened to his palace.[162]

Thévenot also went to Surat, traveling by sea. On his way there, he passes by the Portuguese fortress of Diu, which he describes.[163] On January 10,

[157] The English and Dutch cemeteries are still maintained by the government of India as historical sites.

[158] Probably another reference to the *Gopi Talao,* which actually consisted of two cisterns. See above, pp. 617, 652, 661, and below, pp. 746, 751.

[159] Probably a reference to the *chirah,* the imperial turban reserved to the use of the emperor and the high nobles on whom it had been bestowed as a mark of favor. See Ansari, *op. cit.* (n. 53), p. 11.

[160] The governor's name was Mustafa Khan. See Gokhale, *op. cit.* (n. 15), p. 71.

[161] On the *harkaras* as intelligence agents see Saran, *op. cit.* (n. 90), pp. 184–86.

[162] All the foregoing is based on the translation of Godinho's chapter on Surat in Moraes, *loc. cit.* (n. 150).

[163] In his *Travels into the Levant* (London, 1687), Pt. II, p. 196.

1666, he arrives at the "Bar of Surrat" where the ships must unload. On the following day he and his fellow passengers slowly proceed upriver with the tide in the ship's boat to the customhouse. Thévenot then gives a valuable and detailed description of the entire procedure required of a ship by the customs. The passengers' names are inscribed in a register one by one. The person and baggage of each is closely searched for contraband. If gold and silver are found on the person, a 2½ percent duty is charged. The passengers are then permitted to enter the city, but they must return the following day to collect their goods and to pay whatever duty is owed. On merchandise, foreigners are required to pay 4 percent and natives 5. In spite of all precautions and high fines, jewels are often smuggled in successfully by friends of the Dutch commander.[164]

Thévenot notices that the earthen walls of Surat are in ruins thanks to Sivaji's invasion of the city two years before (1664). New and thicker brick walls are now being built to protect the city against invasions by land. The new wall encloses a smaller part of the city and is built, in Thévenot's opinion, too close to the fortress.[165] The owners of the "cane houses" now outside the confines of the city are asking the government for fair compensation. The fortress, which survived Sivaji's invasion, stands at the south end of the city right on the river and is designed to defend the city from seaborne attacks.[166] Of moderate size and square, it has a large tower on each corner, and several cannons are mounted in its embrasures. The moats on its three land sides are filled with sea water. It is entered on the land side through "a lovely Gate" which opens into the city's principal bazaar. The provincial revenues kept in the fortress are "never sent to Court but by express Orders."

The size of Surat's population is difficult to determine, since it varies greatly from season to season. During the fair-weather months of November to April, when the ships normally arrive, lodgings are hard to find even in the city's three suburbs. While many foreigners congregate there, Christians are relatively few in number. Its "usual population" is made up of those who profess another faith: Muslims both native and foreign, Hindus, and Parsis, who are also called "Gaures" (Persian, *gabr*) and "Atechparest" (*Atash-parast*, or fire-worshippers).[167] Many of the local merchants are very wealthy, especially a Banyan named "Vargivora" (Virji Vora).[168] The En-

---

[164] Sen (ed.), *op. cit.* (n. 2), pp. 1–4.

[165] The new walls, long known as *Sheherpanah* (the Protection of the City) or the inner walls, were apparently under construction for more than a decade. They fell into ruins early in the nineteenth century. See M. S. Commissariat, *Studies in the History of Gujarat* (Bombay, 1935), pp. 82–83. Also see Gokhale, *op. cit.* (n. 15), pp. 11–12. But also see L'Estra's assertion about their good condition, below, p. 748.

[166] The fortress was built in 1540 by Khudawand Khan, the governor of Surat from 1538–46, to protect the city against intrusions by the Portuguese.

[167] *Gabr*, meaning "infidel," is a term of opprobrium.

[168] On this merchant prince see Gokhale, *op. cit.* (n. 15), chap. viii. In religion he was a Jain and a lay leader of his community. Thévenot claims him as a friend, but fails to mention anything about his religion.

glish and Dutch factors have "very pretty Apartments," and there are about one hundred Catholic families in the town.

Housing is expensive in Surat, since there is no local stone. Buildings are generally made of "brick and lime" or wood imported by sea from Damão. The flat houses of the rich are fairly well built and "covered with Tiles made half round," which are white because they are not well baked. These poor tiles but one-half inch thick are laid in double rows on lathes of bamboo. The wooden frame that supports all this "is only made of pieces of round timber." [169] Most building takes place during the rainy season because the scorching sun of the dry season forces the masonry to dry too fast, causing "cracks and chinks in a trice." In rainy weather the masons merely cover their work with "a Wax-cloath" to let it dry slowly. While the streets of Surat "are large and even," they are unpaved. Within the town proper there are no large public buildings, and the homes of the poor are built of bamboo covered with palm fronds. [170]

Christians and Muslims commonly eat beef in Surat. It is the flesh of cows rather than oxen, since the latter are customarily used to pull plows and heavy loads. They also eat mutton, pork, pullets, chicken, pigeons, and all kinds of wild birds. Two types of edible oil are available, from the "wild saffron" and the "Sesamum," the former being better than the latter. [171] Grapes are available from February to April, from which the Dutch make a bitter wine. Large white grapes are brought to Surat from "Naapoura" (Navapur), a small town near Bombay. Local liquors are no better than the wines, a judgment which Thévenot follows with a lengthy discourse on "Tary" (*tari,* or toddy of the *tar,* or the palmyra). Because it is a great international emporium, the weights, measures, and currencies used at Surat are of many kinds. [172]

While in Surat Thévenot learns that its governor is inquiring about the desirability of permitting the newly formed French East India Company to trade there. [173] Seaport gossip, as well as the enemies of the French, had led him to think the French were pirates. The governor finally presents his misgivings about the French to Father Ambrose of Preuilly, the head of the Capuchin mission in Surat. Satisfied himself that the French are legitimate traders, the governor asks the priest to write his comments down in Persian for forwarding to the emperor. The imperial court, evidently content with the Capuchin's declaration, ordains that the French should be welcomed.

---

[169] *Cf.* Gokhale, *op. cit.* (n. 15), pp. 15–16. Thévenot explains that local wood is not used because of the high cost of land transport.

[170] Thévenot in Sen (ed.), *op. cit.* (n. 2), pp. 22–23.

[171] Thévenot's "wild saffron" is a common Indian thistle cultivated for its oil-producing seeds. The other is *Sesamum indicum* whose seeds yield sesame oil. See George Watt, *A Dictionary of the Economic Products of India* (7 vols. in 10; Calcutta, 1885–96), II, 378; VI, 502.

[172] Sen (ed.), *op. cit.* (n. 2), pp. 23–26. Tavernier is far better on these commercial matters. See Ball and Crooke (trans. and eds.), *op. cit.* (n. 1), I, 7–32.

[173] On the formation of the French East India Company in 1664 see above, p. 96.

When the two French envoys arrive, they are received with "extraordinary kindness." Even the English president, a good friend of Father Ambrose, extends his hospitality to "Sieurs de la Boullaye and Beber" on their arrival in Surat.[174]

Surat's cemeteries are just outside the "Baroche" (Broach) gate. The English and Dutch like to build tombs over their graves of "Pyramids of Brick whitened over with Lime." The Indian Christians have square plaster tombs, some topped with domes or pyramids and all with a little window on one side through which the grave may be seen. The Banyans burn their dead on the riverside at a special place also outside the city and beyond the cemeteries. The ashes are left there to be carried away by the sacred waters of the Tapti River. Children who die before becoming two years of age are not burned but buried. "Vartias" (Jains) and Yogis are likewise buried following the orders of "Madeo" (Mahadeoa or Siva), "one of their great Saints."[175]

Near the English cemetery there is a great oblong well built by the charity of a Banyan for the refreshment of travelers. In the direction of the "Daman" (Damão) gate there is a greater reservoir. The gate itself is "covered and encompassed" by a huge banyan tree under which visitors to the tank find repose. The reservoir has sixteen sides, each one hundred paces long. Its bottom is paved with large stones. Stone steps leading "from the brim to the bottom of the Bason" almost completely surround the tank, giving it the appearance of an amphitheater. Where no steps are laid, there are slopes which run into the water, three of which are reserved for animals. In the middle of the tank stands a stone pleasure house which can be reached only by boat. In the rainy season water from the surrounding fields is channeled into the basin. Built by a rich Banyan named "Gopy" (Gopi), this reservoir formerly supplied Surat with water; at present the city is supplied by five wells dug long after the reservoir. The great tank was begun "at about the same time" as the fortress (*i.e.*, around 1546) and reputedly both cost about the same amount to construct. Now this work, worthy of the Romans, is in danger of being silted up for lack of proper maintenance.[176] Just beyond the reservoir is the Garden of the Princess, "so-called because it belongs to the Great Mogul's sister."[177] It includes great plots of trees and shrubs, pleasant walks which form a cross, a small canal, and a square pleasure house.[178] Near

---

[174] Sen (ed.), *op. cit.* (n. 2), pp. 29–31. François de La Boullaye Le Gouz and "a M. Beber" were sent by Colbert to obtain permission from the Mughul emperor to trade at Surat. Le Gouz, the official emissary to Agra, had visited India *ca.* 1648 and had published in 1653 the travelogue of his experiences in the East as *Les voyages et observations*. He arrived at Agra in August, 1666, and obtained from Aurangzib the necessary permission. Beber remained in Surat to lay the groundwork for French commerce there. Two years later the French began to trade at Surat.

[175] Sen (ed.), *op. cit.* (n. 2), pp. 33–34. On the "Vertias" or "Vartias" see *Asia*, I, 459–60.

[176] On the *Gopi Talao cf.* Commissariat, *op. cit.* (n. 165), pp. 97–108, and above, pp. 617, 652, 661, 743. This tank has now all but completely disappeared.

[177] Probably one of the gardens owned by Jahanara Begam, the sister of Aurangzib.

[178] *Cf.* Commissariat, *op. cit.* (n. 165), p. 93.

the garden stands another great banyan tree which the Hindus worship and bedeck with banners (see pl. 127). Under the tree is a temple dedicated to "Mamera" (*Mahāmāyā*) or "a representation of Eve." [179] A Brahman sits at this temple who receives alms from the devout and in return paints a red mark on their foreheads. Here a man (a Jain) is also to be seen who feeds flour to the ants.

The fields around Surat are brown in color and so rich that they never are manured. After the rainy season the people sow their grain in September, and they harvest after February. Sugarcane is planted in deep furrows fertilized with small fish. Good profit is made from the cultivation of rice and palm trees. The Dutch water their fields with well water carried in skins by oxen. The river water is too brackish for watering or drinking; it is used only for bathing. While the Tapti is but a stream in the dry season, it overflows its banks in the rainy months to cause extensive flood damage. Its source is at "Gehar-Conde" (*Gahara Kunda?*, meaning "deep tank") in the Deccan mountains near "Brampour" (Burhanpur). [180]

Trading ships are forced to discharge their cargo at the Bar of Surat because banks of sand prevent their going upriver. They must await the spring tide to go to Surat for careening and repairs. Small barks easily go upriver with all incoming tides. The true port of Surat for oceangoing vessels is at "Soualy" (Suwali) where they ride safely at anchor behind the sand bar. [181] But since it is difficult to control the customs there, no foreign ships have been permitted to land there since 1660 except those of the Dutch and English. Here these two powers have warehouses and are provided with an opportunity to smuggle items of small size. These Europeans have their own harbors for small craft, as well as gardens and houses at Suwali. At the Bar there are always a great many vessels of other nations. At the customhouse in Surat the master is a Muslim appointed by the governor, the clerks are Banyans, and the guards, porters, and other lesser servitors are Muslims known as the "Pions" (peons) of the customhouse. [182]

By the time Thévenot left for Persia in February, 1667, his French countrymen had begun to establish a factory at Surat. François Caron, [183] the Dutch director of the French East India Company, arrived at Surat early in 1668 with a grandiose scheme in hand designed to establish new French trading outposts at Masulipatam and in Bengal, Siam, China, and Japan. Almost immediately he and his French colleagues began to quarrel over the proper trading program to follow. In France itself, perhaps because of the

[179] *Mahāmāyā* is the name of a mother-aspect of Parvati, chief wife of Siva. See G. Liebert, *Iconographic Dictionary of the Indian Religions* (Leyden, 1976), p. 159.
[180] The Tapti rises near Multai in Betul district of Madhya Pradesh. Its name derives from Sanskrit "*tap*" meaning "heat." See B. C. Law (ed.), *Mountains and Rivers of India* (Calcutta, 1968), p. 271.
[181] Suwali is about twelve miles from the city. See plate 12.
[182] Thévenot in Sen (ed.), *op. cit.* (n. 2), pp. 34–38.
[183] On Caron's role see above, pp. 97–99.

crown's deep involvement in this Asian enterprise, very little was published contemporaneously on the problems of the Company in India. The only work of significance was by François L'Estra (1650–97), a young under-merchant of the Company, who landed in Surat in 1671, joined De La Haye's southern expedition in 1671–72, and was captured by the Dutch late in 1672 on the Coromandel Coast. From here he was taken to Bengal, where he waited one month for transport to Batavia. Two years after his return to France, he published at Paris in 1677 his *Relation ou journal* of his experiences in the East.[184]

This book, the work of a young and enthusiastic traveler, is mainly important for what it reports about Surat, Sivaji, the progress and activities of De La Haye's fleet, and the city of Batavia as a commercial center. L'Estra arrived in Surat on October 26, 1671, and stayed there for exactly two months before departing with Caron in the fleet of De La Haye. His observations about the people of Surat are ill-informed and naive. He was there, however, just one year after Sivaji sacked the city for the second time in October, 1670. L'Estra was told that Sivaji headed twenty thousand Mahrattas, who extorted money from Surat's merchants, including the Dutch and English factors, and pillaged the town for eight days. Caron and the French frightened the Mahrattas off by aiming their cannons at the delegation sent to their factory at Suwali.[185] A year after the sack, Surat's walls are in good condition and mounted with artillery.[186] The governor and garrison never leave its fortress, so the factors go there to visit. Europeans of all nationalities feel strongly the hostility of the Muslims. In sum, L'Estra has little that is novel to report about India. His descriptions of the cities of the Coromandel Coast and the Ganges delta are somewhat better, but hardly of special interest.

It was not until 1688, after several successive defeats of the French at San Thomé and in Siam, that the troubles of the Company in Asia were revealed in print to the general public. In that year was published the *Histoire des Indes orientales* (Paris) by Urbain Souchu de Rennefort, a servant of the Company during its early and ill-fated venture in Madagascar.[187] While this book is primarily an attack upon the Company for its abandonment of Madagascar, it contains a journal by an unspecified author (certainly not the author of the book itself) on French activities in India during 1669–70.[188] Rennefort apparently had access to the files of the Company, for he publishes the French

---

[184] For bibliographical data and full title, see above, p. 418.

[185] L'Estra, *Relation ou journal*, pp. 53–57. This is contrary to the reports of the English, who claim that the French bought Sivaji off and that the English and Dutch defended themselves. See Gokhale, *op. cit.* (n. 15), p. 25.

[186] L'Estra, *op. cit.* (n. 185), p. 38. Again this runs counter to the assertions of other contemporary and later observers.

[187] See above, p. 422.

[188] Pt. II, Bk. 2. Rennefort added materials to the original journal appropriated from Thévenot and possibly other French writers.

version of Aurangzib's *farman* of September 4, 1666, granting the French permission to set up a factory at Surat, as well as Caron's letter to the "king of Ceylon" of December 29, 1667. He also provides, without citing his sources, a wealth of detail on the relations of the French merchants with Caron, Father Ambrose (their interpreter), and the governor of Surat. He reports on the departure in May, 1669, for Golconda of the two merchants "Macara" and "Roussel," who hoped to obtain permission to establish a French factory at Masulipatam.[189] Despite its title there is actually very little material in this book on India or its people.

At the end of the rainy season of 1674, Dr. Fryer is ordered to take a ship from Bombay to Surat. Arrived at Suwali, he is lodged in the English compound, a collection of tiled wooden houses, warehouses, and stables, with as much of a garden "as this sandy soil will allow." Here he is plagued by fleas and leech-like Banyan brokers who are licensed by the governor of Surat to act as intermediaries in the trade. The nearby villages of "Damkin" (Damka) and "Mora" (Mora) are "two Nursies for Stews [prostitutes]." The ten miles to Surat is traversed in the Company's "Indian Hackery" (Hindi, *chhakrā*), a "two-wheeled Chariot [cart] drawn by swift little Oxen." Transported across the Tapti River in the Company's barge, Fryer is greeted by a roll of drums and a blare of trumpets emanating from the fortress. His carriage is not examined at the customhouse because it is accompanied by an enclosed coach carrying women. The president of the Company, like the women, is not subject to their ordinarily strict inspections.

The "English House" at Surat is "partly the King's [Emperor's] Gift, partly hired."[190] It is strongly built of stone and timber with heavy and thick cemented floors. Following the "Moorish" (Mughul) style it has "upper and lower Galleries" and neat and convenient places for outdoor dining. The president has "spacious Lodgings" with special rooms for meetings and entertainments. During the shipping season, the whole place is "in a continual hurly-burly" with Banyans, packers, and warehouse men coming and going all day. Besides the president, the English have four principal officers: the accountant of the Company's entire India trade and its treasurer, the keeper of the warehouse, the marine purser, and the secretary. These officials all report directly to the president, for without his approval they cannot "act or do anything." In order of rank, the lesser servants of the Company include merchants, factors, writers, and apprentices.[191] Senior merchants usually become chiefs of the factories subordinate to Surat where they live in "like Grandeur"; then they return to Surat as resident members of the president's council, which usually consists of five men in addition to the president.

---

[189] Aurangzib's *farman* is on pp. 286–88 of the *Histoire,* Caron's letter on pp. 313–14. For the efforts to establish a French factory at Masulipatam see below, p. 1076, n.291

[190] *Cf.* below, pp. 754–55.

[191] Fryer calls the apprentices "Blewcoat Boys." These are charity children who wear the almoner's blue coat.

From this council is selected the deputy governor of Bombay and the agent of Persia. The twenty resident Englishmen who work in the factory are served by a minister, a physician, and a small contingent of English soldiers. Banyans usually act as interpreters, since the Company's servants, despite official encouragement to do so, rarely learn enough of the local languages to carry on business.

The presidency of Surat is in charge of all the English factories in India and Persia.[192] Subordinate inland factories are at Ahmadabad, where silks are purchased, and at Agra, which provides indigo, lac, and textiles. The coastal factories of Bombay and Rajapur buy "Salloos" (Hindi, *sālū*, Turkish red cotton cloths), Karwar purchases "Dungarees" (Dutch, *dongerijs*, a strong, coarse calico), and Calicut collects spices, ambergris, garnets, opium, and saltpeter. No cloth is purchased at Calicut even though its name is used in Europe for all Indian textiles; this misnomer evolved because Calicut was the port at which European merchants first purchased Indian textiles or calicoes. After the ships from Europe are unloaded, the merchandise from the coastal ports is brought to Surat by ship and that from the inland factories by caravan. In the places near Surat the factors oversee the weavers to make certain that a supply of textiles is on hand when the ships arrive from Europe. "On these Wheels moves the Traffick of the East," Fryer concludes.

The Restoration Company has been far more successful than any of the earlier chartered companies in bringing benefits to England. As for the trade of Surat itself, "for some years lately passed [it] has hardly balanced Expenses," even though the English have a far larger share than the Dutch or French. The Dutch sell spices at Surat, purchase small quantities of cheap, coarse cloth, and leave with money in their pockets. The French factory has more merchants than cash; they "live well, borrow money, and make a Shew." The Company indulges its servants by letting them carry on a private trade in diamonds and other precious stones so that they grow rich without harming the Company. French and Dutch jewelers, like Tavernier and his associates, purchase jewels here which they take to Europe for cutting and setting; then they return to India to sell them to the nobles at a profit.[193]

The walls and moat of Surat ordered by Aurangzib in 1664 after Sivaji's first sack are still being built ten years later. The completed portions are high and of well-baked brick. The fortress, while old, is moated by the river, protected by thirty or forty pieces of heavy artillery, and manned by three hundred soldiers. Its independent governor (the *killedar*) is confined to the fortress and dares not enter the town on pain of losing his head. The ruins left by Sivaji in 1670 are still not repaired, and the city lives in fear of a

---

[192] The Presidency of Bantam, founded in 1603, had become independent of Surat by this time. It governed the English factories in the East Indies, the Bay of Bengal, and the Coromandel Coast of India.

[193] Fryer in Crooke (ed.), *op. cit.* (n. 4), I, 210–27. *Cf.* Commissariat, *op. cit.* (n. 149), II, 371–74, on the Surat factory.

renewed attack. To hurry the reconstruction of the wall and to prepare the city's defenses the authorities are collecting a hundred thousand rupees. Seven hundred men are assigned to protect the wall, with Europeans delegated to defend its six gates. On each of its thirty-six bastions six great guns are mounted. Spiked timbers are piled on top of the wall to repel scalers. Every gate is barbed with iron spikes to break an elephant charge. The city's governor has at his command an infantry unit of fifteen men armed with matchlocks, swords, and javelins, as well as two hundred cavalrymen armed with bows and arrows, lances, and swords. The governor keeps forty camels and six elephants armed for war. In his booth-like stables of haircloth, each horse is attended by a personal groom who feeds and courts it "with all the gentleness and kind Speeches imaginable." When troubles develop in 1674 between the governor and the Dutch, the Mughul official issues a "Deroy" (Mahratti, *durāhi,* a decree) forbidding all Europeans to leave the city without his special permission.[194]

At the "Broach gate" of Surat, as at all of its other gates, stands a "Chocky" (Hindi, *chauki,* toll station) at which tolls are collected for the emperor; the Rajputs likewise collect tolls at Surat's gates which are really payments to keep them from preying upon the surrounding villages and roads. The Broach road is lined with Muslim tombs near which is the grave of Tom Coryate (d. 1617), whom the natives call the "English Fakier." Adjoining the Dutch cemetery is a garden in which the Armenians bury their dead and erect "Monuments Coffin-Fashion with a place to burn Incense at the Head." Most impressive is the mausoleum of Sir George Oxenden in the English cemetery. About one mile out of the city on a hill are sepulchers of "Mutanny Pilgrims," probably a reference to local Yogis. Further out is the town of "Pulparra" (Phulpara) which is set apart as a Hindu holy place on the river where they have a seminary for Brahmans. Its two remaining temples have been defaced by the Muslims. As a Hindu place of cremation, Phulpara also has *satī* shrines along the sacred river as well as many emaciated Yogis who look like "walking Skelitons." The road from Phulpara to Surat is lined with shade trees and crowded with all sorts of people. All that remains of Hindu grandeur near Surat is a great empty tank one "mile in Circumference" with rich mausoleums on its brink. Originally it had been filled by aqueducts but is now dry, so that it looks like a huge amphitheater with descending steps.[195]

Pleasant gardens surround Surat in which the people of the town take the air and feast in summerhouses. From step-wells, water is raised in leather bags by oxen and spilled into ditches to water these gardens. Here grow "the Silk Cotton-tree" (*Bombax malabarica,* or the simal tree), the hemp-like plant from whose seeds *bhang* is made, and the beloved "Alluh" (?) tree,

---

[194] Crooke (ed.), *op. cit.* (n. 4), I, 248–52. *Cf.* Commissariat, *op. cit.* (n. 149), II, 376–77.

[195] The *Gopi Talao* was apparently already dry and neglected in 1674. It was completely ruined by 1717.

whose bark is used as medicine. Instead of flowers the people here grow vegetables in their gardens: potatoes, "yawms" (yams), "Berenjaws" (brinjal, or eggplant), pumpkins, cucumbers, and gourds. While roses would grow here, they choose only to cultivate "some wall-flowers" (possibly *Dianthus caryophyllus*), "Culga" (Hindi, *kalgha*, cockscomb), the "Tree Mallow" (*Hibiscus mutabilis*), and several kinds of jasmines. In the fields outside the city grow the "humble Sensitive Plant" (*Mimosa pudica*), tobacco, and sugarcane. The "tree of roots" is called the banyan tree because the Banyans hold it sacred, worship it daily, and make offerings of rice to it. Beside hedges and lanes grow two kinds of bushes used as fences: "Milk trees" (*Euphorbia tiruncalli*) and a kind of privet.

The Tapti River "glides by the Town in swift Tides" and in the spring is deep enough to permit unloaded ships of one thousand tons to come up to Surat's walls. As many as one hundred "good ships" and smaller vessels then lie thickly on the river down to its mouth. The Dutch and English think it unwise to instruct the natives in the art of navigation at sea. Even though the Indians have merchant vessels armed with thirty or forty cannons, these are mostly for show. The emperor also maintains four war vessels and four great ships which carry the pilgrims to Mecca free of charge. The pilgrim ships are "huge unshapen things, and bear both the Name and Model of their old Junks." But for all their preparations, the Indians dare not venture out to sea without European pilots and passes. Their name for a soldier is "Luscar" (*láscar*), for a sailor "lascar" (*lascár*), for a ship's captain "Nucquedah" (Persian, *nā-khudā*), and for a boatswain "Tindal" (Malayalam, *taṇḍal*).[196]

Trading ships arrive at Surat from the Persian Gulf in February and from the Red Sea in August. Like the European ships they buy indigo and textiles; in the main they bring precious metals and pearls as well as lesser-valued dates, drugs, and horses. Most of the world's gold supply ends up in India because of the need for its textiles. Even the proceeds from the spice trade are used to pay for Indian textiles. Surat also profits from the jewel trade. Its artisans cut stones with many fewer tools than the gem-cutters of Europe. All stones except diamonds are cut on a wheel made of lac and a stone obtained only at Cochin.[197] Diamonds are cut "with a Mill turned by Men," but they are mostly sent to Europe for cutting and setting.

Although wealthy from trade, Surat is a "very nasti" city. Since it has no "Privies," every door is a "dunghill." Waste is left to evaporate or to be washed away by the rains. Still, Surat has never suffered from the plague.[198] Common ailments are coughs, catarrhs, tumors of the mouth and throat,

[196] Fryer in Crooke (ed.), *op. cit.* (n. 4), I, 252–69. On the confusing history of the Persian word *lashkari* (soldier) see Yule and Burnell, *op. cit.* (n. 124), pp. 507–9.

[197] More recently, powdered corundum was mixed into the melted lac. Crooke (ed.), *ibid.* (n. 4), p. 284, n. 2.

[198] Plague later broke out, *ca.* 1685, and raged for six years in Surat. See below, p. 755.

rheumatism, and intermittent fevers. Young people contract smallpox "as in all India." Certain diseases prevail seasonally. In the dry and hot months, cholera breaks out sporadically and inflammation of the eyes is common. In the rainy season, cases of dysentery, hemorrhages, and "Distempers of the Brain, as well as Stomach" multiply. The natives use "Hing [Hindi, *hing*], a sort of liquid Assa Foetida," as a medicine; it has a repulsive odor that makes them "smell odiously." [199] For disorders characterized by sleepiness or drowsiness, garlic and ginger are given orally in butter or oil. They use as vesicant a liquid derived from "a certain Nut," which is also employed in making inks and dyes. [200] Cauteries are applied "unmercifully" in cases of cholera and violent fevers.

The English are well treated at Surat because they have received successive *farmans* from the emperor and possess sufficient naval power to protect their freedom. They are regarded much more highly than those who are "harness'd with the Apron-strings of Trade" and who have no special legal status. Private merchants who carry on a trade equal to the European companies enjoy a lower status because they are only "Vackeels" (Arabic, *wakil*, an authorized representative) or factors for rich merchants in the interior. The Europeans fortify their houses, have their own docks and yards, and cultivate their own gardens in the European way. [201] The Portuguese "might have Subdued" India's coastal region had not the English and Dutch come upon the scene. Although from a "Commonwealth" in Europe, the Dutch governor of Batavia behaves like a monarch in the East. The Dutch of necessity maintain a "Tyrannical Government in India" to terrorize the Indians who cannot "be won by any other way then Force." The English, content with their Bombay colony and peaceful trade, "command not that Awe by which these people are best taught to understand themselves." [202]

John Ovington officiated as chaplain of the English factory from September, 1690, to February, 1693. On arriving at Suwali he learns that only European vessels are permitted to anchor in its harbor. Indian ships are required to enter the Tapti River or to berth at its mouth. Close by Suwali harbor stand three wooden rest-houses reserved for the use of the English, French, and Dutch factors when they come down from Surat. [203] The greatest strength of Surat is its fortress, which commands both the river and land approaches. The city's wall, "flankt at certain Distances with Towers and Battlements," now has six or seven gates at which sentinels are posted constantly. In the evening the streets of the city, especially those near the bazaar, are more crowded than those of "any part of London." The governor of the fortress

---

[199] This is indeed asafoetida, a gum resin commonly used in India still as medicine and condiment. See Yule and Burnell, *op. cit.* (n. 124), pp. 418–19.

[200] An astringent derived possibly from the marking-nut tree (*Semecarpus anacardium*).

[201] Fryer in Crooke (ed.), *op. cit.* (n. 4), I, 288–89.

[202] *Ibid.*, II, 114–15.

[203] Rawlinson (ed.), *op. cit.* (n. 3), p. 100.

usually holds office for no more than three years, a long time when it is realized that he may never leave its confines and must be "continually upon his Guard."[204] All imports and exports of precious metals and foreign currencies pay at Surat 2½ percent duty and "other Goods pay more." In all the marts of Asia the Armenians "are as universal Merchants . . . [and] their Language is one of the most general in all Asia." The Dutch alone supply Surat with fine spices and share only the pepper trade with the English.[205]

The civil governor of Surat receives and decides upon petitions and appeals in his residence. About matters of moment he consults and makes decisions jointly with the city's other officials: the kazi, the *vākiahnavis* (or *waqiah-navis*, news-writers), and the kotwal. The kazi is a judge who is well informed on the "Civil Customs" of the empire and on municipal law. The news-writer prepares a weekly report about Surat for the emperor. Another officer, called the *harkāra,* reports to the court on all local news and happenings, "whether true or false . . . of moment or of no account." The *kotwal,* "somewhat resembling a Justice of the Peace," tours the city from nine in the evening until five in the morning to maintain order and to seek out offenders. Although the city hosts many foreigners in addition to its own populace, very few untoward events or minor crimes occur. Indeed over the last twenty years nobody has been punished for a capital crime in Surat. Peace and order are maintained in the country and on highways by a *faujdar* and his aides.[206] Two miles from Surat on the Tapti is the beautiful town called "Pulparrock" (Phulpara), where many "Santones" (Gujarati, *santa,* ascetics) pleasantly while away the time.[207]

According to Ovington, the English factory at Surat is maintained at an annual cost of one hundred thousand pounds. Its factors, who keep the other Europeans from cornering the city's trade, must live in style to be content themselves and to impress the natives and the other merchants with England's wealth and strength. The factory itself is provided by the emperor and "is fitted with the best Accommodations of any in the City." Its president, officers, and factors are paid good annual salaries by the Company, which they supplement by engaging in private trade, a legal privilege which the Dutch factors envy. The factory and the trade are ruled by a council of four which includes in order of rank the president, the accountant, the storekeeper, and the purser mariner; the president has a double vote in making decisions. Factors, secretaries, and apprentices have three- to five-year terms, "or as many as they and the Company have agreed upon at their first coming out." All enjoy free lodging and board and are served by native employees in their business and private affairs. The many native servants,

[204] This assertion about the length of the governor's tenure is correct. See Gokhale, *op. cit.* (n. 15), pp. 70–71.

[205] Rawlinson (ed.), *op. cit.* (n. 3), pp. 129–34.

[206] *Ibid.,* pp. 136–39.

[207] *Ibid.,* p. 210. *Cf.* above, p. 740.

who are noted for their honesty, live outside the factory. All members of the factory are required to obtain the president's permission to leave the factory or to take a trip. Daily at noon a sumptuous meal is served on silver plates. At supper the council meets alone to discuss business and the affairs of the Company. Within the factory English customs and manners are followed, though Portuguese and Indian dishes are served. On holidays the president and "his Lady" invite all factory members to an outing. The Company provides an Indian physician, an English surgeon, and a Christian chaplain to attend to the physical and spiritual needs of its servants. Attendance is required by Company orders at the daily prayers and Sunday services held in the factory's chapel. The chaplain supplements his annual salary with the generous gratuities he receives for officiating at marriages, baptisms, and burials, as well as the income he earns by his private trading activities. While life at the factory is generally placid, the English are confined to its precincts by Surat's governor for brief periods in 1691 and 1692 when falsely charged with conspiring to pirate Turkish vessels. When the Danes prove to be the culprits, the emperor quickly orders the release of the English.[208]

"Six years" ago (*ca.* 1685) the plague broke out among the Indians of Surat and it continues to recur intermittently. Outbreaks are most common just before and immediately after the wet season. At these times as many as three hundred Hindus and Muslims die daily; on one morning alone more than one hundred were carried out of the city to be burned. Just before the onset of the plague, the city suffered a small earthquake which caused alarm but produced no damage or death. The English, who suffered from neither of these natural calamities, are regarded with awe by the natives who believe "that God is among us." At "Balsera" (Bulsar) a short violent attack of the plague killed "Two Hundred Thousand People in Eighteen Days time." Fevers of various kinds are common and Europeans often suffer from them after a "strong Debauch." Cholera, caused most frequently "by an Excess in Eating, particularly of Fish and Flesh together," claims a few victims. Europeans sometimes suffer from "Barbeers" (beriberi), a disease which paralyzes their limbs.[209] Fevers are cured by Indian physicians by administering a "White Powder" or prescribing "Congy" (Hindi, *kanji,* rice gruel). "White powders" against fevers sent to England have been successfully used there as well.[210]

On a brief visit to Surat in February, 1695, Careri, the Neapolitan world traveler, stays in the house of the French director. Located at the entrance to the Bay of Cambay, Surat is "not large" and is enclosed by "a weak wall" built after it was plundered by Sivaji. Its fortress is "no better," though it does command the sea and land approaches to the city. The governor of the fortress commands only its garrison, the city itself being ruled by a nabob

---

[208] *Ibid.,* pp. 225–44; and see the engraving of the English factory as of 1638 facing p. 226.
[209] Probably caused by a deficiency of vitamin B1.
[210] Ovington in Rawlinson (ed.), *op. cit.* (n. 3), pp. 203–5. Probably mercury powders.

"who receives the King's Taxes throughout the whole Province."[211] The city boasts only one dozen "good houses," those belonging to the French, English, Dutch, and Muslim merchants. The Capuchins have a church with a house nearby that is built "after the manner of Europe." The merchants of "the prime Mart of India" are so well furnished with rich goods that they can "load any great Ship out of one of their Ware-Houses." Under the banyan tree of Surat are four Hindu temples, one being a lodging for holy men. In a hospital for birds and beasts a naked man is bound hand and foot so that the bugs may feed on his body. Before the shop of a "Pagan Marchant," a rogue threatens to kill a hen, in order to extort money from the pious Banyans.[212]

4

BOMBAY AND THE PORTUGUESE PORTS

In a lengthy letter of about 1674, Fryer discusses Bombay and its surroundings and provides a sketchy map of its seven islands.[213] These islands "arising as so many Mountains out of the Sea," lie off the "Canarick Coast" (Kanara Coast) midway between Surat and Goa. The island of Bombay itself is the farthest out to sea and faces the Portuguese outposts of Chaul and Bassein on the "Conchon" (Konkan) or low-country coast. A natural bay exists between Bombay island and the mainland, from which is derived the name "Bombaim, quasi Boom Bay."[214] On the north side of the bay are the islands of "Canorein" (Kanheri), "Trumbay" (Trombay), and "Munchumbay" (?). Between these islands and the mainland lie the small islands of "Elephanto" (Elephanta), "Kerinjau" (Karanja or Uran Island), and "Putachoes" (Portuguese, *Ilha de Patecas,* or "watermelon island"). The harbor between these islands and the mainland is "the most notable and secure Port on the Coasts of India." The general name for this cluster of islands is "Salset" (Salsette), a word whose etymology is unclear.[215]

[211] The imperial governors of the *sarkār* of Surat collected the taxes of the *mahāls* (revenue subdistricts) into which the *sarkār* was subdivided. See Gokhale, *op. cit.* (n. 15), p. 51.

[212] Careri in Sen (ed.), *op. cit.* (n. 2), pp. 163–66.

[213] *Cf.* the map as of 1660 in M. D. David, *History of Bombay, 1661–1708* (Bombay, 1973), facing p. 9. Fryer's map (in Crooke [ed.], *op. cit.* [n. 4], I, facing p. 131) is incorrect in details.

[214] Fryer's misapplication of certain general terms, such as Kanara, reflects the uncertainty of Europeans about the extent of the common geographical divisions of the mainland. The old travelers commonly derive the name Bombay from Portuguese "Bom" meaning "good" and "Bahia" meaning "bay." It actually derives from the name of the goddess Mumba Devi, a deity of the Koli fisherfolk. See David, *op. cit.* (n. 213), p. 6.

[215] Salsette, actually a separate island, derives from Mahratti, *shashti,* "sixty-six," for it was supposed to have that number of villages. Fryer's description of the islands, like his map, is incorrect in numerous details. The seven islands are Bombay, Salsette, Trombay, Elephanta, Khanderi, Underi, and Henery. In the seventeenth century they were all separate islands; they are not so now. Kanheri (Kenery or Kennery) is on Salsette Island.

William Baffin and Thomas Roe collaborated to prepare the first modern
map of northern India, which they
called "A Description of East India Con-
teyning the Empire of the Great Mo-
goll." Baffin, the draftsman, was master's
mate on the ship "Anne," on which Roe
returned to England. While in India,
Roe had collected materials on the provinces, chief towns, and major rivers and
routes of the Mughul Empire. In London, Baffin based his map on these and a
few other available materials and issued
a sheet map engraved by Renold
Elstrack which first appeared in print in
1619.[1]

The sheet map was reengraved by
Elstrack and this new rendition was
published six years later in *Purchas His
Pilgrimes* (1625).[2] Elstrack corrected several errors on the original plate but
added nothing substantive. He dropped
the cartouche in the lower left-hand corner, but in the essentials his new map is
an accurate copy of the original. For example, both show prominently "The
Longe Walke" or the lines of trees between the palaces of Agra and Lahore, a
feature that was long to remain on European maps of the Mughul Empire.

The Baffin-Roe map remained the
standard on which most subsequent depictions of the Mughul Empire were
based throughout the seventeenth century. Names were changed over time
and features were dropped or added, but
the debt of subsequent drafters and engravers to the Baffin-Roe map, and
particularly to the version printed in
Purchas, remained clear and obvious
well into the eighteenth century. Cf.
also Dapper's map, our pl. 3.

[1] See S. Gole, *Early Maps of India* (New Delhi,
1976), pp. 48–49. Gole includes a reproduction of
the sheet map, now in the British Library, as her
pl. 7.

[2] *PP*, IV, between pp. 432 and 433.

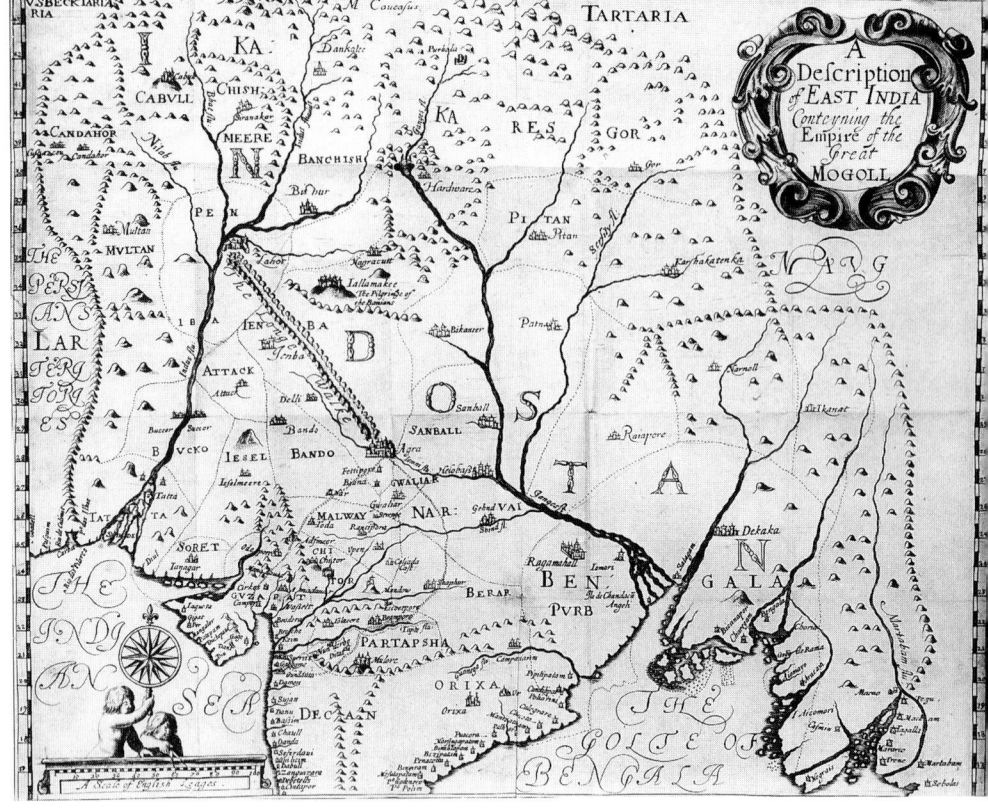

107. THE MUGHUL EMPIRE

From Edward Terry, *A Voyage to East-India* (London, 1655), frontispiece.

A reduced version of Baffin's 1619 map. A number of the provincial names are dropped, such as "Delli" and others to the east. The original cartouches have been omitted and their spaces filled with the caption cartouche and a scale of distances in English leagues.

The engraver was possibly Robert Vaughn, the engraver of Terry's portrait in this same 1655 volume (our pl. 102).

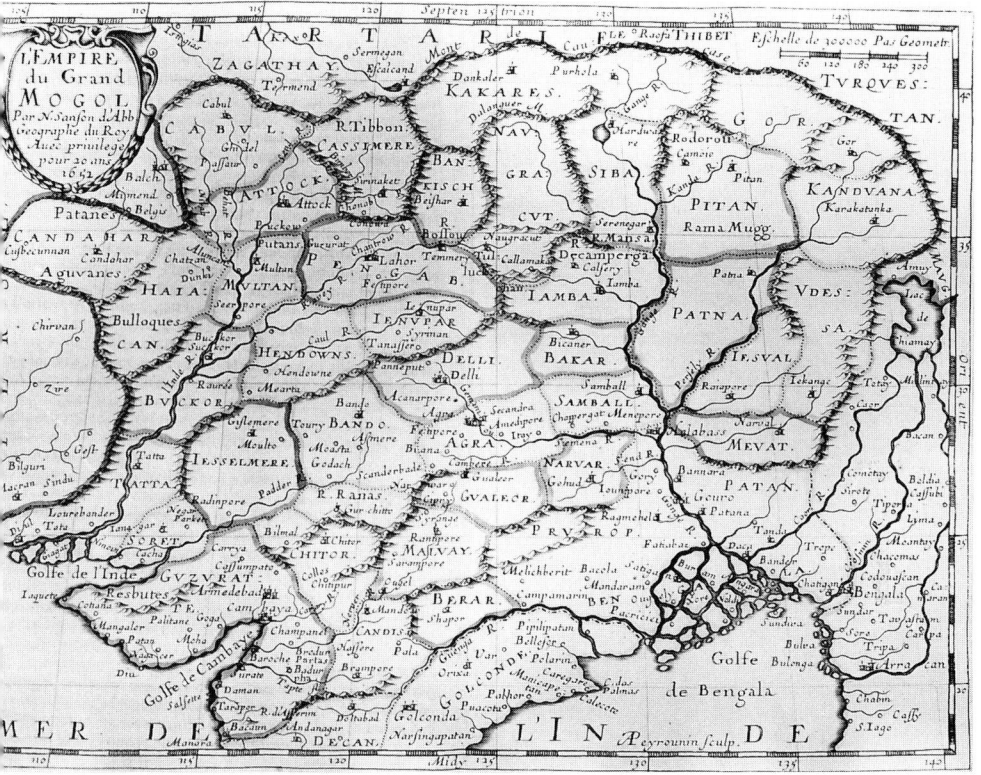

108. THE MUGHUL EMPIRE

From Nicolas Sanson d'Abbeville, *L'Asie en plusieurs cartes nouvelles . . .* (Paris, 1652), following p. 40. Pl. 134 is also from this book.

Engraved by A. Peyrounin.

According to Sanson, Gujarat and Bengal are the best known of the Mughuls' thirty-eight to forty provinces. He gives no sources, but the accompanying text is very well informed for the period when it was prepared.

Sanson, the French royal geographer, certainly followed the Baffin map in many particulars.[1] But it is also more original than most of the other maps of the century. An effort is made to delineate the provincial and imperial boundaries. "Thibet" appears north of the empire and "Golconde," not shown by Baffin, appears prominently on this map. The tree-lined road from Agra to Lahore, so prominent in Baffin, does not appear here at all. The mythical lake from which the rivers of Southeast Asia supposedly rise is shown here but not on Baffin's map.

[1] Susan Gole, in *Early Maps of India* (New Delhi, 1976), p. 50, claims quite incorrectly that this is based on Baffin's map of 1619. She makes no such claim in her book of facsimile maps, *A Series of Early Printed Maps of India in Facsimile* (New Delhi, 1980).

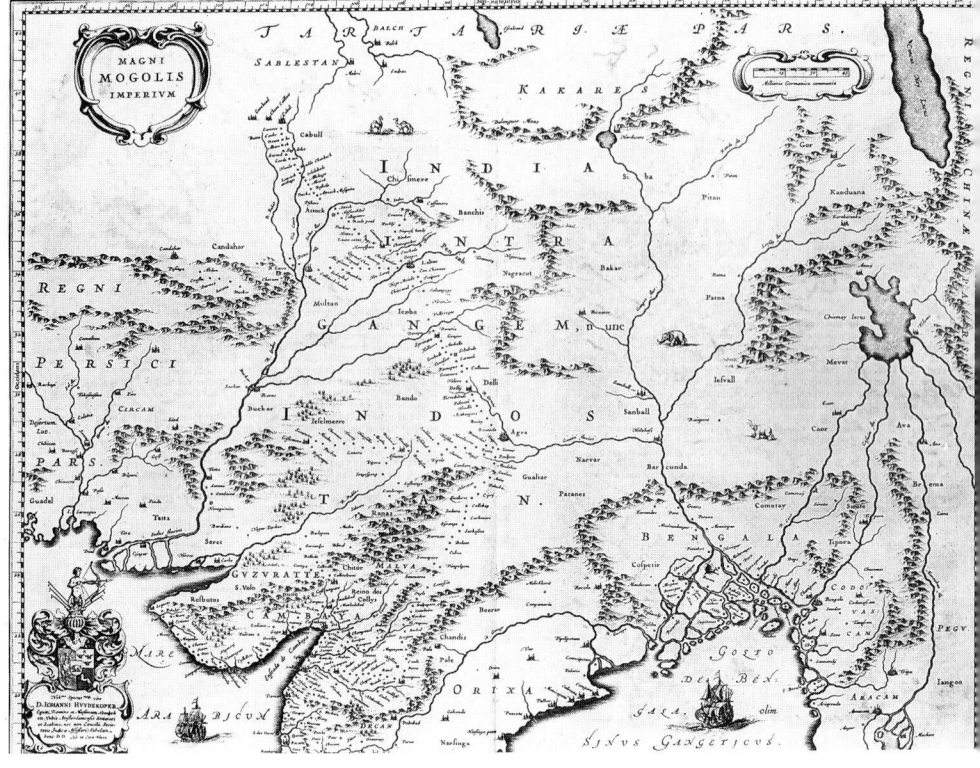

109. THE MUGHUL EMPIRE

From Johan Blaeu, *Asia major* (Amsterdam, 1662), Vol. X, Bk. 1,
between pp. 65 and 66.

This is probably based on the Hondius map of 1629 which itself
owes a debt to Baffin's map and its predecessors of the sixteenth century. It is better on Gujarat, the Deccan, and the major rivers of the
subcontinent than Baffin. Notice the mysterious "Chiamay Lake" in
which the rivers of Southeast Asia were thought to originate ever
since Ortelius put it on the map in 1580. In short, this map seeks to
bring together the maps of the great cartographers of the past and the
more pragmatic picture by Baffin.

Notice also the numerous islands with names at the head of the Bay
of Bengal. This is the "Bengala" of the Portuguese.

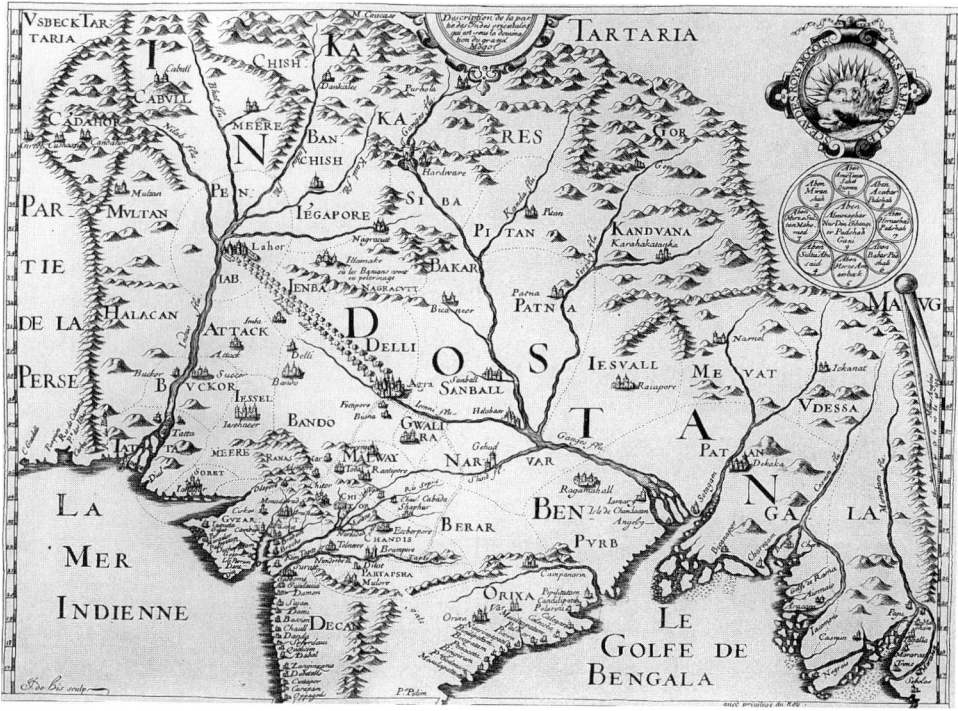

110. THE MUGHUL EMPIRE

From Melchisédech Thévenot (comp.), *Relations de divers voyages
curieux . . .* (TR) (Paris, 1663), I, with Hawkins' voyage, between
pp. 12 and 13. See also pls. 114, 118, 140, 141.

Engraved by J. de Bis.

Based strictly on Baffin's map (1619); but omits the caption from
the lower left-hand corner. Also some English names are translated
into French: "The Golfe of Bengala" becomes "Le Golfe de Bengala."
Cf. the Mughul arms and seal to those in our pls. 117, 118, 120,
and 121.

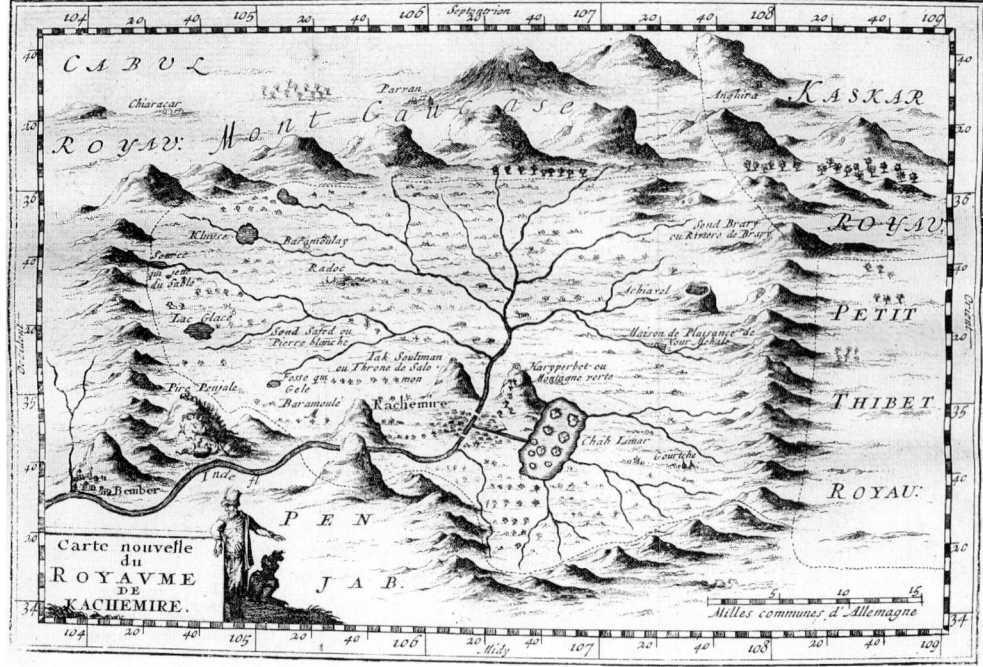

III. MAP OF KASHMIR

From *Voyages de François Bernier* (Amsterdam, 1723), II, between pp. 268 and 269.

Drawn by an anonymous Dutchman to illustrate Bernier's travels, this map uses the name Caucasus for the Pir Panjal range, a designation given to the Himalayas by the soldiers of Alexander the Great. See J. P. Ferguson, *Kashmir: An Historical Introduction* (London, 1961), p. 159.

II2. (FACING PAGE) AKBAR'S PORTRAIT

From Athanasius Kircher, *La Chine illustrée*, trans. by F. S. Dalquié (Amsterdam, 1670), facing p. 212. See also pls. 129, 133, 153–57. The same illustrations appear in both the Latin original (1667) and this French translation.

Based on a Mughul miniature.

"Akbar was famous all over the East, not less for his prowess in warfare than for his discernment. . . . He was a prince of keen insight, although untaught, and not refined in letters. He spoke eloquently with the help only of reason on the various types of religions. . . . Few monarchs had dress of similar beauty, for he exhibited himself to view adorned with a diadem made of gold, pearls, and precious stones of great price, and shining like that of a divinity. His throne was likewise adorned, in his hand he held a sphere, through which he showed himself to be the lord of the world and the greatest power. According to the custom of his ancestors, he sat with bare feet, and they were washed from time to time by his servants with an expensive liquid. Near him was a precious vase containing a liquid for him to drink in warm weather, or whenever he wanted. The fathers sent to Rome a picture or likeness of him in the dress which he used for public audiences" (C. Van Tuyl [trans.], *China illustrata by Kircher, Translated . . . from the 1677 [sic] Original Latin Edition* [Muskogee, Okla., 1987], p. 71). The little dog in the right-hand corner is probably a European symbol for the "Excellent Prince." *Cf.* pl. 311.

113. INDIAN PAINTINGS OF JAHANGIR (SELIM SHAH) AND HIS SON KHURRAM (SULTAN COROOAN) WITH A FEMALE SLAVE

From S. Purchas, *Hakluytus Posthumus* (Glasgow, 1905) (*PP*), IX, facing p. 32. Pl. 117 is also from this book.

This anonymous woodcut copies and combines two Mughul miniature paintings, one of which was by Manohar Das, a famous Mughul painter. See A. K. Das, *Mughul Painting during Jahangir's Time* (Calcutta, 1978), pp. 188–92. The one of Jahangir and the female slave was by Manohar and the other, of Khurram, by an anonymous artist. See A. M. Hind, *Engraving in England in the Sixteenth and Seventeenth Centuries* (Cambridge, 1955), II, 388. The portrait of Jahangir was given to Sir Thomas Roe by the Mughul emperor himself. See Partha Mitter, *Much Maligned Monsters* (Oxford, 1977), p. 72. Jahangir's Persian autograph reads: "The year 1026 [1617], in the town of Mandu. Painted by Manohar [Das]. I was in my fiftieth year" (translation in W. Foster [ed.], *The Embassy of Sir Thomas Roe* [Oxford, 1926], pp. lxxviii–lxxix). Purchas probably was lent the miniatures by Charles, then Prince of Wales, from whom he obtained Edward Terry's manuscript. It is thought that both were given to Charles by Roe on his return from India.

114. MUGHUL MINIATURES IN FRENCH TRANSLATION

From TR, I, "Voyage de Terri," p. 17.

This illustrates how the engravers copied from one another.

SCHACH SELIM

115. PRINCE SALIM, OR JAHANGIR (R. 1605–27)
From Olfert Dapper, *Asia* (Nuremberg, 1681), between pp. 154 and 155. Pls. 116, 125, 130, and 131 are
also from this book.

   This European impression of the emperor typifies
what many Dutch printers prepared as illustrations for
the lavish and expensive encyclopedic books that were
designed to become conversation pieces for the wealthy
and educated of northern Europe.

NURMAHAL

116. NUR MAHAL (D. 1645)

From Dapper, *op. cit.* (pl. 115), between pp. 154 and 155.

Nur Mahal (meaning "Light of the Palace") married Jahangir in 1611. When she was empress, she and her family were immensely powerful at the Mughul court and throughout the empire. Coins were even issued bearing her name.

117. THE SEAL OF JAHANGIR

From *PP,* IV, 468.

    The seal of Jahangir, whose name is in the middle circle. According to Professor C. M. Naim (personal communication), this essentially correct reproduction seems to be some form of the Persian script called *Ta'liq* and to have been prepared in India.

118. THE SEAL OF JAHANGIR, ANOTHER VERSION

From TR, I, following p. 205.

    The French engraver of this plate probably followed Terry's version (pl. 121) rather than the one reproduced in Purchas (above). In Terry's mutilated version the order of the emperors is reversed; Akbar becomes Jahangir's son and so on incorrectly.

pag: 447.

2.ᵈ part lib 1.ˢᵗ page

Ro: Vaughan sculp:

The lively Portraict of the great MOGOL

119, 120, 121. PORTRAIT OF JAHANGIR, HIS STANDARD, AND HIS SEAL

From the edition (1665) of E. Terry, *A Voyage to East India,* that is published in the same volume as the English version of Della Valle's *Travels.* These engravings were probably taken by the publishers from the 1655 edition of Terry, even though each of Terry's versions is by a different publisher.

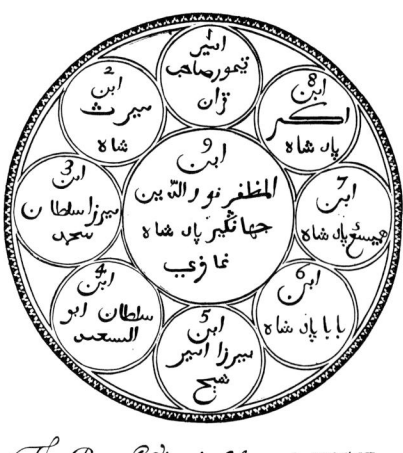

The Royal Signet of ye great MOGOL.

Engraved by R[obert] Vaughan.

The "Lively Portrait" shown here is similar to, but different from, the depiction of Prince Selim (see pl. 113) published in the Purchas collection.

Terry writes: "And now that my Reader may see the great Mogol in a Portrature (which was taken from a Picture of his drawn to the life) I have caused that to be inserted which presents him in his dayly unvaried Habite, as he is bedeckt, and adorned with jewels, he continually wears; . . .

"After this I have set up the royal standard of the great Mogol, which is a Couchant Lyon shadowing part of the body of the Sun.

"And after that I have caused his Imperial Signet, or great Seal to be laid down before my Readers eyes, wherein nine rounds, or Circles, are the Names and Titles of Tamberlane, and his lineal successors in Persian words. . . .

"This Seal (as it is here made in Persian words) the great Mogol, either in a large, or lesser figure causeth to be put unto all Firmaunis [farmans], or Letters Patents. . . . And the words on the Mogols Seal being imbos't, are put upon both sides of his Silver and Gold coin (for there is no image upon any of it" (p. 447).

This seal was prepared by someone whose knowledge of the Persian language and script was more than a little shaky. It was probably written in Europe and is at best a bad imitation of Jahangir's seal in Purchas (pl. 117).

122. AURANGZIB IN CAMP

From Giovanni Francesco Gemelli Careri, *Voyage du tour du monde* (French trans. by M. L. N.; Paris, 1727), II, facing p. 186. Pl. 171 is also from this book.

123. THE MUGHUL COURT AT AGRA

From François Bernier, *Voyages* (new ed., Amsterdam, 1724), I, between pp. 40 and 41.

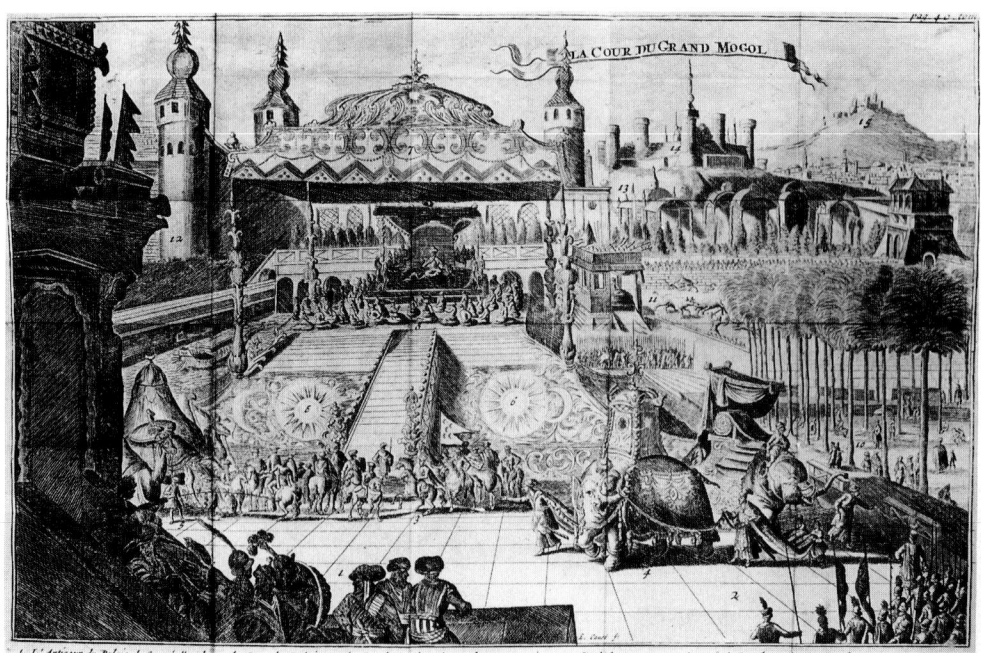

Habitans de Suratte.

124. WOMAN AND MAN OF SURAT

From Gabriel Dellon, *Nouvelle relation d'un voyage fait aux Indes orientales* (Amsterdam, 1699), facing p. 53.

125. THE COURT AND THRONE OF THE "GREAT MOGUL" AT LAHORE (*CA.* 1638)

From Dapper, *op. cit.* (pl. 115), between pp. 142 and 143.

Notice the imperial animal parade.

126. WRESTLERS OF SURAT

From John Fryer, *A New Account* (London, 1698), facing p. 111. Pls. 135 and 145–47 are also from this book.

"The Wrestlers Anoint with Oil, and are Naked, only a Belt about their Wastes, in which they weary one another only by pure Strength and Luctation [struggling], not by Skill or Circumvention; these last use Opium to make them perform things beyond their strength."

Wrestling in western India, especially in Gujarat, dates back at least to the tenth or eleventh century A.D. and remained popular until the end of the seventeenth century.

Fryer's illustration seems to be based on an original Indian representation.

127. FAKIRS UNDER A BANYAN TREE AT SURAT

From J. B. Tavernier, *Les six voyages* (Paris, 1676), II, pp. 376–77.

Later reproduced in Bernard Picart's compilation and elsewhere, with figures being added or taken away.

128. MEANS OF
TRANSPORT IN SIND

From *Les voyages de [Jean de] Thévenot* (Paris, 1689), IV, between pp. 160 and 61. Pls. 139 and 201 are also from this book.

Notice the enclosed palanquin in the background.

129. ELEMENTS OF THE SANSKRIT LANGUAGE

From Athanasius Kircher, *China illustrata* (Amsterdam, 1667), facing p. 162. See also pl. 112.

First page of a five-page summary of the elements of Sanskrit written by Heinrich Roth, S.J. (1620–88). This Jesuit had studied, according to Kircher, the sacred and arcane language of the Brahmans for six years in India. This is the first appearance in a published European book of the *devanāgarī* script and of a Sanskrit grammar.

Roth himself composed the Sanskrit grammar with its characters. His original manuscript was discovered in 1967 by Dr. Arnulf Camps, O.F.M., among the Oriental manuscripts (no. 171) in the Biblioteca Nazionale Centrale Vittorio Emmanule II (Rome). For further detail see B. Zimmel, "Die erste Sanskrit-Grammatik," *Biblos,* V (1956), 48–63, and Zimmel, "Die erste Sanskrit-Grammatik Wiederentdeckt," in *ibid.,* XVI (1967), 219–22. Full information on the grammar and other relevant documents was published in three articles by Camps, R. Hauschild, and Zimmel in the *Zeitschrift für Missionswissenschaft und Religionswissenschaft,* LV (1969), 185–205.

In the estimation of Stephen Neill, Roth's "Elements of Sanskrit" is an "extremely competent piece of work" (*A History of Christianity in India* [Cambridge, 1984], p. 418).

Elementa Linguæ Hanscret.

a   i   u   re   lre   ha   ia   ua   ra   la   nja   ndda na   nga ma

एॅ ऽ ३ ॠ ॡ ‖ ह य ग र ल ‖ ञ ण न ङ म ‖

jha ddha dha gha bha   ja dda da ga ba   kha pha txha ttha tha

झ ढ ध घ भ ‖ ज ड द ग व ‖ ख फ छ ट थ ‖

txa tta ta ka pa   xa kha sa

च ट त क प ‖ श ष स ‖

a   i   u   re lre

Vocales sunt quinq̃ एॅ ऽ ३ ॠ ॡ *quarum ultima vix est in usu. Hæc vocales ut sint Longa vel Breves ita distinguunt*

Vocalis Longæ आ ई ऊ ॠ ॡ : *Breves* अ इ उ ॠ ॡ

Ex Vocalibus nascuntur Diphtongi quatuor ए ऐ ओ औ *e nascitur ex a et i. Ex a et e nascitur ei. Ex a et u nascitur o. Ex a et o fit ou*

Consonantibus conjungunt vocales hoc modo ꝶ G sit littera क *cum Vocali Brevi.* kā ki kŭ krĕ klrĕ क कि कु कृ कॢ *Cum Longis hoc modo* kā ki kŭ krĕ klrĕ का की कू कॄ कॣ

Et sic de aliis consonantibus ex quarum uno facilè colligi potest quo modo vocales prædictæ copulentur singulis ke kei ko kou *Diphtongis sic copulantur* के कै को कौ

Consonantes itidem copulantur inter se quandoq̃, nulla intercedente vocali: Illam enim, quæ Vocali privatur secundum Regulas, vocant Clau dicantem, eúmq̃ solam non ponunt sed alteri sequenti copulatam

Sit pro Exemplo ब *Claudicans* bra bla bma bya bka bxa bsa bna ब्र ब्ल ब्म ब्य ब्क ब्श ब्स ब्न *Et sic de reliquis. Interdum contigit duas privari vocali, et sic ambæ copulandæ erunt cum tertia sequenti Sic* ktra stra tkma क्त्र स्त्र त्क्म *Et sic de aliis*

Sunt aliæ quatuor Litteræ quas copulatas vocant sed in copulatione perdunt suam figuram kfa guia dha xtta क्ष ज्ञ ह्य ष्ट *W. vander Laegh scripsit et sculp.*

Y y

130. HOOK-SWINGING

From Dapper, *op. cit.* (pl. 115), facing p. 118.

"The man who has made a vow to undergo the cruel penance places himself under the gibbet, and a priest then beats the fleshy part of the back until it is quite benumbed. After that the hook is fixed into the flesh thus prepared, and in this way the unhappy wretch is raised in the air. While suspended he is careful not to show any sign of pain; indeed he continues to laugh, jest, and gesticulate like a buffoon in order to amuse the spectators, who applaud and shout with laughter. After swinging in the air for the prescribed time the victim is

let down again, and, as soon as his wounds are dressed, he returns home in triumph" (Abbe J. A. Dubois, *Hindu Manners, Customs and Ceremonies,*

3d ed. Translated by H. K. Beauchamp [Oxford, 1959], p. 598). *Cf.* our pl. 199.

131. YOGI AUSTERITIES

From Dapper, *ibid.,* p. 123. *Cf.* to the Brahman austerities in our pl. 200.

132. THE CELEBRATION IN BENGAL OF THE
MUSLIM FESTIVAL OF HASSAN AND HOSSEIN
From Wouter Schouten, *Reistogt naar en door Oostindien*
(4th ed.; 2 vols.; Amsterdam, 1780), II, facing p. 86.

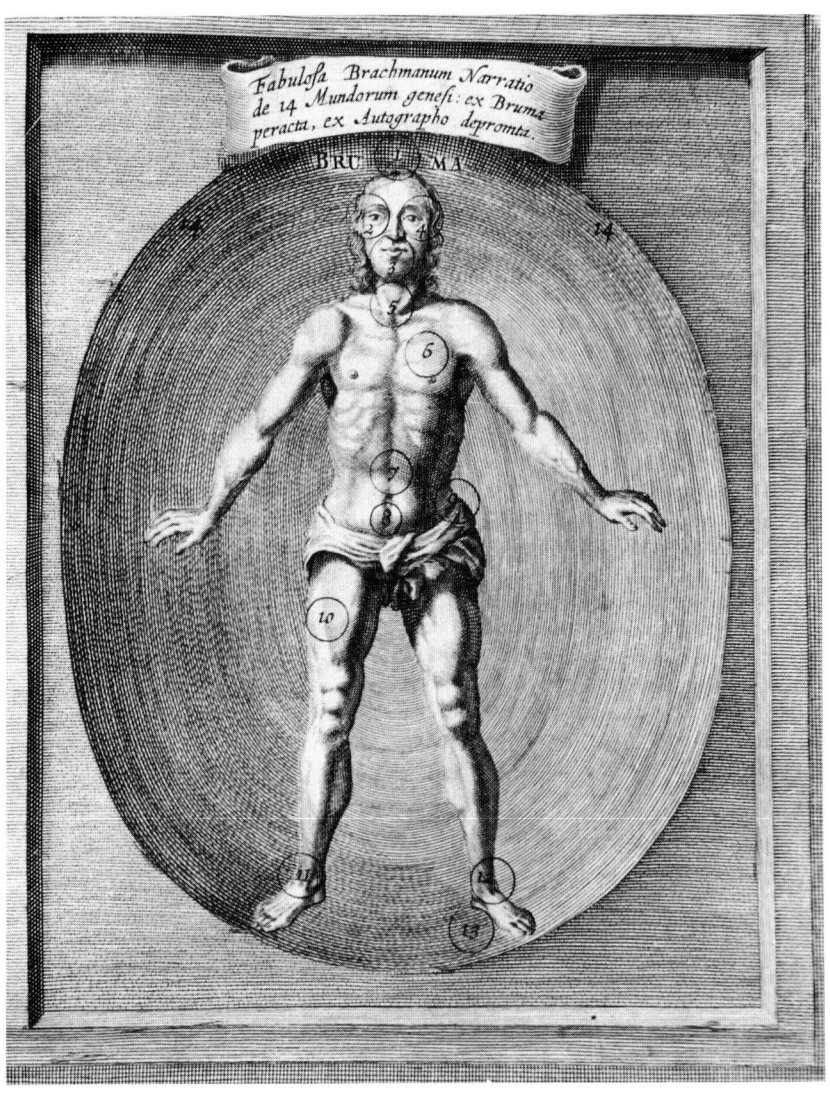

133. THE FABLE OF BRAHMA, THE CREATOR

From Kircher, *op. cit.* (pl. 112), facing p. 212.

    This is a European figure marked with numbers which indicate how each of the fourteen different worlds in the universe was formed from a particular part of Brahma's body. For example, the first and super-celestial world derived from the brain, the second world from the eyes, and so on. Humans derived their particular dispositions or characteristics from these worlds. The first type of human emanates from the first world and is intellectual and wise. Prudent persons are emanations of the second world, etc. While scoffing at these "stupid fictions" and cosmological myths, Kircher nonetheless imparts in brief scope some of the standard features found in the Hindu creation stories. Also see Mitter, *op. cit.* (pl. 113), pp. 56, 60, and pl. 25.

THE PRINTED MAPS OF SOUTH INDIA

South India, unlike the Mughul Empire, was not explored cartographically in the seventeenth century. The maps prepared in Portugal during the sixteenth century had focused on the cities and states of coastal south India and showed little about the interior of the peninsula. In both the sixteenth and seventeenth centuries, the cartographers in Europe continued to produce maps of the peninsula that were no more than modified maps of Ptolemy's India. The best of the newer representations were the sketch maps prepared as illustrations for the books by travelers. Still, as time went on, the major political divisions of south India began to appear, as well as a substantial number of new coastal cities on both sides of the peninsula; the Malabar Coast, as might be expected, was more fully mapped than the Coromandel Coast.

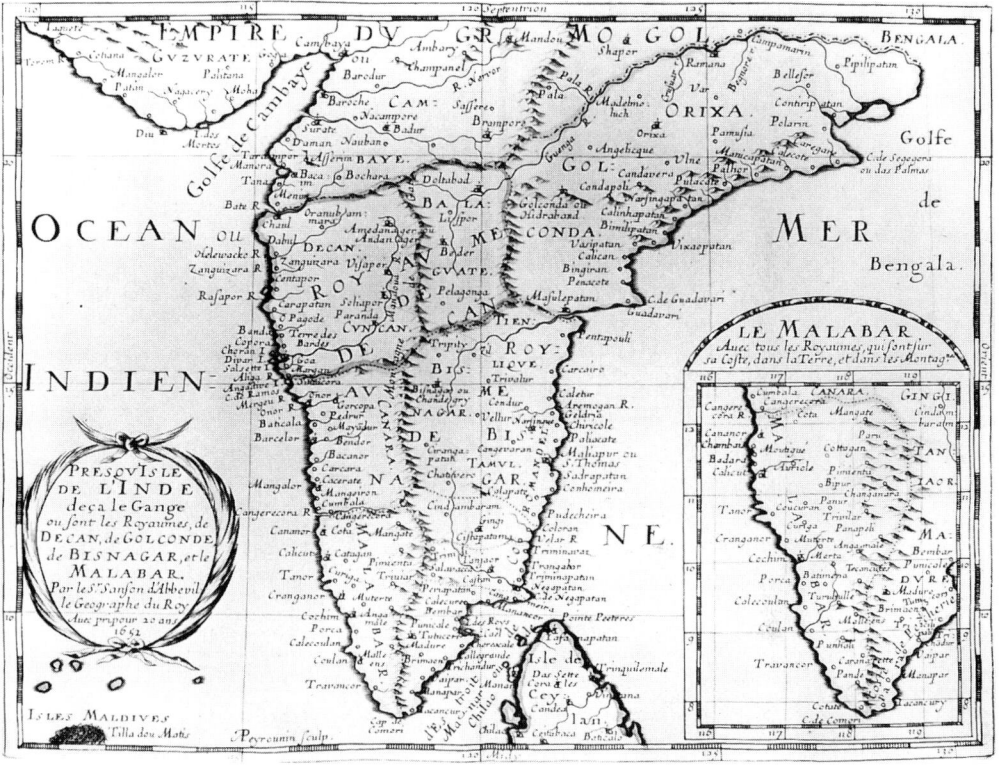

134. SOUTH INDIA

From Sanson d'Abbeville, *op. cit.* (pl. 108).

South India is divided into four principal parts: the Deccan, Golconda, Bisnagar or Vijayanagar, and Malabar.

Sources: Vincent Blanc on Goa. Teixeira on Madura. Cites no other sources, but he certainly used Jesuit letterbooks.

Notice especially the inset map of Malabar.

Indus fl.

Loure Bander

I N D I A

A MAP
of the
Parts of
INDIA
mentioned in
Dr. Fryars Travells.

Chitor

Amadabat

Cambaye

Grambusor

GUZA=
RAT

Boroche

Taquete

Golf de Cambaye

Diu

Swally

Swally R.

Balsore

Surratt

Mulore

Damon

St. Johns

Ieneah

Valentines Peak

Tavapore

Bacim

Tanow

Ven.

Raire

Seva=
Gis

Doltabat

Orengabat or
Aurengabat

Golconda
or
Baynagur

Coular

Canorein

Bonnbaim

Magatan

Tull

Chaul

Panatti

Visapor

Condapoli

Upper Chaul

Danda

Kelfi

Country

Dibul

Rajapor

Carapeten

Medapollan

Mechlapatan

Goulpalan

BarTown

Dere Pt.

Serapatan
or
Cola or
Agoada

Salfet

Norway

Old Goa

Goa

Pettipole

G. de Marmagoin

Curwar

Angediva

Mirja

Bisnagar or
Narsinga

Gundore

Vingula

Onor

Garsopa

Buticalai

Phalapatan

Durmfapatan

Sacrifica I.

Canara

Triblitore

Pellicato or F. Geldria

Barcelor

Gitty Cory

Mangalor

M. Deli

Mala=

bar

Madras & Fort St. Georg

Melipar or St. Thomas

Sadrasapatan

Pordicheri

Cananor

Porto
Novo

Calecut

St. Maria
Major

Madure

Negapatan

Tanore

Cochin

CORMANDEL

Coulan

Coast de la Pescaria

Tutucary

Iaffanapatan

Trincomli

Tangapatan

Molaque

C. Comorin

Columbo

CEY
LON

Pt. Gallo

Maldiviæ Insulæ

Delli

Agra

Aumbegaum

Ieneah Gur

Beelfeed

Dungeness

Oppagaut

Nuny Gaot

Dehir

Moorbar

Wesmure

Purtaabgur

Intwally

Gulleur

Barsta

Raire

Chiblone

Goa

Anchola

Baceim

Puncharra

Gongouli

Nishamport

Gongola

Gocurn

Upper
Chaul

Esthemy

Miria R.

Tudero

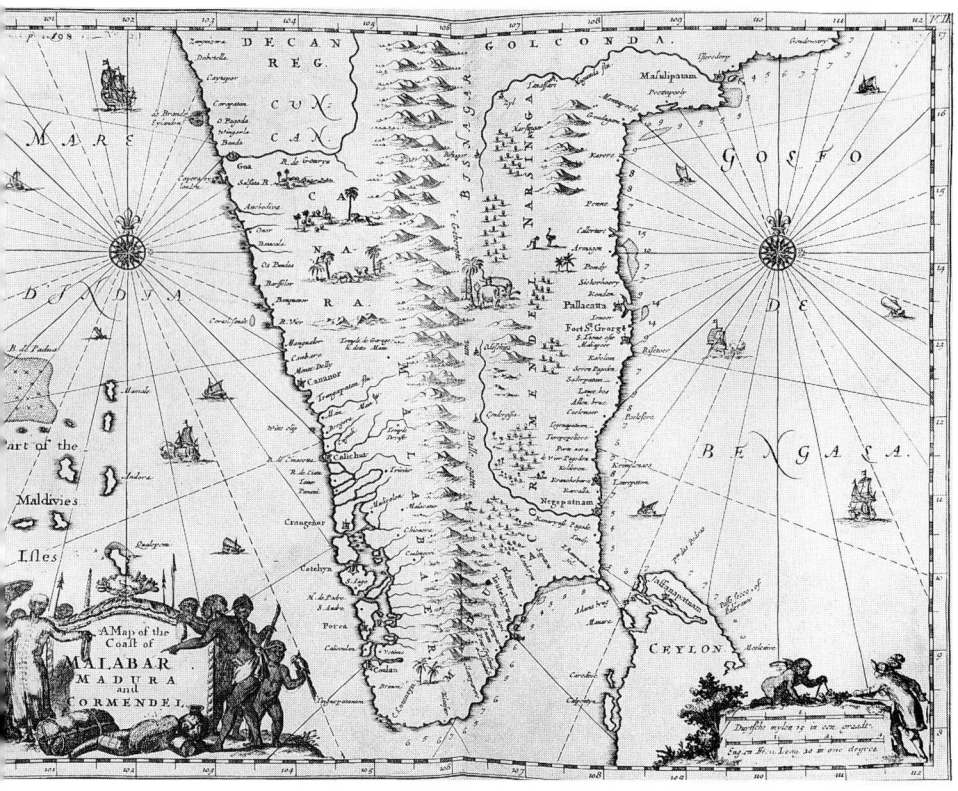

136. SOUTH INDIA AND ITS PERIPHERY
From *CV* (3d ed.; London, 1744), Vol. II, between pp. 196 and 197.
  Reproduces here the text and the maps from Nieuhof's *Reizen*.

135. (FACING PAGE) MAP OF PLACES IN INDIA
From Fryer, *op. cit.* (pl. 126), between pp. 50 and 51.
  Notice that Malabar is divided from Kanara just north of Mount
Deli. Includes Bombay and its neighbors. Inset shows Fryer's travels
in the Deccan.

HORTI
INDICI MALABARICI

AMSTELODAMI, Sumptibus { JOANNIS VAN SOMEREN et JOANNIS VAN DYCK.
HENRICI et Viduæ THEODORI BOOM. Aᵒ cIↄIↄcLXXXII.

137. FRONTISPIECE, *HORTUS INDICUS MALABARICUS*

From the *Hortus* of Hendrik Adriaan van Rheede tot
Drakestein and his collaborators (Amsterdam, 1678),
Vol. I; the frontispiece is dated 1682, although the title
page is dated 1678. Pls. 142–44, 169, and 170 are from
the same book.

The Indians in the lower left-hand corner are placed
before what is clearly a European backdrop. This picture seems to symbolize the cooperation between the
Europeans and the Malabars which was necessary to
produce the monumental *Hortus*. The floral elements
also seem to be of both Indian and European origin.

GULIELMI PISONIS
MEDICI AMSTELÆDAMENSIS

DE

INDIÆ UTRIUSQUE
RE NATURALI ET MEDICA

LIBRI QUATUORDECIM,
Quorum contenta pagina sequens
exhibet.

AMSTELÆDAMI,
apud Ludovicum et Danielem
ELZEVIRIOS.
A⁰. cIɔ Iɔ c LVIII.

138. FRONTISPIECE, *DE INDIAE UTRIUSQUE RE NATURALI ET MEDICA*

The frontispiece of this book by Willem Piso (Amsterdam, 1658), a natural history of the East and West Indies, shows a naked American Indian on the left and a Malay or Javan on the right. Both imaginary and realistic flora and fauna are depicted. By this time, engravings of certain Asian animals, such as the rhinoceros and the dodo bird, were probably kept in stock at the Elzevier and other important printing houses.

FIGURES.	NOMS.	PUISSANCES.
	Les Voielles	
	Aana	*a* breve
	Auena	*a* longum
	Iina	*i* breve
	Iena	*i* longum
	Ououna	*ou* Gallicum breve
	Ouuena	*ou* Gallicum longum
	Ecna	*e* breve
	Eena	*e* longum
	Ayena	*ay* Gallicum
	Oona	*o* breve
	Ouena	*o* longum
	Auuena	*aou* Gallicum
	Akena.	*Non est Vocalis, sed solummodo est signum quietis, sicut quando pronunciamus per, litera r est quiescens, quia pronunciatur cum vocali praecedente, & non habet vocalem sequentem; signum hujus quietis est punctum, superpositum literae.*

CONSONNES.

FIGURES.	NOMS.	PUISSANCES.
	Naana	*nostrum* n.
	Paana	*nostrum* p.
	Maana	*nostrum* m.
	Jaana	J *consonans.*
	Raana	*nostrum* r *simplex, ut in verbe gallico* pere, mere.
	Laana	*nostrum* l.
	Vaana	V *consonans.*
	Raana	*r gras.* — *pronunciatio blasorum qui non possunt pronunciare* r.
	Laana	l *in medio palati tangendo cum extremitate lingua medium palati.*
	Raana	*ç Gregorii aspiratum. nostrum* r *duplex, ut in verbo gallico* terre.
	Naana	*parva differentia pronunciationis hujus literae à pronunciatione nostra n, & non potest bene adverti. illa differentia nisi ab ipsis naturalibus.*

THE
Malabar Alphabet.

139. (TOP) MALABAR (TAMIL) ALPHABET

From Jean de Thévenot, *op. cit.* (pl. 128), III, between pp. 268 and 269.

Modern beginners study the vowels in Tamil as they are given here. The top three in the list of consonants do not belong to the series of eight which follow.

140. (RIGHT) MALABAR (TAMIL) VOWELS

From the English translation (1687) of Jean de Thévenot's *Travels,* III, between pp. 90 and 91.

The column of Tamil vowels is taken from an earlier French edition, but printed upside down. Another example of the way in which engravings were "borrowed" by seventeenth-century printers!

FIGURES.	NAMES.	POWERS.
	The Vowels.	
	Aana	*a* breve
	Auena	*a* longum
	Iinà	*i* breve
	Iena	*i* longum
	Ououna	*ou* Gallicum breve
	Ouuena	*ou* Gallicum longum
	Ecna	*e* breve
	Eena	*e* longum
	Avena	*ay* Gallicum
	Oona	*o* breve
	Ouena	*o* longum
	Auuena	*aou* Gallicum
	Akena	*Non est vocalis, sed solummodò est signum quietis, sicut quando pronunciamus* per, litera r *est quiescens, quia pronunciatur cum vocali praecedente, & non habet vocalem sequentem; signum hujus quietis est punctum superpositum literae.*

Insert this between Pag. 90, and 91. of the Third Part.

THE
Malabar Cyphers.

141. THE MALABAR CYPHERS
From Jean de Thévenot, *Travels*, III,
p. 93.
These are the numerals of old Tamil.
Today Arabic numerals are used in the
Tamil language.

142. LETTER FROM THE BRAHMANS
OF MALABAR
From Van Rheede *et al.*, *op. cit.* (pl.
137), I (1678), prefatory materials.
This and the following two letters
(pls. 143 and 144) are probably the first
examples of the Malayalam language to
be published in Europe. This letter, in
Sanskrit *devanāgarī* script, is from the
three Brahmans of Malabar (Cochin),
called "Ranga Botto, Vinaique Pandito,
and Apu Botto."

143. LETTER OF EMANUEL CARNEIRO
From Van Rheede *et al., op. cit.* (pl. 137), I, (1678), prefatory materials.

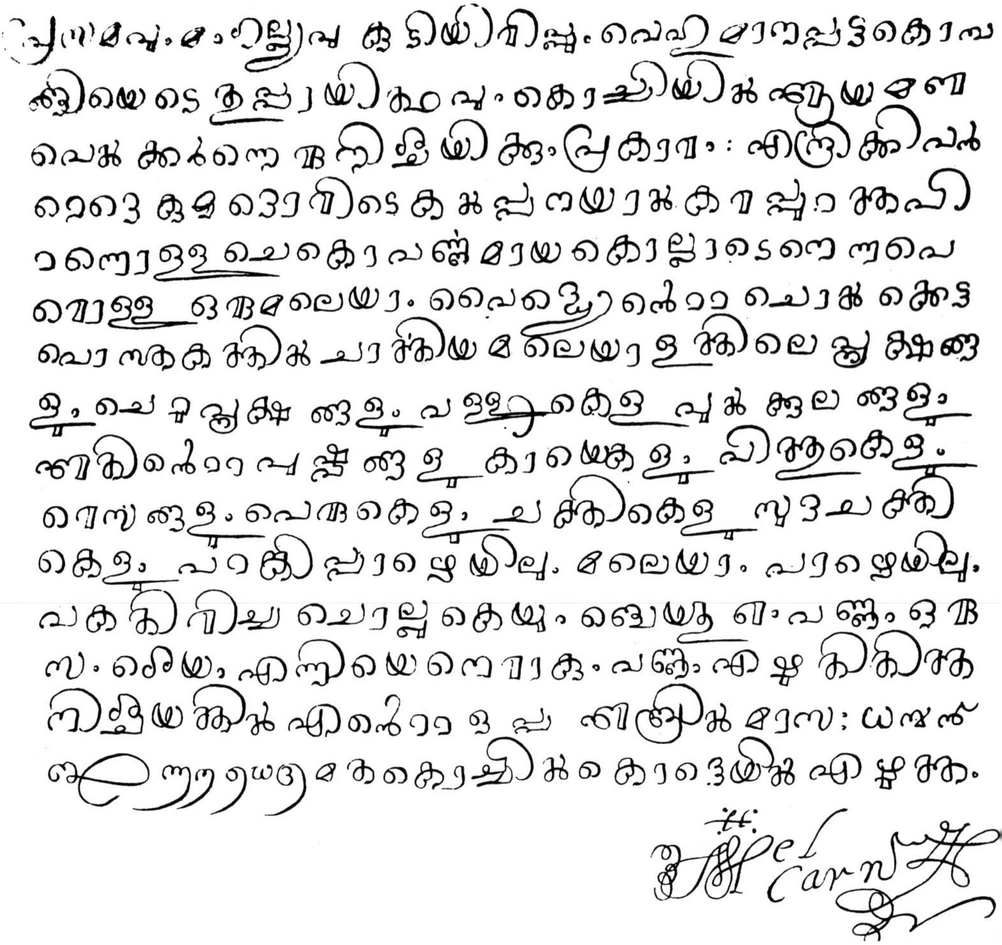

144. LETTER OF "ITTI ACHUDEM," A MALABAR PHYSICIAN OF THE CHEGO CASTE

From Van Rheede *et al., op. cit.,* I, prefatory materials.

JOHANNES FRYER M.D.
Societatis Regiæ Lond. Socius.

145. PORTRAIT OF JOHN FRYER, M.D.
Frontispiece, Fryer, *op. cit.* (pl. 126).
Sketched and engraved from life by R[obert] White.

A

NEW ACCOUNT

O F

Eaſt-India and Perſia,

I N

EIGHT LETTERS.

B E I N G

Nine Years Travels,

Begun 1672. And Finiſhed 1681.

Containing Obſervations made of the *Moral*, *Natural*, and *Artificial* Eſtate of
Thoſe Countries: Namely, Of their Government, Religion, Laws, Cuſtoms.
Of the Soil, Climates, Seaſons, Health, Diſeaſes. Of the Animals, Vegeta-
bles, Minerals, Jewels. Of their Houſing, Cloathing, Manufactures, Trades,
Commodities. And of the Coins, Weights, and Meaſures, uſed in the Prin-
cipal Places of Trade in thoſe Parts.

By JOHN FRYER, M.D. *Cantabrig.*

And Fellow of the R o y a l S o c i e t y.

Illuſtrated with Maps, Figures, and Uſeful Tables.

L O N D O N:

Printed by R. R. for R i. C h i s w e l l, at the Roſe and Crown
in St. Paul's Church-Yard. M DC XC VIII.

146.

147. (BOTTOM) SPECI-
MEN OF THE "MALA-
BAR" SCRIPT USED IN
CALICUT
From Fryer, *op. cit.* (pl.
126), p. 52.
Apparently indecipher-
able, this "specimen"
seems to be written in
Telugu characters and to
show a remarkable re-
semblance to Kanarese or
Old Kannada. Professor
R. K. Ramanujan, of the
University of Chicago,
writes (private communi-
cation): "This certainly
looks like Kannada to
me." See also W. Crooke
(ed.), *A New Account of
East India and Persia . . .
by John Fryer* (3 vols.;
London, 1909, 1912,
1915; in "HS," n.s., XIX,
XX, XXXIX), I, 95,
n. 4; 136, n. 4.

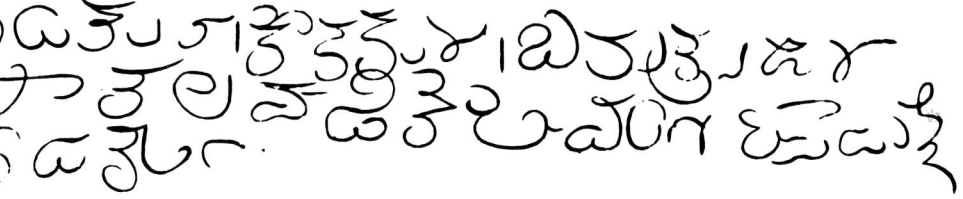

148. SKETCH OF THE ZAMORIN'S PALACE AT CALICUT

From G. Havers (trans.), *The Travels of Sig. Pietro della Valle, A Noble Roman, into East-India and Arabia Deserta* (London, 1665), p. 190.

"I will here present to your view a rough and unmeasur'd Plat-form of the Samori's [Zamorin's] Palace, and the place where he gave us Audience [in 1623]" (p. 189).

149. THE ZAMORIN OF CALICUT AND HIS PALACE

From *BV* (facsimile ed., Amsterdam, 1969), III, "Beschryvinghe van de tweede Voyagie . . . onder . . . Steven van der Hagen," between pp. 8 and 9. Plates 174 and 179 are also from this book.

This is presumably a portrait of the Zamorin (called also the "king of Malabar") who ruled in 1604, the date of Steven van der Hagen's advent in Calicut.

This is probably the same palace where Vasco da Gama was received in 1498. It is said that two pillars still remain of the palace where Da Gama was received. See J. Murray, *A Handbook for Travellers in India, Pakistan, Burma and Ceylon* (18th ed.; London, 1959), p. 441.

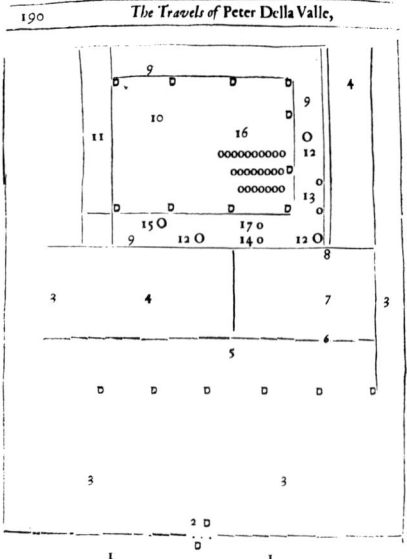

1. The little Piazza without the firſt Gate of the Palace.
2. The firſt Gate guarded with Baliſters.
3. A great Court within the firſt Gate, which ſhould be longer in proportion to the bredth, but is drawn thus in regard of the ſcantneſs of the paper, it hath lodgings about it in ſeveral places.
4. The King's Houſe, and the Apartment of his Women.
5. The Porch of the ſaid Houſe.
6. The ſecond Gate.
7 A dark Room lock'd up
8. A Door

't Hof van den Samorin

Samorin *van* Calicutt, Coninck *van* Malabar.

n.

150. "IXORA" OR ISVARA (SIVA)

From Philippus Baldaeus, *Afgoderye der Oost-Indische heydenen* (Pt. III of *Naauwkeurige beschryvinge;* Amsterdam, 1672), p. 11. Pls. 151, 158–68 are also from *Afgoderye*. See also pl. 173.

A European effort to depict the attributes of Siva. According to Baldaeus, Siva is white in color and has three eyes. The eye in the middle of the forehead represents fire, while the normally placed eyes are the sun and moon. Siva's sixteen hands hold special symbols. Dressed in a tiger skin, Siva carries a noose and wears a garland of skulls around his neck. On his hair Siva wears the crescent of the fifth-day moon.

For a modern summary of Siva's attributes see A. Daniélou, *Hindu Polytheism* (New York, 1964), pp. 213–21.

151. "QUENAVADY" (GANAPATI OR GANESHA), SON OF SIVA, A NATIVE OF THE "SUGAR SEA," WHERE THERE IS A SURPLUS OF EVERYTHING

From Baldaeus, *op. cit.,* p. 20.

Among his many attributes, Ganesha is the kitchen god who makes leftover foods palatable. For Ganesha in Hindu iconography see S. Bhattacharji, *The Indian Theogony* (Cambridge, 1970), pp. 183–84.

152. THE TEN AVATARS OF VISHNU

From Abraham Roger, *Le théâtre de l'idolatrie, ou la porte ouverte* (Amsterdam, 1670), between pp. 366 and 367. Plates 197, 199, and 200 are also from this book.

Engraved sketches of Indian gods had appeared on the title page of Roger's *Open-Deure* (1651) (pl. 196, below). Jean Schipper of Amsterdam, the publisher of its French translation, inserted the collection of avatar pictures shown here. They were sketchily copied from the French edition (1670) of Kircher's work. For a detailed discussion see E. Schierlitz, *Die bildlichen Darstellungen der indischen Göttertrinität in der älteren ethnographischen Literatur* (Munich, 1927), pp. 9–15.

153. "NAREEN," FIRST AVATAR OF VISHNU (ACCORDING TO KIRCHER)

From Kircher, *op. cit.* (pl. 112). (Illustrations 153–57 appear in both the Latin *China illustrata* and the French translation.)

These depictions and stories connected with the avatars (incarnations) of Vishnu were derived by Father Heinrich Roth from an Indian book brought to Rome. Roth explained to Kircher, as best he could, the significance the Hindus attached to these stories and pictures.

There are numerous avatars of Vishnu, but the most important and commonly accepted number is ten, just as Kircher indicates. The ordering, the names, and the stories attached by Kircher (i.e., Roth) to the avatars are for the most part quite different from those given in more recent renditions, such as in Shakti M. Gupta, *Vishnu and His Incarnations* (Bombay, 1974).

The figure shown here is, according to Kircher, identical to one that the Indians depict in their books. It is "Nareen" (*Nārāyana,* a manifestation of Vishnu), the eldest son of "Jagexuar" (?), who was so strong that he killed one thousand elephants with a single stroke of his sword.

He is here depicted with two arms and with a staff in his left hand that he uses to fight against the eighteen arms and many weapons of the warrior king.

This is probably the story of Parasurama or Rama-with-the-Ax that is usually the sixth in order of the avatars (*cf.* the depiction in Baldaeus, pl. 163). Rama restored the social order that had been disrupted by the revolt of the *kṣatriya,* the aristocracy of warriors who sought to wrest control of religion from the priestly caste. See Daniélou, *op. cit.* (pl. 150), pp. 170–71.

154. "RAMCHANDRA" (*RĀMACHANDRA* OR RAMA), THE EMBODIMENT OF RIGHTEOUSNESS

According to Kircher, "Ramachandra," the second avatar, was the "son of Bal which means strength." He delivered the world from the giants through his brother "Laxtman" (Lakshaman) who could kill a thousand men with one arrow. He liberated the world from the tyranny of giants.

This story is usually attached to the seventh avatar, or the story of how Vishnu took the form of a man to kill the ten-headed demon Ravana, the ruler of Lanka, the modern Sri Lanka (Ceylon). This story is the grand subject of the epic *Ramayana*.

155. "NARSENG," THE MAN-LION AVATAR OF VISHNU

In Kircher's fifth avatar, "Narseng" (Narasimha) came to the world to correct impiety. A king who tired of his son calling upon the gods day and night lashed the youth to a pillar. Then the pillar took on the form of a man-lion which slashed open the king's belly. By this act "Narseng" taught the world not to despise those who worship the gods.

The man-lion story is usually the fourth avatar. The above is an overly brief but essentially correct version of the story (cf. the depiction in Baldaeus, pl. 161, below).

156. "BHAVANI," THE GODDESS AND THE NINTH AVATAR OF VISHNU

A symbol of power who transforms herself into a lotus and governs the world. She has four arms which show graphically the power of the four elements.

This is the Buddha avatar.

157. THE HORSE AVATAR OF VISHNU

According to Kircher, the tenth incarnation heralds the advent of the Muslims in India. It is sometimes represented as peacocks or a winged horse.

This is a total misconception of the Kalki avatar. Traditionally it is an incarnation yet to come when Vishnu will appear on a white horse and with his blazing sword punish the evildoers and then destroy the world. From the ruins of the earth, a new golden age will emerge.

158. VISHNU: THE FISH INCARNATION (*MATSYA–AVATARA*)

From Baldaeus, *op. cit.* (pl. 150), p. 45.

This engraving is based on an Indian painting copied by the Dutch artist Philip Angel in his unpublished work on Hindu mythology entitled *Devex Avataars,* which Angel translated from a Portuguese manuscript and illustrated with copies of Indian miniatures.[1] All the illustrations of the incarnations in Baldaeus' book evidently originated from this same source.[2]

Baldaeus learned from his Bengali Brahman convert that "this *Vedam* [Veda], or law book, being inclosed in a Chanki [Sanskrit, *sankha*], or sea horse's horn, the same was found out by Vistum [Vishnu]: whence it is that they say, the prints of the fingers are to be seen in these horns to this day; and that they have put the Saccaram [*chakra*], or sword, and the Chanki, or horn into his hands, as you can see in the preceding draught; though some ascribe the same to Bramma [Brahma]."[3]

Traditionally, this is the first incarnation of the first age, the *satya yuga,* or the Age of Truth. Vishnu in human form emerges from the mouth of a fish which saves Manu, the seventh lawgiver and the rescuer of humanity from the universal deluge. This story is reminiscent of the Noah story in that Manu, on the fish's advice, built a ship to save a remnant from his age with which to start procreation of the next *yuga.*

Vishnu is here pictured with his usual attributes: he has four arms to symbolize his dominion over the four directions, the four stages of human development, and the four aims of life; in his hands he holds the conch which represents the origin of existence, the discus (or wheel) or universal mind, the mace (or sword) or the power of knowledge, and the book or the Vedas. Manu, the recipient of Vishnu's (Matsya's) blessing, is seated on the lotus, a representation of the universe.

[1] See Mitter, *op. cit.* (pl. 113), pp. 57–58, n. 277.
[2] Partha Mitter concurs in this opinion (personal conversation).
[3] *CV*, III, 746. In earlier texts Brahma is sometimes the fish incarnation. See Gupta, *op. cit.* (pl. 153), p. 13.

159. THE TORTOISE INCARNATION (KURMA AVATAR)

From Baldaeus, *op. cit.* (pl. 150), p. 51.

Vishnu appears here in this second avatar in the form of a tortoise to recover some of the valuables lost in the deluge. On its back the tortoise supports Mount Mandara. Gods and genii use the great serpent Vasuki as a rope around Mount Mandara to churn the ocean of milk and to produce the ambrosia, or the essence of life. Later there came forth the divine horse with seven heads, the royal elephant, and the wealth-giving cow, as well as a variety of gods and sacred objects. See Daniélou, *op. cit.* (pl. 150), p. 167.

160. VARĀHA OR BOAR INCARNATION OF VISHNU

From Baldaeus, *op. cit.*, p. 52.

   According to Baldaeus, this is the third avatar, or the one in which Vishnu is depicted as *Varāha*, with boar's head and crown. *Varāha* stands on the body of *Hiraṇyākṣa,* the golden-eyed demon (*asura*) who had cast the earth to the bottom of the sea. After killing this evil genii *Varāha* rescued the earth and divided it into seven continents. *Varāha* is here depicted as balancing the rescued earth on his tusks.

161. MAN–LION INCARNATION (*NARASÍÑHA* AVATAR)

From Baldaeus, *op. cit.* (pl. 150), p. 57.

This fourth avatar (*cf.* the man-lion incarnation in Kircher, pl. 155, above) illustrates the story of *Prahlāda,* the pious boy devoted to Vishnu who suffered severe punishments inflicted by his royal father. To punish the evil king and father, Vishnu appeared as a lion-headed man in a pillar and tore out the entrails of the wicked demon. See A. Daniélou, *op. cit.* (pl. 150), pp. 168–69.

162. THE DWARF (*VAMANA-AVATARA*) OR FIFTH AVATAR OF VISHNU
From Baldaeus, *op. cit.*, p. 61.
   Vamana (Vishnu as a priestly dwarf) stands before Bali, king of the genii (*asura*),
begging for as much land as he can encompass with three steps. In granting this
wish the king pours water over Vamana's left hand. Vamana wears a crown as well as
sandals and carries an umbrella: all symbols of his exalted status.

163. PARASURAMA (RAMA–WITH–THE–AX)

From Baldaeus, *op. cit.* (pl. 150), p. 66.

In this sixth avatar (*cf.* the depiction in Kircher, pl. 153) two-armed Rama uses the ax given him by Siva to defeat the overly ambitious *kṣatriyas* and to restore social order. With the defeat of the *kṣatriyas*, the white cow of plenty returned.

164. RAVANA IN LANKA, OR *RĀMACHANDRA,* THE
EMBODIMENT OF RIGHTEOUSNESS

From Baldaeus, *op. cit.,* p. 77.

Ravana, the symbol of lust, is represented as ten-headed and with
eighteen arms. He carried off Sita, wife of Rama, and was then killed
by that hero. Here Rama (Vishnu, in human form) and Lakshaman,
his inseparable companion, are supported by Hanumant, the monkey-
god, in killing Ravana and rescuing Sita.

Angel's original depiction (see caption of pl. 158, above) is set side
by side with this engraving in Mitter, *op. cit.* (pl. 113), pls. 29, 30.

165. EIGHTH AVATAR OF VISHNU: KRISHNA

From Baldaeus, *op. cit.* (pl. 150), p. 89.

This incarnation belongs to the third age, *dvapara yuga,* when Vishnu manifests himself as Krishna, the embodiment of love. Born in Mathura twenty-five *cos* from Agra, Krishna was the son of "Deuki" (*Devaki*), sister of the cruel king "Ragie Kans" (*Raji Kamsa*). Fearful of Krishna, Kamsa sought many times to kill his nephew. Eventually Krishna killed Kamsa and ruled the kingdom. For Baldaeus' lengthy and important rendition of the complicated Krishna story see *op. cit.,* pp. 88–126.

In this depiction Krishna is shown seated in the background with his two wives. In his four hands he holds the usual symbols of Vishnu.

166. BUDDHA WITH FOUR ARMS ON LOTUS SEAT IN LANKA (CEYLON)
From Baldaeus, *op. cit.*, p. 127. (Treated here as the ninth avatar of Vishnu.)

The two outer hands hold a book and a chank or conch (Sanskrit, *sankha*, a large shell from the Gulf of Manaar prized by Hindus). On either side stand worshippers whose costumes and ornaments are like those on the depictions of Vishnu in Baldaeus.

Compare to the ninth avatar displayed in Kircher (pl. 156, above).

167. THE KALKI OR TENTH AVATAR OF VISHNU

From Baldaeus, *op. cit.* (pl. 150), between pp. 128 and 129.

This is the avatar yet to come. Here Vishnu leads the winged horse which he will ride to destroy the earth. From the earth's ruins a new and better mankind will emerge. *Cf.* pl. 157, above.

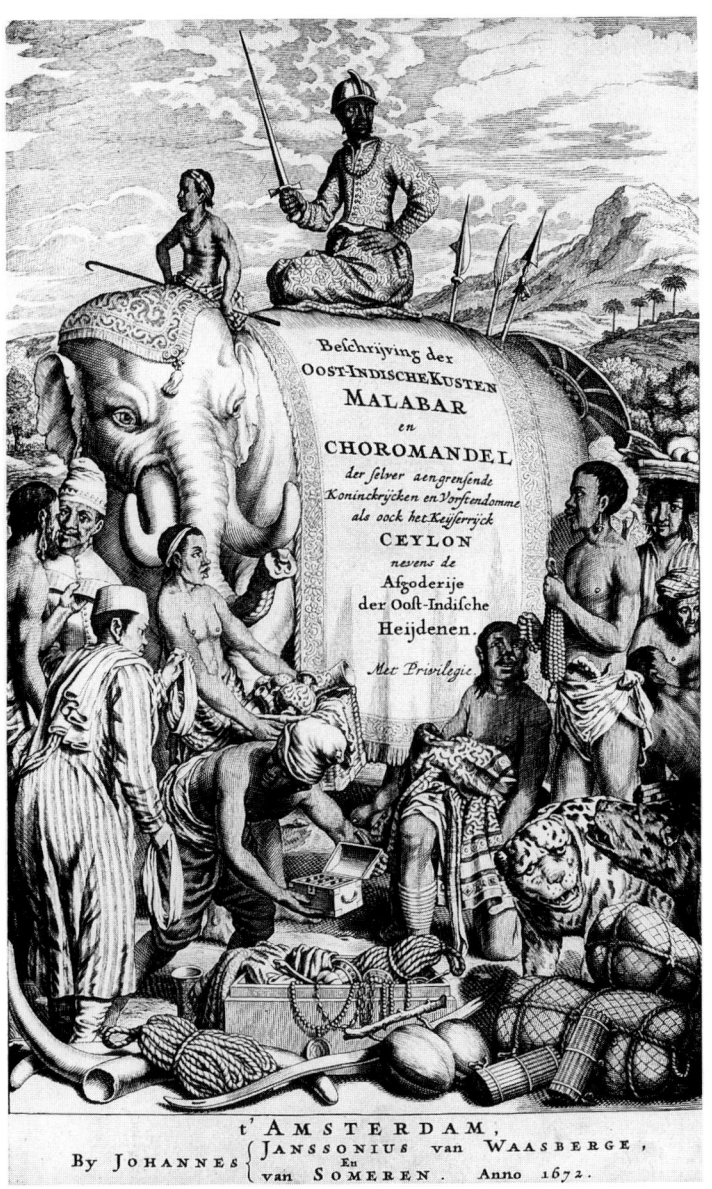

Beſchrijving der
OOST-INDISCHE KUSTEN
MALABAR
en
CHOROMANDEL
der ſelver aengrenſende
Koninckrijcken en Vorſtendomme
als oock het Keiſerrijck
CEYLON
nevens de
Afgoderije
der Ooſt-Indiſche
Heijdenen.

Met Privilegie

t'AMSTERDAM,
By JOHANNES { JANSSONIUS van WAASBERGE,
En
van SOMEREN. Anno 1672.

168. FRONTISPIECE, PHILIPPUS BALDAEUS, *AFGODERYE DER OOST-INDISCHE HEYDENEN*

This is the work from which the preceding Vishnu illustrations are taken.

169. PORTRAIT OF HENDRIK ADRIAAN VAN
RHEEDE TOT DRAKESTEIN
Frontispiece to Van Rheede, *op. cit.* (pl. 137).
   Van Rheede died in 1691. His remains repose under
a huge monument in the Dutch cemetery at Surat.

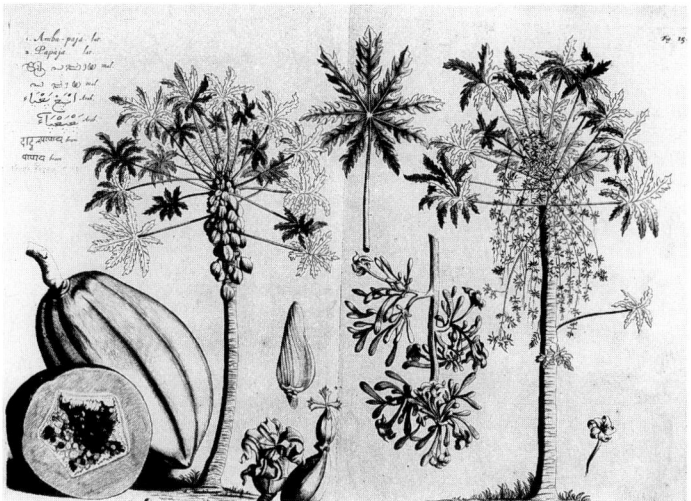

170. INDIAN FRUIT TREES

From Van Rheede, *op. cit.* (pl. 137), I (1678), fig. 23 and fig. 15.

The Indian tamarind (top) and the papaya (bottom), with their Latin, Malayalam, Arabic, and Sanskrit names.

Practically all parts of the tamarind tree are used in India. The pulp of the ripe pod is used as a condiment and an essential ingredient in the curries and chutneys of southern India. Its seeds are widely used in the preparation of textile sizing powder. The leaves and flowers are mainly employed in the preparation of medicines. In the West, tamarind is used in Worcestershire sauces. Our word "tamarind" derives ultimately from Arabic, *tamr-hindi,* date or fruit of India.

Also *cf.* our plate 271.

171. "MOGORIN" OR
THE ARABIAN JASMINE
(*JASMINIUM SAMBAC*)
From Gemelli Careri, *op.
cit.* (pl. 122), II, facing
p. 143.

This beautiful white
flower, sweeter in smell
than ordinary jasmines,
blooms in India from
February to the end of
May, according to Careri.

Father Salvatore Galli
(also Gallo; born in
Milan; d. 1697), superior
of the Theatine house in
Goa beginning in 1673,
told Careri that earthen
pots of these plants had
been sent to the court of
Lisbon and also to the
Grand Duke of Tuscany
(presumably Cosimo III,
r. 1670–1723).

The *mogra* or *motia,* as
it is called in India, is a
climbing shrub that also
grows in Burma and
Ceylon. It is cultivated
for its fragrant flowers
that are made into oils
and into medicines. The
double varieties, such
as the one in this illus-
tration, are sacred to
Vishnu. In Ceylon the
double jasmine was culti-
vated and reserved to the
ruler. See George Watt,
*Dictionary of the Economic
Products of India* (6 vols. in
9 plus index, Delhi, 1972,
reprint of 1893 edition),
IV, 544–45.

172. SNAKE–CHARMER OF MALABAR
From *CV* (3d. ed., London, 1744), Vol. II, between
pp. 230 and 231.
    Engraved by Gilliam (also Willem) van der Gouwen,
who worked around 1650 at Haarlem, and who also
engraved pl. 247, below.

173. LEARNING TO WRITE THE ALPHABET

From Baldaeus, *Naauwkeurige beschryvinge* (Amsterdam, 1672), I, p. 193. Pls. 151, 158–68, 175, 184, and 185 are also from this work.

Children are here being taught to write the letters of the Malabar language (Tamil) in the sand. Baldaeus informs us (p. 192) that he himself learned to write Tamil by this same method.

174. MAP OF CEYLON (*CA.* 1602)

From *BV* (facsimile edition; Amsterdam, 1969), II, "'t Historiael Journael," between pp. 42 and 43. Pls. 149 and 179 are also from this book.

Notice that although the map is labeled with west to the left and east to the right, the map itself is "flipped," with the towns and features of the west coast on the right (*e.g.,* Chilau, Negombo, and Colombo), and the east on the left. See our Note to Illustrations (following Table of Contents) for a discussion of flipped images.

This illustrates the account of Spilbergen's first voyage, 1601–4.

175. MAP OF JAFFNA AND ADJACENT ISLANDS
From Baldaeus, *op. cit.* (pl. 173), II, between pp. 154
and 155.

Notice that many of the smaller islands are named
for Dutch cities.

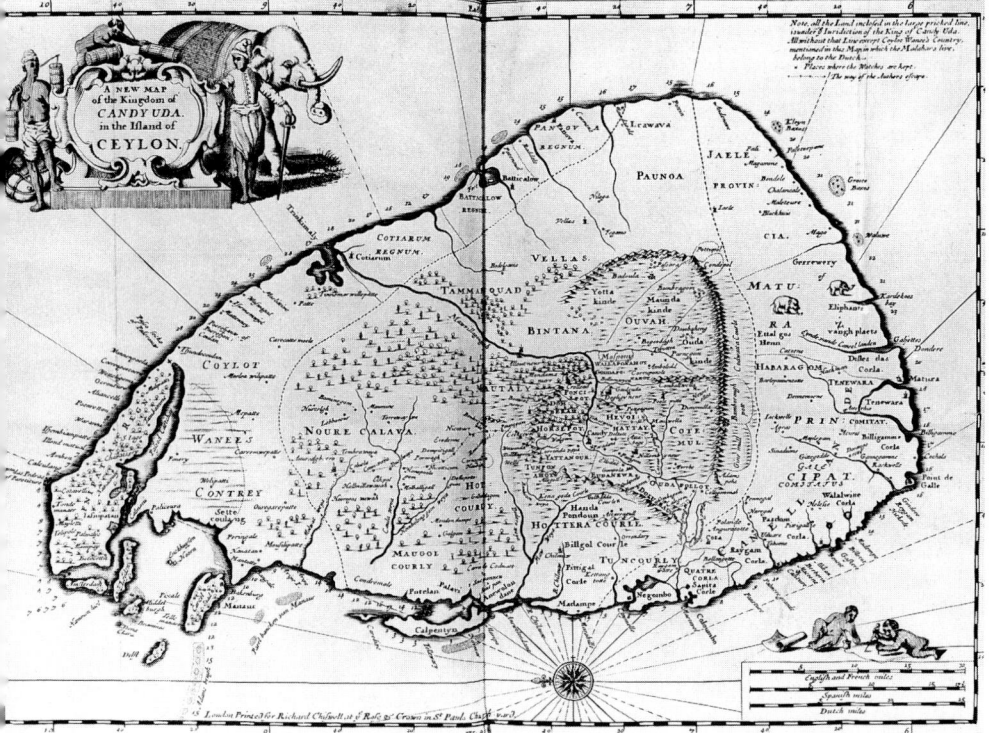

176. MAP OF KANDY ON CEYLON

From Robert Knox, *An Historical Relation of the Island
Ceylon in the East Indies* (London, 1681), frontispiece.
Pls. 182, 183, 186–88, and 190–95 are also from this
book.

 South is to the right and north is to the left on this
map. Kandy is the land within the dotted line. The rest
is controlled by the Dutch, except for the "Coylot
Wanee's Contrey." Notice Kandy's entryway to the sea
at Leawava, a land with no river for transport.

177. THE MALDIVES AND CEYLON

From Robert Morden, *Geography Rectified* (London, 1688), p. 428.

Text cites no sources. It is evident, however, from his rendition of certain of the place-names that at least one of his sources was Portuguese.

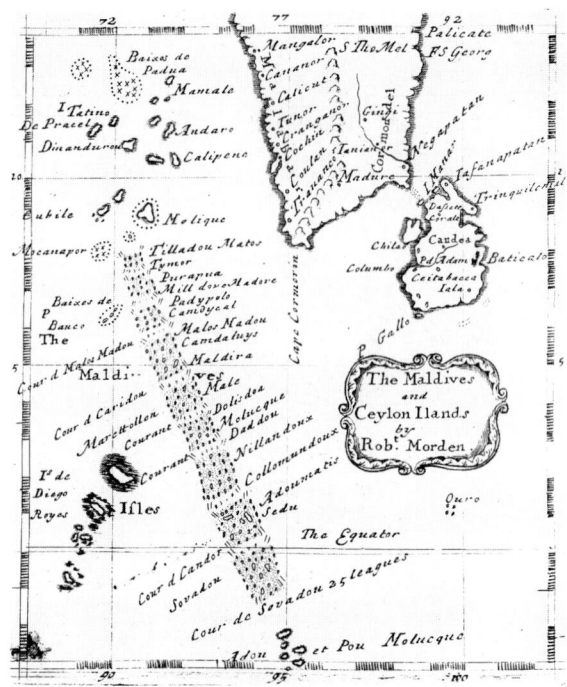

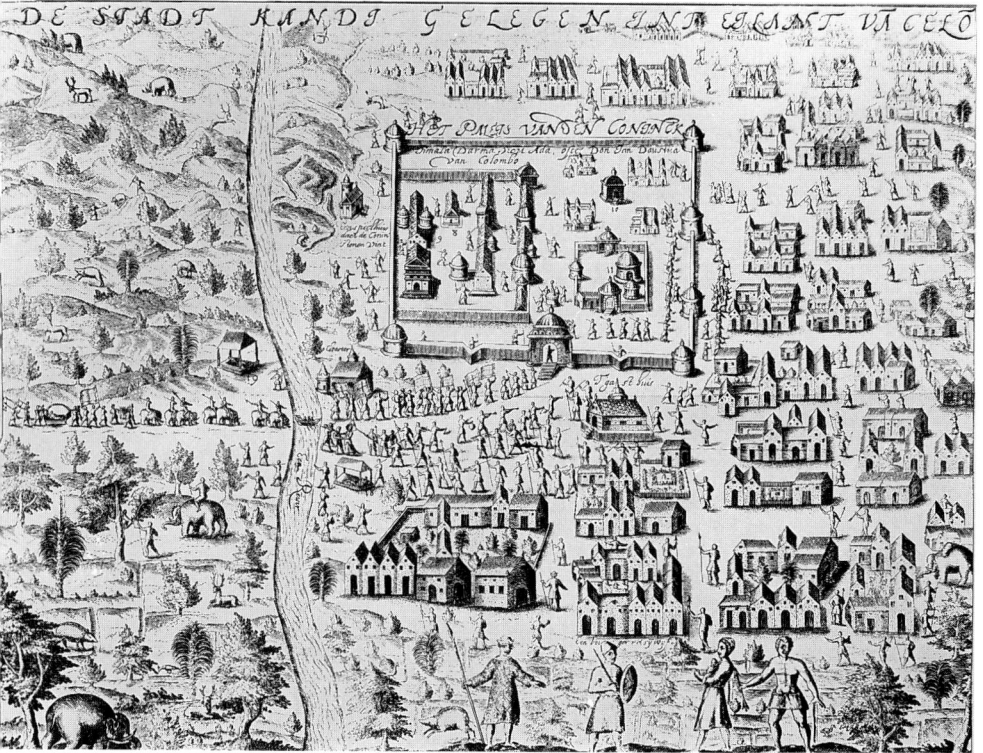

179. THE CITY OF KANDY IN 1602

From *BV* (facsimile edition, Amsterdam, 1969), II, "'t Historiael
Journael," between pp. 30 and 31. Pls. 149 and 174 are also from this
book.

Portrays the reception of Spilbergen at the court of "Fimala,
Darma, Suriada" (Vimaladharmasuriya).

178. (FACING PAGE) SPILBERGEN AND VIMALADHARMASURIYA
(R. 1592−1604), KING OF KANDY, IN 1602

From Cornelis Vennip, *De reis van Joris van Spilbergen naar Ceylon, Atjeh en Bantam,
1601−1604*, ed. Wouter Nijhoff *et al.*, "WLV," XXXVIII (The Hague, 1933), facing
p. liv. Pls. 180 and 181 are also from this book.

The portrait of the king, according to the caption, was executed from life in
Ceylon. It was certainly drawn by an artist who accompanied Spilbergen. The engraver, Floris Balthasar of Delft, combined the king's portrait with an engraving
made after the painted portrait of Spilbergen (see pl. 105) to produce this remembrance of their meeting. See P. H. Pott, "The Orient Reflected Our Views on the
East throughout the Ages," in P. W. Pestman (ed.), *Acta orientalia Neerlandica*
(Leyden, 1971), pl. 2, following p. 8. For a detailed analysis of the king's costume
and of its authenticity see G. P. Rouffaer and H. H. Juynboll, *Batik-Kunst in
Nederlandsch-Indië en haar geschiedenis* (Utrecht, 1914), pp. 159−63.

d'Wapen ende Cachet vanden Coninck van Celon.

SONET.

Die Reysen breet en wijt door de Zee vaerlijcke
    Sien de wonderen Gods, seyt David wel claerlijck daer
    Hy s'Heeren genaad' groot / Wanneer hen den noodt druckt swaer/
    Over haer uytghebzepdt / thoont: Op dat wy te g'lijcke
Sijnen Naem maecken groot : u die ons Geloof-Rijcke
    Maeckt / daer ghy thoont Gods-macht/ niet in het gantsch stercke/ maer
    Het swack' te verschijnen / tot roem sy dit gheseght naer:
    Dat even alst Canneel, dweick ghy terst uyt den Rijcke
Van Celon (daert wast) bzacht / verstercht de herten slouwe/
    Oock u Hope in Godt, als een Ancker meest trouwe
    Stercht onse zielen daer/ Wy ons vermoghen achten
Ydel en nietich gantsch' / en hem gheven die Eere:
    Dat hy t Fortuynen Radt / door een Oog-wincken keere/
    Waer over wy in hem meer wonders door u wachten.

                                              Kamp en eere.

180. THE ARMS AND SEAL OF THE KING OF
CEYLON
From Vennip, *op. cit.* (pl. 178), facing p. 88.

HIOB. CAP 75. VAERS

SONET.
Op de Reyfe vanden Generael Speilberg int Coninckrijck van Celon ghedaen.

I Anus twee-aenfichtich heet men Noah b'Eerts-bader
Die fach de wereld oudt en nieuwt / met onderfchepden:
f'Daer ghp Kepfer meer wijft/ Die bpna b'epn ot ban bepden
Hae-ght/ daermen focht t'verftandt in H' Behemoths Cop / nader
Cempt den Name Ianus: Daer d'outw'/ het d'nieuw' tegader
Ghp (door D'Licht opghegaen boven Phoebi claerhepden/
En d'upter hellen-hoeck ghecomen dupfterhepden/
Claerlijck onderfchepden/ ons comt als doen d'Eerts-bader.
Dien Gheeft die doen u als een Welt heeft ghebzeven/
Door tflantbaftich ghemoet/ en s'hert flerck u ghegheven
Daer ghp gaeft de eer' hem / bander Fozupms dpunighe/
En met en weerckt in noodt/ Die will' u foo verftercken
In u boozuemen goet / Dat wp fijn wonder-wercken
f.Piet bzeucht aenfchouwen meer / door uws levens derlinghent.

Der dinghen Opmerck'.   P. D. K.

181. THE GOD OF THE KING OF "MATECALO"
(BATTICALOA) ON CEYLON
From Vennip, *op. cit.,* facing p. 64.
    "This is the god to whom they pray for wisdom,
riches, and health."

Rajah Singah the King of Ceylon.

182. RAJA SINHA (LION-KING) OF KANDY
(R. 1635–87)
From Knox, *op. cit.* (pl. 176), facing p. 33.

"He bears his years well, being between Seventy and
Eighty years of age; and tho an Old man, yet appears
not to be like one, neither in countenance nor action.
His Apparel is very strange and wonderful, not after
his own Country-fashion, or any other, being made
after his own invention" (pp. 33–34).

A Noble Man.

183. NOBLE OF KANDY
From Knox, *op. cit.*, facing p. 89.

**184. CINNAMON HAR-
VESTING IN CEYLON**
From Baldaeus, *op. cit.*
(pl. 173), II, p. 195.

185. (FACING PAGE, TOP) BUTTER MAKING BY
THE "BELLALES" (*VELLALAS*) IN CEYLON
From Baldaeus, *op. cit.* (pl. 173), II, p. 178.
  Notice the ears of these women cultivators.

186. (FACING PAGE, BOTTOM) SINHALESE
PREPARING FOR RICE PLANTING
From Knox, *op. cit.* (pl. 176), facing p. 10.
  "Their Ploughs bury not the grass as ours do, and
there is no need they should. For their endeavor is only
to root up the Ground, and so they overflow it with
Water, and this rots the Grass" (pp. 9–10).

The Manner of their Ploughing.

The Manner of Smoothing their Feilds.

**187. (ABOVE) ON SMOOTHING
THEIR FIELDS**
From Knox, *op. cit.* (pl. 176), facing
p. 10.

"They have a Board about four
foot long, which they drag over their
Land . . . not flat ways, but upon the
edge of it. The use of which is, that it
jumbles the Earth and Weeds together,
and also levels and makes the Grounds
smooth and even so that the Water (for
the ground is all this while under water)
may stand equal in all places" (p. 11).

The Manner of treading out their Rice.

189. TREADING OUT THE RICE INDOORS BY "BELLALES" (*VELLALAS*)
From Baldaeus, *op. cit.* (pl. 173), II, p. 177.

188. (FACING PAGE, BOTTOM)
TREADING OUT THE RICE
From Knox, *op. cit.,* facing p. 11.
    "They use not threshing, but tread
out their Corn [grain] with Cattel,
which is a far quicker and easier way.
They may tread out in a day forty or
fifty Bushels at least with the help of
half a dozen Cattel" (p. 11).

An Execution by an Eliphant.

190. EXECUTION BY ELEPHANT
From Knox, op. cit. (pl. 176), facing p. 22.
Notice the authentic elephant hook.

The manner of burning their Dead.

191. CREMATION IN CEYLON
From Knox, *op. cit.*, facing p. 116.

The Talipat.
Tree

The Manner of
their Eating and Drinking

192. DRINKING CUSTOM IN CEYLON

From Knox, *op. cit.* (pl. 176), facing p. 87.

"When they drink they touch not the pot with their mouths, but hold it at a distance, and pour it in. They eat their Rice out of *China dishes* or Brass Basons, and they that have not them, on leaves. The *Carrees* [curries] or other sorts of Food which they eat with their Rice, is kept in the Pans it is dressed in, and their wives serve them with it, when they call for it" (p. 87).

Their manner of Fishing.

193. SINHALESE POND FISHING

From Knox, *op. cit.,* facing p. 14.

"They have a kind of Basket made of small sticks. . . . It is broad at bottom and narrow at top, like a funnel . . . ; these baskets they drop down, and the ends stick in the mud, which often happen upon a Fish; when they do they feel it by the Fish beating it self against the sides. Then they put in their hands and take them out" (p. 28).

A Vadda or Wild Man

194. A WILD MAN OF CEYLON
From Knox, *op. cit.* (pl. 176), facing p. 61.
  "The Land of Bintan is all covered with mighty Woods, filled with abundance of Deer. In this Land are many of these Wild-men; they call them Vaddahs [Veddas], dwelling near no other Inhabitants. They speak the Chingulayes [Sinhalese] Language" (p. 61).

The manner of their sheltring themselvs from the Raine by the Tolipat leafe.

195. A TALIPOT PARASOL OF CEYLON

From Knox, *op. cit.*, facing p. 14.

"One of these I brought with me into England, and you have it described in the Figure" (p. 15).

For many years this leaf was one of the natural rarities displayed in the Ashmolean museum at Oxford.

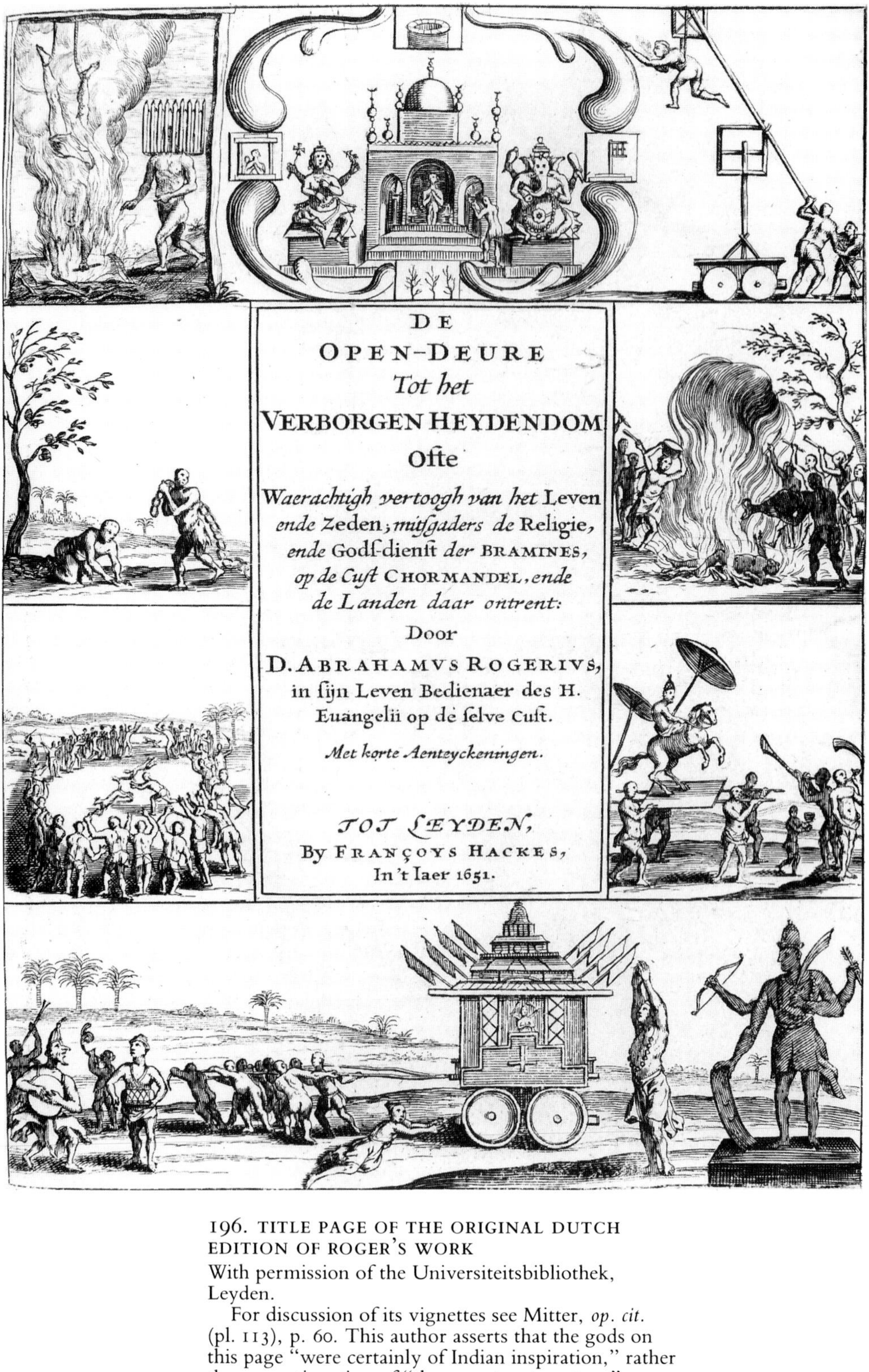
DE
OPEN-DEURE
Tot het
VERBORGEN HEYDENDOM
Ofte
Waerachtigh vertoogh van het Leven
ende Zeden; mitsgaders de Religie,
ende Godsdienst der BRAMINES,
op de Cust CHORMANDEL, ende
de Landen daar ontrent:
Door
D. ABRAHAMVS ROGERIVS,
in sijn Leven Bedienaer des H.
Euangelii op de selve Cust.
Met korte Aenteyckeningen.
TOT LEYDEN,
By FRANÇOYS HACKES,
In't Iaer 1651.

196. TITLE PAGE OF THE ORIGINAL DUTCH EDITION OF ROGER'S WORK

With permission of the Universiteitsbibliotheek, Leyden.

For discussion of its vignettes see Mitter, *op. cit.* (pl. 113), p. 60. This author asserts that the gods on this page "were certainly of Indian inspiration," rather than a continuation of "the monster stereotype" so well known in European depictions. Also *cf.* pls. 199 and 200.

197. FRONTISPIECE, ROGER, *THÉÂTRE
DE L'IDOLATRIE OU LA PORTE OUVERTE*,
THE FRENCH TRANSLATION OF *DE OPEN-DEURE*

198. TITLE PAGE OF D. HAVART'S BOOK
(AMSTERDAM, 1693).
With permission of the James Ford Bell Library,
University of Minnesota.
   Pls. 203, 204, 207, and 208 are also from this book.

199. HOOK-HANGING

From Roger, *op. cit.* (pl. 152), p. 246.
Propitiation of the devil Ganga on the
Coromandel Coast by being hanged.
(Also see *ibid.*, p. 249.) *Cf.* our pl. 130.

200. BRAHMANS IN 1640 ACQUIRING MERIT WITH SIVA BY
SUBJECTING THEMSELVES TO DEPRIVATION AND TORTURE
From Roger, *op. cit.* (pl. 152), p. 259. *Cf.* our pl. 131.

201. SEPULCHRE OF
THE KINGS AND
PRINCES OF
GOLCONDA

From Jean de Thévenot,
op. cit. (pl. 128), IV, between pp. 298 and 299.

    About five miles
west of Golconda city
(Hyderabad) stand the
necropolis and tombs of
the Qutb Shahi rulers
(1507–1687).

    At first sight, this de-
piction appears quite
European in conception,
but in fact it would seem
to agree with a later de-
scription: "The general
plan of the tombs is a
dome standing upon a
square base, which is surrounded by an arcade of
pointed arches. . . . The
prevailing colour is
white, in some cases
picked out with green"
(John Murray [publ.], *A
Handbook for Travellers in
India, Pakistan, Burma,
and Ceylon* [London,
1959], p. 375). Notice the
crescent, also.

202. MUGHUL [?] MIN-
IATURE PORTRAIT OF
SULTAN MUHAMMAD
QUTB OF GOLCONDA
With permission of the
Rijksmuseum-Stichtung,
Amsterdam; portrait
dated *ca.* 1630.

Muhammad Qutb
ruled from 1612 to 1626,
and is known to posterity
as a peace-loving ruler
and an able poet in Per-
sian. See H. K. Sherwani,
*History of the Qutb Shahi
Dynasty* (New Delhi,
1974), chap. v.

Quo plus sunt potæ, plus sitiuntur aquæ.

Soo niet uw dwaas gemoed, aan't goud, en aan't gesteente,
Zeer vast gebonden, en genageld was geweest,
Zoo niet de geld-zucht had bezeeten uw gebeente,
Gy zoud de beste Vorst (van wien men ergens leest)
Ia als een vader zyn geweest voor uw gemeente. D. Havart.

203. SULTAN ABDULLAH QUTB SHAH OF
GOLCONDA (R. 1626–72)
From D. Havart, *op. cit.* (pl. 198), II, facing p. 210.
With permission of the James Ford Bell Library,
University of Minnesota.

    Probably based on a Deccan miniature painting
brought from Golconda to Holland in 1686 by Laurens
Pit. See H. Goetz, "Notes on a Collection of Historical
Portraits from Golconda," *Indian Arts and Letters*, X
(1936), 12–13, 15.

Nemo felix ante obitum.

Hy was een Koning in de naam, niet inder daad,
Quam tot die waardigheyd van de alder laagste staat.
En liet door andere, zig zelf, en 't Ryk bestieren,
Een dom onnozel Mensch, niet Vorstlyk in manieren.
Toen nu 't geluk met hem een tyd lang had gepopt,
Wierd hy door eygen schuld van Kroon en Throon geschept,
Kroop in het zant, vrat stof, moest zig als slaaf vermind'ren,
Wee zulken land, alwaar de Koningen zyn kind'ren.
D. Havart.

204. SULTAN ABU'L HASAN, THE LAST RULER OF
THE QUTB SHAHI DYNASTY
From D. Havart, *op. cit.* (pl. 198), II, facing p. 214.
With permission of the James Ford Bell Library,
University of Minnesota.
"He was a king in name but not in deed," accord-
ing to the verse beneath the portrait. He ruled from
1672 to 1687. This depiction is based on a Deccan min-
iature painting brought back to Holland in 1686 by
Laurens Pit.

205. PERSIAN MINIATURE PORTRAIT OF
ABU'L HASAN
With permission of the Rijksmuseum-Stichtung, Goetz
B 33 (23) in the Witsen Collection (Amsterdam).
    In spite of Islamic injunctions against figure and por-
trait painting, Deccan painting blossomed in the reign
of Abdullah Qutb Shah (r. 1626–72). See Sherwani,
op. cit. (pl. 202), pp. 540–43.

206. PORTRAIT OF AKKANA OF GOLCONDA
With permission of the Rijksmuseum-Stichtung,
Amsterdam.
    Deccan work. See Goetz, *op. cit.* (pl. 203), p. 16.

De Konink van Golconda komt bij de Hollanders in haar Kerk.

207. SULTAN ABU'L HASAN OF GOLCONDA VISITS
(1678) THE DUTCH CHURCH AT MASULIPATAM
From D. Havart, *op. cit.* (pl. 198), I, facing p. 191.
With permission of the James Ford Bell Library,
University of Minnesota.

1. de Konink van Golconda Sultaan Aboe-il-hassan Kotbsjah. 2. den grooten Colonel Rustamrou, 3. de Bramine Piesprat Wenkatt. 4. beschikker van het Hof. 4. het Geschenk, synde een curieus Goud stuk werk. 5. de Heer Ambassadeur Laurens Pit, presenteerende zyn Last Brief, 6. Gevolg van den Ambassadeur.

208. LAURENS PIT AND THE SULTAN

From D. Havart, *op. cit.* (pl. 198), II, between pp. 158 and 159. With permission of the James Ford Bell Library, University of Minnesota.

Presentation of Laurens Pit, Dutch ambassador, to the Sultan of Golconda, "Aboe-il-hassan" (Abu'l Hasan) in 1686.

Bombay and the Portuguese Ports

The Portuguese, who had presented Bombay to England in 1661 as a dowry for King Charles II's bride, were at first reluctant to abide by the terms of their contract and wished to give up only the separate island of Bombay. A fleet of five royal warships had to be sent from England before the Portuguese resignedly gave over control of the bay and its seven islands in 1664. Upon taking over, the English discovered that Bombay Island was virtually unfortified. Because of the expense involved in fortifying the island, the king in 1668 turned it over to the Company. Thereafter its merchants, required to take over the defense and administration of Bombay, became worried as to "how they will manage the Sword as well as the Quill." The first appointee of the Company to be governor of Bombay was Sir George "Oxendine" (Oxenden), who resided generally at Surat and left the governance of Bombay to his deputy "Mr. Goodyeer" (John Goodier). On Oxenden's death in 1669 a commission of five ruled Bombay for a few months during which "this Body Politick grew up into an Anarchy." Gerald Aungier, the new president in Surat, dissolved the committee and appointed Matthew Gray as deputy governor of Bombay. His successor, Philip Gyfford, went on for three years rapidly building fortifications until he was replaced by Captain John Shaxton and "an handsome Recruit [troop] of Soldiers." Fearing a continuation of the long-term feud between soldiers and merchants, Aungier came to Bombay to take charge himself in 1671.[216]

The Dutch are the best witnesses to the progress made by the English in fortifying Bombay (see pl. 15). In the spring (1673) before Fryer arrived, the Dutch launched a surprise attack which misfired. They quickly retreated to their ships when it became apparent that the fort was heavily protected with artillery and manned by around twelve hundred well-armed soldiers. Several thousands of "Bandarines" (Mahratti, *bhandārī*) who constitute a militia also could "make a Shew" although they could not generally be relied upon in a pinch.[217] Three "Men of War" rode in the harbor, the largest mounting thirty guns. Bombay was further strengthened by the arrival of Fryer's ship. Work was thereafter begun immediately on building a moat between the fort and the sea as well as "Hornworks" for its better security.[218]

At a distance from the fort lies the town of Bombay with its mixed population of English, Portuguese, "Topazes" (Luso-Indians), Hindus, Muslims, and "Cooly" (Koli) Christians who are mostly fisherfolk. A stretch of a full mile is occupied by the town's low thatched houses, most left by the Portuguese and a few built by the Company. The customhouse and the warehouses are tiled or plastered buildings with windows whose panes are squares of polished oyster shells. In a field on the edge of the town the Portuguese

[216] For a listing of the governors and deputy governors of Bombay from 1664 to 1715 see David, *op. cit.* (n. 213), Appendix A. Fryer's list is generally correct but not complete.

[217] *Bhandārī* tended the cocopalms, made toddy, and acted as militia.

[218] Crooke (ed.), *op. cit.* (n. 4), I, 157–71. Hornworks are single-fronted outworks designed to occupy advantageous ground not included within the original fort.

"have a pretty House and Church, with Orchards of Indian fruit adjoining."
The English have only a cemetery with a few tombs in it.

Most of the town's drinking water comes from wells and nearby tanks.
The best water comes from a spring at "Masseqoung" (Mazagong) which is
"up the Bay a mile." It is a fishing village noted for its catch of "Bumbelo"
(bummelo, from Mahratti, *bombīl*) which the poorer natives eat along with
"Batty" (Mahratti, *bhāt*, Kannada, *bhātta*), "a coarse sort of Rice."[219] Around
Mazagong they grow "Batty," and the Portuguese have there another church
and a house of the Franciscans. Nearby is the town of "Parell" (Parel), with
another church and a residence of the Jesuits, as well as the village of "Siam"
(Sion), whose fields are cultivated by "Columbeens" (*Kunbis*). At Sion also
live the "Frasses," a caste of porters (Arabic, *Farrāsh*, one who spreads carpets, superintendent of tents, etc.). Each of these castes is superintended by
a "Mandadore" (Portuguese, *mandador*, commander), a member of the caste
who keeps his fellows in line and reports on them to the English authorities.
Along the coasts, pits are dug to catch the tidal waters which then evaporate
in the sun and leave sea salt encrusted on the sand.[220] At one place there is an
inlet through which the sea periodically floods "40,000 Acres of good Land"
so that it will grow nothing but "Samphire" (St. Peter's herb, a plant that
grows on tracts otherwise barren). At "Maijim" (Mahim) the Portuguese
have another church and house and the English their customs building and
guardhouse. Here the Muslims have erected a tomb to a "Peor" (Persian, *pir*,
saint) who by his prayers is said to have saved the Prophet's tomb from fire.
At the farthest end of this bay is "Salvesong" (Salveçam) where the Franciscans maintain a convent and church, and also "Verulee" (Worli) where the
English have a watchtower. Across the bay a great point "abutting against
Old Woman's island" is called Malabar Hill. At the crest of this rocky,
woody, and grassy hill a Parsi tomb has but recently been built.[221] On its
seaside are the ruins of a temple built near a tank to which the Malabars once
made pilgrimages.[222]

Fugitives and refugees from the mainland are attracted to English Bombay by hope of gain and by reason of its toleration of all religions. Around
sixty thousand persons live here, or six times more than when it was controlled by the Portuguese. Dependent on imports for its food, Bombay is
nonetheless well supplied with grain and meat at reasonable prices. More
meat is consumed here in one month than in Surat during one year. Since
the government is English, the soldiers live under military law and the free-
men under the common law. The administration is headed by the president

[219] Bummelo is a small fish (*Harpodon nehereus*) which, when dried, becomes the well-known
"Bombay Duck."

[220] The *kunbis* were the salt-makers. See David, *op. cit.* (n. 213), pp. 381–82.

[221] This is the first Parsi Tower of Silence; probably built between January, 1672, and April,
1674, it still stands on Malabar Hill. See *ibid.*, pp. 434–35.

[222] Crooke (ed.), *op. cit.* (n. 4), I, 171–77. The ruins are those of the ancient *Wālkeshwar* (Lord
of Sand) temple and tank.

and his council at Surat. Beneath the president is "a Justiciary" (Court of Judicature), a Court of Common Pleas, and a Committee for Regulation of Affairs and Complaints. The president maintains a separate council and staff in Bombay. When visiting the islands, he lives in viceregal splendor and parades from place to place with a splendid escort.[223]

Climate and other conditions at Bombay make it an unhealthy place. At first it was thought that the use of fish for manure contributed to disease, but even after this practice was prohibited, conditions did not improve. To prevent the spread of disease by "Foul Women," the Company sends out English women to propagate its colony. These imported women "beget a sickly Generation," and, as the Dutch have learned, the offspring of a European father and an Indian mother are far healthier. The English women, not always being of the highest type, "spoil their milk" in these tropical places by indulging too freely in wine and strong drink. While the mortality rate among the English is high, the more temperate natives and Luso-Asians live to "a good Old Age." The English in Bombay are "exotic plants" not able to adjust to their new environment. Despite these drawbacks the Dutch still "cast an envious Eye" on the colony. The Banyans prefer it to Surat since life is freer and taxes lower.

Of major concern to Bombay are its relations with the Portuguese, Sivaji, and the Mughuls. Peace with the Portuguese and Sivaji is necessary to protect the islands' food supplies; better relations with the Mughuls are required to encourage commerce. The rivalries of these three continental powers make it difficult to establish good relations with one without offending the others. The Portuguese, who maintain neutrality in the continental wars, are angered by Bombay's willingness to sell weapons to the combatants which might one day be turned on Christians.[224]

The nearby island of Salsette is seventy miles in circumference, twenty in length, and fifteen in width.[225] Its rich soil produces sugarcane, rice, and local fruits. The peasants are required to till as much land as necessary to pay the taxes in rice demanded by the lords of the villages, their landlords. If the peasants take land to till in their native place, they pay no other taxes. If they flee from one village to the other, their landlords bring them back by force. These villages are awarded by the Portuguese crown to veteran soldiers, other deserving persons, and the church. The gifts to the church are in perpetuity, while those granted to others are "for three Lives [generations]." Careri makes Bombay part of Salsette since only a fordable channel divides one from the other.[226] On Salsette proper there are Portuguese forts at Bandra and Vesava; Thana has five forts around it. The weavers of Thana

---

[223] *Ibid.,* pp. 177–78. On the judicial system see David, *op. cit.* (n. 213), pp. 326–49.
[224] Fryer in Crooke (ed.), *op. cit.* (n. 4), I, 178–82.
[225] Careri in Sen (ed.), *op. cit.* (n. 2), p. 179. Its area is 236 square miles. Both Fryer and Careri also use Salsette as a general name for the whole cluster of islands.
[226] Today the two are connected by a bridge and causeway.

produce textiles in quantity which are used as table linens.[227] The Jesuits, who reputedly derive more revenues from India than the king of Portugal, own "the best part of Salsette, especially its eastern spur."[228] Its Jesuit college is in a building similar to "those of our Universities" but defended by seven cannons. Salsette's port of Bandra is a large town of tiled houses. Four miles from Bandra stands a magnificent rural church in the midst of the country seats of the Portuguese gentry. The next town is "Magatana" (Magathan) with two more churches. Nearby is the famous ancient, but now ruined, city of Kanheri "all cut out of a Rock."[229] Thana, the island's chief city, has seven Catholic churches and colleges, the main one belonging to the Jesuits; the Portuguese permit only Christians to reside in Salsette. A fertile and well-watered island, Salsette exports vegetables and fruits to its neighboring islands and to Goa.[230]

According to Fryer, Bassein is a coastal town encircled with a stone wall pierced by gates which open to the four directions.[231] On its outwalls and on the circular fort in the center of town a total of forty-two "great guns" are mounted. Bassein's fortifications are sufficiently strong to protect the town from the Indians but too weak on the seaside to stand off a European attack. Near the market stands the State House, where each morning the governor consults with his nobles; "toward Evening they meet there to Game." Within its walls there are also six churches, four convents, and two colleges. One of the colleges belongs to the Jesuits and the other to the Franciscans. The Jesuit college is a fine structure, but its students live in town. Within the college there is a library, a refectory, a chapel, and the cells of the Jesuits. The classes, evidently held in the library, deal with "Historians, Moralists, Expositors, and no more." Three-quarters of the city is devoted "to their [the Jesuits'] use." Only Christians live within the city, the Banyans residing mainly in the suburbs. The Portuguese nobles have stately dwellings within the city "with covered Balconies and large Windows [of oyster shell or lattice] two Stories high." Bassein is surrounded by flat land on which sugarcane, rice, and other grains are cultivated. Many of the villages and churches outside the city have recently been destroyed by pirates from Muscat in Arabia.[232] Such raids occur frequently in retaliation for earlier Portuguese attacks on Muscat and despite the efforts of the Portuguese to sweep marauders off the seas with their annual fleets.[233]

By 1695 Bassein has eight fortresses, though some are still unfinished.

---

[227] *Thanusi,* or Thana cloth, is a striped cotton material.
[228] Careri in Sen (ed.), *op. cit.* (n. 2), pp. 179–80.
[229] On the Buddhist cave temples of Kanheri see below, pp. 796–98.
[230] Fryer in Crooke (ed.), *op. cit.* (n. 4), I, 182–89.
[231] From 1534 on, Bassein was the northern capital of Portuguese India. See *Asia,* I, 394.
[232] In 1674 six hundred Arab pirates landed unopposed to pillage this region, an indication of the growing weakness of the Portuguese.
[233] Fryer in Crooke (ed.), *op. cit.* (n. 4), I, 189–94.

One-third of the city on its north side is unpopulated because of "the Plague which some Years rages in it." [234]

Behind the city for fifteen miles are the "Cassabo" (Arabic, *qasaba*, towns or large villages) with their pleasure houses, gardens, and orchards. [235] Their soil is cultivated by Christian, Muslim, and Hindu peasants from nearby villages. To keep this garden spot green and fruitful, the cultivators water it "with certain Engines." Here they grow an abundance of sugarcane which they make into white sugar by pressing the canes between two heavy wooden rollers turned by oxen. The juice is boiled in cauldrons and cooled in earthen vessels in which it hardens into sugar. A Dominican parish church on the road to "Cassabo" houses the image of *Nossa Senhora dos Remedios*. [236] Five years ago (*ca.* 1690) this church was burnt by "Kacagi" (Kakaji), a Hindu subject of the Mughuls who plunders villages and towns on the west coast. [237] In addition to the Jesuits the Dominicans, Franciscans, and Hospitallers (Brothers of St. John of God) have in 1695 their own churches and monasteries, the Franciscans building theirs in the European style. While priests are plentiful, there are no trained lawyers in these Portuguese settlements. Civil cases are handled by "Canarins" (probably Konkanis or Luso-Asians), who are so ignorant that they sometimes "Plead both for Plaintiff and Defendant" before judges untrained in the law. Careri is asked to stay on at a high salary to act as advocate for the monasteries. Not wanting to live in these hot places, he declines the offer. [238]

North of Bassein is Damão, a small but attractive Portuguese town and fortress on the north bank of the Damanganga. Built "after the Italian manner," new or Portuguese Damão is regularly laid out with straight and broad intersecting streets lined with single-storied, detached houses. It has four modern, well-built fortresses, but they are not well supplied with cannon. A good garrison, governed by a Portuguese captain, is maintained at Damão; a royal factor manages its customs and trade. [239] Its inhabitants are Portuguese, Luso-Asians, Hindus, and Muslims; only its Christians are allowed freedom of worship. In addition to a parish church, Damão has monasteries of the Jesuits, Franciscan Recollects, and Augustinians. On the other side of the river is old Damão where Hindus and Muslims live in mud-and-thatch huts. The harbor between the two settlements can be entered by ves-

---

[234] Probably a reference to the plague of 1689. Between 1685 and 1696 there were severe outbreaks of plague in western India. See David, *op. cit.* (n. 213), p. 405.

[235] On the "*Cacabe de Bacaim*" see J. Gerson da Cunha, *Notes on the History and Antiquities of Chaul and Bassein* (Bombay, 1876), pp. 157–58. Other Portuguese coastal settlements had similar suburbs.

[236] *Cf.* below, p. 809.

[237] Kakaji was the ruler of Jawhar state in the *Koli* country south of Surat. He was called the "Koli King" by the Portuguese. See Da Cunha, *op. cit.* (n. 235), p. 164n.

[238] Sen (ed.), *op. cit.* (n. 2), pp. 166–70.

[239] Damão was taken by the Portuguese in 1558 and it thereafter became one of their permanent establishments on India's west coast.

sels "great or small" only at flood tide; it is defended by a small fortress located in old Damão. The Mughuls have tried unsuccessfully several times to take Damão; the most recent attempt was a siege by an army of eighty thousand, which took place fifty-five years ago.[240]

The high-living Portuguese of Damão are served by many slaves. When traveling about the city, the Europeans, including priests and women, are carried in palanquins. In rainy weather, they travel in another kind of conveyance called an "Andora" (Portuguese for litter), which has a palm leaf covering, with windows and doors on both sides. On the palanquins the bamboos are bent, so the rider may sit up; on the "Andora" they are straight, so the rider must lie down (see plate 128). Meat and fish are scarce in Damão, but the breads, including those made of rice, are extraordinarily good. Native fruits and European vegetables are readily available. Particularly good are the roots of the cassava, which have the size and taste of a chestnut. Game is abundant, particularly various sorts of deer, wild boars, and birds. Europeans must eat regularly and lightly or run the danger of contracting an incurable disease such as cholera. Experience has shown that European medicines are of no use in curing the local diseases. Consequently European physicians in India must learn from their Indian colleagues "to be fit to Practice." The Portuguese of Damão build ships called "Galavetta" (gallivats or *jalia*, a kind of galley) which are "all Pinn'd with Wood, and Caulk'd with Cotton."[241]

Ovington, who visited Bombay during the worst part of the year in 1690, and immediately after its occupation by the Mughuls, is most pessimistic about the colony's future.[242] The monsoon is so violent on this coast that "it hinders all Navigation, and puts a general stop to all Journeys by land" from late May to mid-September. At the end of this season, the Banyans throw gilded coconuts into the sea to pacify it for navigation.[243] Violent thunderstorms called the "Elephant" herald both the onset and departure of the southward monsoon.[244] Once the monsoon ends, the dry season sets in and the weather becomes progressively hotter over the next eight or nine months. At Bombay more Europeans die after the monsoons in September and October "than generally in all the Year besides." Its rank air and foul water

---

[240] A reference to the siege of 1638 when Aurangzib was viceroy of the Deccan. The siege of four or five months failed; still, the Portuguese continued to pay rent to the Mughuls.

[241] Careri in Sen (ed.), *op. cit.* (n. 2), pp. 158–62. On gallivats see Roy, *op. cit.* (n. 133), pp. 59–60.

[242] For a modern map of its harbor see Rawlinson (ed.), *op. cit.* (n. 3), facing p. 80. In the 1696 edition (opposite p. 146) there are two prints of the citadel and fort of Bombay as of 1678.

[243] The Hindu festival of *Nārali Purnima*, or Coconut Day, when the sea is worshipped and fairs held along the west coast. See R. M. Lall, *Among the Hindus: A Study of Hindu Festivals* (Cawnpore, 1933), pp. 149–51.

[244] The "Elephant" is the Hindu constellation *Hasta* (thirteenth lunar mansion) which coincides with the end of the southwest monsoon. *Hasta* is Sanskrit for "hand." From it is derived indirectly Hindi *hāthī*, or elephant, since the trunk of the elephant is its hand. See Yule and Burnell, *op. cit.* (n. 124), p. 412, under Anglo-Indian "Hatty." Also see above, pp. 639–40, and below, p. 1145.

make Bombay a very unhealthy place. Fatalistically the English say that "Two Mussouns are the Age of a Man." In the malignant air of the monsoon spiders, frogs, and toads grow to an immense size. Wounds and bruises heal only slowly, if at all. The Company encourages matches between its factors and English women, but the offspring of these marriages rarely survive infancy in Bombay.[245]

The governor of Bombay resides in its fort and from there presides over military and civil affairs.[246] Both the English and the Portuguese possess fine dwellings which beautify the island. The Portuguese freely practice their religion in their own chapels. Because of the war with the Mughuls, the English have not completed their church but hold twice-daily services in a room especially set aside in the fort.[247] The Hindus likewise enjoy freedom of worship in their small temples. The occupation by the Sidis forced many English to leave the island and wrecked its coconut production, the source of a "staple income." Difficulties between the Mughuls and the English began because Aurangzib arbitrarily raised the duty from 2½ to 4 percent. When the English refused to pay these new exactions, his officials systematically harassed the Company's servants. After a number of forays at sea, Sidi Yakrut brought a land army to a Bombay totally unprepared to meet such a challenge. Although the Mughuls outnumbered the English ten to one, they were able only to besiege the fortress. Once English ammunition began to run out, the governor sued for peace. Governor Child died before terms could be arrived at, and his successor George Wildon quickly married his widow and heiress. While the English fought for their lives in Bombay, the Jesuits supported the Mughuls with money and supplies as they urged the Sidis to exterminate the Protestants.[248]

5

THE DECCAN WARS, RAJPUTS, AND SIVAJI

Mughul expansion southward to the Deccan had begun early in Akbar's reign. He and his successors continued this drive by fits and starts, becom-

[245] Rawlinson (ed.), *op. cit.* (n. 3), pp. 81–89. The Company's policy of sending out English women was gradually abandoned.

[246] The seat of the Company was moved from Surat to Bombay in 1687, when John Child was in charge. Ovington stayed with George Cook, its deputy governor during the presidency (February 4, 1690–May 10, 1694) of Bartholemew Harris.

[247] Bombay church (now St. Thomas' Cathedral) was planned by Governor Aungier. It was not completed until 1718. In February, 1689, Sidi Yakrut, the Mughul admiral, landed on Bombay with twenty thousand men. He forced Governor Child out of office and exacted tribute from the Company before withdrawing in May, 1690. Sidis, originally African Muslims, worked as mercenaries for Indian princes. The Sidi ruler of Janjira, an island on India's west coast, was the admiral of the Mughul fleet based at Surat.

[248] Rawlinson (ed.), *op. cit.* (n. 3), pp. 90–96. In 1691 and thereafter the Company confiscated the lands of those who had not remained loyal to its government, including the Jesuit estates.

ing especially active when not faced by more pressing problems in the north. Their main efforts were directed against the Muslim states of Khandesh, Berar, Bihar, Ahmadnagar, Bijapur, and Golconda; the early Mughul drives were sometimes abetted by the benevolent neutrality or active support of the independent Hindu rajas of Rajputana. Aurangzib while prince first became viceroy of the Mughul Deccan in 1637. Throughout the remainder of his long career he was more actively and successfully engaged in the conquest of this region than his predecessors had been. While he was successful in conquering the two large Muslim states of Bijapur (1686) and Golconda (1687), he also aroused the resistance of the Hindu rajas and the Mahrattas to his rule.[249] Sivaji (1630–80), the Mahratta leader, created a Hindu resistance to Aurangzib's southward movement which ultimately frustrated the emperor's plans. Sivaji also established a Deccan state based in Poona, over which he officially became raja in 1674. As a result of the constant wars which followed between the Mughuls and the Mahrattas, the Deccan was desolated and impoverished by the end of Aurangzib's era.[250]

The European merchants and travelers based in Surat, Bombay, and other west-coast ports watched closely the power struggle in the Deccan. Trade, they thought, would benefit, and their own precarious coastal positions would be rendered safer, by a resolution of these internal struggles. Even Bernier, in distant Delhi, reports on the Deccan wars early in Aurangzib's reign. He writes that these wars have been raging "during more than forty years" and involve the Mughuls, Golconda, Bijapur, and several lesser states. The Shiite Muslim kingdoms of the Deccan, once united, are now divided among themselves and act in concert only to prevent a Mughul conquest. For a long time Golconda preserved its independence by using its wealth to finance Bijapur's army and to bribe the Mughul generals. But ever since Aurangzib as prince invaded Golconda, it has been a vassal of the Mughul Empire.[251] The ruler of Golconda has "lost all mental energy and has ceased to hold the reins of government." He never ventures out of the fortress of Golconda and permits his nobles to "exercise a disgusting tyranny." In 1667, when Bernier visits Golconda, the Mughul ambassador and Aurangzib's other representatives exercise an "uncontrolled authority" there. Unlike Golconda, Bijapur "still preserves the name of an independent kingdom." It lies behind a series of almost impregnable mountain fortresses and its capital city is especially well defended. Bijapur is, however, "verging towards dissolution," for the fortresses of "Paranda" (Parenda) and "Bidu" (Bidar) have fallen to the Mughuls and it now faces a succession crisis. Sivaji profits from these unsettled conditions to capture fortresses and to ravage the countryside "from Surat to the gates of Goa," while he laughs at the

---

[249] On Bijapur and Golconda see below, pp. 855–63, 1021–28.
[250] On these wars see Sarkar, *op. cit.* (n. 17), chaps. x, xi, xiv, xv. Also see Hallissey, *op. cit.* (n. 65).
[251] See above, pp. 698–99; and, below, pp. 1073–75.

threats of Bijapur and the Mughuls. He attracts to his side the unemployed soldiers of the Deccan and constantly harasses the Mughuls. He unintentionally serves Bijapur well by distracting the attention of the Mughuls "by his bold and never-ceasing enterprises"[252]

While he still lived, the fame of Sivaji began to reach Europe through the reports of European factors and travelers and in the incidental references to his activities in the writings of Tavernier and Bernier.[253] Thévenot was the first author, European or Indian, to attempt a biographical sketch of this Hindu rebel, general, and statesman. Impressed by what he heard and saw with respect to Sivaji's siege (January, 1664) of Surat, Thévenot attempts a history of his early career to 1666. Son of a captain of Bijapur, Sivaji was born at Bassein.[254] Possessed of a turbulent spirit, he rebelled while his father was still alive against the sultan of Bijapur. Putting himself at the head of a rebel band, Sivaji established himself strongly in the mountains of Bijapur and regularly turned back the forces sent against him. The sultan, believing that the father was traitorously conspiring with his rebellious son, threw the former into prison. When his father died in prison, Sivaji swore revenge against Bijapur.[255] He plundered its countryside, seized certain of its towns, and attracted many new followers to his standard. By the time of the sultan's death, Sivaji had created a "little State" of his own, the Mahratta kingdom. The queen regent of Bijapur, failing to quell his activities, agreed to the peace terms he presented to her.[256] Raja Sivaji then attacked places belonging to the Mughuls; a large force was subsequently sent against him led by "Chasta-Can" (Shaista Khan), the uncle of Aurangzib and the local governor.[257] Sivaji was driven into the mountains by the superior Mughul forces who then occupied his kingdom.

Impatient to regain his kingdom, Sivaji duped the Mughuls into accepting his services. Once he had won Shaista Khan's confidence, the raja boldly attacked Shaista Khan's tent in 1663 and carried off his treasure and his

---

[252] Constable (ed.), *op. cit.* (n. 1), pp. 191–98. Sarkar fails to include Bernier among the European sources on Sivaji. See Sarkar, *op. cit.* (n. 22), pp. 190–94. On the decline of Golconda see below, pp. 1090–94.

[253] See Sen (trans. and ed.), *op. cit.* (n. 6), pp. 1–2.

[254] Actually he was born at Shivner near Junnar. For Thévenot's account of Sivaji see Sen (ed.), *op. cit.* (n. 2), pp. 38–43.

[255] His father was called Shahji Bhonsle. On his quarrels with the 'Adil Shahs of Bijapur see Sarkar, *op. cit.* (n. 22), pp. 64–67. Shahji did not die in prison as Thévenot asserts. He was killed many years later while hunting.

[256] Sivaji's rise to power occurred during the reign of Muhammad 'Adil Shah (1627–56). His independent Mahratta state was carved out of Bijapur's territory. Muhammad was succeeded by 'Ali 'Adil Shah II (r. 1656–72), a youth of eighteen who ruled under the queen regent, Bari Sahib, sister of the Qutb Shah of Golconda. Bijapur, constantly under pressure from the Deccan armies of the Mughuls, hereafter was caught between Aurangzib and Sivaji as it desperately struggled for survival. See M. A. Nayeem, *External Relations of the Bijapur Kingdom, 1489–1686 A.D.* (Hyderabad, 1974), pp. 25–27. *Cf.* the biography of Sivaji by Fryer in Crooke (ed.), *op. cit.* (n. 4), II, 59–61.

[257] Shaista Khan was the maternal uncle of the emperor; he was appointed viceroy of the Deccan in 1659.

daughter. On the payment of a ransom, the daughter was shortly returned to her father. Meanwhile Sivaji warned Shaista Khan he would certainly not escape with his own life unless he withdrew from the Mahratta lands. Realizing that the cost of tracking Sivaji down in the mountains was too high, the emperor ordered the withdrawal of Shaista Khan's occupying army. To revenge himself on the Mughuls, Sivaji prepared to attack Surat and to plunder its vaunted riches. Disguised as a fakir, Sivaji himself reconnoitered the city in 1664. Once he had decided upon his strategy, the raja returned to his headquarters between Bassein and Chaul. Taking four thousand men, he secretly advanced on Surat and set up camp before its Burhanpur gate. To mislead its governor about his intentions, Sivaji asked for guides to conduct him to another place. Without responding, the governor retired to the fortress and sent for assistance. The town's inhabitants fled to the country, while Sivaji's men entered the city and plundered it for four days. Several houses were burned and many pillaged. The English and Dutch saved their places by mounting their cannons before them. Without artillery of his own, Sivaji did not dare to attack either the Europeans or the fortress. Fearful that a siege would take valuable time during which assistance might arrive, Sivaji withdrew his forces and took with him as booty only that which had been pillaged from the populace. On his orders the monastery of the Capuchins and the homes of the Christian converts went untouched.[258]

While the emperor was shocked by Sivaji's boldness, he was then otherwise occupied and so determined to postpone his revenge. Pretending to admire Sivaji's valor, the emperor invited him to court in 1666. After an imperial safe conduct was issued, the raja and his son went to the court. For the first few months of the stay he met with a warm reception, for the emperor knew that Sivaji had many friends among the Hindu rajas at court. When the emperor's attitude began to cool, Sivaji boldly announced that if he were killed, many there would revenge his death. Fearing an insurrection of the other rajas, Aurangzib protested that he had no intention of killing Sivaji but merely wanted his cooperation. Not trusting the emperor's reassurances and promises, Sivaji with the aid of his friends managed to effect an escape. "This Raja," writes Thévenot, "is short and tawny, with quick eyes that shew a great deal of wit." In 1664, when he pillaged Surat, "he was but thirty-five years of age."[259]

Carré, an ardent admirer of Sivaji, assiduously gleaned from others the details about the earlier career of "one of the greatest men the East has ever seen." Like Gustavus Adolphus of Sweden, Sivaji is renowned for "his courage, the rapidity of his conquests, and his great qualities." He spared the foreign factories in anticipation of someday being allied with the Euro-

---

[258] Bernier corroborates this story of sparing the Capuchin house. See Constable (ed.), *op. cit.* (n. 1), pp. 188–89. Thévenot gives a brief account of Father Ambrose's activities in Sen (ed.), *op. cit.* (n. 2), pp. 44–45.

[259] Sen (ed.), *op. cit.* (n. 2), pp. 38–43. The following material on Sivaji from the Abbé Carré is translated into English in Sen (trans. and ed.), *op. cit.* (n. 6).

peans. Facing almost no organized resistance, Sivaji's sack of Surat lasted "three days and three nights." With new war funds in hand, Sivaji mobilized a large army. He occupied unprotected places in Bijapur, especially along its coast, thinking they would be easier to protect and would open the sea to him. He ordered the governors of these maritime places to treat the Europeans well. His tactic was to move against the interior forts and then quickly switch his efforts to cause havoc at some distant place. He ravaged the Portuguese territories near Goa and took the island of Bardez (in 1667). He cultivated and propagandized tradesmen and artisans to win their support. Aurangzib, apprehensive of Sivaji's growing strength, replaced his Deccan general with "Jesseingue" (Jai Singh I). The new general of the Deccan was instructed to win over Sivaji to the Mughul cause by offering him great honors. Since Aurangzib wanted Sivaji to lead an army against Persia, the emperor invited him to court.

While honors were heaped upon Sivaji in Agra, a plot was contrived to kill him. In fear of his life, Sivaji escaped from Agra and returned to his army determined to found a lawful kingdom of his own. With the support of his officers, he founded a state based on his earlier conquests. To consolidate his kingdom, he required new funds. He resolved once again therefore to sack Surat. With some twelve thousand men he entered (in 1670) this city of four hundred thousand inhabitants without meeting serious resistance. He conspired with its governor and was able to plunder the city without a fight. Again he spared the Europeans. Once Aurangzib learned of this second sack, he had Surat's traitorous governor poisoned.

The sequel to Sivaji's history is based on what Carré learned during his second voyage of 1672 to 1674. Through guile and bribes, Sivaji won over Romton Jaman, a Bijapur general and provincial governor. The traitor was replaced by "Abdelkasn" (Abdul Khan), a voluptuary and former friend of Sivaji, who had the two hundred women of his harem killed before departing for the army.[260] When Abdul Khan's army finally confronted Sivaji, a conference between the two generals was held. Sivaji drew a concealed dagger from his vest and stabbed to death his former friend. His army then fell upon the disorganized forces of Bijapur, half of whom surrendered and came over to Sivaji. Thereafter Sivaji's enlarged army occupied many important places in Bijapur which were incorporated peacefully into his growing kingdom. Using the loot from his new conquests, Sivaji prepared an army for campaigns in Gujarat. He entrusted this new command to his son, whom he himself had trained in the profession of war. The soldiers had as much respect and regard for the son as they had for the father.[261] While the

---

[260] This is a local tradition. Abdul Khan, better known as Afzal Khan, had his palace just northwest of Bijapur city. Adjoining the palace is a mosque next to which stand eleven rows of identical tombs of females. See Murray (publ.), *op. cit.* (n. 40), p. 387. For the sequel to Carré's history see Sen (trans. and ed.), *op. cit.* (n. 6), II, 1–85.

[261] This evaluation of Sambhaji, the son, runs directly counter to the Mahratta tradition which depicts him as a wicked rebel. See Sarkar, *op. cit.* (n. 22), p. 195.

prince advanced in Gujarat, Sivaji sent another army to attack the western ports between Chaul and Surat and to depose their quasi-independent rulers. After three difficult campaigns, Sivaji's army subjugated most of these petty princes. Sivaji then assigned governors and garrisons to these restive conquests.[262] The Portuguese of Damão hoped that Sivaji's conquest would relieve them of paying annual tribute to these local rulers. But Sivaji had other plans. Once his forces had occupied the entire coast and the backlands from Damão to Chaul, he himself led an army to conquer the region between Chaul and Goa. By this expedition he drove the Portuguese from Chaul and made himself master of an additional number of opulent trading towns. Upon returning inland he left governors and garrisons in these coastal places.

Carré meets the governor of Chaul in 1673 to obtain a safe conduct to pass through Sivaji's territory to Rajapur, where the French had a factory. The governor tells him that Sivaji is a man whose unbounded vision is exceeded only by his capacities as soldier and politician. He is portrayed as a close student of warfare, fortification, and the geography and topography of India. He spends money lavishly to keep informants and spies in other courts. Sambhaji, his son, is now in Gujarat trying to conclude a secret understanding with one of Aurangzib's discontented sons. Sivaji deliberately does not invest and garrison the unfortified coastal places but leaves them to the Portuguese and others to encourage trade and to discourage resistance to his authority.

In crossing the peninsula from Chaul to San Thomé, Carré receives nothing but courtesy from Sivaji's officers and troops.[263] Sivaji, after leaving defeated Bijapur, learns of the death of its king ('Ali 'Adil Shah II) and of the regency set up for his young heir.[264] While Sivaji is occupied on the west coast, "Cavescan" (Khawas Khan), the regent, receives an embassy from Aurangzib which seeks an alliance between Bijapur and the Mughuls directed against Sivaji.[265] In the meantime Sivaji threatens to attack one place or the other while driving his troops hither and yon to keep the enemy off balance. It is feared in particular that he plans to attack Ahmadabad, "one of the richest and strongest towns of the Mogol." Instead he surprises them all by appearing in Golconda, while its troops are engaged in the siege of San Thomé, to demand a ransom of its ruler. Unable to resist Sivaji, Golconda saves itself from being sacked by paying the ransom asked.[266] With his new funds Sivaji retires to his kingdom to rest his troops and to build and rebuild

---

[262] This is a reference to Moropant's conquest in 1672 of Jawhar and Ramnagar.

[263] Carré was carrying royal orders to Admiral de La Haye who was besieged at San Thomé in 1673–74 by the Dutch and the forces of Golconda.

[264] 'Ali 'Adil Shah II died in 1672 when his heir, Sikandar, was but four years old.

[265] These negotiations of 1673–74 proved to be abortive because of the overthrow of Khawas Khan. See Nayeem, *op. cit.* (n. 256), pp. 173–74.

[266] Sivaji arrived at Hyderabad in 1672 with a large Mahratta force and took back to Rigarh a huge sum of money. See H. K. Sherwani, *History of the Qutb Shāhī Dynasty* (New Delhi, 1974), p. 636.

his fortifications. While the great warrior relaxes, Bijapur continues frenziedly to prepare itself for a major onslaught by Sivaji.[267]

Thévenot visits the Deccan himself on the way to Golconda. "Doltabad" (Daulatabad), the capital of Balaghat before its conquest by the Mughuls, was once a great center of trade. It has been superseded by Aurangabad through Aurangzib's endeavors when he was governor of the Deccan.[268] Daulatabad, a town of moderate size, stretches from east to west and is surrounded by sound walls, battlements, and towers in which cannons are mounted. It is, however, the citadel which "makes it accounted the strongest place belonging to the Mogul." The fortress is located on an oval hill that rises from the middle of the town. At its base the hill has "a Wall of a natural smooth rock." On its summit is a "good Citadel . . . whereon the King's Palace stands." While Thévenot made these observations from outside the town's walls, he later learned more about the fortress from a Frenchman who had lived in it for two years. Besides the citadel there are three other forts further down the hill called "Barcot," "Marcot," and "Calecot," the word "Cot" meaning fort "in Indian."[269]

From Daulatabad, Thévenot and his companions start out for "Calvar" (Kalavaral), the last town belonging to the Mughuls at the frontier with Golconda. On the way he passes through eight villages and towns and a heavily populated countryside. At the town of "Ambar" (Ambad) he sees and describes a stately tank and notices a small underground Hindu temple to which many worshippers flock. Near the town of "Nandier" (Nander on the north bank of the Godavari) he is diverted by juggling and gymnastic acts, which he describes at length. After some days' travel, he arrives at "Indour" (Indur) "which belongs to a Raja who owes the Mogul no more than he thinks fit" and who sides in the wars between the Mughuls and Golconda "always with the strongest."[270] In Indur's vicinity there is an ornate stone temple on a hill called "Chitanagar" (Sitanagar) which he compares in its interior organization to the eighth-century Kailasa temple at Ellora.[271] At the foot of the hill is a partially finished palace and a lengthy reservoir. Both the temple and the residence had been built by "a Rich Raspouti" who died before their completion.[272] At the next town of "Indelvai" (Indalvai), iron is

---

[267] Cf. D. G. Keswané, "Shivaji through Foreign Eyes," in N. H. Kulkarnee (ed.), *Chhatrapati Shivaji, Architect of Freedom* (Delhi, 1975), pp. 182–98; and V. G. Hatalkar, "French Sources for the History of Shivaji," in *ibid.*, pp. 199–205. For Sivaji's activities in the vicinity of Goa, see below, pp. 853, 861.

[268] In 1636 it was taken from the Nizam Shahi king when Ahmadnagar was merged into the Mughul Empire. See Sen (ed.), *op. cit.* (n. 2), pp. 107–8.

[269] The stronghold of Daulatabad dates from the eleventh century and is one of the best-preserved Hindu fortresses of India. For a modern description, illustrations, and photographs see Toy, *op. cit.* (n. 138), chap. vii.

[270] Sen (ed.), *op. cit.* (n. 2), p. 110. Indur is the modern Nizamabad.

[271] On Ellora, see below, pp. 795–796.

[272] This "modern" temple, Thévenot observes, is like the ancient temples in that "the Architectors make the Basis, Body, and Capital of their Pillars, of one single piece [of stone]." See Sen (ed.), *op. cit.* (n. 2), p. 112. No traces of these structures seem to exist today.

mined which is fashioned into swords, daggers, and lances known throughout the Indies. For the moment this town is nearly depopulated because
Sivaji's brother has invaded its precincts.[273]

In the rainy season of 1673 the Mughul fleet under Admiral "Siddy" (Sidi
Sambal), a former "Lord of Ducaan" (Deccan), winters in Bombay harbor.
In reality he is part of the general Mughul effort to recover the seacoast
taken by Sivaji.[274] But Sivaji defies these naval efforts and remains safely en-
sconced in his strong fortress at "Dan de Rajapour" (Danda Rajpuri). In
fact, he is preparing to be installed as maharaja at his court of "Rairee" (Rairi
or Rajgad). To regularize their relations with Sivaji, the governor of Bombay sends an embassy to Rairi.[275] Fryer obtained a copy of the ambassador's
journal which he summarizes in his own book and with his own romaniza-
tions of Indian names and terms.[276]

From Bombay, the embassy proceeds to Portuguese Chaul and then to
"Upper Choul" (Muslim Chaul), a mart formerly of importance in the Deccan trade but now ruined by the wars. They make a goodwill visit to its
"Subidar" (Persian, *shahbandar,* or *sūbahdār,* governor), who commands the
ports and towns on the coast directly opposite Bombay. Then they sail up
the Chaul River to "Estheny" (Astarni), "Nishampore" (Nizampur), and
"Gongouly" (Gongavali). On the way to Rairi they learn that Sivaji is at the
moment on a pilgrimage to "Purtaabgur" (Pratapgad) to worship at the
shrine of "Bowany" (Bhawani) prior to his coronation.[277] They must await
his return before being allowed to enter the city. While waiting, the English
show their letters and presents to his "Procurator" to win his cooperation in
presenting their case. Informally they urge a peaceful resolution, in the interests of trade, of the differences outstanding between Sivaji and Bijapur.
They are told that such a conclusion might be forthcoming after the coronation, since Bijapur is weary of the war and has already made overtures of
peace.[278]

Finally the English receive word of Sivaji's return to Rairi and are soon
granted permission to ascend the hill. Fortified by nature, Rairi is reached
by a single road protected by two narrow gates and lined by high walls and
ramparts; the rest of the mountain "is a direct Precipice." On its summit

---

[273] Sen (ed.), *op. cit.* (n. 2), pp. 113–15.

[274] On the English relations with Sidi Sambal see Roy, *op. cit.* (n. 133), pp. 147–49.

[275] In 1674 Governor Aungier sent Henry Oxinden, two English factors, and an interpreter to
Rairi to settle the damages claimed by the British when Sivaji took Rajapur in 1659–60, to
obtain permission to trade in the ports he controlled, to get a guarantee of freedom to trade
between those ports and the marts of the Deccan, to work out an agreement for the free circulation of English money in his dominions, and to bring up the question of the disposal of shipwrecks. For Oxinden's instructions see Sen (trans. and ed.), *op. cit.* (n. 6), pp. 288–303.

[276] For the original text of Oxinden's *Journal* see *ibid.,* pp. 307–15. For Fryer's version see
Crooke (ed.), *op. cit.* (n. 4), I, 198–209.

[277] Bhawani was the favorite goddess of his family.

[278] After Sivaji's coronation on June 5, 1674, he actually continued a languid war against Bijapur while assuming the role of protector of the Deccan against the Mughuls. See Nayeem, *op.
cit.* (n. 256), pp. 204–5.

stand three hundred buildings, including the palace and the residences of the ministers. The entire settlement, two and one-half miles in length, is located on an arid spot without trees or cultivation. Four days after their arrival the English delegation is received by Sivaji, even though he is busy preparing for his coronation and marriage. After assuring the envoys of his goodwill, he turns their documents over to his chancellor, "Moro Pundit" (Moro Trimal Pingle, a Deshest Brahman), for examination and review. To speed the negotiations, the English are advised to present appropriate gifts to the various officers of the court.

While the English press for action, they witness the weighing of the raja against gold. They attend the coronation rites and present a diamond ring as their gift of congratulation. They observe that Sivaji sits on a magnificent throne and that his son "Samba Gi Rajah" (Sambhaji) and an eminent Brahman sit "on an Ascent under the throne." Many emblems of dominion and government hang on each side of the throne upon gilded lances. On the right hang two large fish with golden heads and large teeth;[279] on the left hang several "horses Tails" (yak tails) and a pair of golden scales as an emblem of justice. As they leave the palace, they see the figures of two small elephants, one on each side of its gate and two horses with golden trappings. Two days after the coronation Sivaji, without ceremony, marries his fourth wife. A few days later he signs the agreement with the English granting all their requests except for the right to use their money in his lands.[280]

As part of Governor Aungier's diplomatic program, Fryer in 1674 is sent to work as a physician at "Jeneah" (Junnar, a Mughul hill fortress near Poona) in the Deccan.[281] He goes by way of Thana and Bassein to "Gullean" (Kalyan) where Sivaji's jurisdiction begins. Quickly granted a pass, he leaves Kalyan and "the most Glorious Ruins of the Mahometans in Duccan." This city, once a major emporium, has been a victim of the wars waged in its vicinity by the Portuguese, the Mughuls, and Sivaji. The road to "Intvally" (Titvala), seven miles in length, as well as the village itself, has suffered a like devastation. From here he proceeds by night to the "poor village of Moorbar" (Murbad), whose inhabitants are "ignorant Idolaters and Husbandmen"; their pitiful harvests are reaped by Sivaji's men. Conditions improve as he moves towards the "lofty mountains" of the Western Ghats. The town of "Dehir" (Dehir) at the foot of these mountains is an armed camp awaiting trouble at any time. Sivaji stables his best horses here and one of his "Halvadars" (*havaldār*, commander), or petty generals, runs the town. From here the mountain fortresses and watchtowers of Sivaji can be seen. The ascent to these lofty garrisons is up a tortuous and narrow footpath laid hap-

[279] Fish are often regarded as holy. These are known as the *māhī wa marātib*. See Sarkar, *op. cit.* (n. 22), p. 192.
[280] On the Mahratta-English treaty of 1674 see David, *op. cit.* (n. 213), pp. 214–16.
[281] Junnar is about fifty-six miles north of Poona and about sixteen miles east of the crest of the Western Ghats. Its fort was built in 1436. Sivaji plundered it in 1657, but its Mughul garrison soon returned.

hazardly with stone steps so steep as to require clambering on all fours. On the mountain's summit is a "sad Starving Town" where a toll station is located. At the end of a deep and circuitous valley further on is "Aumbegaum" (Ambegaon), a town on the Ghod River. The long uphill road to Junnar ends at "Beelseer" (Belsar), a town which faces a vast plateau with Junnar at its opposite end. From this fortress base, war has long been waged in the Deccan by the Mughuls.

Arrived at Junnar at the end of April, 1675, Fryer is lodged outside of town in a palace with a "compleat Garden, adorned with Cypress Trees (not usual in India)" as well as tanks, waterways, and walks.[282] On May 1 he is received by the governor at a durbar held in his own apartment within the fortress. The governor sits in "a Seat of State" with his nobles to his right. Since the floor is cushioned by a soft mat covered with white calico, Fryer takes off his shoes. Then he delivers the letter from his president and is seated on the governor's left in the place of honor. Those who follow perform the following salutations: salaam, receive permission for an audience, leave their slippers below, mount the "Buchansia" (Hindi, *bichhauna*, the padded cotton flooring of the durbar hall), bow "by first putting their Hands to their Heads, then to the Feet" in the salute prescribed for approaching "Cauns [khans] or Dukes."[283] Persons of distinction sit cross-legged in the governor's presence, while those of lesser rank kneel and sit on their heels.

The fortress itself, a "large, but rude" structure of "raw brick," is more like a camp than a bastion. It is not prepared to endure a siege by Sivaji; should such an eventuality occur, its defenders would have to either flee or join the main Mughul army of forty thousand horsemen stationed permanently three days' journey away at "Pergom" (Pedgaon) under the command of "Badur Caun" (Bahadur Khan).[284]

On an auspicious day Fryer is admitted to the harem to examine one of the governor's four wives. Standing beside her curtained bed, the physician is permitted to take the lady's pulse and talk to her through an interpreter. Pleased with Fryer's treatment, the governor invites him to return the next day to bleed another of his wives. On this occasion the lady extends her arm through a curtain which covers the entry to a room. The curious women (the governor had more than three hundred concubines) accidentally pull down the curtain in their eagerness to have a peek at this strange man. "Fluttering like so many Birds," the women put their hands over their faces and "continue looking through the wide Lattice of their Fingers." Before the

[282] Cypresses are planted as garden trees in northwest India.

[283] Though his names for the traditional salutations are indecipherable, Fryer knows that different ranks are entitled to different modes of salutation. The rules of salutation were fixed by Akbar.

[284] Crooke (ed.), *op. cit.* (n. 4), I, 306–26. Later called *Khān Khānān,* Bahadur Khan was commander-in-chief and acting viceroy of the Deccan from January, 1673, to August, 1677. See Sarkar, *op. cit.* (n. 17), p. 213.

curtain is replaced, Fryer glimpses a room where the women have been at work preparing foods and doing needlework like good housewives. Their cloister is run by "Toothless Old Women and Beardless Eunuchs" who guard, serve, and spy on them. The women are entertained by "Singing Wenches" who are dressed like men except for the veils they wear when outside the harem.[285]

Once he is on friendly terms with the governor, Fryer inquires as to why the Mughuls do not pacify the Deccan and open direct trade with Bombay. While the governor maintains that Sivaji's strength is underestimated, Fryer is convinced that the Mughul generals do not want to win the war, since they and their soldiers would then be unemployed. After this unsatisfactory conversation, Fryer begins to visit the environs of Junnar. One of the local sights is a garden given "by a common Strumpet" which includes a tomb dedicated to her memory and a wellspring from which aqueducts conduct water to the city.[286] Nearby is a ruined palace where Aurangzib lived as an avowed fakir during his father's reign. On another occasion Fryer visits "Dungeness" (Ganesh Dongar), a city of "like Antiquity and Workmanship as Canorein [Kanheri]." It is cut out of "a Mountainous Rock, with a Temple and other Spacious Halls."[287]

Fryer also inspects the "Gur" (*garh*, hill fort) of Shivner where the Mughuls maintain a garrison and large numbers of horses and camels. Here stand the tombs of former rulers and a mosque of polished marble. Its governor is a poor but learned official named "Nishambek" (Nizam Beg). He knows Persian and Arabic and is intrigued by European dress, customs, weapons, and military discipline. In the fortress are vast granaries and food enough for one thousand families to endure a siege of seven years' duration. For weapons they have a few small pieces of artillery but depend mainly on stones which they roll down the precipice to halt an enemy attack. From these heights can be seen the many caves which honeycomb the hills surrounding Junnar.

Sivaji, because Shivner was his birthplace, is determined to regain control of its fortress.[288] He has made efforts to bribe its governor and to lure away its ill-paid—often unpaid—defenders. Religion does not prevent Hindu soldiers from deserting to the Mughuls or Muslims from joining Sivaji's plunderers. Cavalrymen are generally Mughuls and the infantrymen Hindus.

---

[285] Crooke (ed.), *op. cit.* (n. 4), I, 326–28. On the status of women in Mughul India see M. Yasin, *A Social History of Islamic India, 1605–1748* (2d rev. ed.; New Delhi, 1974), pp. 105–9; on harem life and the aristocracy see P. Ojha, *North Indian Social Life during the Mughal Period* (Delhi, 1975), pp. 141–44.

[286] Still known as Uma's garden. This area is renowned for its deep springs which rise in pools.

[287] Crooke (ed.), *op. cit.* (n. 4), I, 328–32. The Buddhist caves are north of Junnar. For a thorough discussion of the Junnar caves see J. Fergusson and J. Burgess, *The Cave Temples of India* (London, 1880), Pt. II, chap. v.

[288] Shivner was granted to Sivaji's grandfather in 1599 and it is said that the raja himself was born there. During the Mahratta wars it was often taken and retaken.

Soldiers are taught little except marching; cavalrymen ride in wide saddles and hold to the horse with the calves of their legs. They wear no spurs and they bring their horses up abruptly with a thorny bit which is injurious enough to halt the wildest horse in its tracks. The infantrymen are armed with matchlock muskets. The Mughul governor pays the officers, who in turn pay the men, "every one having their Snips" in the process. The nobles reserve the imported steeds for themselves and to all others are left the fiery and flashy native breeds. Fryer has little respect for Indian soldiers and puts forth the opinion that the best soldier is the one who runs fastest; the officers are "good Carpet-Knights" who prefer their beds to the battlefield. All of them would rather polish their weapons than use them.[289]

Governor "Mucklis Caun" (Mukhlis Khan) of Junnar lives sparingly and not as well as the governor of Surat, even though he receives a salary twice as large. He is also permitted much more independence and latitude because he must constantly be prepared for a new onslaught by Sivaji. To increase his own income, this governor, like others all over the empire, actually maintains in his service only half of the numbers for which he is paid. These frauds are commonly overlooked by the "Vocanoivice" (*waqiah-navīs*, reporters) in their reports, since they receive a stipend from the governor in addition to an imperial salary. Their reports to the emperor also minimize the defeats and magnify the victories of local commanders. Junnar is a half-ruined city, most of whose inhabitants have fled. Because trade is at a standstill, its bazaar offers only provisions, some of which are taken by force from the poor farmers of the area.[290]

On the advice of the governor, Fryer takes a different route back to Bombay to avoid Sivaji's men. He returns by way of "Nunny Gaōl" (Nana Ghat), a pass which is "far shorter and easier" than the one through which he had come.[291] This road is provided with "charitable Cisterns of good Water" and shaded by "beautiful Woods" at the mountains' foot. Soon he arrives back at Murbad and takes the road on the level land over which he had come. At "Bafta" (Barvi) the *Kunbis* who dwell there are unable to protect their buffalo herds against the vicious wild beasts of the neighborhood. The *Kunbis* work in the teak forests and thatch their round hovels with the broad leaves of the teak trees. The "coolies" (*Kolis*) from Bombay in Fryer's party favorably compare their life under the English to the hardships suffered by the poor *Kunbis* of this ravaged region. Back in Kalyan, Fryer sees near his lodgings "a great Tree full of stringy red Flowers, set in open Calices upon a long Stalk, like budding Grapes," which drops its blossoms upon the ground in showers. This tree strangely blooms at night and sheds by day.[292] Here he also enters a mosque whose walls are plain except for an

---

[289] Crooke (ed.), *op. cit.* (n. 4), pp. 333–43.

[290] *Ibid.*, pp. 343–45.

[291] On his way to Junnar he had crossed the difficult Avapa pass.

[292] Probably the *Hibiscus mutabilis*, a native of China now commonly cultivated in Indian gardens.

Arabic inscription which hangs over a raised pulpit (the *mimbar*) "where the Priest expounds." Supported by carved wooden pillars, its wooden roof has a square hole in it over the pulpit. Beneath the pulpit are vaults. Stone stairs nearby lead to a deep tank where a "priest" is making cotton rags into paper by steeping them in water, beating and slicing them into sheets, drying them in the sun, and glazing them for use.[293]

The Mughuls, who formerly received rich revenues from Gujarat, are now facing a revolt there and losses of income. The Rajputs and the governor of Gujarat, the son of Mir Jumla, are conspiring to overthrow Aurangzib.[294] The Mughuls "engaged over Head and Ears in Wars" have been forced to ask the ruler of "Brampore" (Burhanpur) for aid. Mughul involvement in the Deccan with the Rajputs provides Sivaji with an opportunity to threaten Surat again. Fear of another sack of the city sends its merchants scurrying in 1679, even though Surat's new walls are complete and ready to stand off a strong attack. The merchants have no confidence in the Mughul governor of the city, who is "a better Politician than Warrier" and unwilling to take the field against Sivaji. To stop Sivaji from ravaging the surrounding country, Aurangzib sends a new governor and reinforcements in May. Immediately upon his arrival he launches attacks against Sivaji's "pilfering Troops." Unable to defeat Sivaji and the Rajputs by arms, Aurangzib wreaks his revenge on the Hindus by taxing them heavily. Those who cannot pay these exactions are compelled to become Muslims or leave the empire.

As the rainy season ends in 1679, Aurangzib is preparing to leave Delhi at the head of one hundred thousand men to subdue the Rajputs.[295] Sivaji in the meantime turns his attention to the English at Bombay by landing several hundred men on the twin islets of Khanderi and Underi on the pretext of protecting the English against the incursions of Sidi forces.[296] Two naval engagements follow with the English which result in the rout of Sivaji's ships. Anxious to avoid further trouble, the English make no effort to retake the twin islets but let the Sidis and Sivaji fight over them. In response to Sivaji's depredations, Aurangzib doubles the exactions demanded of the Hindus, destroys more of their temples and idols, and forbids them to worship openly. On June 1, 1680, Sivaji dies.[297] His son, "Sambu Ge Raja" (Sambhaji

---

[293] Crooke (ed.), *op. cit.* (n. 4), I, 345–52. This is a rough description of a papermaking process still in use in India.

[294] Fryer in *ibid.*, II, 160–62. Governor Muhammad Amin Khan ruled Gujarat from 1672 to 1682. Aurangzib's efforts to conquer the Rajputs began in 1679. If a conspiracy between the Rajputs and the *shahbandar* existed, it was not of long duration. See Commissariat, *op. cit.* (n. 149), II, 177–79.

[295] Crooke (ed.), *op. cit.* (n. 4), III, 160–65. The emperor arrived in Ajmer on September 25, 1679, to assume personal command of the operations against the Rathors of Merwar. See Hallissey, *op. cit.* (n. 65), p. 56, and G. N. Sharma, *Merwar and the Mughal Emperor, 1526–1707* (Agra, 1954), pp. 171–72.

[296] Both being rising naval powers, the Sidis of Janjira and the Mahrattas were permanently at war. See Roy, *op. cit.* (n. 133), pp. 144–46.

[297] The correct date is April 4, 1680. See Sarkar, *op. cit.* (n. 17), p. 224.

Raja), presides over the funeral rites before continuing the military activities
of his father. The deaths of "Raja Jessinsins" (Raja Jaswant Singh, d. 1678),
the Rajput lord, and of Sivaji have left the Hindus disorganized and at the
mercy of the hated Mughuls. After a succession battle at Sivaji's court,
Sambhaji eliminates his opponents and emerges as "Maw Raja [Maharaja],
or the lawful Heir to his Father's Conquests."

Delhi meanwhile experiences a crisis of its own. Aurangzib, "jealous of
his Eldest Son," had sent him to "Goualar" (Gwalior).[298] Two of his other
sons are defiant and have refused new assignments given them. The emperor, however, must swallow his resentment, since he is so heavily engaged himself in the Rajput war. Within the past year he has conducted two
campaigns without being able to engage his sons' forces; both times his armies have been obliged to withdraw "distressed by Famine." At court the
emperor openly favors his youngest son "Sultan Eckbar" (Akbar) as his
successor.

Aurangzib, determined to defeat the Rajput Hindus, has ordered the governor of Ahmadabad to join him. The Rajput succession crisis which developed following Jaswant Singh's death continues to involve his widow (the
Rānī) in various conspiracies directed against Aurangzib.[299] In his frustration
the emperor orders the destruction of the Hindu temples in captured Ajmer
and Chitor, the celebrated Rajput fortress near Udaipur in Mewar.[300] Because of their repression the Brahmans predict a drought for this year and
people carry signs through the streets which call on the gods for rain. An
ominous sign in the heavens appears on November 20, 1680, in "the Rise
and Fall of the most prodigious Comet I ever was witness to."[301]

On his way to Chaul by sea in 1695, Careri passes by the coastal territories and fortresses held by the Mahrattas and Sidis. The latter have been
given the coast between Bombay and Chaul by the emperor to defend it
against the depredations of the Mahrattas. The Sidi ruler maintains at his
own expense two thousand infantry and cavalry and forts at "Undrin" (Underi) and "Canderin" (Khanderi).[302] Chaul itself is a Portuguese fortress
town six miles from the sea and about six miles in length, which stands be-

[298] Sultan Muhammad died on December 5, 1676, in the prison of Gwalior.

[299] Fryer's account of this confused period in Mewar is derived from hearsay and is inaccurate.
For Mewar's relations with Aurangzib in 1679–80 see Sharma, *op. cit.* (n. 295), pp. 160–70.

[300] Fryer includes an engraving of the fortress of "Chetore" based on a drawing made by an
English gunner, "an Eyewitness both of its Glory and Destruction." Crooke (ed.), *op. cit.* (n. 4),
III, 172. On this occasion in 1679 sixty-three temples were demolished. For a modern descrip-
tion of the famous fortress see Toy, *op. cit.* (n. 138), pp. 84–90.

[301] Fryer in Crooke (ed.), *op. cit.* (n. 4), III, 166–75. This comet of 1680 is generally called
"Newton's comet," because from observing it he was able to prove that comets revolve around
the sun in elliptical orbits. This was the first comet discovered and tracked in Europe by tele-
scope. See G. W. Kronk, *Comets. A Descriptive Catalog* (Hillside, N.J., 1984), p. 12.

[302] The struggle between the Mahrattas and the Sidis began in 1648. The Sidi base at Janjira
had originally been established by Bijapur, but in 1670 the Sidis transferred their allegiance to
Delhi. Although the Mahrattas occupied the hinterland, the Sidis retained control of this
coastal strip for the remainder of the seventeenth century.

tween the Mahratta forces to its south and those of the Sidis to its north. The entire coast from Chaul to Goa is controlled by the Mahrattas, as well as the hinterland as far east as Bijapur. The present Raja "Ramrão" (*Rājārām*) is trying to capture the entire west coast. His subjects are "Robbers both by Sea and Land" who prey indiscriminately on Mughuls, Portuguese, and all others who pass by their forts.[303] All ships are forced to travel in convoys to be protected from the Mahratta and Malabar pirates who terrorize this coast. Even the former Portuguese town of Dabhol is subject to the marauding Mahrattas.[304] Further south is Sivaji's fortress of "Maliandi" (Malvan), just to the north of Goa.[305]

After a brief stay in Goa, Careri departs overland, determined to visit the court and camp of Aurangzib.[306] He is accompanied by a Kanarese bearer from Goa and by an interpreter, a young native of Golconda. He leaves the Portuguese citadel by the Pass of Daugim to cross over the Mandavi River to the mainland. On his first night of the overland trip he is unable to sleep because of the noise being made by celebrants of "Siminga" (Mahratti, *Shimga*, the Holi festival). In the village of Mardol he visits a famous Hindu temple which is entered by means of a covered bridge. Much of this village has been destroyed in the wars between Sivaji and the Mughuls.[307] At Ponda (Phonda) he meets a detachment of Mughuls who had accompanied a newly appointed imperial *dīwān* (revenue collector) to his post. While the populace madly celebrates Holi, the formal installation of the new *dīwān* takes place despite the objections of the local *shahbandar*. Phonda town, situated among many mountains, is protected by an earthen fortress and a garrison of about four hundred commanded by this *shabandar*. Its previous fort on higher ground was destroyed twelve years ago (1683) in the wars between Sivaji and the Portuguese.[308]

Pushing eastward from Phonda through the rough North Kanara country, Careri again arrives in Mughul-controlled territory at "Alcal" (probably Haliyal).[309] He then proceeds northward via "Mandapur" (Mamdapur in Belgaum) to Aurangzib's camp at "Galgala" (Galgala) on the north bank of the Krishna River.[310] Here he is lodged with the European Christian gunners and their native Christian priests. The tents of the imperial quarters cover an area three miles in circumference. Encircled by a red cotton textile barrier, the camp is defended by palisades, ditches, and five hundred light cannons.

---

[303] Rajaram, who was in Gingee and on the east coast from 1689 to 1693, centered his activities thereafter on the west coast. See Sarkar, *op. cit.* (n. 22), chap. xvi.

[304] Dabhol fell to Sivaji in 1662. The Portuguese thereafter sacked Dabhol a number of times but never occupied it permanently.

[305] Sen (ed.), *op. cit.* (n. 2), pp. 183–85. Sivaji had his naval base and arsenal at Malvan.

[306] For his remarks on Goa see below, pp. 853–54.

[307] Mardol is north of the town of Phonda.

[308] Careri means Sambhaji, the son of Sivaji. *Cf.* the account of Sambhaji's war with the Portuguese in Sarkar, *op. cit.* (n. 17), pp. 281–82.

[309] See map of his itinerary in *ibid.*, p. 277.

[310] Galgala is a large village thirty-two miles southwest of Bijapur.

The Empire of Aurangzib

Careri is told that the forces massed here include sixty thousand cavalry, seven hundred thousand infantry, fifty thousand camels, and three thousand elephants.[311] Five hundred of these elephants belong to the emperor, the remainder to his nobles.[312] When all the camp followers are included, this camp is a "moving city" thirty miles in circumference, with a population of five hundred thousand. The princes of the blood and the "Omrahs" serve as generals, each one commanding his own troops and being subordinate only to the "Gium-Detol-Molk" ('Umda-al-Mulk, Pillars of the State, the title of great nobles). These forces, "being lazy and undisciplined," fight "when they please."[313] The Europeans serving in this army are paid well and enjoy their employment, since they lose nothing more than one day's pay whenever they miss one day's action. They feel no sense of honor or duty when serving "a Barbarous King, who has no Hospital for the Wounded Men." While Europeans may become rich in the imperial service, it is hard to obtain a legal discharge and consequently they must escape "to enjoy what is got."

On the morning of March 21, 1695, Careri has a brief personal interview with Aurangzib, following which he attends the public audience. In the first court of the imperial enclosure there is a large tent which houses the musical instruments sounded at "certain Hours of the Day and Night."[314] There is also here a "Gold Ball . . . hanging by a Chain" which is carried on the march as the imperial insignia.[315] In the imperial tent, "adorn'd with Silks and Cloth of Gold," Aurangzib is seated "after the Country manner, on Rich Carpets." Careri is accompanied to the audience by a "Christian of Agra," who acts as his interpreter. The emperor inquires about his homeland, his travels, and the reason for his visit. To the last point he responds that he has come "only out of curiosity to see the greatest Monarch in Asia . . . and the Grandeur of his Court and Army." Aurangzib then asks about the war being waged in Hungary between the Turks and Europeans.[316] These polite questions being answered, Careri is dismissed and escorted to the adjoining tent of public audiences.

The audience court is enclosed "with painted Calicos," and its main tent, supported by two great poles, is covered on the outside with "ordinary red Stuff [material]," and on the inside with a finer cloth and "small Taffeta Curtains." Within the tent is a square platform of several levels, on top of which stands a square throne of gilded wood. Aurangzib enters the tent "leaning on a Staff" and preceded by many courtiers. The emperor wears a "white Vest" which is tied under the right arm to distinguish him from the

[311] On the size of Aurangzib's armies see Puhl, *op. cit.* (n. 80), pp. 132–34.
[312] Akbar introduced the system of requiring certain nobles to look after particular grades of elephants, ordinarily the baggage carriers. See *ibid.*, pp. 68–69.
[313] Aurangzib was noted for the severe punishments he meted out to his nobles and generals.
[314] The instruments were played eight times in twenty-four hours as a rule. *Cf.* Puhl, *op. cit.* (n. 80), p. 218.
[315] The *Kaukabah.* See *ibid.*, p. 208.
[316] The war of 1683 to 1699 by which the Turks lost their dominion in Hungary.

Hindus who tie it under the left. His turban of the same white cloth is tied with a gold veiling on which a huge emerald and four smaller ones sparkle. A silk sash covers the "Catari" (*katārī*, dagger) which hangs on his left side. Aurangzib is "of a low Stature, with a large Nose, Slender, and stooping with Age."[317] Still he is a cheerful, commanding figure and able to read and write "without spectacles." He is vigorous in war and in administering his empire. Whatever he eats is first tasted by his daughter and several nobles. He drinks exclusively water from the Ganges that possesses the "singular quality of our River Thames, that it never remains corrupt long." While he formerly "admir'd the Fair Sex," he now remains at a distance from his harem.[318]

After reviewing the petitions handed him, the emperor inspects the elephants. Then the imperial princes enter, make their obeisances, and sit on the lower levels of the platform; the "Omrahs" stand throughout the ceremony. Outside the tent, on the right, stand "100 Musketiers and more Macebearers" who carry on their shoulders clubs topped with silver globes.[319] To the left of the tent the "Royal Ensigns" are held aloft on spears by nine attendants. The person in the middle holds a sun, the two on either side of him hold "two gilt Hands," and the next two hold "Horse Tails dy'd Red."[320] The other four attendants merely have their spears covered. Outside the imperial enclosure several companies of cavalry and infantry stand guard. With them are elephants who carry kettledrums that are beaten throughout the ceremony.[321]

6

RELIGIOUS BELIEFS AND PRACTICES

Despite his ignorance of Sanskrit (a handicap he admits), Bernier investigated the Hindu classics and tried to understand their teachings. Partly at his suggestion, his patron employed a celebrated pandit who had previously worked for Dara Shikoh, the son of Shah Jahan.[322] This pandit was Bernier's

[317] He was eighty years old (see pl. 122).

[318] Rawlinson (ed.), *op. cit.* (n. 3), pp. 126–27. On the emperor's character see Sarkar, *op. cit.* (n. 17), pp. 437–99.

[319] Mace-bearers (*yasāwals*) were imperial messengers who carried maces of steel as their insignia. They were always in attendance upon the emperor. See Puhl, *op. cit.* (n. 80), p. 106.

[320] Collectively these ensigns were called the *gur* (cf. pls. 120–21). The sun (*āftāb*) was adopted as a standard when Timur conquered the fire-worshippers. The gilt hand (*panjah*) represented the hand of Ali. (Ali is revered by Shiites as the true successor of Muhammad; he lost his hand in battle.) The tails (*chartroq*) were yak tails which adorned a small standard. See Irvine, *op. cit.* (n. 28), pp. 31–35.

[321] Sen (ed.), *op. cit.* (n. 2), pp. 217–22.

[322] Dara, when governor of Bengal in 1656, had employed a large staff of pandits from Benares to make a Persian translation from Sanskrit of fifty-two Upanishads, called *Sirr-i-Akbar* (the Greatest Secret) in Persian; this translation was rendered into a Latin version by An-

"constant companion over a period of three years," a time when the French physician was also engaged in translating Descartes' philosophy into Persian for the edification of his patron.[323] He was also acquainted with other pandits who came to visit his companion. Although Bernier and his patron questioned the pandit on Hinduism, they finally "became disgusted both with his tales and childish arguments." Bernier conversed about Hinduism with Father Heinrich Roth, S.J. (1620–1667), the German missionary "who had made great proficiency in the study of Sanskrit" (see pl. 129 for his Sanskrit grammar). He also consulted the writings on Hinduism of Henry Lord, Abraham Roger, and Father Athanasius Kircher, the polyhistor of Rome. Many of the materials he collected on Hinduism himself were already organized and arranged systematically in these earlier European writings. Consequently Bernier decided only to "touch briefly" on Hinduism in his book and "in a general and desultory manner."[324]

Hindus believe that God, called "Achar" (*Achara*), is "Immovable or Immutable." From him they received the "Beths" (Vedas), four books which include "all the sciences." These works enjoin that the people should be divided, as they effectively are, into four "tribes" (orders): Brahmans or interpreters of the law, "Quetterys" (Kshatriyas) or warriors, "Bescué" (Vaisya) or merchants, commonly called "Banyanes" (Banyans), and "Seydra" (Sudras) or artisans and laborers. Members of these castes may never intermarry. The Hindus believe in the transmigration of souls and forbid the eating or killing of any animal, to avoid the heinous crime of consuming an ancestor. It is particularly sinful to eat cows or peacocks. Their peculiar respect for the cow rests upon its holy character and its extraordinary usefulness as provider of milk and butter. Also, since pasturage is scarce, the cows of India would disappear completely if they were consumed in anything like the numbers eaten in France and England. On at least two occasions the Brahmans have petitioned the emperor to outlaw completely the slaughter of cows because of their growing scarcity. They even offer Aurangzib considerable sums of money to issue an edict forbidding cowkilling to all his subjects.

The Vedas oblige every Hindu to pray three times in each twenty-four hours with the face turned to the east. The whole body must be washed three times daily or at least before each meal. It is more meritorious to wash or pray in running than in still water, a custom to be understood in terms of the hot climate of Hindustan where regular ablutions are necessary and easy

---

quetil-Duperron and published at Paris in 1801 as *Oupnekhat (id est, Secretum Tegendum) opus ipsa in India rarissimum*. . . . See A. Ahmad, *Studies in Islamic Culture in the Indian Environment* (Oxford, 1964), p. 192.

[323] Translation of Western philosophical materials into Persian was Bernier's principal scholarly occupation during five or six of his years in Delhi.

[324] Constable (ed.), *op. cit.* (n. 1), pp. 323–25, 332–34. On Lord see above, pp. 569–70, 645–51; on Roger see below, pp. 1029–57. On Roth and Kircher, the Jesuits, see above, pp. 415–86, 527–28.

to perform. The pandits agree that such customs are for India alone, and bemuse Bernier by asserting that their religion is not meant for universal acceptance. As a consequence, no foreigner may become a Hindu, since God ordains different religions to meet the needs of different peoples. Hindus, on their part, therefore, do not accuse Christians or Muslims of practicing a false religion.

God, once having determined to create the world, first brought into existence three perfect beings who were to effect creation: Brahma, or the penetrating spirit; "Beschen" (Vishnu), or that which exists in all things; and "Mehahdeu" (Mahadeva or Siva), or the mighty lord. Through Brahma God created the world, Vishnu upholds it, and by Mahadeva it will be destroyed. Brahma, following God's command, issued the four Vedas and consequently he is sometimes represented as an idol with four heads. With his Christian background showing, Bernier seeks to find a correlation between these three gods and the Christian Trinity. He is assured by Father Roth that Hindus teach that Vishnu "has been nine times embodied in the flesh" to deliver mankind from its ills. According to popular tradition the tenth incarnation of Vishnu will emancipate humanity from the tyranny of Islam.[325]

Since he does not want to repeat what other Europeans had already written about Hindu doctrine, Bernier adds to their contributions by commenting on Hindu education and thought. At Benares, the "Athens of India," is located the "general school" of the Hindus at which Brahmans and other devotees undertake their studies. There are no colleges or regular classes here like those in European universities. The teachers live in private houses in various parts of the town, "principally in the gardens of the suburbs, which the rich merchants permit them to occupy." Here they ordinarily meet with a few disciples, never more than twelve to fifteen at a time. Normally the disciples study "under their respective preceptors" for ten to twelve years. Instruction proceeds slowly, since most of the students "are of an indolent disposition" due to diet, heat, and little hope of honors or rewards.[326]

Sanskrit, which means "pure language," is the first subject taught. It is the ancient and holy language of the Vedas and differs totally from the vernaculars of Hindustan. It is a difficult language because it lacks a good book of grammar. In addition to sacred texts, Sanskrit literature includes works on philosophy, tracts on medicine in verse, and "many other kinds of books, with which a large hall at Benares is entirely filled." After acquiring Sanskrit, the students study the "Purane" (*Purāna*), an abridgment of and gloss

---

[325] Constable (ed.), *op. cit.* (n. 1), pp. 325–33. Father Roth was one of the first Catholic writers to comment on the avatars of Vishnu. But also see Roger and Baldaeus, below, pp. 915–17, 1046.

[326] An ancient seat of Hindu learning, Benares suffered severely from the early Muslim conquests. Its revival, usually dated from the time of Akbar, attracted great *āchāryas* (renowned scholars) from all over India. Over the remainder of the Mughul period Hinduism was revitalized at Benares. See R. B. Pandey, *Varanasi. The Heart of Hinduism* (Varanasi, 1969), p. 121.

on the Vedas. The four Vedas are bulky books and difficult to find because the Brahmans, fearing their destruction, do their best to keep them concealed from the Muslim officials. Students next turn to philosophy, a discipline in which the Hindus have six great schools or sects.[327] A seventh heterodox sect now exists called "Bauté" (Buddha or Buddhism) which has spawned twelve subsects of its own. Not as numerous as the Hindus, the Buddhists are hated by them and live "a life peculiar to themselves."[328]

For traditional Hindu learning Bernier exhibits little patience or understanding. While their sacred books speak of first principles, they hardly ever agree on what those are. Some see matter as composed of small, indivisible atoms, others vaguely talk about matter and form, others refer to four elements which emerge from nothing, and still others claim that light and darkness are the first principles. While they agree in their belief that all these first principles are eternal, they fail to address the problem of how something derives from nothing. About medicine they have a few small books "which are rather collections of recipes than regular treatises." Their methods of treatment differ from those prevailing in Europe, but they are nonetheless efficacious in Hindustan.[329] It is not surprising that the Hindus know nothing of anatomy, since they will dissect neither man nor beast. Nonetheless they ignorantly allege that the human body contains exactly five thousand veins. In astronomy they have slightly greater learning. With the aid of tables they are able to predict eclipses with great accuracy. They mistakenly believe that the moon is further away than the sun and that it secretes a vital liquid which enables the human brain and the members of the body to perform their respective functions. All the planets and stars are thought to be gods. Night comes on when the sun retires behind "Someire" (*Su-meru*), "an imaginary mountain placed in the center of the earth."[330] Their geography is equally fabulous, for they believe the world is flat and triangular in shape. It is divided into "seven distinct habitations [*lokas*]" each of which is surrounded "by its own peculiar sea." The first "habitation" is that closest to Mount Meru and it is peopled by "Devitas" (*devatās*, minor gods) of great perfection. The populations of each subsequent "habitation" are less and less perfect. The earth, populated by humans, is the least perfect and the furthest in distance from Mount Meru. The whole of this world is supported "on the heads of a number of elephants, whose occasional motion is the cause of earthquakes."

While in Benares in December, 1665, Bernier visits the chief pandit "in

[327] The Nyaya founded by Gautama, the Vaisheshika by Kanada, the Sankhya by Kapila, the Yoga by Patanjali, the Mimamsa by Jaimini, and the Vedanta by Badarayana.
[328] Probably a reference to Buddhism in Bengal. Buddhism elsewhere in India was in regression by the seventh century and soon thereafter disappeared completely. The most virulent opponents of Buddhism were the Brahmans, as Bernier suggests.
[329] *Cf.* the Paracelsian notion that different treatments are required for different climates, times, and peoples. See *Asia*, Vol. II, Bk. 3, p. 424.
[330] Golden Meru, the Olympus of the Hindus.

that celebrated seat of learning."[331] This eminent scholar, who had previously been a pensioner of Shah Jahan, had lost his state income when Aurangzib came to power. Thereafter he regularly visited Bernier's patron in hopes of winning that official's support in his effort to regain the pension. Consequently the French physician formed "a close intimacy" with this distinguished pandit. On Bernier's visit to Benares the pandit gives him "a collation in the university library" in the company of "the six most learned Pandets [pandits] in the town." Bernier asks this gathering to explain why learned Hindus are not scandalized by the prevalence of idol worship. They reassure him that Hindus do not worship the idol itself but rather the deity it represents. They explain that it is easier to pray with devotion when "there is something before the eyes that fixes the mind." They go on to declare that "God alone is absolute" and omnipotent, an assertion which Bernier suspects is designed "to correspond with the tenets of Christianity."[332]

Bernier then turns the conversation to the subject of chronology and learns from their discussion of the four "Dgugues" (Sanskrit, *yugas*, or ages) that "the world is astonishingly old" by their reckoning. Questioned on the nature of their "Devitas" (*devatās*), the pandits say that some are good while others are evil or morally neutral. Certain philosophers believe they are formed of fire, while others argue that their essence is light. Many believe they are composed of "Biapek" (*vyāpaka,* the all-pervading), the essence of God and the soul. Others hold that the gods are "only portions of the divinity," while still others claim that they are "certain species of distinct divinities, dispersed over the surface of the globe!" From Bernier's viewpoint these sages are as unclear as ordinary pandits when discoursing on the nature of the "Lengue-cherire" (*Linga vīrya,* the male essence?). This is the idea that the seeds of plants, trees, animals, and men receive no new creation but exist from the world's beginning as perfect miniatures requiring only life and nourishment to develop into their mature and full-grown forms.[333] While hardly clear in his understanding of Hinduism, Bernier learns from these discussions that the Hindu pandits themselves are divided in their beliefs and readily resort to parables or invoke the authority of the Vedas when asked to support or explain their differing viewpoints.

A new sect of mystics "has latterly made great noise in Hindoustan" because of its appeal to Dara Shikoh and Sultan Shujah, the sons of Shah Jahan who had lost out in the succession wars to Aurangzib.[334] Like many ancient

---

[331] Bernier was accompanied on this excursion by Tavernier, from whose account this date is derived. The jeweler provides a valuable description of the great temple of Benares dedicated to Siva which was destroyed in 1669 by order of Aurangzib. See Ball and Crooke (trans. and eds.), *op. cit.* (n. 1), II, 180–83.

[332] Constable (ed.), *op. cit.* (n. 1), pp. 333–43. On monotheism and polytheism in Hinduism see A. Daniélou, *Hindu Polytheism* (New York, 1964), pp. 8–11.

[333] On the *linga* see Daniélou, *op. cit.* (n. 332), chap. xviii.

[334] Aurangzib's brothers were attracted to Sufism, a form of mysticism popular in Persia and elsewhere in the Islamic world. Upon coming to power, Aurangzib, a staunchly orthodox

philosophers of the West, these Indian mystics, both Hindu and Muslim, hold that all living creatures are but so many parts of the "great life-giving principle."[335] In Persian poetry, the teachings of Sufism are set forth in the "Goul-tchen-raz" (*Gulshan-i-Raz*, or Mystic Rose Garden) in "very exalted and emphatic language."[336] These Indian mystics contend that *Achara*, their name for the Supreme Being, has produced everything "material and corporeal" from his own substance as a spider exudes its web from itself. Destruction "is merely the recalling of that divine substance and filaments into Himself" on the final day of the world which they call "maperlé or pralea" (*Mahā-pralaya*, day of annihilation). The everyday world in which we live is therefore nothing more than an "illusory dream" in which there is "nothing real or substantial." The varieties of our sensory experiences are illusions, for all are "one only and the same thing, which is God himself."[337]

Bernier, like other Europeans, comments on the "strange customs" of the Hindus. While in Delhi, he observes from the roof of his house their reactions to the solar eclipse of 1666 and he compares their behavior to the "childish credulity" exhibited by the people of France at the eclipse of 1654.[338] He reports that Hindus of all ages and ranks flock to the Jumna to await the beginning of the eclipse. Once it starts they plunge "the whole body under water several times in quick succession," and then lift their hands and eyes to the sun while praying. Finally they begin to throw water at the sun while performing various other antics. The natural phenomenon ending, they come out of the water and put on new clothes. They then throw "pieces of silver" into the river and give alms and their old clothes to the waiting Brahmans. From his informants Bernier learns that these same ceremonies are observed at the eclipse festivals celebrated at all other rivers and "Talabs" (tanks). At the tank of "Tanaiser" (Thanesar) more than 150,000 Hindus congregate, because its waters are "considered on the day of an

---

Muslim, executed Dara and persecuted other Sufis. See *The Cambridge History of India,* IV, 210, 232; and Ahmad, *op. cit.* (n. 322), pp. 196–97.

[335] The Hindu mystics here referred to are the proponents of Bhakti, an ancient cult stressing devotion to a personal god. Aurangzib feared that these two pantheistic sects, Bhakti and Sufism, might act together to wipe out the differences between Hindu and Muslim or at least challenge the predominance of Islamic orthodoxy. Dara and his son were executed in 1659 on charges of heresy and infidelity, and for describing Hinduism and Islam as "twin-brothers." See S. A. A. Rizvi, *A History of Sufism in India* (2 vols.; New Delhi, 1983), II, 128.

[336] This is a work composed in 1317 A.D. in response to fifteen questions on Sufism propounded by Amir Syad Hosaini, a celebrated Sufi. Very little is known about its author, Muhammad Shabistari.

[337] Constable (ed.), *op. cit.* (n. 1), pp. 343–49. For a brief account of Sufi beliefs and practices see G. A. Herklots and W. Crooke (trans. and eds.), *Islam in India or the Qānūn-i-Islām . . . by Ja' Far Sharif* (reprint of 1921 ed.; New Delhi, 1972), chap. xxxi.

[338] Tavernier also reports on this eclipse, which he saw in Patna. It occurred on July 2, 1666, at 1:00 P.M. He comments also on the ceremonies at the Ganges. See Ball and Crooke (trans. and eds.), *op. cit.* (n. 1), II, 192–94.

eclipse [to be] more holy and meritorious than those of any other."[339] These rites are followed, according to Hindu teachings, to drive away a wicked *devatā* who wants to take possession of the sun.[340]

Among the other "wild extravagancies" of the Hindus, Bernier includes the annual festival held at "Jagannat" (Jagannath) in Orissa.[341] During the "eight or nine days" of this festival more than 150,000 pilgrims participate in the ceremonies. Most spectacular is "the superb wooden machine" which carries the idol from temple to temple in this town on the Bay of Bengal.[342] It is set on "fourteen or sixteen wheels . . . and drawn or pushed along by the united exertions of fifty or sixty persons." On the first day, when the idol called Jagannath (*Jagannātha*) is put on display, pilgrims are crushed to death in the press that surrounds it. As the car carries the idol about the streets, fanatics throw themselves under the heavy wheels "without exciting the horror or surprise of the spectators." During this festival the Brahmans select a "beautiful maiden" to become the bride of Jagannath. She returns with the idol to the temple, where the unsuspecting girl is ravished during the night by a Brahman posing as the god. The next morning she accompanies her idol-husband in the car and publicly answers questions about what she heard from her spouse during the night. Throughout the festival, public women perform lascivious dances in the streets and temples "which the Brahmans deem quite consistent with the religion of the country."[343]

On suttee and other death customs, Bernier is an excellent witness. He concludes that the reports of earlier travelers certainly exaggerate the number of suttees and avers they are fewer "now than formerly." The Muslim rulers seek by indirect means to suppress this "barbarous custom," for no woman may legally sacrifice herself "without permission from the governor of the province in which she resides." Such a permission is not granted until all possible efforts have been made to dissuade her from self-immolation.

---

[339] Thanesar, about one hundred miles north of Delhi, is an ancient town and a famous place of Hindu pilgrimage at the center of the *Dharmakshetra* (Holy Land). Its *Kurukshetra* (the Place of God) tank, an oblong sheet of water over three thousand feet in length, is surrounded by temples. At an eclipse of the sun the Hindus believe that the waters of all other tanks visit this particularly sacred tank. Consequently anyone who bathes in its waters during a solar eclipse receives the merit of bathing in them all and at the same time washes away the sins of his ancestors. As many as one-half million worshippers have been known to assemble here for an eclipse festival. See Murray (publ.), *op. cit.* (n. 40), p. 258.

[340] Constable (ed.), *op. cit.* (n. 1), pp. 300–304. It is the antigod Rahu, the Boar, who tries to devour the sun. See Daniélou, *op. cit.* (n. 332), pp. 99, 166.

[341] *Cf.* above, pp. 677, 683.

[342] For a description of the idol called "Kesora" (Kesavi Rai, or Krishna) and his companions see Tavernier in Ball and Crooke (trans. and eds.), *op. cit.* (n. 1), II, 176–78.

[343] Constable (ed.), *op. cit.* (n. 1), pp. 304–6. It is not clear from this account that Bernier was actually present at one of these festivals. He seems rather to be relating stories told him. In 1697 Aurangzib ordered the destruction of the temple and idols of Jagannath. The temple was damaged, desecrated, and its idols confiscated. See R. D. Banerji, *History of Orissa from the Earliest Times to the British Period* (2 vols.; Delhi, 1980), II, 60.

Still, the number who persist remains considerable, especially in the territories of the rajas where there are no Muslim governors. Bernier himself was present at numerous suttees and was even involved in convincing the wife of his patron's clerk from burning herself on her husband's pyre. He provides eyewitness accounts of suttees in the territories of the rajas and at Surat and Lahore. He explains the persistence of the custom of suttee by insisting that the Hindu males, especially the Brahmans, inculcate the females, beginning in childhood, with the belief that "it is virtuous and laudable in a wife to mingle her ashes with those of her husband." The males adopt this tactic "as an easy mode of keeping wives in subjection, of securing their attention in times of sickness, and of deterring them from administering poison to their husbands." Certain women, particularly those wives who are young and pretty, escape the flames at the last moment by throwing themselves on the mercy of the sweepers who frequent cremation places. Such an act of self-preservation results in the widow's being utterly dishonored, excluded from her caste, and the slave of her rescuers. While the Portuguese occasionally give succor to widows, the Muslims are generally afraid to offer them asylum or to contribute directly in any other way to their safety. In certain other regions of India the Brahmans bury the suttee up to the neck in her husband's grave, and then choke her to death.[344] Along the Ganges, certain Hindus partially burn the corpse and cast the charred remains into the river to become prey to crows, fish, and crocodiles.[345] Others carry a deathly sick person to the river's edge, put the feet into the water, and then let the whole body gradually slide into the river.[346]

Hindustan is full of holy men, both Hindu and Muslim, who may be seen day or night lying under trees near tanks or loitering around temples. "Jauguis" (yogis), a name which means "united to god," affect long and shaggy hair and practice numerous austerities. Some keep their arms lifted perpetually over their heads until they wither and become useless. Others walk unabashedly nude through countryside, town, or the capital itself.[347] Some stand immobile and upright for a week or so until their calves swell to the size of their thighs. It is said that yogis torture themselves in this life "in the confident hope they will be Rajas in their renascent state." Some are reputed to be perfect yogis and truly united to their god. They supposedly have renounced the world, live in seclusion in a remote place, and lose themselves in profound meditation or ecstasy. Certain ones are able to induce trances by

[344] For other descriptions and analyses of suttee by other Europeans see above, p. 656, and below, pp. 866, 885, 1044. Also see Tavernier's description in Ball and Crooke (trans. and eds.), *op. cit.* (n. 1), II, 162–72. On the burying of *satīs* in Coromandel see below, p. 1026.

[345] Usually done by those too poor to pay for an ordinary cremation.

[346] Constable (ed.), *op. cit.* (n. 1), pp. 306–16.

[347] Although it is now illegal, nude holy men may still be seen walking around central Delhi. Aurangzib, after repeated warnings, had a celebrated *fakir* decapitated for walking about nude in Delhi. *Cf.* Tavernier in Ball and Crooke (trans. and eds.), *op. cit.* (n. 1), II, 153–58.

long fasting and by fixing the eyes steadily on the nose. Both yogis and Sufis also have secret means of provoking states of ecstasy and trance.

Other less saintly yogis roam the countryside claiming "to be possessed of most important secrets." The people believe these men know how to make gold and how to administer mercury as a digestive and restorative. Some are sorcerers who compete in performing magical tricks. Others are mind-readers as well as magicians. Despite his profound personal interest in these soothsayers and sorcerers, Bernier was never "to witness any marvellous performance" and remained convinced that their reported marvels were merely sleight of hand or gross deception. Clean and well-dressed yogis modestly walk about two by two carrying an earthen pot while seeking alms. They freely enter Hindu households where they are given a hearty welcome, "their presence being esteemed a blessing to the family." Often they take advantage of the female members of the house, a custom of the country, "and their sanctity is not the less on that account." [348]

According to Godinho, yogis besmear themselves with ashes of cow dung and wash themselves in cow urine. Without house or bed they sleep on the bare earth. Some bury themselves by the roadside and get their air, food, and water through a reed. Still others mount columns, fall into a trance, and leave their perch only after death. On feast days certain yogis "hang themselves from poles by pointed hooks" (see pl. 130). A yogi of Surat who held his arms above his head for ten years finds it impossible now to lower them. [349] These yogis, unable to feed or otherwise take care of themselves, are attended by the younger yogis. The Hindus revere these yogis as saints, who do penance "for all the sins of mankind, and control the wrath of God with those hands lifted." When a yogi approaches a hamlet, he sounds a trumpet to have the people bring food to him. If a yogi's wish is not heeded, he curses the offenders. To avenge a wrong against one of their numbers, the yogis "will collect together and stand in defence of the honour of their Order." More feared than respected, the yogis in congregation elect a chief, usually a man of high lineage. In most Hindu states there are princely yogis who possess both social and political power and influence. Bahadur Khan of Gujarat, the third son of Muzaffar, was "at first a fakir [Muslim holy man]" before usurping the kingdom from his two older brothers. [350]

---

[348] Constable (ed.), *op. cit.* (n. 1), pp. 316–23. Because he lived mainly among Muslims of the court, Bernier seems to share their disdain for Hindu customs. His Hindu informants also ordinarily worked for his patron or other Muslim courtiers.

[349] For a twentieth-century recital of the marvels performed by yogis see R. S. Gherwal, *Lives and Teachings of the Yogis of India. Miracles and Occult Mysticism of India* (Santa Barbara, Cal., 1939), Vol. II.

[350] Bahadur as prince was favored by the fakirs. On the death of Muzaffar Shah II in 1526, succession wars ensued from which Bahadur Khan emerged victorious as they had foretold. On the "scramble for the throne" see J. Chaube, *History of Gujarāt Kingdom* (New Delhi, 1975), chap. viii.

Even Aurangzib was helped to power by the fakirs. All yogis are "great sorcerers" and they pretend to be physicians "though in truth they are only herbalists." They prepare what is known as the cobra stone "which is the best anti-venom for the bite of any poisonous animal." Placed on the wound, the stone adheres to it until the venom is absorbed; the stone is cleansed by immersing it in milk.[351] In Madura and Mysore the Jesuits "dress themselves as honest Yogis to have easier access to, and be held in higher esteem by the natives."[352]

In the many towns and villages of the province of "Caboul" (Kabul) the people are mainly Hindus. They celebrate a feast called "Houly" (Holi) which lasts for two days.[353] At that time the people fill the temples, feast, dance in the streets, wear dark garments, visit their friends in masquerade, and light bonfires at night. The celebration ends with the destruction of the image of a giant by a child shooting arrows at it. This is a drama depicting Krishna on earth as a child who destroys the great giant who threatens him.[354] The Hindus of Kabul dig wells and build inns along the roads as acts of charity.[355] Hindus in the Deccan observe with great strictness all customs about washing, bathing, eating, and fasting. Some drink coffee and tea in their water. One day each year Brahmans eat pork, and at another feast they eat a cow made of paste and filled with honey. In all the Indies the Hindus have no religious communities reserved to a particular caste.[356]

The Banyans, the merchants at Surat and elsewhere in India, are so horrified by the sight of blood that they have no "thoughts of war." Although they are the richest of all Hindus, the Banyans believe in transmigration and are devout. Two days each month they fast from sunrise to sunset, children as well as adults.[357] Hindus who do manual labor sing sacred ballads while at work. They are "constant in their washings" and careful about drinking after others. They religiously abstain from taking the life of any creature and denounce those who do so for their inhumanity. Close to Surat they maintain a hospital for the sick and old animals and another for bugs, flies, and ants. They will buy animals to enable them to die a natural death. On one of their solemn fast days, they drink nothing in the morning but cow's urine.[358]

---

[351] On the snakestone see Yule and Burnell, *op. cit.* (n. 124), pp. 847–49.

[352] Father Godinho in Moraes (trans.), *loc. cit.* (n. 150).

[353] The Hindu carnival of Holi is celebrated, according to the lunar calendar, during the ten days preceding the full moon of Phalgun (in January or February), a period dedicated especially to Krishna.

[354] A vague reference to Krishna's battle with Kamsa, a cruel king. This demon-king and uncle of Krishna became in legend a killer of children. So it is only proper that a child should destroy him by assuming the role of Krishna. See Daniélou, *op. cit.* (n. 332), p. 176.

[355] Thévenot in Sen (ed.), *op. cit.* (n. 2), p. 81.

[356] Fryer in Crooke (ed.), *op. cit.* (n. 4), I, 256–57. These last reports of Hindu customs are singular and are not found in other European accounts.

[357] The *Ekadashi*, or the eleventh day of each half of the Hindu month.

[358] Rawlinson (ed.), *op. cit.* (n. 3), pp. 163–209. In this lengthy discussion of "the Bannians of

Fryer is particularly outraged by the rudeness, insolence, and unwar-
ranted demands of the Muslim fakirs of Surat who prey upon foreigners,
Hindus, and even rich Muslims. Other natives are "very respectful" unless
they become intoxicated on toddy or bhang. The best houses in town belong to Muslim merchants, although a rich Parsi, the broker of the "King"
of Bantam, has a "sumptuous house." There are three inns, intended by the
donors to provide free lodgings for strangers, which are now rented to foreign merchants. Ordinarily the Banyans live in cramped and humble dwellings with windows of oyster shells or lattice. A few rich houses have sash
windows of expensive painted glass from Venice that comes over the land
route by way of Constantinople. The customs of Surat Muslims resemble
those of the Shiites of Golconda more than those of the ruling Sunni Mughuls. The Sunnis are more puritanical than the Shiites and, like the Arabs,
respect four expositors of the law: "Hanoffi" (Hanafi), "Shoffi" (Shafi'i),
"Hamaloch" (Hanbali), and "Maluche" (Maliki).[359] Sunnis refuse to eat
with persons of another persuasion.

About intermarriage between different types of Muslims there are some
restrictions and also much confusion. Muslims are distinguished from one
another by the degree of their relationship to their Prophet. The "Siad"
(Sayyid) are direct descendants; they wear a green vest and a turban.[360] Their
distant cousins are the "Shiek" (Shaikh), a group to which all new converts
are admitted. Others are classified according to their place of birth, for example, Mughul, Pathan, or Tartar Muslims.

In Surat there are but two important mosques with minarets; next to one
stands the residence of their "Xeriff" (Arabic, *sharīf*, eminence). Muslims
strictly observe their hours of prayer and prepare for them by donning
simple clothes and by washing their hands and feet. While performing their
devotions, they prostrate themselves; after rising they invoke their guardian
angels. Boys are circumcised at eight years of age by a barber. After the rite
is performed, they celebrate by carrying him around joyously and by feasting.[361] Girls are taught to pray within their homes. Marriages are arranged
by the parents and performed by the "Cazy" (kazi). The marriage is sometimes celebrated for several weeks. Houses are illuminated at night, garments are dyed with saffron, and the bride's dowry is paraded through the
streets.[362] If they can maintain them, Muslims take four wives; the one bear-

---

Suratt" Ovington, although a Protestant minister himself, lumps together Hindu and Jain
practices. In fact, he is not as well informed on these religions as Henry Lord was sixty years
earlier.

[359] See Fryer in Crooke (ed.), *op. cit.* (n. 4), I, 229–32. These are the four orthodox schools
of law interpretation among the Sunnis. See Herklots and Crooke (trans. and eds.), *op. cit.*
(n. 337), pp. 15–16.

[360] They are sometimes called "wearers of green." See Herklots and Crooke (trans. and eds.),
op. cit. (n. 337), p. 303.

[361] Cf. *ibid.*, chap. v.

[362] Cf. *ibid.*, chap. viii. Saffron is associated with fertility; *ibid.*, p. 66.

ing the first son becomes the chief wife.[363] Divorces are obtained by petitioning the kazi. Midwives are seldom called for deliveries, although women do practice that profession; they are known by the tufts of silk they wear on their shoes or slippers. After a birth the mother goes through a forty-day period of purification during which the child is named without much ceremony. At funeral services the mullahs preach a sermon on a text from the Koran. Corpses are buried north to south, rather than east to west "as we do."[364] A great outcry by the women accompanies every death, mourners are hired, and the begrieved neither eat nor change their clothes until the corpse is buried. In the same period the relatives neglect their clothes and do not wash or shave. Every noon the widow goes to the grave with a friend "to repeat the doleful Dirge, after which she bestows *Holway* [Arabic, *halwā*, halva], a kind of Sacramental Wafer," and prays for the departed's soul.[365] The dead are never buried in mosques but rather in adjoining places where they build tombs; financial foundations for the tombs insure that the mullahs will pray for the departed. Others are buried near the roads to remind travelers to pray for the dead.[366]

Every three hours the mullahs with their fingers in their ears call the people to prayer from "the Steeples of their moschs."[367] The mullahs pray five times daily and preach a sermon on the Koran every Friday. To be pure on the holy day of Friday "they are not to lye with their Women." The Muslims have a hierarchy headed by a "Xeriff," who is followed in rank order by the kazis, the mullahs, and the scribes or teachers of Arabic. The fakirs have become much more prominent and powerful in the reign of Aurangzib, since he was one of their number before becoming emperor. Most are vagabonds who profess poverty while begging, forcing alms, or taking whatever they want. Because of their numbers they terrorize the public and defy the governor.

The Muslims of Surat celebrate the advent of the new moon, especially the first one to appear in November. This event inaugurates the festival of *Ramazān* (Ramadan), or the Islamic Lent, which is observed strictly and solemnly by all the devout. For one month, they rigorously fast and abstain from water from sunrise to sunset. On this occasion the mullahs spend their nights in the mosque "chanting alowd alternately their Divine Hymns."[368] At its end, Fryer reports, the governor and the other officials of the city lead

[363] *Cf. ibid.*, pp. 85–86.

[364] "They lay the body on the back with the head to the north and the feet to the south, turning the face to the westward towards Mecca, the *Qibla*." *Ibid.*, p. 97.

[365] *Halwā* is a sesame-seed sweet. For the recipe see *ibid.*, p. 324.

[366] Fryer in Crooke (ed.), *op. cit.* (n. 4), I, 233–39. *Cf.* Ovington's description of their costly funerals in Rawlinson (ed.), *op. cit.* (n. 3), p. 146.

[367] Fryer provides a somewhat abbreviated version of the summons to prayer in Romanized Arabic and in English translation. Crooke (ed.), *op. cit.* (n. 4), I, 239.

[368] Ovington in Rawlinson (ed.), *op. cit.* (n. 3), pp. 144–46.

a great procession outside the wall to a special holy site set apart in the queen's garden.[369] On the way the governor throws rupees to the crowd as he rides in the midst of his soldiers on a little female elephant. After prayers and ceremonies are over, the officials return to the city for a feast. At the new moon before the new year the governor again goes in procession to the holy place to sacrifice a ram or billy goat in remembrance of the offering of Isaac. Other Muslims perform like sacrifices at this time and sprinkle the blood on the doors of their houses.[370] At about this time the Muslims observe ten days of mourning in remembrance of "Hosseen-Gosseen" (Hasan-Husain), two of their martyrs who died in the desert while fighting Christians.[371] On this occasion jars of water are placed at every street corner. The devout run in groups up and down the streets calling out the names of the martyrs and laying about them with swords, clubs, and staves. When two such groups meet, "they seldom part without bloody Noses." On the last day they prepare two coffins which they carry to the river and put into the water "with a loud Cry." Aurangzib, shocked by the unseemly excesses of the mourners, has sought "to reduce the Celebration" on grounds that such behavior is a scandal to the faith and a bad example to unbelievers.[372]

The emperor, being determined to bring the entire populace over to his faith, has instituted severe head taxes which fall most heavily on Brahmans and other Hindu castes.[373] In reaction, some of the Hindu rajas have revolted, and refugees are crowding into the Portuguese centers and Bombay to escape this heavy tax.[374] By their political power the Muslims forbid suttee and the governors exact from the Hindus "large Gratuities" for the right to carry on publicly their festivals and weddings.[375] Consequently the Hindus are not "totally denied their Feasts" which, in contrast to Muslim festivals, are times of "Jollity and Pomp." At the first moon of October the Banyans celebrate "Dually" (*Divālī*, feast of lamps), a festival of much kind-

[369] The governor offers prayers on this occasion at the *'īdgāh* (place of prayer), usually a building erected outside of town for this purpose. See Herklots and Crooke (trans. and eds.), *op. cit.* (n. 337), p. 145.
[370] This is the Baqar 'Id Festival or "the cow festival." *Cf. ibid.,* pp. 214–17.
[371] This is the Muharran festival, lamenting the martyrdom of the sons of the Imam Ali in A.D. 680. They were not fighting Christians but other Muslims. The festival is celebrated annually during the first month of the Muslim calendar. *Cf. ibid.,* chap. xiv. For its celebration elsewhere in India see above, p. 664, and below, pp. 1075–76, as well as plate 132.
[372] In 1669, because of a fatal riot at Burhanpur, Aurangzib ordered his governors to forbid the making of the imitation tombs and certain of the processions. As a strict Sunni, Aurangzib also disliked this Shiite festival. See Commissariat, *op. cit.* (n. 149), p. 379.
[373] The *jizya,* or poll tax on non-Muslims, was reimposed in April, 1679, during Fryer's second visit to Surat. It was designed to curb Hinduism and to spread Islam by making unbelievers pay a price for the imperial indulgence. See Sarkar, *op. cit.* (n. 17), pp. 148–49.
[374] It increased by fully one-third the direct taxes paid by Hindus. *Ibid.,* p. 149.
[375] *Zimmis* (non-Muslims) were under legal disabilities with regard to the public performance of rites and marriages. No doubt a gift to the proper official would have the effect of reducing the offensive character of Hindu public ceremonies. See *ibid.,* p. 141n.

ness, mirth, and banqueting.[376] At the next new moon the Hindu women bathe in their sacred wells "where they say, it is not difficult to persuade them to be kind." March begins with a "Licentious Week of Sports and Rejoycing."[377] Banyans show their beneficence by feeding ants and flies and by being "constant Benefactors" to the myriad dogs which roam the streets.[378]

The division between Sunnis and Shiites is so deep that one will neither talk nor eat with the other. Muslim merchants profit more from the preeminence of their religion than from their adeptness in trade. While they "imitate a noble pomp," the Banyans do their work. Muslim women are no more than the "Chief Slaves" of their husbands. In short, "the Moguls Feed high, Entertain much, and Whore not a little." Even their fakirs are dissolute; some wander about the country terrorizing the people and spying for any prince who will employ them.[379] In government the Muslims are appointed to the best and most lucrative offices, while the Hindus are encouraged by the authorities "just to follow their several Manual Occupations, or Merchandize."[380]

According to Thévenot, the great highway whch runs from Agra to Lahore is lined with "Achy" (ash) trees whose "long and thick branches" cover the road and make traveling on it pleasant.[381] On this road are many temples, "especially toward the Town of Tanassor [Thanesar]."[382] In that town stands a convent of the "Vartias" (Jains).[383] This sect reputedly is more than two thousand years old. In the Indies it boasts at present more than ten thousand monasteries, "some of them more Austere than others." Some Jains worship the spiritual God and disdain idols. In their convents they live under a rule and a hierarchy of superiors. They take a vow of "Obedience, Chastity, and Poverty" and follow it rigorously. Certain "brothers" are appointed to beg for the others; all eat but once daily.[384] They have no fixed time for the novitiate, elevation being the prerogative of the superiors. They follow the Golden Rule even in their treatment of animals. They obey "without murmuring" the most trifling order, never look a woman in the face, and make no response if reviled or reaction if attacked. They wear nothing but a loincloth and a coif. They wait patiently each day to eat until food is brought by their mendicants. They eat "but a handful of Rice" and refuse

[376] *Cf.* above, p. 672.
[377] Holi, the spring festival.
[378] Fryer in Crooke (ed.), *op. cit.* (n. 4), I, 269–78.
[379] *Ibid.*, II, 110–14.
[380] Ovington in Rawlinson (ed.), *op. cit.* (n. 3), p. 140.
[381] The *Fraxinus excelsior* are native to north India. See R. N. Parker, *A Forest Flora for the Punjab with Hazara and Delhi* (New Delhi, 1973), p. 314.
[382] Thanesar in the Punjab is a sacred place in the Holy Land of *Kuruksheta* (the place of God). See above, p. 690.
[383] Thévenot probably learned about this monastery from the Jains of Gujarat.
[384] Those designated mendicants must be well versed in Jain scriptures and are required to make their rounds in pairs or groups. See S. B. Deo, *A History of Jaina Monachism* (Poona, 1956), p. 413.

anything more when offered it. All their food must be prepared elsewhere, for they will have no fire lest a fly should be burned in it. They eat rice and drink a little water at noon each day and touch neither food nor drink until the following day at the same time. The rest of the day they spend praying and reading. They go to sleep at sunset, all lying on the floor of the same dormitory. Once they have taken their vows, they may never leave the order. If they break any of their vows, the punishment is expulsion from both their order and caste. Monks move to a new convent every three months, the superiors every four. Superiors hold office for life, and generally appoint their own successors. The Jains also have orders of nuns "who live very exemplarily." [385]

Certain Brahmans (Jain monks) never marry for fear of crushing an animal to death "by their mutual Embraces." To maintain the succession in their priesthood, a son from a lay family with several boys is chosen for consecration. These priests speak very little for fear of killing some small or invisible creature. They sweep the places where they sit down with a brush to avoid crushing insects. Also to keep from taking life they wear a cloth across the mouth, never bathe, and refuse to drink cold water. They never cut their beards or shave their heads but pull all hair out by the roots as soon as any grows on the body. They accept each day cheerfully as it comes, take no thought of tomorrow, and freely distribute to others whatever they do not need since they trust Providence to take care of the following day. [386]

The Jain merchants of Surat are the Jews of India. They respect religion highly and follow strictly the rites and customs of the country. They observe omens and will travel ten miles out of their way to avoid encountering an inauspicious convoy of asses. When it rains they will not ride in a coach for fear of killing insects caught in the ruts or puddles. Even while conscientious in following the tenets of their religion, the Jain brokers and merchants are the greatest cheats in the world when dealing with other people. They take as much advantage of their own artisans as the tax collectors do.

The Parsis live in the vicinity of Surat for forty miles along the coast and not more than twenty miles inland. This alien folk from Persia sought refuge here before the Muslims became masters of India. They were accepted as free citizens by the Hindus and were permitted to live among them on condition that they would not kill living creatures and would conform to many Hindu customs. [387] Once the Muslims came to power, the Parsis no longer felt obliged to observe their arrangements with the Hindus. Now they eat fish and meat and drink wine. Parsis worship the sun, and at "Nun-

[385] Thévenot in Sen (ed.), *op. cit.* (n. 2), pp. 85–87. On the Jain practice of "touring" see Deo, *op. cit.* (n. 384), pp. 386–92; on their order of nuns *cf. ibid.*, chap. iv.

[386] Ovington in Rawlinson (ed.), *op. cit.* (n. 3), pp. 195–96. On *Ahiṁsā* (the doctrine of non-violence and respect for all life) *cf.* Deo, *op. cit.* (n. 384), pp. 205–6, 432–33.

[387] According to their tradition the Parsis arrived at Diu and Sanjan islands in A.D. 716. For their version of the compact with the Hindus see S. K. H. Katrak, *Who Are the Parsees?* (Karachi, 1965), p. 110.

sarry" (Navsari) they maintain an eternal fire which was originally kindled by the sun.[388] They hold all the elements to be sacred and will not defile clean water by urinating in it; they quench a fire with dust or sand rather than water.[389] The Parsis expose their dead "in round Tombs" to be eaten by carniverous birds. The nearest relatives of the departed watch to see which part of the body is first attacked. From this observation they predict the future of the deceased.[390] Parsis are somewhat whiter than most Indians. They live together as an extended family in compounds and greatly revere their father, or the eldest son if he is head of the household. Occupationally they are cultivators rather than merchants.[391]

According to Ovington, the Parsis venerate the cock as much as the Hindus do the cow. They worship fire because it is the emblem of the sun. A Parsi servant will not plunge a hot iron into punch because the heat from fire will be unnaturally extinguished. Zoroaster, their great lawgiver, brought fire from heaven which he commanded his followers to worship. They revere a single supreme being and dedicate the first day of each month to devotions. Other days are set aside for public prayers. To their festivals in the suburbs each believer brings food which all partake of. They are devoted to their fellows, assist the poor, and give comfort where it is needed. No member of their sect is a beggar or is ever "destitute of Relief." They are not as abstemious in their diet as the Hindus, but refrain out of respect from eating beef.[392] Industrious and diligent, they bring up their children to know the meaning of work. Parsis are the main weavers of the silk and other textiles produced in Surat. Their high priests are called "Destoor" (*Dastūrs*) and their ordinary priests are known as "Darvos" (*Dārus*) or "Harboods" (*Harbads*).[393]

Their marriage ceremonies are similar to those of the Banyans. Their dead they expose to be eaten by birds of prey. Several days after death they take the bier into the open fields. A piece of bread or cake is placed in the corpse's mouth which they hope a dog will eat. If the dog is not revolted by the corpse and eats the bread, this is a certain sign that the "Condition that he died in was very happy."[394] Once the dog's part in the ceremony is over, two *Dārus* stand at a distance from the bier and with joined hands repeat by heart a lengthy prayer. These services ended they carry the body to a nearby

[388] The Parsis settled at Navsari in A.D. 1142 and established a chief fire temple there.

[389] For the purity of water in their rituals see J. J. Modi, *The Religious Ceremonies and Customs of the Parsees* (2d ed.; Bombay, 1937), pp. 253–54.

[390] While this assertion is dubious, the Parsis do believe in paradise and hell. See *ibid.*, pp. 479–80.

[391] Fryer in Crooke (ed.), *op. cit.* (n. 4), I, 293–95. Today most Parsis are involved in commerce and business at Surat and Bombay.

[392] Even today only a small percentage of Parsis will eat beef, even though their religion has no prohibition against eating the flesh of animals.

[393] Ovington in Rawlinson (ed.), *op. cit.* (n. 3), pp. 216–18. *Dāru* is an ordinary prefix to a priestly name. Priests are of three classes: *Dastūrs, Mobeds,* and *Harbads.*

[394] *Ibid.*, p. 215. This is a vague reference to the ceremony called the *Sagdid,* or "the sight of the dog." See Modi, *op. cit.* (n. 389), pp. 56–57.

circular tower. The mourners follow the bier two by two with joined hands.[395] After leaving the corpse in the sepulchre, they purify themselves by washing in a stream. A day or two later they return to the tower to inspect the corpse, particularly to see which of its eyes was taken first. If they find the right eye was seized first, "this bodes undoubted Happiness"; misery is foretold if the left is taken first.[396] The Parsis each year take the hair cut off from their heads and beards to this sepulchre for decent burial.[397]

Certain of the artificial cave temples and monasteries of the western Deccan were visited and described by Thévenot, Ovington, Fryer, and Careri. Cave temples began to be cut into the hills and valleys along the trade routes of the Deccan during the second and first centuries B.C.[398] While in Aurangabad, Thévenot decided to make a side-trip to "Elora" (Ellora), whose temples he had heard about. Unable to locate an interpreter, he made the journey with just four bearers and an oxcart. Once atop a steep mountain near "Doltabad" (Daulatabad), the French adventurer sees a broad plateau of well-cultivated land dotted with villages. After an hour's travel he observes a number of "very fair Tombs several stories high."[399] A little further on he passes a great tank and then alights at a small mosque. Pushing onward, he and his bearers climb down a rock to a lower level where there are "very high Chappels" cut out of the "dark grayish stone." On each side of a porch stands a "Gigantick figure cut out of the natural Rock." The walls are "covered all over with other figures in relief, cut in the same manner."[400] Inside is a square court, "an hundred paces every way," with high walls that are "cut as smooth and even, as if they were Plaster smoothed with a Trewel." In the middle of the court stands a chapel whose walls are covered with carved beasts in relief, on either side of which is a "Pyramide or Obelisk" with inscriptions engraved in it. Beside one of the obelisks stands a life-sized rock elephant whose "Trunck has been broken."[401] At the end of the court, two staircases cut into the rock go up to another level "full of stately Tombs, Chappels, and Temples . . . cut in the Rock." One of the great temples, "built in the Rock" has in its interior a flat roof supported by "eight rows of Pillars in length, and six in breadth." The temple is divided

[395] On the importance of the number two in Parsi funeral ceremonies see Modi, *op. cit.* (n. 389), p. 61.

[396] According to Parsi beliefs, the soul of a dead person remains in this world for three days after death. On the ceremonies for the soul of the deceased see *ibid.*, pp. 73–82.

[397] Rawlinson (ed.), *op. cit.* (n. 3), pp. 218–22. Ovington follows this with a morbidly graphic description of the half-eaten carcasses in the Tower of Silence. The burying of the hair is a purification ceremony. *Cf.* Modi, *op. cit.* (n. 389), p. 161.

[398] See V. Dehejia, *Early Buddhist Rock Temples. A Chronology* (Ithaca, N.Y., 1972), pp. 30–31. On Fryer's visit to the Buddhist caves of Ganesha Lena near Junnar see above, p. 773.

[399] Probably the tombs at Rauza near Ellora.

[400] Evidently a reference to the two gigantic *Divarapalas* (doorkeepers) at the north entry to the court of the Kailasa or Rang Mahal temple.

[401] On either side of the detached porch of the Kailasa temple there is a pillar (*dhvajastambha*) flanked by two elephants.

into three sections; the first and main part comprises two-thirds of its length. A second and narrower part resembles a "Quire" (choir). At the end of the temple is a small chapel-like part, in the middle of which stands "a Gigantick Idol, with a Head as big as a Drum, and the rest proportionable."[402] The walls of the chapel are decorated with stone sculptures of huge figures; in the other smaller chapels round about, the sculptured figures are of ordinary size. Nearby is a temple of three stories which has a single facade for all three.[403] In this entire region nothing else is to be seen but these rock temples dedicated to "some Heathen Saints." Although he spent but two hours surveying the cave temples, Thévenot concludes that "they are Works surpassing humane force" and that the men who made them must not have been "altogether Barbarous, though the Architecture be not so delicate as with us."[404]

In 1695 Careri traveled south from Bassein by boat to the large island of Salsette with the intention of visiting and describing the cave temples of Kanheri. As "one of the greatest wonders of Asia," these cave temples exhibit an "incomparable Workmanship, which certainly could be undertaken by none but Alexander." It is Careri's quite incorrect belief that he is the first European to write a description of them.[405] He does provide, however, the most graphic and accurate general description published in his century.

One mile from "Monoposser" (Mandepeshwar) on the island of Salsette a temple is cut in the rock on which stands a college and monastery of the Franciscans.[406] The sides of the cave temple are the natural rock, "only the Front is made by Art."[407] At the top of the craggy rock a great temple is cut out with other smaller caves beside it.[408] Two large pillars stand in front of its veranda; the bottom third of each pillar is square, the middle octagonal, and the top round. They support a stone architrave cut out of the same rock.

---

[402] The Kailasa temple of the eighth century "is by far the most extensive and elaborate rock-cut temple in India, and the most interesting as well as the most magnificent of all the architectural objects which that country possesses." J. Burgess, *Report on the Elura Cave Temples and the Brahmanical and Jaina Caves in Western India*, Vol. V of the *Archaeological Survey of Western India* (reprint of the 1882 ed.; Varanasi, 1970), p. 26. For a brief description of this gem of Indian sculpture and architecture see J. Burgess, *Elura Cave Temples* (Varanasi, 1972; originally publ. 1885), pp. 29–39.

[403] This is the *Tin Thal*, the twelfth and the last of the series of Buddhist cave temples at Ellora. See Burgess, *Report* (n. 402), p. 16.

[404] Sen (ed.), *op. cit.* (n. 2), pp. 104–7. Thévenot was probably the first European to publish a description of some of the thirty-four cave temples of Ellora (*ibid.*, p. xix).

[405] Orta, Linschoten, Do Couto, and Fryer (Crooke [ed.], *op. cit.* [n. 4], I, 186–87) had written about them earlier. Do Couto's account is translated into English by W. K. Fletcher in *JRAS, Bombay Branch*, I (1844), 35–40.

[406] This temple was originally dedicated to Siva. The Franciscan college was built by the missionary Antonio de Porto.

[407] This is one of the smaller of the 128 caves of Kanheri. They are excavated from a bare bubble-like hill of basalt situated in the midst of forest country. Careri refers to such small excavations as "grottos." The Kanheri *caitya* was excavated some time between A.D. 152 and 181. See Dehejia, *op. cit.* (n. 398), pp. 30–31, 183–84. See also Fergusson and Burgess, *op. cit.* (n. 287), p. 348.

[408] This is Cave No. 1 of the Kanheri series.

Three porticoes open into a hall at the end of which are three doors over which other doors and windows and grottoes are cut out of the same rock. Ten paces to the right is a kind of grotto open on two sides and surmounted by a cupola. Here the figure of an idol is cut in half relief which seems to hold something in its hand. By it stand two figures in a submissive posture over whose heads are two small angel-like figures. Below are two other little statues with two children by their sides in a praying posture.[409] In a second room there are four great figures carved in half relief and representations of many of their attendants.[410] Deep within the rock are two statues sitting in the same way and with their hands placed the same way as those in the reliefs.[411]

On the same side of the rock is the most famous of the Kanheri cave temples.[412] At the entrance to this temple is a circular room which holds many sculptured statues, some sitting and others standing. Two columns stand before the entrance. The capital of one supports three statues of figures, and the other, two lions and a shield.[413] Beyond these columns at the entrance to a grotto stand two great statues looking at each other.[414] Nearby are other larger and smaller statues. Three tall doors of equal size open into a veranda. To the right of the doors is an inscription in "unknown Letters worn with Age." Within this place, besides several small figures, stand two statues of "giants," in whose ears are "Pendents after the Indian Fashion." Statues, including some of women, stand on either side of and above the temple's great portal. Over the door's arch is a window the width of the temple. Inside and to the left of the portal is another inscription. Thirty pillars, in addition to the four at the portal, divide its arched nave into three aisles. Seventeen have capitals and figures of elephants on them, the rest are octagonal and plain.[415] At the end of the nave is an empty round cupola (*stupa*) whose use we "cannot guess at."[416]

At a somewhat higher elevation on the mountain, there is another "handsome" temple which fronts upon an open area with a cistern in its center and little benches around it. The temple itself is a square excavation with a rela-

---

[409] This is a sculpture of Buddha and his attendants. The Buddha is seated on the lotus. For a reproduction see Fergusson and Burgess, *op. cit.* (n. 287), pl. LVI.

[410] There are only three main figures in this Buddhist litany. See *ibid.*, pl. LV.

[411] Statues of Buddha and Padmapani, the procreator, who is portrayed with a lotus in his hand.

[412] The great Chaitya cave or No. 3 in the series. For a plan of it and the adjoining caves see Fergusson and Burgess, *op. cit.* (n.287), pl. LIII. For photographs of the facade and interior see Dehejia, *op. cit.* (n. 398), pls. 75–79.

[413] These two columns are known as the "lion pillars."

[414] Two standing Buddhas, each about twenty-three feet high.

[415] "The temple is 86½ feet long by 39 feet 10 inches wide from wall to wall, and has thirty-four pillars round the nave and the dagoba, only 6 on one side and eleven on the other having bases and capitals of the Karlé Chaitya-cave patterns . . . while fifteen pillars round the apse are plain octagonal shafts" (Fergusson and Burgess, *op. cit.* [n. 287], p. 352).

[416] In the early Buddhist caves a hemispherical *stupa* was a symbol of the Buddha and an object of worship.

tively low roof. Over the entrance and on its walls are more than four hundred sculptured figures "but all worn with Ages, which destroys everything."[417] In this temple's vicinity are numerous grottoes and cisterns which "it is likely . . . were the Dwellings of the Priests." In descending the mountain one sees grottoes, cupolas, pillars, statues, and temples which are cut into or stand forth on the hillside.[418]

Fryer, after he spends a week in Bassein, makes a visit to "Elephanto" (Elephanta), an island which gets its name "from a monstrous Elephant cut out of the main Rock, bearing a Young one on its Back."[419] Near to the elephant stands the statue of a horse half buried in the earth.[420] On the crest of the island's highest hill is "a miraculous Piece [cave] hewed out of solid Stone." It is an open square structure supported by "Forty-two Corinthian Pillars." In it stands a carved statue with three heads "crowned with strange Hieroglyphicks."[421] On its north side an altar rises from a high portico; it is guarded by statues of giants and enclosed within a square wall. Huge giants, some with eight hands, line the other walls. This place seems to be of more recent date than "Canorein" (Kanheri) even though it has been defaced by the Portuguese on the island.[422]

That the earlier Portuguese reports of Elephanta had aroused the interest of the court in England is attested by Ovington, who alleges that "the present Queen Dowager" (Catherine of Bragança) expects all returnees from India to give some account of it."[423] Ovington himself is most impressed by the "Pout Gheda" (Persian, *butkadah*, idol house, or temple) cut into the solid rock of the island's high hill.[424] Its central room is about eighteen feet high and "an Hundred and Twenty Foot Square," and adjoining it are several rooms or recesses.[425] Sixteen stone pillars three and one-half feet in diameter and spaced sixteen feet apart seemingly support "this weighty Building." Forty or fifty statues of men, each twelve to fifteen feet in height, stand along its sides. Some of these huge stone figures have six arms, others have three heads, and others have fingers larger than the ordinary person's leg. Some wear crowns and others hold scepters. Above the heads of others

[417] This is Cave No. 67.

[418] Sen (ed.), *op. cit.* (n. 2), pp. 171–79.

[419] *Cf.* Garcia da Orta's visit to Elephanta in 1535. See *Asia*, I, 405. Orta's was the first description published in a European language.

[420] The horse disappeared completely in the eighteenth century.

[421] A famous statue of the *Trimūrti*, the Brahmanical Trinity.

[422] The caves of Elephanta are of the eighth or ninth centry A.D., or about three centuries later than those of Kanheri. See Crooke (ed.), *op. cit.* (n. 4), I, 194–95.

[423] Catherine introduced almost everything Portuguese to the English court, including a consuming interest in India and a taste for China tea. She returned to Lisbon in 1693 and became regent in 1704 for her ill brother Pedro. She died in the following year.

[424] This is the Hindu temple which Fryer—and every other visitor to Elephanta—marvels at. In its plan it resembles Sita's bath at Ellora. See R. S. Wauchope, *The Buddhist Cave Temples of India* (New Delhi, 1981), p. 81.

[425] The height actually varies from fifteen to seventeen feet and the area is 130 × 130 feet. See Murray (publ.), *op. cit.* (n. 40), p. 21.

are reliefs in which "multitudes of little People [are] represented in a posture of Devotion." These figures, according to Ovington, represent "the first Race of Mortals, which, according to the Account of their Chronicles," were originally giants, but then the race shrank in size because of "an Universal decay of Humane Nature."[426]

7

ECONOMY AND SOCIETY

Shortly after his return to France in 1669, Bernier addressed a letter to J. B. Colbert, superintendent of finance and one of Louis XIV's most influential ministers. This letter was designed to let the Mercantilist minister know about the economy and administration of Hindustan.[427] In it he stresses the vastness of a country whose north-south extent from the border of Golconda to Qandahar is "five times as far as from Paris to Lyons." A large part of this state is extremely fertile and productive, particularly Bengal, which surpasses Egypt in grain yields and in the fabrication of articles for trade.

Because of its quantity of exports and its central location in the international trading system, "gold and silver, after circulating in every other quarter of the globe, come at length to be swallowed up, lost in some measure, in Hindustan." India is "an abyss for gold and silver" because so much is used in fabricating jewelry, ornaments, and brocades; most of it, however, is withdrawn from circulation because of the habit they have of secretly burying it.[428] Hindustan is destitute of mines, so the precious metals must be paid for by the export of commodities produced in the country. Hindustan mainly imports copper, lead, fine spices, elephants, horses, fresh fruits, cowries, ambergris, rhinoceros horn, ivory, slaves, musk, porcelain, and pearls. Like gold, these imports are exchanged for native products. Most overseas imports are brought in by European ships and merchants.

A continuous ridge of mountains runs from the Himalayas south to divide India's two coasts from each other.[429] The rivers originate in springs and are swollen by the rain running off the mountains. Among the innum-

[426]Rawlinson (ed.), *op. cit.* (n. 3), pp. 97–99. The figures actually represent Siva and Parvati, the Hindu Trinity, and similar religious subjects. For the myths depicted in this "home of Siva" see W. D. O'Flaherty, George Mitchell, and Carmel Berkson, *Elephanta, the Cave of Shiva* (Princeton, 1983), pp. 27–39.

[427]On Colbert's role in the foundation and establishment of the French East India Company, see above, pp. 95–100. This long letter was published, along with letters to other Frenchmen, in Bernier's book.

[428]Many contemporary European writers, including Tavernier (Ball and Crooke [eds.], *op. cit.* [n. 1], II, 159), explain the seeming absorption of gold in India by reference to a custom of burying it secretly to conceal the owner's wealth. Hoarding of treasure was certainly common among nobles and merchants. For Bernier's comments see Constable (ed.), *op. cit.* (n. 1), pp. 202–5, 223–24, 226.

[429]Fryer in Crooke (ed.), *op. cit.* (n. 4), II, 95. In fact there are two ridges, the Eastern and Western Ghats, and they are not connected to the Himalayas at any point.

erable rivers, the Ganges is especially famous for its many navigable distributaries and for the sanctity of its water. Reservoirs and ponds conserve rain water. Deep wells are dug at great expense by charitable donors to keep their names alive. Most remarkable are those dug to serve the hill fortresses. Mineral waters are scarce but there is a hot spring at "Rajapore" (Rajapur). The lowlands are rich in all necessities except for those pastures that dry up in the hot season. Forage for animals is consequently harvested and stored during the other two seasons. Rice grows best while swimming in water until harvest. At that time the water is let out of the fields by drains. Other grains and cotton want drier ground.[430]

The emperor is the sole proprietor "of every acre of land in the kingdom excepting some houses and gardens which he sometimes permits his subjects to sell" or otherwise dispose of.[431] Much of this vast land is "little more than sand, or barren mountains, badly cultivated, and thinly peopled." Even much of the good land remains untilled because of labor shortages. Unable to pay the heavy exactions laid upon them by their governors, the peasants abandon the land and seek "a more tolerable form of existence" in other occupations. Some even flee from Mughul territories to the lands of the Hindu rajas to escape oppression. The lesson to be learned from the experience of the Mughuls is "Take away the right of private property in land, and you introduce, as a sure and necessary consequence, tyranny, slavery, injustice, beggary, and barbarisms."[432]

The natives "have less the appearance of a moneyed people than those of many other parts of the globe." They live in a debased state because of the land and revenue system. As sole proprietor, the emperor makes grants of land to military and civil officials in lieu of cash and in support of troops on condition that they pay to the imperial treasury all surpluses produced by the assigned lands. The imperial domains are let out to contractors who pay an annual rent for their use. This system leaves the assignees and contractors with "an authority almost absolute over the peasantry, and nearly as much over the artisans and merchants of the towns and villages within their district." Cultivators pay one-half their crop in taxes. To encourage trade, the merchants in port cities and commercial centers are permitted to own their own places and to pass them on to their descendants. Despite his absolutism Aurangzib will listen to the petition of "the meanest Man," a circumstance which "makes the Omrahs very circumspect of their Actions, and punctual in their Payments." Since the capture of Bijapur and Golconda in 1686–87,

---

[430] *Ibid.*, pp. 96–97.

[431] Bernier, unlike many other European observers of the time, qualifies his assertion about the exclusive imperial ownership of the land. For a criticism and analysis of the assertions of European writers about imperial proprietary rights see I. Habib, *op. cit.* (n. 92), pp. 112–14. Also see the same author's statements in *The Cambridge Economic History of India* (see n. 19), I, 235.

[432] Constable (ed.), *op. cit.* (n. 1), pp. 204–5, 238.

Aurangzib claims to own their diamond mines. He has shut them down, abandoned the system previously employed for digging diamonds, and ordained that all stones exceeding a certain size belong to the crown.[433]

According to Bernier, no system of justice exists to which the oppressed may turn for redress of the wrongs they are forced to endure. Abuses of authority are not as merciless near the capitals or the seaports as they are elsewhere far from the kazis. These oppressive conditions obstruct the development of commerce and touch every individual's way of life. Nobody wants to invest in trade or manufacturing when he knows that the fruits of his labor may be snatched away by some local tyrant. The land-revenue system produces such deep misery and exhaustion for the peasants that they have few or no children, not wishing to see them die of starvation. Many emigrate to neighboring states or take employment as servants in the army. "As the ground is seldom tilled otherwise than by compulsion" and the ditches and canals rarely repaired by willing and able hands, "the whole country is badly cultivated and a great part rendered unproductive from the want of irrigation." Houses are left in a dilapidated condition and are neither repaired nor replaced.

Most towns are in an advanced state of decay with their inhabitants living in mud huts. Under these conditions the arts cannot flourish freely. Through the patronage of the emperor and the leading "Omrahs," certain artists continue to work, some stimulated by hope or reward and others by fear of the "korrah" (whip). Rich merchants, who are themselves protected by powerful patrons, help also to preserve the arts by paying higher wages to skilled workers. Ignorance is profound and universal in a country where it is impossible to establish properly endowed academies and colleges. As a consequence the emperor has no reservoir of loyal and talented subjects to call to his service but must surround himself by ignorant, brutal, and parasitical men. Revolts against this oppressive regime occur regularly and are prevented from spreading only by paying a large army to keep the people in subjection. Misery is constantly being aggravated by the selling of power and influence for hard cash or expensive presents. Impelled by blind ambition and an insatiable thirst for power, the country's rulers "grasp at everything until at length they lose everything." About the only thing which works in such a despotism is the legal system. It produces swift justice, especially among those who have neither the means nor the power to corrupt the judges![434]

[433] Ovington in Rawlinson (ed.), *op. cit.* (n. 3), pp. 120–21.
[434] Bernier in Constable (ed.), *op. cit.* (n. 1), pp. 200–238; *cf.* Ovington in Rawlinson (ed.), *op. cit.* (n. 3), pp. 113–15. Bernier's highly critical analysis of the Mughul economy continues to be widely quoted and seriously qualified by modern scholars. *Cf.* Habib, *op. cit.* (n. 92), pp. 325–26; and Tapan Raychaudhuri in *The Cambridge Economic History of India* (see n. 19), I, 172–75.

The European authors who write about Aurangzib's reign are preoccupied, like their predecessors, by Gujarat. After an initial stay of about three weeks in Surat, Thévenot starts on February 1, 1666, for Ahmadabad.[435] Two hours after leaving through the Broach gate, he crosses the Tapti in a boat while his oxcart is carried across by eight men. His first important halt is at Broach, whose ancient and neglected hill fortress he describes as "large and square." The town on the side and foot of the hill is surrounded by stone walls flanked by regularly spaced large round towers. The chief market at the foot of the hill sells the locally woven *baftas*, or cotton cloths, that are exported to all the Indies. The water of the Narbada River has properties which are excellent for bleaching the cloths which are brought there for whitening even from distant places.[436] The Dutch maintain a factor at Broach to clear their dutiable merchandise as quickly as possible through its customs. The country around Broach abounds with peacocks. After Broach Thévenot stops at "Debca" (Dabka), a large village next to a forest. Its inhabitants were formerly "Merdi-Coura" (Persian, *mardumkhor*, or cannibals) and "it is not many years" since human flesh was sold in its markets. Now these people are armed with swords and rob the unprotected for a living. After crossing the Mahi River, Thévenot stops at "Gitbag" (Jitbag in modern Jetalpur) on the outskirts of Ahmadabad. Here he meets on the road a great many "Colies" (*Kolis*), Hindu migrants who pick and clean cotton. The royal garden of "Gitbag" runs along the side of a reservoir and is filled with monkeys and peacocks. Its buildings, including the royal house, are badly in need of repair.[437]

On arriving in Ahmadabad, Thévenot lodges at a caravanserai. After a brief repose, he goes to visit the Dutch factors to present his letter of introduction from their commander at Surat. They invite him to lodge in their factory "in the fairest and longest Street of the Town."[438] From their factory the "Meidan-Chah" (*Maidān-i-Shāh,* or royal square) is entered through "three large arches." Four hundred paces in width and seven hundred in length, this rectangular *Maidān* is enclosed by the trees planted on its sides. Opposite the triple-arched entrance is "the Gate of the Castle" to the west.[439] The gate leading to the caravanserai on the south is protected by six or seven pieces of artillery.[440] The caravanserai, a two-story building, contributes much to the beauty of the courtyard, for it is "a Square of Freestone" var-

[435] For his route see Commissariat, *op. cit.* (n. 165), p. 109, n. 2.

[436] *Cf.* Tavernier in Ball and Crooke (trans. and eds.), *op. cit.* (n. 1), I, 54.

[437] Sen (ed.), *op. cit.* (n. 2), pp. 8–11. On the Jitbag, or garden of victory, see Commissariat, *op. cit.* (n. 165), p. 111.

[438] On the Dutch factory see Commissariat, *op. cit.* (n. 165), p. 112, n. 1.

[439] The *Tin Darwaza,* or Three Gateways, are of carved stone reputedly built by Sultan Ahmad in the early fifteenth century. They lead into the outer court (*Maidān-i-Shāh*) of the *Bhadar,* a citadel built in 1411. Murray (publ.), *op. cit.* (n. 40), p. 162.

[440] The caravanserai was built in 1637 by Azam Khan, the viceroy of Gujarat from 1636 to 1642. It is sometimes wrongly designated as Azam Khan's palace. See Commissariat, *op. cit.* (n. 165), p. 113.

nished to look like marble. Within the court are several smaller square build-ings, which are halls of justice governed by the kotwal.

The royal citadel (the *Bhadar*) nearby is entered through a very high gate between two large towers. Walled about with freestone, the interior of the castle "is as spacious as a little Town." Over the gate is a large balcony where the royal musicians play concerts in the morning, at noon, in the af-ternoon, and at midnight. The royal apartments are decorated with "several Ornaments of Folliages, where Gold is not spared." "In the middle of the town," perhaps as seen from the citadel, stands the English factory with its warehouses full of the textiles of Lahore and Delhi "with which they drive a great trade."[441]

Many large and small mosques dot Ahmadabad, the chief of which is the "Juma-mesgid" (*Jami Masjid*). It stands on the same street as the Dutch fac-tory and is entered "by several large Steps" which lead into a great and al-most square court "adorned with twelve Domes."[442] Three great arches form the entryway to the enclosure and on the other two sides of the court are "two large square gates." Outside each gate there is a high minaret with four balconies from which the "Muezins" (Arabic, *mu'azzin*, or crier) call the faithful to prayer. In the main cupola is the chair of the "imam" (*imām*, leader) and to its right the royal gallery, which is shut off from the mosque by a perforated plaster screen that runs from floor to ceiling.[443] Thévenot also mentions Aurangzib's desecration of the Jain temple of Chinataman, built by Shantidas, when he converted it into a mosque *ca.* 1645.

The "Chaalem" (Shah 'Aalam's mausoleum) is the sepulchre of a wealthy man who is regarded as a magician by the Hindus and a saint by the Mus-lims. On each side of this square building are small cupolas "which set off a great one in the middle." Its entire facade is taken up by seven entrances. On the interior is a square chapel paved with marble and decorated with mother-of-pearl and crystals. Its windows are covered with copper lattice "cut into various Figures." The tomb in the middle of the chapel "is a kind of bed" covered with a cloth of gold and six or seven different-colored canopies. Muslim pilgrims visit the tomb daily and make offerings of white flowers.[444] On the other side of the court there is a similar structure where other of their saints lie buried.[445] Nearby there is also a mosque with chambers for lodging the poor, which has a large garden at its rear.[446]

The royal garden (*Shahi Bag*) outside the city and next to the river is stud-

---

[441] The English factory was well established as early as 1620. For the history of the *Bhadar* see Commissariat, *op. cit.* (n. 165), pp. 113–14.

[442] It stands on the south side of the main street called *Mānik Chauk*.

[443] *Cf.* the description of the *Jami Masjid* in Murray (publ.), *op. cit.* (n. 40), pp. 160–61.

[444] For a photograph of this mausoleum and a summary of its history see J. Burgess, *The Muhammedan Architecture of India* (2 pts.; London, 1900, 1905), Pt. II, pp. 15–23.

[445] See *ibid.*, p. 20.

[446] This mosque was built by Muhammad Salih Badakhshi, probably in the early seventeenth century. *Ibid.*, facing p. 15 for a photograph of the mosque and its court.

ded and lined with all the varieties of trees native to the Indies. It is laid out on many levels, the highest of which is "a Terasse-Walk" overlooking the surrounding villages and countryside. Long walkways are cut through these gardens, along which stretch beds of flowers. In the center of four walks which form a cross stands, next to a tank, a pleasure-house covered with green tiles where young city people gather "to take the fresh Air." [447] Nearby is the mausoleum of a king of Gujarat, a square structure covered with a great dome and five smaller ones on each side. [448] A few streets away stands another domed sepulchre dedicated to a cow buried there.

Outside Ahmadabad is the small town of "Serquech" (Sarkhej) which reputedly was the ancient capital of Gujarat. [449] It enjoys such a reputation because of the vast number of royal tombs found there. [450] One of these, reminiscent of "Chaalem" (Shah 'Alam's tomb), is likewise dedicated to one of their saints. [451] Near the royal tombs stands a mosque flanked by a great tank. In its chapels are the tombs of Gujarati royalty "to which they descend by several Steps of very lovely Stones." Most of the tombs are built along the same general lines and are all full of "marks of the Peoples Devotion," both Muslims and Hindus. Closer to Ahmadabad is a "lovely Well" covered with "seven Arches of Freestone." At each end are staircases which lead underground to the well's six levels. Each level has a gallery of freestone supported by sixteen pillars. At the bottom are three wells, the opening of the third being octagonal in shape. This splendid well was reputedly built at great expense and "at the charge of a Nurse of a king of Gujarat." [452]

In Ahmadabad itself there are hospitals for sick and wounded birds and animals. Some are bought from Christians and Muslims by the "Gentiles." If they prove to be incurable, the beasts are maintained in the hospital for the rest of their lives; if they recover they are sold but only to "Gentiles" and nobody else. "Panthers" (cheetas) for hunting are reserved to the governor who has them trained before sending them as gifts to the emperor. The commodities most traded in Ahmadabad are satins, velvets, taffetas, and tapestries "with Gold, Silk, and Woolen Grounds." Most of the cotton textiles sold there come from Delhi and Lahore. Major exports include indigo from Sarkhej, dried and preserved ginger, sugar, cumin, lac, myrobolans, tamarinds, opium, saltpeter, and honey. The Dutch buy most of their

---

[447] Cf. *ibid.,* pp. 57–60. These gardens were built by Shah Jahan when viceroy between 1610–23.

[448] The tomb of Ahmad Shah, first king of Gujarat. Also see pl. 201.

[449] The ancient capital was Anhilvada (Patan).

[450] Cf. Burgess, *op. cit.* (n. 444), Pt. I, pp. 46–51.

[451] Dedicated to Shaik Ahmad Khattu, the mausoleum was built in the mid-fifteenth century.

[452] The famous step-well at Aswara, outside the walls of Ahmadabad, was built in 1499–1500 by Bai Shri Harir Sultani, the female superintendent of the *Zanana* of Sultan Mahmud I Begara. It is commonly known as the well of Dada Hari. See Commissariat, *op. cit.* (n. 165), p. 115, n. 1.

chintzes here, but they are of coarser quality than those of the Coromandel Coast.[453]

On February 17, 1666, Thévenot leaves the Gujarati capital for Cambay, a distance of "but two days easie Journey." Situated on a gulf of the same name, Cambay is equal in area to Surat but not so populous.[454] It is encompassed by brick walls topped at irregular intervals by towers. The "large streets" of Cambay terminate at gates which are closed and locked at night. Its houses are tall structures of sun-dried bricks. The shops of Cambay sell perfumes, spices, silks, and other textiles. Its artisans make "vast numbers" of ivory bracelets as well as cups, chaplets, and rings of agate. These agates, "no bigger than ones fist," come from the quarries of the nearby village of "Nimroda" (Limroda). The governor's castle is large "but not at all beautiful." The town is overrun with monkeys, but its outskirts are adorned with public gardens. In one of these stands a ruined marble tomb "which a King of Guzerat raised in Honour of his Governor,"[455] as well as many tombs of princes.[456] Indigo is processed in Cambay's extensive suburbs. The sea, which formerly came up to the town, is now "half a League [almost two miles] distant from it," as a result of the silting up of the gulf. As a consequence its trade has declined, for large oceangoing vessels must anchor at too great a distance and must contend with the swift tides of the Bore, as well as the violent storms of September.[457]

Any of three routes may be followed from Cambay to Surat. A sea passage by "almadie" (Portuguese, *almadia,* native canoe or boat) takes the least time, usually about twenty-four hours. It is, however, an exceedingly dangerous passage because of the tides and the Malabar pirates who lurk in the gulf. At low tide the edge of the gulf may also be traversed by cart, but this is likewise an uncomfortable and somewhat dangerous trip. Thévenot finally decides to make the usual journey by land. Because of the omnipresent danger of brigands on this route, he is advised to hire for protection a "Tcheron" (*Chāran*) guide and a woman of this same caste. The members of this caste live mainly in Broach, Cambay, and Ahmadabad and are highly regarded by the Hindus of the region. A *Chāran* guide protects the traveler by threatening to mutilate or kill himself if a robber dares to harm one in his custody. Any Hindu who causes the death of a *Chāran* is expelled from his caste. While *Chārans* have actually killed themselves in the past, they report-

[453] All of the above on Ahmadabad derives from Thévenot in Sen (ed.), *op. cit.* (n. 2), pp. 11–17. On Ahmadabad as an economic unit see B. G. Gokhale, "Ahmadabad in the Seventeenth Century," *Journal of the Economic and Social History of the Orient,* XII (1969), 187–97.

[454] Mandelslo (see above, p. 671) in 1638 found it to be "much greater than Surat." The quick growth of Surat and the consequent decline of Cambay in the interim is the major reason for these differing estimates.

[455] The tomb of Umar bin Ahmad al Kazaruni, who apparently died in 1333.

[456] To 1400 Cambay was the capital of a Muslim state.

[457] Thévenot in Sen (ed.), *op. cit.* (n. 2), pp. 17–18.

edly now work with bandits with whom they divide the loot. As a consequence, Thévenot decides not to use their services.[458] At the passage of the Mahi River, he and his coachmen merely pay a toll to the "Gratiates" (*garasia*s) whose chieftain controls the villages and roads from Cambay to Broach. In return this raja guarantees as best he can the safety of the lone traveler or caravan.[459]

Shortly after returning from his Gujarat tour to Surat in February, 1666, Thévenot sets out in company with "Monsieur Bazou," a French merchant, across the heart of India to Masulipatam on the east coast. For this journey he hires two carts, one for himself and the other for his guide and the luggage; two Rajput servants are also employed to walk beside his cart. On the road southeastward from Surat to Aurangabad, the country is replete with trees and wild animals. Most of the land along the way is arable and produces the best rice in the Indies, especially the aromatic variety which grows around "Navpoura" (Navapur).[460] Cotton and sugarcane also grow here and in many places there are sugar mills and furnaces. Along the highways guards called "Tchoguis" (*chaukī*s) ask for money even though they do not perform services for it. In the towns are many temples and tanks as well as caravanserais too dirty to be satisfactory hostels. While encamped at "Setana" (Satana), halfway to Aurangabad, Thévenot and his companion meet the Bishop of Heliopolis who is on the way back to France from his post in Siam.[461]

At the end of 1679 Dr. Fryer is back from his travels in Persia. Soon after his return he is called to Broach to take care of an English merchant in the factory there. Broach can be approached from Surat by sea or land. The sea route runs directly from Suwali to the mouth of "Broach's River" (the Narbada). Fryer takes the land route, which runs over a spacious plain and can be traversed by coach or on horseback. He contrasts this route to those in Persia. There the traffic is light, whereas in Gujarat the road is always crowded with caravans of heavy wagons drawn by teams of oxen as well as all sorts of other traffic. Guides are needed in Persia while guards are more important in Gujarat. In Persia the roads are safe and open at all seasons, while in Gujarat travelers "must observe the set times, and move with a good Force." Inns, so numerous in Persia, are hard to find on the Broach road; shelter is where it can be found. But rivers and other sources of water are more plentiful in Gujarat as well as provisions of all sorts.

Fryer's two-wheeled "chariot" is drawn by two large white oxen with brass-tipped horns, scarlet collars, brass bells around their necks, and bri-

---

[458] The Gujarati *Chāran*s, a community related to the *Bhāt*s, still exist. For their role in former times as guards attached to travelers see Commissariat, *op. cit.* (n. 165), pp. 120–23.

[459] Sen (ed.), *op. cit.* (n. 2), pp. 18–21.

[460] *Cf.* Tavernier in Ball and Crooke (trans. and eds.), *op. cit.* (n. 1), I, 41.

[461] Thévenot in Sen (ed.), *op. cit.* (n. 2), pp. 102–3. On Bishop François Pallu see above, pp. 231–33, 241–52.

dles in their nostrils. The bed of the wagon sits on the main axle, supports a "Foursquare Seat," and has pillars at each corner to hold up the sides and roof. Its interior is covered with carpets and lined with cushions to support the riders who sit cross-legged. The driver perches on the tongue of the wagon and carries a goad instead of a whip. In the rainy season "when they rarely stir," the wagon is covered with a "Mumjuma" (Persian, *momjāmah,* waxed cloth).[462]

The road northward from Surat is lined with flourishing fields of grain as well as tobacco plantations. A ferry carries the traveler across the Tapti to "Bereaw" (Barião). It takes from sunrise to midnight to reach "Uncliseer" (Anklesvar), one of the southernmost towns in Gujarat. Here a toll is paid before proceeding to the Narbada River. This broad, swift, and deep river is crossed, somewhat dangerously, in a boat, whose pilot must avoid the shoals. Large vessels can be brought up the river to the walls of Broach, where they are loaded with salt, grain, and cotton textiles. Before the Mughuls took Gujarat, Broach was a place of great importance, strategically located on the highways to Lahore, Delhi, Agra, and Ahmadabad. Its walls were razed because the city refused to permit free passage to Shah Jahan's army.[463] From the ruins it can be seen that there was a strong double wall and entrenchment pierced by nine gates.[464] Within the fort stands a former Hindu temple which has been converted into a mosque.[465] A mile outside the city is the tomb of "Mahmoody," the last of the independent Gujarati rulers.[466]

While Thévenot's personal travels were confined to central India, he systematically sought information on other parts of the Mughul Empire from native informants and other itinerant Europeans. Much of this material duplicates the comments and conclusions of earlier European writers. But because Thévenot was a tireless observer and researcher, he provides occasional new materials in his systematic surveys of the imperial provinces. In these synoptic accounts he ordinarily places the province geographically, lists its most important towns and products, and ends by estimating its annual contribution to the imperial purse.[467] Tucked into these methodical paragraphs are occasional sidelights and acute observations which are novel. He also departs every so often from provincial organization to summarize what he has learned of castes, costumes, conveyances, and animals.

The castes of India are said to total eighty-four, divided into "an infinite

[462] Crooke (ed.), *op. cit.* (n. 4), III, 155–58. To Fryer this conveyance is comical.

[463] Because Broach aided Dara during the wars of succession, Aurangzib in 1660 ordered a part of its wall to be razed. See Commissariat, *op. cit.* (n. 149), II, 163, n. 26.

[464] According to tradition Broach's wall is of the late eleventh and early twelfth century. It was rebuilt and strengthened by Bahadur Shah (r. 1526–36).

[465] The Jami Masjid, or Principal Mosque, stands on the site of an old Jain temple.

[466] Crooke (ed.), *op. cit.* (n. 4), III, 158–60. The tomb is that of Mahmud II (d. 1554); the sultanate was actually ended by the victory of Akbar's forces in 1572.

[467] See above, pp. 738–39.

number of sects."[468] All members of a caste follow a particular occupation; the children must follow the same one. For example, Brahmans "profess Doctrine and so do their Children." Kshatriya or Rajputs, the second caste, are soldiers who claim to be descendants of princes. Actually some members of this second caste are merchants, and in Multan, Lahore, and Sind, some are weavers.[469] The third caste is called "Souder" (Sudra) or "Courmy" (Kurmi) and they are the tillers of the soil. Some also serve as guards or foot soldiers. The Sudra is the biggest caste in terms of numbers.[470] The fourth is the caste of Banyans and they are "all Merchants, Bankers, or Brokers, and the expertest People in the World for making Money of [from] anything." In ancient days these four were the only castes, but over time any group following the same occupation constituted itself a caste: "Colis" (Kolis) are "Cotton-dressers;" "Teherons" (Charans) traveler escorts; "Covillis" (probably Kolis) carry palanquins. There are also occupational castes of bow and arrow makers, "Hammer-men" (who include armorers, smiths, and masons), woodworkers, prostitutes and dancers (including tumblers and jugglers), tailors, and coach and saddle makers.[471]

The *Kunbis* are peasants who till the soil and harvest the grain "with no remarkable Difference from other Nations." Their plow of hardwood pulled by oxen turns the thin soil without the aid of a sharp "iron Colter." Hindus thresh grain with a stick rather than a flail; Muslims have their oxen tread upon it in the open fields before carrying it home.[472] The "Bengiara" (Banjaras) are bearers, painters, and artisans.[473]

The polluting castes are the "Piriaves" (Pariyans) and the "Der" (Dher) or "Halalcour" (Persian, *Halālkhor*). The Pariyans are leatherworkers, while the Halalkhors, called "sweepers" in English, are the town scavengers; for their services they receive a monthly wage.[474] Halalkhors perform necessary functions others will not consider doing: sweeping houses and offices, cleaning streets, "carrying away the Dirt and Dung," and washing dead bodies and carrying them in funerals.[475] They are not permitted to carry on their own funerals and marriages in the presence of others. They are considered to be

[468] Probably confused with the common Hindu belief that the soul has to pass through eighty-four forms of life before reaching perfection. The castes, large and small, must have numbered in the thousands during the seventeenth century. See above, pp. 655–56.

[469] The "merchants" are probably Khatri, a trading caste of the Punjab and northwest India who claim Kshatriya origin. See J. H. Hutton, *Caste in India* (4th ed.; Oxford, 1963), pp. 66, 285.

[470] Actually the Sudra is the fourth order of the Hindu scriptures. On the relationship of the concept of *Varna,* or the division of Hindu society into four orders, and the caste system of reality see M. N. Srinivas, *Caste in Modern India and Other Essays* (Bombay, 1962), chap. iii.

[471] Sen (ed.), *op. cit.* (n. 2), pp. 88–89. Thévenot provides no names for these occupational castes.

[472] Modes of threshing vary according to locality and the kinds of grain and not according to religion.

[473] On the Banjaras see Hutton, *op. cit.* (n. 469), pp. 21, 277. Thévenot, because of his lack of personal experience elsewhere, limits his description to the castes of northwestern India.

[474] In modern India these two are referred to as "exterior castes."

[475] Ovington in Rawlinson (ed.), *op. cit.* (n. 3), p. 223.

unclean because they eat meat of all sorts, as well as the leavings of others. Another caste called "Baraguy" (Bairagi) dislike the color yellow and wear a white rather than the usual red mark on the forehead.[476] Members of all these castes worship in the same temples, each worshipping the idol or god of choice. Intermarriage beween members of different castes does not occur. All castes are status conscious, so that Banyans yield to Kurmis, Kurmis to Rajputs, and all to the Brahmans. Those Brahmans who practice medicine pay a "yearly tribute" to their caste for the right to pursue an occupation not appropriate to a Brahman. Their main gods are Rama and his wife Sita, whom they often confuse with the Virgin Mary. Many Hindus visit Portuguese Bassein to make offerings to an image of the Virgin known as "Our Lady of Remedies."[477]

According to Fryer, Brahmans are of two basic types: "Butts" (*Bhat*) and "Sinais" (Mahratti, *chhianave,* ninety-six).[478] Because of a famine in the lowlands, the latter type took up the eating of fish to fend off starvation. Although they are utterly despised by the undefiled Bhats, they still wear the Brahmanical cord.[479] The Bhats live according to a rule, study and teach law and ceremonies, and practice as physicians. The "Sinais" take posts as civil servants, physicians, accountants, secretaries, and interpreters. Both groups keep their "pious Secrets" in a language known only to themselves. Those who are learned are highly revered even though they are rigidly dogmatic in their teaching of the people. They believe that God is "uncomparably Good," and in some of their languages a term for "Hell" does not exist. Instead of immortality of the soul, they believe in transmigration.

The Brahmans study magic and astrology principally. Some are masters of their numerous languages: Persian, Hindustani (Hindi and Urdu), Arabic, Sanskrit or "Holy Language," Portuguese, Deccani, Mahratti, Konkani, and "Canatick" (Kanarese or Kannada). Their sonnets and poems are written mainly in Kannada since that language is "softer and more melting than the others." They understand something of physics and metaphysics, and are not "quite ignorant" of medicine even though they have only a slight understanding of its rationale. Their music seems "loud and barbarous; yet

---

[476] They are Hindu mendicants and recluses found mainly in the Punjab and the central provinces. See the listing in E. J. Kitts, *A Compendium of the Castes and Tribes of India* (Bombay, 1885), p. 2.

[477] Sen (ed.), *op. cit.* (n. 2), pp. 88–92. The church of Nossa Senhora dos Remedios is near Bassein and many miracles are attributed to its patroness.

[478] Among the Mahrattas the Bhat are a mendicant and learned Brahman group held in high regard. "Sinais" probably refers in a general way to all other types of Brahmans. For a discussion of the Bhat see William Crooke, *The Tribes and Castes of the North-Western Provinces and Oudh* (4 vols.; Calcutta, 1896), II, 20–29. In recent times the Brahmans of Gujarat include 160 subdivisions. See P. Thomas, *Hindu Religion, Customs, and Manners* (4th rev. ed.; Bombay, 1960), p. 13.

[479] Abbé Dubois in H. K. Beauchamp (trans. and ed.), *Hindu Manners, Customs, and Ceremonies* (3d ed.; Oxford, 1959), p. 110, talks of the fish and egg-eating Konkani Brahmans of the north.

they observe Time and Measure in their Singing and Dancing." They dislike European music and feel that our laments are "fit to play to Bears." While European stringed instruments do not appeal to them, they will listen in rapture to the organ. They have a natural propensity for arithmetic and quickly do difficult calculations in their heads. In some places they write on palm leaves with an iron stylus. Secretaries write on paper with a reed pen and ink, which they keep in a brass case that they carry in their girdles.[480]

Physicians are not trained in schools or licensed, but simply follow traditional methods of treatment. Brahmans treat patients free of charge expecting only acknowledgment as the patient's sole physician. Indian physicians, even the Muslims who follow the Arabic tradition, know nothing of anatomy, since dissection of the human body is illegal. Since they do not understand the system of veins, they cannot practice phlebotomy. Instead of blood-letting they martyr patients by clapping on hundreds of leeches which suck blood until they drop off by their own weight. Surgery and pharmacy are in an equally parlous condition. Amputation is "an horrid thing," while medicines are compounded by the physicians themselves or by untrained apothecaries. They "pretend to understand the Pulse" but will never examine the urine. Fevers, including malaria, are treated with powders of "Natural Cinnabar" (mercuric sulphide) which work infallibly and as well as "the Peruvian Bark" (cinchona). Poor women deliver their own children without much difficulty or loss of time from work; only the "Rich and Lazy" employ midwives. Instead of going to physicians for treatment, some ill persons consult sorcerers or seek "the Advice of Old Women."[481]

The common language of the Indian Muslims is different from that of the Hindus and has no alphabet of its own. In writing this language they borrow their letters from the Hindus, the Persians, or other nations.[482] The Persian court language is used by all nobles and "Persons of Ingenuity and polite Conversation." The introduction of Persian and the growth of a Muslim common language is helpful in completing the conquest of a nation which continues to maintain zealously its old traditions and languages. While the Brahmans continue to uphold Sanskrit as the language of Hindu religion and learning, it is so difficult to learn that "several of themselves therefore understand [it] not."

The paper books in common use are long scrolls, sometimes ten feet long and one foot wide, which are sewn together at the top.[483] Pens are made of reeds and are often kept in inkstands with the ink. Ordinary paper is shiny and smooth, and that used for official correspondence is gilded on the sur-

---

[480] Fryer in Crooke (ed.), *op. cit.* (n. 4), II, 100–104.

[481] *Ibid.*, I, 285–88. Preparations of mercury are still used for fevers by native physicians.

[482] Urdu, a dialect which became widespread under the Mughuls, is a mixture of Hindi and Persian. It was written in Persian or Sanskrit characters indifferently. Urdu includes many loan words from Persian and Arabic.

[483] This probably refers to the account books of the merchants.

face and ornamented with flowers.[484] Official letters are sent in a hollow bamboo, the open end of which is sealed. "Chops" (Hindi, *chhāp*, seal-impression) are seals engraved on gold, silver, or carnelians with characters which generally represent the owner's name. Letters are generally sent by a "Pattamar [Konkani, *pātamār*] or Foot Messenger" no matter what the distance. While they do not adopt European printing techniques, they "imitate a little the English manner of Binding Books."[485]

Hindus follow a lunisolar calendar in which the months are reckoned by the moon; every third year they insert an intercalary month in August "and count it double." Each year is divided into twelve months beginning in March, and Fryer gives their Sanskrit names in a recognizable romanization of his own devising. Their weeks are divided into seven days, Sunday being a holy day to the Hindus.[486] Day and night are each divided into twelve hours throughout the year, no allowance being made for varying periods of light and dark in the different seasons. Indians, not having watches or hour glasses, measure time by the outflow of water from a brass basin. Each basin holds a "Ghong" (*gong*) of water which takes something less than one-half hour to drain out. When the basin is empty, they strike it once to announce the expiration of the first "Ghong." The process is repeated until they reach eight "Ghong," which is equivalent to the first "Pore" (Hindi, *pahr,* a watch or one-fourth of a day or night). Each day and night is thus divided into sixty-four "Ghongs" or eight "Pores."[487] Instead of dividing the year into four seasons of three months each, they have three seasons of four months each: "Mew Colla" (Hindi, *Menh Kāl*) or the rainy season, "Ger Colla" (*Jārā Kāl*) or the cold season, and "Deup Colla" (*Dhūp Kāl*) or the hot season. The rainy season begins with the first full moon in May and ends in September; the cold season comes next and ends around February 1; the hot season therefore includes February, March, April, and May. Fevers rage in the first part of the rainy season. At its end the first crop of rice is harvested. The cold season is healthier, and at its end they harvest a second crop. During the hot season the leaves drop from the trees but are quickly replaced. Since this season is also excessively dry, only those who irrigate may glean a lean crop. They keep their crops alive by drawing water from wells in buckets raised by oxen, by lever (the *dhenklī*), or on a wheel. The water is conducted into the fields by aqueducts.[488]

Wealthy Indians, according to Thévenot, usually travel in comfortable

[484] Paper-making was first introduced in India in the fourteenth century. See G. Watt, *The Commercial Products of India* (London, 1908), p. 863.
[485] Ovington in Rawlinson (ed.), *op. cit.* (n. 3), pp. 147–50; *cf.* Qaisar, *op. cit.* (n. 36), p. 145.
[486] Fridays are the days when Hindus usually go to their temples to pray.
[487] Actually each quarter (*pahr*) was divided into *gharis* of twenty-four minutes each, or sixty *gharis* for a day and a night. This is exactly the reverse of the Western system of twenty-four hours, each sixty minutes in length. See Qaisar, *op. cit.* (n. 36), p. 68.
[488] Fryer in Crooke (ed.), *op. cit.* (n. 4), II, 90–94. Most of these observations relate to Surat and its vicinity.

palanquins rather than in carts or coaches. In Thatta, the port of Sind, palanquins are like couches suspended by ropes from two great bamboos. The
couch itself has a short railing on either side and a backrest at its head. It is
equipped with a canopy to keep off the sun and rain, with mats and cushions
to repose upon, and with silk straps attached to the bamboo to help the pas-
senger move about. Such luxurious palanquins are expensive and their owners decorate them, each according to his individual taste. Porters, four to the
conveyance, are relatively inexpensive.[489] Persons of lesser means travel generally in the two-wheeled carts of Thatta. The bed of the cart is flat and
even, and enclosed by a railing and short posts. Leather thongs are inter-
woven netlike through the posts to keep the passengers from falling out. Its
two wheels have eight spokes each, but often do not have metal bands around
the rim. The wheels of freight-bearing carts have no spokes and are but
"one whole piece of solid wood." The beds of these carts are also of heavy
wood. Ordinarily heavy loads are drawn by eight to ten oxen. Caravans
commonly include more than two hundred such carts.[490]

As artisans the Indians are ingenious both in their originality and in their
ability to copy European products and patterns. Weavers of silk imitate European patterns exactly. Shipbuilders at Surat will produce "the Model of
any English vessel . . . as exactly as if they had been the first Contrivers."
They build these vessels of a superior hard wood (teak) that will not splinter
when hit by a bullet. Tailors fashion clothes according to all prevailing
styles. They refuse, however, to mend old clothes in the morning and will
do it only in the afternoons. While the Indians make no attempt to produce
European clockworks, the Chinese have begun to study and work with mechanical clocks. European dyers are unable to paint cloths to match the
brightness and the "life of the Colours" of the chintzes of India. The gold-
rimmed carnelian rings made in India that are inlaid with precious stones
cannot be successfully reproduced elsewhere. The Indians cleverly carry
water in earthen pots called "Kousers" (Persian, *kūza*), which keep it cool
and fresh.[491]

In connection with his discussion of Agra, Thévenot digresses on
Mughul costume, a subject on which his own experiences make him a firsthand authority. For, as he says, "there is a pretty great uniformity in the
manner of apparel" throughout the empire. Muslim males differ in dress
from other Indians only by the distinctive headcloth they wear. All Indian
men wear cotton breeches which end between the calf and the ankle. The
rich wear long, colored and striped pajamas of silk, which are pleated on
the leg to keep them from dragging on the ground. A shirt is worn over the
breeches, many of which, following Muslim custom, are "open from top to

[489] Cf. Ovington's description in Rawlinson (ed.), *op. cit.* (n. 3), p. 152. See pl. 128.
[490] Sen (ed.), *op. cit.* (n. 2), pp. 75–76; cf. Qaisar, *op. cit.* (n. 36), pp. 37–38.
[491] Ovington in Rawlinson (ed.), *op. cit.* (n. 3), pp. 166–67, 174–75.

bottom." These shirts are worn also by non-Muslims, because they are cooler and more easily "put on and off." In cold weather an "Arcaluck" (Turkish, *arqualiq*), a coat with sleeves, is worn over the shirt. Ordinarily, it is a quilted cotton coat covered on the outside with chintz or painted cloth. Sometimes they wear a "Caba" (Arabic, *qabā*, vesture) over the coat. This is a tunic-like upper garment which is pleated from top to bottom to keep it from spreading out too much. It is tied together with bands of the same white cotton material. When these clothes are not warm enough, they don another outer garment called a "Cadeby" (?). For the outdoors they wear a "Chal" (Hindi, *shāl*, or shawl) of Kashmir wool which they drape across the shoulders, tie the two ends together across the stomach, and let the rest fall down the back. Others wear these shawls like a scarf; those of the poor are "of plain Cloath." The turban of the Indian Muslim is always white and the head is shaved. The other Indians wear them over the hair and tie them higher behind than in front. Indians wear no stockings or socks. Their thin leather slippers are called "Papouches" (Persian, *pā-posh*). The rich have borders of gold on their flat-heeled and open sandals. Banyans have heels in their slippers, for as businessmen they must "walk with freedom." Rich Banyans wear slippers covered on the top with velvet that is embroidered "with great Flowers of Silk."

The Mughul women, who wish to be different from other ladies, dress almost like their men. But the sleeves of their shirts never fall below the elbow, so they are free to wear jewelry on the forearms.[492] The ordinary bodices (*cholis*) of other Indian women end at the waist as do their outer waistcoats. From the waist to the feet they wrap themselves in a length of cloth (*sārī*), one end of which reaches "up to their Head behind their Back." On their feet they wear "high Pattins [footwear]." They wear rings in their ears and nostrils, as well as on their fingers. Among their many rings, they always have one inset with a small mirror so that they can see themselves.[493]

Hindus are distinguished from one another by the cut of their beards, by the various modes of marking their bodies and foreheads, and by the way they tie their turbans. Hindus wear little beards and shave around them, while Muslims have great beards which they trim only slightly. Barbers seldom work in shops but travel around the city "with a Chequered Apron over their Shoulders, and a Mirror in their Hands." They also carry a razor "not an inch long," a small brass basin, and a piece of Castile soap. They dip the soap into the basin of water and then rub the wet soap over the face or head. They give good shaves, especially of the head. They clean the ear with one end of an iron tool and trim the nails with its other end. Even the poor bathe daily, "both Men and Women," and anoint their bodies with oil. The

---

[492] Mughul ladies and other Muslim women were distinguished primarily by their *shalwars* (breeches) and shirts with sleeves to the elbow. See Ojha, *op. cit.* (n. 285), p. 30.

[493] Thévenot in Sen (ed.), *op. cit.* (n. 2), pp. 50–53.

poor use rank coconut oil which, combined with the "Hing" (asafoetida) and garlic they eat, makes them reek offensively "before one be accustomed to them."[494]

On holidays public entertainments are put on by dancing girls called "Quenchenies" (Hindi, *kanchani*) who by their amorous looks and calculated charms often entrap the unwary European male.[495] Some performers amaze spectators with the Indian rope trick and others magically produce in an hour or so a mango tree with ripe fruit upon its branches. Others take their recreation by playing chess. Snake charmers are a common sight as they play a pipe to make their snakes dance. A tame snake brought to the English factory is so huge that it is able to swallow a chicken whole. The snakestone of Diu, or a burning coal, is used as a specific to counteract the venom of snakebites, which are frequent. Cures for a variety of ailments are effected by the Maldive coconut (*Coco de Mer,* or double coconut) and the rhinoceros horn.[496]

Parsis are "straw Coloured," Ethiopians "Black and Frizled," and the Indians a long-haired mixture of the two, who vary in darkness from region to region. Indian infants are white but soon become the brown color of their parents. Their women are small, wide-hipped, and shorter than the men. They mature earlier than European women and "leave off Childbearing sooner."[497] Indian women are neat, well-shaped, "obsequious to their Husband," quick in labor, and affectionate to their children. They bind their breasts carefully, carry their naked offspring on their hips, and are unashamed "to shew the Motion" of their well-proportioned bodies. Clean both in cooking and in personal grooming, they pluck out their pubic hair to keep "their privities . . . as smooth there as the back of their Hands." The hair of their head grows out in tresses which they decorate with gold ornaments, rich jewels, and jasmine flowers. Their attire does not change in style nor is it made by a seamstress or tailor. They merely throw a "Lungy" (Hindi, *lungi,* a bodycloth or a waist cloth) loosely over their shoulders and tie it between their legs; beneath it they wear a short waistcoat to hold up their breasts.[498] They never wear shoes or stockings. Widows who survive their husbands are shaved, deprived of their jewels, condemned to wear a red "Lungy," and treated worse than the lowliest servant.[499] Babies are not wrapped in swathings and there are very few deformed or stunted children. They live temperate lives and when they grow old their hair becomes gray. Wives cook, fetch water, and grind grain. Hindus bake their thin wafer-like

[494] Fryer in Crooke (ed.), *op. cit.* (n. 4), II, 108–9.

[495] *Kanchani,* or "Nautch-Girls," were both Hindus and Muslims. See Yule and Burnell, *op. cit.* (n. 124), p. 295.

[496] Ovington in Rawlinson (ed.), *op. cit.* (n. 3), pp. 153–59.

[497] On early marriage and childbearing *cf.* Ojha, *op. cit.* (n. 285), pp. 123–26.

[498] Ovington in Rawlinson (ed.), *op. cit.* (n. 3), p. 161. *Cf.* Ojha, *op. cit.* (n. 285), pp. 27–28.

[499] Hindu widows are still subjected to persecutions and humiliation and are considered to be ill omens at marriages. See Thomas, *op. cit.* (n. 478), p. 60.

bread of rice on "round Plates or Stones"; Muslims plaster the dough of their thicker wheat bread on the sides of a furnace to bake.[500] The common foods of the ordinary people are boiled rice, "Nichany" (Mahratti, *nachani*, ragi, or raggy millet) and millet; in times of famine they eat "Grass-Roots." Contentedly they finish off their simple meals with a pipeful of tobacco.[501]

Hindus eat grapes and drink unfermented grape juice. Most of their native edible fruits, however, are unknown in Europe: pineapples, custard apples (*Anona squamosa*), and mangoes. Europeans as well as Indians eat mangoes in vast quantities "for pleasure and delight." When they are green, the mangoes are pickled and "Mango Achar" (chutney) is sent to England. Watermelons are large, delicious, and rich but are surpassed in delicacy, taste, and fragrance by the muskmelons of Ahmadabad. At any time of the day the Banyans brew and drink large quantities of coffee and China tea. Tea is drunk as much by the Dutch as by the Indians. Often they mix hot spices, sugar-candy, "small Conserv'd Lemons," or arrack in the tea. Banyans ordinarily do not drink water from wells or rivers, only that which "falls from Heaven" in the monsoon rains. At noon Indians usually eat "Dye" (*dahī*, curd), a thick sweet milk product mixed with boiled rice and sugar. "Kitcheree" (*khichri*, or kedgeree, buttered rice with split peas) is cooked over fires of wood or dried cow dung. No heat is required in dwellings, so firewood for cooking is bought in small quantities only. Banyans prepare most food at home and rarely buy cooked food from shops. They eat their major meals around 8:00 A.M. and 5:00 P.M., it being too hot at noon to eat very much. During the heat of the day they rest and sleep.[502]

Indian Muslims often eat meat, especially in mixed dishes. "Dumpoked" (Persian, *dampukht*, steamed food cooked in sealed pots) is meat garnished with spice in butter; "Pullow" (Persian, *pulāo*) is a stew of rice and butter which may include meat, poultry, or fish. They also like fruits, relishes, pickles, and sweets. When entertaining Christians, they order separate dishes. Between meals they serve coffee, tobacco, and *pan* (betel), and "drown" their guests and themselves with expensive scents. While they drink no wine publicly, they tipple in private with "sack" (for example, sherry) or brandy right out of the bottle. They meet strangers at the entrance of their homes, and invite them to remove their shoes or slippers. After the usual greetings, all sit down in "Choultris" (Malayalam, *chāwati*, a hall) spread with carpets and cushions and overlooking a tank. They sit cross-legged on the carpets with the pillows bolstering "their Back and Sides"; they think it rude to expose their legs while sitting. The ceilings and posts of their rooms are adorned with colorful cloths. Men dress neatly and walk gravely; in their girdle they usually carry a dagger. Their women

[500] Hindus baked on a *tāwā*, or griddle; Muslims in a *tanur*, or oven. But now there is no distinction.
[501] Fryer in Crooke (ed.), *op. cit.* (n. 4), II, 114–19.
[502] Ovington in Rawlinson (ed.), *op. cit.* (n. 3), pp. 179–85.

wear unbecoming drawers and silver and pearl head ornaments, bracelets, earrings, and nose rings on which jewels hang. They do not use gold because it is "Nigess" (Arabic, *najiis,* unclean).[503]

Thévenot, perched in a window to get a better view, describes the Muslim wedding of the governor of Surat's daughter to the son of an "Omra."[504] About two weeks before the appointed Wednesday, the bridegroom announces his forthcoming marriage by entertaining the public with musical concerts. Around eight on the evening of the ceremony a procession forms of torchbearers, musicians, and dancing girls. The bridegroom rides immediately behind on horseback "his face covered with a Gold-Fringe" which hangs down "from a kind of Mitre" on his head. He is followed by twelve horsemen, two elephants with their riders, and two camels carrying musicians. After parading about the city for two hours, the bridegroom is brought to the governor's house, into which he retires. Then bonfires are lighted on the river bank in front of the house. The river itself is illuminated by barks full of lamps and by candles put into the water near "Rendell" (Rander) on the other side of the river, which float gently with the ebb tide toward the sea.[505] A lavish display of fireworks is put on for almost an hour. Finally the marriage is performed in the governor's house by a mullah; then the bride is carried off on an elephant to her husband's dwelling. While observing the procession, Thévenot sees some "Hermaphrodites," persons who are obliged "to wear upon their Heads a Tuban like Men, though they go in the habit of Women."[506]

He also describes the Muslim festival of "Choubret" (Persian, *Shab-i-Barāt* or Night of Record), a night of reckoning by the angels of the good and sinful actions of men. They celebrate it with illuminations, bonfires, fireworks, and feasts.[507]

Hindus wed girls of six or seven years of age but wait until the girl is eleven or twelve to consummate the marriage.[508] The courting of the young girl by her husband is conducted during these years, and it involves frequent visits, presents, and amorous looks and sighs. To prepare the bride for the conjugal state she is fed great quantities of boiled milk. The new husband prepares himself by drinking ghee. A widow who fails to burn herself on her husband's pyre may not remarry even if she is only six or seven years of

[503] Fryer in Crooke (ed.), *op. cit.* (n. 4), I, 234–36.

[504] In 1666 the governor was Muhammad Beg Khan.

[505] Once an important port, Rander, according to Thévenot, was daily falling into ruins. The Dutch nonetheless maintained a factory there.

[506] Sen (ed.), *op. cit.* (n. 2), pp. 31–33. On Muslim marriage customs see Yasin, *op. cit.* (n. 285), pp. 57–59.

[507] Sen (ed.), *op. cit.* (n. 2), p. 44. This is sometimes called the "Guy Fawkes Day of Islam." For a more detailed description of its meaning and celebration see Yasin, *op. cit.* (n. 285), pp. 51–53.

[508] Child marriages are now illegal but many continue to be arranged by orthodox Hindus. Wealthy families will pay a fine to follow this ancient custom. See Thomas, *op. cit.* (n. 478), pp. 59–60.

age and still a virgin. Husbands may remarry and may have several wives at once. Many men nonetheless restrict themselves to one wife because of the feuds and jealousies that reign in a polygamous household. There are no secret or private marriages at Surat, for all parties participate in public ceremonies, including a procession through the city on horseback. The wedding takes place at the bride's home: the couple sits opposite each other on chairs with a table between them. While they join hands over the table, a Brahman covers each of their heads with a "Pamarin" (Mahratti, *pāmari,* a silk scarf) and prays for their happiness. This wedding ceremony being completed, "mirth and Festivity follow." Guests are sprinkled with rose water and other perfumes. Outer garments are colored yellow with saffron as a symbol of gladness. Since marriages are performed only on auspicious days, sometimes "two or three hundred" will be celebrated on the same day. All wedding ceremonies end with a banquet to which all guests are invited. The sumptuous banquets of the wealthy will sometimes last for over a week. Brahmans marry even though they are priests.[509]

Pregnant women are encouraged by others to be serene and cheerful so that the child when born will be happy. For ten days after childbirth a new mother is touched by none but a "dry Nurse." Forty days must pass before she is allowed to prepare food. Indian cradles are "more convenient than ours" since they are hung by strings from a beam or post and are swung easily and quietly just by a touch of the hand.[510] The Hindus name their children ten days after birth. For this ceremony they assemble twelve boys, who hold a large sheet while standing in a circle. A Brahman pours rice into the middle of the sheet and lays the unnamed infant down upon it. The boys shake the child and the rice for at least fifteen minutes. Then the father's sister, the infant's aunt, advances to the sheet and names the child. In the absence of a father's sister, this privilege devolves upon the father or the mother. A month or two after it has received a name, the child is taken to the temple for its religious initiation. A Brahman of the temple puts on the child's head a mixture of sandalwood shavings, camphor, cloves, and perfumes. By this rite the child officially becomes a "Member of their Religion."[511]

Hindus burn their dead and sometimes the seriously ill thought to be beyond recovery, or mistaken for dead. The corpse is carried on a bier accompanied by relatives and friends who chant "Ram, Ram," as they walk along the road. When a raja dies, his subjects mourn by cutting off their beards and shaving their heads. After the death of a friend, the Banyans put on expensive feasts which last for two or three days. Similar observances occur on the twelfth, twentieth, thirtieth, and fortieth days thereafter and once each

[509] Ovington in Rawlinson (ed.), *op. cit.* (n. 3), pp. 189–95.

[510] *Ibid.,* pp. 197–98.

[511] *Ibid,* p. 197. The Naming Ceremony is still celebrated in this manner in Gujarat. For further details on *Nāmakarana* (Name Giving) see Thomas, *op. cit.* (n. 478), p. 76.

quarter over the following year. Anyone who appears to be parsimonious in putting on these feasts is considered by others to be "the most sordid Miser in the World."[512] The Mughul authorities have almost wiped out the custom of suttee in their provinces. Self-immolation is rarely seen except for rajas' wives. While most Hindus burn their corpses, a few appear to bury theirs in small tombs.[513]

Their buildings and dwellings reflect the region and the condition of its inhabitants. The poor live in houses whose roofs and walls are made of thatched teak leaves or palm boughs and leaves. Those Hindus who are better off live in single-story mud huts with dried cow dung as flooring. Here they live in one room with their cattle and household goods. They plaster cow dung before their doors to keep the entry clean, and there on a shrine of mud they grow the "Tulce" (*tulsi*, or holy basil) which they worship every morning. Richer Hindus and Muslims build their dwellings with stone and mortar, sometimes with brick. Plain on the outside, these several-storied houses are "delicately contrived within" and have tanks, airy halls, private recesses for the women, and terraces on top. Their furnishings are movable carpets and cushions. Indoors they have no chairs, but at the door they sometimes place "large Elbow Chairs" on which they sit and smoke "in State." Most spend their entire and lengthy lives in the same dwellings.

Careful about what they eat, the Hindus also observe certain proprieties in their toilet habits. Sunrise and sunset are the set times when both sexes go to particular places to defecate. Men go to one place, women to another. At other times of the day they squat almost anywhere to urinate. Once they have finished, they wash themselves with the left hand, the right being used for eating. Cows usually eat their excrements. Although these practices defile particular places, it is not to be assumed that the Hindus are dirty personally. They wash their entire bodies before performing religious rites or eating. To keep their private parts clean they use depilatories on chests, armpits, and the groin, shave their heads and beards, cut their nails, wash their mouths, and rub their teeth until they look like ivory. Washers of both sexes, "the best in the World," keep their clothes clean for a slight charge. Clothes are washed in pits of water and then beaten on a rock until clean; in this process cheap labor is used instead of expensive soap. Family clothes are starched with "Conges" (rice water) and taken home when dry. Clothes for commerce are bleached in the sun before being starched and delivered to the packers.[514]

[512] Funerals, like weddings, were heavy financial drains on families, who often had to provide feasts for the whole caste. Poor Hindus sometimes borrow money to meet these expenses. See N. A. Thootl, *The Vaishnavas of Gujarat* (Calcutta, 1935), p. 152.

[513] Ovington in Rawlinson (ed.), *op. cit.* (n. 3), pp. 200–202. Possibly he is here referring to cenotaphs erected sometimes on the site of cremations.

[514] *Ibid.*, pp. 119–22.

Both Muslims and Hindus revel in sports, games, and contests; Muslims especially enjoy hunting. Both compete in riding, tilting, "Gerseding" (Arabic, *jaridah,* or dart-throwing), archery, footracing, and wrestling. Wrestlers are naked except for a belt around the waist; they anoint their bodies with oil and take opium for extra strength.[515] Tiger-hunting is a dangerous sport, as is the chase of wild bulls, buffaloes, and boars. Nobles hunt with Persian greyhounds the "Colum" (Hindi, *koonj,* or great grey crane), a large bird that rises slowly.[516] Animal fights are favorite amusements, especially encounters between large beasts such as buffaloes, rams, and elephants. Duels between men wielding bamboo bludgeons go on until "they warm one another." Hindus compete at chess, backgammon, and in "Banyan fights," quarrels limited to tongue-lashings and scoldings. Their chief pleasure comes from cheating one another, especially by cuckolding their neighbors.[517] The punishment most repellent to Banyans is "Slippering." A person who feels offended removes his slipper, spits on it, and then strikes the offender with its sole. This is considered to be more disgraceful and detestable than spitting in the face of another is "among us."[518]

Hindu boys are first taught to write their letters and numbers by tracing them in the dust. As they advance they are given a plastered board to write on. Once they have learned to write well they are given paper. The proud but lazy Muslims scorn letters. They dare not entrust their youths to teachers "for fear of Sodomy." As a consequence very few of their great merchants are literate. Most retain a Hindu secretary to keep their accounts and a Banyan to bargain for them. Even though they discuss the bargain openly, they finally clasp fingers under a cloak to let each other know silently and secretly the actual bargain struck.[519]

Since animals are rarely killed, they exist everywhere in great variety and numbers. Besides the animal fights staged regularly at court, it is common for lesser folk to entertain their friends by putting on fights of smaller animals: goats, rams, cocks, stags, antelopes (commonly called blackbucks), and quails. The Indian antelope is prized for its spiralled horns, which holy men piece together and make into an iron-tipped, two-ended staff.[520] Pigeons, commonly green in India, and wild parakeets are snared by fowlers who hide behind a screen to keep out of their sight. Waterfowl are captured by fowlers who swim or walk with their heads above water "which they

---

[515] See the engraving of wrestlers in *ibid.,* facing p. 279. On the popularity of wrestling see Ojha, *op. cit.* (n. 285), pp. 62–63. Also see pl. 126.

[516] Probably the common crane (*Grus grus lilfordi*), which is still hunted. See S. Ali, *The Book of Indian Birds* (7th ed.; Bombay, 1964), p. 87.

[517] Fryer in Crooke (ed.), *op. cit.* (n. 4), I, 278–81.

[518] Ovington in Rawlinson (ed.), *op. cit.* (n. 3), pp. 208–9.

[519] *Ibid.,* pp. 281–82. On silent bargaining elsewhere see below, pp. 977, 1076, 1803.

[520] On the Indian antelope (*Antilope cervicapra*), see S. H. Prater, *The Book of Indian Animals* (2d ed.; Bombay, 1965), pp. 270–71.

hide with a Pot full of holes, to let in the air and give them sight." With this feather-covered pot on his head, the fowler catches the feet of the bird and pulls it beneath the water.[521] Hunters from Agra make a "five Days Journey" to a mountain called "Nerouer" (Narwar) to "catch a kind of Wild Cow which they call Merous [merus]."[522] The Muslims of Surat spend much of their free time in hunting wild game. Since they have to import hunting dogs, they train other animals to be hunters.[523] "Leopards" (cheetahs) are trained to leap from carts and to hold fast to antelopes and deer. Falcons from Persia clamp their talons onto the head of the antelope, blinding it until the hunters come. Large groups of men surround the game and beat the ground to raise it. Trained oxen are ridden like stalking horses when fowling. On land the fowler often stalks his prey from behind a walking blind made of boughs in the shape of a small bush.[524]

At Delhi there is a veritable menagerie of "all sorts of Beasts that are known," including camels, dromedaries, mules, asses, elephants, rhinoceroses, stags, lions, and leopards. While there is a good native breed, horses are imported from Uzbekistan and Persia but "those of Arabia are most esteemed." Since they are fed neither oats nor barley, the foreign horses have a hard time adjusting to the Indian regime of equine care. Each horse has a groom who curries him an hour before daybreak and gives him water to drink when it becomes light. At seven o'clock he feeds the horse five or six balls of "Donna" (Persian, *dāna*, grain). These balls made of flour, ghee, and jaggery sugar are forced down the throats of the newcomers until they learn to like them. The horse is then fed grass at regular intervals during the day. In the late afternoons he is fed dried peas mixed with water. Just before nightfall the groom prepares a litter of dried horse dung for his charge. The saddles and trappings of these prize horses are embroidered and sometimes set with precious stones. Their "finest Ornament" is "six large flying tassels of long white hair," four of which are attached to the saddle and the other two on each side of the head.[525]

Elephants of several kinds are kept at Delhi, those of Ceylon being preferred to all other types "because they are the stoutest," even though smaller than the others. The sure-footed elephants are generally used as pack animals. Elephants isolated from their group are dangerous, especially to lone travelers. Because they are so expensive to maintain, the great lords keep

---

[521] Thévenot in Sen (ed.), *op. cit.* (n. 2), p. 54. This method of duck-hunting is described by several other foreign writers. See *ibid.*, pp. 300–301, n. 12a. Also *cf.* Ovington in Rawlinson, *op. cit.* (n. 3), pp. 161–63. It is sometimes also ascribed to the Chinese; see *Asia*, Vol. II, Bk. 1, pp. 92–93 and pl. 47.

[522] Narwar is in Gwalior State in central India. *Meru* is the Mahratti name for the Sambar (*Cervus unicolor*), the largest Indian deer. See Prater, *op. cit.* (n. 520), pp. 290–91. The above based on Thévenot in Sen (ed.), *op. cit.* (n. 2), pp. 53–55.

[523] See Qaisar, *op. cit.* (n. 36), pp. 151–53.

[524] Ovington in Rawlinson, *op. cit.* (n. 3), pp. 161–63.

[525] These are yak tails.

only a few elephants, and the emperor himself has but five hundred for the use of his household and not more than two hundred for his army.[526]

In the region of the city of Ajmer a small animal is found which "yields most excellent Musk." The "bladder" of this beast is removed to obtain the musk it holds.[527] In this area there are also "Pullets whose skin is all over black, as well as their Bones," but the flesh is white.[528] Here are also poisonous scorpions whose venom is removed from a person by the application of a burning coal.

Because the country is rocky, they shoe the oxen for long journeys. Oxen are sometimes ridden like horses, but are generally used to pull carts and wagons. Oxen come in various sizes, the smallest of which "go very fast, and serve to draw small Waggons." White oxen are expensive and highly prized for their strength and good looks. While oxen are common, the best ones are given great attention and ornamental trappings by their owners. They are curried daily, fed straw and millet, and enjoy the fodder of good horses.[529]

In Bengal and Golconda there is a bird called "Meina" (Hindi, *maina,* starling) which looks like a blackbird and they "teach it to speak like [we do] a Starling."[530] An extraordinary bat is native to Malwa which Thévenot describes in great detail from a specimen he examined at a friend's house.[531]

The animals of Surat are both of local and foreign origin. Certain pigeons, in leaving their roost, tumble three or four times before taking wing.[532] Another variety of pigeon is taught to carry messages. From Siam the ships have brought the little "Champores" (Bantams), cocks "with ruffled Feet, well armed with Spurs."[533] Here are also seen turtle doves from Basra, cockatoos and lory parrots from Bantam, and the cassowary "that digests Iron." Small cage birds "spotted with White and Red" from Ahmadabad sing admirably in chorus. Strong rats the size of pigs burrow under houses and prey on poultry.[534] The mongoose is much like a ferret. Squirrels streaked black and white run about on houses and terraces. Muskrats contaminate houses and water jars with their scent. A crocodile-like creature

[526]Thévenot in Sen (ed.), *op. cit.* (n. 2), pp. 62–65.

[527]A reference to the small Indian civet (*Viverricula indica,* Desmarest). Thévenot's "musk" is the secretion of its scent glands used in India for perfume and medicine. See Prater, *op. cit.* (n. 520), p. 88.

[528]For a lengthy commentary on this mysterious bird, see Sen (ed.), *op. cit.* (n. 2), pp. 306–8, n. 3. The "black chicken" is still frequently used in both India and China for food and medicine. Lach has eaten this "chicken" in Taiwan; its flesh is white and its skin and bones are black. See A. Lach, "Dining on the Rim of the Pacific Plate," *The World and I,* March, 1988, p. 322.

[529]Thévenot in Sen (ed.), *op. cit.* (n. 2), pp. 72–73. Elephants are treated likewise.

[530]The Indian grackle. *Ibid.,* p. 96.

[531]This bat is the flying fox (*Pteyopus medius*) common throughout India. *Ibid.,* pp. 98–99.

[532]Probably the common green pigeons which feed in flocks in banyan and pipul trees when they are in fruit. See Ali, *op. cit.* (n. 516), p. 73.

[533]Possibly from Champa in Indochina originally.

[534]The bandicoot rat (*Bandicota indica*). See Prater, *op. cit.* (n. 520), pp. 211–12.

called "Guiana" (iguana) is used by robbers who allegedly hold onto their tails to get into houses.[535] Centipedes, scorpions, and huge spiders often bite people. Poisonous snakes live in the fields and man-eating crocodiles or alligators infest the rivers. The Brahmans claim that they charm the crocodiles of their sacred rivers to keep them from harming people. This is important because great crowds of Hindus bathe in the river twice daily.

In Surat the main pack animals are buffalo and oxen, since horses are used mainly for war or pleasure. "Milk-White Oxen" have curved horns that the owners encase and tip with silver, gold, or brass. They put a rope through the oxen's nostrils and load its neck with collars. The smaller oxen like the others have a "Bunch on their neck." Oxen are not castrated, but the same result is obtained by bruising the testicles of the young animal. Buffaloes are brown in color and generally as big as the largest oxen. Wild buffaloes trample or butt men to death. Their horns can do little harm since they lie too flat on the back of the head. The butter from the milk of domesticated buffaloes is boiled to make it less "Rank" and is kept in "Duppers" (Hindi, *dabbā*, a vessel of buffalo hide) throughout the year.[536] In the local marshes they raise many cattle of all kinds. The mutton is inferior in taste to that of England and the wool not even comparable.

The Indians grow carrots, beets, turnips, radishes, melons, coleworts, and a few cabbages. For food grains they have wheat "as good as the world affords," rice, barley, millet, and "Nuchanny" (Mahratti, *nachani*, or raggy millet). In addition to peas and beans, they raise rape for lamp oil. Their salad greens include purslane (portulaca), sorrel, lettuce, parsley, tarentine (?), mint, and "Sog" (Hindi, *sāg*, pot herbs), a kind of spinach. Asparagus flourishes here, as do limes, pomegranates, apples, and grapes. The sea provides oysters and fish, especially mackerels and sole. Wild fowl, particularly geese, cranes, and ducks, abound around pools and lakes.[537]

Like so many seventeenth-century travelers, Careri is intrigued by the flora of India. He lists a number of them with their Portuguese names; the original Italian edition of his work contains engravings of most of those discussed.[538] He gives in excellent detail the varied uses of the cocopalm and its fruit, as well as the areca, the banana, and the mango trees. This is followed by brief descriptions of many other fruit-bearing trees and plants, some of

[535] The word *iguana*, the usual name for this crocodile-like lizard, is taken from the vocabulary of the West Indies. The "Guiana" (Hindi, *goh*) is apparently more correctly called a monitor; it is a riverine scavenger which may grow to be three meters in length. See J. and K. MacKinnon, *Animals of Asia* (New York, 1944), p. 75. A legend exists in India to the effect that iguanas were used by soldiers to scale fortress walls thought to be impregnable. Crooke (ed.), *op. cit.* (n. 4), I, 291, n. 9.

[536] Ghee is held and transported in dried and stiffened buffalo hides.

[537] Fryer in Crooke (ed.), *op. cit.* (n. 4), I, 295–98.

[538] These illustrations are poor, compared to those of Van Rheede. See below, pp. 926–27. Much of Careri's information on plants comes from Vincenzo's work. See Magnaghi, *op. cit.* (n. 8), p. 35. On Vincenzo see below, pp. 891–909.

which are probably derived from Linschoten and other earlier writers. He reports that samples of the "Mogoreira" (*mogra*, or *Jasminium sambae*) plant were sent in earthen pots to Lisbon and to the Duke of Tuscany "who had a great Mind to them."[539] The Spaniards, in imitation of the Indians, make up a mixture for chewing of the bonga-fruit, betel leaves, and lime which they call "buyo." Betel-chewing makes the lips so "red, fine and beautiful" that Italian ladies would pay an equal weight of gold if they could obtain it. In addition to native fruits and vegetables, many plants imported from Persia and Europe grow well in India.[540]

In 1675 a huge "Sea Tortoise" (*Chelone imbricata,* the hawk-bill turtle) is brought to Dr. Fryer at the fort at Surat for him to examine. Six feet in length, its body is shielded by a large and tough brown shell. This kind of turtle is able to carry three men on its back without difficulty. While the head is sheathed with scales, its long neck is "soft and undefensible." It swims and crawls on four fins which it has instead of legs. The belly is covered with a breastplate which is soft and white when compared to the backplate; the tail is short and curled. Turned on its back, this animal becomes helpless. The females lay eggs as big as hen's eggs and in large numbers at once. They go ashore to bury their eggs in the sand for hatching. Its eggs and flesh are eaten on board ships and also used medicinally in the treatment of scurvy and venereal disease, and as a tonic. On dissecting the turtle Dr. Fryer finds that, contrary to popular lore, it has but one heart and not three.[541]

In the lowland forest live solitary "Satyrs" called "Men of the Woods." Fryer sees two of these creatures in a cage and notes that they sleep by day and "Sport and Eat" at night.[542] There are also "Men of the Rivers," who die as soon as they are captured.[543] The most ferocious tigers in the world live in India; its few lions are "feeble and cowardly."[544] Other wild animals are "Balus" (Hindi, *bhālu,* the sloth bear), wild cats, monkeys, and wild dogs "whose urine blinds the venison on which they prey."[545] In addition there are squirrels, jackals, mongooses, wild bulls, elephants, rhinoceroses, buffaloes, and bears. Game animals include the antelopes, deer, boars, and elks (probably the sambhar stag). Birds of prey include eagles, vultures, kites, "Newries" (Malay, *nuri,* parrot), and crows which are plagued by a

[539] Cosimo III, grand duke of Tuscany from 1670 to 1723. See pl. 171.

[540] Careri in Sen (ed.), *op. cit.* (n. 2), pp. 199–206.

[541] Crooke (ed.), *op. cit.* (n. 4), I, 305–6.

[542] Probably a reference to the slow or slender lorises, who are creatures of the night that live in dense forests and are seldom seen. See Prater, *op. cit.* (n. 520), pp. 43–45.

[543] Probably the dugong, or sea cow, which is sometimes thought to resemble a man or woman. See *ibid.,* pp. 315–16.

[544] The Asiatic lion was once found generally in northern and central India as far south as the Narbada. It is now restricted to the Gir Forest in Kathiawar. *Ibid.,* p. 67.

[545] It is still commonly believed in India that "wild dogs sprinkle bushes with urine, and drive their quarry through the bushes to blind them with the acrid fluid" (*ibid.,* p. 112).

small bee-like creature which attaches itself to the bird's breast and pierces it.[546] Game birds are of numerous types and abundant. Ocean fish are innumerable, the best known being sharks, whales, sea snakes of the coastal waters, pilchards, porpoises, oysters, crabs, tortoises, swordfish, cuttlefish, ink-fish, and mackerel. Snakes are found in river and field, some large enough to devour a pig "if the Natives may be believed." In the rainy season, large biting flies are driven off with a "Mirchal" (Hindi, *morchhal,* a fly whisk of peacock's feathers). Ants will swarm to any edibles left about. The greatest pest is the mosquito. Bugs bred in the cotton fields are impossible to exterminate once they have infested a house.[547]

Over the course of the century the European sources revealed, as if in a kaleidoscope, an evolving picture of the Mughul Empire. In the first generation, Jesuit letters and commercial reports from India appeared in the great collections of Guerreiro (in Portuguese), Purchas (in English), and De Laet (in Latin). During the remainder of the century sixteen separate accounts by individual authors kept the picture changing. At least one such observer and commentator was in India during each decade of the century. Of the independent narratives five were by English authors, five by French, two by Portuguese, two by Italians, one by a Dutchman, and one by a German. All were published in Europe during the century, and most were translated and printed in other languages. Eight were written by merchants or commercial attachés, four by clergymen, two by physicians, and one by a lawyer. Five were prepared by independent travelers—Della Valle, Tavernier, Bernier, Thévenot, and Careri—with no official connection to European states, companies, or churches. De Laet and most of the other independent authors knew the writings of their predecessors and frequently borrowed from them, sometimes with acknowledgment and sometimes without. All adopted quite naturally a European and Christian stance in their appraisals.

The northern European authors of the seventeenth century, like the southern European commentators and historians of the sixteenth, initially introduced India to their readers by concentrating on its physical aspects, political conditions, and strange customs. Many of their comments were limited by lack of geographical range. Manrique and Bernier had traversed the entire empire during the mid-years of the century, but Bruton was confined to Orissa and the delta of the Ganges, and all the other authors to the west coast, the Deccan, and the Agra-Delhi region. In the accounts of the latter half of the century, stereotypes appeared with respect to certain general categories which regularly received attention: social customs, religious rites, costumes, dwellings, staple foods, and popular diversions. Most of the

[546] A puzzling assertion. Perhaps it is a reference to the king crow or black drongo which rides on the backs of grazing cattle to eat the insects disturbed by the animals' movements. See Ali, *op. cit.* (n. 516), p. 23.

[547] Crooke (ed.), *op. cit.* (n. 4), II, 96–99.

authors commented, sometimes adversely, on early marriage, caste, trans-migration of souls, the excessive respect of the Jains for animal life, suttee, yogis and their austerities, Parsi funeral practices, cow worship, polygamy, and astrology.[548] But they also commented approvingly on the religious tolerance prevailing in India and implicitly contrasted it to the intolerance of Christian Europe. They admired Indian building skills as exhibited in architectural masterpieces, tanks and wells, fortresses, palaces, roads, inns, and gardens. Many wrote with great appreciation of the courtesy, modesty, and compassion of the Hindus, while others denounced their beliefs as "super-stitions" and reviled the Banyans for their craftiness and the Bengalis for their servility.

While all the reports contained independent observations, they also related bazaar gossip and often accepted it as accurate. In some instances, as in Bernier's famous account of the civil wars attending Aurangzib's rise to power, "gossip" was the only source available. But this was "gossip" related by contemporaries who were often participants in, or witnesses to, the civil wars. Bernier and other European authors were sometimes conscious of the limitations of their sources and would so indicate in their remarks. Several who knew Persian examined the historical records in that language or had them translated. Others collected information from the Mughul records on imperial and provincial revenues and on the size of armies. Lord and Bernier sought to learn about Hinduism from conversations with Brahman pandits. Della Valle, who came to India determined to learn about its pre-Muslim religions and traditions, was disappointed in that all he was able to do was observe the externals. Despite their limitations these contemporary European sources still remain indispensable for the reconstruction of seventeenth-century Mughul India. Although they contain bias, distortions, and mistakes in fact and interpretation, they generally relate the unvarnished truth as their authors understood it and report with meticulous care many seemingly unimportant matters "which a native of India would have ordinarily dismissed as commonplace."[549]

By looking at these sources in chronological order, we can see how Europe's image of Mughul India evolved, reflecting changing conditions. The European reader was made aware of the rise of Delhi as the great imperial center, paralleled by the decline of Agra and Lahore as court cities and artistic hubs. As Gujarat was unveiled by degrees, the eclipse of Cambay by Surat could be clearly observed. For a reader following the changing fortunes in the Deccan wars, light was thrown on the rise of the Hindu resistance under Sivaji and the beginnings of Mughul naval power on the west coast. At a more detailed level, it was possible to follow the sieges of Surat, the rebuilding and strengthening of its walls, and even the slow desiccation

---

[548] *Cf.* Sen (ed.), *op. cit.* (n. 2), p. xlii.
[549] *Ibid.,* p. xliv.

of its Gopi tank. Descriptions were provided of Akbar's tomb and the Taj Mahal under construction and after completion. And even in those categories of Indian life which became increasingly stereotyped, new materials were added, finer distinctions made, and sharper conclusions drawn. For example, not satisfied merely to describe the immolation of widows, the European authors expatiated on the background and rationale of suttee, its legality, and the attitude of the Mughuls and the Portuguese toward it and the widows who refused it.

By century's end, most of the empire's provinces had been visited by one or the other of these authors, even distant Kashmir and Qandahar. Internal land routes were pioneered by Fitch and the early English merchants: from Surat to Ahmadabad, Agra, Lahore, and Kabul; from Agra to Allahabad, and down the Ganges. Manrique explored the river route from Lahore to Thatta and the land route from Multan to Qandahar. In the middle years of the century Tavernier followed these same general routes and provided further detail on them. The route best known to the Europeans was the tree-lined highway which linked together the imperial capitals. They also learned from Brother Goes about the route from Lahore to China, and observed that it functioned until about 1640 when difficulties with Baltistan forced a shift to the route from Patna on the Ganges to Lhasa. In the process the Europeans learned much about the rivers of northern India and the organization of travel, particularly the milestones, tolls, road guards, guides, and inns. They also learned that travel was virtually suspended during the rainy season because of flooded roads. In the hot season, travel was made dangerous and uncomfortable, particularly in Gujarat, by bandits and heavy dust. Caravans usually included ox-drawn carts as well as baggage-carrying elephants and camels.

The lands so traversed were generally seen to be agriculturally productive, especially in Bengal. Staple crops were rice, cotton, wheat, barley, indigo, sugarcane, sesame, and tobacco. Because domesticated and protected animals were everywhere in profusion, there seemed to be insufficient pasturage, especially during the dry season. Fresh and dried fruits, both domestic and imported, were available most of the year. Many of the fruits, trees, and flowers were unknown to the Europeans. Flowers grew throughout the year but were not as fragrant as those of Europe.

While the land was considered to be basically rich, it was not well cultivated. The farmer with his oxen and plow was a victim of an exploitive land-revenue system. All land being owned by the emperor, it was parceled out to non-cultivating assignees and contractors, who ruthlessly oppressed the cultivators to squeeze all possible profit from their holdings. Exhausted by this system, the peasant left the empire or moved off the land to processing centers. Fearing starvation for his family, the farmer had few children. Shortages of farm labor resulted in a lack of maintenance and losses in yields. Merchants and artisans, while harassed and exploited by the state, were better off than farmers. The recurrent internal wars had, however, ruined many centers of commerce, especially in the Deccan and Bengal. The Europeans saw the domestic economy suffering everywhere from disrepair, dislocation of peoples, and official neglect.

Despite this dismal economic picture, the empire enjoyed a favorable balance of payments in international trade and was not itself dependent on imports. Few of its imports could be classed as necessities; they were generally luxury items for the consumption of the court and the nobility. The empire exported worldwide its silk and cotton textiles, processed indigo, scented oils, diamonds and semi-precious stones, saltpeter, opium, and leather goods. In return the world funneled its precious metals and cowries into India to pay for its products, especially cotton textiles. Most of this international trade was carried on with a minimal expense to the empire, since the empire bore none of the cost of ocean carriage or protection: the overseas trade, with the exception of the annual pilgrim ships, was carried in foreign bottoms on seas protected by European navies. While the rich native merchants of Surat owned fifty armed trading ships (in 1663), their commerce was largely confined to the coast, and they regularly had to employ European pilots and obtain passes from the European naval powers. The Mughul governors nonetheless claimed all the returns salvaged from shipwrecks, and the emperor prohibited the export of precious metals from his realm.

The structure of the imperial government was first outlined by Roe (at court for three years) and later in Aurangzib's early reign amplified and corrected by Bernier (at court for eight years). Both saw the emperor as a ruler whose personal will was law. Firm with his nobles, the emperor generally administered fair justice to all. The predecessors of Aurangzib were generally tolerant in religion; his imposition of special disabilities on Hindus was generally viewed as a reaction to the Hindu resistance sparked by Sivaji. The emperor as sole owner of the land parceled it out to nobles and contractors of his personal choice. Under the Mughul law of escheat all a noble's lands and acquisitions reverted at his death to the emperor. The emperor's treasure, variously estimated by Hawkins, De Laet, and Bernier, clearly established him as the richest ruler in the world.

The emperor was, however, a victim of his own absolutism. He had to maintain an inflexible daily schedule to reassure the nation that he was well and in charge. He personally had to hear petitions and claimants, make judicial and administrative decisions, and receive foreign embassies. He presided over lavish court festivals held for special celebrations, for his birthday, and for the new year. Factional disputes had to be settled by his intervention. Unable to trust the loyalty of his sons, he had to resort to the unfatherly practice of playing one off against the other and to punishing recalcitrants and rebels by imprisonment, mutilation, or death.

All the emperors meted out justice swiftly and inflicted cruel punishments. They kept the imperial prisons full, especially those at Ranthambor in Jaipur, at Gwalior fort, and at Rohtas in Bengal. The families of nobles were often held as hostages at court while the noble himself was away on military or administrative assignment in the provinces. All the emperors were personally avaricious and expected gifts on every occasion and with every request. They encouraged their courtiers to flattery and imitation of themselves. They played favorites without qualm or question and withdrew favors on whim. Akbar, although illiterate, kept himself well posted by having official communications read aloud. He was curious about religious matters, even about Hinduism. Jahangir was addicted to drink. He collected paintings, especially portraits; he was ever anxious to possess paintings of renowned personages, including Europeans. While avowedly a strict Muslim, he enjoyed debates between Christian priests and the court mullahs. Shah Jahan, born at Lahore of a Hindu mother, made his reputation as the builder of Delhi and the Taj Mahal. He was reputed to be lascivious and too much under the influence of his daughter. Aurangzib, who imprisoned his own father during his climb to power, was reserved and subtle as a youth and a complete master of trickery. While he proved to be an orthodox and puritanical Muslim, Aurangzib was also a commanding and cheerful personality. At the age of eighty he walked with a cane but could read without spectacles.

The Mughul aristocracy was essentially a military peerage organized by ranks based on the number of horses commanded. The emperor decided on the number each noble should maintain and paid a stipend accordingly. To augment their incomes the nobles inflated the number of horses officially maintained and held back money from each man's pay. Nobles were of two types: horsemen who received *mansab* pay (based on the number of horses) and specific honors and titles, and *rozindārs*, a less elevated class paid a daily wage. Cavalrymen and artillerymen received higher pay than infantry soldiers. All ranks were often paid according to the whim of the commander. Through this *mansabdār* system the Mughuls kept large armies permanently employed at the court and in the provinces. Even in relatively quiet periods the imperial forces included at least two hundred thousand effectives. On campaigns their numbers were swollen greatly by the vast throng of camp followers who served the armies.

The imperial provinces were first delineated, somewhat confusedly, by Roe and Terry and in Baffin's map. Bernier more correctly indicated that they were twenty in number and divided into *sarkārs* and *parganas*. Headed by a governor or viceroy, the provincial government was a replica in miniature of the imperial administration. The names of many of the provinces were the same as those of the capital cities. Gujarat was the province best known to the Europeans, who occasionally visited its governor in Ahmadabad and frequently mentioned his name and relationship to the emperor. All the provinces suffered periodically from disorders and food shortages. Gujarat suffered especially in the drought of 1630 and its aftermath of the following several years. Bengal was the province which proved most difficult to subdue and to integrate into the Mughul system of control.

The European visitors were particularly impressed by the numerous large cities of the empire. Agra, a new city in Akbar's time, replaced the nearby abandoned city of Fatehpur-Sikri as the imperial capital. Built in crescent shape, Agra covered more area and was twice as populous as Delhi. While it lacked the planned character of Delhi, its noble houses were finer. Delhi, with its traditions of empire, was built anew by Shah Jahan into an imperial seat called Shahjahanabad. While the Red Fort became its main administrative and artistic center, the rest of Delhi preserved the temporary appearance of an armed camp. In mid-century it was as populous as Paris, that is, a city of about three hundred thousand inhabitants. Under Aurangzib, Lahore was allowed to languish, for the emperor mainly concentrated his attention on Bengal and the Deccan. None of these imperial cities boasted large private estates in the suburbs. Because of the law of escheat, nobles rarely built establishments which would be confiscated at their death.

Surat was the city best known to the European merchants. According to Thévenot its population was hard to estimate because so many of its inhabitants were temporary residents who lived there only in the trading season. Other less cautious observers estimated its population at one hundred thousand (in 1662) or "more than Evora [in Portugal]" and at four hundred thousand (in 1670). At the beginning of the century Surat was smaller than Cambay, but by the end of the century it had outstripped Cambay both in commercial importance and population. The new city of Surat, however, was a "nastie city" when compared to Ahmadabad, capital of Gujarat and an ancient center of art. Almost as large as London, Ahmadabad was the most impressive city in the western part of the empire, with its many monuments, tombs, and fine public buildings. Limited descriptions were given of ten other western cities, a list to which Bombay was added by century's end with its population of "60,000." To the east of the Agra-Delhi region, the Europeans gave their attention to Benares, Rajmahal, Patna, Dacca (population, three hundred thousand), Cuttack, Hugli, and Pipli, a port city which has since disappeared. To the Europeans, the leading Mughul cities were, in order of size, Agra, Delhi, Lahore, Ahmadabad, Dacca, and Surat.

This wealthy and well-armed empire was threatened by no foreign power except Persia on its northwestern frontier. Its main military problems were related to the pacification of Bengal, revolts of the princes, and the conquest of the Deccan. The Europeans, sometimes as eyewitnesses but more often by hearsay, reported on Akbar's successful siege of Asirgarh (1601), Khusru's rebellion of 1606, the Bengal revolt of 1612 to 1620, Shah Jahan's occupation of Hugli (1631–32), the continuing struggle with Persia for control of Qandahar, the succession wars of 1656 to 1661, and the expeditions in the east against Assam (1661) and Arakan (1662).

But it was the Deccan wars of Aurangzib that they wrote about most authoritatively and fully. These wars were seen as threats to the trade of Surat because they cut off and disrupted internal production and commercial routes, especially the land connection between Surat and Masulipatam. So long as the Mughuls did not press aggressively southward, trade went on around the sporadic battles of the earlier half of the century. But when Aurangzib determinedly set out to conquer Bijapur and Golconda, the Europeans felt that their precarious footholds were also threatened. The rise of Sivaji and the Sidis brought the war to the west coast and directly endangered the new English colony of Bombay. The spreading war, which involved naval combat, also seemed to presage a threat to the maritime supremacy on which the European positions rested.

Because of their concern for the trade, the Europeans pressed both Sivaji and the Mughuls for guarantees. They sent emissaries, official and unofficial, to both camps urging a peaceful or a quick military resolution to the Deccan struggle. In the process they visited and described in some detail the situation and the condition of the hill forts of Asirgarh, Parenda, Bidar, Junnar, Daulatabad, Rairi, Shivner, and Chitor. They observed from a distance, and commented upon, the gradual deterioration and the final conquests of Golconda and Bijapur. They hailed the rise of Sivaji as a Hindu hero, and Thévenot and Carré wrote biographies praising his accomplishments. Others followed closely the extent of his southward conquests to the very gates of Goa. The occupation of Bombay by the Sidis in 1689–90 brought the war directly into the center of the European coastal outposts and threatened the Portuguese as well as the English positions. In 1695, Careri expended great effort to find Aurangzib's camp on the Krishna in order to interview the greatest living military leader in Asia.

The military power and potential of the Mughuls were always of interest to the Europeans. Reports about the enormous size of their armies stimulated the Europeans to make their own estimates. Whenever possible they based these estimates on Mughul records rather than hearsay. Estimates were made (some of which are still cited by modern scholars) by Hawkins, De Laet, Van Twist, and Bernier. The French physician estimated the Mughul effectives, excluding camp followers, as being more than three hundred thousand as of 1665. In 1695 Careri estimated Aurangzib's tent city at Galgala to include a total of five hundred thousand persons. The Europeans were overwhelmed by the incredible expense to the empire of maintaining such vast numbers of armed forces, but explained that the disunity of the empire and the military ambitions of its rulers required such expenditures. While powerful on land, the Mughuls remained powerless at sea even after a west coast naval force under the Sidis came into being. The Europeans studied Mughul tactics, troop movements, fortifications, and weaponry. They even celebrated as military heroes such great leaders as Pratap Sah, Aurangzib, Mir Jumla, and Sivaji.

Naturally the European authors wrote extensively about their own coastal footholds and their relations with the Mughuls. The Jesuits in 1602 obtained a *farman* from Akbar officially permitting his subjects to become Christians. They also successfully enlisted his aid in preparing and financing Goes' overland journey to China. Manrique and others described the unofficial Portuguese-Augustinian outpost at Hugli, its occupation by the Mughul forces in 1632, and its establishment as an imperial port. Thereafter the Dutch and English became more involved in the trade of Bengal, and the Dutch eventually set up their own silk factory at Qasimbazar. On the west coast, meanwhile, the English and Dutch traders congregated at Surat. After mid-century the Dutch concentrated much more on their new conquests and the trade in Ceylon and the Malabar coast. Soon thereafter the French obtained permission to open a factory at Surat. The Portuguese in the meantime continued to operate their northern stations at Salsette, Bassein, Damão, and Dabhol. The cession of Bombay to the English, while opposed by many Portuguese in Asia, posed no immediate threat to the Portuguese in the north. They followed a strict neutrality with respect to the continental wars as the Jesuits continued to increase their authority over these cities. The Portuguese and Dutch were more inclined to marry natives than the English, who often married women specially sent out from England. The English Company officially allowed its servants to increase their incomes through private trade and in its dealings with the natives pursued a much more flexible policy than the Dutch. Several good descriptions of the English factory at Surat were published by its former servants. The Europeans reported that they sent or carried exotica to Europe including Indian costumes, books, medicines, and even potted plants.

As Christians most of the European authors forthrightly expressed their hostility to the "Moors." Fryer inquired more than the others about their beliefs and practices in India. Islam, the official faith of the emperor, was maintained strictly only by Aurangzib. Like his predecessors, Aurangzib gave preference in his appointments to Muslims and during the course of his reign exempted them from certain duties and taxes. Sunnis, being more puritanical and orthodox than Shiites, respected and upheld four schools of law. Muslims were distinguished from one another by the degree of their relationship to the Prophet; the Sayyids were the most highly regarded. Newcomers to the faith were added to the numbers of the Shaiks. Muslims were also divided according to place of origin into Pathan, Tartar, and Mughul groups. The Muslim hierarchy was headed by the sharīf who was followed in rank order by kazis, mullahs, and scribes. In social practices the Muslims of Gujarat resembled more the Shiites of Golconda than the Sunni Mughuls. They were permitted four wives, circumcised their sons at eight years of age, and had green as their favorite color. They buried their dead with the head to the north and the feet to the south in tombs separated from the mosques or along roadsides. Wives were virtually slaves and were forbidden to wear gold because it was thought to be unclean. Annual pilgrimages to Mecca were encouraged and sponsored by the state. Annually they held religious festivals: *Muharram* (Shiite), *Ramazān* (Islamic Lent), and *Shab-i-Barāt* (Night of Record). Muslim fakirs were a general menace and a potent political force highly respected by true believers. Aurangzib, while in debt politically to the fakirs, opposed Sufism because it was too close to Hindu Bhakti, its "twin brother." Like Christians, the monotheistic Muslims denounced Hinduism as superstitious nonsense. Nonetheless many Muslims unwittingly adopted Hindu customs and viewpoints. The Europeans, hostile as they were to Islam, commented in some detail and admiringly on the great mosques of Delhi and Ahmadabad as well as many Muslim tombs and gardens.

The main commentators on Hinduism were Lord and Bernier. Both received their information from pandits and their own observations. Bernier, because he had read about Hinduism in the writings of earlier European authors, confined his remarks largely to education and to principal beliefs and ideas. Lord, on the instructions of the English Company, investigated the religious beliefs of the Banyans, the native merchants through whom much of the Company's business was conducted. Lord, for all his researches, never realized that the Banyans were both Jains and Hindus in religion. Van Twist was the earliest of the European writers to make this distinction. Bernier, who knew Persian well, learned from the pandits at Delhi and Benares that the Hindus have six philosophical schools, that their idols merely represent deities and are not gods themselves, and that the pandits are divided about the correct interpretation of the Vedas. Most surprising to Bernier was their assertion that Hinduism was the religion of Indians solely and laid no claim to universality.

Most of the other Europeans emphasized the externals and understandably could make no sharp distinctions between the social customs and religious rites of the Hindus. Several of them were impressed by what they saw or heard about the great pilgrimages to Jagannatha, Benares and the Ganges, Awadh, and Allahabad (Prayag). Cow and tree worship attracted a disproportionate share of their attention. They reported that marriages were always great affairs presided over by Brahmans, priests who were usually married themselves. Many brides were children whose marriage ceremony ended with lavish and overly expensive banquets. The marriage of a child bride was normally not consummated until she had achieved puberty. After childbirth the mother was unpure for forty days; ten days after birth a naming ceremony (*Nāmakarana*) was held and shortly thereafter the child was taken to the temple for the first time. Hindus burned their dead ritually on a pyre by the sacred waters of a river, or in some cases merely put them into the river. Widows, even child brides, were expected to become suttee or to face disgrace. Under the Mughuls suttees became fewer. Aurangzib pursued an active anti-Hindu policy by destroying temples, forbidding festivals, and imposing special taxes. Nonetheless the majority stiff-neckedly continued to follow the faith of their fathers, to give alms to Brahmans, and to respect the Yogis. The river and tank ceremonies followed in connection with the solar eclipse of 1666 were rivaled in superstitious awe only by the reaction of the French people to the eclipse of 1654. Hindus followed a lunisolar calendar that differed from that followed by the Muslims.

The Jains, finally identified as an independent religious group, attracted general comment because of what was esteemed to be their ridiculously excessive respect for life of all sorts. Thévenot realized that Jainism was more than two thousand years old, that it included both laymen and monks, and that its major centers were in Gujarat. Jain monasticism was distinguished by the touring of its monks; Jains had thousands of monasteries as well as a few nunneries. The Parsis, or Zoroastrians from Persia, were better understood by the Christians. Aware of the history of their flight to the region around Surat, the Europeans were quick to dub them sun- or fire-worshippers. Most importantly the Europeans learned about their oral traditions and hierarchy by interviewing certain of their clergy. They noted the social compact concluded between the Parsis and Hindus, and were especially curious about their death rites and Towers of Silence. Early in the century, the merchants reported that the Sikh guru had supported Khusru's rebellion in 1606; but no further mention of the Sikhs appeared in these sources. Bernier told of the hatred of the Brahmans for the Buddhists, probably referring to those few Buddhists remaining in Bengal.

In the empire's coastal provinces and internal centers of commerce lived many foreigners from neighboring countries, the Levant, Europe, Southeast Asia, and China. The most important Asian foreigners were the Christian Armenians. The Mughuls, who favored light-skinned persons, recruited many foreigners, especially Persians, for the court and their armed forces. As a result, a variety of languages was current throughout the empire. In the European sources transliterations were given of Indian words derived from Sanskrit, Persian, Arabic, Turkish, Portuguese, Urdu, Hindi, Mahratti, and Gujarati. Roe had a smattering of court Persian, but Pelsaert and Bernier evidently knew enough of it to read and converse readily. Manrique knew Urdu, and other Europeans, such as Della Valle, had acquired unspecified amounts of Persian, Turkish, and Arabic during their travels elsewhere. Portuguese was probably the main language of commerce in the west. In their comments the Europeans asserted that Sanskrit was hopelessly difficult and Urdu easy to learn. Educated natives used Persian, Arabic, Sanskrit, and Hindi in addition to their provincial or regional languages. Urdu, the Mughul popular language of conquest, borrowed its alphabet from Persian and Hindi. The native chronicles were known to be very limited in number, Kashmir being the only province to possess a written history of its own.

Information on pre-Mughul history had to be obtained from native informants learned in the oral traditions of Delhi, Gujarat, and Bengal. Mughul history could be learned from the Persian chronicles available in the court cities.

The Europeans were most impressed by the great constructions, some in ruins, to be seen in so many different places. Thévenot provided the first written description of the cave temples of Ellora; Ovington and Fryer commented on Elephanta; and Careri produced a veritable guide to Kanheri. They described many edifices since destroyed, such as the great Hindu temples of Mathura and Benares. Akbar's tomb and the Taj Mahal at Agra were described both while in construction and in their finished states. They also commented, often in detail, on other Mughul masterpieces: the ruins of Fatehpur-Sikri, the bridge at Jaunpur, the Red Fort and the Jami Masjid in Delhi. The gardens and great tanks and wells of Gujarat, the canals of Delhi and Srinagar, and the hill fortresses of the Deccan likewise excited their admiration. The Indians, like the Romans, were clearly seen to be great builders.

Other aspects of Indian culture and learning were not as highly regarded. The Jesuits, Roe, and Bernier were interested in Mughul paintings, especially miniatures; but they were dissatisfied with portraits, which generally showed the faces only in profile. Indian instrumental music, singing, and dancing were strange arts which became appealing to Europeans only after lengthy exposure to them. Admittedly the Indians knew how to observe time and measure, but their music seemed to lack harmony and melody. Their instruments, while of curious construction, were recognized as belonging to the string, wind, and percussion families. Parenthetically, the Indians showed little interest in Western instruments; only the organ seemed to appeal to them. Indian secular learning appeared primitive. Their geography, based on fabulous religious ideas, made the world flat and triangular. Their astronomy, limited to the accurate prediction of eclipses, was used too exclusively for astrological forecasting. An isolated few showed an interest in Western learning; Bernier's patron, for example, read Descartes and Gassendi in the Persian translations prepared by the French physician. The Kashmiris were reputedly the equals of the Persians in poetry and the sciences.

Public education and literacy were both seen as limited. Muslims paid no attention to the schooling of their children. Adult Muslim merchants often were illiterate and had to hire Banyans to read, write, and keep accounts for them. Hindu children were taught the three R's by Brahmans. At Benares the Brahmans were prepared by pandit tutors in Sanskrit, religion, and philosophy. Medicine was not formally taught, but Brahmans often practiced as physicians. While they had medical books, they were mainly collections of traditional recipes for making medicines. They understood very little about anatomy because of religious prohibitions against dissection. Native treatments and medicines nonetheless worked well, according to both Drs.

Bernier and Fryer. Indeed most European physicians in India freely admitted that they had much to learn about local diseases and treatments from their Indian colleagues. The English East India factory in Surat even retained an Indian physician on its staff. Although they were thought to be quick learners in arithmetic and reckoning, the Indians trained no sea pilots. The emperor, who maintained four war vessels and four pilgrim ships at Surat in 1674, was forced to hire Europeans to pilot them on the high seas.

Hindu castes reputedly were, depending on the European source cited, from eighty-two to eighty-four in number. This is perhaps a vague reference to the eighty-four forms the soul must pass through to attain perfection. The Vedas prescribed that society be divided into four classes or groups. These orders were then further divided over time into castes and subcastes by occupation. Brahmans, the first of the great orders, were divided into orthodox Bhats and other less rigid groups. Twenty-seven occupational subcastes existed among the Banyans. In addition, the Europeans mentioned the names, and frequently the occupations, of ten other castes of northwestern India.[550] They commented favorably on the three polluting castes for performing necessary social functions which others refused to do. Hindu caste practices were unwittingly adopted and followed by Muslims, Jains, and Parsis.

Indian costume of all types were unsewn; cloths of various kinds were simply wrapped skillfully around the body in one way or the other. Styles never changed and male costume was everywhere similar. Mughul women always wore trousers to distinguish themselves from Hindus and all others who wrapped themselves in saris or lunghis. The Europeans, many of whom wore Indian male dress while in the interior, considered it to be clean, convenient, and comfortable.

Housing styles varied regionally, although everyone was permitted to live in any style or level of grandeur. Hindus intentionally lived simply, often below their means, to avoid inviting special exactions from the Mughul officials. Rich urban homes had two stories, terraces, and often courtyards. Their interiors were carpeted and furnished mainly with pillows, cots, and other easily portable items. No portraits or paintings ever decorated the homes of Muslims. The poor in both town and country lived in one-room hovels with their cattle and household idols. Most Indians lived out their entire lives in the same poorly maintained dwelling. In most households women did the gardening, cooking, and serving; laundry was sent out to a caste of washers. In the cities there were public Turkish baths, but people usually washed themselves in rivers, streams, and tanks. Most food was prepared in the home, with major meals being served at 8:00 A.M. and 5:00 P.M. Because of the heat, the noon repast was limited to *dahī* (curd). The diet of the poor consisted mainly of boiled rice, raggy millet (ragi), and

---

[550] See appendix on castes, following chap. xiii, below.

grass roots. Hindus ate kedgeree, several types of wheat bread, salad greens, cassava root, eggplant, and various fruits. They drank grape juice, lemonade, tea, coffee, and occasionally toddy. Muslims ate and drank all these as well as meat dishes and a sweet called *halwā*.

Common diseases were dysentery, fevers, venereal disease, catarrhs, scurvy, coughs, rheumatism, smallpox (particularly among children), cholera, tumors, beriberi (particularly among Europeans), and inflammation of the eyes. To treat these diseases native physicians used mercury powders, asafoetida, garlic, rice gruel, ginger, cauteries, cinchona, snakestone, rhinoceros horn, Maldive coconuts, and turtle eggs. European treatments were generally less effective than the native medicines. Brahmans treated people free of charge and certain Yogis were traveling herbalists. Indians practiced good hygiene and had a constant regimen in toilet habits and bathing. At Rajapur there was a hot spring for mineral baths.

Artisans, too often exploited by the authorities, were capable of good work when encouraged. They were deemed to be superior to Europeans in textile design, weaving, and dyeing, as well as in inlay work, ivory carving, and the setting and working of agates and carnelians. Although they cut and set diamonds, the Europeans were thought to be their superiors in this craft. Indian weavers were adept at imitating European textile designs and Indian shipbuilders skillful in copying European-type craft. Indian muskets rivaled those of Europe but their cannons were decidedly inferior. The Indians were particularly proficient in water control by tanks, canals, and aqueducts. They were also able to make paper from rags and to operate sugar mills and devices for watering gardens and fields. Their palanquins and two-wheeled coaches were practical and sometimes attractive conveyances. They were extremely skillful in minting coins and their Banyan money changers kept records in proper account books and had foreign correspondents as far away as Constantinople. Indians had no interest in adopting European printing techniques and mechanical clockworks. In cities they kept time with waterclocks. They divided the day into sixty units of twenty-four minutes each, or the reverse of the European division into twenty-four units of sixty minutes each. Their year was divided into three rather than four seasons.

Hindus and Muslims reveled in sports, games, and contests. Mughuls and other Muslims hunted the numerous animals and birds everywhere available. Because they lacked hunting dogs, they trained other animals for the chase. Delhi was a veritable imperial menagerie and the scene of regularly staged animal fights for the entertainment of the court. In Bengal they taught birds to speak and everywhere caged birds were on display. Pigeons were taught to carry messages, and snakes were charmed in the streets. Horses were used mainly for riding and war, oxen for riding and transport. Great care was lavished on all transport animals. Wrestling was a common pastime, but personal quarrels rarely went beyond scoldings, tongue-lashings, and slipperings. People of all ages played chess and card games. Children played with tops, horns, and fireworks. Most spare time was spent, however, in idle conversation and in chewing *pan* (betel).

Indian servants were strictly honest because the punishment for theft was so severe. Thieves were hanged in trees along roadsides as an example to others. The skulls of corrupt or disobedient officials were exposed on columns placed along the highways.

Indian women matured earlier than their European sisters and were more sensual than the men. Hindu widows were often forced into prostitution. Muslim women were not as chaste as Hindus, most courtesans being Muslims. Polygamy was legal to all, and polyandry was practiced in Ladakh and other northern places. Muslim men were reputedly addicted to sodomy. At the festivals of Holi and Diwali, license and easy morals reigned. Eunuchs maintained morals in the harem. Wine was officially forbidden to Muslims, but Mughul nobles drank in secret. Addiction to opium was common in Bengal, where the poppy was grown; it was recognized as an addiction injurious to mind and body. In the port cities, especially Surat and Sind, prostitutes and even transvestites were common. But most Indians were devoted to parents, affectionate towards children, and compassionate to the sick and dying.

CHAPTER XI

From Goa to Cape Comorin

Viewed from Europe as of 1600 the area of southwestern India from Goa to Cape Comorin was the part of the subcontinent seen in greatest detail. The Portuguese authorities of both state and church had their main offices at Goa. From here their economic, military, and ecclesiastical tentacles extended as far south as Travancore. Cochin, in between, was suffragan to Goa in religious affairs and its partner in the economic and political direction of Portuguese India. The viceroys in Goa still had occasional relations with the rulers of the Deccan, especially the 'Adil Khan of Bijapur, and with the princes of Kanara. During the sixteenth century the Portuguese chroniclers and the Jesuit letter-writers and historians had cataloged the coastal towns, had furnished rich materials on ports, products, and trading conditions, and had commented on the strange social and religious customs of the natives.[1] A few adventurous souls had visited the Hindu empire of Vijayanagar and several of the Muslim rulers of the Deccan. The sixteenth-century commentators on these inland places had, for the most part, talked about the best-traveled land routes, the centers of trade and government, and the military strength of the various rulers. Except for a few Jesuits, they had ignored the languages, customs, and religions of the interior and given the impression that except for Vijayanagar and the Fishery Coast these hinterlands were not worthy of much attention. The Jesuits of Goa and the port cities had shown more interest than the secular writers in Hinduism, but mainly for the purpose of exposing its "errors." A few members of the Society had made efforts to learn the local languages, especially those who worked in Malabar and on the Fishery Coast. The Jesuits in Malabar had concentrated most of

[1] *Asia.*, I, 347–69.

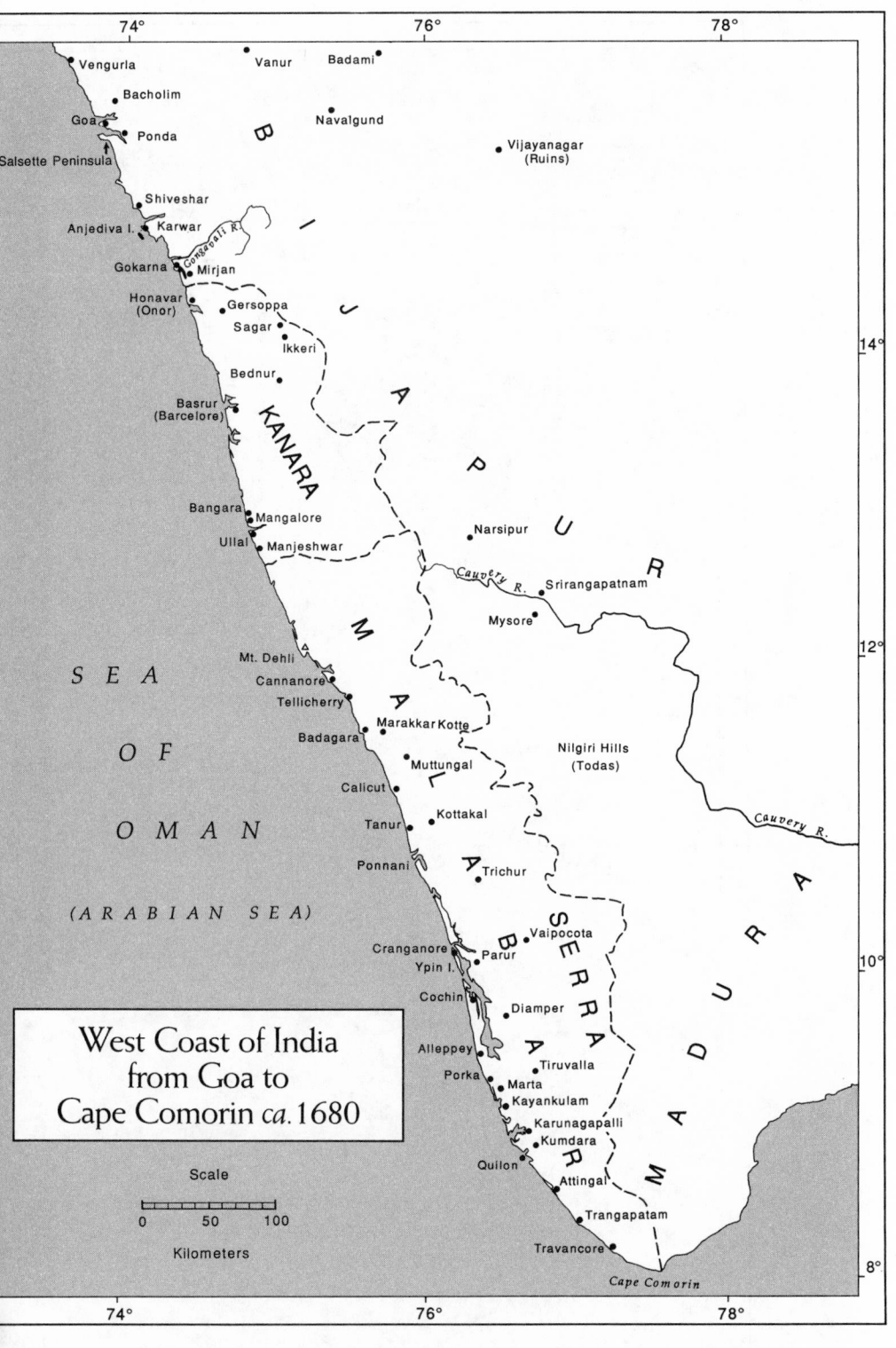

74° 76° 78°

Vengurla
Vanur   Badami

Bacholim
Navalgund

Goa
Ponda   Vijayanagar
(Ruins)

Salsette Peninsula

Shiveshar

Anjediva I.   Karwar

Gokarna   Mirjan

Honavar   Gersoppa
(Onor)
Sagar
Ikkeri   14°

Bednur

Basrur
(Barcelore)

Bangara   Mangalore
Ullal   Manjeshwar   Narsipur

Cauvery R.   Srirangapatnam

Mysore   12°

Mt. Dehli
Cannanore
Tellicherry
Marakkar Kotte
Badagara
Muttungal   Nilgiri Hills
(Todas)
Calicut
Kottakal
Tanur
Cauvery R.
Ponnani   Trichur

Vaipocota
Cranganore   Parur   10°
Ypin I.
Cochin
Diamper

Alleppey
Tiruvalla
Porka   Marta
Kayankulam
Karunagapalli
Kumdara
Quilon
Attingal

Trangapatam

Travancore

Cape Comorin   8°

B I J A P U R

K A N A R A

M A Y S U R A

M A D U R A

S E R R A   B A D A G A R A

S E A

O F

O M A N

(A R A B I A N   S E A)

West Coast of India
from Goa to
Cape Comorin *ca.* 1680

Scale

0   50   100

Kilometers

74°   76°   78°

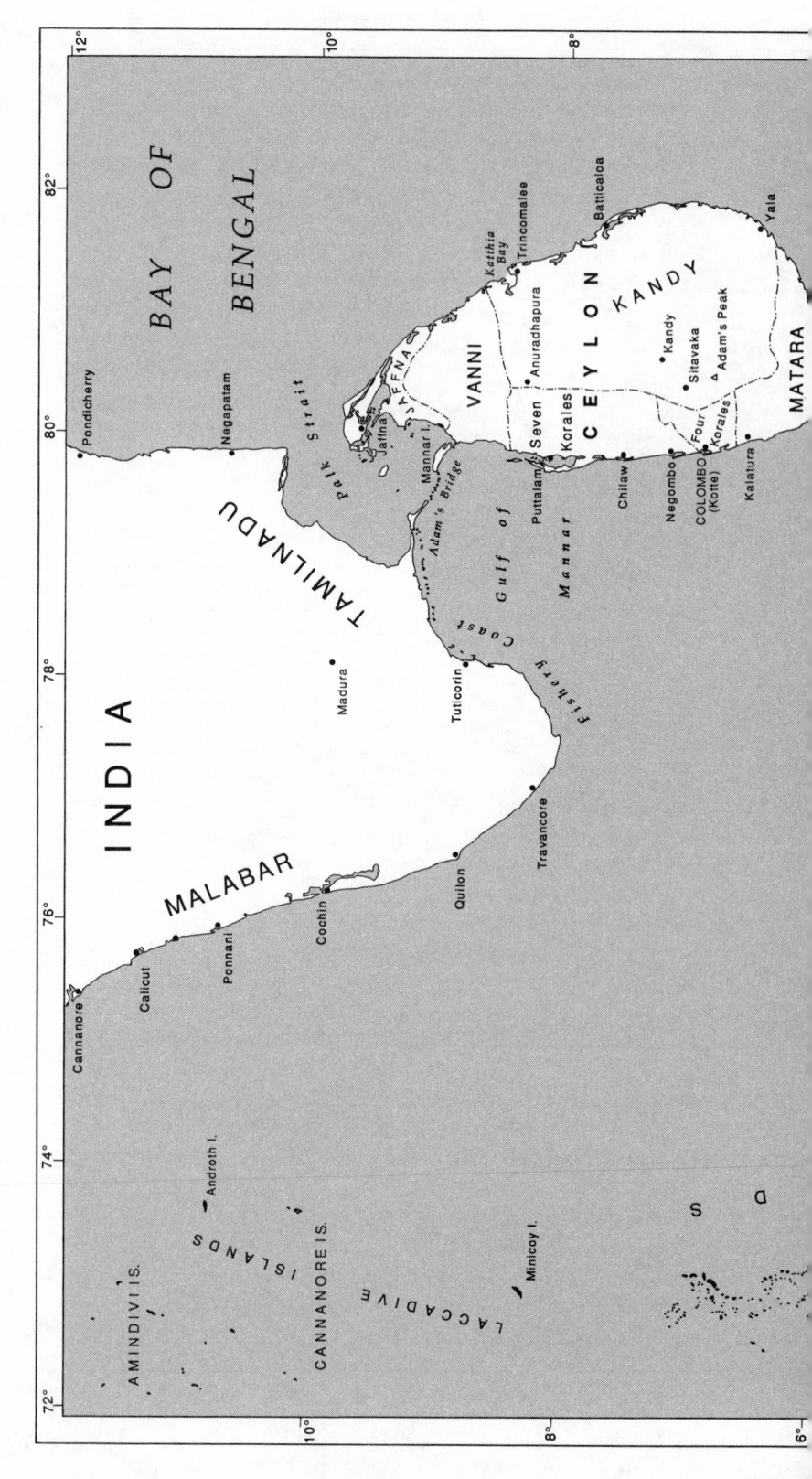

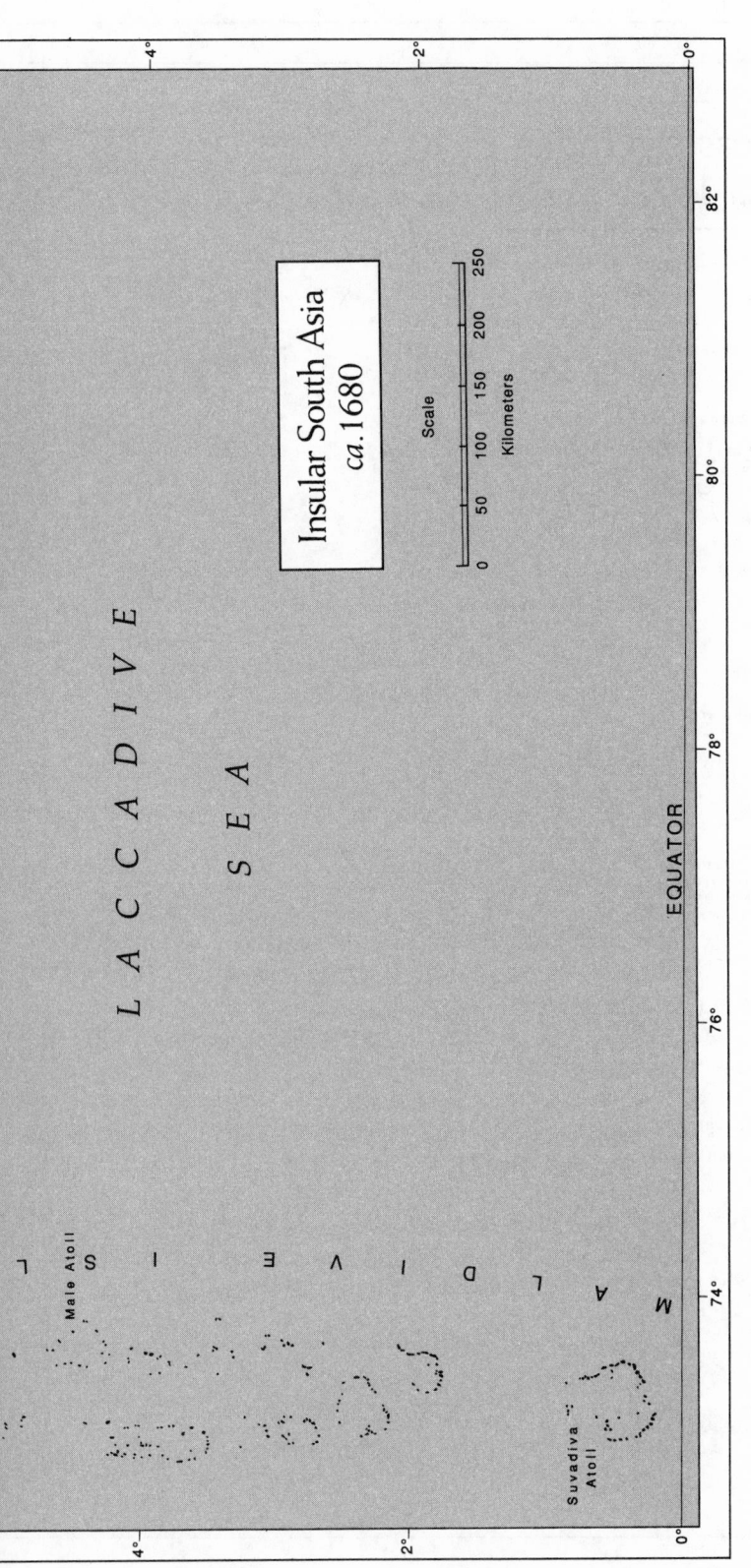

Insular South Asia
*ca.*1680

Scale

0   50   100   150   200   250

Kilometers

LACCADIVE

SEA

EQUATOR

MALDIVE ISLANDS

. Male Atoll

Suvadiva
Atoll

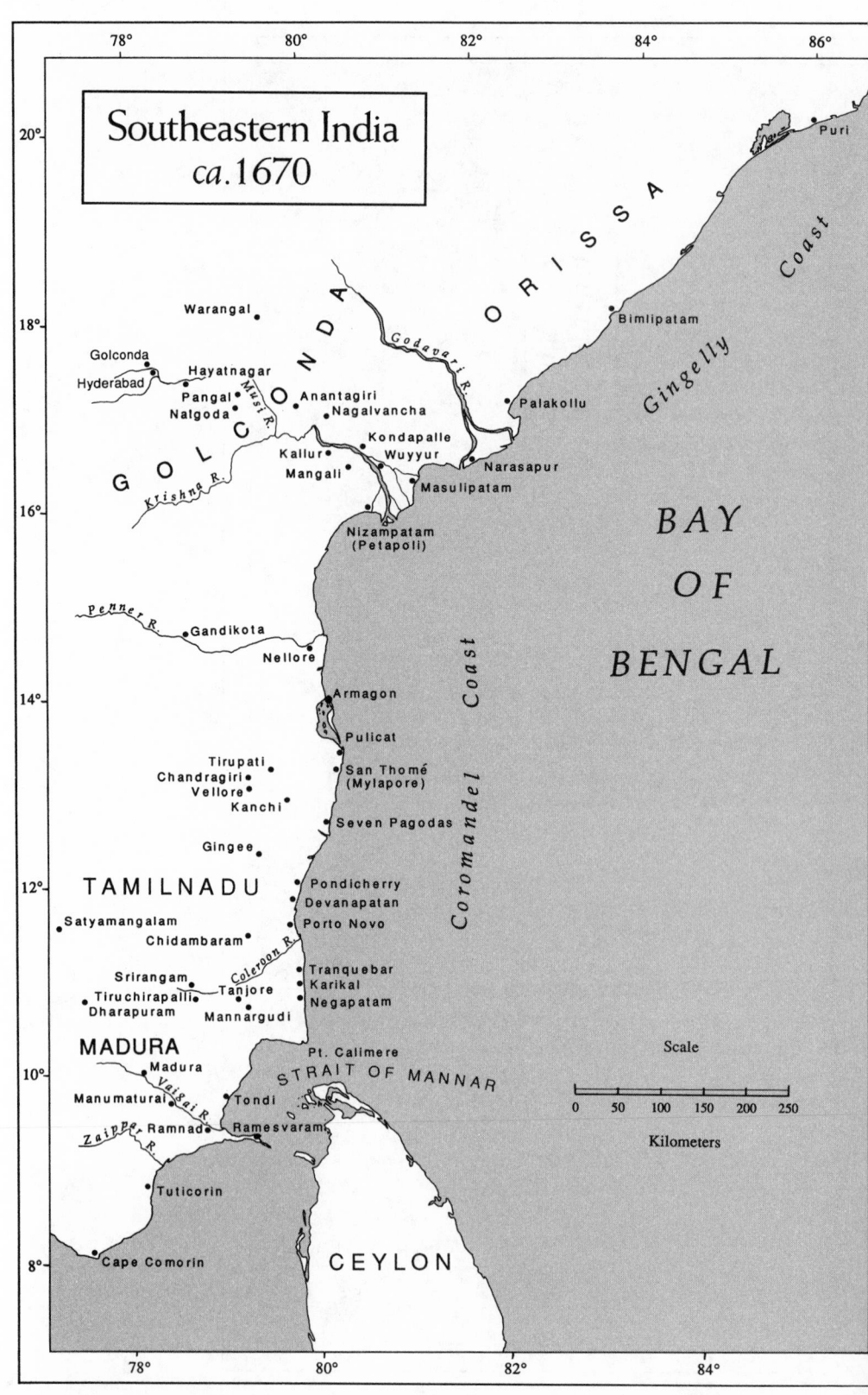

Southeastern India
ca. 1670

their attention upon the St. Thomas Christians for the purpose of realigning them with the Latin church. The best materials on *fin de siècle* Goa, its environs, and the Malabar towns had been published by Couto and by non-Portuguese authors, especially Linschoten.[2]

Between 1613 and 1619 Samuel Purchas (1575?–1626) published four editions of his *Pilgrimage*. It contains a summary of what he knew about India based on the sixteenth-century sources, with additions from the writings of a few identified and unidentified seventeenth-century authors. While his account of southwestern India is mainly retrospective, the good Rector of St. Martin's (Ludgate) tantalizes the careful reader by introducing an occasional new and intriguing bit of information. For example, he reports that "Stephanus de Brito [Estaban de Brito, S.J.] speaks of the *Maleas* [Malayars, or hill tribes of Malabar] which inhabit small Villages in the Mountaynes, which are hunters of elephants."[3] This is the earliest notice of these hill tribes on record and is based on the eyewitness account of Brito.[4] Purchas also exhibits knowledge of the studies of Hinduism being contemporaneously carried on at Calicut by the Jesuit Father whom he calls "Fenicim" (Jacome, or Giacomo, Fenicio), a piece of information he also extracted from the Jesuit writings. In brief, the *Pilgrimage,* despite the fact that it relates mostly to the Americas, contains a good summary of sixteenth-century sources on India and includes stray bits of new information about the early years of the seventeenth century extracted from materials of Purchas' own day.[5] *Purchas His Pilgrimes* (1625) contains important retrospective material as well. For example, it includes a lengthy report on Goa—its jurisdictions, parishes, budget, laws, and wages—as of 1584 prepared by Viceroy Duarte de Meneses (r. 1584–88) and translated into English for Purchas' collection.[6]

The major seventeenth-century European materials on the region from Goa to the Cape are fuller than the sixteenth-century sources with respect to interior places, flora and fauna, and Malabar Hinduism in its numerous aspects. Ten important authors and several lesser lights visited this area over

---

[2] *Ibid.*, pp. 482–88.

[3] The *Pilgrimage* is a very rare work and should not be confused with *Hakluytus Posthumus, or Purchas His Pilgrimes* (1625), a collection of texts by other authors. For the Indian matter in the *Pilgrimage*, see J. Talboys Wheeler (ed.), *Early Travels in India* (Delhi, 1975). For Purchas' description of southwestern India see pp. 103–35; for the "Maleas" see p. 134.

[4] See K. P. Padmanabha Menon, *A History of Kerala Written in the Form of Notes on Visscher's Letters from Malabar* (3 vols.; Ernakulam, 1933), III, 524–25. In 1600 Brito (1567–1641), rector of Vaipocota, went on a three-month's mission to the "Maleas." His letter from Cochin of October 13, 1600, was sent to Europe by Visitor Pimenta and published in Pierre Du Jarric's *Histoire des choses plus memorable advenues tant ez Indes Orientales. . . .* (3 vols.; Bordeaux, 1608, 1610, 1614), III, 686–91. See Streit, V, 2. It was probably from one of these two printed works that Purchas obtained his information on the "Maleas." Many European maps of the seventeenth and eighteenth centuries place the "Maleas" in the mountains behind Calicut.

[5] For a summary of Fenicio's ideas on Hinduism in Purchas' works see Wheeler (ed.), *op. cit.* (n. 3), p. 118. On Fenicio see below, pp. 874–76, 911–12.

[6] *PP*, IX, 118–96.

the course of the century and published extensive accounts, ordinarily of more than one of its divisions. For the first sixty years of the century, the best accounts appear in the mission materials and in the works of Pyrard (first published in 1611), Della Valle (1650–53), and Mandelslo (1658). For the last generation of the century the indispensable sources are Vincenzo (published in 1672), Baldaeus (1672), Nieuhof (1682), Dellon (1685), Van Rheede (1678–1703), Fryer (1699), and Careri (1699–1700).[7] These are supplemented by sources of lesser depth and breadth: Couto (*Década* V, published in 1612), Van Twist (1645), Philippe de Sainte-Trinité (1649), and Poser (1675). The most striking feature of this list is the dearth of Portuguese names, though many of the Jesuit letters were written by Portuguese fathers.[8]

I

GOA, THE METROPOLE

As the Portuguese administrative and ecclesiastical capital of the Estado da India, Goa had been described in detail during the sixteenth century. In the first decade of the seventeenth century the Jesuit letters continue to chart Christian progress there. Seventy-two Italian and Portuguese Jesuits land safely at Goa in 1602 under the leadership of Alberto Laerzio (1557–1630); they are followed by fifteen more in the next year. Between 1603 and 1607 more than six thousand converts are baptized, including a Muslim prince of Ormuz. In the peninsula of Salsette near Goa more than forty-five thousand native Christians worship in fourteen churches. Between 1604 and 1607 a separate house is constructed in Goa proper for the Jesuit novices. By 1609 thirty-seven persons live in Goa's Jesuit House of the Professed, ninety-two in the College of St. Paul, and thirty-three in the new House of the Novices. From these figures, whatever their accuracy may be, the impression was conveyed to Europe that the Christian tree planted in the sixteenth century was bearing a bountiful harvest.[9] But strangely, after these initial optimistic reports of the new century, the Jesuit letters remain relatively silent about Christian progress in Goa.

François Pyrard de Laval, the French traveler, arrived in Goa during June, 1608, and remained there until February, 1610. Although he was kept in prison by the Portuguese during the first month of his stay, the Jesuits and other priests quickly won his release. For the next eighteen months or so he remained in Goa as a free man and an occasional mercenary with the Por-

[7] For bibliographical details on the works of these authors see above, chaps. iii–viii.
[8] See above, pp. 315–18.
[9] See A. Viegas (ed.), *Relação anual . . . pelo Padre Fernão Guerreiro* (3 vols.; Coimbra, 1930), II, 347–58; III, 1–3.

tuguese fleets. According to Pyrard, the Portuguese maintained two great armadas, each composed of fifty to sixty war galiots (small galleys with one mast), a number of merchant vessels, and one or two great galleys. One fleet plys between Goa and Ormuz and the other between Goa and the Cape. Many recruits are levied in Portugal by towns or parishes for a seven-year term as a *soldado* in India. Some youths are impressed, particularly the children of poor peasants. At Lisbon they are paid in advance for the whole passage and are maintained on shipboard at the king's expense. Once they arrive in Goa, they are on their own; those too young for military service are hired as pages. To return to Portugal they must pay their own passage back; consequently many marry and remain in India with their families. Mestizos recruited in India must serve for eight years. In Goa there are from four to five thousand Portuguese soldiers (though the Portuguese try to keep their numbers secret), as well as innumerable Indian soldiers. While the pay is meager, the soldiers and sailors are permitted to trade on their own account. A few make fortunes, and all the Portuguese recruits assume honorable titles to enhance their importance in the eyes of the colonials and the Indians.[10]

Of Goa itself Pyrard provides a number of memorable descriptions comparable only to those recorded a generation earlier by Linschoten;[11] indeed, it is not outside the realm of possibility that Pyrard borrowed from, or was inspired by, Linschoten's vivid accounts of Portuguese life in Goa. But a number of his descriptions and facts were certainly not drawn from Linschoten or other earlier European commentators. For example, his description of the royal hospital (Misericordia), where he was a patient, is the best extant account and more detailed than anything before provided. This institution, well endowed by the king and the local *fidalgos,* is run by the Jesuits. As many as fifteen hundred European Christians are served within its confines by a bevy of Indian Christians and slaves. It has separate departments for the various ailments, regular mealtimes, and established visiting hours. Its plates, bowls, and dishes are of Chinese porcelain. A separate hospital is maintained for the Indian Christians, which is endowed by the townsfolk. Most of the doctors are Indian Christians who use both native and European treatments. The most common ailments are fevers, dysenteries, and mental derangements. Venereal diseases are prevalent, but only in places frequented by the Portuguese. One of the most serious diseases is called "Mordesin" (Konkani, *modashī,* or cholera). It comes on suddenly with terrible headaches and vomiting; most often the patients die of it. Cases of poisoning and bewitchment lead to lingering illnesses and deaths.[12]

[10]This is a fascinating account of a soldier's life in the East. See Albert Gray (trans. and ed.), *The Voyage of François Pyrard of Laval to the East Indies, the Maldives, the Moluccas, and Brazil* (3 vols.; "HS," o.s., LXXVI, LXXVII, LXXVIII; London, 1887–90), II, 16–31.

[11]See *Asia,* I, 482–88.

[12]Gray (trans. and ed.), *op. cit.* (n. 10), II, 5–15. Also see M. P. de Fígueiredo, "The Practice of Indian Medicine in Goa during the Portuguese Rule, 1510–1699," *The Luso-Brazilian Review,* IV (1967), 51–60.

Pyrard is impressed by what the Portuguese have been able to construct in Goa over just one century and by the good order they maintain in a heterogeneous metropole. His general remarks on its castes and foreigners add nothing to what Linschoten reported earlier. While he was there, Pyrard met Father Nicolas Trigault, the Flemish Jesuit, who was on his way to China for his first tour of duty there. Jean Mocquet (b. 1575), the French voyager, apothecary, and collector of curiosities, arrived in Goa on May 26, 1609; he met Pyrard shortly thereafter and saw him often.[13] Pyrard told Mocquet about the Maldives and his own experiences in those islands. He also comments on most of the other nationals who appear in Goa, and contentedly notes that "there are very few" Castilians. Because Goa has grown by two-thirds over the past century, it has spread out beyond its original walls and gates. Indeed, it has no strong fortress and is really protected only by the surrounding waters, a serious problem now that the Dutch have begun to appear off its shores.

The Portuguese live like noblemen in Goa. They alone possess the legal right to bear arms. In making their progress through the city's streets and byways, they travel on horseback or in palanquins followed by great numbers of pages, lackeys, and slaves dressed in livery. Their wives and concubines travel about in similar fashion. Only the Portuguese are permitted to hold offices and benefices; the soldiers of the garrison all come from the Iberian peninsula. The merchants and artisans are Indians who pay taxes on both their shops and wares. Porters are called "Boye" (Konkan, *Bhūi,* a caste of carriers); they carry everything on a thick bamboo pole slung across their shoulders. The grooms of Goa are all Muslims of the Deccan who are experts with the horses of Arabia and Persia and excellent teachers of riding. At the slave auctions the Portuguese buy, in particular, the black females of Mozambique, whom they use as house servants. If a son by the master is born to one of these slaves, the child is legitimate and the woman becomes free. Although she may not leave without the master's consent, on his death

---

[13] See Gray (trans. and ed.), *op. cit.* (n. 10), pp. 274–75. For confirmation of their friendship see Jean Mocquet, *Voyages en Afrique, Asie, Indes orientales et occidentales* (3d ed., Rouen, 1645), p. 352. Mocquet, who had been apothecary to the court of King Henry IV, left France in 1601 to collect specimens for the royal cabinet of curiosities. He made five voyages, the fourth taking him to Goa on a Portuguese vessel, where he served for a period as an apothecary in the royal hospital there. He lodged with an Indian physician who was married to a Chinese woman (*ibid.,* p. 221). His impressions of Goa, however, are fleeting and unsystematic, for he was restricted in his effort to keep a diary. The Portuguese suspected him of being an agent of France intent on learning vital details about the sea voyage to India; consequently they kept him under surveillance (*ibid.,* pp. 349–50). Both Pyrard and Mocquet report on hearing about the visit to Goa of the Sieur de Feynes, the Comte de Montfort, early in 1609. This traveler, whose account first appeared in English as *An Exact and Curious Survey of All the East Indies* (London, 1615), was long suspected of being a charlatan. For his work see above, p. 554, and Gray (trans. and ed.), *op. cit.* (n. 10), II, 279, n. 1. The independent testimonies of Pyrard and Mocquet about his visit to Goa have laid to rest whatever suspicions may remain about the veracity of De Feynes' overland trip to Goa. His account of Goa is mainly a diatribe against the Portuguese.

she remains free and cannot be sold. After sunset a thieves' market is quickly set up where stolen goods are sold at low prices.[14] Public brothels are not allowed, but it is legal to gamble in the special houses run by the city. Elsewhere gambling is prohibited.[15]

Viceroys are sent to Goa every three years. When a new appointee arrives, the emissaries of the Indian "kings" friendly to the Portuguese quickly come to welcome him with gifts and promises of support. In his turn the viceroy dispatches couriers to the friendly native "kings" to reconfirm their allegiances. The Indian Christians of Goa pledge allegiance to each new viceroy, parish by parish. When a viceroy dies in office, an established order of succession is followed, which Pyrard details. He was easily able to make observations on the succession issue since he "saw four that had been appointed one after the other." He also comments on the salary, revenues, and peculations of the viceroys who "take more pains to enrich themselves than to protect and preserve the state." Pyrard observes, in a manner reminiscent of Linschoten's declarations, about the viceroy's three-year term of office:

For in the first year, it is all they can do to learn the details and forms of government, know the various peoples, and dispatch fleets and armies. The second year they fill their purses. . . . The third year in some cases he employs in visiting all the fortresses of the Indian coast with a large force. . . . But he draws large profits from these voyages, as well from the captains and governors, as from the other officers, and from the countries visited although the king is debited with the whole expense. So it is no wonder these viceroys enrich themselves so much, nor that their servants and officers, who to the number of fifty or sixty live at the palace, do the same. . . . So it is, they say, with the viceroys, for the gorged depart and the hungry arrive.[16]

When Pyrard arrived in Goa in 1608, Aleixo de Meneses, third archbishop of Goa and first Primate of the East (r. 1595–1610), was about to complete his term as thirty-sixth governor of India (1607–9). Meneses and his servants are esteemed to be prodigiously rich, since they derive large sums annually from both their ecclesiastical and secular benefices. For charity and almsgiving Meneses "has a great reputation." He often eats in public and entertains at his table a dozen or so poor Europeans, occasionally including Pyrard. Although he is supreme lord of Goa, Meneses is in trouble with Lisbon for burning the prince of Ormuz at Goa and with Rome for his conflicts with the Jesuits. Under his regime the Inquisition of Goa became more severe than the Inquisition in Portugal, especially in its persecution of rich New Christians. While Hindus are not subject to the Inquisition, the Indian and European Christians are dealt with most rigorously since the fathers of the Inquisition act as both accusers and judges. Nobody dares to speak in public against the Inquisition.

[14] Gray (trans. and ed.), *op. cit.* (n. 10), II, 64–79.
[15] *Ibid.*, pp. 110–16.
[16] *Ibid.*, pp. 85–87.

A vast number of ecclesiastics of all orders make private gains in addition to their salaries from the king. This includes many priests of the orders who act in India as secular priests and administer the sacraments. Some natives are ordained as priests, both secular and regular, but never as Jesuits. Christian feast days are celebrated with rich processions and public burnings of those condemned to death by the Inquisition.[17]

In 1622, the Italian Pietro della Valle (1586–1652), called "Il Pellegrino" because of his extensive independent travels in the Near East, was on an English ship in the Persian Gulf on his way to Surat.[18] After brief junkets to Ahmadabad and Cambay, Della Valle arrived at Goa in 1623. Here he notices, perhaps because he himself experienced the wars in the Gulf of Ormuz between the Portuguese on one side and the English and Dutch on the other, that the splendor of life in Golden Goa is beginning to tarnish. While the Portuguese of Goa continue "to avoid submitting to such Employment as they judge unbecoming their gravity," they "have not much wealth, but are rather poor; . . . in secret they endure many hardships."[19] Most of Goa's population is made up of black and ignorant slaves who are "rather a disparagement than an ornament to the City." On his arrival in Goa, Della Valle is welcomed by the colleagues of the Discalced Carmelites[20] and Jesuits he had known in Persia. He is particularly impressed as an Italian by the many Jesuits there who are natives of Italy "of which Nation, the Society makes frequent use, especially in the Missions of China, India, and many other places in the East."[21] The Italian pilgrim is intrigued by the different modes of transportation used within the narrow confines of Goa, such as "andors" (litters), palanquins, and "retes" (net hammocks). The "rete" is "a net of cords ty'd at the head and feet [of the individual being transported], and hanging down from a great Indian cane" carried by two men. He reports at length on the "rete" because "they are unknown in our Countries, although I remember to have seen in Italy the Effegies of a Net or Rete, engraven in certain maps of the world, and if I mistake not, amongst the ways of travelling in Brazil."[22] Hindu pilgrims come on foot and in all sorts of conveyances to "Nave," near Goa, for a two-day festival,

[17] *Ibid.*, pp. 89–104.

[18] See Pieter G. Bietenholz, *Pietro Della Valle (1586–1652). Studien zur Geschichte der Orientkenntnis und des Orientbildes im Abendlande* (Basel and Stuttgart, 1962), p. 77. For bibliographical details on his *Viaggi*, first published at Rome in 1650–53, see above, p. 380.

[19] See Edward Grey (ed.), *The Travels of Pietro della Valle in India from the Old English Translation of 1664 by G. Havers* (2 vols.; "HS," o.s., LXXXIV, LXXXV; London, 1891–92), I, 157.

[20] Members of this order had worked in Goa since 1607. For more on their activities see below, pp. 891–92.

[21] Grey (ed.), *op. cit.* (n. 19), I, 159–60, 163. He mentions the following Italian Jesuits as being resident in Goa in 1623: Vincenzo Sorrentino, Antonio Schipano, Cristoforo Borri, Giuliano Baldinotti, Alessandro Lessi, Giacinto Franceschi, Flaminio Carlo, and Brothers Joseph Masagna and Bartolomeo Pontebuoni, "a good painter" from Tuscany.

[22] *Ibid.*, I, 183–84. See pl. 128.

beginning on August 17, 1623, during which they "bathe in the sea and perform ablutions."[23]

On Della Valle's return trip to Goa, early in 1624, after his trip to the south, he traverses Salsette and observes that the Jesuits own "perhaps a third part of the Island." The inhabitants of Salsette "acknowledge more Vassallage to the Jesuits than to the King himself." After remarking that the Franciscans' hold on Bardez is similar, Della Valle concludes that "it may justly be said that the best, and perhaps too the greatest part of this State is in the hands of the Religious Orders."[24] On January 25, 1624, the Jesuits of Goa begin to celebrate the canonization of Loyola and Xavier with a series of masses, processions, masquerades, and plays which go on until February 18.[25] While there is constant talk and preparation in Goa for the recapture of Ormuz, Della Valle is skeptical about the success of such an enterprise, since the Persians can supply the city on the gulf so easily from the continent and since the morale of the Portuguese is so low. He also believes that Goa is too far away from Ormuz and the sea-lanes unsafe for the Portuguese. Five days before Della Valle left Goa, news arrives there on October 31, 1624, of Malik Ambar's descent upon Bijapur.[26]

The French Carmelite Philippe de Sainte-Trinité (Philippus a SS. Trinitate; 1603–71) observed the increasingly tense political situation in western India from his cloister in Goa. After a two-year overland journey from Rome, Philippe had arrived at Portugal's eastern metropole in 1631 at the end of a terrible famine in northwestern India. He remained in Goa for the next eight years, finally reappearing in Rome *ca.* 1640. At Lyons in 1649 he published in Latin his *Itinerarium orientale* which records in ten books his travel experiences and observations of India. In his treatment of western India, Philippe concentrates on the activities of the Europeans, especially the missionaries, and on its strange flora and fauna.[27]

Philippe adds just a few significant points to what Europeans had earlier written about Bijapur and its relations with Goa. He was there in the period during which friendly relations were maintained under the terms of the treaty of 1633. The city of Bijapur is then divided into three parts, and the kingdom includes many other towns: "Dabul" (Dabhol), "Reisapor" (Rajapur), and "Panda" (Ponda), the last being just behind Goa to the south.

---

[23] Possibly a reference to the annual festival held at Naroa on Divar Island. See R. G. Pereira, *Goa. Hindu Temples and Deities* (trans. from Portuguese by A. V. Conto; 2 vols.; Goa, 1978), I, 51.

[24] Grey (ed.), *op. cit.* (n. 19), II, 392.

[25] *Ibid.*, pp. 402–4.

[26] *Ibid.*, pp. 415–17, 442–43. On events at Bijapur see D. C. Verma, *History of Bijapur* (New Delhi, 1974), pp. 99–100.

[27] For bibliographic details see above, p. 407; in what follows we cite the German translation of 1671: *Orientalische Reisebeschreibung, warinnen unterschiedliche Begebenheiten seiner Reise vielerley Orientalischen Landschaften . . . , so darinnen geherzschet. . .* (Frankfurt). Materials about India are on pp. 49–52, 121–55, 269, 287–318, 351–60, 522–51, 570, 586.

While the 'Adil Shah of Bijapur regularly keeps an ambassador in Goa, the viceroy sends emissaries to Bijapur only when needed. Two Carmelites were sent to Bijapur when Philippe was in Goa, one of whom (Father Leander ab Annuntiatione) died there in 1631. The 'Adil Shah and his nobles are Muslims but the majority of the people are Hindus. Beginning in 1635 an epidemic sweeps the city of Goa, and food, especially bread made from Persian wheat, becomes scarce. The Dutch blockade of Goa begins to ruin Portuguese trade and business after 1636. A rich nobleman of Goa called "Ramacani" concludes in 1638 a secret agreement to deliver Goa to the Dutch by treachery. After he had a few Portuguese galleys burned in the harbor, the traitor is caught and exiled. The crusade against the Dutch heretics is led by Father Dionysius a Nativitate (1600–1638), the renowned student of the Goa Carmelites who was eventually "martyred" by the Dutch in Sumatra.[28]

Like many of its other inhabitants, the Carmelite seems to assume that peace will prevail and prosperity endure in Goa forever. He sees Goa, a city the size of Avignon, as a Christian enclave in a heathen world seriously infected by Islam. In Goa itself there are seven Christian parishes and in the entire Portuguese enclave about thirty parishes.[29] On Salsette there are more than twenty churches as well as a Jesuit college at Rachol. Along the banks of Goa's two rivers, pleasure-houses dot the palm groves. Miscegenation is common, as the Luso-Asians become darker with each generation of intermarriage with Indians and lighter when one parent is Portuguese. There is a small community of Jews in Goa, a fact which seems not at all to disturb Philippe's Carmelite serenity. He rejoices in the new cloister on a hill where he lives, works, and looks out over Goa.[30] He gives specific detail on state and church administration and is especially good on justice and punishment. Among his best friends are the exiled king of the Maldives and his family. Life in Goa becomes dreary during the rainy season, when the eucharistic wafers become soggy and grass grows on the roofs of the houses.[31] About the rest of western India, Philippe has little to add to earlier accounts, although he reports that yogis assemble every year on a given date in the upper city of Cannanore to elect a superior.[32]

Early in 1639, while Philippe was preparing to leave for Europe, Johann Albrecht von Mandelslo (1614–44) visited Goa.[33] After a tour of north-

---

[28] *Ibid.*, pp. 123–24, 522–47, 585. Dionysius was a native of Honfleur in Normandy.

[29] *Ibid.*, p. 143. He gives their names.

[30] In 1620 the Carmelites obtained permission to build a cloister in Goa; thereafter a church and a cloister were built with alms from the faithful. *Ibid.*, p. 522.

[31] *Ibid.*, pp. 131–35, 139–55, 299–310.

[32] *Ibid.*, pp. 354–60. *Cf.* above, pp. 786–88. Yogis do not assemble to elect heads. This probably refers to the annual meetings held by the heads of the five monastic orders of the Krishna cult. At these meetings, usually held in Udippi, they select one of their number to be the chief for the next year.

[33] See above, pp. 522–23.

western India, Mandelslo left Surat in the company of William Methwold, the retiring president of its English factory. The Englishman was leader of an embassy to the 'Adil Shah and the viceroy of Goa to obtain trading rights in Bijapur and to settle outstanding financial affairs in Goa.[34] Mandelslo's reports of Bijapur and Goa are based generally on personal observations; they were first published in 1645, and they appear not to have suffered unduly from additions or emendations by Olearius and later editors and translators.[35]

Mandelslo and Methwold stayed in Goa for ten days during January, 1639. While being royally entertained by Viceroy D. Pedro da Silva and the Jesuits, the German traveler concludes that the Dutch blockade has not affected Goa's easy life. Goa itself "is not able to sustain anything," but provisions continue to be brought in at low prices from Bardez, Salsette, and the continent. Coastal trade also remains unaffected by the Dutch attacks on the great ships plying the major sea routes. The "Indians of Goa" who go into the mainland are "marked on their arms for identification." The Portuguese tolerate the idolatry of the Hindus and the Inquisition has no power over them. Hindu physicians are so highly regarded "that they are permitted to have their umbrellas carried with them." The local artisans, metalworkers, and jewelers are "incomparably better than ours." Many of them lease the royal lands in Bardez and Salsette; when they become involved in lawsuits over their enterprises "they are so well vers'd in the Lawes and customes of Portugal, that they need no Advocates to plead their causes." Clearly, in Mandelslo's estimation, the Hindus of Goa are becoming a respected element in the civil life of the island.[36]

The "Canarins" of Goa are farmers, fishermen, or palm cultivators; other "Canarins" are restricted to washing clothes.[37] The Jews "have there their Temples and Synagogues, and enjoy an absolute liberty of conscience." Some Jews are native to India, while others are immigrants from Palestine; "these last for the most part, speak the Spanish tongue." The Muslims who live in Goa trade in spices, mainly to the region of the Red Sea. From 7:00 to 9:00 A.M. daily the Goa market is held. "Public criers, whom they call

[34] On the English legation to Bijapur see below, pp. 858–59.

[35] On the various editions and translations of Mandelslo's reports see above, pp. 522–23. In what follows the references are to John Davies (trans.), *The Voyages and Travels of the Ambassadors Sent by Frederick Duke of Holstein to the Great Duke of Muscovy, and the King of Persia . . . Whereto Are Added the Travels of John Albert de Mandelslo (a Gentleman Belonging to the Embassy) from Persia, into the East Indies . . . in III Books* (London, 1662). On Methwold see above, pp. 568–69, and below, pp. 1020–21.

[36] *Ibid.*, pp. 98–106; also see M. N. Pearson, "Indigenous Dominance in a Colonial Economy, the Goa Rendas, 1600–1700," in J. Aubin (ed.), *Mare Luso-Indicum* (2 vols.; Paris, 1972), II, 61–73; and T. R. de Souza, S.J., "Glimpses of Hindu Dominance of Goan Economy in the Seventeenth Century," *Indica*, XII (1975), 27–35.

[37] The term "Canarin" is used in two different senses by the Goans and the early observers. It may refer to natives of Kanara or simply to the Konkanis resident in Goa. See H. Yule and A. C. Burnell, *Hobson-Jobson: A Glossary of Anglo-Indian Colloquial Words and Phrases* (new ed., New Delhi, 1968 [orig. publ. London, 1886]), p. 154.

'Laylon' [Malayalam, *lèlam;* Portuguese, *leilão,* auction] sell there by out-cry."[38] Each type of merchant and artisan works on a street assigned to his occupation, "so the Silk-men are not shufled in among Linnen Drapers." Merchants buy and sell slaves of both sexes, but they make their greatest profit in the exchange of currencies. They buy reals at 10 to 12 when the fleet arrives in the autumn, and "in April when the ships sail for the Moluccas and China they sell them at 25 to 30," thus realizing at least 100 percent profit in six months.[39] Like the merchants, the viceroy enriches himself through trade and speculation.[40]

In 1641 Jean Baptiste Tavernier, French traveler and jewel merchant, arrived in Goa for a one week's stay. During his next voyage to the East, Tavernier remained in Goa for nearly two months during 1648. At no time did he personally visit the west coast of India south of Goa. On his later trips to Surat and northern India he heard stories and rumors about events in the south, including the Dutch capture of Cochin in 1662–63, which he dutifully recorded. Back in France in 1668, Tavernier wrote *Les six voyages . . . qu'il a fait en Turquie, en Perse, et aux Indes* which was eventually published at Paris in 1676.[41] What this work contains about the region from Goa southward to Cape Comorin is a composite of Tavernier's personal experiences in Goa and Bijapur and a number of events he learned about at second hand from other Europeans in India.

From Surat to Goa, according to Tavernier, the best route is by sea, even though there is the constant risk of falling into the hands of the Malabar Muslim pirates who prey upon coastal shipping and "are very cruel to Christians." On his way to Goa in 1648, Tavernier took a Dutch ship at Surat which brought him to Vengurla. The Dutch, now that they no longer use Vengurla as a base for their vessels blockading Goa, keep this port mainly for supplying food and water to their trading ships. Goa itself as a port rivals Constantinople and Toulon, "the three finest ports of our great Continent [Eurasia]." Tavernier is much impressed by its houses and the viceroy's palace, permanent reminders of the wealth and magnificence of Goa's past. With the arrival of the Dutch in western India, the Portuguese "have lost the sources of their gold and silver, and are altogether come down from their former splendour." Now, previously wealthy persons, especially women, beg alms secretly from strangers. The Portuguese in Goa are reduced to "so low a condition" because they tried to maintain too many fortresses and were originally too contemptuous of the Dutch to take proper precautions. Their viceroys and governors previously made huge fortunes from the rich posts and other assignments they were able to "bestow." Once

---

[38] See *ibid.,* p. 621. See pl. 14.
[39] On the importance of the differentials in silver prices to the Asian trade see above, pp. 27–28, 116.
[40] Davies (trans.), *op. cit.* (n. 35), pp. 107–8.
[41] For bibliographical details see above, pp. 416–18.

they have passed the Cape of Good Hope the Portuguese of every station become *fidalgos* and add "*Dom*" to their ordinary names. After changing their status, they become cruel and vindictive swaggerers who abide by no laws. When trials are held they "never come to an end." Legal affairs are entirely in the hands of Kanarese lawyers who are "cunning and subtle." Otherwise the Kanarese hold no offices and are kept in subjection to the Portuguese. Nonetheless "these blacks [natives] have much intelligence and are good soldiers." Their children "learn more in the colleges in six months than the Portuguese children do in one year, whatever the science may be to which they apply themselves." The Portuguese vindictively confiscate Hindu religious relics and often destroy them. In addition to many secular clerics, Goa hosts Dominicans, Augustinians, Cordeliers, Discalced Carmelites, Jesuits, and Capuchins. The Augustinians run "two houses of nuns." The Christians, despite their numbers and influence, have let Goa's renowned hospital deteriorate seriously.[42]

Like many non-Iberian Europeans, Tavernier was intrigued and perhaps baffled by the operations of the Goa Inquisition. Even though he acknowledged that he was a Protestant, Tavernier was granted a two-hour interview with the Inquisitor and his aides and invited three days later to a dinner at the Carmelite residence. It is in connection with his story of the capture of Father Ephrem of Nevers, a French Capuchin, that Tavernier relates something about the reputation of the Goa Inquisition in coastal India generally.[43] Seized at San Thomé on the Coromandel Coast by agents of the Inquisition, the venerable priest was carried off to Goa a prisoner. News of his seizure reached Surat and was relayed to Father Zeno, his former companion and friend of Tavernier. Zeno, in Tavernier's estimation, was taking a great risk in his determination to go to Goa to aid his fellow Capuchin. Tavernier claims that anyone who protests on behalf of a prisoner of the Inquisition "is regarded as more criminal than him for whom he wished to speak." Nobody, not even the archbishop or viceroy, who are outside the Inquisition's jurisdiction, would dare to interfere with the work of the Holy Office. Once seized, a prisoner of the Inquisition is searched and his possessions taken; for those of little value he is given a receipt, but things of great value are not inventoried. The inquisitors never let the accused confront or even know the names of the witnesses against him. Ephrem's imprisonment by the notorious Inquisition created a sensation at San Thomé, in Europe, and in Golconda, whose ruler had long been seeking to retain Ephrem's services at his court. It was only when Golconda threatened to take San Thomé itself from the Portuguese that enough pressure was placed upon the Inquisition

[42] See V. Ball and W. Crooke (trans. and eds.), *Travels in India by Jean Baptiste Tavernier* (2 vols.; London, 1925), I, 148–60. Many of the European writers refer to the natives as "negros" or "blacks," meaning thereby that they are not Europeans or Luso-Asians.

[43] On Ephrem's career see above, pp. 257–58. Dellon (see below, pp. 850–52) read Tavernier's account of the Inquisition before writing his own.

to obtain Ephrem's release. In Tavernier's words, the good Capuchin claimed that he was most distressed "by the ignorance of the Inquisitor and his council when they examined him, and he believed that not one of them had ever read the Holy Scriptures."[44]

Philippus Baldaeus (1632–72), the Reformed Minister who was with the Dutch forces attacking Malabar, traveled up and down the west coast of India in the late 1650's and wrote about most of its port cities.[45] About Goa itself Baldaeus adds nothing of merit to the descriptions supplied by earlier European authors. He remarks that the Dutch were content to blockade Goa around 1640, since they were not interested in capturing it. He gives considerable detail on the negotiations between Goa and Batavia which resulted in the ten-year truce of 1642 and the subsequent special agreements worked out over the following five years. He notes that the contest between Bijapur and Goa for control of Anjediva Island ended in a stalemate, the Portuguese finally tearing down their own fortress and leaving the island deserted. Thwarted by the Dutch and Bijapur, the Portuguese begin to concentrate upon controlling the rich rice-producing regions in the interior of Kanara.

Quite different is the story of Gabriel Dellon (b. 1649), an employee of the French East India Company and a medical practitioner. He left France in the spring of 1668 and arrived at Surat in 1670, having spent one year on the way in Madagascar. After working for a time on the ships of the Company, he was assigned to its factories on the Malabar Coast during 1671 and 1672. In 1673 he resigned from the Company because of differences with the head of the French factory at Tellicherry. From here he went north to Damão, a port city run by the Portuguese, where he started a private medical practice. It was not long before the twenty-four-year-old physician ran afoul of the Portuguese authorities. On orders of the Inquisition he was arrested for heresy and soon transferred to Goa. After two years of examination and imprisonment, Dellon was condemned to the Portuguese galleys for five years. He was sent to Lisbon in 1676 and was eventually released in 1677 by the Inquisitor-General on the condition that he return to France immediately. In 1685 Dellon published his *Relation d'un voyage fait aux Indes Orientales* (Paris), most of which relates to his experiences on the west coast of India from 1671 to 1673.

On February 1, 1672, Dellon arrives in Goa. In his description of the Portuguese metropole he adds just a few new items of interest. Both African and Indian slaves are well treated because they can escape so easily to the continent. More native priests serve Goa's Christians than true Portuguese fathers. "Savagi" (Sivaji) controls Vengurla and a place on the mainland

[44] Ball and Crooke (trans. and eds.), *op. cit.* (n. 42), I, 162–64, 176–86.
[45] For bibliographical details on his *Naauwkeurige beschryvinge* . . . (1672) see above, pp. 493–95, and below, pp. 911–18.

where "there is a beautiful fountain under the trees to which the ladies [of Goa] go to divert themselves."[46]

On his second visit to Goa, as a prisoner of the Inquisition from 1674 to 1676, Dellon spent most of his time in "the neat and light cells of the Holy Office." His *Relation de l'Inquisition de Goa* (Leyden, 1687) was first published with the approval, and perhaps the encouragement, of King Louis XIV of France. In the following year it was reprinted at Paris and appeared at London in an English translation; in 1689 a German translation was issued.[47] The French court—like the Protestants of England, Holland, and Germany—was at odds at this time with the papacy, which possibly accounts for the aversion the northern Europeans generally felt towards the Goa Inquisition and all its works.[48] More practically, they were all directly or indirectly involved in undermining and destroying the Portuguese empire in India and were probably grateful to have at hand a work of moral stricture to help legitimize their own activities in India. Although Dellon's work has frequently been denounced as a convenient fabrication, recent scholarship has shown that he was a prisoner of the Inquisition in Goa and that he was tried and sentenced by it.[49] That Dellon, a French Catholic, writes critically about the Inquisition and its practices is scarcely surprising, since his view was, after all, that of a long-term prisoner charged with heresy.

Dellon's description of the Inquisition and of the practices of its officials and their collaborators is the only source available on the functioning of that institution by a contemporary who saw it from the inside. He starts by describing in detail the physical appearance, both exterior and interior, of its extensive and magnificent palace. In discussing the treatment of prisoners, he admits that they are "tolerably well kept," with the whites being "treated more delicately" than the blacks. They are all fed adequately and the sick receive "every necessary attention." At Goa there are two inquisitors, the Grand Inquisitor, who is always a secular priest, and his aide, a Dominican. They are assisted by numerous deputies of all orders, who participate in preparing the cases and in rendering the final decisions. Other officials, who do not participate in the trials, are in charge of examining and reporting on "works," probably meaning books and art, which are suspected of containing something "contrary to the purity of the Holy Faith." Advocates are provided for the prisoners who request them. The Familiars of the Holy Office, some of whom are high-ranking secular officials or nobles, are

---

[46]Gabriel Dellon, *Relation d'un voyage fait aux Indes Orientales* (Paris, 1685), pp. 191–215 *passim.*

[47]For bibliographical details see above, p. 421–22. In what follows the references are to the English translation of 1812 as it appears in A. K. Priolkar, *The Goa Inquisition* (Bombay, 1961), Pt. II, pp. 3–85. The translation of 1812, comparison shows, is essentially the same as the English translation of 1688 except that the former is couched in nineteenth-century English rather than seventeenth-century English.

[48]On the religious disputes in France see above, pp. 244–46.

[49]Priolkar, *op. cit.* (n. 47), Pt. I, pp. 35–49.

deputized to arrest the accused. They serve without wages and "deem themselves sufficiently rewarded by the honour conferred upon them in serving so holy a Tribunal." Finally there are secretaries, jailers, guards, and other service employees of the Inquisition.[50]

The prisoners, generally kept in separate cells, are required to keep "a perpetual and rigid silence" on pain of being beaten by the guards. About once in every two months the prisoners are visited by inspectors who inquire if they have any complaints, an act "made for no other purpose than to display that justice and goodness, of which there is so much parade in this Tribunal." In the public mind this tribunal "dispenses justice with more leniency and charity than any other known jurisdiction." In reality, however, this is not the case. Witnesses never confront the accused and are not carefully screened as to their relation to or interest in the case. Depositions are sometimes extracted from witnesses by torture. The accused himself, "confessing on the rack of crimes of which he is guiltless, is also reputed as a witness." Those accused of "Judaism," especially the New Christians, and those charged with sorcery suffer most from the persecution of the inquisitors. Christian converts who lapse into Hindu practices or participate in native ceremonies are also handled roughly.

The Inquisition of Goa, one of the four sovereign Portuguese tribunals, exercises authority over the entire Portuguese East. It reports only to the Grand Council and the Inquisitor-General in Lisbon. Revenues for the Goa Tribunal come from the sale of the effects and properties of prisoners and from the royal treasury. All inquisitors are nominated by the king and confirmed by the pope. The Grand Inquisitor of Goa is more respected than either the archbishop or viceroy. This is so because all Christians except the archbishop, his grand vicar, and the viceroy are subject to his jurisdiction. Upon appeal to Portugal for the necessary authority he can even have these high officials arrested. Ordinarily the Goa Tribunal meets every fifteen days unless an extraordinary occasion causes it to meet oftener. Subordinate councils meet twice daily. When final decisions are taken, the archbishop or bishop is present and presides over the proceedings. After recounting his personal experiences with the Inquisition, Dellon concludes with a graphic description of the *auto da fé* in which he participated as one of the prisoners.[51]

While Dellon languished in prison, Dr. John Fryer spent from September, 1675, to December, 1676, in Goa and its environs, a region which he calls the "Canatick-Country."[52] He was first in Goa during the Christmas season of 1675. In its harbor he sees three great carracks rotting and ready to fall apart for "want of cargo" to take back to Europe. He describes Goa's

[50] *Ibid.*, Pt. II, pp. 23–26.

[51] *Ibid.*, pp. 27–69.

[52] W. Crooke (ed.), *A New Account of East India and Persia. Being Nine Years' Travels, 1672–1681 by John Fryer* (3 vols.; "HS," 2d ser., XIX, XX, XXXIX; London, 1909–15), II, 1–88. Also see above, pp. 580–82.

churches and other ecclesiastical buildings and observes that the Jesuit establishment dominates the scene just as the Society does the city's administration and economy. The English physician surveys the royal hospital and declares that the care given there to the sick is "commendable." The Jesuits prepare and sell the "Goa stone," a medicine in high repute during the seventeenth century.[53] In the governor's palace he sees the portraits of the viceroys and is introduced to Luis Mendoça de Albuquerque, the viceroy (r. 1671–77) then governing. He distinguishes between pre-Portuguese Goa ("Old Goa"), a country town, and the metropole created by the Portuguese three miles inland.[54] Like Dellon he is shocked by the powerful and omnipresent Inquisition. Goa, he avers, is suffering meat shortages and an interruption of its diamond commerce as a result of the activities of Sivaji in north Kanara. Manpower shortages mean that Goa's many priests must be prepared to fight, "there being in the Convents more [men] than in the Garisons."[55]

Like other non-Portuguese commentators, Fryer sees Goa as a "Rome in India," where clerics and nobles flaunt their status and lord it over all others. The majority of its people are "Canorein" who are "Portuguezed" in speech and manners; even so, they cringe before white men. Women, "both White and Black," are kept indoors and jealously guarded. They devote themselves wholly to their homes, a fact which renders them "unfit for Conversation." The epidemics of Goa are treated by feeding mangoes to the patients. In addition to the best mangoes in India, Goa produces cashews and pineapples in abundance. Its bakers make excellent wheat bread. Wax is formed into tapers there for the city's many altars. Arrack from the nearby village of Nerul is the main ingredient of the five put into a punch made by the English on this coast.[56]

Twenty years later Giovanni Francesco Gemelli Careri, the Neapolitan world traveler, was in Goa on two occasions (February 26 to March 3, and April 5 to May 15, 1695).[57] From its viceroy, Careri learned about the city's history and its recent decline "to a miserable Condition."[58] Goa's population has fallen to no more than twenty thousand and the Portuguese from Europe are the fewest in number of the city's diverse peoples. Luso-Indians are more numerous and mulattoes, the children of whites and blacks, constitute roughly one-quarter of its inhabitants. The Konkanis of Goa are descended from Brahmans, Banyans, and "Charados" (*Kárádás*). Members of the two higher castes are sharp-witted, ingenious, and apt learners. They work in

---

[53] See Yule and Burnell, *op. cit.* (n. 37), p. 379.

[54] *Cf.* J. N. da Fonseca, *An Historical and Archaeological Sketch of the City of Goa* (Bombay, 1878), pp. 120–21n.

[55] Crooke (ed.), *op. cit.* (n. 52), II, 10–25.

[56] *Ibid.*, II, 25–28, 84–85. On "punch" see above, p. 736, n.124.

[57] For his accounts see S. Sen (ed.), *Indian Travels of Thevenot and Careri* (New Delhi, 1949), pp. 186–94, 269–73. Also see above, pp. 386–88.

[58] Dom Pedro Antonio de Noronha, Conde de Villa Verde, was viceroy from 1693 to 1698.

the professions as priests, lawyers, and secretaries. Because they are diligent and loyal, they are in great demand as servants. The lower-caste Konkanis, even when Christian, are disloyal thieves and ruffians. Occupationally they are cultivators, fishers, rowers, and bearers. These lazy workers respond only to thrashings. Indeed they derive much pleasure from beatings; it is even the custom for relatives to whip bridal couples on their wedding night. Most of Goa's merchants are Hindus and Muslims who live in their own sections of the city. No non-Christian group may practice its faith publicly. The Portuguese buy many black slaves imported from Africa to have as household servants and personal attendants. These Africans, originally idolaters, quickly accept baptism.[59]

The island of Goa includes thirty villages while the peninsula of Salsette boasts fifty villages numbering 50,000 souls. The peninsula of Bardez has twenty-eight villages. Salsette is governed by the Jesuits. The religious life of Bardez is watched over by other clergy. While describing the sights of the Portuguese city of Goa, Careri observes that the "little Church of the Theatins is built after the Model of S. Andrew della Velle in Rome."[60] He decides that Goa's renowned royal hospital is badly administered. On his return trip to Goa, Careri is granted special permission to see the "decayed" body of St. Francis Xavier which the Jesuits have not displayed publicly for nine years. They are awaiting "a noble tomb of Porphiry Stone, from Florence, order'd to be made by the Grand Duke."[61] In the mint, located in the main viceregal palace, they make coins of "Tutunaga" (tutenag), a metal from China unknown in Europe.[62] Before sailing for China himself, Careri has his own gold changed into silver "Pieces of Eight, because there is a great deal lost by carrying Gold into China."[63]

From this quick review it can readily be seen that Goa retained its prominence and glamor until about 1623 for European missionaries and travelers. The loss of Ormuz in 1622 inaugurates the rapid decline of Goa as the bastion and metropole of the Portuguese East, at least in the estimation of Della Valle. In these years it is still, however, a crossroads to which all European voyagers eventually make their way. The powers of the viceroys and the other authorities of the state gradually erode, however, as the religious orders become increasingly prominent in the management of Goa, Salsette, and Bardez and in leading the fight against the Dutch heretics. At the same time the parishes there are served more and more by native secular priests. Business affairs and professional services begin to slip away from the Portuguese into the hands of native merchants, lawyers, and physicians. In the process the royal hospital and other Portuguese charitable institutions no

[59] Sen (ed.), *op. cit.* (n. 57), pp. 186–89.
[60] The Theatines first came to Goa in 1640. Their convent and church of St. Cajetan was built after 1655. See Fonseca, *op. cit.* (n. 54), pp. 248–50.
[61] For a detailed history of Xavier's tomb see *ibid.*, pp. 286–301.
[62] It was known in Europe. See *Asia*, II, Bk. 3, p. 426.
[63] Sen (ed.), *op. cit.* (n. 57), pp. 190–95, 268–73.

longer function efficiently. The economic pressure of the Dutch blockade leads to the truce of 1642 by which Goa is forced to tolerate the Dutch presence in western India. Ultimately the loss of Malabar in 1663 shows up the awful weakness of Goa for the world to see. Fearful that Goa itself might fall to internal enemies in league with outside powers, the Inquisition becomes increasingly repressive throughout the latter half of the century. By its end, Golden Goa, though it still remains Portuguese, has become just one of several important ports on India's west coast.

2

BIJAPUR

When Pyrard was in Goa (1608–10), the Portuguese had come to enjoy good relations with the "Dealcan" ('Adil Khan, or 'Adil Shah) of Bijapur, their erstwhile enemy in the Deccan.[64] In 1570–71, and again in 1583, the Muslims of Bijapur and their allies had besieged Goa with vast armies that had been turned back by Portuguese cannons. In the process both sides came to realize they needed each other to survive. Bijapur required the trade that came through Goa, and the Portuguese were heavily dependent upon Bijapur for provisions. Gradually they came to agree that the Portuguese might live peacefully in Goa according to their own laws and customs, providing that they should not encroach upon Bijapur's territory in any other way. Further, it was understood that the more than twenty thousand Hindus in Goa's territories might practice their own religion while observing Portuguese law. These Hindus were not to have their own temples and were required to pay a small head tax for every male member of a family. Portuguese and Indian Christians were permitted to live in Bijapur but were not allowed to build churches or practice Christianity publicly. Refugees from Goa might not be followed into Bijapur's territory or refugees from Bijapur be taken into custody in Goa's territory by Bijapur's officials. With these conditions settled, regular diplomatic relations were established which obtained during Pyrard's stay in Goa.[65]

The ruler of Bijapur, Ibrahim 'Adil Shah II (r. 1580–1627), is no tyrant, but an amiable and peaceful prince who is "a friend of all foreigners, and of his neighbors who are at peace with him." An ambassador from Goa is always at his court. There are also some Jesuits there "who are well received by him, and they make some use of their opportunities but secretly. . . ."

[64] On their relations in the mid-sixteenth century according to the Jesuit letters see *Asia*, I, 434–35.
[65] Pyrard in Gray (ed.), *op. cit.* (n. 10), II, 131–33. On the implications of the various treaties between Bijapur and Goa see M. A. Nayeem, *External Relations of the Bijapur Kingdom (1489–1686 A.D.)* (Hyderabad, 1974), pp. 225–28.

The Portuguese who reside and work there are able to practice their religion under the protection of the ambassador and the Jesuits. Bijapur also "keeps an ambassador in ordinary at Goa." He is recognized as a person "of dignity and importance" and he practices his own religion in his residence. When he travels around the city, he is accompanied by an entourage of his servants, merchants from Bijapur, and a few of his own guard. Forty years before, according to the local tradition, a prince of Bijapur came to Goa and became a Christian. When his father died, he avoided fighting with his brothers over the succession by accepting as his share Bardez, Salsette, and three or four other small islands around Goa. When this prince died without heirs, he left these lands to the king of Portugal, and they now help to feed the island of Goa.[66] The "king" of Bijapur, who owns many elephants, sends one as a gift now and again to the king of Spain. They are kept in Goa, where they are managed by trainers from Bijapur. Bijapur is plagued by a surfeit of tigers and huge serpents; still it produces diamonds and cotton textiles for export. Its people dress in trousers "and large coats of silk and cotton, with turbans—straight, high, and pointed and not round like those of the Turks and Arabs." While most of the people of Bijapur are Muslims, the Hindus who reside there also dress in this way. Many of these people enter Goa daily to sell provisions. Several royal refugees from Bijapur live in Goa as well as the exiled king of the Maldives who receives a regular pension from the king of Spain.[67]

Pyrard and the Portuguese of Goa were well aware of the mounting threat of the Dutch in Indian waters during the first decade of the century. The Mughuls were another threat, and the Portuguese were determined to be on good terms with Bijapur to keep a barrier between the expanding Mughul Empire and Goa.[68] Still the failure of the Dutch efforts to blockade Goa effectively in 1603, and subsequently, permitted the Portuguese the luxury of living contentedly, if somewhat anxiously, in Golden Goa, at peace and in alliance with Bijapur for the time being. Ibrahim 'Adil Shah II, like his predecessors, never gave up hope of regaining Goa despite the treaties with the Portuguese. Not able to blockade Goa effectively, the Dutch made a few weak efforts to push into coastal Karnatak, or into small ports weakly held by Bijapur, with the idea of bringing greater pressure upon the Portuguese. But it was not until 1617–18, when the Dutch received permission from the Mughuls to trade from Surat inland, that they once again made efforts to work out an alliance with Bijapur directed against Goa.[69]

---

[66] This is a truncated, pious, and misdated version of the story of Meale Khan's collaboration with the Portuguese in 1555. See F. C. Danvers, *The Portuguese in India* (2 vols.; London, 1894), I, 503–5.

[67] Pyrard in Gray (ed.), *op. cit.* (n. 10), II, 134–39. On the exiled king of the Maldives see below, pp. 934–35, 943.

[68] See Nayeem, *op. cit.* (n. 65), pp. 228–29.

[69] See the appropriate articles from the *farman* of the Khan Khanan in Ann B. Radwan, *The Dutch in Western India, 1601–32* (Calcutta, 1978), p. 37.

That the Dutch sought closer relations with Bijapur is indirectly attested to by Heinrich von Poser (1599–1661), a German nobleman and traveler who visited the Deccan in 1622. While in Agra, Poser met Wouter Houten, the Dutch resident, who apparently suggested a trip across the Deccan to Masulipatam, possibly with the idea of buying diamonds cheaply. Poser started this journey by wending his way from Aurangabad in the Nizam-shahi kingdom, to Sholapur, Bijapur, and Hyderabad. In Bijapur, Poser was summoned to meet Ibrahim 'Adil Shah, who was then celebrating the fortieth year of his reign. Here Poser witnessed an elephant fight and saw his first crocodile. He stayed on there for more than one month with a German mercenary soldier. Poser's diary, first published at Jena in 1675, is particularly valuable for the detailed itineraries it provides and for the indications it gives of growing Dutch interest in the Deccan around 1622.[70]

Despite the considerable successes enjoyed in northwestern India by the Dutch and English, the uneasy Portuguese-Bijapur alliance functioned until 1636 as a barrier against both Mughul and Dutch expansion. In that year Bijapur made peace with the Mughuls and began to push its dominion southward and westward. Bijapur also showed a new independence by violating a treaty obligation to send pepper only to Portuguese ports. A vessel was sent out from the Bijapuri port of Dabhol destined for Persia and Mecca. Determined to maintain their monopoly of the pepper trade, Portuguese from Goa attacked the ship and murdered its crew. This incident set up a hostile situation from which the Dutch immediately sought to derive profit. In 1637 they instituted the policy of blockading Goa each year during the season favorable to the dispatch of armadas to Europe. In January, 1637, the VOC sent Johan van Twist from Batavia on an embassy to Bijapur. He was instructed to procure trading rights at Dabhol and to conclude a military alliance directed against Goa. Successful in his mission, Van Twist obtained *farmans* granting the Dutch free trade in Bijapur, the promise of landside military support for a joint seizure of Goa, and orders to fortify Vengurla as a base for the VOC's blockading fleet.[71]

Van Twist's report of his mission to Bijapur was first published at Amsterdam in 1645 in the *Begin ende voortgangh* collection compiled by Isaac

[70]After his meeting with Houten in Agra, Poser enjoyed the hospitality of Dutch residents in Hyderabad and Masulipatam. He generally traveled around India on Dutch ships and lodged on land with Dutch merchants until his departure from Surat in November, 1623. He traveled overland to and from India with the aid of Dutch merchants, and apparently learned enough Persian from them to get along. He returned to Breslau in 1623 after an absence of five years, with his Latin diary. It was translated into German at his son's behest as . . . *das Tagebuch seiner Reise von Constantinopel aus durch die Bulgarey, Armenien, Persien, und Indien aus Licht gestellet.* . . . For further detail on his book see above, pp. 534–35. A copy of this extremely rare work is in the British Library. For an English translation of his Deccan journey with commentaries by leading Indian scholars, see Gita Dharampal (trans.), "Heinrich von Poser's Travelogue of the Deccan (1622)," *Quarterly Journal of the Mythic Society*, LXXIII (1982), 103–14.

[71]On these negotiations see Nayeem, *op. cit.* (n. 65), pp. 252–55; for the failure of the Dutch Bijarpuri alliance see Verma, *op. cit.* (n. 26), pp. 59–60.

Commelin.[72] It begins with a geographical description of the western Deccan, of "Visiapour's" (Bijapur's) placement therein, and of Goa's vulnerability from the landside. Van Twist notes that "Mamedh Idelxa" (Muhammad 'Adil Shah, r. 1627–56), Bijapur's ruler, was but twenty-four years of age in 1637.[73] He tells in some detail "the tragic story of 'Chavas-Chan' [Khawas Khan]," Muhammad's regent and adviser ever since his advent to power. Fifteen or sixteen months before Van Twist's arrival in Bijapur, Khawas Khan was murdered. The minister, a former slave, had ruled the country well until he angered the 'Adil Shah by sleeping with the queen and antagonized the "Great Mogul" by robbing the tribute caravans. Khawas Khan engaged in further conspiracies against the ruler and his other advisers and so was assassinated. Now Muhammad continues to pay tribute to the Mughuls but enjoys absolute power within his own domain. He no longer has open enemies, but his kingdom is plagued by the depredations of the robber rajas of "Rasbouten" (Rajputana). He also has troubles with the Portuguese, who in 1635 began to persecute his subjects in Goa and to prey on pilgrim ships bound for Mecca. (Possibly one of these vessels was the same one called a "pepper ship" by the Portuguese.) The city of Bijapur itself is an impregnable fortress protected by large cannons. The farm population, made up largely of "Canarijns" (Kanarese), is very poor and lives in straw huts for the most part. Van Twist ends his discussion with a description of the route from Bijapur to Goa, with details on each of the cities on the road as well as on other Deccan towns. While Van Twist may be inaccurate in his dates and dependent on others for some of his descriptions, his account of Bijapur at this turning point in that state's history deserves more attention than it has hitherto received from both foreign and native historians.[74]

According to Mandelslo, "the kingdom of Dicam [Deccan], or rather Cuncam [Konkan], for so it is more commonly called, though from its Metropolis it sometimes gets the name of Visiapour [Bijapur], reaches all along that Coast, from Ingediva [Anjidiv Island or Anjediva], which lies within twelve leagues [forty-eight miles] of Goa, towards the South to a place named Siffarde [Shiveshar, north of Karwar]."[75] Its chief ports are "Geytapour" (Jaitapur), "Rasapour" (Rajapur), "Carrpatan" (Kharepatan), and

---

[72] For bibliographical details see above, pp. 472–73; for the section on the Deccan and Bijapur see *BV*, I, 69–83.

[73] If correct, this would make the 'Adil Shah fourteen years old when he ascended the throne. Nayeem, *op. cit.* (n. 65), p. 25, declares that he began his reign "at the comparatively young age of sixteen years."

[74] Exceptional are the works of P. M. Joshi, "John Van Twist's Mission to Bijapur, 1637," *Journal of Indian History*, XXXIV (1956), 111–37; and Nayeem, *op. cit.* (n. 65), pp. 252–55.

[75] Davies (trans.), *op. cit.* (n. 35), p. 89. This definition seems to include the southern frontier region officially claimed by the 'Adil Shah before the Portuguese intrusion. Before mid-century the desolate island of Anjediva was, like many of the other islands in the vicinity of Goa, under *de facto* Portuguese control. Nayeem, *op. cit.* (n. 65), p. 24, writes: "The Kingdom in 1605 extended along the West Coast from Bankot in the north to about Bhatkal in the south (except Ankola, Gersoppa, Honavar)." By Nayeem's definition Bijapur included inland territories to the south of the fourteenth parallel.

"Dabul" (Dabhol).[76] Bijapur, the metropole and capital, is inland "eighty leagues [320 miles] from Dabul, and eighty-four [336 miles] from Goa." It is a fortified city with high stone walls, a surrounding moat, and more than one thousand mounted cannons of brass and iron. The royal palace stands in the center of the city and is itself surrounded by a double wall and two encompassing moats.[77] The man who commands the palace guard of two thousand men and the city's garrison of five thousand is called "Nammouth Chan"; he is an Italian born at Rome. Most of the merchants resident in Bijapur live in its five suburbs.[78] Besides the ordinary Indian merchant groups, there are in the Konkan those called "Venesars" (*banjārās*), rice and wheat merchants who drive caravans of oxen and cows from place to place.[79]

Mandelslo gives in detail the route from Goa to Bijapur and follows it with the route from Bijapur to Dabhol, in which he carefully notes the names of towns, rivers, products, and sights.[80] Dabhol on the "Kalewacko" (Kalewacka) River is one of the most ancient cities of the region. It possesses no wall or fortifications, but boasts "a white tower which serves as a temple or mosque that pilots observe [as a landmark] at sea."[81] The Hindu and Muslim merchants of Dabhol trade mainly in salt and pepper, but their business is suffering a depression. Other local people are goldsmiths and workers in brass. The people dress in the manner of "Benjans" (Banyans, or Gujarati traders) except that their shoes, called "alparcas," are made of wood and tied on the instep with leather straps. Like Van Twist, Mandelslo comments on the death of "Chauas–Chan" (Khawas Khan). The German, however, sees the regent as a usurper of the 'Adil Shah's powers. While domestic conflict is now resolved in Bijapur, war with Goa appears to be imminent. In case of such an eventuality the 'Adil Shah is well prepared, since he is "strongest in artillery of all local princes." He is also supported by the Dutch who have a factory at "Fingerla" (Vengurla) "within four leagues (sixteen miles) of Goa."[82]

Because of the common enmity of the VOC and Bijapur to Goa, Baldaeus evidently spent his time in this region at Vengurla, the Dutch outpost in Bijapur. As of around 1660, he reports that Bijapur "borders to the south of

[76] The first three of these ports are close together and far to the south of Dabhol. They are about midway between Dabhol and Goa. See I. Habib, *An Atlas of the Mughal Empire* (Delhi, 1982), map 14B.

[77] For a modern confirming description of the city and its castle walls as well as the ruins of the cannons see Henry Cousens, *Bijapur, The Old Capital of the Adil Shahi Kings* (3d ed., Poona, 1923), pp. 8–11; and Sidney Toy, *The Strongholds of India* (London, 1957), chap. vi.

[78] See Davies (trans.), *op. cit.* (n. 35), p. 91. Mandelslo gives the names of the suburbs and notes that in "Schanpar" (Shahapur) "live most of the Iewellers."

[79] *Ibid.*, p. 93. For this identification see Yule and Burnell, *op. cit.* (n. 37), pp. 114–15. Van Twist writes of the "Venesares" as raiders and robbers.

[80] Davies (trans.), *op. cit.* (n. 35), pp. 90–92.

[81] Probably a reference to its beautiful mosque, "the only specimen of pure Saracenic architecture in the Southern Konkan" (*Imperial Gazeteer*, under Dabhol). Also see above, p. 777.

[82] Davies (trans.), *op. cit.* (n. 35), pp. 92–98.

Wingurla [Vengurla] upon the river Mirsee [Mirjan], the boundary of the country of Carnatica in the territory of Sivipaneyk [Sivappa Nayaka of Ikkeri]." To the north of Vengurla lies the seaport of "Danno" (Dahana) at the boundary between Bijapur and the Mughul Empire "about ten leagues [south] from Damam [Damão]." But the Portuguese control the mouths of most of the eight rivers belonging to Bijapur. Besides Bijapur city, its other cities of note are "Sintapour" (Jaitapur), a seaport, "Razapour" (Rajapur), "Banda" (Banda), "Rajebaag" (Raybagh), "Arec" (Achra), "Asta" (Ashta), "Tamba" (Tamba), and "Wingurla" (Vengurla).[83] Economically Bijapur is important to the Dutch for the saltpeter it exports.[84]

In 1641, Tavernier had traveled overland from Goa to Bijapur, a journey "which one generally accomplishes in eight days." The French traveler claims that of Bijapur's three main ports the best of all is "Crapatan" (Kharepatan) with its protecting mountaintop fort. While Bijapur no longer (*ca.* 1648) pays tribute to the "Great Mogul" and is at peace with Goa, its ruler is confronted by the rebellion of "Nair Sivaji" (Sivaji). This rebel rapidly and efficiently put together an army. The death of Bijapur's previous ruler and the subsequent disruption enabled Sivaji to gain control over its ports, from Rajapur in the south to Dabhol in the north, and in the process to obtain treasure for the payment of his forces. In the meantime the queen of Bijapur adopted a boy whom she has elevated to the throne. Ultimately Sivaji and the young king conclude a treaty by which Sivaji retains his conquests as a vassal of Bijapur. Half of the revenues collected by Sivaji are assigned to Bijapur.[85] With Sivaji's rise in this region, it was not long before Bijapur became enmeshed in the struggle between the Mahrattas and the Mughuls.

Dr. Fryer, who visited Vengurla in the autumn of 1675, describes its parlous condition. Caught in the Deccan wars and preyed upon regularly by the hit-and-run attacks of Malabar pirates, Vengurla is a partially ruined town and port. It is ruled by a Hindu governor appointed by Sivaji, who

---

[83] See Habib, *op. cit.* (n. 76), map. 14A.

[84] Baldaeus in *CV* (3d ed., 6 vols.; London, 1744–46), III, 545. Baldaeus also gives the names of the eight rivers belonging to Bijapur.

[85] Tavernier in Ball and Crooke (trans. and eds.), *op. cit.* (n. 42), I, 142–48. This is typical of the way Tavernier puts his *Voyages* together. He uses a reference to his trip of 1641 to Bijapur as an opportunity to talk about political events which occurred subsequently. He obviously learned of the rise of Sivaji on his later journeys in northern India, or during his trip of 1648 to Goa. The history of the rise of Mahratta power as an independent, or nominally dependent, state is intimately involved with the final decade of Muhammad 'Adil Shah's reign. In 1646 Muhammad fell seriously ill and for the next ten years his wife Bari Sahiba ruled in his stead. It was generally believed that Muhammad died in 1646, a popular supposition taken up by Tavernier. On his actual death in 1656 his adopted son 'Ali 'Adil Shah II was established on the throne. In the succession crisis which ensued both Aurangzib and Sivaji took advantage of the situation to take territory and treasure from Bijapur. Sivaji plundered Bijapur city in 1660; two years later, he agreed to a truce to give himself an opportunity to push into Kanara. Six years after Sivaji's death in 1680, Aurangzib annexed Bijapur to his realm. See Verma, *op. cit.* (n. 26), pp. 28–32; and for more detail see Nayeem, *op. cit.* (n. 65), pp. 186–210.

permits the Dutch to maintain a fortified factory there.[86] Unlike earlier European observers, Fryer denounces Sivaji's "Tyrannical Government. . . where all Barbarous Customs are exercised." He is particularly appalled by the "Linguits" (*lingāyats*) of "Hubly" (Hubli) who bury their dead standing in an upright position. Suttees are buried alive to the shoulders, their necks are then wrung, and they are quickly covered with earth. Between Vengurla and Goa, Sivaji governs "Norway" (Naroa), a place famous for its courtesans.[87]

After his coronation in 1674, Sivaji wages a languid war in the vicinity of Goa against the divided and irresolute leaders of Bijapur. Although Sivaji reassures the Bijapuris that he will protect them from the Mughuls, they fear his embrace will cost them dearly. While the Bijapuri leaders irresolutely seek allies, Sivaji's forces freely range over Bijapur in all directions between Surat and Ponda just to the south of Goa. "Bullul Caun" (Bahlol Khan), the Afghan regent (1675–77) of Bijapur, mistrusts Sivaji's promises and attacks his allies among the Bijapuri factions. In response to this affront, Sivaji negotiates a truce with "Badur Caun" (Bahadur Khan), the Mughul general whom Bahlol Khan and his Pathan levies have twice defeated in his efforts to take Bijapur city. Despite the setbacks suffered in the Deccan wars, Bijapur in 1675 remains "a spacious Kingdom," in Fryer's estimation, which stretches north to Junnar and south to Porto Novo on the Coromandel Coast; on the east it is bounded by Golconda and on the west by the ocean. When pressed too much by the Mughuls, "unsettled and ill-governed" Bijapur is rescued by money from Golconda, paid out in bribes to Sivaji or to the Mughul generals. The Mughuls, particularly the nobles and generals, are satisfied to keep Golconda and Bijapur as vassals from whom money can be regularly extorted. The Mughul emperor, although constantly busied by problems on the northern frontier, is still able to maintain a minimum of forty thousand horsemen in addition to infantry in the Deccan wars. These forces would be sufficient to bring Golconda and Bijapur into total subjection were it not for the duplicity of the Mughul nobles, officials, and military officers.[88]

Although Bijapur is a hereditary monarchy, its 'Adil Shah rulers are now dependent for their sovereignty upon retaining the support of noble factions. The Deccan kingdoms, unlike Hindustan, possess a hereditary nobility whose lands and acquisitions pass on to their sons and do not revert to the king. These nobles act as petty lords; they build forts and make peace

---

[86] The Dutch factory, first established in 1638, was destroyed by Sivaji in 1664 and again by the Mughuls (Sidis) early in 1675. Fryer visited a newly constructed and fortified factory.

[87] Fryer in Crooke (ed.), *op. cit.* (n. 52), II, 16–19. Hubli was sacked and occupied by Sivaji's forces in 1673 with considerable loss to its English factory. Old Hubli is centered around a plain stone temple (possibly eleventh century) which contains a lingam. Naroa is on Divar Island. (See under Naroa in *Imperial Gazetteer*.)

[88] Fryer in Crooke (ed.), *op. cit.* (n. 52), II, 43–51.

and war against one another and even their sovereign. Traditionally they are supposed to make their obeisances to the "king" at appointed times. When they fail to perform this or other acts of vassalage, the "king" appoints foreigners as regents whom these lords fear or resent. The regent of Bijapur, "Hobsy Caphir" (Habshi Kafir), an Abyssinian and a Sidi, was an excellent general. Addicted to drink, Habshi was blamed by the feuding nobles for the sad plight of Bijapur. He was killed by Bahlol Khan, who now runs the kingdom for its ten-year-old ruler.[89] Fryer lists the 'Adil Shahs of Bijapur and estimates the holdings of its greatest nobles.[90]

Sivaji, Bijapur's "diseased limb," benefits the state by his attacks upon the Mughuls and undermines it by "rewarding himself most unconscionably." He maintains himself in the mountains and descends to the lowlands only to rob and pillage; Aurangzib calls him "his Mountain Rat." Sivaji has irreparably damaged Bijapur by taking the Konkan coast and blocking its western ports. After reviewing Sivaji's biography and military exploits to 1675, Fryer makes a final estimate. A strict Hindu, Sivaji is under the influence of the Brahmans and swayed by them. While most of his followers are Mahratti Hindus, a few are Muslims. He can put thirty thousand cavalry and innumerable infantry into the field. His soldiers are "Hardy Brave Fellows, fit for the Mountains"; on the sea and flatlands he is no stronger than his neighbors. He will permit no females to accompany his armed forces. Merchants have little use for Sivaji, probably because he disrupts trade and inspires other discontented nobles to revolt. Of the commoners Sivaji says: "Money is inconvenient for them; give them Victuals and an Arse-Clout, it is enough."[91]

Bijapuris and other Deccanese are warlike and "apt to dislike Government." These "Swarthy or Olive" peoples are "Proud and Brave" and delight in splendid military displays. The interior of the country is rich and fruitful, whereas the mountainous coastal regions produce only wood, cattle, rice, and coconuts. The mountaineers are rough while the lowlanders are given to soft and easy living. The lowlanders "will rather escape than pursue a Foe" but fight better in pitched battles than Sivaji's raiders. Important cities are usually named for the local lord. Bijapur's major markets are at "Hubly" (Hubli), "Rabag" (Raybagh), and "Huttany" (Athni). The Portuguese blockade the port towns of "Gulleau" (Kahjan in the Thana district) and "Bimly" (Bhimdi in the Thana district). Sivaji has occupied its ports of "Rajapour" (Rajapur), "Dabul" (Dabhol), "Vingula" (Vengurla), and "Carwar" (Karwar). Porto Novo in Coromandel produces large revenues, but in 1675 it is the only eastern port still controlled by Bijapur.[92]

[89] Sultan Sikandar, a young child of four at his succession, was the titular ruler until the demise of Bijapur in 1686.
[90] Crooke (ed.), *op. cit.* (n. 52), II, 52–57.
[91] *Ibid.*, pp. 57–67. *Cf.* the more favorable estimates of Sivaji, above, pp. 765–75.
[92] Fryer in Crooke (ed.), *op. cit.* (n. 52), II, 66–68. On Bijapur's expansion to the Coromandel region see Nayeem, *op. cit.* (n. 65), pp. 142–44.

Despite the occasional support received from Golconda, the 'Adil Shahs finally succumbed to the imperial Mughul forces in 1686.

3

KANARA

Goa, dependent on Kanara for its pepper supplies, began in the seventeenth century to cultivate relations with the ruler who most nearly controlled the pepper-producing areas of its interior. Rice from Kanara also helped to feed Goa's population. At this period the leading political power in Kanara was the nayak of Ikkeri, one of those south Indian rulers who began as provincial governors in the Vijayanagar empire and with its decline assumed an increased independent authority. At its zenith the Ikkeri state controlled most of the coast and much of the hinterland in the region between Goa and Cannanore. Its Hindu ruler also maintained formal relations with Goa. Many people from Kanara worked at either permanent or temporary jobs in Goa.[93]

The most novel of the materials in the letters of Della Valle relate to his experiences on a trip south of Goa from October to December, 1623. After a rather lengthy stay in Goa, the Italian pilgrim wanted "to see some country of the Gentiles where they themselves bore sway, and observe their Rites without any subjection to Christians or Moors. . . ."[94] To this end he received permission to accompany "Fernandez Leiton" (Fernandes Leitão), the Portuguese ambassador and his friend, on a mission to the court of "Venktapa Naieka" (Venkatappa Nayaka I, r. 1586–1629) at Ikkeri. The Portuguese, who had forts at Mangalore, Honavar, and Barcelore (Basrur) along the coast of Kanara, were eager to promote good relations with Ikkeri and other states which controlled the major pepper production centers of the interior. Under Venkatappa Nayaka I the semi-independent princelings of Kanara, whom the Portuguese had previously intimidated or played off against one another, were becoming increasingly hostile, independent, and demanding with respect to deliveries of pepper. Fernandes Leitão, because of Goa's recognition of the new power of Ikkeri in north Kanara, was delegated to investigate the situation and to negotiate an agreement with Venkatappa.[95]

The Portuguese mission was accompanied and guided by Vithula Sinay, Ikkeri's envoy to Goa. On October 14 the two ambassadors and their entourages left by sea for "Onor" (Honavar). Here they remained for almost two weeks awaiting orders to proceed inland to Ikkeri. Honavar, they report, is "a good port of indifferent capacity" formed by two branches of the Shira-

[93] See J. Gerson da Cunha, "The Portuguese in South Kanara," *JRAS, Bombay Branch*, XIX (1895–97), 249–62.

[94] Grey (ed.), *op. cit.* (n. 19), I, 190.

[95] See K. D. Swaminathan, *The Nāyakas of Ikkēri* (Madras, 1957), pp. 41–42, 46.

vati River which "meet at the Fortress, and are discharg'd with one mouth into the Sea." Its fortress, the walls of which are "not very well designed," was originally a native bastion that the Portuguese simply took over. The dwellings in the town "are rather Cottages than Houses." The Portuguese for the most part live in houses within the spacious fortress, which "stands upon a high Hill of freestone"; it also includes two churches and a great public square. Just outside of Honavar is a hot spring used for bathing and for watering the nearby fields. On October 24 the Hindus celebrate "Davali" (Divali) which Della Valle compares to a festival of lights he had witnessed in Persia. This festival delayed the embassy as did news from Ikkeri telling of the death of Venkatappa's chief queen, an aged woman named "Badra-Amà" (Bhadramma). Both the nayak and his queen are "Lingavant" (Lingayats), or worshippers of Siva. Della Valle learns that "twelve or thirteen years since" Venkatappa took a Moorish woman as a paramour. The queen, on learning of his defilement by "a strange Woman of impure Race," took an oath that she should henceforth be daughter rather than wife to the nayak. Although she persisted in this decision to her death, she retained the love of her husband and had considerable influence over him.[96]

Finally the delegation leaves Honavar for Ikkeri around November 1. On the way they pass through "Garsopa" (Gersoppa) in one of India's best pepper-growing regions. Before being conquered in 1606 by Venkatappa, Gersoppa was ruled by Queen Bhairadevi, known to the Portuguese as the "*Reyna da Pimenta*." This queen, so the story goes in Della Valle, "fell in love with a man and a stranger into whose power she resigned herself together with her whole kingdom." When he tried to overthrow her, the queen appealed for help to the Portuguese; he, in his turn, asked for aid from Venkatappa. The prince of Ikkeri responded swiftly, drove out the Portuguese, took the queen prisoner, murdered the traitor, and burnt Gersoppa along with its royal palace. Thereafter Honavar and other Kanarese ports, as well as most of the pepper exports of the region, came under the control of Ikkeri.[97]

Along the road, Della Valle notices how little boys study arithmetic in village India. Without the supervision of a teacher, they write their problems in the sand and sing their lessons aloud in small groups to keep from forgetting their assignments.[98] On painting the interior of houses with cow dung he writes:

Indeed this is a prety Curiosity, and I intend to cause tryal to be made of it in *Italy*, and the rather because they say for certain that the Houses whose pavements are thus

---

[96] Grey (ed.), *op. cit.* (n. 19), II, 202–3, 207–9. This story of the erring nayak and his queen is quoted verbatim in Swaminathan, *op. cit.* (n. 95), p. 51.

[97] Grey (ed.), *op. cit.* (n. 19), II, 218–21; also see Swaminathan, *op. cit.* (n. 95), pp. 42–43.

[98] Grey (ed.), *op. cit.* (n. 19), II, 227–28. See pl. 173.

stercorated, are good against the Plague, which is no despicable advantage. . . . The Portingals use it in their Houses at Goa and other places of India; and, in brief, 'tis certain that it is no superstitious custom, but onely for neatness and ornament.

At "Ahinali" (Honnali), the first populous center on the route, the Italian lodges, as a yogi might, on the porch of a Siva temple. Its deity, called "Virenà Deurù" (Virana), "the latter of which words signifies God, or rather Lord," stands "in a dark place with Candles before him." There is also "a Brahmà with five heads, which in their language they call Nau Brahma" (the new Brahma, or the four-headed Brahma; Siva cut one head off) and another called "Naraina" (Narayana, an epithet of Siva). Della Valle describes a procession he witnessed here and concludes his lengthy discussion with a sketch of the temple's ground plan.[99]

The city of Ikkeri, where Della Valle arrived on November 8, 1623, is "seated in a goodly Plain" and encompassed by two circuits of bamboo fence and "a Wall, but weak and inconsiderable." While it is a city of "good largeness," Ikkeri's "Houses stand thinly and are ill-built." At the formal reception of the embassy, Venkatappa is presented with cloths, a lance, and a horse. Della Valle, the sophisticated Italian and experienced traveler, is unimpressed both by the Portuguese' handling of the mission and by the nayak and his court. He understands that Venkatappa, who was "sometime vassal and minister of the emperor of Vijayanagar [has] become absolute Prince of that part of the State whereof he was Governour."[100] Thereafter he warred against the other princes of Kanara until his power was recognized even by the Portuguese.[101] Della Valle nonetheless concludes that Venkatappa

deserves not the Appellation of King; and the less because he pays tribute to Idal-Sciah ['Adil Shah], who although a greater Prince is but small for a King and payes Tribute to the Moghol. . . . The Portugals, to magnifie their affaires in India . . . give the title of King to all those petty Indian princes.[102]

During the remaining two weeks of his stay in Ikkeri, Della Valle concentrates his attention upon the daily life of the Hindu city and its vicinity. He visits the new city of "Sagher" (Sagar) being built just to the north of the capital. The nayak's palace there is finished and he frequently visits it. A new temple at Sagar is "built upon a great Artificial Lake, [as well as] a house for his Nephews and other Grandees." In Ikkeri itself the leading temple is dedi-

---

[99] *Ibid.*, pp. 234–41. Apparently this is the first Hindu temple to which Della Valle had time and opportunity to give his full attention. It was dedicated to Vikramadeva, according to Swaminathan, *op. cit.* (n. 95), p. 237.

[100] Grey (ed.), *op. cit.* (n. 19), I, 190. Venkatappa certainly acknowledged the suzerainty of Vijayanagar until about 1613. See Swaminathan, *op. cit.* (n. 95), p. 41.

[101] Ikkeri controlled the west coast of Kanara from Gersoppa in the north to Tuluva in the south. Swaminathan, *op. cit.* (n. 95), p. 41.

[102] Grey (ed.), *op. cit.* (n. 19), II, 243.

cated to "Agore Scuara" (*Aghōrēśvara,* or the Nonfearful Siva) and served by "Giangami" (*Jangami,* or Lingayat priests).[103] Siva is here represented as a man with thirty-two arms. The *Jangami* are married "Indian Fryers" who smear their faces with ashes and wear "certain extravagant habits, with a kind of peaked hood, or cowl, upon their heads . . . [and] with many bracelets upon their arms and legs fill'd with something that makes a jangling as they walk." The chief of the *Jangami* is clad in white, rather than in the saffron-colored robes of the others, and travels about "sitting in an handsome *Palanchino* [palanquin] with two white umbrellas held over him, one on each side." His procession is led by soldiers, accompanied by musicians, and followed by a great throng of "other Giangami clad in their ordinary habits." Della Valle also witnesses a funeral procession in which the corpse is carried seated in a chair, presumably to be buried in a sitting posture. A lavish and somewhat tipsy performance by *devadāsis* is put on for the Portuguese delegation which includes dancing, singing, and a ballet.[104] On November 20–21, Della Valle witnesses the New Moon festivities in which the nayak and his family participate during the second day.[105]

Most poignant is Della Valle's encounter with a widow who is intent upon becoming a suttee.[106] The Italian meets a woman one night riding on horseback "with face uncovered, holding a looking glass in one hand and a lemon in the other." While gazing into the glass, she sings or wails a lament accompanied by doleful drumbeats; she is escorted by "many other women and men on foot." She is clothed in white, with a garland of flowers on her head, and is bedecked with many jewels; in short, she is dressed in wedding costume, "talking and laughing in conversation as a bride would do in our countries." Several days before her death, and nineteen days after her husband's demise, Della Valle visits the widow in hopes of dissuading her from self-immolation. Her husband, a drummer, had also left two other older wives who intended to make no such sacrifice out of concern for their many children. Della Valle tries to persuade the thirty-year-old widow to abandon her plan for the sake of her two children. She declines and claims that she is doing it voluntarily and joyfully as a "Masti" (from *Mahāsatī,* or a very virtuous one).[107] Apparently Della Valle chose not to witness her death, for he writes nothing about it.

Just before leaving Ikkeri on November 23, Della Valle is presented with a

[103] For recent photographs of the sixteenth-century *Aghōrēśvara* temple and for a verbal description of it see Swaminathan, *op. cit.* (n. 95), figs. 1–8, and pp. 225–28.

[104] Grey (ed.), *op. cit.* (n. 19), II, 260–61, 265, and 268–73.

[105] *Ibid.,* II, 279–85. These lengthy descriptions of processions and festivals are cited verbatim in Swaminathan, *op. cit.* (n. 95), pp. 216–19. They are particularly valuable because of the perspicacity and enthusiasm of the author and because native sources almost never bother to describe such mundane events.

[106] *Satī,* "a woman who is pure" because she is faithful. On the various aspects of suttee see Edward Thompson, *Suttee* (Boston and New York, 1928), p. 15.

[107] Grey (ed.), *op. cit.* (n. 19), II, 266–67, 273–77.

palm-leaf book "in the Canara language [Kannada]" by Vithula Sinay. He had requested the former ambassador to obtain a book for him, "not finding any to be sold in the city," since he wanted one "to carry as a curiosity to my own Country for ornament of my Library." On horseback and accompanied by bearers, Della Valle then goes overland to "Barcelor" (Basrur); he gives the names of the places on the route and notes that the "High Ways . . . are very secure." From "Barcelor" he takes a ship southward to Mangalore "at the mouth of two rivers," [108] and in the middle of the bay. The Portuguese fort there, captured in 1596, is "the worst built of any I have seen in India." [109] On December 1 he visits "Banghal" (Bangara), just north of Mangalore and at that time within the jurisdiction of Ikkeri. During the conquest of Venkatappa its palace and fort were destroyed so that only a bazaar remains there. [110]

Always eager to observe the novel, Della Valle was especially interested "to see the person of the Queen of Olala [Ullal], whose History and many valiant exploits I read of when I was in Persia." On December 2 he sets out for Ullal by crossing the river's mouth a few miles southwest of Mangalore. Since the queen is not there, he contents himself with describing her palace before searching her out. On December 4 he goes upriver to interview her at "Manel," a place of refuge. Black, corpulent, and about forty years of age, the queen is named "Abag-devì Ciautru [Abaga Devi], of which words *Abag* is her proper name." Queen Abaga, who had been married for many years to the ruler of "Banghal," had fought her husband and his Portuguese allies with aid from Ikkeri. Once she and her ally had emerged victorious, Ikkeri assumed control over her and her territory, and now exacts tribute. Her son, "Celuna Rairu" (Saluva Rairu) is raja in name only, for she continues as *de facto* ruler. Della Valle visits Raja Saluva at his royal lodge, presents the young ruler with a small map of the world in Italian, answers his numerous questions about the outside world, and satisfies his curiosity about European eating habits by dining in his presence with cutlery and table linen. At "Manel" the Italian visits the royal shrine dedicated to the propitiation of the local devils and is intrigued, as other Europeans were, by the numerous evil spirits the Indians seek to placate. In all, he judges "Olala" to be a wretched place. [111]

Back in Mangalore, Della Valle visits on December 11 the hermitage of "Cadiri," probably a Jain temple on Kadiri hill, as well as the residence of

---

[108] "The Netravati, with its affluent the Kumaradhari, and the Gurpur river . . . have a common backwater and outlet at Mangalore" (S. D. Misra, *Rivers of India* [New Delhi, 1970], p. 119).

[109] Some walls of this ruined fort can still be seen. See Swaminathan, *op. cit.* (n. 95), p. 55.

[110] Grey (ed.), *op. cit.* (n. 19), II, 290–302. The war may have taken place towards the end of 1615. See Swaminathan, *op. cit.* (n. 95), p. 54.

[111] Grey (ed.), *op. cit.* (n. 19), II, 289, 303–40. For more details on "Olala's" history at this time see Swaminathan, *op. cit.* (n. 95), pp. 64–65.

"Batinato" (probably *Bhāt Nath,* or Lord of a Vaishnavite temple), who is called "king of the Gioghi [Yogi]." [112] He describes in some detail this tiny principality on a hill whose "Batinato" is fearful of being forced to pay tribute to Ikkeri. Another petty city-state north of Mangalore is called "Carnate" (Karnad). Its queen accepted vassalage to Ikkeri without putting up a fight. While Della Valle planned to visit "Carnate," a Portuguese fleet arrived at Mangalore on December 18, 1623, on its way to Calicut, and so he left with it on the following day. [113] Della Valle remarks while on shipboard: "at Mangalor ends the Province of Canara and that of Malabar begins." [114]

Vincenzo Maria di Santa Caterina da Siena, a barefoot Carmelite from Rome, was on India's west coast during 1657–58. In his *Viaggio* (1672) Vincenzo expresses his admiration for the prosperity and order prevailing in the Hindu-controlled states, especially Kanara. [115] All flat country and lying next to the sea, Kanara is densely peopled right up to the mountains. Its land is irrigated by numerous rivers and so fertile that its farmers harvest copious crops of high quality rice three times annually. They gather the grubs of silk worms and make so much material that even the common people wear silk. In the dense jungles they feed herds of animals. Their forests are full of peacocks as well as many wild beasts, mostly tigers and monkeys of extraordinary size and numbers. The roads are so well constructed that they resemble garden paths, being flat, spacious, and lined with shrubs. Every so often one finds a refreshment stand maintained at the king's expense where sour milk and pure water are freely offered to the traveler. No matter how much treasure is carried, it is always safe to travel in Kanara. Its people look out for the travelers' well-being because they fear the royal ire should a traveler be set upon. [116] On the first of his trips around Kanara in 1657, Vincenzo slept outdoors near a vast temple in "Cagnarotta" (?). In the temple itself slept many of its prostitutes. From here he went to "Olalla" (Ullal) where he was courteously received in the marketplace by the governor of the capital city and his secretaries. When in Mangalore, he stayed in the hovel of a Brahman's widow who was living in perpetual disgrace and had to serve everyone. From Mangalore he went overland to Barcelore, noting on the way the temples, fortresses, and mud huts he passed by.

The people of Kanara are judicious, wise, and generally courteous and friendly to strangers. Ordinary men wear tight, short pants and little else; the lords wear long gowns, and still others wear loose loincloths. The women

[112] On the existence of Jain monuments in the Ikkeri state see Swaminathan, *op. cit.* (n. 95), pp. 238–39. According to Grey (ed.), *op. cit.* (n. 19), II, 345–52, the "Batinato" was probably a *Mahant,* or abbot of the *Kanphattis* (Split-Ears), a sect of Hindu ascetics.

[113] Grey (ed.), *op. cit.* (n. 19), II, 352–55; also see Swaminathan, *op. cit.* (n. 95), p. 58.

[114] *Cf.* below, p. 880, n. 164.

[115] For details on Vincenzo and his book see above, pp. 383–84, and below, pp. 891–909.

[116] Vincenzo, *Il viaggio* (Rome, 1672), p. 312. *Cf.* the letter of Reverend Visscher in Padmanabha Menon, *op. cit.* (n. 4), I, 22.

more sedately wear a skirt from the waist to the knees and a shift of another color from the shoulder to the flank which only partially covers the back and breasts. They artfully shape a tuft of hair on the left side of the head in which they wear flowers, gems, and other precious things. Their king is of Brahman stock, prudent, and of good moral character.[117] His justice is quick and severe. Muslims are treated most rigorously and are required to shave their heads and wear Turkish costumes, presumably to make them more easily identifiable. Verbal affronts and fights between individuals are not punished. Two soldiers who wish to fight must have the prince's permission. If they fail to obtain it and fight anyway, both are condemned to death. Soldiers are well disciplined and able to keep petty princes and neighboring states from challenging the royal authority. Kanara was even able within the space of a few years to limit the Portuguese activities at Honavar, Barcelore, and Mangalore.[118]

Vincenzo and his companion, Giuseppe di Santa Maria Sebastiani, also surveyed the condition of the Christians scattered throughout Kanara. Many of Goa's Christians had emigrated to Kanara after the establishment of the Inquisition in 1560. Jesuits and Augustinians based in the Portuguese ports of Kanara had followed these fugitives into the interior to minister to them and to seek new converts. But these endeavors did not prosper. When Della Valle visited Kanara in 1623, he found there only three churches and three priests, two Franciscans and a secular. Beginning around 1630, the Franciscans launched a new initiative that fared better, since they were well received by the nayak of Ikkeri. The Jesuits renewed their activities at mid-century, and by 1660, when Vincenzo traveled in Kanara, its scattered Christian communities included around six thousand believers. He and his companion reported back to Rome, however, that the state of Christianity in Kanara nonetheless continued to be deplorable.[119]

On January 20, 1672, Gabriel Dellon, while still employed by the French East India Company, left Tellicherry on his way north to Goa. Four days later he arrived at "Mangalor" (Mangalore), one of the most important places in Kanara. It has a good harbor served by a deep and wide river where ships find shelter during the southwest monsoon. On an elevated place stands a large market town of Hindus and Muslims where the Portuguese have their factory. The "king" of Kanara and most of his subjects are Hindus whose castes and customs differ from those of the Malabar Hindus. Their manners and dress are more like those of the Hindu subjects of the Mughul emperor, to whom the "king" of Kanara is a tributary. Constantly

---

[117] Most of Kanara was then under the control of Sivappa Nayaka (r. 1645–60) of Ikkeri, the most distinguished ruler of his dynasty. See Swaminathan, *op. cit.* (n. 95), p. 88.

[118] Vincenzo, *op. cit.* (n. 116), pp. 420–22.

[119] Material from Vincenzo's and Sebastiani's books, summarized in S. Silva, *History of Christianity in Canara* (2 vols.; Kumta, 1959–61), I, 48–59.

at war with the Malabars, the Kanarese follow better order in battle than do the Malabars, but they are less determined to win.[120] Their merchants freely leave the country to make money elsewhere. Those who remain at home spend too much time and effort in their devotion to processions and festivals. Nonetheless its farmers produce rice which is exported to foreign marts as far away as Acheh in Sumatra and Mozambique. Criminals in Kanara are tied, laid out on the sand, and allowed to die slowly in the heat, attacked by ants.

After a three-day stopover at Mangalore, Dellon went on to the port of "Mirseou" (Mirzapur) where the French had previously maintained a factory. He talked with "Cojabdella," its governor, who expressed his displeasure with the decision of the French company to abandon his port.[121]

Dr. Fryer, who arrived at Karwar in September, 1675, with an English trading mission, relates vividly how the wars of Sivaji had spilled over into north Kanara. Karwar, "Anchola" (Ankola), "Pundit" (Ponda), "Cuderah" (Kadra), and "Semissar" (Shiveshar, or Halekot) have now been taken from Bijapur and are subject to Sivaji. When Sivaji burned Karwar and occupied its fort, the inhabitants fled into the interior. The English, who were originally granted the right to build a factory at Karwar by the 'Adil Shah, are permitted by Sivaji to continue their activities. But commerce, particularly the diamond trade of Goa and Karwar, is cut off by Sivaji's incursions in the area. In his method of governing these towns Sivaji continues the practices of Bijapur by appointing individual governors for town and fortress who are superintended by "a Commander with a Flying Army." All offices, both civil and military, are filled by Brahmans and other Hindus interested mainly in lining their own pockets. Under Sivaji's maladministration the "Desies" (Mahratti, *desāi,* district headmen) are forced to rent land for which they pay twice the previous price. Moneyed men, even Brahmans, who refuse to pay these prices are thrown into prison where they are tortured until they reveal the location of their hoards.[122]

In February, 1676, Fryer made a pilgrimage from Karwar southward to "Gocurn" (Gokarna). On the way he and his companions cross the mountains of Ankola to its flatlands. The town itself is half-burned and almost deserted. Ankola's fortress commands the surrounding countryside as far south as the "Gongole" (Gongavali or Bedti) River, where Sivaji's dominion ends in the south. On the south side of this river is Gongola, the first town which remains under the jurisdiction of Kanara. Its people look cheerful and "live in Peace under a quiet Government."[123] The next day the trav-

---

[120] On the wars at this time of the Kanarese and Malabars see K. G. Vasnath Madhava, "Kēladi Nāyakas in Malabar (1669–1763), Part II," *Journal of Kerala Studies,* I (1974), 429.

[121] Dellon, *op. cit.* (n. 46), pp. 195–200.

[122] Fryer in Crooke (ed.), *op. cit.* (n. 52), II, 2–5, 25.

[123] Kanara and Bednur, its capital, was then ruled by Queen Cannammaji (r. 1671–96). On her reign see Swaminathan, *op. cit.* (n. 95), chap. xi.

elers arrive at the Hindu center of Gokarna where they change into Mughul costume so that they can observe the "tomasia" (Hindi, *tamāsha,* spectacle) without "being taken notice of."[124]

Gokarna, formerly a splendid city, is now most famous for its Hindu temples and relics. Like Benares, it has a "University of the Brahmins" which is well endowed. Throughout the city are many ancient temples, most of them in ruins. Only two that remain "half-standing" are worthy of comment. They are both ancient constructions of "good Workmanship in Stone." At the far end in the interior is the idol, before which lighted lamps burn constantly. Some of the worshippers bathe and anoint the idol before placing their offerings of oil, rice, and frankincense at its feet.[125] Hindus from all parts of India make pilgrimages to Gokarna at this time of the year to attend the fair and to gain merit. Its temporary bazaar consists of long rows of sheds which line the streets connecting the two functioning temples.

Tides of people sweep from the bazaar to a "large oblong stone Tank" surrounded by steps and with a temple in its center. Both sexes wash in its waters and give rice and money to Brahmans. The tame fish which swim in the tank are held to be sacred. Mourners offer hair as part of their funeral rites. A barber, while standing in the water, shaves the hair off the head and face of the bereaved. It is wrapped and handed over to a Brahman who brings a cow and a calf into the water to receive the offering of hair. The mourners are then taken to the temple, which they enter barefooted with their offering for the idol. On leaving the temple they strike a bell, pick up their slippers on the porch, and wash themselves in the tank.[126] Near the tank stands a temple around which yogis concentrate. Some, covered with ashes, wear their own plaited hair as turbans.[127] One of the yogis wears a gold ring "fastened into his Viril Member."[128]

At the marketplace of Gokarna a procession of idols passes by. Two "cars" decorated with paintings and streamers carry the idols and their attending Brahmans. The "cars" are accompanied by musicians, dancing girls, and ensign-bearers. Five hundred armed men precede and two hun-

---

[124] Fryer in Crooke (ed.), *op. cit.* (n. 52), II, 30–33. The "spectacle" they had come to see was the annual fair held in February. See the *Imperial Gazetteer,* XII, 307.

[125] The great Mahabaleshwar temple is built in the Dravidian style and is renowned because it contains a fragment of the original lingam given to Ravana by Siva. More than one hundred lamps burn perpetually at this shrine.

[126] Fryer in Crooke (ed.), *op. cit.* (n. 52), II, 33–34. This is probably the *Kotī* pool, in the center of which a lingam stands. Shaving of hair by mourners is not permitted for ten days after the death. With the permission of the Brahmans the chief mourner and his near relatives are thereafter shaved. *Cf.* the eighteenth-century observations of the Abbé Dubois in H. K. Beauchamp (trans. and ed.), *Hindu Manners, Customs, and Ceremonies by the Abbe J. A. Dubois* (3d ed., Oxford, 1959). Today this is not a mourning rite, but a votive offering of hair by both men and women asking for special favors. The temple sells this human hair.

[127] The matted hair is the *Jata* or Siva's knot, which represents Vayu, the lord of wind. See A. Daniélou, *Hindu Polytheism* (New York, 1964), p. 215.

[128] *Karalingī,* a practice followed by certain ascetics of Siva.

dred follow the nayak's conveyance. This entourage is followed by a medley of male drummers and dancers. As the "cars" pass from one temple to the other, the procession is followed by the "Gentry in Cavalcade," who pay their respects to the idols and bring the ceremony to an end by discharging their guns. As the formal ceremony proceeds, devotees run about as if possessed and compete with one another in exhibitions of religious fervor. While the ruins of Gokarna are innumerable, one figure escaped destruction and is "therefore highly venerable." The height of a man, with four heads and hands, it is a "Piece of Admirable Work and Antiquity" cut out of black marble.[129]

Although Gokarna is the seat of a Hindu university, it boasts no library to compare to the Bodleian or the Vatican. Their books are generally old manuscripts of religious texts which include nothing about the history of Gokarna. The students and teachers do not live in colleges but in separate houses with their families.[130] Celibacy is not required of their divines. However, a house of the "Sinai" (Mahratti, *chhianave,* meaning ninety-six) caste is headed by a celibate old man who is attended by a great many ascetics and Brahmans who spend their lives in prayer and abstinence.[131] They count their prayers on a rosary of cowries and wear red caps. The most rigorous and purest of the Brahmans are those called "Butt" (*Bhāt*). All Brahmans are distinguished by the sacred thread they wear, and some, accompanied by music and dancing girls, go to the tank three or four times daily to fetch water for the idols. Dancers, both males and females, are recruited from the caste called "Dowlys" (Mahratti, *devalī,* son of a woman devoted to an idol). The eldest son and daughter of each family in this caste become dancers dedicated to the temple. They may not dance elsewhere. They receive "large Dispensations concerning their Marriage, or the Liberty of getting Children, being common to all."[132]

Just south of Gokarna is "Tudera" (Tudri), a small town at the mouth of the "Mirja" (Mirjan) River. Slightly upriver is the town of Mirjan, which has an old but excellent fortress with a wide moat around it. Once subject to a Muslim governor (probably of Bijapur), Mirjan is now ruled by the "Canatick Ranna" (Queen Cannammaji of Bednur). The town is a market center and possesses a Muslim cemetery and an "ample Aquaduct of good Stone."[133] At this town Fryer is told by the natives that Kanara stretches along the coast from the Gongavali River southward to the borders of Calicut and inland to the "Pepper-Mountains of Sunda [Sonda] and the Precinct of Sergi Caun [Sheriza Khan, a general of Bijapur]." The capital and resi-

---

[129] Possibly a reference to the well-carved figure of Brahma which stands to the south of the Mahabaleshwar temple.

[130] *Cf.* Bernier's description of the "university" of Benares, above, p. 781.

[131] Probably a *sannyasi,* a holy man, and his followers. See below, p. 1035.

[132] Fryer in Crooke (ed.), *op. cit.* (n. 52), II, 33–39. The females are usually called *devadāsi.* On the *devadāsi cf.* Abbé DuBois in Beauchamp (trans. and ed.), *op. cit.* (n. 126), pp. 584–87.

[133] Mirjan no longer exists. Fryer's description is one of its few remains.

dence of the "Ranna" (queen) is at "Bedmure" (Bednur, now Nagar in My-sore).[134] The queen is the widow of "Sham Shanker Naìg" (Somasekhara Nayaka I [r. 1664–71]) who was murdered by his own nobles.[135] She rules the country during the minority of her son "Bassepae Naig" (Basavappa Nayaka I [r. 1696–1714]) with the support of "Timi Naig" (Timmanna), her general and protector.[136] Timmanna has concluded an alliance with "Sergi Caun" (Sheriza Khan) of Bijapur and it is rumored that the Kanara general is about to become a Muslim.[137]

In Kanara the leading nobles are called *nāyaka*. The prevailing language is Kanarese, probably the primitive tongue of the coastal region from Malabar to Surat. Other dialects of this area are variations on it. Names of places change with the fortunes of war. Wild elephants, betel nuts, and wild nut-meg, used as a dye, grow in Kanara. The world's best pepper grows in Sonda; it is known in England as Karwar pepper. The raja of Sonda, a tribu-tary of Bijapur, sells most of his pepper in India, so that little of it arrives in England. The raja of "Saranpatan" (Seringapatam or Mysore) must not be passed by in silence. Since it is against his faith to kill, he trains his soldiers in the use of an instrument to cut the noses of his enemies so as to deform them. He is generally feared and he controls a vast territory east of Cali-cut.[138] The Kanarese delight in arming birds with razors for cockfights. Eu-ropeans hunt and fish to obtain meat in this Hindu world. Fryer even has an opportunity to dissect a local tiger and a number of apes. He also provides semi-scientific descriptions of bamboo, the "Cassia Fistula Tree" (Indian Laburnum), the *Cassia lignia* (false cinnamon), tamarind trees, teak trees, and other trees. In their fields the Kanarese grow rice, various millets, and flax; in enclosures they cultivate turmeric and ginger. Potatoes are served at their banquets.[139]

Despite all the blessings conferred upon them by a generous nature, some Hindus "sink below Brutes" in their superstitions. These "dregs" will wor-ship stalks and make oblations to devils. At "Semissar" (Shiveshar) frenzied women copulate with the idol.[140] Priests of the god are welcomed into the homes of the devout "to do the Wife a Kindness."[141] Under the banyan tree they sacrifice a cock to placate the devil with blood. Snakes are brought into

[134] The capital of north Kanara was moved around 1640 from Ikkeri to Bednur by the Keladi ruling house.

[135] On his last days see Swaminathan, *op. cit.* (n. 95), p. 115.

[136] *Cf. ibid.*, pp. 117–18. Basavappa was her adopted son.

[137] Fryer in Crooke (ed.), *op. cit.* (n. 52), II, 39–42.

[138] *Ibid.*, pp. 42–43. Chikka Deva (r. 1672–1704) of Mysore was notorious for his cruelty. *Cf.* also below, p. 1061.

[139] *Ibid.*, pp. 68–76. The potato (*Solanum tuberosum*) was probably introduced to western In-dia by the Portuguese. That they would serve it at banquets is probably an indication of its rarity.

[140] Lingam worship.

[141] Refers to the Jangama priests of the Lingayat sect. *Cf.* Abbé DuBois' remarks in Beau-champ (trans. and ed.), *op. cit.* (n. 126), p. 117.

the house to protect the family from devils. The better sort of people acknowledge a god, live by their caste rules, and follow more "Innocent Rites." At the spring festival of Holi, they cut down a tree, strip it, erect the remaining pole near the temple, decorate it with pennants, and bind straw around it which they set on fire. From study of the flame the Brahmans pronounce their auguries. Then they offer rice and flowers, paint their bodies with the ashes, and depart in procession to the accompaniment of drums. In addition to those who believe in the works of the devils and the gods, there are atheists who perversely and wrongly attribute everything to chance.[142]

Kanara, like Goa and Bijapur, suffered after 1660 from the raids of Sivaji and the civil wars that swept the Deccan and the entire coast of Kanara. The retreat of the Portuguese from Malabar in the 1660's likewise brought about a shift in the pepper-trading centers so vital to Kanara's export trade. Throughout the remainder of the century the Portuguese were generally successful in maintaining good relations with Ikkeri despite the efforts of the Dutch and Cochin to sever this connection. In Europe by century's end Goa, Bijapur, and Kanara belonged to the past and were associated only with the days of Portuguese glory on India's west coast. Under Dutch and English influence the attention of Europe was drawn almost entirely to the Mughul Empire and the Malabar and Coromandel coasts.

4

MALABAR AND THE PORTUGUESE

At the dawn of the seventeenth century most of what Europe learned about Malabar was relayed by religious writers, since there were few, if any, secular accomplishments to boast of. Fernão Guerreiro reports that the Jesuit Vice-Province of South India (then including Malabar, the Fishery Coast, Coromandel, Malacca, and the Spiceries) is ruled by the College of Cochin.[143] The Catalonian Jesuit Francisco Roz (Ros) is newly consecrated as bishop of the Serra with the assigned task of imposing the terms of the Synod of Diamper (1599) and of uprooting the Nestorian errors still stubbornly retained by many St. Thomas Christians. An alliance of 1598 between the Zamorin of Calicut and his old enemy, the Portuguese, results in the defeat of the Kunhali Marakkars (Muslims) in 1600 and permits the Jesuits to open a mission at Calicut in 1602, which they do under the leadership of Giacomo Fenicio (*ca.* 1558–1632), an Italian Jesuit.[144] Three years

[142] Fryer in Crooke (ed.), *op. cit.* (n. 52), II, 77–82. These "atheists" are perhaps the *Pāsanda*, heretics who deny all Hindu doctrines. *Cf.* below, p. 1035.
[143] In Viegas (ed.), *op. cit.* (n. 9), I, 26–31.
[144] By the terms of the 1598 treaty, the Zamorin guaranteed that his subjects might become Christians. On the fall of the Kunhalis see K. M. Panikkar, *Malabar and the Portuguese* (Bombay,

later a residence is established at "Tanor" (Tanur), just to the south of Calicut, whose raja had become a convert for a short time in 1545.[145]

In Malabar the Jesuits confront many more physical problems than they are at that time experiencing in Goa: epidemics, typhoons, and earthquakes. According to Jesuit figures, there are two hundred thousand Christians in Malabar at the beginning of the century. In 1609 their colleges at Cochin, Cranganore, and Quilon, including dependent annexes and residences, are served by more than one hundred Jesuits. At the seminary of the Serra in Vaipocota (Chengamangalam) a handful of Jesuits teach doctrine and Syriac as well as Latin rites to the sons of leading St. Thomas Christians. In the Serra there are around eighty thousand St. Thomas Christians, with their own native priests called "Cacanares" (Malayalam, *kattanāra;* cattanars in English).[146] The resistance of these Christians to the Latin rite is aided and abetted by the king of Cochin, who is outraged by the recent Portuguese alliance with Calicut, his traditional enemy. He makes his subjects take an oath not to become Christians on pain of death.

In an effort to win over the St. Thomas Christians, Rome elevates Ros in 1608 to the status of archbishop of Cranganore to place him on a par with the archdeacon sent to the Serra by the patriarch of Alexandria. But the king of "Mangate"[147] is disrespectful to Ros and defends the rebels in their efforts to uphold the Nestorian heresies. While the Jesuits receive the political and military support of the Portuguese, they nonetheless continue to be faced by the recalcitrance of the St. Thomas Christians and by the hostility of the Malabar Muslims, many of the court Brahmans, and the vengeful "amoucos."[148] Periodically the Malabar rulers flirt with the Dutch, turn against the Portuguese, and persecute the native Christians, especially those of Quilon and Travancore. Wherever they go in Malabar, the priests warn the native rulers about the dangers inherent in negotiating with the Dutch.

Because the St. Thomas Christians are widely scattered, some well into the interior, the Jesuits and their aides begin to penetrate inland. This infiltration of new regions is also advanced by the periodic exile of the local Christians from the coastal towns to places out of the reach of hostile native rulers. Around 1603 the fathers follow the Christian exiles from Travancore

---

1929), pp. 140–45; on Fenicio see Joseph Wicki, S.J., "Portuguese Works of Frs. J. Fenicio and Diogo Gonçalves on Malabar (1609–1615)," *Journal of Kerala Studies,* IV (1977), 555. Fenicio remained in Calicut until 1617.

[145] On the Jesuits at Tanur and the relation of this mission to Fenicio's, see D. Ferroli, S.J., *The Jesuits in Malabar* (2 vols.; Bangalore City, 1939), I, 249–66.

[146] See S. R. Dalgado, *Glossário Luso-Asiático* (2 vols.; Coimbra, 1919), I, 161. Seventeenth-century estimates on the number of St. Thomas Christians vary between seventy and eighty thousand.

[147] The Hindu raja of Mangatti (Alangad), a petty state near Cochin, supported Archdeacon George of the Cross in his rebellion of 1608–9 against Ros. See Joseph Thekkedath, *History of Christianity in India* (6 vols.; Bangalore, 1982), II, 77–78.

[148] On the special character of the Malabar amuck runners, their hostility to Christianity, and their dedication to revenge see *Asia,* I, 450.

into the villages near Cape Comorin, whose inhabitants survive by selling cut wood. At "Paru" (Parur) in the Serra they find Christians of St. John whose sacred texts are in neither Syriac nor Chaldean.[149]

In Calicut, meanwhile, Fenicio and a Portuguese Jesuit named Hilaire study Hinduism with a native teacher who comes daily to the house.[150] There is little else for the two Jesuits of Calicut to do; Christians are few and converts hard to make since the city's trade is dominated by Muslims. The Zamorin and his nobles are nonetheless intrigued with Fenicio who willingly talks to them of European mathematics and astrology. He serves as a political emissary of the Zamorin, and even acts as an intermediary between Calicut and Cranganore. Well-versed in Malayalam, Fenicio is asked to seek out certain former St. Thomas Christians who live in the mountains behind Calicut at a place called "Sodomala" (Todamala).[151] Accompanied by some nayars and a "Principe Erari," nephew of the Zamorin, Fenicio late in 1602 journeys into the Nilgiri hills to hunt for the "Todares" (Todas). Once in this high country, Fenicio meets a native priest called a "Palem" (*palol*) who has a live buffalo as both his object of worship and his temple. From this informant Fenicio learns something about the beliefs and customs of the Todas. It was not until the nineteenth century that Europe was to hear much more about the existence of these hill people whose lives and religion revolve around buffaloes and dairies.[152]

In Europe meanwhile there appeared in Portuguese (1606) and French (1609) an apologetic history of the Synod of Diamper and the role played by Aleixo de Meneses, Augustinian primate of the East, in realigning the Christians of St. Thomas with Rome.[153] It was written by António de Gouvea (*ca.* 1575–1628), an Augustinian Eremite and one of the few non-Jesuit priests to write about India at this period. It was translated into French by Jean Baptiste de Glen (1552–1613), a fellow Augustinian, and issued at Antwerp

---

[149] Possibly a reference to the Malabar Jacobites, rather than to disciples of St. John the Evangelist. This monophysitic sect was founded in the sixth century A.D. by Jacobus Baradai, bishop of Antioch. Eight hundred thousand followers survive today in India. On the Malabar Jacobites see *The New Catholic Encyclopedia*, I, 954.

[150] On Fenicio's understanding of Hinduism see below, pp. 911–12.

[151] The decrees of the Synod of Diamper (1599) include a command to send priests to "Tadamalla" to bring these ancient peoples (Todas) who live behind Calicut back into the Christian fold. See James Hough, *The History of Christianity in India from the Commencement of the Christian Era* (2 vols.; London, 1839), II, 646.

[152] All of the above discussion of these Jesuit activities derived from A. Viegas (ed.), *op. cit.* (n. 9), I, 26–31, 328–50; II, 155–63, 334–46; III, 67–75, 106–13. For the materials on the Todas see *ibid.*, I, 344–47. The Fenicio letter of April 1, 1603, on which this account is based, is preserved in manuscript in the British Library. For its text see Jarl Charpentier, *The "Livro da Seita dos Indios Orientais"* . . . *of Fenicio* (Uppsala, 1933), pp. lxxxvi–xcv. For an English translation of it see W. H. R. Rivers, *The Todas* (Oosterhout, 1967; reprint of the edition of 1906), pp. 721–30. The prince who accompanied Fenicio as interpreter and guide was a Christian of the Errari or cowherd caste (*ibid.*, p. 721, n. 2).

[153] On the synod see *Asia*, I, 268–69.

and Brussels in 1609.[154] This Augustinian publication program, inaugurated by J. Gonzales de Mendoza with his 1585 book on China,[155] was part of a general effort being made by the order to challenge the Jesuit supremacy in the Asian missions. In Malabar, where the Portuguese and the Jesuits needed all the help they could get, Meneses was praised by the men in the field for his zeal in promoting the decrees of the synod and for his cooperation with the Society.[156] Despite this propaganda drive, the papacy refused to recognize the legality of the synod. Nonetheless in India its decrees became the constitution for the Latins in their dealings with the St. Thomas Christians.

Gouvea's *Jornada* is a paean of praise to the pious work of Meneses in bringing the St. Thomas Christians back to the obedience of Rome within a period of less than one year. The synod itself is portrayed as a placid assembly of Christian brothers who proceed in an orderly fashion to work out their differences by consultation and discussion. The cattanars and the laymen, it is said, were permitted to speak freely and openly. Whenever possible their suggestions were followed, particularly with respect to secular customs and local practices. A few of the commentators, especially Archdeacon George of the Cross, repeatedly displayed stiff-necked, heretical tendencies in the opinions they expressed about the decrees submitted to them for consideration. In the end the decrees were signed by all the participants, without any serious objections being raised. This veneered version of the proceedings corresponds not at all to the letters sent to Rome by the Jesuits or even to the descriptions of subsequent events summarized above from the *Relaçam* of Fernão Guerreiro covering the years from 1600 to 1610.[157]

While the *Jornada* is clearly a work of special pleading, it may also be read as a valuable source for Christian accommodation policies, both Syrian and Roman, as well as for Malabar customs.[158] In the acts and decrees of the synod the practices expressly prohibited, permitted, or commanded are of

---

[154]For bibliography see above, pp. 320–21. Glen published separately *La messe des anciens Chrestiens dicts de S. Thomas* . . . (Antwerp, 1609) as revised by Meneses; it includes a Latin translation of the purged Syriac mass in an effort to show the heretical Calvinists or the uncertain Catholics of the Low Countries how "mother Church" realigns those who have wandered too far from Rome. Later in the century Michael Geddes, chancellor of the cathedral church of Sarum, of the Church of England, translated the acts from the Portuguese of Gouvea and published them together with a history entitled *The History of the Church of Malabar . . . , giving an Account of the Persecutions and Violent Methods of the Roman Prelates to Reduce Them to the Subjection of the Church of Rome together with the Synod of Diamper . . .* (London, 1694). Geddes' translation of the decrees of the synod has been reprinted in Hough, *op. cit.* (n. 151), II, 511–683.

[155]See *Asia*, I, 743–44.

[156]See the letter of Pimenta to the General of 1604 as cited in M. K. Kuriakose, *History of Christianity in India: Source Materials* (Madras, 1982), pp. 44–45.

[157]See Thekkedath, *op. cit.* (n. 147), II, 65–70; and Jonas Thaliath, T.O.C.D., *The Synod of Diamper* ("Orientalia Christiana analecta," No. 152; Rome, 1958), pp. 92–96.

[158]On the assimilation of Hindu social customs by the St. Thomas Christians see Ninan Koshy, *Caste in the Kerala Churches* (Bangalore, 1968), pp. 16–17.

particular interest. It is proclaimed that the St. Thomas Christians through their long association with Hindus have clearly imbibed "errors." Condemned are the tendencies of the Malabar Christians to believe in transmigration of souls, in fatalism, or in the equal validity of all religious persuasions. Children are permitted to study with heathen teachers so long as they are not obliged to conform to their masters' idolatries. Christian schoolmasters are forbidden to set up idols in their schools for their Hindu or Muslim pupils. Reading of Syrian books, particularly those on religious subjects, is prohibited. All such blasphemous books must be corrected or destroyed. Priests may not preach to the people without license and must recant publicly the errors and fabulous stories they have previously taught. All children are to be baptized within eight days after birth, including those of infidel slaves. Christian slaves, including those newly baptized, may not be sold to infidels. Hindu children abandoned or exposed and left to die by their superstitious parents must be rescued whenever possible by their Christian neighbors. All Christian children, contrary to older custom, must now have godparents and must be given names from the New Testament and not from the Old Testament or from Hindu mythology.

The matter in the sacrament of the Holy Eucharist must be wheaten bread and grape wine and not rice bread or a substitute for wine. The king of Portugal will be asked to send wine annually for sacramental purposes. No one is to receive the sacrament without prior confession, a neglected sacrament in this land where there are so many public sinners: witches, common women, and men who keep concubines. The Roman mass is to be translated into Syriac and must be said in that language. All heathen musicians who play for religious festivals must leave the church during mass. Leprous and other undesirable priests may not celebrate mass. All forms of exorcism are forbidden except for those sanctioned by Rome. Marriage dates are not to be set by the superstitious custom of determining propitious and unpropitious days by astrology. Priests must be temperate and sober, must eat only with Christians, and must never frequent taverns or public eating establishments. Priests must always wear clerical habits, must never engage in business or trade, must never hold a secular office or fight as mercenary soldiers, and must not marry. Simony is strictly forbidden, because the sale of spiritual things for money has too long been a common practice. The clergy is to be supported by church and state rather than from gifts and barter.

Marriage, since it is a sacrament, must be celebrated in church and before witnesses, and never entered into clandestinely. A man may not marry before the age of fourteen or a woman before the age of twelve, to prevent the Christians from imitating the Hindu custom of marrying at earlier ages. Marriages and separations not sanctioned by the church are declared null and void. Polygamy and heathen marital rites are strictly outlawed. Heathen festivals, fasts, ordeals, oaths, and ablutions are not to be observed. Heathen superstitions commonly followed by Malabar Christians are forbidden, in-

cluding washing the dead, encircling a bridal couple with rice, and remov-
ing a thread from a cloth when it is cut. Because life would otherwise
become unbearable, the Christians may observe the practice of not touching
inferiors for fear of pollution, so long as they recognize it as a superstitious
heathen vanity without validity in Christian teachings. All witchcraft, con-
juring, and charms are forbidden. Since too many Christians have traditionally engaged in usury, legitimate interest is limited to ten percent or the
common rate. Christians may not ordinarily buy or sell Christian children
unless they do so to keep them from being enslaved by non-Christians. Men
must not bore their ears to make them large but Christian women may continue the practice since this custom is a universal ornament with females.
Christians may not drink, sell, or trade "Orraca" (arrack) because of the de-
bauchery its use leads to. In default of male heirs, females shall be entitled to
share in the estate of the parents. Adoption of sons is forbidden if there are
legitimate children; too often the children of slaves are adopted to disinherit
rightful heirs. Finally, the synod expresses the wish that Christians should
live in separate villages to be more closely bound together and more tightly
insulated against infidel beliefs and practices.[159]

While the Christians continue generally to denounce Hinduism for its
"errors," a new trend in European learning begins to appear. Diogo do
Couto, the archivist and chronicler of Goa, provides a brief discussion in his
fifth decade (published in 1612) of what he presents as the four Vedas of Hinduism.[160] In fact what he summarizes here are the Saivite ritual texts called
Agamas.[161] As Couto indicates these are mostly verses in Sanskrit designed
as manuals of worship and sectarian practices. While these verses provide
only a superficial and sectarian introduction to Hinduism, Couto is nonetheless basing his discussion on native texts—the first European to make
such an effort. He relates the teachings of Hinduism to the education of the
young, the worship of idols, and the devotion of the natives to holy days,
processions, and pilgrimages. While not very illuminating about the tenets
of Hinduism, these brief chapters forecast what is to become a preoccupation for Europeans in their understanding of India, namely, an effort to
comprehend from native texts and informants what Hindus believe.[162] Still,
until mid-century, most of his contemporaries, like Couto himself, continue to be more interested in social than in theological and philosophical
concerns.

Pyrard, the Frenchman who had been shipwrecked in the Maldive Is-

---

[159] Based on Hough, *op. cit.* (n. 151), II, 511–633. *Cf.* discussion in Cardinal E. Tisserant,
Eastern Christianity in India (Bombay, 1957), pp. 164–72. Also *cf.* Meneses' Latinizing policy to
the adaptation policy followed by Nobili in Madura. See below, pp. 1012–17.

[160] *Da Asia*, Decada V, Liv. VI, Cap. iii and iv. In the Lisbon reprint of 1974 it is in Vol. XIII,
pp. 23–48. For bibliographical details see above, pp. 314–15.

[161] See Charpentier, *op. cit.* (n. 152), pp. xxxiv–v.

[162] See below for the better-informed discussions of Hinduism in the works of Roger and
Baldaeus, pp. 912–17, 1029–57.

lands,[163] was in Malabar from April, 1607, to May, 1608. He is the only European to write extensively about conditions in Malabar during the early seventeenth century, and he is particularly good on Cannanore and Calicut. From his lengthy experience in the Maldives he had acquired much information about the trade of the region as well as a knowledge of Portuguese and Arabic, two of its most important commercial languages. Like Linschoten earlier and Mandelslo later, Pyrard sees Malabar as extending northward from the cape to "Barcelor" (Basrur), the northern limit of the Malayalam country.[164] This region includes numerous political entities, "yet they are all of one language, law, and religion [?], of like governments, classes, and ranks of men . . . and above all of the same manners."

Pyrard first landed at "Montinqué" (Muttungal), a Muslim-dominated harbor between Cannanore and Calicut close by the Kotta River, a "refuge for the Malabar corsairs and pirates."[165] Here he stayed for several days with a "Moplah" (*Māppiḷa*, or Malayali Muslim) family. He mentions the nearby corsair ports of "Chombair" (Chombal) and "Badora" (Badagara) and notes that all three Muslim harbors are well fortified. He discourses on the "Jangay" (*jangada*s or Nayar guides) "who are found at the gates of towns to act as escorts to those who require them," or as guards against those other Nayars who live from highway robbery. The Malabar Muslims, who are corsairs at sea, "do no robbery by land." They are prone to maintain blood or family feuds (*kuḍuppu*) for as long as seven years; the dreaded Nayars are assigned by the king to restrain the feuding parties. These Malabar Muslims are almost all pirates, sea warriors, or dry-land merchants. Theirs is a relatively equal and open society with no noble class, very few slaves, and "a free table for all comers." Their loot from piracy is sold on land by their merchants, and whenever they take a "good prize," donations are given to the poor. As in the Maldives, the Muslims of Malabar worship at "Ziares" (Arabic, *ziyarat,* or place of visitation) presided over by "priests" dressed in Arab fashion entirely in white. These "priests" officiate in the mosques and at marriages, but "they have no hand in administering justice." They are the associates of men called "Abedalles" (Arabic, *abdāl,* servant of god, or

[163] For his Maldive experiences see below, pp. 934–44.

[164] Gray (trans. and ed.), *op. cit.* (n. 10), I, 369–70. Modern scholars, as well as some other seventeenth-century writers, usually make Deli Point the northernmost point in Malabar. "Barcelor" is much farther north, about halfway up the Kanara coast. The problem of the northern boundary of Malabar at this period is a long-term question, and some, like Dellon (see below, pp. 922–25), even claim that Malabar includes the entire coast from Surat southward. In John Thornton's maritime chart (1703) of "The Coast of Malabar" the northernmost town given, as in Pyrard, is the port of "Bassalore or Bodven Factory." Recent students of language, on the other hand, place the northern frontier of the Malayalam region just north of Deli Point at the Nieleswara River. See Gita Dharampal (trans.), "On Kanarese Language and Literature [written by Reverend Weigle of Tübingen]," *Quarterly Journal of the Mythic Society,* LXXII (1981), 3. On map 16A in Habib, *op. cit.* (n. 76), a compromise solution is adopted by placing the northern frontier of Malabar as of 1707 between Deli Point and Basrur.

[165] Gray (trans. and ed.), *op. cit.* (n. 10), I, 336.

fakir),[166] ascetics who have taken a vow of poverty and roam about the world. Occasionally thirty or forty of them will congregate in one place, but usually they travel alone or in small groups. They live from alms and sleep in the mosques. Some accept great austerity and would sooner die of hunger than to ask for alms; others are not so reticent. Because they know many languages and have seen much, they are judged to be "the best company in the world." Pyrard seems to make no distinction between these Muslim ascetics and the yogis, and so treats them together.[167]

While in Badagara for fifteen days, Pyrard learned more about the Mappilas and their activities. The three Mappila harbors already mentioned lie around the bay of "Cangelotti" (Kangirota, or modern Cassergode in South Kanara) and another of their ports further to the north is close to "Barcelor." These corsairs rule most of the lands and people along this lengthy stretch of coast and inland. The ports on the bay cooperate with one another in keeping watch for the passing Portuguese fleets and in preparing and maintaining the barriers to obstruct an enemy landing. When they launch a maritime expedition, the Malabar Muslims appoint a commander of the fleet who holds office for that voyage alone. Upon their return he takes up his former position and may be given a special reward for his services if the spoils warrant it. The rest of the booty is equally divided among the participants. They treat Pyrard well in the hope that he may be of aid to them in their activities in the Maldives.

Pyrard traveled into the interior behind the bay, sometimes in the company of the ruler of Badagara. On his way overland to Calicut he visits "Marcaire Coste" (Marakkar Kotte), a Mappila chiefdom, in the country of the "Cognialy" (Cunhale or Kunhali) and stops there for at least ten days. This is the seat of the Kunhali family whose leader had worked as admiral of Calicut until he tried to become the independent "King of the Malabar Moors" in the 1590's. Defeated by Calicut and its Portuguese allies in 1600, the Kunhalis remain at peace with both their former enemies. While the district remains legally subject to the Zamorin, the son of the defeated Kunhali retains the title of "Marcaire" (Malayalam, *Marakkān,* or viceroy) and is held in great respect by all the Malabar Muslims. Officials of Calicut run the custom house in Kotte as well as other government offices. Most of Kotte's inhabitants are Mappilas, many of whom retreat here periodically from the coast; its permanent dwellers sometimes "join the others on the coast in piracy." The victories of the great Kunhali are commemorated in paintings kept in the mansion of one of the local grandees.[168]

At the beginning of May, 1608, Pyrard returned to this Muslim region

---

[166] See Dalgado, *op. cit.* (n. 146), I, 5.

[167] Gray (trans. and ed.), *op. cit.* (n. 10), I, 337–43.

[168] *Ibid.,* pp. 344–56; for an effort to place some of Pyrard's observations of this region into a broader setting see S. F. Dale, *Islamic Society on the South Asian Frontier. The Māppiḷas of Malabar, 1498–1922* (Oxford, 1980), pp. 44, 47–48, 53.

and spent three or four days at Cannanore, a town which he had briefly visited just after his arrival in Malabar the year before. The Portuguese, now at peace with "Aly Ragea" (Ali Raja or "sea king"), are permitted to maintain a small fort at Cannanore which contains a church and a Jesuit college. Ali Raja, a Muslim, is the *de facto* ruler of Cannanore, and he also holds control over the Maldive Islands.[169] Far into the interior behind Cannanore city "there is a *Nāyar* king" who has "no authority nowadays" though he is often at war with Ali Raja.[170] The Muslim corsairs of Ali Raja operate on the sea against the Portuguese during the six summer months each year; the rest of the time they act as respectable merchants who sell the loot captured at sea. The Malabar Muslim merchants are identifiable by their dress; they wear a skull cap of red scarlet with a turban-like kerchief wound about it called a "Mondou" (Malayalam, *mundu*, cloth). The hair of the head is kept short with "the beard half-shaved and without mustaches." To conceal their money they tie it into other pretty kerchiefs. Pyrard has much more understanding for these Muslim corsairs and their relations to Cannanore and Cochin than most of his European Christian contemporaries, because of his lengthy and relatively happy experience with the Muslims of the Maldives.[171]

Pyrard came to Calicut around the end of June, 1607, and stayed there for the next eight months. He describes its "Alfandique" (Portuguese, *alfandega*), or the customhouse, as "a great square building of stone, with galleries above and below, . . . [and] with a large number of rooms and warehouses for keeping all the different sorts of goods separate." Over the door to each storage place is written the name of the goods kept there. The owners and a royal official have the only keys and one cannot enter without the other. Both exports and imports pay customs. Goods may not be removed from the warehouses until the duties are paid. Pyrard is taken by the hospitable customs officers into the town, and from there, soldiers of the royal guard escort him and his companions to an interview with the Zamorin at his palace.

Since it is after nightfall, the audience is conducted in a lower hall lighted by oil lamps suspended on silver rods held aloft by royal attendants. The Zamorin, who "never sits in public," stands before the foreigners while holding a small child in his arms. Talking through a Portuguese interpreter, the Zamorin questions the foreigners at length before telling them that the Dutch had been there a month earlier with thirteen ships. The Dutch had traded for nine or ten days and gone away with a permit to build a fortress.

[169] On the relationship of Cannanore to the Maldives see below, pp. 944–45. The Arakkal dynasty of Cannanore came into prominence and began to act independently in the mid-sixteenth century as a maritime power. See K. K. N. Kurup, *The Ali Rajas of Cannanore* (Trivandrum, 1975), chap. i.

[170] Probably a reference to a scion of the deposed Kolattiri rajas who opposed both the Mappilas and their unofficial Calicut ally. See Dale, *op. cit.* (n. 168), p. 66.

[171] Gray (trans. and ed.), *op. cit.* (n. 10), I, 441–49. On his Maldive experiences see below, pp. 934–44.

The interpreter, a "Banian" who had helped the Dutch carry on trade at Calicut, was assigned to be the permanent companion of Pyrard and his friends while they were in Calicut. He found them a lodging at the custom-house and quickly became their friend and informant. From him they learn that the Zamorin is the most powerful ruler in Malabar and frequently at war with the "king" of Cochin, who claims to be his equal. Since "Coilan" (Quilon) is so far south of Calicut, its "king" retains "more of his sover-eignty than the rest."[172]

The state of Calicut covers a large area between Cannanore and Cochin and its principal town is named for it. The land is fertile and flat and pro-duces all the necessities of life except rice. It exports pepper, gems, cotton, and white cotton textiles (calicoes) as well as "divers kinds of painted and patterned tapestry"; rice is Calicut's only import. The Brahmans of Calicut wear a "Libasse" (Arabic, *libās,* garment) or "Cabaye" (Arabic, *kaba,* vest-ment) of white cotton cloth which falls to the heels. Under it they put on a white cotton garment (*dhoti*) that hangs down to mid-thigh and they en-circle the waist with a belt of the same fine white cloth of which their turbans are made.[173] All wear their hair long, suspend pendants from their ears, and throw a piece of white or colored cloth around their shoulders. The distin-guishing mark of the Brahman "is a cord of three strands of cotton which they wear next to the skin." Some Brahmans "serve in arms with the Nairs [Nayars]" while the rest are priests or merchants. Industrious, learned, adroit, and experienced, the Brahmans "besides being soft and pacific in temper . . . [are] men who keep inviolate their faith and word." The Zamo-rin himself is a Brahman who wears the cord.[174]

Pyrard digresses on details of footwear. The Brahmans of Malabar wear red slippers; the slippers of the "Canarins" (people from South Kanara and the Konkan) of Malabar are also red but "much pointed in the front, the point being raised somewhat high, with a knob of the same leather." In Goa the "Canarins" wear "Alparcas" (Arabic, *pargat,* sandals), a hempen shoe held on with gilded leather straps which pass between the toes and over the foot. While the shoes worn in Goa may be practical enough, the white cos-tumes worn there require constant washing, since they are always being stained by the island's red mud and dust which is like "bolarmeny" (*i.e.,* "Armenian bole," or *terra sigillata*). Returning his attention to the Brahmans of Malabar, Pyrard notices that the most important of them, as well as "other Gentiles," have attendants when appearing in public, one of whom carries a parasol, another a silver box of betel, and the third a silver flagon of

---

[172] Gray (trans. and ed.), *op. cit.* (n. 10), I, 361–70.

[173] Turbans and *dhoti* were often of the same flimsy white material. See J. B. Bushan, *The Costumes and Textiles of India* (Bombay, 1958), p. 27.

[174] Gray (trans. and ed.), *op. cit.* (n. 10), I, 370–74. This seems to be a generalized description of Brahman occupations. For the differing opinions on the caste of the Zamorin see *Asia,* I, 353–54, n. 104; for sixteenth-century treatments of the Malabar Brahmans see *ibid.,* pp. 360–62.

water for washing. Since the Brahmans always wash or bathe before eating, they are clothed only in a breechcloth when they dine. Their food must always be prepared by themselves or by another Brahman. While the other castes will eat what has been touched by the Brahmans, "yet in no case do superiors prepare food for those who are beneath them." The wives of the Brahmans, "Banians," and "Canarins" wear nose jewels, toe and finger rings, ear plates "as large as little saucers," and bracelets "from the hand up to the elbow"; the wives of other groups do not wear such a diversity of ornaments. [175]

The Nayars of Calicut, who "are all nobles," have no "other exercise but that of arms." [176] They live in the countryside on their royal pensions and payments. Physically they are handsome men and "the best soldiers in the world." Many of them assemble daily around the Zamorin wherever he may be. While they always carry arms, they are "of competency only on land" and never fight at sea. Some employ themselves in hunting tigers, while others study astrology and related sciences. They act as escorts to travelers and make good companions, for they are courteous, cultivated, and "most gentle and humane in conversation." The most respected Nayars are the "teachers of arms" (*pannikars*); they are distinguished from the others by a thick gold bracelet they wear on the right arm. Other great lords also wear such bracelets "but of a different pattern." The ordinary Nayars wear a bracelet of buffalo horn, dilate and decorate their ear lobes, cover themselves from the waist down with a breechcloth of fine silk or cotton, never cut their hair, and wear no head covering or shoes. They may eat anything, but must dine only with members of their own caste. It is only with the Brahmans that "they live without difference or ceremony" though these two high castes do not intermarry. Every Nayar woman "may have as many as three husbands at once if she likes," but the men may have but one wife. All husbands contribute to the wife's support, each giving his proportionate share for her maintenance. As a consequence of this practice, the fathers "are not succeeded by their children but by their nephews, the sons of their sisters, this being a more certain line." Nayars are not depraved people, as Pyrard's European readers might conclude from his account of their marital practices, but live morally within their own matrilineal system. "Sodomy and incest are never heard of." These people laugh but little, for laughter is regarded as "a great incivility and indiscretion."

About the other castes of Calicut, Pyrard has much less to say than the Portuguese writers of almost a century earlier. [177] He notes that the "Moucois" (Mukkuvans), a fisher caste, have quarters of their own outside of Cal-

---

[175] Gray (trans. and ed.), *op. cit.* (n. 10), I, 374–77.

[176] *Ibid.*, p. 380; for the more detailed, sixteenth-century Portuguese descriptions of this caste see *Asia*, I, 362–65. What follows supplements the Portuguese accounts. Although Sudras by caste, the Nayars are treated as Kshatriyas.

[177] See *Asia*, I, 365–68.

icut next to the sea and in other remote places. Their wives and daughters perform all sorts of menial services on land, including prostitution. They and the "Tiva" (Tiyan) women are the only public women found in the city. Their mothers sell them at the earliest age possible into prostitution, "a commoner practice there than anywhere else in the world." The Tiyans are sometimes artisans as well as toddy drawers and the "Coulombin" (possibly Komarthans, who are barbers to the Tiyans) are cultivators "who marry one with the other, albeit there are certain grades and distinctions among them." [178] In terms of caste status the tillers are the most respected of the common people, followed by the artisans and then by the fishers. All these lower-caste men are attired in the same way, naked except for a breechclout made of cloth, leaf, or bark, and with their hair cut except for a tuft on the crown of the head. Their women wear a skirt to the knees and leave their hair long. Neither sex may have ear lobes more than three fingers in length. The tuft of hair and the shorter ear lobes distinguish them from the higher castes. The Zamorin appoints certain of their chiefs to rule over these lower castes. Many of them do menial work for the Nayars, but never indoors. They have their own temples which are set apart and separate from other temples. In appearance they are "less comely," darker, and smaller than the members of the higher castes. [179]

The Zamorin tolerates all religions, but in the interest of public peace will permit no debates about religion. If a Hindu becomes a Christian and his wife does not, she is required to behave as if she were a widow, except that she does not burn herself alive. If a Muslim becomes a Christian and his wife does not, she is free after three months to remarry. All Hindu corpses, including that of the Zamorin, are burned and the ashes divided among the relatives. [180] The widows of Nayars, probably because of the matriarchal kinship system, are not expected to perform suttee and may even marry again. Since the widows of common men are not required to burn themselves, it appears that Brahman widows were the only ones of whom suttee could be expected. While in Calicut, Pyrard saw five or six self-immolations but still concludes that most widows seem to prefer infamy to suicide. [181] Ordinarily the Malabars wear no mourning. But when the Zamorin dies, all the males shave the hair off their heads and faces as a sign of respect for the dead ruler. Members of both sexes suffer from elephantiasis ("Cochin leg"), a congenital disease which is not painful or severely handicapping in Pyrard's estimation. [182]

[178] The "Coulombin" are not mentioned by the sixteenth-century European authors.

[179] On the Nayars and the lower castes see Gray (trans. and ed.), *op. cit.* (n. 10), I, 380–89.

[180] Ashes may be taken by different relatives to various holy rivers.

[181] Some modern commentators contend that suttee was forbidden in Malabar. See Thompson, *op. cit.* (n. 106), pp. 29, 69.

[182] Gray (trans. and ed.), *op. cit.* (n. 10), I, 390–94. For a quite different description and reaction to this dreadful disease see the remarks of the eighteenth-century Dutch chaplain J. C. Visscher in Padmanabha Menon, *op. cit.* (n. 4), p. 3.

Calicut is the Malabar state which has regularly given the greatest trouble to the Portuguese "and does so daily still." Its second city is "Panany" (Ponnani), a fortress town on the river which serves as the frontier between Calicut and Cochin. Most of the time the Zamorin resides there because he is perpetually at war with Cochin. The Zamorin's permanent court is in the town of Calicut, which is, "as it were, a summary of the whole kingdom." It is full of merchants and in its bazaars people of all races conduct business daily in three large enclosures. While security is generally excellent, the warehouses and shops are barred at nightfall and locked with heavy iron padlocks. The port itself is little more than a roadstead, so it provides no protection for the market. Calicut is nonetheless an important international emporium, since the merchants of all nations are accorded freedom and security there. The Zamorin, unlike most Indian rulers, does not confiscate shipwrecks or the possessions of refugees. In earlier times the Portuguese had "two towns and fortresses" in Calicut, but conflicts with the Zamorin deprived them of these footholds. Even now, when they are at peace, the Portuguese are not trusted, though they do their best to cultivate the Zamorin by favors and gifts. A Portuguese factor and a clerk live in Calicut presently with their families to issue licenses (*cartazes*) to merchant ships sailing the Arabian sea.

Two Jesuit fathers, an Italian (Fenicio) and a Portuguese (Hilaire) have been well received by the Zamorin and granted a royal pension for their living and maintenance above and beyond what they get from the king of Portugal. The fathers have constructed "a very handsome and large church, with an enclosure and cemetery attached, near the seashore, on ground presented by the king." They have a fine house and garden. They may preach publicly in their church but not elsewhere. Still, the Jesuits have made a number of converts, who live near the church in houses which they themselves have built. "Among these new Christians," Pyrard believes, "none will be found to eat the flesh of a cow." Even though the Jesuits "had the ear of the king," Pyrard is warned by the men of Calicut "not to eat or drink with them, for fear lest they should poison us." The Portuguese and the Jesuits were evidently troubled and puzzled by Pyrard's appearance in Calicut and by the favors shown him and his companions by the Zamorin. In Calicut "the Jews have their own quarter and synagogues which none enter but they." Foreign Muslims, except for the Persian Shiites, worship freely in the mosques of the Mappila. The "Banians," while Hindus in religion, have their own temple and Brahmans, and they do not go to the temples of the Malabar Hindus. The Brahmans of Malabar nonetheless freely enter their temple "as having common rights with them." [183]

In this diverse society, justice is administered freely and equitably by the Zamorin. It "proceeds from him alone, and . . . there is no other judge."

[183] Gray (trans. and ed.), *op. cit.* (n. 10), I, 395–407.

When he is absent, justice is administered by the chief officers of state. Complaints lodged by members of the lower castes and foreigners are settled by the first Nayar to appear on the scene. Punishments include imprisonment, mutilation, and death. The prisons are all at the Zamorin's palace. Executions are often performed by throwing the accused to the tigers or elephants.

All the "kings" of the Malabar coast accept the Zamorin's authority except for the ruler of Cochin, who asserts his independence because of the aid he receives from the Portuguese. The Zamorin can readily put 150,000 Nayars into the field. Like most Indian rulers, the Zamorin has no regular navy, but he may count on help at sea from the Muslim corsairs, "whose services he can command." His royal palace in Calicut is heavily guarded at all times, for it serves as the command post for the military. In the palace stands a great bell which is sounded only in an emergency to assemble the Nayars for the Zamorin's protection. An arsenal is maintained in the palace, but the chief arsenal is at Ponnani, the main base for the land operations being carried on against Cochin.

In 1607 the Zamorin is about fifty years of age and has reigned for about thirty-five years. He has but one wife and no children. He dresses like a Nayar, except for festive occasions, and is constantly in their company. In his personal daily habits the Zamorin follows Nayar customs: he prays to the sun on rising, oils his body, bathes, and is dried and well oiled again by his attendants. His valet marks his face with paste and smears ashes on his head. While these ablutions are being performed, the royal pavements and apartments are being cleaned and painted with cow dung. The Zamorin then goes to pray in the small palace temple before eating breakfast. His main meal at noon usually occupies him for three hours. Thereafter he holds court, receives visitors, or watches exhibitions put on for his entertainment by Nayar swordsmen or buffoons and actors. After a light supper he retires at a late hour. His "queen" never eats with him and is seen but rarely. In her daily habits and dress she also follows Nayar customs. She is nude above the waist except for jewels and other ornaments; her dilated ear lobes fall to the nipples of her breasts. Pyrard claims, as seems possible from the intimacy and detail of his descriptions, that he was regularly at court, "where I was much beloved and caressed by the king, and by all the other lords and other Gentiles."

While the Zamorin often tours his kingdom seated on an elephant and escorted by a great entourage of armed men, his principal residence is the "handsome and well built palace" in Calicut town. The palace is enclosed with good walls and a well-filled moat that can be crossed only by a drawbridge. The four gates of the palace are guarded around the clock by large numbers of soldiers. The straight avenues that run inward from the four exterior gates are each controlled by three interior gates, all well guarded. Sentries block the doors leading immediately to the Zamorin's apartment. Within the large courtyard of the palace there are blocks of well-built houses of several stories as well as flower beds, orchards, tanks, fishponds, and canals. The Zamorin's officials and clerks live in these houses. The "queen" has a separate residence which is linked to the "king's" palace by a communicating gallery.

On the outside the palace is surrounded by barriers and palisades to keep the public from blocking the gates. In front of the palace there is a great square where a market is opened daily at 7:00 A.M. to sell and exchange local products. There are little tables around the bazaar, on which men are perched "whose only duty it is to give fresh water to all the thirsty that ask it." A bell sounds to open the market and the Zamorin's servants enter to buy produce for the palace. When they are satisfied, the bell is rung again to call in other purchasers. But before they are permitted to enter, the merchants must pay taxes on their goods, indeed on even the smallest items. The merchants, seated on the ground with their produce around them, carefully guard themselves and their wares from pollution. If anyone other than a Brahman or a Nayar touches merchandise he must buy it. Buyers and sellers cautiously avoid personal contact unless they happen to be of the same caste or faith. This market lasts for about three hours. Those who do not sell out their merchandise here move their stand to the great market which is "held all day every day" in the town proper.

The road which runs from the palace to the town is straight and lined with fine mansions on either side. Near the square where the market is held stands the royal mint. Gold pieces called "Phanans" (*fanams*) are struck here with the Zamorin's portrait on one side and a silhouette of a temple or idol on the other.[184] Not far from the palace stands the royal temple, the principal religious center in a land where Hindu temples are numerous. In the palace itself and in other nearby buildings the royal secretaries and clerks do their jobs. Many men keep the royal accounts in orderly and systematic palm-leaf registers. Some enter into these books all goods arriving on the Zamorin's account; others record the dues and taxes paid each day; others keep account of the expenditures of the royal household; others note down all incidents, judicial proceedings, and general news of the day. Certain clerks even keep lists of foreigners, for the Zamorin "has everything registered" by his highly efficient bureaucracy. Reports are also periodically sent to Calicut from the provincial record offices which function in "all towns, ports, harbors, and frontier passages."[185]

At the urging of Fenicio, Pyrard and two of his companions left for "Christian Cochin" at the end of February, 1608, on a Portuguese bark. They carried with them letters of introduction from the Jesuit; but these

---

[184] Coinage was issued in Malabar by the rulers of Cannanore, Cochin, Travancore, and Calicut. The reference here is probably to the *vira rayen puṭiya*, the new gold *fanam* of the Zamorin. See C. J. Brown, *The Coins of India* (Calcutta, 1922), p. 66; and W. Elliot, *Coins of Southern India* (London, 1886), p. 137.

[185] Gray (trans. and ed.), *op. cit.* (n. 10), I, 407–21.

meant little to the suspicious Portuguese, who immediately took the Europeans prisoner. After landing at "Chaly" (Chaliyam) "whose king is a friend of the Portuguese," they were taken overland to "Tanar" (Tanur) where "the Portuguese have a church, also a Jesuit father, a factor, and some other Christians, as at Calicut." Sent to Cochin by sea, they were marched through its streets to the local prison. After ten days they were released and placed in the custody of the Jesuit college. For the next six weeks they remained in Cochin while awaiting a ship for Goa.

Cochin is similar in most ways to Calicut except for the domineering presence of the Portuguese. The old town of Cochin is somewhat inland and that is where the "king" resides; the new town is closer to the sea at the mouth of the river which serves both towns, and it belongs to the Portuguese.[186] The Portuguese town has "the same order of government as at Goa" with a governor, a bishop, many churches and convents, a Jesuit college, and a royal hospital. On the small island of "Vaypin" (Vypin, a rock formation between the backwater and the sea) at the mouth of the river, the bishop has his splendid residence. While Hindus may not practice their religion in Portuguese Cochin, many "rich Jews" live there and worship in their own way. Between the two Cochins are "continuous houses like suburbs." The "king" of Cochin levies taxes on the market in old Cochin and on all imports from abroad. The Portuguese collect duties on all exports destined for Europe or elsewhere and they pay "certain tribute" to the "king," as well. In the new town the Nayars give way to the Portuguese in passing, and in old Cochin the reverse practice obtains. Portuguese justice and custom prevail in new Cochin, for the "king" has no jurisdiction there. Elsewhere the traditional Malabar justice obtains. Criminals who flee from Portuguese jurisdiction may not be followed beyond the limits of new Cochin; likewise criminals who seek sanctuary with the Portuguese cannot be followed or taken into custody by the "king's" officials. The "king" buys, collects, and stores the pepper produced in Cochin. Sometimes he keeps it for two or three years before selling it. The Portuguese, who buy most of Cochin's pepper, cooperate by causing "it all to be brought there." Strangely, Pyrard has nothing to say about the "king's" hostility to Christianity, a matter constantly complained of in the Jesuit letters of this time. He does admire the workmanship and art on the shields carried by the Nayars.[187]

When Della Valle left Mangalore on December 18, 1623, the Portuguese fleet with which he sailed had aboard an emissary from Goa who was trying to arrange a new peace treaty with the Zamorin. At Calicut, while the Zamorin delayed giving his reply to this peace overture, Della Valle had time to look around the city and to conclude, perhaps incorrectly, that its people were mostly Muslims. He was present at a lengthy but infor-

---

[186] For the description of Cochin in the sixteenth-century European sources see *Asia*, I, 352, 447–48, 472, 488.
[187] Gray (trans. and ed.), *op. cit.* (n. 10), I, 433–38.

mal meeting of the Zamorin and the Portuguese. He describes the palace and gives a sketch of its groundplan (see pl. 148). The Zamorin is of the "Vikira" (Vikrama) family, a young man of thirty to thirty-five years of age, "of a large bulk of body, sufficiently fair for an Indian and of a handsome presence with a full beard." On the way to Goa, Della Valle spent Christmas day, 1623, on shore at Cannanore. Here he saw the residence of "Aga Begel" (Aga Bey), then the dominant political figure of the region "by authority from a King of this Country . . , who resides far from the sea."[188] After another long stay in Goa, Della Valle left India for Europe early in November, 1624.[189]

While the Dutch continued to menace the Portuguese on the high seas and in their outposts, not all was serene within Malabar, either. The truce worked out by Archbishop Ros around 1610 with the St. Thomas Christians began to fall apart around 1640, contemporary to the loss of Portuguese Malacca (1641) and the shift of Dutch attention to the strongholds of Ceylon and coastal south India.[190] The conciliatory and aged Archbishop Estaban de Brito, S.J. (r. 1624–41), had maintained the Latin ascendancy over the St. Thomas Christians while working cooperatively with Archdeacon George of the Cross and the older cattanars who had guided the destinies of their religious communities through the realignment required by the Synod of Diamper. In 1640 the archdeacon died and Brito appointed as his successor Thomas Parampil (or Thomas de Campos), George's young nephew. At the end of 1641, Brito himself died and was succeeded by the Portuguese Jesuit Francisco Garcia, archbishop of Cranganore from 1641 to 1659. Almost at once a stuggle for power ensued between the archdeacon and the archbishop, which culminated in a general rebellion of the Serra in 1653 against the Jesuits directly and against the Portuguese indirectly. The new archbishop proved to be harsh, inflexible, and insensitive to the traditions and pride of the St. Thomas Christians; the new archdeacon was impetuous, unscrupulous, and equal to Garcia in resolution and determination. Around 1645 each began to search for allies in anticipation of a final showdown. This came in 1653 with the "Coonan Cross" episode, when the leaders of the St. Thomas Christians solemnly swore that they would proclaim their archdeacon as archbishop of the St. Thomas communities.[191]

The rebellion of the Serra against Archbishop Garcia also produced diffi-

[188] Grey (ed.), *op. cit.* (n. 19), II, 355–83.

[189] *Ibid.*, pp. 442–43.

[190] See above, pp. 162–65.

[191] See Joseph Thekedathu, S.D.B., *The Troubled Days of Francis Garcia, S.J., Archbishop of Cranganore (1641–59)* (Rome, 1972), pp. 18–82; for the St. Thomas view that this was a rebellion against the Jesuits and the *Padroado,* and not an effort to escape the jurisdiction of Rome, see A. M. Mundadan, "History of St. Thomas Christianity in India to the Present Day," in George Menachery (ed.), *The St. Thomas Christian Encyclopedia of India* (3 vols.; Madras, 1982), II, 49.

culties for Lisbon and Rome. Goa and Cochin urged conciliation, since Portugal already had enough enemies in India. The other religious orders, long jealous of Jesuit domination of the *Padroado,* argued the case for the St. Thomas Christians both in Goa and Lisbon. Archbishop Garcia in 1654 sent his secretary and confessor, Giacinto (Hyacinth) de Magistris, S.J. (1605–68), to Lisbon and Rome to plead his case. In Rome the Propaganda, long critical of the *Padroado* and the Jesuits' role in it, acted swiftly to heal the schism in India. Two Italian Carmelite priests, Giuseppe di Santa Maria Sebastiani (1623–89) and Vincenzo Maria di Santa Caterina da Siena (alias Antonio Murchio, 1626–79), were sent in 1656 by the Propaganda to investigate the situation and to recommend remedial measures. Magistris did not leave Rome for the return to India until 1657. It was not long before the schism of the Serra was brought to the European public in books prepared by the antagonists. In 1661 Magistris published his *Relatione della Christianità di Maduré* (Rome), which celebrates the successes of the Jesuits in south India.[192] Five years later Sebastiani published his *Prima speditione all' Indie Orientali* (Rome) followed six years later by his *Seconda speditione* (Rome). In this same year, 1672, Vincenzo published *Il viaggio all' Indie Orientale* (Rome), a lengthy book which is far more informative on India than the other European publications which grew out of the St. Thomas controversy.[193]

Sebastiani and Vincenzo left Naples on February 22, 1656, to take the overland route to Surat. They went to Chaul and then to the Dutch factory at Vengurla. They avoided Goa and the Portuguese by taking an Indian *parāo* (Malayalam, *pāṛu,* a boat or small craft) to Malabar. On their way they were joined at Banda, inland just north of Goa, by another Discalced Carmelite called Matthew of St. Joseph (d. 1691), a natural scientist who would later contribute to the *Hortus indicus malabaricus.*[194] After landing at "Parur" (Paravoor) in Malabar they went on February 5, 1657, to Edapally to interview the archdeacon. Once Sebastiani understood something of the difficulties facing the Carmelites, he sent Vincenzo on to Cochin and Cranganore to present their credentials from the pope to the ecclesiastical authorities in those places. The Portuguese secular officials, who had just lost Colombo to the Dutch, were prepared to accept the good offices of the priests in helping to bring peace to the Serra. Even Archbishop Garcia promised to help them. But these bright prospects soon dimmed as the archdeacon and the archbishop continued to suspect the motives and to challenge the powers of the two Carmelites. After a series of tempestuous assemblies, Sebastiani returned to Rome to make his report. On January 7, 1658, Sebastiani and Vincenzo began their long return journey via Goa to Rome. They arrived there

---

[192] See below, pp. 1057–63.

[193] For bibliographical detail on these works see above, pp. 382–84.

[194] See below, pp. 925–27. This meeting occurred early in January, 1657, at which time they also met Bishop Matheus de Castro, the first vicar apostolic appointed by the Propaganda.

over one year later on February 22, 1659, after traversing the land route again.[195]

Vincenzo's *Il viaggio* (1672) is far more than an itinerary of the Carmelite mission to India: Book I tells of the journey to Malabar; Book II is about the St. Thomas Christians; Book III is on the political, religious, and social life of Malabar; Book IV, probably prepared with the aid of Father Matthew, describes the plants of Malabar, tells of the return trip to Europe, and includes a description of Goa. While he cites a number of earlier European commentators on India, his description of Malabar, where he lived for almost one year (February, 1657, to January, 1658), is original and perceptive. Perhaps a bit of freshness is added to his account in that he and Sebastiani were forced out of the conventional Portuguese-Jesuit mold because of the nature of their mission. Since they did not have a command of Malayalam, they relied for information on non-Jesuit religious and priests as well as native informants and translated books. They spent very little time in the port cities and came to know interior places rarely frequented by Europeans. Since Sebastiani acted as the negotiator, Vincenzo apparently had both the time and opportunity to inquire about more general matters and to record his findings. Finally, when he returned to Europe, Vincenzo rose rapidly in the ranks of his order until he became procurator-general for India. His book may therefore be seen as a call for volunteers and as a manual for prospective Carmelite missionaries to Malabar.[196]

After discussing India in general terms, Vincenzo attempts to give the political divisions of Malabar. "Cananor" (Cannanore), the first one he visited, is the most highly regarded of the Malabar states. It is separated from Kanara on the north by a wall that runs from the mountains to the sea;[197] it extends southward to the "Capucate" (Kappata) river, a short distance from Calicut. Cannanore is divided into 444 jurisdictions, all owing allegiance to a Brahman king of the Kolattiri dynasty. To prevent landward invasions there are numerous mountain fortresses in the interior, guarded by 200,000 Nayars. Its king unwisely spends most of his time and money in venerating idols. Several years before, he divided his kingdom among his fifty sons. Vincenzo met the Kolattiri ruler on two occasions and notes that he wears a golden tiara as a singular privilege of his high status. His land is rich in rice,

[195] For further detail on the first Sebastiani mission see Thekedathu, *op. cit.* (n. 191), pp. 107–27.

[196] Sebastiani returned to India, arriving in 1660, to set up the Vicariate of Malabar. After the Dutch captured the Malabar ports a few years later, Sebastiani returned to Europe. Other Carmelite missionaries simply faded into the interior. Father Matthew of St. Joseph, the botanist, even collaborated with the Dutch governor Van Rheede in compiling the *Hortus indicus malabaricus*. Gradually other Carmelites were tolerated by the Dutch, and by 1700 the Vicariate of Malabar had again come under the administration of Carmelite prelates and the Propaganda. But the Dutch still excluded all priests native to Portugal.

[197] This wall shows up on a number of seventeenth- and eighteenth-century European maps of South Asia.

ginger, pepper, and cardamom. Most of its inhabitants are Hindus, but a few Muslims live on the coast. Five or six households of Jews live near "Monte de Li" (Mount Deli), who smelt metal and manufacture large brass drinking vessels.[198]

The second state of Malabar that Vincenzo mentions is Travancore, an arid and sterile land. Situated next to the cape, it enjoys greater security than the other states and is the one most feared. Third, Calicut, the land of the Zamorin, stands between Cannanore and Cochin on the coast and borders in its mountainous hinterland on the territory of Cranganore and the principality of "Curito" (Koratti). In the city of Calicut there is the royal palace called "Talam" (Tali) where the Zamorin lives whom they call "Quetris" (*Khetri*),[199] that is to say, knight, or hero. This prince commands 150,000 soldiers and in case of need can still call for help from the Muslim pirates who live along the coast. The fourth state, Cochin, is stronger than the other Malabar states because of its permanent alliance with the Portuguese. It extends from the "Aicotta" (Alicot?) river to above "Mutano" (Muttam?). Within this region are many small principalities which pay tribute in pepper to the Cochin ruler. When they proclaim the accession of this king, all the notables of the realm assemble at "Odiamper" (Diamper) for a tiger hunt. Once it is over the assemblage swears allegiance to the king and reaffirms the traditional alliance with Portugal. The fifth state of Malabar is "Tecancuti" (Tekkumkur) in the mountains behind Travancore. There are at least fifteen other identifiable principalities in Malabar which pay tribute to the larger states and maintain small forces of Nayars.[200]

While conscious that practices differ from place to place, Vincenzo hereafter writes in general terms about the government, peoples, products, castes, and beliefs of Malabar.

Governance in India, whether by Hindu or Muslim, is despotic and arbitrary. All lands belong to the prince, who ordinarily parcels them out to his chief captains. They, in turn, farm them out to individuals who agree to maintain and develop the holdings assigned to them. The prince may give or take back gifts of land at his pleasure. Succession is by direct inheritance,

[198] Vincenzo Maria di Santa Caterina da Siena, *Il viaggio all' Indie Orientali* . . . (Rome, 1672), pp. 222–23. *Cf.* the sixteenth-century accounts in *Asia*, I, 350–51. On the high social status of the Kolattiri rulers see P. K. S. Rajā, *Mediaeval Karala* (Chidambaram, 1953), p. 61. They were nominal rulers over numerous small principalities, as Vincenzo indicates. On Jews at Mount Deli see Padamanabha Menon, *op. cit.* (n. 4), I, 15.

[199] A Konkani or Malayalam word derived from Sanskrit, *Kṣatrya*, the name of a military caste. See Dalgado, *op. cit.* (n. 146), II, 235–36, for a thorough rundown of its usage in European literature.

[200] Vincenzo, *op. cit.* (n. 198), pp. 223–25. For a survey of the confused political geography of Malabar, when the Dutch replaced the Portuguese in the 1660's, see T. I. Poonen, *Dutch Hegemony in Malabar and Its Collapse (A.D. 1663–1795)* (Trivandrum, 1978), pp. 10–14. Tekkumkur, though not usually included among the principal states, was an independent kingdom of substantial area and population.

but if a line fails a system of adoption is instituted.[201] If the king dies without heirs, the queen adopts a successor and commends him to an assembly of the Brahmans. Once the Brahmans swear allegiance, the new ruler goes to live with the queen as her son. The prince has his own chancellor, but the Brahmans direct the affairs of state. Everyone offers betel to the prince ceremonially, but otherwise formalities are few and simple in Hindu royal courts. Muslim rulers follow more ceremonies and rituals both at court and in their ostentatious processions. Justice and punishment are meted out quickly and harshly. Trials are not held; both civil and criminal cases are handled administratively. Trials by ordeal are used frequently to extract the truth. In Malabar sentences of imprisonment or exile are most common. Murders are avenged by the "Amouchi." They customarily follow a certain law called "Ketrither" which prohibits fights of two on one, or of the armed against the unarmed. Even princes follow this custom scrupulously. One prince does not aid the other with soldiers, but may provide only arms and money; anything more is considered dishonorable.[202]

Physically the Indians are straight, almost tall, and not often fat. Spinal curvatures, common in Europeans, are rarely seen. In color the people are swarthy like sun-tanned farmers and not black like Abyssinians. All have black eyes, the whites being tinted with blood. The black hair of the head is straight and not at all kinky. Except for Moors and Gujaratis, natives of all classes tend to be effeminate, soft, and little inclined to work. They are sweet and loving, not at all barbaric. Much of their time is spent in talking, chewing betel, and washing themselves. Merchants are astute, sagacious, and self-interested. Not all the Gentiles profess the same faith. Some are descended from the Persians (Parsis) and worship fire, eat meat, drink wine, and keep to themselves.[203]

Malabar is well watered by rivers and inlets, making cultivation and navigation easy. All grains yield one or two crops annually without fail and the harvests are more bounteous than those in Europe. Great quantities of cotton are produced, from which they make thread and textiles for both domestic and foreign consumption, their cloths being much better than the linens of Holland. They produce enough pepper to satisfy the whole world. In the south, rice is harvested two and sometimes even three times annually. There are three types of rice: red, large-grained but not very white, and small-grained and white. The first is the food of slaves and cultivators, the second of commoners, and the third of the rich.[204] Malabar also produces

---

[201] On the role of adoption in Cochin see Rajā, *op. cit.* (n. 198), pp. 147–48; and Padmanabha Menon, *op. cit.* (n. 4), I, 188–89.

[202] Vincenzo, *op. cit.* (n. 198), pp. 235–38. "Amouchi" is perhaps a confusion with *amoucos,* amuck runners, or possibly refers to *arachar,* hangman; "Ketrither" is possibly *Kshatriyam,* the code of behavior of the *Kshatriyas.*

[203] *Ibid.,* pp. 231–34.

[204] In modern times red rices are preferred in Kerala. See R. L. M. Ghose *et al., Rice in India* (rev. ed., New Delhi, 1960), p. 13.

palm products, tamarinds, sea salt, tobacco, and sugar. Poultry and fish are abundant; fish is cheap, since the Indians generally will not eat fish.[205]

Novelty in dress is despised, each following the styles of his region, class, or office. Ordinary houses are very poor and mostly of one story. In Kanara they are of mud covered with a black bitumen which makes them shiny. In Malabar they are of wood and mud bound together with palm fronds. Every two years or so they have to be rebuilt. No matter how rich the owner, his social level determines the type of house he may build. Their furnishings are as poor as their hovels. The interior walls are bare and painted with cow dung. Their utensils are limited to drinking vessels and pots for cooking rice. Benches and chairs are never used, for they sit and work on the bare ground. Their food is unsalted, spare, and limited to rice, vegetables, milk, butter, and fruits. They make a number of different rice dishes, the best being one called "Puto" (*pūttu*).[206] While eating they sit cross-legged in a circle on the floor and eat with their hands. They never drink while eating, but once satisfied they wash their hands and drink the same water they wash with. The Portuguese and the native Christians eat well and learn to use creatively the local spices, fruits, and vegetables. Meat of all kinds is cheap, but wine from Portugal is limited and expensive. Both the natives and the Portuguese drink palm liquors.[207]

Malabar has many castes and subcastes based on profession, craft, or some other distinction. In caste, lineage is all that matters; there is very little communication between persons of different castes. The Brahmans of Malabar are known as "Namburi" (*Nambūtirī*) and they are of nine levels. The "Tirinamburi" are high priests similar to bishops and are venerated as saints.[208] They are the guardians of the idols and they alone may offer sacrifices in the temples.[209] They never marry, and they claim to be chaste.[210] A second group, the "Patadesi Namburi" (*Ādyhan*?), are royal advisers.[211] The "Ciatada Namburi" (*Chittal Namburi*) are the philosophers and religious instructors who settle debates and prescribe ceremonies. They are followed in order by the ordinary "Namburi" (*Sāmānyu*), who aid the others in performing their rites and functions. The fifth group, called "Pateres" (*Paṭṭar*), perform in certain ceremonies where they repeat the names of the god being

---

[205] Vincenzo, *op. cit.* (n. 198), pp. 225–28.

[206] Layers of rice and coconut are steamed together in a bamboo tube.

[207] Vincenzo, *op. cit.* (n. 198), pp. 238–46. On food habits *cf.* Francis Day, *The Land of the Perumals, or Cochin, Its Past and Its Present* (Madras, 1863), pp. 407–10.

[208] Does the "Tiri" in "Tirinamburi" derive from the Malayalam word *Tiru*, which means "holy" or "saintly"?

[209] "The *Tampurākkal* [high priest] . . . possesses unquestioned supreme spiritual authority over all Nambūtiris." Padmanabha Menon, *op. cit.* (n. 4), III, 35.

[210] Actually they form an endogamous community with the *Ādyhan*, the second subcaste. See *ibid.*

[211] The *Ādyhan* form eight families. "They are the constituted gurus of the temple priests and are the final authorities in all matters of temple ritual" (E. Thurston, *Castes and Tribes of Southern India* [7 vols.; Madras, 1909] V, 165).

invoked.[212] The "Eulunambi" (*Elayathu?*) carry the idols in their processions.[213] The "Pecilla Pateres" (*Piccha Paṭṭar?*) participate in processions by attending the idol's palanquin. The eighth group, called "Embrandeci" (*Emprāntirī*), are custodians of the temple treasury and collect temple offerings.[214] The ninth and final subcaste named "Eleda" (*Ilayathu*) performs death rites.[215] The first four of these subcastes perform only those functions here noted; the others all engage in trade as well.[216] Obviously Vincenzo's grasp of the various types of Nambutiri is incomplete and faulty. He is, however, the first European writer to make an effort to identify and understand these distinctions.

The second great caste is that of the soldiers called "Nairi" (Nayar) in Malabar.[217] They are divided into fifteen subcastes according to military rank or specialty.[218] Five of these groups are in commerce. The eighth group raises cows, the ninth fishes with nets, and the twelfth sells oil. Only the thirteenth group is permitted to exchange money. In terms of occupational types, Vincenzo's listings correspond to a certain extent to the divisions given in modern listings.[219]

The third caste, commonly called "Cegos" (*Chegos*) or "Bandarine" (*Paṇṭāram*, sellers of garlands), are palm cultivators. The first subcaste, named "Paellacumarere" (*Palla-kumārar*) cultivates the palm and gathers the nuts. The second called "Tiveri" (*Tiuuers* or *Tiyan*) draw the toddy or *sura* and distill it into "Oracha" (arrack) and nipa (palm) wine. The third subgroup called "Bati" (?) or "Canacas" (*Cāṇar*) make white and black jaggery. Each group has its own chief called "Tendana" (*tanṭān*) who is selected by the prince. He does no menial work, superintends the others, resolves disputes, and punishes delinquencies. He has a deputy called "Panicke" (*panikkan*).[220]

Unlike his European predecessors, Vincenzo distinguishes between the *Chegos* and the lower castes of Malabar. Goldsmiths and jewelers (*Taṭṭan*)

---

[212] *Paṭṭar* are foreign Brahmans who usually live on charity. See Day, *op. cit.* (n. 207), p. 308.
[213] On the *Elayathu* see Padmanabha Menon, *op. cit.* (n. 4), III, 46.
[214] See *ibid.*, pp. 3–4.
[215] According to *ibid.*, p. 4, the *Ilayathu* are priests to the Sudras.
[216] Vincenzo, *op. cit.* (n. 198), pp. 246–47.
[217] On the Nayars according to the sixteenth-century Europeans see *Asia*, I, 362–65.
[218] Most of the names Vincenzo gives do not correspond at all to the sixteen chief divisions of the Nayars listed in Thurston, *op. cit.* (n. 211), V, 297–300, or to the fourteen in L. K. Anantha Krishna Iyer, *The Tribes and Castes of Cochin* (3 vols.; 1981 reprint, New Delhi [orig. publ. 1962–64]) II, 15–18. The Italian Carmelite itemizes them as follows (*op. cit.* [n. 198], p. 247): "Manerli" are captains. They are followed in rank by lower-grade officials called "Balati" and "Agastigernadu." The "Cittari" constitute the royal bodyguard. In order follow the "Patramanichare," "Bellacatatterra," "Beltoa," "Cananaimar," and "Andinaimar." The tenth group "Paliciani" (*Pallichan*) carry the royal palanquin. Everything is lawful to the "Brandanaimar," "Undiela," "Parmaniati," "Tatengerati," and "Nicitigethiere."
[219] See Padamanabha Menon, *op. cit.* (n. 4), III, 192–95, who gives eighteen subdivisions with their occupations.
[220] Vincenzo, *op. cit.* (n. 198), p. 247. On the *Chegos* see Padamanabha Menon, *op. cit.* (n. 4), III, 424–46.

work with few tools and still achieve excellent results. Next come the "Giari" (*Ācāri*), or carpenters, who are divided into subgroups of those who carve and those who build. Fishermen are "Mucuas" (*Mucuar*), the most important of whom fish at sea and are called "Caramucuora" (?). Those who fish the rivers are divided into subgroups according to the type of boats or nets they use. All fishermen are ruled by a captain called the "Aremar" ('*arayan*).[221] In rank they are followed by the barbers called "Ambutere" (*Ampaṭṭan*), the sawyers called "Muggiaci" (*Muchi?*), and the blacksmiths called "Colloni" (*Kollan*).[222] Those who gather honey are "Doladas" (*Ul-ladan*), and they eat snakes, as well as everything else.[223] Shoemakers are called "Tacciare" (*Tayyallār*). Washers named "Belle" (*Vēlan*) beat drums at festivals. Those who make shields of leather are called "Garippi" (*Tōle Kuruy*). The "Othigala" (*Ōdaṭṭu*) are bricklayers, the "Cregianen" (*Ka-lamkoṭṭi?*) are potters, the "Cacoreas" (*Kakkalam*) are clowns or medical quacks. Those who make a profession of magic or enchantment are called "Cagner" (*Kanian?*). Certain soldiers who live like gypsies are the "Marua" (*Maravan*); similar unarmed nomads are known as "Tottias" (*Toṭṭi*). Finally, the diggers and peasants are known as "Pulias" (*Pulayan*) and they are of five sorts: "Boroas" (*Paṟayan*) are riceworkers, "Corombinis" (*Kuṟumbar*) are cultivators of vegetables, "Patysulias" (*Pasu Pulayan*) are foresters, and then there are "Faras" or "Pareas" (*Parayan* or Pariahs), who are detested because they eat cows. This last subgroup has a chief called the "Baloin" (*palavān?*).[224]

Traditionally, according to Vincenzo, caste rules are traced back to a Brahmanical book on the creation of the world. The first man "Ruthren" (Rudra) had a daughter called "Sattiabadi" (Satyavathi). She bore sixty sons, to each of whom she taught a particular profession in the order of their birth; she further ordained that they and their progeny should rigorously follow it forever. Over time the Malabars have observed this admonition most faithfully, while the Kanarese have not.[225] In both religious and social terms, the educated Brahmans of Malabar dominate society; the lower classes, so far as they are permitted, imitate their practices and respect the standards they set. The Brahmans study and follow the Vedas, books of law in which everything about social relations is ordained. In religious terms the Brahmans are rivaled in influence only by the "Gioqui" (yogis), who believe in poverty and penitence. These wandering mendicants impose unbelievable penances upon themselves. Those who are called "Ruxis" (rishis, hermit

---

[221] See Thurston, *op. cit.* (n. 211), V, 106–12.
[222] On the blacksmiths see Day, *op. cit.* (n. 207), p. 324.
[223] See A. A. D. Luiz, *Tribes of Kerala* (New Delhi, 1962), p. 231.
[224] Vincenzo, *op. cit.* (n. 198), pp. 247–48. Modern students of caste usually treat the *Parayan* as a separate group. On the internal structure of the Pulayans, see Anantha Krishna Iyer, *Social History of Kerala* (2 vols.; Madras, 1968), I, 96–97.
[225] "Kerala is one of the most caste-ridden parts of India," according to Krishna Iyer, *op. cit.* (n. 224), II, 46.

sages) or "Hioboli" (?) always stay far from human habitations and live solely on wild leaves, berries, and fruits. These contemplatives sleep on the bare earth, think only of their gods, keep chaste, and flee from the sight or touch of women. To ward off temptations they always carry a stock or cane. They follow Vishnu and are the most revered of all holy men.[226]

In contracting marriages the castes follow ancient customs and ceremonies, which vary from group to group and place to place. The Brahmans, who abhor polygamy, negotiate a rigid and perpetual contract. Vincenzo then compares the ceremonies followed by the Brahmans of Malabar to those of the Brahmans of Gujarat. Among the Nayars the woman chooses a husband not for cohabitation but for support and protection. The *Chegos,* or cultivators of palms, practice "true marriage," but only for as long as the relationship works.[227] The fisher castes feast during the entire day of the wedding. At sunset they sit down in a circle. After a brief discourse by the groom, the bride runs around the circle followed by the groom. He slaps her on the shoulder three times while saying "Maiuren" (*Mayuram,* peacock). To this she responds only with a reverent smile. They then go to the river, submerge themselves three times, and change their clothes. While returning to the house on a litter, he ties a gold thread around her neck and again slaps her on the shoulder while repeating the word "Maiuren." Members of the *Pulayan* caste must have permission to marry from the master for whom they work. In concluding a marital agreement they are not permitted to exchange gold or any other metal, a simple cord binding them in their promises. Divorce is a simple matter of breaking the cord. Everyone may remarry at will.[228] No caste may marry children to blind or other permanently disabled persons.[229]

The Brahmans deserve the reputation they enjoy in Europe of being intellectually talented. They show great respect and reverence for learning and for teachers. Most of their education relates to transcribing and reading their ancient books, knowledge of which provides them with a nucleus of learning. They add nothing of their own speculations to received knowledge except fables and chimeric inventions. Elementary reading and writing are taught in open-air schools where the students may be watched by everyone. Youngsters learn their lessons by repeating in a high voice, while perpetually moving their heads and chests, whatever they wish to commit to memory. They have more letters of the alphabet than we do: the Gujaratis with thirty and the Malabars with thirty-eight, most of which they palatalize. Their thin books have pages of cotton cloth, bamboo, or palm leaves. Gu-

[226] Vincenzo, *op. cit.* (n. 198), pp. 249–54. He compares the "Ruxi" to the cloistered religious of Gujarat, in what is apparently a reference to Jain monachism.

[227] Possibly a reference to the real marriage that follows a mock wedding, rather than to divorce. See Padmanabha Menon, *op. cit.* (n. 4), III, 439.

[228] Cf. Krishna Iyer, *op. cit.* (n. 224), I, 100–101.

[229] Vincenzo, *op. cit.* (n. 198), pp. 258–60.

jaratis write with a pen, the Kanarese with a sharpened white stone, and the Malabars with an iron stylus.[230] In the Malabar language there are three types of scripts: those in common use, the "Sampsahardam" (*Granthakshara?*) and the sacred letters of Tamil.[231] They are all quite distinct and difficult to copy. To write in ordinary characters to a prince, or about matters of law, is considered improper. Since they use special ornaments and forms in their higher language, an "olla" of the prince, a public document, or a contract is authenticated by the writing itself and does not require a signature or seal. Grammar is not taught. Some apply themselves to the study of certain linguistic affectations which slightly resemble rhetoric. They employ metaphors, comparisons, and illustrative stories to embellish and liven discourse. They compose verses in which they exhibit an understanding of cadence and the music of words. These verses are composed of seventy-two syllables. Sometimes they compose rhymes based on ancient stories and beliefs.[232]

Their natural philosophy is short in precepts and long in opinions based on conjecture. Solid reasoning and demonstrations of their understanding of nature are rare; they are much more adept at exploring human talents and inclinations. They discourse on the elements; some include the wind or the heavens among them. Their discussions of generation and corruption show their imperfect understanding of nature. They admit the concept of the soul's immortality and concede that the world was created in time. Their physicians have no professional schooling but gain their positions of esteem or respect by birth and heredity.[233] The Malabars use many unguents, some so harsh they ruin the complexion. Most of their remedies are jealously guarded secrets. One of their medical books fell into Vincenzo's hands, but it proved to be of little use to him in using the roots and simples of India as medicines. The Malabars never bleed patients, but limit their treatments to herbs, decoctions, and exorcisms.[234]

Many profess the study of moral philosophy. Like most of their learning, it is unordered and dispersed throughout their ancient books in the form of good maxims. Perusal of these aphorisms reveals that they recognize all the evils of concupiscence and disdain riches. They adulate poverty, respect chastity, and greatly praise virginity. Human happiness is not found in temporal possessions or in sensual gratification but in contemplation. While for the most part they study religious aphorisms, they also teach several forms

---

[230] On writing materials *cf.* Dubois in Beauchamp (trans. and ed.), *op. cit.* (n. 126), p. 429.

[231] In the seventeenth century the two traditional scripts were the Vattezhuth and the Kolezhuth, both derived from Brahmi. Tamil was used in court records and official documents. The modern Malayalam alphabet based on the spoken language and on the Tamil-Sanskrit character called Granthakshara was introduced in the seventeenth century by Tunjatta Eluttachchan. See W. Logan, *Malabar* (3 vols.; Madras, 1951), I, 105–6.

[232] Vincenzo, *op. cit.* (n. 198), pp. 262–63.

[233] On learning through family instruction rather than by study in public institutions see Dubois in Beauchamp (trans. and ed.), *op. cit.* (n. 126), pp. 377–78.

[234] Vincenzo, *op. cit.* (n. 198), p. 263.

of systematic theology. Their theologies, however, are much too legalistic and devoid of content; they all commence with fables, chimeras, and errors. Religious study is divided into four parts, each part into six members, and each member into eighteen articles.[235] The first part deals with the efficient cause of the universe, the angels, how this world was formed, the transmigration of souls, rewards and punishments, and what the sins are and how to be redeemed. The second treats of the three gods as rectors of heaven and earth and how the gods were created. The third is full of morality, good precepts, and advice for living in secular society or in solitude. The fourth deals with rites, observances, and ceremonies.[236]

Always curious about Hindu beliefs and traditions, Vincenzo hired a guru to instruct him in the meaning of the ancient texts. From Francisco Garcia, the archbishop of Cranganore, he obtained copies of six such texts, and perhaps others as well, which had been translated into Portuguese by Garcia himself, probably sometime before 1630.[237] In Vincenzo's ordering, the first of these is a series of thirty-two moral stories for the guidance of princes based on the fabulous life of "Vicramaditi, King of Uzini" (*Vikrāmaditya, king of Ujjayini*).[238] The second relates to "Aricando, King of Aiodi" (*Harischandra, king of Ayodhya*), his consort "Tarmati" (*Tamarati*), and a son who is an exemplar of fortitude, constancy, and fidelity.[239] The third includes twenty-four maxims, some secular and others moral, which are epitomized in diverse fables of animals reminiscent of the Aesop stories.[240] The fourth text relates the life story of "Pralado" (*Prahlāda*), son of "Hiranea Cassipri" (*Hiranya-kasipu*), who is a giant in strength and stature and an exemplar of constancy and piety.[241] The fifth is the life of "Vppemanio"

---

[235] Four Vedas, six Vedangas, and eighteen Puranas. *Cf.* A. L. Basham, *The Wonder That Was India* (3d rev. ed., London, 1967), p. 164.

[236] Vincenzo, *op. cit.* (n. 198), pp. 265–66.

[237] Vincenzo probably examined a Portuguese version of Garcia's translations which was slightly different from the collection of Garcia's translations brought to Rome in 1660 by Giacinto de Magistris (see below, pp. 1057–63), onetime secretary to Garcia and Jesuit procurator for Malabar. Magistris presented these translations to Daniello Bartoli, the historian of the Society. This manuscript collection of 173 pages is preserved in the General Archives of the Society of Jesus (Opp.NN,192); it has been edited and published by J. Wicki, S.J., in *O homem das trinta e duas perfeições e outras histórias* (Lisbon, 1958).

[238] This is obviously a version of the *Vikramcharita*, a collection in which each of thirty-two divine statues tells a story about the wonderful deeds of King Vikrama, a quasihistorical popular hero in India. It is an Indian example of the literary form known in Europe as a "mirror for princes." For a modern scholarly translation see F. Edgerton (trans. and ed.), *Vikrama's Adventures, or the Thirty-Two Tales of the Throne* ("Harvard Oriental Series," ed. C. R. Lanman, XXVI; Cambridge, Mass., 1926). For the edited Portuguese text which reproduces the version preserved in Rome see Wicki (ed.), *op. cit.* (n. 237), pp. 63–160.

[239] This legend is related in various forms in the Aitareya Brahmana, the Mahabharata, and the Markandeya Purana. For Garcia's possible source see Wicki (ed.), *op. cit.* (n. 237), pp. xx–xxi; for the edited Portuguese text from the Roman version see *ibid.*, pp. 1–62.

[240] Probably stories extracted from various Indian collections. See Wicki (ed.), *op. cit.* (n. 237), p. xxv.

[241] This story relates to the appearance of Vishnu in his Man-Lion incarnation and is from Book I of the Vishnu Purana. For the edited Roman version see *ibid.*, pp. 255–58.

(*Upamanyu*), the son of a poor Brahman.[242] Finally, there is the story of "Zanarzenū" (*Janārdana*, or Vishnu as "Giver of Rewards"), son of King "Vrana Caranū" (*Uttāna-charana*, ordinarily called *Uttāna-pāda*), who retreated to the desert to live a contemplative life.[243]

From his guru Vincenzo learned the opinions of the Brahmans about the first cause and the formation of the universe. Although the Hindus have a multitude of gods, they believe in one supreme god who is eternal and infinite. From him all the other gods receive their existence. The supreme god created only heaven, earth, and the principal gods; everything else was created by the other gods. Some believe the first god to be spirit, but others question how pure spirit could create matter. The first cause is contained in everything and is divided into diverse spheres according to the members of its body (see pl. 133). Wisdom proceeded from its brain, prudence from its eyes, eloquence and good discourse from its mouth, and so forth. Wide differences of opinion exist as to how the other gods were created, though it is generally agreed that Brahma, Vishnu, and "Parmissera" (Paramesvara or Siva) were their progenitors. While the first cause has no name of its own, the Malabars worship it under the name of "Shibba" (Siva). The "Patares" (*Pattars*, or foreign Brahmans) give it many other names, more than sixty, each of which refers to a particular aspect and possesses a special symbolism—strength of the tiger, splendor of the horse, fecundity of the cow.[244]

In the beginning it was not possible to discern time, places, substance, or laws. Only a nameless person existed unaware of everything as if in an egg. The egg, when it split, divided into two substances.[245] Then the five elements were created, heaven (ether), air, fire, water, and earth, followed by the three principal deities. Brahma created substance and time and decorated the heavens with stars. He brought into existence a mountain called "Brudia" (Vindhya?) across from a sea called "Sindu" (*Sindhu*, ocean), in the middle of which he placed an island called "Cugniran" (?). Then he mixed his own blood and a little mud together to make "Rutrun" (Rudra), the first man.[246] The earth was so well watered at first by rivers that it produced fruits in great abundance without rain or human labor. But since men were discontented and inconstant, God substituted downpours for rivers and

[242] An ascetic revered by the Saivites whose hermitage in the Himalayas became a sanctuary for all kinds of animals. *Cf.* chapter 36 of the Sama Purana. For the edited Roman version see *ibid.*, pp. 235–39.

[243] One of the avatars of Vishnu from the Vishnu Purana. For the edited Roman version see *ibid.*, pp. 219–35. For Vincenzo's excerpts and summaries of these six translations see *op. cit.* (n. 198), pp. 265–81.

[244] Vincenzo, *op. cit.* (n. 198), pp. 281–83.

[245] That is, one part of the shell became silver and the other gold. See Daniélou, *op. cit.* (n. 127), p. 248.

[246] For this identification and for the story of "Rutrun" (Rudra) see the old Portuguese text of the late seventeenth century as translated into Dutch in W. Caland and A. A. Fokker, "Drie oude Portugeische Verhandelingen over het Hindoeisme," in *Verhandelingen der Koninklijke Akademie van Wetenschappen te Amsterdam, Letterkunde*, n.s., XVI (1915), No. 2, pp. 166–75, 211. The father of Rudra was Prajapati, lord of progeny.

forced men to work for their harvests. Brahma provided man with his powers of intelligence and speech. On earth Brahma has no temples, only immortal descendants or Brahmans. In Malabar the people use twenty names for Brahma, and the author lists eighteen of them in his own inimitable transliterations.[247]

"Vistnù" (Vishnu) is a highly acclaimed deity who governs and administers everything. He descends once a year from his habitat in the sea of milk to reward or punish according to the merits or demerits of each person. In Malabar he is known under twenty-three different names, which the author lists.[248] "Parmissera" or Siva was born from the mouth of the first cause and was married to another god named "Paravati" (Parvati). "Parmissera" possesses a variety of attributes and is particularly associated with the tiger named "Kanauasù Sheoffarabali" (?).[249] All three of the principal gods are manifestations of the "Perabrahma" (*Parabrahman*) or the Supreme Being. Vincenzo then lists the twenty-three avatars of Vishnu common to Malabar and comments on some of them.[250]

After the principal deities, Vincenzo gives place of preference to "Ganavedi" (*Ganādhipa*, an epithet of *Ganęśa*, Ganesha, "lord of the gaṇas"). This is the god of greed and gluttony to whom most of the temples are dedicated (see pl. 151). The Brahmans tolerate in this god the liberty and license condemned so roundly in their scriptures. That he is held in such high esteem by the common people is much to the profit of the priestly caste. The Malabars say that Ganesha is the son of Siva while the Gujaratis claim him for Vishnu. Both depict him in a rotund and deformed human body and with the head of an elephant. He has four arms as symbols of his strength. According to the Malabars, Ganesha is depicted in this monstrous fashion because his father and mother wanted to recall the joys of playing in the forest with the animals. In Malabar he is always seated on a throne with two arms raised and with the other two resting on his knees.[251]

The second of the lesser gods is "Ramani" (Ravana), chief god of the Sinhalese and prince of the giants. He is always shown as having twenty arms and ten heads in each of which there is a mouth with two huge teeth. He ruled "Lenga" (Lanka, or Ceylon) for fifty-three epochs. He assumes the form of a toad called "Bandadin" (?) and rides easily in the air on a wooden horse named "Teru" (?). The third of the minor gods is "Narando" (Narada),

[247] Vincenzo, *op. cit.* (n. 198), pp. 283–87.

[248] *Ibid.*, p. 287.

[249] The tiger is the symbol of nature's power. Since Siva is beyond nature's power, he carries the tiger's skin as a trophy. See Daniélou, *op. cit.* (n. 127), p. 216.

[250] *Op. cit.* (n. 198), pp. 287–89; also see below, pp. 914–17. The Bhagavata Purana lists twenty-two avatars. See Daniélou, *op. cit.* (n. 127), p. 165.

[251] Ganesha is misrepresented here. He is generally revered as the god of good luck, prosperity, and blessings. On the literature and iconography of Ganesha see S. Battacharji, *The Indian Theogony* (Cambridge, 1970), pp. 183–84. On his place in popular Hinduism see the remarks of Dubois in Beauchamp (trans. and ed.), *op. cit.* (n. 126), pp. 631–32.

son of Vishnu and the symbol of chastity and perpetual virginity.[252] He is depicted as a young Brahman of good appearance and serene countenance. The fourth of the lesser deities is "Dessu" (Devasenapatti, who originates from the third eye of Siva), god of weapons and of war worshipped by the military to instill an aggressive spirit. He is followed by "Cuberù" (Kubera), god of wealth and helper to Siva, who gives him control over all the gold and silver in the universe and in their distribution.[253] The sixth is "Calanidru" (Kala [time] as Yama), god of death, who can grant immortality and alter transmigrations. "Dessesù" (Sesha) is the god of snakes, under whose dominion fall all the poisonous beasts. In his kingdom of "Patale" (*Pātāla*) he keeps the "Amruta" (*amṛta*) or nectar of the gods. The eighth of the minor gods is "Emù" (Yama), god of hell, to whom they attribute the execution of justice. He has a scribe called "Kioruguputù" (Citraputra) who tours the universe registering man's actions and deeds.[254] In Calicut they show a special regard for "Anomager" (Arumgham, literally "six faces"), also called "Armagi" (Arumghi), who is depicted as a youthful warrior with six heads and twelve arms. He is armed with bows and arrows to fight the giants. The tenth of the lesser gods is "Aiapn Ciartava" (Ayappan Sastav), god of hunters and son of Vishnu. He is depicted in the nude with bow, arrow, and horn. Hunters implore his assistance before going on a hunt. Occasionally he is transformed into a female.[255] "Cadagarana" (*Kāttawarāyan*?) is related to the goddess Kali and is shown with one thousand and eight arms.[256] The Hindus deify beasts as well as men. Those who believe the story of "Selirama" (Sri Rama, the embodiment of righteousness) revere a monkey called "Animan" (Hanumant), the son of Siva and a relative of the wind. Hanumant rescued the goddess "Sida" (Sita) from "Ramanu" (Ravana, the demon enemy of Rama) as he went from India to "Lenga" (Lanka) in one great jump. He is much venerated by soldiers. On the gate of the fortress of "Decla" (?), the key to the state of Kanara, as well as in various other places, they erect images of this brutal beast, which they worship before entering. To add to all this confusion, they revere the serpent of "Baguzzi" (Vasuki, where Sesha dwells) on which Vishnu reposes in the sea of milk. They also worship a bird "Karera" (Khagesvara, lord of birds, an epithet of Garuḍa, or "Wings of Speech") who is the carrier of Vishnu.

The Brahmans also venerate goddesses. They assign women to each of their gods to gratify their beastlike sensuality. The first is "Shiath" (Sati, the faithful), wife of Vishnu, who succors supplicants. In Bijapur between the

[252] Narada was the son of Brahma, and an avatar of Vishnu.

[253] *Cf.* Daniélou, *op. cit.* (n. 127), p. 136.

[254] *Cf. ibid.*, pp. 132–35.

[255] Ayappan, the son of Siva and Vishnu, is transformed into Mohini, the enchantress and a female incarnation of Vishnu.

[256] See W. Caland (ed.), "Ziegenbalgs Malabarisches Heidenthum herausgegeben und mit Indices versehen," *Verhandelingen der Koninklijke Akademie van Wetenschappen te Amsterdam*, n.s., XXV (1926), No. 3.

towns of Banda and Vengurla there is a sumptuous temple dedicated to her where pilgrims go in large numbers hoping for miracle cures. The second goddess is "Paranni" (Bharati), called by others "Saraspati" (Sarasvati), who is the guardian of the sciences and the schools and is worshipped by students and teachers. She is depicted half-nude with a spear in her right hand and a palm-leaf book in her left. Her feast day is celebrated in December.[257] "Lozemi" (Laksmi) is the goddess of chance or fortune who sits to the right of Vishnu. Her feast of plenty, called "Bhiriva" (?), is celebrated on the first day of the year. The fourth goddess is "Parmidabi" (Shakambari?), who cares for trees, shrubs, and the fruits of the earth. She sits at the feet of Vishnu. She is depicted as an ordinary woman with skin saffron-color, clear, and resplendent. Her head leans on the world as if on her depended the conservation of everything. The fifth is "Paruati" (Parvati), wife of Siva and mother of "Ganavedi" (Ganesha). She is the mother deity. Her image is especially revered in the kingdom of "Porcha" (Porka). "Gengudiva" (Gangadevi) is goddess of the sea, the intimate and favorite of the first cause or the unknown god.[258] The seventh is "Sida" (Sita), the wife of "Selirama" (Sri Rama), who was born in "Lenga" (Lanka), the fertile island.[259] The last is "Cali" (Kali), who was created by Vishnu to punish the insolence of "Taride" (Dhaksha?) who had gravely affronted his wife "Shiatti" (Sati).[260] Kali is shown with two closed eyes and an open eye in the middle of her forehead. Her hair is wild and she is armed with sword and shield. She is propitiated by those with smallpox, a disease especially virulent in Malabar.[261]

In addition to these gods and goddesses the Brahmans revere the sun, moon, and elements, as well as demi-gods, many of whom are imaginary people of the kingdom of "Amaravati" (*Āmarāvatī*) who live as happy immortals.[262] Their chief is "Indù" (Indra), or "Divendren" (Devendra), a god who is continually consumed by jealousy. He has a ship on which he has imprisoned the four mists or clouds, possibly a reference to his role as the ruler of the sphere of space and the sky. The sun, moon, and planets, while not really gods, are held in the highest esteem. When the sun rises, Hindus begin the prayer called "Pangiaxeron" (?) which goes: "Hom namo pagabato, Hom Shilem, Hom Brehma, Hom Visnu, Hom Saruna Issverache-

---

[257] On Sarasvati also see Daniélou, *op. cit.* (n. 127), pp. 259–60. Her feast day is now celebrated on the ninth moon, between mid-September and mid-October.

[258] Gangadevi (Ganges) originates from the big toe of Vishnu and flows into the matted hair of Siva and thus becomes the consort of Siva.

[259] Sita was found in the ground by Janaka, king of Mittila, while he was plowing for a religious sacrifice.

[260] Kali was not created by Vishnu. Kali is the fierce form Parvati (Sati) takes to correspond to the fierce form her husband, Siva, took to punish Dhaksha (father of Parvati) for insulting her.

[261] Vincenzo, *op. cit.* (n. 198), pp. 290–96.

[262] Amaravati is the "Immortal City" of Indra. See Daniélou, *op. cit.* (n. 127), pp. 84, 110.

sana." [263] Every month the Hindus celebrate the new moon and the full moon with solemn processions. The five elements exist in perpetuity since, being uncreated, they are eternal and independent. Each is an attribute of its own divinity: fire from "Vuonrsnù" (?), ether from "Gandarinù" (?), water from "Veaschu" (Varuna), earth from "Parmidavi" (Prithivi?), and wind from "Vaiu" (Vayu). Each element has its own kingdom, and Vincenzo goes on to describe them briefly. [264]

The gods are infinite in number and vary from place to place both in importance and character. Representations of them are especially numerous in Kanara, Mansul, and Madura. Everywhere in public places and private homes they display tutelary deities. The "Thodri" (Todas) even worship the buffalo, who nurses them. In the kingdom of the "Nair" (Nayars) behind Cannanore, priests at "Gurugelar" (Garagoli) serve the cult of a god named "Basti" (?). This god is represented as a male, completely shaved and nude except for a band of peacock feathers around his loins. He has a brass vase in his hands of the sort the Indians drink from. His priests dress in a similar fashion, follow an austere life, and sleep nude on a slab of black stone. [265] In Goa they worship certain infamous gods to whom mothers unite their daughters in marriage; such a temple is called the "Galego" by the Portuguese. In Malabar at a place called "Bareati" they worship an idol called "Patragaif" (Bhadra-Kali), who looks like a woman with a forelock and three eyes, the third being in the middle of her forehead. Her birthday is celebrated in November. Many of the lower castes worship at the sepulchre of their dead, which they build in front of their houses. Almost everybody worships a plant called "Colo" (Malayalam, *Kala-toolsie,* or the tulasi plant, holy basil) which they grow around their houses and temples. They revere another called "Barè," probably a form of borage called Darbha grass. [266] The Brahmans also have great reverence for the cow, since in its horns live the daughters of Siva, in its eyes the sun and moon, in its ears the two consorts of Brahma, in its tongue Siva himself, in its nostrils Vishnu, in its hide the "Ruxis" (rishis), and in its feet the four laws (Vedas). Its milk is ambrosia and its urine the "Tirta" (*tirtha*) which erases sins. If one meets a cow first thing in the morning it will be a happy day. This peaceful beast also keeps the peace among the other animals. Before their temples they even build stone and wooden images of cows. [267]

[263] "Hom" is Aum, or the sacred word of Hinduism, perhaps the symbol of the union of the three principal gods. This is one of the chief mantras used by all Hindus.

[264] *Op. cit.* (n. 198), pp. 297–99. He is somewhat confused in these designations. Fire is from Agni, ether from Akasa, water from Varuna, earth from Prithivi, and wind from Vayu.

[265] Possibly a reference to the Jain monks of the Digambara cult. On the Malabar map of H. A. Chatelain in his *Atlas historique* (Paris, 1719), a "Temple de Garagoli dette Matte" is shown in the interior of the kingdom of Cannanore.

[266] On Darbha grass see Dubois in Beauchamp (trans. and ed.), *op. cit.* (n. 126), pp. 651–52.

[267] Vincenzo, *op. cit.* (n. 198), pp. 299–303.

A few of India's many temples are tall, magnificent, and sumptuous structures, but usually their grandeur is confined to exterior decorations. Ordinary temples are low and unimpressive. In their interiors they are all dark, dirty, and reeking. The smoke from the lamps, the oil and butter smeared on the walls and on the idols, the cow dung on the floors, and the great number of worshippers combine to produce a stench.[268] While in Vengurla, Vincenzo was permitted to enter its main temple as well as two or three lesser ones, through the influence of his Dutch friends. All temples are maintained by returns from properties and alms. Particularly wealthy are the temples of "Trevilar" (Tiruvalla) with their incredible horde of gold and diamonds.[269] There is also a rich temple at Cranganore which is covered with gold.[270] At the ruins of another old temple it is still possible to see five iron boxes full of money. All worshippers, except the king, must remove their sandals or shoes before entering the temples. Conversation and spitting are prohibited. Each person must quietly and composedly await his turn to perform his devotions. Offerings to the idol are presented each morning; processions are almost always held at night.[271]

The Hindus, like all other peoples, solemnize certain days of the year in honor of their gods. Since the gods are many in India, festivals are numerous. Among the principal ones, the first is that of the New Year, called "Bericaeranze" (*Chaitramasam?*), that is to say, festival of the first day of the year.[272] On this occasion the Hindus congregate at the temple, light many lamps and fireworks, perform military exercises, and give fencing demonstrations. On the following nights all the houses are decorated with lights. Their second important festival occurs in March; it is dedicated to Brahma for the security from danger he provides.[273] The festival of "Shiverastir" (*Sivarātri*) or "Cwalateri" (*Kolathiri*), takes place in April. On this occasion they fast, sleep by day, and dance and stargaze at night. They are supposed to contemplate the greatness of the first cause as symbolized by huge representations of Brahma and Vishnu. The fourth festival, called "Biriva" (an epithet of Laksmi?), celebrates good fortune and the efficacy of augury. On that day superiors give gifts to inferiors. In June they celebrate "Pulentulela" (?), or the festival of snakes, an event that is dedicated to "Dessesù" (Sesha). Women offer the idol flowers and water, while Brahmans play music and

[268] *Cf.* the similar reaction of Dubois in Beauchamp (trans. and ed.), *op. cit.* (n. 126), p. 581.
[269] See below, pp. 1047–50.
[270] Possibly a reference to the temple of the Devi at Cranganore, or to the Sri Mahadevar temple of Ettumanoor, one of the richest temples in Kerala. See V. Meena, *Temples of South India* (Kanyakumari, n.d.), Nos. 46, 49.
[271] Vincenzo, *op. cit.* (n. 198), pp. 304–6.
[272] The Malayalis follow an agricultural year known as *Kollam Andu.* The first day of the year in this calendar falls in late August or early September. See P. V. Jagadisa Ayyar, *South Indian Festivities* (Madras, 1921), p. 67.
[273] Possibly a reference to the festival of *Meena Bharani.* See *ibid.*, pp. 128–29.

sing in the atrium of the temple.[274] The sixth, celebrated in August, is called "Onna" (*Onam*). It occurs on the day when Vishnu visits the earth. They remember his bounty by feasting and wearing new clothes. Soldiers put on a military display before the temple and receive the gift of a blanket from the prince.[275] Because the country abounds in wizards and magicians, they celebrate for nine days the festival of magic called "Churotnichnù" (?). They then display the image of a satyr with horns on its head, chinchilla-like teeth, and its whole body covered with hair. In December they celebrate "Kodieri" (*Kodiettam*), which goes on for nine days.[276] On the last day they hold a huge procession. Immediately after this festival, they have another dedicated to "Parani" (Bharani), the god of science or learning.[277] Aside from these principal festivals, many others are celebrated at particular temples and at other public places. While several on the list of Vincenzo's festivals are not readily identifiable by moderns, it should be remembered that popular names vary and practices change over time, and that India probably has more festivals than any other country.[278]

In their offerings to the gods the Malabars follow certain standard practices. For illnesses, particularly of the eyes, they offer rice flour with eggs and milk.[279] For good fortune at the beginning of a new project, they present coconuts. To obtain sons or to patch up marital relations, they offer uncooked rice and saffron. Of all their sacrifices, the most important is that of the fire called "Homù" (*Homam*). This sacrifice is made in one of three forms: lighting of odoriferous woods on an altar; shaking capsules of cinnamon, sandal, and other precious materials into the fire; or filling a trench with wood and giving to its fire some butter, oil, rice, honey, milk, sugar, bunches of flowers, and other sweet-smelling things. Once such a fire sacrifice is completed, those who have offered it give alms to the Brahmans who have chanted and sung while the rite was being performed. Blood sacrifices of animals, especially chickens, are made to obtain forgiveness of sins.[280] Prayers are short, but are repeated for a long time. Worshippers cover their foreheads with ashes of cow dung mixed with water as a sign they recognize the dependency of mortals on the three principal gods. For prevention of illnesses they apply ashes to other parts of the body as well.

The next acts of piety in importance are alms-giving and rigorous peni-

---

[274] Ordinarily called the Nagapanchami festival. On the snake cult in Malabar see Krishna Iyer, *op. cit.* (n. 224), II, 114–21. Sesha is the name of the great serpent on which Vishnu reclines.

[275] Today Onam is the most popular festival of the year in Kerala. See *ibid.*, II, 123–25.

[276] This is a flag-raising ceremony which inaugurates the festival of Navaratri.

[277] This is the *Bharani Kirthika Deepam,* in honor of Siva. It is held in South India at the full moon between mid-November and mid-December.

[278] Vincenzo, *op. cit.* (n. 198), III, 636–40.

[279] Eggs not probable, according to Cyriac Pullapilly.

[280] Only in Kali temples and ordinarily by the lower castes.

tence. In "Mogor" (Mughul Empire) and "Idalchan" (Bijapur) beggars commonly travel in groups seeking alms. But in Malabar and Kanara, such wandering bands are not seen, probably because the southern temples are more numerous, richer, and dedicated to charity. All comers receive rice and other edibles at these temples. But even more important are the public houses and hospitals called "Annasettra" (*Annakshetra*) or "Darmasetta" (*Dharmakshetra*) which provide food and shelter to those who need it.[281] The southern princes (Hindus) are generous in alms-giving and many people are fed at the numerous festivals of Malabar. Finally, food is more abundant in the south and the weather is so warm that clothes are not a necessity.

Yogis travel constantly and practice rigorous austerities. They undertake a fast called "Masa Vpasa" (*Māsa Upavāsa* or forty-day fast) which involves voluntary fasting from time to time over a period of several years.[282] At the end of October they put on fresh garments and fast until December 10. During this forty-day fast they chant and praise the gods and every day tour 101 times around the temple; the most devout do it 1,001 times. The following year, beginning on December 10, they fast again for forty days and carry out the same ceremonies. Successively each year thereafter they perform identical austerities until they have completed a fast totaling twelve months. By this means they believe that they receive divine grace and freedom from all sins.[283]

The Vedas, like the Decalogue, first of all command the worship of god. To make their daily devotions the Hindus need not actually go to the temple, for rocks, plants, and other objects may be given offerings as if they were visible deities. They often take the names of the gods in vain, even as we do in Europe, but they accept unquestioningly the tenets of their faith. Since religion is a simple given, they never debate about it among themselves. They respect and honor their parents by never sitting in their presence and by never speaking until spoken to. If punished by their parents they reverently kiss the hand which chastizes and never hold resentment. Homicide is a grave sin as in Europe. In India the murderer of a Brahman or a cow pays for his offense with his own life. While their commandments denounce sexual immorality, adultery is the only such transgression actually punished.[284]

There are many ways of obtaining forgiveness for breaking commandments. The first is to call out the name of "Naraim" (the holy names Nara and Narayana). The second is to think about and remember the gods. The third is to wash in a tank or sacred river. The fourth is to make a pilgrimage to the Ganges or to another sacred place. The most sacred of all places of

---

[281] Common rest and welfare houses, called *Samuhamadhams*, existed in the seventeenth century in every important village and town. See K. V. Krishna Ayyar, *A Short History of Kerala* (Ernakulam, 1966), p. 130.

[282] Twelve forty-day fasts (*Māsa Upavāsa*) in twelve years constitutes the *Maha Upavāsa*, or "Great Fast."

[283] Vincenzo, *op. cit.* (n. 198), pp. 311–12.

[284] Cf. Dubois in Beauchamp (trans. and ed.), *op. cit.* (n. 126), pp. 308–11.

pilgrimage is "Casson" (*Kāsī* or *Vārānasī*) in the mountains of the "Tauro" where there is a cliff named "Shibba" (Siva) which looks like the head of a cow. Here the Ganges has its origins.[285] Yogis often carry the ashes or relics of important persons to the Ganges.[286]

The Hindus believe that after death the soul separates from the body and is judged before Vishnu, who determines its fate; the souls of tyrants go into tigers, the false into wolves, the wanton into pigs, and the jealous into dogs. Generous souls go into elephants and the sincerely religious into cows. Since these beliefs prevail commonly, it is no wonder Hindus hold that every living thing has a rational soul and should not be molested or killed. Consequently, they protect snakes, ants, birds, and all the weaker animals. Those castes who eat cows are universally detested. In Cambay and elsewhere they have hospitals for animals and are more charitable to them than to humans. They pay ransoms to have hunters and foreigners release captured animals. They even permit animals to eat freely of their crops and sometimes plant especially for them.

Indians follow very specific death rites, especially the relatives of dying Brahmans. The Malabars and Kanarese bring a cow to the dying man. He squeezes its tail during his last throes thinking thereby to facilitate the soul's passage from his body. They divest the corpse of its old clothes and attire it in new apparel. They also provide it with gold and silver for the passage. Then they carry it to the burning ground called "Massana" (*Smasāna*). This field is especially set aside for this purpose, and is never cultivated. In the midst of the field they erect a column near which they burn the corpse. To display their grief the relatives sing and make loud noises. After the corpse has been consumed, they collect the ashes and other remains and carry them to the river. Some keep the ashes until they can be taken to the Ganges.

Hindus recognize heaven for reward and hell for punishment. All pain and happiness in the hereafter are purely physical, according to their beliefs. Vincenzo then goes on to repeat certain lengthy descriptions of the glories of heaven and the tortures of hell extracted from their books. Relatives mourn the dead person by sitting in front of his house for five days occasionally uttering sounds of bereavement. At the end of the mourning period they wash themselves and take an oath not to wear ornaments or jewels and to eat rice but once each day for one year. When Nayars die, the relatives mourn for sixteen days, eat only once each day, drink only coconut water, and sleep on the ground. All the other castes have their own death and mourning ceremonies and may not practice those followed by Brahmans and Nayars.[287]

---

[285] The Ganges originates above Gangotri in the Garhwal Himalayas. For the identity of *Kāsī* and *Vārānasī* see S. M. Bhardwaj, *Hindu Places of Pilgrimage in India* (Berkeley, 1973), p. 97.

[286] Vincenzo, *op. cit.* (n. 198), pp. 313–15. Today only relatives carry ashes.

[287] Vincenzo, *op. cit.* (n. 198), pp. 317–23. On the funeral ceremonies of Brahmans cf. Dubois in Beauchamp (trans. and ed.), *op. cit.* (n. 126), pp. 482–89, and E. Thurston, *Ethnographic Notes in Southern India* (2 parts; reprint of 1906 edition, New Delhi, 1975), I, 133–36.

5

Malabar and the Dutch

Admiral Steven van der Hagen led a VOC fleet to the Malabar Coast in 1604 as part of an early Dutch effort to undermine the Portuguese position in western India by establishing friendly relations with its native rulers. In November of that year he concluded an offensive and defensive alliance with the Zamorin, the aim of which was to drive the Portuguese out of India. While this early agreement failed to topple the Portuguese centered at Cochin, it did lay the basis for future joint action by the Dutch and the Zamorin. Over the next half century the agents of the VOC nibbled away at the Portuguese monopoly of the pepper trade by concluding contracts and agreements with those princes of Malabar, including the Zamorin, who were not regular in their pepper deliveries to the Portuguese at Cochin. Beginning in 1647 the Dutch began to establish factors at Kayankulam and at other of the southern Malabar ports. In 1650 they built a warehouse at Quilon as part of Batavia's new program designed to challenge directly the Portuguese control of Malabar's foreign trade by establishing permanent, fortified settlements of their own along its coast. Once the twelve-year truce with Goa expired in 1652, the VOC launched the military conquest of Ceylon and Malabar. Colombo fell to the Dutch in 1656 and two years later the remainder of Portuguese Ceylon. After a series of rebuffs, the Dutch completed their expeditions in Malabar by the capture of Cochin and Cannanore early in 1663.[288]

According to Tavernier, the Dutch, after their capture of Ceylon in 1658, raised the price of cinnamon so high that the merchants began to go to Cochin to buy its lower-priced wild cinnamon. To cut off this traffic the Dutch sent forces in 1662–63 to capture Cochin, many of whom were Sinhalese soldiers. The old queen of Cochin, a Portuguese puppet, was taken alive and placed in the custody of the Zamorin. In return for his cooperation the Zamorin was given Cranganore, but only after the Dutch had demolished all its fortifications. In cleaning up Cochin the Dutch were aided "by the Chinese who were in their service." The Dutch governor from Batavia places heavy taxes on food, drink, and tobacco, to the point that prices come to be double those obtaining under the Portuguese. The Dutch also have a bad reputation for treating with cruelty the mercenary soldiers in their employment, many of whom are banished to hard work in Ceylon for minor infractions. Escape from Cochin to Madras or Goa is made extremely difficult by a lack of easy overland routes, the ubiquitous leeches, and the unwillingness of the Hindus to house or feed polluting foreigners.[289]

[288] Based on Poonen, *op. cit.* (n. 200), chaps. ii and iii.
[289] Tavernier in Ball and Crooke (trans. and eds.), *op. cit.* (n. 42), I, 187–203.

In 1672, the same year as Vincenzo's *Viaggio,* there appeared at Amsterdam the *Naauwkeurige beschryvinge* of Philippus Baldaeus.[290] Divided into three parts, this large book deals with the personal experiences of the Dutch minister on the Malabar and Coromandel coasts and in Ceylon. In addition to his own observations, Baldaeus includes materials garnered from other European authors, the files of the VOC, and native informants. The third part, on the idolatry of the East Indian pagans, is Baldaeus' attempt to provide Europe with a rounded and systematic account of Hinduism in its south Indian form. This last part, along with the writings of Faria y Sousa, Abraham Roger, and Vincenzo, gave to European readers of the next two centuries a basis for understanding, or misunderstanding, many of the fundamental precepts and practices of Hinduism.[291]

While Baldaeus generally acknowledges his debt to published materials, he is not so scrupulous in giving credit to his manuscript sources.[292] The third part of his book, which has the separate title *Afgoderye der Oost-Indische heydenen,* is basically an unacknowledged translation of the manuscript *Livro da seita dos Indios Orientais* (1609) of Fenicio.[293] This Portuguese work, now kept in the British Library (Ms. Sloane 1820), was written by its Jesuit author to provide Catholic missionaries with an introduction to Hinduism and a handbook to consult in debating with the Brahmans and other learned

---

[290] *Naauwkeurige beschryvinge van Malabar en Choromandel . . .* (Amsterdam, 1672); for bibliographical details and a brief synopsis of this encyclopedic publication see above, pp. 493–95.

[291] On Roger's work see below, pp. 1029–57. The original Dutch edition of Baldaeus was translated into English in the eighteenth century as *A True and Exact Description of the Most Celebrated East India Coast of Malabar and Coromandel as also of the Isle of Ceylon . . . Also a most Circumstantial and Compleat Account of the Idolatry of the Pagans in the East Indies . . . With the Draughts of their Idols, Done After their Originals.* It is included in *CV* (3d ed., 6 vols.; London, 1744–46), III, 509–793. A verbatim comparison of the original and the Churchill translation reveals that the translation is generally faithful and accurate. The discrepancies which occur are mainly minor omissions or precise summaries. Allusions to classical European authorities, as well as to Christian theologians and their controversies, are sometimes omitted totally or reduced in number. Comparisons of Hindu beliefs with non-Indian religions, as well as the moralistic asides of the preacher-author, are generally dropped, cut, or briefly summarized. There are occasional misprints, especially of numbers, and a few translation inaccuracies. One, at least, of the original engravings has not been reproduced. Since the English version is full and accurate, in what follows our references are generally to this translation, interspersed with occasional references to the critical edition by A. J. de Jong (ed.), *Afgoderye der Oost-Indische Heydenen . . .* (The Hague, 1917). On the sources of the Baldaeus illustrations see Partha Mitter, *Much Maligned Monsters* (Oxford, 1977), pp. 297–98, n. 277.

[292] He cites a number of sixteenth-century published works from Varthema to Linschoten, as well as a number of European authors of the first half of the seventeenth century. But he is especially dependent on Pedro Teixeira, *Relaciones de Pedro Teixeira d'el origin, descendencia y succession de los reyes de Persia y de Harmuz* (Antwerp, 1610); Jan (Johan) van Twist, *Generale beschrijvinge van Indien* (Amsterdam, 1648); Abraham Roger, *De open-deure tot het verborgen heydendom* (Leyden, 1651); D. Godefridus Carolinus, *Het hedendaagsche heidendom, of beschrijving van de godtsdienst der heidenen* (Amsterdam, 1661); A. Kircher, *China . . . illustrata* (Antwerp, 1667). For a complete rundown of his published sources see the introduction to De Jong (ed.), *op. cit.* (n. 291).

[293] On Fenicio at Calicut, see above, pp. 874–76, 886.

Indians. Fenicio's was but one of several such guides to Hinduism prepared by the missionaries of the seventeenth century.[294] By one route or the other, Fenicio's manual fell into the hands of Faria y Sousa,[295] of Philip Angel (a Dutch artist), and of Baldaeus. The Dutch preacher apparently supplemented the Fenicio manuscript he used with materials on the avatars of Vishnu taken almost word-for-word from an anonymous Dutch manuscript (Sloane 3290). Possibly Baldaeus' only original contributions to the *Afgoderye* are some of his descriptions of Hindu customs and temples.[296]

Baldaeus' account of Hinduism, even though mainly derivative, is a systematic review of the Siva and Vishnu traditions and of a number of the stories and beliefs connected with each. The "Ixora" (*Īśvara* or Siva) legend begins with the egg story of the world's creation. Once the egg was broken and the world begun, a triangular substance called "Quivelinga" (*Śivalinga*) stood on the mountain named "Calaga" (*Kailāsa*). The "Quivelinga," or the "members of generation of both sexes," is the divinity called "Ixoretta" (*Īśvaratā*), the "original of all created things." According to the Brahmans, this infinite figure was transmuted into the three primary gods—Brahma, Vishnu, and Siva—who were commissioned to rule the world as viceroys. Siva resides in "Calaga," Vishnu in the sea of milk, and Brahma in "Sattialogam" (*Satyaloka*) or the highest place in heaven.[297]

"Ixora" (Siva) is as "bright and white as milk," with three eyes, the third of which is in the middle of the forehead. Everything the third eye looks at is consumed by its fire. "Ixora" is gigantic and has no fewer than sixteen

---

[294] For example, *cf.* the more elaborate work of the Benedictine Clemente Tosi, *Dell' India orientale descrittione geografica et historica . . . con la confutatione, dell' idolatrie, superstitioni, et altro loro errori* (2 vols.; Rome, 1669). It is designed to help missionaries refute heathen beliefs throughout Asia and was probably prepared at the behest of the Propaganda. It was reprinted in 1676 with a slightly different title: *L'India orientale. . . .* Most of the Jesuit handbooks, like that of Fenicio, apparently circulated only in manuscript.

[295] In the *Asia portuguesa* (3 vols.; Lisbon, 1666–75) of Manuel de Faria y Sousa (1590–1649) there is an important description of the religions of India, Ethiopia, Japan, China, Ceylon, and the St. Thomas Christians. The author, with Fenicio as his source, uses the Hinduism of Malabar to "inform us of the Religion and Government of all the rest [of India]." Consult the modern edition of Manuel Perusquets de Aguilar (trans.), *Asia Portuguesa por Manuel de Faria e Sousa* (6 vols.; Porto, 1945–47), IV, 215–67. A comparison of the materials on Hinduism in the original with the English translation by John Stevens, *The Portugues Asia* (3 vols.; London, 1694–95), II, 375–411, reveals that Stevens omits sentences and proper names, sometimes for no apparent reason. He does convey, however, the general sense of the original description. We have preferred Baldaeus' description, since the Dutchman had actually visited Malabar whereas the Portuguese author had worked exclusively in Iberia. Baldaeus' rendition is also much more complete than that of Faria y Sousa. For more on Faria y Sousa see above, pp. 354–55.

[296] For a detailed comparison of the Fenicio and Baldaeus texts see Charpentier, *op. cit.* (n. 152), pp. lxxxiii–lxxxv. On Angel's role see Mitter, *op. cit.* (n. 291), pp. 57–58. Also see Wicki, *loc. cit.* (n. 144), pp. 545–52, who makes the additional point that Diogo Gonçalves' manuscript *Historia do Malavar* (1615), preserved in the Roman Archives of the Society of Jesus (Codex Goa 58), is an independent work, even though some earlier scholars thought that it, too, was derived from Fenicio.

[297] See Baldaeus in *CV* (1744–46 ed.), III, 734–35; De Jong (ed.), *op. cit.* (n. 291), pp. 3–6. And on *Kailāsa* see *ibid.*, pp. 213–14.

hands, which hold "a heart, chain, fiddle, bell, a porcelain basin, Brahma's head, a trident, rope, axe, fire, gold, a drum, beads, staff, iron wheel, and a serpent with a crescent on its forehead." He wears a tiger skin, a cloak of elephant hide, and a collar of leather from the animal called "Maudega" (Sanskrit, *mandha?*, meaning gazelle), on which a bell hangs of the sort put on buffaloes. Around his neck he also has three chains.[298]

"Ixora" has two wives: "Grienga" (*Gaṅgā*), goddess of the seas, and "Chagtti" (*Śakti*) who is also called "Paramesceri" (*Parameśvara?*). This second wife dies and revives once each year; when she dies her husband takes one of her bones to put into the chains around his neck. The attendants of "Ixora" are called "Pudas" (*Bhūta*, or wandering souls), "Pixaros" (*Piśāca* or monsters), and "Pes" (Tamil, *Pey*, the equivalent of Sanskrit, *Bhūta*).[299] A "Puda" is represented as a short, fat person with a large paunch and with serpents hanging down from his head. On his left arm he wears a bracelet and on his thighs two rings of serpents. In his right hand he carries a staff. The "Pixaros" and "Pes" are presented as being much taller, and they hold torches in their hands which are lighted at night. "Ixora" is a destroyer and he has imparted part of himself to his wife "Paramesceri," otherwise "Parvati" (*Pārvatī*), and she has given of herself to him. Thus in some dispensations they are thought to be hermaphrodites and are sometimes represented as such. Certain Brahmans called "Tirimpini" (Tamil, *Tiru?* or ascetics) are set apart in that they refuse to look at women and are often escorted through the streets by persons who tell women to move out of the way.[300]

The residence of "Ixora" is on the silver mount *Kailāsa* just to the south of the famous mountain called "Mahameru" (*Mahāmeru*, Mount Meru). In an adjacent forest live "Mumis" (*muni*, or wisemen) or "Rixis" (rishis, or sages) who spend their time offering daily sacrifices to their gods. Inside the mountain there live "Jexacquinnera" (*Yakṣa Kiṃnara*, or heavenly spirits) and "Quendra" (*Gandharva*, or other heavenly spirits), who are trouble free and spend their days contemplating and praising the gods. In a contest over primacy among the three principal gods, a story sung by many of the Malabar poets, "Ixora" cuts off one of Brahma's four heads. To atone for the grave offense of killing a Brahman, "Ixora" becomes a mendicant for twelve years. During this period of penitence he is attacked by the "Mumis." From these contests "Ixora" acquired many of the trophies he customarily holds in his hands. Ultimately he was released from his mendicancy by Vishnu.

"Ixora" fathered three sons and one daughter. The eldest named "Quena-

---

[298] For the engraving which illustrates this description see pl. 150. For the textual description see *CV* (1744–46 ed.), III, p. 735.

[299] See the article on devil worship in Yule and Burnell, *op. cit.* (n. 37), p. 308.

[300] *CV* (1744–46 ed.), III, 735–36. Baldaeus injects this comment here, followed by a quotation from Roger on the *Sannyasi*. Siva and Sakti unite to form the hermaphrodite called *Ardhanārīśvara*. See Daniélou, *op. cit.* (n. 127), p. 203.

vady" (*Gaṇapati,* also called Ganesha) has the hands, feet, and face of an elephant because his parents imitated elephants in their copulation. Since this son was castrated by "Ixora," elephants are born without testicles. "Quenavady," considered to be voracious and insatiable, is worshipped by artisans and workers. "Quenavady" curses the moon on August 4 and so the Malabars will not go outdoors on this evening or on the next day for fear of suffering from this curse. The third son, "Superbennia" (*Subrahmaṇya*), has six faces and twelve arms, and he rides a peacock. The second son, the true god called "Egasourubum" (a deity whose name seems to be composed of *eka* [eleven] and *sura* [?],[301] is represented with an elephant's head and eleven hands. He is supposed to be worshipped only by Brahmans, though others make offerings to him also. Next to him stands "Ceuxci" (?) who has an elephant's head and two hands. Another son of "Ixora," named "Siri Hanuman" (Sri Hanumant), was born as an ape because his parents were imitating apes when he was conceived.[302] Many odd stories are told about him in the fable of Rama, and many temples are dedicated to him.[303]

"Patragali Pagodi" (*Bhadrakāli*),[304] the daughter of "Ixora," is shown with eight faces, sixteen hands black as coal, and teeth like the tusks of a boar. To avenge her father, "Patragali" cut off the head of "Darida" (*Daridrā*), the goddess of poverty. This vengeful daughter is also responsible for spreading smallpox to the people. They propitiate her in behalf of the sick. Her chief residence is in the great temple of Cranganore, to which pilgrims flock.[305] The "king" of Cochin sends soldiers to rob and prey upon the pilgrims. When the father and mother of "Patragali" were shipwrecked and lost all their riches, she sent her husband out to sell her golden footrings. A traitorous goldsmith of Pandy robbed and killed her husband. In searching for her husband, "Patragali" has nine famous adventures. Once she located her husband's body, "Patragali" called in "Raxaxos" (*rākṣasa,* or evil spirits) to avenge his death.[306]

Vishnu, the second in rank among the gods, has two wives: "Leximi" (*Laksmī*) and "Pumi Divi" (*Bhūmidevī*), the goddess of the earth. In presenting the avatars of Vishnu, Baldaeus compares and supplements Fenicio's account with materials from Kircher's *China illustra* (Pt. 3, ch. vi), which had been sent from India to Rome by the Jesuit Heinrich Roth, and from the list of Abraham Roger.[307] Baldaeus, like Fenicio, is more concerned than

---

[301] See De Jong (ed.), *op. cit.* (n. 291), p. 229.

[302] Hanumant was the son of Vayu, god of the wind, and Anjana, a celestial maiden.

[303] *CV* (1744–47 ed.), III, 736–41. Many more details on the sons of Siva are included in the original version of Baldaeus' book than are found in the English translation. For a portrait of "Quenavady" (Ganesha) see our pl. 151.

[304] On the use of the word "Pagodi" in connection with the names of idols see Yule and Burnell, *op. cit.* (n. 37), pp. 652–57.

[305] This shrine of Kali still exists. See Padmanabhan Menon, *op. cit.* (n. 4), p. 133.

[306] *CV.*(1744–46 ed.), III, 741–44. This shipwreck story has nothing to do with Bhadrakali. It derives from the *Silapadhikāram,* a Tamil classic.

[307] *Cf.* below, p. 1046; also pl. 152.

Roger or Kircher with the stories connected with the avatars, and is less intent upon determining their exact number and names. Like Roger, he tries to relate Vishnu's transformation to the Indian eras. The first avatar, for example, "now stood 250,000 years." Of the ten transformations of Vishnu, nine have already been accomplished.

First of all, Vishnu materialized as a fish, specifically as a shark to rescue the four law books which had been stolen and dropped into the sea. The fish is named "Mat" or "Mathia" (*Matsya*), but the "Banians" and Malabars call it "Zecsis" (Sanskrit, *Jhasa?*, or sea monster). The first of the recovered Vedas "treats of the souls of the blessed, second of the vagabond souls, third of good works, and fourth of bad works." Although Roger reports that the fourth Veda is lost, Baldaeus is not convinced that it really is. He consulted a "certain Brahman who coming from Bangala, settled at Jaffnapatam" about Roger's book, the last Veda, and the avatars of Vishnu.[308]

Vishnu in his second transformation appears as a tortoise in order to raise "Mahameru" (Mount Meru) from the sea. Baldaeus gives at length the story of the tortoise current in the south, which he has drawn from Fenicio.[309] In discussing the third transformation, into a hog, Baldaeus gives both the north and south Indian traditions.[310] He follows this with the strange story of "Agassia" (Agastya, a rishi or sage). Once Vishnu rescued the earth from the sea, "Agassia" restored its balance. To prevent a future disaster of this sort, Vishnu ordered the great serpent "Sisnage" (Seshanaga) to wind itself about the seven worlds and seven seas. And he appointed eight guardians to watch over the earth whom the Malabars call "Indra," king of the celestial spirits; "Vanni" (*Vahni* or *Agni*), god of fire; "Pidurpati" (*Pidurpati* or *Yama*), king of the evil spirits; "Nirurdi" (*Nirṛtī*), king of the infernal spirits; "Varunna" (*Varuṇa*), the god of the sea; "Marel" (*Marut* or *Vayu*), the god of the winds; "Cubera" (*Kubera*), the god of riches, otherwise called "Bassirouem" (*Vaiśravana*); "Ixanonam" (Siva as governor of *Īśa* or *Īśāna*) or "Ixora" (Siva) himself.[311]

In his fourth avatar Vishnu appears as half man and half lion.[312] Associated with this incarnation is the story of the giant "Renaicran" (Hiranyakasipu) who made himself master of the whole earth and ordained that nobody else should be worshipped. This story is told in many ancient works and Baldaeus tries to indicate some of the differences between its south and north Indian versions.[313]

In his fifth transformation Vishnu assumes the form of a dwarf Brahman

---

[308] *CV* (1744–46 ed.), III, 745–46. See pl. 158.
[309] For an engraving of the tortoise avatar see pl. 159.
[310] For an engraving see pl. 160.
[311] *CV* (1744–46 ed.), III, 748–49. Siva, as the ruler *Īśāna*, is the All-Enjoyer. See Daniélou, *op. cit.* (n. 127), p. 104.
[312] For an engraving see pl. 161.
[313] On the story of the man-lion see Daniélou, *op. cit.* (n. 127), pp. 168–69. Also see pl. 155.

called "Vanam" (*Vāmana,* or dwarf). "Mavaly" (*Mahabali*), called "Bebragie" (*Baliraja*) by the "Banians," was the great king who provided men with all their needs and erased poverty. Vishnu as the dwarf-priest tricked him and took over the rule of heaven, earth, and the nether regions. The great god in return permitted "Mavaly" to act as doorkeeper of paradise from which station he overlooks the earth.[314] Then Vishnu divided mankind into rich, poor, and middle classes, "which were to have a reciprocal dependence on one another." He also founded the feast of "Ona" (*Onam*) celebrated in August.[315]

In his sixth incarnation Vishnu appears as "Camdoga" (*Kāmadughā*), the cow of plenty. Related to this transformation is the story of the Brahman and his wife who could not have children. Vishnu gives them three descendants: "Reneca" (*Renukā*), "Siamdichemi" (*Jamadagni*), and "Prassararam" (*Paraśu-Rāma*), son of the first two offspring. "Reneca" was jealous of the wife of a great raja. Vishnu as "Cambdoga" provides entertainment for the raja and his court. The Malabars say that in this avatar Vishnu took the form of "Siri Parexi Rama" (*Sri Paraśu Rāma*).[316]

Vishnu becomes Rama in his seventh avatar. Baldaeus then goes on, following Roger's account, to give the Rama story in considerable detail.[317] In his eighth incarnation Vishnu appears as "Kisna" (Krishna), the cowherder. Roger had given this story in a very abbreviated form,[318] but Baldaeus, following Fenicio, provides an accurate and detailed version of this famous tale which is of more than passing interest to modern students of Indian literature.[319] This avatar, in Baldaeus' opinion, "is accounted of the greatest moment above the rest; for . . . in all the others Vistnum [Vishnu] appeared in the world with some part of his divinity; but in doing this he carried with him the whole substance of it so that he left his place vacant in heaven." In what follows an account is given of Krishna's parents, birth, education, and marriage. Many of his "miracles" are related, until finally, his work on earth being completed, Krishna returns to heaven.[320]

The ninth incarnation is that of "Boudha" or "Bodhe" (Buddha). He came into this world with neither father nor mother. He is ordinarily invisible, but in his rare appearances he is shown with four arms.[321] In Vishnu's

---

[314] Vishnu allowed Mavali to visit his kingdom once each year. Mavali's annual visit is celebrated as *Onam.*

[315] *CV* (1744–46 ed.), III, 749–52. Cf. the myth of the dwarf incarnation in Daniélou, *op. cit.* (n. 127), pp. 169–70. For an engraving see pl. 162.

[316] *CV* (1744–46 ed.), III, 752–54. For an engraving see pl. 163. This story of Renuka is partial and confused. Renuka is ordinarily presented as the wife of Jamadagni and the mother of Parasu-Rama. See Daniélou, *op. cit.* (n. 127), p. 172.

[317] *CV* (1744–46 ed.), III, 755–62. For an engraving of the ten-headed Ravana see pl. 164.

[318] See below, p. 1046.

[319] De Jong (ed.), *op. cit.* (n. 291), p. lxvi.

[320] *CV* (1744–46 ed.), III, 762–81. For an engraving called "The Deliverance of Kishna" see pl. 165.

[321] See pl. 166.

final transformation, which has not yet taken place, he will materialize as a white horse. Balancing itself on three legs, the horse will stamp the earth with its raised leg and bring an end to the world. Once this happens, the first era will begin again, "for it is observable, that all the eastern pagans believe [in] the eternity of the world."[322]

Following a summary of the Hindu cosmology and a comparison of the general Indian conceptions of creation and transmigration with those held by the believers of other religions, Baldaeus gives a brief account of Hindu daily religious rites.[323] He notes that the temples of Malabar are most commonly built of marble covered with copper and adorned "with balls gilt on the top." Aside from purification rites performed either inside or outside the temple, the Hindu avoids pollution and sin by following a series of rules: never touch inferiors, a dead body, a woman in childbirth, a newborn child, a menstruating woman, or anyone who is polluted. It is a mortal sin to eat unpurified rice or rice prepared by an inferior, or to have sexual intercourse with a woman of low extraction. Pollution also occurs if Brahmans eat with one another or consume leftover rice. Baldaeus gives a few details on the ceremonies observed and the formulas repeated in performing ablutions. He lists their fast days: "Egadexi" (*Ekādaśī*), or the eleventh day after the full moon; "Quiverasiri" (*Śivarātri*), or Siva's night, in February; "Tirinadira" (*Tirivadira*), kept by women only, on December 27, commemorating the death of "Canteven" (*Kāmedēva*), the god of love who was killed by Siva;[324] and "Masaupasa" (*Māsaupavāsa*) a Vishnu fast held on the last day of October. Baldaeus disdains talking about suttee, "that most barbarous custom of some of these pagans."[325]

Like Vincenzo, Baldaeus regards Cannanore as the best state of Malabar. The finest pepper comes from there, as well as small quantities of bezoar stone, saltpeter, and lac. At Cannanore the Dutch sell opium, textiles, fine spices, metals, and "coarse porcelains." Opium is used frequently by the Nayars when they go to battle. The residence of the "king" of Cannanore is in the interior up the "Balipatan" (Balliapatam) river. His state extends from "Montedely" (Mount Deli) in the north to "Bergera" (Badagara) in the south. Its port city of Cannanore is populated mainly by rich Muslims who previously traded with Surat and the ports of the Red Sea. "Termapatan" (Trangapatam), south of Cannanore city, is ruled by a Muslim and is protected on its land side by a "good wall." There are many pirates at "Bergera" who sell passports to those wishing to traffic in the waters of Cannanore.

---

[322] *CV* (1744–46 ed.), III, 782–83. See pl. 167. Baldaeus observes that dark-skinned Indians seem "to have a peculiar esteem for the white colour," as in white cow, elephant, and now horse.

[323] *CV* (1744–46 ed.), III, 785–89. These routines are related more clearly and accurately by Roger. See below, pp. 1041–43.

[324] Tirivadira is the day Siva danced the cosmic dance; it does not commemorate Siva's killing of Kamadeva.

[325] *CV* (1744–46 ed.), III, 784–93. On fasting and fast days *cf.* Dubois in Beauchamp (trans. and ed.), *op. cit.* (n. 126), pp. 269–72.

This information is followed by a lengthy account of the Dutch efforts to evict the Portuguese from the fortress of Cannanore, which they finally succeeded in doing in 1663–64.[326]

Calicut, the second state of Malabar, extends from just south of "Bergera" to the river of Cranganore. In 1662 Baldaeus saw its Zamorin, the most powerful of the independent rulers of Malabar. Not above fifty years of age, the Zamorin suffers mentally from his excessive use of opium. In 1607 the Dutch had inaugurated negotiations with Calicut at "Panane" (Ponnani), following the alliance Steven van der Hagen had concluded with the Zamorin three years before. The Dutch also sought the support of Cranganore, whose ruler was enemy to both Calicut and the Portuguese. In December, 1661, the Dutch captured "Coulang" (Quilon) and immediately undertook the siege of Cranganore. Baldaeus participated in these actions, and after the takeover of Cranganore on January 15, 1662, went ashore to preach a sermon of thanksgiving. He mentions that Cranganore was once the seat of a Roman archbishop and the site of a Jesuit college and library.[327]

The capture of Quilon and Cranganore were necessary preliminaries to the Dutch attack on Cochin, the Portuguese stronghold lying in between. In 1662 the Dutch built a fort on Ypin Island prior to their two sieges (1662–63) of Cochin, a town not nearly as large as Batavia. In connection with these sieges and the town's final capitulation, most Portuguese churches and buildings were destroyed by the Dutch. The church and monastery of the Franciscans was the only sizable Catholic building to remain standing. But, since many Dutchmen were also Catholics, the VOC, while determined to eliminate Portuguese-Jesuit influence root and branch, took a somewhat more benign attitude towards the non-Portuguese Catholics and the St. Thomas Christians. The Carmelite Giuseppe de Santa Maria was treated kindly by the Dutch before his return to Rome. Baldaeus was delighted to learn about the St. Thomas Christians and to advise the VOC on how to handle them. Baldaeus also had an audience with the "king" of Porka, a man of about twenty-four years of age, in 1664.[328] The English had a factory at Porka which the Dutch were intent upon shutting down as part of their effort to monopolize the trade of Malabar.[329]

Baldaeus' Dutch contemporary, Johann Nieuhof (1618–72), was also involved in the conquest of Malabar by Van Goens and the forces of the VOC. After the capture of Quilon in 1661, Nieuhof was appointed its governor, a post he occupied continuously for the next two years. After a stay at Tuticorin in 1664–65, he was recalled for another brief stint of service at Quilon. Thereafter he was in Colombo for more than one year before re-

---

[326] *CV* (1744–46 ed.), III, 563–65. Includes an engraving of the Cannanore fort.

[327] *Ibid.*, pp. 565–68.

[328] *Ibid.*, pp. 569–82. See engravings of Cranganore and Quilon.

[329] At this point, the Dutch sought exclusive control over the import of opium and the export of pepper. See Poonen, *op. cit.* (n. 200), p. 33.

turning to Batavia. No longer in the service of the VOC, Nieuhof nonethe-less spent the next three years in Java before returning to Holland in 1670. Here he turned over the papers and documents relating to his voyages to his brother Hendrik, and shortly sailed for the East again. He disappeared with a landing party on Madagascar in 1672. His brother put his voluminous notes and papers together in reasonable form and in 1682 published the *Zee-en Lant-reize door verscheide gewesten van Oost-indien* as Part II of *Gedenkwaer-dige zee- en lant-reizen* (Amsterdam).[330]

Nieuhof's account is particularly valuable for the light it sheds on Quilon and the petty states in its environs. The city of "Kolany" (Kollam or Qui-lon) is divided like most Portuguese outposts on India's west coast into a "Malabar" or native town and a Portuguese town closer to the sea. In the upper or inner city called "Colang China" by the Portuguese the king and queen of the state of Quilon ordinarily reside. Portuguese or lower Quilon clusters around an extremely strong fortress "built some hundred years ago by the famous engineer Hector de la Costa." When the Dutch took Quilon they razed its seven Portuguese churches and the Franciscan and Jesuit resi-dences while leaving untouched the church of the St. Thomas Christians. Nieuhof himself occupied the castle of the Portuguese governor and super-intended its repairs. Quilon is built at the mouth of the "Kalchan" (Kallada?) or "Mangal" (Manali?) river about four miles away from the great river "Eguick" (Achenkoil?), both of which waterways often flood the flatlands during the rainy season. In the bay of Quilon are "three vast rocks laying altogether in a ridge."

While the Dutch besieged Cochin at the end of 1662, its deposed king called "Momadavil" (the *Mūtta Tāvali* prince) stayed with Nieuhof at Qui-lon.[331] While in Nieuhof's charge, the prince became ill and died. The Dutch turned to his brother as his legitimate successor, and in 1663 crowned him king of Cochin with a "crown which was of gold having the cypher of the East India Company graven on its side." As Dutch rule of Malabar became centered at Cochin, Nieuhof was delegated by James Hustaert, then the governor of Malabar, with the delicate task of negotiating alliances with the queen of Quilon and the rulers of neighboring regions in southern-most India.[332]

On January 21, 1664, Nieuhof began making his assigned rounds. On his way to Porka (Purakkad) the Dutch emissary received a friendly reception at "Kalkolang" (Kayankulam). He then proceeded to Porka, whose king is "a person of 39 years of age, very stately and well made." His territory is bor-

[330] For bibliographical details see above, pp. 500–501. An English translation of the India portion may be found in "Mr. John Nieuhoff's Remarkable Voyages and Travels to the East Indies," in *CV* (1744–46 ed.), II, 203–50.

[331] This was Vira Kerala Varma of the Mutta Tavali branch of the Cochin royal family whom the Portuguese had deposed in 1646. He had immediately fled to Colombo to seek Dutch help in regaining his throne. See Poonen, *op. cit.* (n. 200), p. 27.

[332] Nieuhof in *CV* (1744–46 ed.), II, 203–10.

dered on the north by Cochin, on the south by "Kalkolang," and on the northeast by "Takken Berkenkar" (Tekkumkur and Vadakkumkur). Over his territories this prince is an absolute ruler "acknowledging no superior, every foot of the country being his own, and at his disposal." He administers justice and punishes theft most severely. Roman Catholicism was introduced in 1590 "though St. Thomas Christians had long been here." When Nieuhof first arrived, the king was out of the city at his palace called "Kudda Malair" (Kudamalur?) near a village of St. Thomas Christians. This palace, in process of being constructed over a period of twenty years, is described in some detail. The "king" receives the Dutch favorably and orders the English to leave. He refuses, however, the request to visit Hustaert in Cochin, although he agrees to meet the Dutch governor at any time or place in his own territories. Nieuhof himself returned to Porka in February to complete these negotiations. On this occasion the king refuses to have his pepper weighed at Cochin, but expresses a willingness to reach an agreement on pepper deliveries to the Dutch at Porka. Once Porka is clearly subservient to the Dutch, Nieuhof observes that its chief strength now lies in its ability to muster large numbers of boats for transportation when the fields and roads are flooded and impassable.[333]

In February, 1664, Nieuhof visits Marta (Marutukulannara) just south of Porka. Here the Dutch emissary ran into resistance from Muslim merchants who opposed the Dutch efforts to monopolize the trade of Marta. Its raja, a prince of about sixty years of age, resides at "Carnopoly" (Karunagapalli). Marta is almost as large as "Kalkolang." It controls the port called "Panderatoutle" (Pantaratturuttu) by the natives and "Pesse" (Peza) by the Portuguese, the town where the Dutch finally set up a factory with the "king's" consent. Another city belongs to Marta called "Maulikara" (Mavelikkara), while other places are owned jointly by Marta and "Kalkolang," "a thing not usual on this coast." In 1581 Roman Christians had been permitted by its ruler to work in Marta, long a stronghold of St. Thomas Christians.

From "Carnopoly" Nieuhof goes on to "Attingen" (Attingal), the seat of the raja of Travancore. On February 12 he meets with the chief official of the Travancore court who wants "Gondormo" (*Gōdavarma*), the fugitive "king" of Cochin, to be recognized by the Dutch as a member in good standing of Cochin's ruling family. While Travancore resists the Dutch proposal of an alliance, Nieuhof observes his surroundings in Attingal, a city which has "hitherto not been describ'd by any that I know." He comments on the red soil of Travancore and its terraced rice culture.[334] To the east Travancore is bordered by Madura and to the west by "Peretaly" (Perakattavali) and "Allage" (Alwaye?). In all it boasts twenty-nine great cities and villages, the most important of which are in the interior and the most famous of which is

---

[333] *Ibid.*, pp. 210–12; also see Poonen, *op. cit.* (n. 200), pp. 50–51.
[334] The soils of this region are red and lateritic and comprised of clay and sand. See Ghose *et al.*, *op. cit.* (n. 204), p. 30.

"Paru" (Parur, now Paravur), the seat of the queen of "Singnaty" (Desinganad). Many of its villages are peopled by Muslims or by members of the fisher caste.[335]

"Kalkolang" (Kayankulam) is a very large city in a relatively large territory. Situated on a high hill, it is inland three leagues (twelve miles) from Tengapatam and twelve (forty-eight miles) from Quilon. On the east it is protected from Madura, its neighbor, by inaccessible mountains and on the west it is fortified by a wall. Its ruler maintains a garrison of ten thousand men to keep Madura at arm's length. The royal commanders are called "Mandigals" (*manthrikals*, or ministers), and the councillors are known as "Pullas" (*pulas*). The land is watered by the "Mannikorin" (*Mannikudi?*) river, and it produces the best cinnamon grown in Malabar.

By March, 1664, Nieuhof had managed by promises, gifts, and threats of war to create a federated alliance which included Quilon, Marta, "Singnaty," "Goernu" (Kumdara), Travancore, and "Barrigetta Pule" (the Pula of Bariatla or Barrigate). By its terms they agreed to grant a trade monopoly to the Dutch with deliveries at fixed prices and without payment of customs. While Quilon and Travancore balked for a time on the issue of customs, Nieuhof left his post at Quilon to his successor in good condition and departed on good terms with the queen of Quilon and the other local rulers.[336]

Following the account of Nieuhof's diplomatic mission, there is included in this work a substantial dissertation on Malabar's location, peoples, ceremonies, and products. These generalized statements seem to have been extracted almost entirely from earlier European descriptions, perhaps by Nieuhof's brother. Certainly many statements, names, and facts in this section either contradict or fail to relate to the materials furnished in the account of the mission. The description of the mourning ceremonies followed after the death of a Malabar king repeats almost word for word that written by Duarte Barbosa in 1503, or about 175 years earlier.[337] The generalizations about Brahmans, Nayars, and especially "Mohammedan Malabars" have evidently been pieced together from earlier European accounts, especially that of Pyrard de Laval.[338] The same seems also to be true of the long list of flora and fauna native to the region. In brief, the account of Nieuhof's mission is original, reliable, and informative; the remainder of the materials on Malabar appear to be mainly derivative and clearly add very little to what can readily be found in earlier European accounts. There are a few exceptions to this generalization, one of the most significant being Nieuhof's description of the "Malleans" (Malayars, or hill people).[339] While Purchas had

[335] *CV* (1744–46 ed.), II, 212–16; also see Poonen, *op. cit.* (n. 200), pp. 51–55.

[336] *CV* (1744–46 ed.), II, 216–20; also see Poonen, *op. cit.* (n. 200), pp. 55–57.

[337] *CV* (1744–46 ed.), II, 220–44. Compare p. 228 with M. L. Dames (trans. and ed.), *The Book of Duarte Barbosa* (2 vols.; London, 1918, 1921), II, 12–15.

[338] Much of the material on the Brahmans and Muslims of Malabar is taken from Pyrard's account. See above, pp. 880–86.

[339] *CV* (1744–46 ed.), II, 231; also see Padmanabha Menon, *op. cit.* (n. 4), III, 525–26.

included a Jesuit description of these people in his 1626 collection, the account of them in Nieuhof is certainly different and appears to be original. He notes that their center is in a region called "Priata" (?), which is a plateau near the boundary of Madura; there they also have a Christian church. While this is an important exception to the rule, certainly students of Indian or Malabar history should not unquestioningly accept as primary the assertions made in these pages.[340]

Scholars should also notice that the materials on Goa and Malabar attached to the 1666 travels of Jean de Thévenot are only in the slightest degree personal observations and recollections. Rather, these accounts appear to be based in large measure on what he learned about the south from informants in other parts of India. His two engravings, "Malabar Cyphers" and "Malabar Alphabet" (see pls. 139–41) might have been acquired at Surat or elsewhere in the north, where Thévenot spent much more time. At any rate, though he claims to have been in Cochin, Thévenot's accounts of Goa and Malabar add nothing substantial, except for the engravings of the Tamil characters, to what was readily available elsewhere in Europe.[341] In brief, the general materials on Goa and Malabar in the works of Nieuhof and Thévenot should be utilized as sources for seventeenth-century history only with the clear understanding that they are basically derivative, though in different ways. Nieuhof's essay appears to have been put together in Europe, possibly from some of his personal papers, and certainly from already published accounts; Thévenot seems to have gathered materials himself from printed works and from informants in north India, which his editors in Europe possibly rounded out with materials garnered from other literary sources.

In 1685 Gabriel Dellon published his *Relation* in Paris; this deals for the most part with what he did and saw on the west coast of India while in the service of the French East India Company.[342] The youthful Dellon had arrived at Surat in 1670, just three years after the establishment of the first French factory there. He was one among the French pioneers sent to the Malabar coast by François Caron to secure a footing for the Company in its commercial centers. Dellon's group, headed by François de Flacourt, the company's chief on the Malabar coast, was first located at "Baliepatan" (Balliapatam) within the territory controlled by "Prince Onriti" (Onthuruthi?) of Cannanore. Since they were dissatisfied with conditions at this place, the French were permitted by "Onriti" to transfer their operations to

---

[340] Padmanabha Menon, among others, has accepted at face value and as contemporary observations all the statements included in this section. See the appendices to Vols. II and III, *op. cit.* (n. 4).

[341] His *Relation de l'Indoustan* (Paris, 1684), the third part of his *Voyages* (Paris, 1689), is in an edited English version by Sen (ed.), *op. cit.* (n. 57). On pp. 120–30 may be found the descriptions of the Deccan, Goa, and Malabar.

[342] For bibliographical detail see above, pp. 421–22. The references which follow are to the Amsterdam reprint of 1699. Also see above, n. 46, and accompanying text.

nearby "Talichere" (Tellicherry). While the local population opposed their presence, the French at "Talichere" held on tenaciously with the help of "Onriti" and some Nayars they hired as guards.[343]

Dellon generalizes about conditions in Malabar on the basis of his experiences in the state of Cannanore. He has very little to add to what earlier European writers have already related about local matters, most of what he has to say being either trivial or the repetition of the same thing with a different emphasis. Like Vincenzo and Baldaeus, he recognizes that Cannanore, even though its territories are not as extensive as those of Calicut, is the most important of the Malabar states since the natives accord to its crown the name of "Colitri" (Kollattiri).[344] Like so many of his contemporaries, Dellon shows a particular interest in the strange flora and fauna of Malabar.[345] He notes that cardamoms grow on a mountain (Cardamom Hill) in Cannanore and that they are used in Asia as a spice and in Europe as a medicine. Nayars guard houses as well as travelers. Disgraced daughters of Brahmans are sold as slaves to foreigners. Thieves often wear shackles until they die, for stealing is the most serious of all crimes except murder. One of the most intelligent of the king's subjects is chosen to be "lieutenant-General," the most important official in the state. Upon his appointment, the king retires to a tranquil life and is consulted only when vital decisions need to be made. Princes are paramount in political affairs but are subject to the Brahmans in religion. Rich temples have grounds consecrated to the gods where it is a crime to spill blood. If a criminal escapes after committing a crime against the gods, his nearest relative is executed in his stead.

The Muslims of Malabar control foreign trade. The richest Muslims live on the coast and at the river deltas in villages called "Bazars" (bazaars). Muslim corsairs have large ships called "Paro" (*parão,* a Portuguese word used on India's west coast for Muslim merchantmen)[346] which carry as many as four to six hundred men, even trading into the Red Sea. Ten percent of the loot from piracy is paid to the king. Brigandage on land is severely punished. The corsairs are more belligerent and ferocious than other Muslims. In general, they follow local customs except for those which conflict directly with their religious beliefs. They are distinguished from Hindus only by their beards, turbans, and jackets. In south Cannanore there is a great "Bazar" commanded by a Muslim called "Aliraja" (Ali Raja), who also rules several of the Maldive Islands. The Muslims of "Bargara" (Badagara) and "Cogualy" (Kunhali) are especially hostile to the French at Tellicherry.[347]

[343] Dellon, *Relation d'un voyage fait aux Indes Orientales* (Amsterdam, 1699), pp. 153–54, 157–61.

[344] The Kollattiri ruled Kolattunad (Cirakkal), the territory between the Kottakal River on the south and the Nileswaram River on the north at the frontier of Kanara. See Poonen, *op. cit.* (n. 200), p. 11.

[345] Dellon, *op. cit.* (n. 343), pp. 88–121.

[346] See Yule and Burnell, *op. cit.* (n. 37), p. 733.

[347] Dellon, *op. cit.* (n. 343), pp. 82–161 *passim.*

The enemies of the French were scared off by the appearance in May, 1671, of a fleet which brought supplies, guns, and ammunition. Caron, on his way to Bantam, was on one of these vessels. After talks with "Onriti," Caron ordered De Flacourt and Dellon to explore the possibility of setting up a French office at "Sirimpatan" (Srirangapatnam), an important city in the interior behind Tellicherry.[348] The two Frenchmen left Tellicherry on June 16, 1671, for the long overland trek with their guides and Nayars. Feeling frightened and useless, Dellon abandoned this entourage and tried to return to Tellicherry by himself. He was captured by Muslims and taken to Kunhali as a slave. Its chief, a vassal of the Zamorin, soon ordered his release, since Calicut was then seeking French support in its conflict with the Dutch. Once De Flacourt returned from Srirangapatnam in November, he learned of the Zamorin's desire to conclude a treaty with the French. De Flacourt had also learned that the overland journey to Srirangapatnam required thirty-five days of steady travel and that cloths, natural saltpeter, and plenty of sandalwood were available there at good prices.[349] When a French squadron arrived at Tellicherry in February, 1672, De Flacourt informed its commander of the Zamorin's hopes. A treaty was quickly signed by which the French agreed to support the Zamorin in return for the cession of the small settlement of Alicot and for the right to maintain a permanent agent at the court of Calicut.[350]

After Dellon's desertion of the mission to Srirangapatnam, he took off on his own on a reconnaissance trip southward to Calicut and "Tanor" (Tanur). His route took him overland through the village of "Meali," a place inhabited only by "Tives" (the caste of Tiyans). At "Bargara" (Badagara), on the southern border of Cannanore, the real ruler is a Nayar, a vassal of the "Colitri." In this region the Muslim corsairs are insolent and dominant, at one time having even dared to revolt against the Zamorin. In the local language, Calicut itself is called "Coi-cota" (*Kozhikode*), or "cock-fortress," a name which relates to the Malabar tradition that in earlier times the territory of the Zamorin extended no further than a cock's crow could be heard.[351] As a trading center, Calicut's importance has declined with the rise of Goa and Surat. Frequent floods during the rainy season have submerged its old Portuguese fort as well as an installation of the English. Since the Zamorin no longer lives in Calicut, its royal palace is occupied by a governor called "Rajador" (*rajadoothor?*). In its court can still be seen a great bell and some cannons taken from the Portuguese fortress. The English provided lodging for Dellon in their new factory in Calicut.[352]

[348] In 1610 the raja of Mysore had taken Srirangapatnam from its Vijayanagar governor and had elevated it to be his capital city.

[349] See Dellon, *op. cit.* (n. 343), pp. 190–91.

[350] *Ibid.*, pp. 161–63; also see S. P. Sen, *The French in India* (Calcutta, 1947), pp. 105–8.

[351] This is the tradition. See under "Calicut" in the *Imperial Gazeteer*.

[352] Dellon, *op. cit.* (n. 343), pp. 175–82.

From Calicut, Dellon went south by sea to "Tanor," a small, square kingdom whose ruler is not a vassal of any of the larger Malabar states. Its port
city, from which the state gets its name, has no river and its harbor functions only during the dry season. It is mainly inhabited by rich Muslim merchants, though nearby there are two large villages of fishers, one Hindu and
the other Christian. "Tanor's" land is fertile, but most people there live off
fish and seafood. The "king" resides inland and maintains a governor in the
town to administer justice to Hindus and Muslims; the Christians are ruled
by their own leaders and he has no authority over them. "Tanor's" "king"
has cultivated the Portuguese ever since their arrival in India and is a bitter
enemy of the Dutch. The Jesuit superior at "Tanor" is "Mathias Fernandes,"
a veteran of seven or eight years of service there, who speaks the local language perfectly. From "Tanor," Dellon went northward to Balliapatam to
see the English who had recently arrived there and to hear news from Europe and Surat. Bored with his job and estranged from De Flacourt, Dellon
resigned his post shortly after returning to Tellicherry.

Throughout the seventeenth century great progress was made both in
Asia and Europe in cataloging and describing the exotic plants of the East.
For this endeavor a rich heritage existed in the herbals of Garcia da Orta and
Cristobal de Acosta, who described the plants of India on the basis of
their many years of personal experience in the East. Beginning in the mid-
sixteenth century the most eminent botanists of Europe began to plant
exotic specimens in their gardens. In his *Pinax* (1623) Gaspard Bauhin
(1566–1624), a Swiss botanist who collected dried specimens of exotic
plants, described them and endeavored to discover a universal system of
plant classification based on taxonomic affinities.[353] Dutch physicians, both
in Asia and Europe, continued thereafter to collect specimens of Asian
plants and to classify them generally after Bauhin's system. The *De medicina
Indorum* of Jacob de Bondt, or Bontius (1592–1631), a physician for the
Dutch East India Company in Batavia, was published at Leyden in 1642.
His plant descriptions were incorporated into Willem Piso's *De Indiae utriusque re naturali et medica libri XIV* (Amsterdam, 1658).[354] Lay observers in India, especially in Malabar, began in the latter half of the century to include
large descriptive sections on flora in their writings. Philippe, Thévenot,
Vincenzo, Nieuhof, and Dellon (who also includes fauna) were particularly
close students of nature and included in their works whatever they were able
to learn about India's flora.

Most of what Vincenzo published about Malabar's flora in his Book IV
was based on information gathered by his fellow Carmelite, Matthew of St.
Joseph. A young man skilled in medicine and Arabic, Matthew arrived in
India during 1657 with the first Carmelite expedition. Unlike the other Car-

---

[353] See also *Asia*, Vol. II, Bk. 3, pp. 427–45.
[354] For further bibliographical detail see above p. 457.

melites of his day, Matthew seems to have remained in Malabar until his death at Cochin. After the Dutch conquest of Malabar in the 1660's, he continued with both his religious work and his botanical collecting.

Finally, in 1671 Hendrik Adriaan van Rheede tot Drakestein (*ca.* 1637–91) took over as Dutch commander of Malabar with headquarters at Cochin. Shortly thereafter this genial amateur and Maecenas enlisted the help of Matthew and Joannes Casearius, the Reformed chaplain of Cochin, in preparing sytematically an investigation of the flora of Malabar. A team was put together to collect and to sketch and paint floral specimens before they had time to wither. In this enterprise the Europeans were aided by three Konkani Brahmans and an Ayurvedic physician of the Izhava caste named Itty Achutan. The Indian collaborators made lists of the plants they knew, collected specimens of them, and took them to Cochin, where Matthew and three other artists sketched them.[355] Casearius laid out the plan of the work and rendered into elegant Latin the information relayed to him by the others and by his Luso-Asian translator Manuel Carneiro, a Roman Catholic. Van Rheede, who remained at Cochin until 1677, was the moving spirit behind the investigation in India and its publication in Europe.

Van Rheede's *Hortus indicus malabaricus* was published at Amsterdam between 1678 and 1703 in twelve folio volumes with 794 copper-plate engravings.[356] It is dedicated to Joann Mastsuyker, Dutch governor-general of the East Indies. Volume I begins with prefaces by Casearius, Matthew, Carneiro, Itty Achutan, and the three Brahmans. These statements, all dated from Cochin as of April 20, 1675, provide in brief the early history of the Van Rheede enterprise and of the role played by the original participants. The statements by the Indians and Carneiro appear in both Malayalam and Latin, the first printing in Europe of the Malayalam language (see pls. 142–44). The three Brahmans "used Konkani Nagara lipi [script]; Itty Achutan used Vattezhuthu lipi; and Emmanuel Karnol Roy [Carneiro] used Malayalam lipi."[357] A sixth preface by Arnold Seyn, professor of botany at Leyden and the European editor, indicates that he collated the information from the Van Rheede group with that of earlier European commentators and added as far as possible the Latin names of plants following Bauhin's system. While Casearius died before the first volume was printed and Seyn before the second was issued, publication went ahead in Europe and was con-

---

[355] The three Brahmans were called Ranga Bhatter, Appu Bhatter, and Vinayaga Bhatter. See M. O. Koshy, "Dutch Impact on Kerala Society and Culture," *Journal of Kerala Studies,* IV (1977), 566.

[356] We have consulted the copy in the Crerar Collection, in the Special Collections of the Regenstein Library at the University of Chicago. For its early publication history see Marjorie F. Warner, "The Dates of Rheede's Hortus Malabaricus," *The Journal of Botany British and Foreign,* LVIII (1920), 291–92.

[357] Koshy, *loc. cit.* (n. 355), p. 566. The Nagara is basically the Sanskrit script. The Vattezhuthu (literally "rounded script") was used in Kerala until the mid-nineteenth century and was very similar to Tamil script. The Malayalam script given here is very close to the present-day Malayalam script still used in Kerala. From a communication of C. K. Pullapilly, July 29, 1988.

tinued even after Van Rheede died in 1691. During the history of this ambitious cooperative scholarly project probably more than one hundred persons were involved in it at Cochin, Negapatam, Batavia, and in Holland.[358]

Volume I, which sets the pattern for the rest, includes fifty-seven copper plates of line drawings showing the whole plants, life-size or in proportion to their natural sizes, with special sketches of their roots, fruits, leaves, and seeds, sometimes in cross sections. The name of each plant is given in Malayalam, Sanskrit, Arabic, and Latin. This is followed by a thoroughgoing botanical description in Latin which includes, where appropriate, the economic and medical uses made in India of each plant. The scholarly world of Europe was quick to recognize the value of this new work and to be inspired by it. The first three volumes, published respectively in 1678, 1679, and 1682, are acclaimed by the *Philosophical Transactions of the Royal Society* as "excellent, admirable, and laudable." The anonymous reviewer is impressed especially by the prefaces of the native participants whose testimonials "have certified to the World the truth of these Relations."[359] That Van Rheede's was a work of enduring importance to the botanical world is testified to by Linnaeus himself. In his *Species plantarum* (1753), the great Swedish botanist lists the *Hortus* of Van Rheede as one of five works he considers true "flora" from the 192 he cites. He also commemorates Van Rheede himself in the name of the monotypic exotic genus called *Rheedia*.[360]

In Amsterdam Jan Commelin (1629–92) and his nephew Caspar (1668–1731) cultivated and studied exotic plants at the university's botanical garden and prepared a catalog with superb illustrations of their collections.[361]

Politically the coastal tract from Goa southward was divided during the seventeenth century into at least twenty-four identifiable states. The Portuguese enclave of Goa bordered the independent Muslim state of Bijapur on the north and west until the Mughuls overran Bijapur in 1686. On Goa's southern side lay Kanara, its northern half dominated by the Hindu nayaks of Ikkeri and its southern half divided into a series of petty principalities subject to intermittent spoilation by Portuguese, Malabar Muslims, or the forces of Ikkeri. Malabar, the scene of the greatest amount of European activity, was dominated from Cochin southward by the Portuguese until 1663; they also held a fort at Cannanore, but little else. The replacement of the Portuguese by the Dutch put a more effective European control into place and subjected Travancore to a vassalage of a strictness the Portuguese had not seen fit to impose. Throughout the century the Zamorins of Calicut

---

[358] See H. Terpstra, *De Nederlanders in Voor-Indië* (Amsterdam, 1947), pp. 193–98.

[359] *Philosophical Transactions of the Royal Society,* XII (1683), 100–109.

[360] See S. A. Bobroff, "Exotic Plants in Carl Linnaeus' *Species Plantarum* (1753)" (Ph.D. diss., Dept. of History, University of Chicago, 1973), pp. 30, 74, 107–8.

[361] *Horti medici Amstelodamensis rariorum . . . plantarum . . . descriptio et icones* (2 vols.; Amsterdam, 1697, 1701).

retained their independence of European control by keeping constant military pressure on Cochin, by maintaining an unofficial alliance with the Muslim corsairs, and by making agreements to supply pepper to Europeans who could not buy at Cochin. Calicut's policy of expediency based on shifting alliances was supported on land by a standing army of 150,000 Nayars and at sea by the forays of the Muslim corsairs, who plundered hostile shipping. The returns from these maritime enterprises supported the Ali Rajas of Cannanore and helped its Kollathiri family to remain in the interior and safe from European dominance. The role of the Malabar Muslims as a buffer between the Europeans and the Malabar Hindus emerges with particular clarity in the accounts of Calicut.

The fact that the European sources do not always agree in detail on political boundaries conveys a sense of their ill-defined character and the shifting of demarcations over time. The northern boundary of Malabar, for example, is placed at Deli Point by some, by others at Mangalore, by others at Basrur, and by Dellon at Surat. Between Kanara and Cannanore a wall stands as a permanent boundary; similar walls separate certain Malabar states as well. The Europeans also provide information on routes of inland travel from Goa to Bijapur, Bijapur to Dabhol, Honavar to Ikkeri, and Ikkeri to Mangalore, as well as many other roads between coastal places. They report that Srirangapatnam in Mysore can be reached from Tellicherry, that the Toda people reside in the Nilgiri hills behind Calicut, and that Tekkumkur is an independent Malabar state. In accounting for the decline of Bijapur and Goa, the European writers record the southward expansion of Bijapur after 1635, the rise of Sivaji around 1648, and the succession crisis in Bijapur preceding the Mughul takeover. In brief, the careful reader of these sources would have been able to conclude that the region was not of one piece politically, that European military dominance prevailed only in a few coastal towns, and that life was turbulent even for the Queen of Ullal.

Individual centers receive varying degrees of attention in the European materials. Goa's wealth and decline is described by several non-Portuguese authors. Early in the century, Pyrard de Laval, like Linschoten before him, marvels at what the Portuguese have been able to construct in Goa over only a century's time. He is likewise impressed by the city's material prosperity, its cosmopolitan character, and its numerous and heterogeneous population. This sunny picture has shadows cast over it in the 1620's after the fall of Ormuz and the apparent efforts of the Dutch to combine with Bijapur to tighten a circle around Goa. Once the Dutch inaugurate their naval blockade in 1637, the character of the city changes. In a declining economy, the religious orders and the Inquisition are less subject to secular authority. Those who were formerly rich and powerful begin to seek alms, Hindus and Luso-Asians become more prominent and influential in business and the professions, and non-Portuguese Europeans, especially the clerics sent out by the Propaganda, are much less welcome in what has become a beleaguered city.

Goa's charitable institutions, especially its royal hospital, share in the city's general decline.

Calicut, too, favorably impresses the Europeans, and it receives high marks for its tidy appearance and its material prosperity. It is an independent Hindu state with an orderly economy and government. Its port, while not boasting a fine natural harbor, is frequented by all nationalities except the Portuguese. The Zamorin of Calicut maintains and runs efficiently a customhouse, warehouses, and regular markets for the conduct of international trade. In his mint he produces his own coinage, which is thought to be clearly an attribute of sovereignty on this coast. He administers justice personally, rules arbitrarily, and heads an efficient bureaucracy which keeps careful records of everything pertinent to the management of the state. The best evidence for the effectiveness of Calicut's fine organization is its ability to sustain what is almost a continuous war against Portuguese-supported Cochin. To preserve internal harmony, the Hindu Zamorin tolerates all faiths, including European Catholics and their local converts. He always seems ready to receive European visitors; Della Valle took advantage of an audience in 1623 to sketch a ground-plan of the palace (see pl. 148). From time to time, as political conditions change, the Zamorin will permit the Portuguese and later on the Dutch monopolists to maintain representatives at Calicut to issue licenses for ships. Calicut's grasp on small neighboring states and ports is weakened with the appearance of the Dutch in its waters. As a trading center, Calicut's importance declines as the Dutch monopoly tightens and as more international trade is attracted to Cochin and Surat.

Most of the European writers are likewise impressed by the prosperous condition and good order prevailing in other Hindu-controlled states. Kanara and Cannanore, like Calicut, are hospitable to foreigners and maintain a social order in which travelers and their belongings are absolutely safe. These rajas and their servitors rule arbitrarily and despotically. Theft and murder are severely and quickly punished by a harsh system of justice strictly administered by the ruler personally. Goa, the Europeans realize, becomes increasingly dependent on Kanara for provisions and labor as its relations with Bijapur and the Dutch deteriorate after 1635. While Goa declines precipitously as a trading center at mid-century, it begins to recover somewhat after the Dutch capture of Cochin, since the forced concentration of the Portuguese at Goa lessens its military responsibilities in southern India and strengthens its hand in northern trade. This is particularly the case after the fall of Bijapur in 1686. Goa's involvement in trade with the continent likewise increases and it becomes a regular supplier of Surat and Bombay with products and goods from the mainland. Outside of Goa Europeans are employed in Bijapur and Malabar, primarily in military capacities. Communities of Jews, some Spanish-speaking, are found in Goa, Cochin, and at Deli Point. Muslims can be seen everywhere, but most especially in Calicut.

On social conditions the Europeans are most detailed on Malabar and

Kanara. They generally project to an entire region the observations made at a particular place, especially at Cannanore. The Indians are described as being swarthy with straight black hair and erect posture. One group is distinguished from the other by costume and ornament. The members of a particular caste or faith do not alter their dress or decoration to satisfy individual tastes; novelty in dress is generally frowned upon. In Hindu states Muslims are required to dress so as to be readily identifiable. Housing is generally poor; social level rather than personal wealth determines the type of abode that one may build. On the castes of Malabar and Kanara several of the Europeans explain that they differ in name and function from place to place. Vincenzo enumerates many more caste names and practices than any of his predecessors or contemporaries in Malabar. Most notable is his listing of nine levels of Nambutiri and fifteen ranks of Nayars. He also, perhaps for the first time in European literature on castes, treats the Chegos (palm cultivators) as an independent caste with subcastes of its own. The Chegos are described by Vincenzo as an intermediate caste set apart from the lower castes distinguished by their crafts. A number of the Europeans indicate that marriage, burial, and mourning customs differ from place to place and from caste to caste, and most commentators describe ceremonies and practices they have personally observed.

European writers comment on open-air elementary education, and the fact that at all levels, education is confined to the study of ancient texts and manuals based on them. Both Vincenzo and Baldaeus employed gurus to instruct them in the traditions and learning of Hinduism; Baldaeus' teacher at Jaffna was a Bengali Brahman and a Christian convert. Six Hindu texts were translated into Portuguese for Vincenzo. These were mainly moral tales and compilations of aphorisms culled from basic Sanskrit texts. While detailing the avatars of Vishnu, Baldaeus relays to his European readers a valuable version of the story of Krishna. Thévenot provides samples of Tamil script in the engravings he provides of its letters and numbers. Vincenzo discloses that Malayalam is commonly written in three scripts and that a literature, especially poetry, exists in that language. The Jesuits in Malabar learn both Malayalam and Tamil to carry on their missionary work more effectively; they also compile and circulate vocabularies. Three Malayalam letters, in three different scripts, were printed in Europe in 1678 as prefaces to Van Rheede's *Hortus*. Indeed, this great work of botany, as the prefaces indicate, was a cooperative Indo-European project, perhaps the first such international scientific endeavor ever undertaken and brought to a highly successful conclusion.

Religious toleration exists everywhere to a greater or lesser degree. Non-Christian religious practices are closely watched and sharply restricted at Goa and Cochin. In Muslim Bijapur, Christians are tolerated, even Jesuits, but missionizing is prohibited. As Goa declines, its Christian authorities become increasingly intolerant of Jews, New Christians, and converts who continue to be overly attached to Hindu customs. The Catholic orders and the Inquisition are constantly on the watch for heresy, heretical tendencies, and sorcery. The secular arm is used ruthlessly against Christians and Jews to carry out the judgments of the Inquisition. The missionaries of the Propaganda generally avoid Goa and Cochin on their way to and from the Serra to work with the St. Thomas Christians. To mid-century an accommodation between the Latin and St. Thomas Christians based on the Diamper decrees seems to make slow if unsteady progress. The revolt of the Serra in 1653 brings a quick end to these efforts. Rome thereafter sends Propaganda priests, generally Carmelites, to Malabar in hopes of working out a new accommodation. When the Dutch take over Malabar, the Portuguese priests are quickly exiled. But their converts and the St. Thomas Christians, and even some of the Carmelites, are tolerated by the Dutch. Once the Dutch are safely in charge of the economic and political situation, an association develops in Malabar among the various Christian groups reminiscent of the religious freedom enjoyed in Holland itself during the late seventeenth century. The Muslims continue to worship at their mosques, and their wandering ascetics, as well as their mullahs, enjoy a practical freedom of conscience and the liberty to observe the tenets of their faith.

It was Hinduism and its extraordinary beliefs and customs which most intrigued the European observers. Pyrard, Della Valle, Mandelslo, Nieuhof, Dellon, and Fryer were beguiled and bewildered by its many idols, temples, and public celebrations. Vincenzo and Baldaeus, the Carmelite monk and the Reformed minister, sought to learn whatever they could from gurus, Jesuits, and earlier European writers about Hinduism's cosmology and theology as well as its practices. Despite their obvious Christian biases, both understood Hinduism to be a systematic religion based on ancient scriptures that were taught and interpreted by the priestly caste of Brahmans. They both readily observed that, while practices differed widely, and while the same gods had many different names, the basic beliefs of Hinduism were universally understood and respected. To make Hinduism comprehensible to themselves and their readers, both Christian authors introduce into their discussions references to comparable ideas and beliefs from other religious persuasions, including Judaism and early Christianity.

At the beginning of the century Couto had provided a sketchy description of Hindu beliefs based on the Saivite Agamas. This summary, while interesting in itself, was not widely diffused in Europe outside of Portugal. Hinduism was first relayed to Europe at large in the writings of Giacomo Fenicio, Abraham Roger, and Athanasius Kircher, all of which were used (or misused) by Baldaeus in preparing his book.[362] Vincenzo's account, published in the same year (1672) as Baldaeus', appears to owe much less to other European commentators. Still, it is striking to see how much the

---

[362] On Roger and Kircher see below, pp. 1029–57; on Fenicio see above, pp. 911–12.

two descriptions supplement, complement, and confirm each other in what they say about Hindu ideas of one creating God, traditional cosmology, and the eternity of the world. They differ radically on the number of avatars assigned to Vishnu, as do many Indian writers on this subject. Inevitably they expend much space on the names, iconography, and attributes of the numerous gods, goddesses, cultural heroes, and anti-gods. They are both impressed and repelled, as are many of the other European writers, with the universal propitiation of evil gods and spirits. Hindu temples are considered to be ornate and beautiful on the exterior and dark, dirty, and foul-smelling on the interior. The Europeans give the names of many Malabar festivals and generally a few details on how they are celebrated; all agree that *Onam* is the most popular Malabar festival. Hindus worship daily, repeat many prayers, and make regular sacrifices to their gods. They all believe in omens, portents, and auspicious days or times of day. Brahmans fast periodically and regularly receive food and alms from others. Yogis appear to be organized and to hold general meetings on fixed dates at particular places; they are renowned and revered everywhere for the austerities and extreme penances they perform. Both Hindu and Muslim ascetics seem to attract the attention of the Europeans by their nudity or semi-nudity, by their conspicuous dedication to religion and religious rites, and by their moral ideals.

CHAPTER XII

Insular South Asia

India's influence spread in ancient times to islands as close to the subcontinent as Ceylon and as far to the southwest as the Laccadive and Maldive
archipelagoes. The Sinhalese people, who probably originated in north India, had colonized these insular regions at an early date; in fact, the Maldive
language is a dialect of Sinhalese. Buddhism was introduced into Ceylon in
the third century B.C., and despite Muslim, Christian, and Hindu encroachments it continues today to flourish there. Dravidians from Malabar had
meanwhile emigrated to the archipelagoes just as Tamils moved into northern Ceylon from the Coromandel Coast. Social customs, especially in
Ceylon, were much affected by the regular contacts between Buddhists and
Hindus. The advent of Arab traders in the ninth to twelfth centuries brought
Islam to the archipelagoes. Close trading relations thereafter developed between the Muslims of Malabar (Moplahs) and those of the Maldives and
Laccadives. Ibn Batuta, the famous Muslim traveler, lived and worked in
the Maldives for more than a year in the fourteenth century.

After rounding the southern tip of Africa, the Portuguese had quickly
learned about the strategic importance of these islands to Asian trade. Barros,
the great Portuguese chronicler, was the first to introduce this maritime
world to European readers.[1] The Portuguese in the field were regularly harassed by Muslim traders as they sought to break into this trading region
with their ships, merchandise, and factories. In Ceylon they became involved in commerce as early as 1505. They soon set up other factories on the
island of Anjediva, in the Laccadives, and in the Maldives. Unable to main-

[1] See *Asia*, I, 342–47.

tain these shaky footholds in the archipelagoes, the Portuguese of Goa were forced to trade and carry on relations in the atolls on terms prescribed by the native rulers. By the middle of the seventeenth century the Laccadives and the Maldives became the vassals of the Malabar and Muslim city-state of Cannanore. After the Dutch ousted the Portuguese from Ceylon and after they captured Cannanore in 1663, the archipelagoes paid tribute to the VOC. Today Ceylon and the Maldives are independent republics, and since 1956 the Laccadives have been constituted as a Union Territory of India known as Lakshadweep.

I

THE MALDIVE AND LACCADIVE ARCHIPELAGOES

The Portuguese and Jesuit chroniclers and commentators of the sixteenth century recorded very little about these atolls that lay around four hundred miles southwest of Ceylon (see map 6). Barbosa and Barros, though more specific materials were probably available in Lisbon, provide only incidental references to the islands and a general description of their placement, peoples, beliefs, and trade.[2] Neither writer even distinguished clearly between the Laccadive and Maldive chains.[3] Maffei, the Jesuit historian, provides only tantalizing references to the prevalence of Islam and its practices in the islands. Linschoten repeats much of what had been reported earlier by the Portuguese writers.[4] Well aware of their strategic importance to trade in the Indian Ocean, the Portuguese sought on numerous occasions over the course of the sixteenth century to extend their authority over Male, the island seat of the sultan of the Maldives. Successive efforts were repelled until the middle of the sixteenth century when the Portuguese took advantage of a revolution in the islands to give refuge to the deposed sultan.

Sultan Hassan, who had abdicated in 1550, fled to Cochin, where he and his family two years later converted from Islam to Christianity. The Portuguese meanwhile took advantage of the tumult in the Maldives to occupy Male and to establish there a puppet ruler to govern in the name of Hassan. This Portuguese protectorate remained effective over the next decade. There-

[2] That other materials were then available in Lisbon became clear during the nineteenth century when many of the Portuguese documents were printed. A manuscript description, prepared as early as 1505, is reproduced from the Peutinger Codex (Munich) in M. A. H. Fitzler, "Die Maldiven im 16. und 17. Jahrhundert," *Zeitschrift für Indologie und Iranistik*, X (1935–36), 249–55.
[3] Possibly this is because the name Laccadives (*Laksha-diva*, the Hundred Thousand Islands) as used in India evidently included the Maldives.
[4] See A. C. Burnell and P. A. Tiele, *The Voyage of John Huyghen van Linschoten to the East Indies from the Old English Translation of 1598* (2 vols.; "H. S.," o.s., LXX–LXXI; London, 1884, 1885), 74–76. On Linschoten see *Asia*, I, 482–90.

after control over the trade of the islands slipped into the hands of Muslim merchants of Cannanore. The Portuguese, who needed the coir (coconut fiber) of the Maldives for rigging their ships, took as protection money one-third of the coir paid as tribute to the exiled Hassan.[5] After the death in 1583 of Hassan, or Dom Manoel as he was known to his fellow Christians, his descendants remained under Portuguese protection for the next eighty years, still claiming to be the legitimate sovereigns of the Maldives. A native ruler, Ibrahim (r. 1584–1607[?]), maintained an uneasy truce with the Portuguese and continued as governor of the islands into the seventeenth century.

The Portuguese chroniclers of the seventeenth century—notably Diogo do Couto, Faria y Sousa, and Antonio Bocarro—have next to nothing in their works pertaining directly to past or contemporary events in the Maldives. The Spanish friar Antonio San Román de Ribadeneyra gives a brief description in 1603 concerning the placement and products of the Maldives based on Barros' work and on the *Trattado* (1578) of Cristobal de Acosta.[6] Otherwise the Iberian commentators, whose writings were published during the seventeenth century, have nothing new to add.

What seventeenth-century Europe learned about the Maldives came exclusively from the pen of François Pyrard (d. 1621) from the Norman town of Laval. Shipwrecked on the Maldives in 1602, Pyrard remained in the islands under protective custody until he was taken to Chittagong in 1607 by an invading Bengali fleet. The story of his experiences in the East was published first at Paris in 1611 and in two revised and amplified editions of 1615 and 1619.[7] It records all that he learned about the Maldives during his approximately five years (1602–7) residence in the islands. His edition of 1619 includes a vocabulary of Maldive words and their meanings.[8] Like most of his contemporaries, Pyrard evidently did not know when he wrote his book that the Parmentier brothers of nearby Dieppe had reached the Maldives back in 1529.[9]

On the placement and geographical features of the Maldives, Pyrard reports at length and in accurate detail. The natives informed him that the chain included twelve thousand islands, and he rightly concludes that this figure is not meant to be exact but merely a conventional way of indicating "an incredible number."[10] The archipelago is divided by nature into island

---

[5] Also see F. C. Danvers, *The Portuguese in India* (2 vols.; London, 1894), II, 293.

[6] *Historia general de la Yndia Oriental* (Valladolid, 1603), pp. 322–24.

[7] For its publication history in brief see above, pp. 396–97.

[8] See Albert Gray and H. C. P. Bell (trans. and eds.), *The Voyage of François Pyrard of Laval to the East Indies, the Maldives, the Moluccas, and Brazil. Translated into English from the Third French Edition of 1619* (2 vols. in 3 nos.; "HS," o.s., LXXVI, LXXVII, LXXX; London, 1887, 1888, 1890). For his dictionary of Maldive words see LXXX, pp. 405–22.

[9] See *Asia*, I, 178.

[10] Gray and Bell (trans. and eds.), *op. cit.* (n. 8), I, 95. For figures given by the early European authors see *ibid.*, n. 1. The modern Republic of Maldives includes 1,087 small islands, of which 219 are inhabited. Their population in 1985 numbered 181,453.

groupings called atolls." There are thirteen atolls, each containing "a great number of little isles," each separated from the rest by a considerable distance, and each surrounded on all sides by a round or oval bank of stone." Each atoll has its own name and each is a political unit." Most of the islands in the archipelago are uninhabited, some have vegetation and others are "merely shifting sands" that sometimes wash completely away. The archipelago lies parallel to the Indian subcontinent, about 150 leagues to the west (actually 350 to 400 miles), its length being about 200 leagues (470 miles) and its width from 30 to 35 leagues (around 70 miles)."

Because the islands lie in the equatorial zone, the climate is excessively hot and the nights and days of roughly equal length at all seasons. Winter begins in April and summer in October. During the winter, when the winds are stronger from the west, it rains continually. In the summer extremely hot winds from the east parch the islands and no rain falls. The nights are cool and dew is abundant; thus it is possible for animals and humans to survive the summers. The winds are commonly known as monsoons, those seasonal winds on which sailors depend. The currents in the surrounding seas run for six months eastward and during the next six months in the opposite direction. Navigation in the vicinity of the islands and between the atolls is made treacherous when the currents reverse their flow." Four channels are navigable by the large foreign vessels which pass through the Maldives."

Tradition has it that the Maldives were colonized by people from Ceylon." Pyrard doubts the veracity of this oral tradition because the Maldivians are not "black and ill-shapen" like the people he later saw in Ceylon." In contrast to Barros, who held the Maldivians in low esteem, Pyrard describes the people as being adroit in crafts, skilled in arms, and law-abiding. The women are olive in color, are attractive, and pride themselves on their long,

---

"From Maldive *atoln*, perhaps the only word from the Maldive language which has become a fixture in the European languages. *Ibid.*, pp. 93–94, n. 2.

"*I.e.*, a coral reef, typical of those that lie in a belt between south Africa and south India. For a modern scientific description of these coral formations see J. S. Gardiner, *The Fauna and Geography of the Maldive and Laccadive Archipelago* (2 vols.; Cambridge, 1903), I, 13, 172–83.

"For their names in Pyrard's and in modern transliterations see Gray and Bell (trans. and eds.), *op. cit.* (n. 8), I, 97–99.

"*Ibid.*, p. 93.

"*Ibid.*, pp. 100–101, 104, 257, 279–80.

"*Ibid.*, pp. 103–4. Six channels are recognized in most modern sailing directories.

"Little reliable information is available on this subject. The origins of the Maldivians are constantly being pushed farther into the past. It is now thought that Dravidian, Veddoid, and Sinhalese peoples from India and Ceylon began to settle in the islands at some unspecified time during the pre-Christian era. See T. L. Stoddard *et al.*, *Area Handbook for the Indian Ocean Territories* (Washington, D. C., 1971). The explorer Thor Heyerdahl, an advocate of the seas as highways rather than impediments of migration, has recently excavated ruins in the Maldives which seem to point to the existence of a culture in the atolls as far back as 2000 B.C. See *Chicago Tribune*, March 14, 1983. In the 1970's and 1980's others studied the sherds of Chinese pottery of the ninth to the nineteenth century which lie scattered through the coral sands of Male.

"Gray and Bell (trans. and eds.), *op. cit.* (n. 8), I, 105.

thick, black hair. The heads of children are clean shaven to the age of eight or nine years, the girls being distinguished from the boys by leaving a rim of hair around their heads. Nobles, soldiers, and royal officials are permitted to wear their hair long, but are not obliged to. Men who cut off their hair give or sell it to the women who make it into switches to fill out their own long tresses even more. The males, who pride themselves on their body hair, shave their chests and stomachs to "look like a slashed doublet" and sport beards that are shaven away from the mouth since hair pollutes meat or drink. Every adult tends to his own hair and carries after the age of fifteen a private set of implements—razor, scissors, and copper mirror. Cuttings of hair, as parts of the body, are always buried.[19]

To the age of eight or nine, the boys wear no clothing or shoes. They are clothed in a breechcloth after circumcision. Girls wear a breechcloth at all ages and don a top when they begin to form breasts and become eligible for marriage. The men wear a loincloth covered by colored drawers that fall to the knees, and a silk or cotton robe (sarong) held together by a sash; on their heads they wear turbans, or kerchiefs if the hair is long. The women wear petticoats which cover them from the waist to the ankles; over this they wear a full-length robe of taffeta or fine cotton cloth decorated with blue and white borders. All men wear steel knives in their girdles, but are forbidden to carry other weapons. The women wear many heavy bracelets, often of silver, as well as silver and gold chains around the waist and neck. Garments and ornaments of gold may be worn only by those of royal blood or by those who have paid for the privilege. Those who have made a pilgrimage to Mecca wear a special white costume. People of all stations in life go without shoes.[20]

Fishing is the chief form of employment and everyone is free to fish anywhere. For export they fish for tuna and bonito in the deep seas; inshore fishing around the reefs provides fresh food for domestic consumption. Fishing is also a sport comparable to hunting in Europe.[21] Two types of millet are cultivated, from which they obtain two harvests each year. They make flour from this grain, as well as from roots that grow wild in the islands. Certain roots are cultivated which are cooked and then preserved in honey and palm-sugar. They have in abundance coconuts as well as other tropical fruits: limes, oranges, bananas, and pomegranates. They also eat the leaves of wild trees which do not produce fruits. Sea birds and their eggs, pigeons, and ducks supplement fish as fresh meat. Each of the atolls, alleges Pyrard, yields different produce; the plants native to one will not grow on any other. Living is still easy, for food is plentiful and cheap. Life has

[19] *Ibid.*, pp. 106–11. Today women of all ages still wear their hair in long tresses; most men are clean shaven. See Stoddard, *op. cit.* (n. 17), p. 33.
[20] Gray and Bell (trans. and eds.), *op. cit.* (n. 8), I, 161–69.
[21] *Ibid.*, pp. 188–90.

its little miseries brought on by pesty crows, bats, mosquitos, rats, mice, and ants.[22]

Each craft is practiced on specific islands and only by the peoples of those islands. Like plants, the craftsmen, whether weavers or goldsmiths, do not migrate. Since every person has his own boat, the Maldivians travel easily from atoll to atoll trading their produce and wares or practicing their crafts. They never navigate after nightfall and so spend every night on land. Their rafts and fishing boats are made from planks of very light native lumber called "Candou" (Maldive, *kadu,* pronounced *kandu*). With these corklike planks they construct a device to lift stones and other heavy objects from the seas. They rub together sticks of this wood to make a fire.[23]

Their principal island is Male, and its name is combined with the word "Dives" (*divehi* is the Maldivian word, "the islands") to yield the word "Maldives." Located centrally, the island and city of Male is the site of the royal residence and the main emporium for both natives and foreigners. While its land is the most fertile to be found in the islands, its climate and water supply are bad. Water has to be imported from other islands where the supply is better, but scarcity of fresh water is general. The city of Male is the most heavily populated center and is clean, well organized, and divided into distinct districts. All the houses and warehouses are elevated to keep out vermin and pests. The common people build their houses of coconut wood thatched with palm fronds; the residences of the kings and nobles are built of stone and elevated above the shallows of the sea. The people of Male are fairer and more genteel than those of the south because of intermarriage with foreigners.[24]

During the years of his forced sojourn in Male, Pyrard learned the spoken language and was consulted by the sultan and his courtiers about Europe, the art of making paper and parchment, and Western navigation.[25] To carry on such discussions his command of the Maldive tongue (*Divehi*) must have been far from superficial. The Maldive words in his vocabulary of almost three hundred words and in the text itself are rendered phonetically. Most of the words are nouns or adjectives relating to everyday life: days of the week, parts of the body, military and marine terms, articles of trade, and numerals. He makes clear that two languages are in regular use: Maldive for ordinary secular matters, and Arabic for religion and science, "just as Latin is employed by us." The court dialect of the Maldive language is quite different from the southern dialect prevailing on Suvadiva. In Male itself he heard, as languages of commerce, Cambay, Malay, Gujarati, and Portuguese.[26]

Arabic is the language of religion because Islam "is the religion and there

---

[22] *Ibid.,* pp. 111–17.
[23] *Ibid.,* pp. 119–22.
[24] *Ibid.,* pp. 105, 117–19.
[25] *Ibid.,* pp. 242–44.
[26] *Ibid.,* I, 122–23; and for the vocabulary *ibid.,* vol. II, pt. 2, pp. 405–22.

is no other throughout the islands save among the foreigners."[27] Stone mosques with wooden superstructures are called "mesquites" (Maldive, *miskítu*); these stand in the middle of a walled square in which they bury the dead, and face west towards Mecca. The chief mosque at Male is called the "Oncouru mesquite" (Maldive, *Hukuru miskitu*), or "Friday mosque."[28] Each of the numerous mosques dotting the islands is served by a priest called a "Moudin" (*mudému*) who manages the mosque, teaches religion, and instructs the children in reading and writing in Arabic and their own language.[29] All men of fifteen and older pray in the mosque each day at daybreak, noon, mid-afternoon, sunset, and 10:00 P.M. These prayer sessions constitute "a heavy tax on their time," for on each occasion they stay in the mosque for thirty minutes or so. Women never enter the mosques but say their prayers at home.[30]

Every Friday is a holy day celebrated communally with great ceremony. The ablutions always performed before entering the mosque are more elaborate on Fridays. Trumpets announce the celebration, work ceases, and the people don their finest clothes. Similar festivals are held to celebrate each new moon and the circumcision of a son at age seven. The greatest occasion of the year is Ramadan, which commences in December and lasts for about one moon. At the end of Ramadan they take the annual census and pay their head-taxes to the mosque for its support and for poor relief. A minor festival follows which features games, sports, and fencing matches.[31]

Marriage, like other customs, is ruled by religion. A husband may have as many as three wives at once, but only if he can afford to support them. Women may not marry until fifteen years of age and are forbidden to wed their brothers or first cousins. A husband may divorce a wife at will; the wife can leave only with the husband's consent. Divorced persons may marry or remarry, but only for a total of three times. Like marriage customs, the rules governing burial emanate from a mixture of native and Islamic tradition. Everyone, including the ruler, must be buried where he died, for a corpse may never be transported from one island to the other.[32]

Like most foreign observers, Pyrard is fascinated by customs of everyday

---

[27] *Ibid.*, I, 123. Muslim Arabs began to settle in the islands during the ninth century. Under their influence Sunni Islam gradually supplanted Buddhism and in 1153 became the official religion of the sultanate. The process of religious transformation was probably slow and tortuous, for Ibn Batuta, the Arab traveler who visited the islands in 1343–44, complained that many non-Islamic customs and practices were still being followed. See Stoddard *et al.*, *op. cit.* (n. 17), p. 27.

[28] In 1674 a new mosque, one that Pyrard could not have seen, was built at Male. For its ground plan see Gray and Bell (trans. and eds.), *op. cit.* (n. 8), I, facing p. 126.

[29] The Maldivian language has two alphabets: Tana, from the old Sinhalese Sanskrit-based alphabet, and an adaptation of the Arabic alphabet. Both are still taught in the schools. See Stoddard *et al.*, *op. cit.* (n. 17), p. 28.

[30] Gray and Bell, *op. cit.* (n. 8), I, 123–28.

[31] About these Muslim ceremonies Pyrard has much to say and in detail. He clearly understands that life is governed by a lunar calendar. See *ibid.*, pp. 128–50.

[32] *Ibid.*, pp. 150–61.

life which differ from his own. Men and women never dine together, nor do men of different stations. They sit on the floor cross-legged on a mat and eat with their fingers the food presented on banana leaves. Their dishes are locally made of lacquered wood and are covered to keep the ants off the food. Their vessels are imported earthenware from Cambay or porcelains from China. Porcelains are "very common," obviously to the surprise of the Frenchman. Coffee and cocoa beverages are served in covered copper cups. At meals they are not permitted to cough, spit, eat with the left hand, or converse. They have no fixed hours for meals, and the women and girls do all the cooking. Men who cook are treated as females.[33]

The Maldivians are meticulous about personal grooming, bathe frequently, and regularly oil their skin. Everyone chews betel and areca, so all have red teeth and "deem it a beauty." They are great believers in omens and signs especially with respect to fishing and seafaring. Daily sacrifices are made to the "kings" of the seas and winds in the form of miniature boats and ships that are set afire before being cast into the water. They wear charms called "Tauide" (*tavídu*) that are enclosed in little boxes which they purchase from a sorcerer. These charms, which correspond to the *huniyam* of Ceylon, are worn to procure luck, illicit sexual intercourse, and good health.[34]

Problems of health are common. Their only doctors are the sorcerers, who try to rid them of the evil spirits thought to cause illnesses. "Maldive fever," known under this name throughout the Indies, is very common and foreigners are particularly susceptible to it.[35] Many die of it and of periodic epidemics of smallpox. Of the common tropical diseases they suffer most from night blindness, ringworm, and the itch. They have no toothaches because of the habit of chewing betel. Syphilis, which is not common despite their addiction to lechery, is called the French or European disease and is cured with China wood (*Smilax china*).[36] Adultery, incest, and sodomy are common despite the severity of the penalties prescribed by Islamic law for these offenses. Many Maldivians eat opium "to practice their lechery" with greater strength and abandon.[37]

Formal education begins at the age of nine when the children first learn how to read and write. They particularly study the Koran "to know how they have to live." Pyrard claims that they are taught three sorts of letters: a modified Arabic alphabet, their Maldivian alphabet, "and a third which is common to Ceylon and to the greater part of India."[38] The children practice

[33] *Ibid.*, pp. 170–73.

[34] *Ibid.*, pp. 175–80.

[35] Mosquitoes are the vector for this variety of malaria. It is a debilitating rather than a fatal disease. See Stoddard *et al.*, *op. cit.* (n. 17), p. 32.

[36] Gray and Bell (trans. and eds.), *op. cit.* (n. 8), I, 180–84.

[37] *Ibid.*, p. 195.

[38] The second is a reference to the "island letters," an alphabet of twenty-five letters written from left to right. The third is a possible reference to the *Gabuli tana* which became popular

writing on wooden boards sprinkled with sand. Later they whiten little wooden tablets with clay and write on them with ink. When finished, they wash the tablet clean and rewhiten it. Permanent writings are incised on the large leaves of a particular tree and bound together to make books "which last as long or longer than ours, without decaying." Aside from religious subjects, they cultivate mathematics and astrology. Nobles have a school where they teach the use of weapons: sword, bow, pike, and arquebus.[39]

The political organization of the archipelago is founded on geography. The thirteen atolls constitute thirteen provinces, each of which is ruled by a "Naybe" (Arabic, *naib*), an ecclesiastic who is in charge of religion, education, and justice. Their subordinates, the "Catibe," rule the individual islands that are inhabited. Four times each year the "Naybe" inspects the islands within his jurisdiction and collects taxes. The "Naybes" report to a superior located at Male called the "Pandiare" (Maldive, *Fadiyaru*), who is advised by a council of four or five men of learning. He administers the island of Male personally and the other twelve provinces through the "Naybes." The "king," who is the one on whom everything depends, is advised by his own council of six lords. Royal tax collectors are stationed in each province to levy and collect taxes for the sultan and for Goa, a reference which indicates that in Pyrard's time the Maldives were still paying tribute to the Portuguese.[40]

In a lengthy discussion of legal practices, Pyrard again reveals the degree to which native and Islamic traditions intermingle in the Maldives. Of particular interest is his treatment of human bondage, the most common type of which is debt slavery. A debtor becomes the bondsman of his creditor until the debt is paid. If payment is not forthcoming, the descendants of the debtor continue in bondage. Slaves of any sort may not bear witness or marry more than one wife. In trials or judgments nothing is ever written down except for deeds to property. The testimony of one man is equal to that of three women. Only the sultan can decree a death sentence. The usual punishments for most crimes are banishment to the desert islands of the south, mutilation of a part of the body, or scourging.[41]

Society is divided into four classes: royal family, royal appointees and ministers, nobles by birth or royal appointment, and the common people. The first two classes are furnished with rice by the sultan. The revenues from certain islands are granted to the royal ministers as salaries and pensions. Nobles are numerous throughout the islands, because "the king enobles whom he will." To be well regarded a noble must serve the sultan in an administrative or military capacity. The royal guard includes six hundred

---

during the seventeenth century in India and Ceylon and is written from right to left. See *ibid.*, pp. 184–85n.

[39] *Ibid.*, pp. 184–87.
[40] *Ibid.*, pp. 197–201.
[41] *Ibid.*, pp. 201–7.

men in six companies of one hundred each, commanded by six elders. In addition, the militia consists of ten other companies (presumably of one hundred each also) who are commanded by ten of the greatest lords. Men of substance purchase their position in the militia from the sultan. Slaves, coco workers, and illiterates may not serve. Persons of all classes have but one name, usually Muhammad or some other Islamic name. To distinguish one from the other they add the rank to the name. All commoners are termed "Callo" (Maldives, *Kalo*) and are distinguished by the addition of their occupation or condition.[42]

The sultan's court in Male consists of several stone buildings elevated three feet above the ground. The royal halls are decorated with silk tapestries and other wall hangings from China and India. At court everybody sits cross-legged on mats, the sultan on an elevated platform. Nobles sit in rank order, the highest being closest to the sultan. A special mode of speech is reserved for addressing the sultan and is never employed otherwise. Visitors to the court are obliged to present a gift to the ruler. The sultan and his wives alone are permitted to wear leather slippers sewn with gold thread, from Arabia. The chief symbol of majesty is the royal umbrella or parasol. Whenever the sultan leaves the palace, he is accompanied by a company of the royal guard. Generally he walks or is carried on a litter, since animals for riding do not exist in the islands.[43]

The sultan's revenues derive from a variety of sources. His domain consists of many islands which he holds as crown lands. Dues in kind are paid by his subjects: a fifth of all grain harvested, a percentage of the coconut and lemon crops, a fixed annual amount of palm-sugar, coir, dried fish, and shells called "Boly" (cowrie). Those who hold rank or office pay in cash rather than in kind. Each year the sultan provides certain of his subjects with raw cotton which they are obliged to make into cloth and return to him. Everything found on the seashores, including shipwrecks, as well as all of the precious ambergris and sea coconuts (*Lodicca seychellirum,* or Seychelles nuts) belong to the sultan. The crown monopolizes the grey and black amber, as well as the black coral, and employs people to gather it. Foreign vessels which call in the Maldives must declare their cargo, sell to the sultan whatever he wants at a price he will agree to pay, and remainder the rest to the people at a price higher than that paid by the crown.[44]

The Maldives import rice, white cottons, raw silk and cotton, coffee, body oil, areca, porcelain, gold, and silver. Gold and silver bars are never reexported, for they make currency and trinkets from these metals. Exports include cordage (coir), coconuts, and other coco products, up to more than one hundred shiploads annually. Great quantities of dried fish, bonito, and

---

[42] *Ibid.,* pp. 208–17.
[43] *Ibid.,* pp. 218–27.
[44] *Ibid.,* pp. 227–31.

tuna are sent to Acheh in Sumatra. Thirty to forty shiploads of cowries, gathered twice a month by women from the beaches and shallows of the sea, are exported annually to Bengal where they are "ordinary money." A virtual monopoly of the Maldives, the cowries are purchased by most of the states on the Bay of Bengal and by the Portuguese, English, and Dutch. The Europeans reexport them to Africa and the West Indies where they are also accepted as currency.[45] The Maldivians pack twelve thousand of them in little cocobaskets, an amount equal in exchange to one Maldive *larin,* a silver piece struck in the islands and stamped with the sultan's name in Arabic letters. Cowries are stored in treasure troves in Bengal and set in furniture manufactured in India as if they were precious stones. A certain kind of tortoise shell, found only in the Maldives and the Philippines, is exported to Cambay, where it is made into bracelets and other knickknacks. They also enjoy a brisk export trade in "rush mats of perfect smoothness" and in patterned and figured cotton cloths in various colors.[46]

Pyrard reconstructs the history of the Maldives from 1550, when Sultan Hassan abdicated and fled to Cochin, to the Frenchman's own departure early in 1607. Based on the oral tradition current in the Maldives, he states that Hassan from his exile called upon his subjects to become Christians. On their refusal, the Portuguese attacked Male, killed the usurper, built a fort, set up a garrison, appointed a native governor, and required that tribute be sent to Hassan. After a decade of Portuguese rule, a native resistance movement was organized in the southernmost islands. With the help of Malabar corsairs, the father and uncle of the sultan reigning in Pyrard's day ousted the Portuguese and became masters of the islands. After turning back several Portuguese attempts to retake Male, the Maldivians concluded a peace arrangement which "has endured to the present day." By its terms the Portuguese agreed to leave the Maldives in peace, in return for the payment of a pension to the sultan in Cochin and for agreeing to purchase Portuguese passes for their ships sailing to foreign ports. One-third of the ex-sultan's pension was to be paid to the king of Portugal. Despite this peace agreement, Pyrard asserts that "they still bear a deadly hatred to the Portuguese."[47]

The two brothers reigned in peace for the next twenty-five years. To establish their legitimacy the new rulers married members of the exiled sul-

[45] Tavernier declares that the cowries are found nowhere else in the world. Because of their scarcity they are used as currency "even to the islands of America." See V. Ball (trans. and ed.), *Travels in India by Jean Baptiste Tavernier* . . . (2 vols.; London, 1889), I, 28.

[46] *Ibid.,* pp. 232–42; on p. 232 there is a picture of the Maldivian *larin.* See our pl. 35 for a cowrie. Pyrard saw other coins of iron, Malayan tin (Malay, *kalang*) and the Spanish real. He notes that silver is more highly valued than gold in Male. Maldive fish, still a delicacy in Ceylon and India, accounts today in value for 90 percent of the export trade. Fish processing and coir making are still the most important industries. For discussion of the modern economy see Stoddard *et al., op. cit.* (n. 17), pp. 42–47.

[47] Gray and Bell (trans. and eds.), *op. cit.* (n. 8), I, 244–51. No record of this treaty has yet been found in the Portuguese sources.

tan's family. Because they were commoners by origin, they had constantly to be on the watch for rebellion. To prevent revolt, soldiers who leave Male for other islands are required to leave their firearms behind in the royal magazine. Only a specified number of soldiers are permitted to leave the capital at one time and others may not leave until the absentees have returned. Permissions to leave are granted only during the winter when the westerly winds prevail, a rule which was evidently enacted in the knowledge that Portuguese or other invading forces from the east could not sail against the monsoon. Clearly, even in Pyrard's time, the rulers of the Maldives feared that an internal threat to their regime was present and that foreign forces might take advantage of a revolt to gain ascendancy over their strategically important atolls.[48]

Diplomatic contacts were maintained with Goa and the Malabar city-states. About one year before Pyrard left, an emissary from Goa, Adrian de Gouveia, appeared in Male to negotiate about a law suit involving the Christian Maldivian princes in India. He was left to cool his heels for four months before being received at court. Evidently the Maldivian government was then stocking firearms and cannons against possible internal subversion or invasion from without. In February, 1607, a Bengali fleet invaded Male, ostensibly to capture the stockpile of cannons. Ibrahim, the ruler in Pyrard's day, fled southward but was captured and killed by the Bengalis. Pyrard, who remained behind in Male, instructed the Bengalis in the use of the cannons and informed them about the islands. After the withdrawal of the Bengali fleet with Pyrard aboard, a civil war ensued in the islands. Peace was restored by a fleet sent to the Maldives by Ali Raja, ruler of Cannanore in Malabar. At this point Cannanore controlled most of the trade betweeen Malabar and the Laccadive and Maldive archipelagoes and stood to profit from peace.[49]

The Bengali fleet sailed north from the Maldives to the island of Minicoy, today a part of Lakshadweep, itself a territory belonging to India. Pyrard describes it as being at one time part of the Maldive realm and as using "the same customs, manners, and language as those of the Maldives."[50] Pyrard was received by a "queen" who "holds it of the King of Cahanor [Cannanore] for the sake of greater security." From here Pyrard sailed further northward to what he calls "Divandurou," the Anduru, or Androth, Islands, a designation derived from Androth, the largest of the Laccadive group and its leading Muslim center. The peoples of these five islands, who are ruled by Cannanore, are Muslims who follow the customs and use the language (Ma-

---

[48] *Ibid.*, pp. 251, 275.
[49] *Ibid.*, pp. 293, 310–23.
[50] *Ibid.*, p. 323. This assertion is still generally correct, for the people on this island are the only group in Lakshadweep who use the Maldive language.

layalam) of Malabar. "These islands are, as it were, a half-way house for merchandise between the mainland and the Maldives and Malecut [Minicoy]."[51]

About these islands off Malabar and Ceylon the Portuguese writers of the first half of the century have almost nothing to say, probably because the Portuguese protectorate, if such a thing existed, could not be administered effectively as the power of Goa waned. Clearly the trade of the islands was in the hands of Ali Raja, the Muslim ruler of Cannanore, who styled himself "sultan of the Laccadives." The Dutch sent ships to the Maldives from their factories on the Coromandel Coast to purchase cowries for their trade in the Bay of Bengal.[52] From the middle of the century onward, cowries became a regular import of Amsterdam, where they were sold to the Dutch West India Company.[53] As the Dutch extended their control over Ceylon and the Malabar cities, they assumed a protectorate over the Maldives and placed them under the government of Ceylon. Cannanore, whose fortress fell to the Dutch without resistance in 1663, maintained friendly relations with the Dutch and was probably permitted to continue its trading activities in the islands.[54] The Portuguese meanwhile removed the exiled Maldivian princes from Cochin to Goa to keep them from falling into the hands of the Dutch. Like the Portuguese, the Dutch commentators of the seventeenth century have nothing to add to Pyrard's invaluable description of the Maldives and the Laccadives.[55]

2

CEYLON

From the mid-sixteenth century publications of Barbosa, Barros, and Castanheda, an interested European could have obtained an accurate but limited picture of Ceylon's placement, physical features, political divisions, trading centers, and leading products (elephants, cinnamon, and precious stones).[56] Linschoten, from his vantage point in Goa, supplied at the end of the century later information on the Portuguese military position at Colombo and

[51] *Ibid.*, pp. 323–25. Laccadives were called the "Mammale islands" by the Portuguese from the name of the great merchant of Cannanore who controlled their trade. On Cannanore's rule see Murkot Ramunny, *Laccadive, Minicoy, and Amindivi Islands* (New Delhi, 1972), pp. 17–18.
[52] See T. Raychaudhuri, *Jan Company in Coromandel, 1605–90* (The Hague, 1962), pp. 86, 89.
[53] K. Glamann, *Dutch-Asiatic Trade, 1620–1740* (Copenhagen, 1958), pp. 22–23.
[54] See P. C. Alexander, *The Dutch in Malabar* (Annamalainager, 1946), pp. 159, 162. The Dutch maintained only a small garrison at Cannanore.
[55] Christoph Schweitzer, a German in the employment of the Dutch, apparently had some acquaintance with the Maldivians living in Colombo in 1681. See R. Raven-Hart (trans. and ed.), *Germans in Dutch Ceylon* (Colombo, n.d.), pp. 74, 78.
[56] See *Asia*, I, 342–45. Only one-half the area of New York state, this small tropical island is remarkable in the variety of its landscape, climate, flora, fauna, and products.

on additional items of trade produced in Ceylon.[57] From the secular and religious accounts available in Europe at the beginning of the seventeenth century, Friar San Román de Ribadeneyra compiled a general description of the island in the context of reporting on its "discovery" by the Portuguese.[58]

As Linschoten notes, the Portuguese had tried with varying success during the sixteenth century to take over the kingdom of Kotte and the rest of Ceylon's western coastal plain. The Portuguese went on the defensive in the 1580's and were practically confined to their fort at Colombo. The attempted subordination of Kotte by the Portuguese had been paralleled by the rise of the kingdom of Sitavaka, which led the native resistance to the encroachments of Portuguese arms and the Catholic religion. Raja Sinha (r. 1581–93), ruler of Sitavaka, had annexed the interior kingdom of Kandy by 1582 and had gradually come to control most of the lands formerly belonging to Kotte. In 1587–88 he had besieged Colombo and threatened seriously the entire Portuguese position in the island. To relieve the pressure on Colombo, the Portuguese had sent an expeditionary force from Mannar against Kandy led by Konappu Bandara (known in Goa as Dom João of Austria). Once in power at Kandy, Konappu had turned against his Portuguese allies and thereafter had assumed leadership in the war against them. The Portuguese meanwhile had defeated by 1594 the forces of Sitavaka in the western lowlands and had established dominion there and in part of the northern kingdom of Jaffna. Over the next half century the Portuguese tried unsuccessfully to reduce Kandy to submission.[59]

A. SOURCES

As part of their forward policy in Ceylon, and because they now controlled more territory on the island than ever before, the Portuguese brought an end to the Franciscan monopoly of missions and opened the field in 1602 to the Jesuits. Soon a few Augustinians and Dominicans also began work in Colombo. In an effort to avoid mission competition from developing, as it had in Japan, the authorities of church and state sought, but without much success, to create specified zones of activity for the orders.[60] In Portugal, Guerreiro let it be known by 1606–7 that ten Jesuits were operating a College at Colombo and that three dependent residencies existed in the towns of "Cailor" (Kalatura?), "Chilau" (Chilaw), and "Cardiva" (Karativu) on an island between Chilaw and "Putulão" (Puttalam). The fathers also were

[57] See Burnell and Tiele (eds.), *op. cit.* (n. 4), I, 76–81; II, 292–94.

[58] San Román de Ribadeneyra, *op. cit.* (n. 6), pp. 104–6. The Ceylon section depends heavily on Maffei's work.

[59] Based on Tikiri Abeyasinghe, *Portuguese Rule in Ceylon, 1594–1612* (Colombo, 1966), pp. 9–15.

[60] See *ibid.*, pp. 197–99.

reportedly acting as chaplains to the Portuguese troops attacking Kandy.[61] Guerreiro encouraged Pierre Du Jarric, the Bordeaux Jesuit, to write his widely circulated *Histoire des choses plus memorables advenues tant ez Indes,* a three-volume work (1608, 1610, and 1614) which includes substantial sections on Portuguese activities and Jesuit interests in Ceylon.[62]

The Dutch were well aware from the beginning of their activities in the East of the strategic importance of Ceylon to Asian and Portuguese trade. Joris van Spilbergen, a native of Antwerp, led an expedition to Ceylon in 1602. On May 29 he landed at Batticaloa on the eastern side of the island, a long distance from the Portuguese fort at Colombo. Here he was given a friendly reception by the "Modeliar" (Sinhalese and Tamil, *mudaliyār*), the local captain. After communicating with the king of Kandy called "Fimala Derma Suriada" (Vimaladharmasuriya, who reigned from 1592 to his death in 1604), Spilbergen departed for the interior kingdom in July, 1602. On the way the Lowlanders halted at "Vintane" (Bintenna) on the river of Trincomalee. Arrived in Kandy, Spilbergen presented gifts to the king, including a portrait of Prince Maurice of Nassau in full battle dress. During his stay of five days in Kandy, Spilbergen assured the king that the Dutch were enemies of the Portuguese and willing to cooperate with Kandy in driving them out of the island. This business concluded, Spilbergen returned to Batticaloa and sailed for Acheh in Sumatra on September 3, 1602.

The story of Spilbergen's embassy was recorded by Cornelis Janszoon Vennip, a native of Enkhuizen who kept a journal until his death at sea on the return voyage. This book, *'t Historiael journael,* published at Delft in 1604 by Floris Balthasar, was the first Dutch work on Ceylon prepared by an eyewitness. It went through six printings in the seventeenth century.[63] It provides more than a record of the progress of the embassy, for Vennip clearly endeavored to learn as much as possible about the island from reading Linschoten and by his own observations. He reports that the "king" of Batticaloa is named "Dermuts Iangadare" (?), that he rules tyranically, and that he pays tribute to the Portuguese. The rulers of "Settavaca" (Sitavaka), he asserts correctly, are vassals of Kandy, and the Portuguese areas of political dominance are limited to Colombo and Mannar. He describes the Buddhist temples and cloisters of Bintenna and goes into detail about the dress and the processions of the monks. He reports accurately on the early career of the king of Kandy while in the hands of the Portuguese, on his return to

[61] A. Viegas (ed.), *Relação anual . . . nos annos de 1600 a 1609 . . . pelo Padre Fernão Guerreiro* (3 vols.; Coimbra, 1930, 1931, 1941), II, 344–45. Guerreiro (I, 325) repeats the story common in his day that Xavier himself had visited Ceylon. Actually he had gotten no further south than the Fishery Coast.

[62] For the publication history of Du Jarric's work see above, p. 396. For a translation of materials from it to 1600 see E. Gaspard, S. J. (trans. and ed.), "Ceylon according to Du Jarric," *Ceylon Antiquarian and Literary Register,* III (1917–18), 163–73; IV (1918), 5–18; V (1919), 49–57.

[63] For bibliographical details see above, pp. 443–44.

Kandy around 1590, and on his marriage to Doña Catherina, the Christian daughter of the former king. He notes that the king is interested in Western civilization, that he speaks Portuguese well, that he dresses his children in Western clothes, and that he wants to learn Dutch. Vennip reports that the king's ceremonial guard includes soldiers and musicians of many nations, including Portuguese prisoners and deserters. Balthasar, the publisher, added fourteen copper plates to Vennip's text (for some of these, see pls. 180–81), probably engraved by himself. One of these, the portrait of Spilbergen with the "king of Kandy" (see plate 178) was copied by the engraver from a drawing actually made in Kandy.[64]

The early English voyagers were well aware of the importance of both the Maldives and Ceylon to eastern navigation and trade. But they report little in print. Purchas included in his *Pilgrimes* (1625) a summary account of the early Dutch voyages and a reproduction of Hondius' map of Ceylon "for the Reader's further delight, and because I find little Trade of our English of this Iland."[65] Purchas also includes a notice of the mission of Sebald de Weert to Batticaloa in November, 1603, just somewhat more than three months after Spilbergen's departure.[66] He was received by the king of Kandy, who promised to besiege Colombo if the Dutch would prevent the Portuguese from bringing in help from Goa. De Weert received reinforcements from Acheh, but the proposed siege of Colombo never occurred. The Dutch soldiers angered the Sinhalese by killing cows and otherwise misbehaving. As a consequence De Weert and forty-nine of his men were killed and the rest fled to Acheh. About which event Purchas remarks: "some forsooth, imagined that the soules of the oxen (had themselves any) thus slaine were precipitated to hell."[67]

The Portuguese, fearing a Dutch alliance with Kandy, prepared to meet a joint attack on Galle, which was the island's southernmost port, and was of greater importance to navigation than Colombo. They hurried to fortify Galle and prepared for a new invasion of Kandy before Dutch help could arrive. The Portuguese attack on Kandy was turned back shortly before Spilbergen arrived in Ceylon.[68] Dutch naval support never arrived, and Vimaladharmasuriya died in 1604 without having realized his dream of forcing the Portuguese to leave Ceylon. His successor, Senerat (r. 1604–35),

---

[64] Wouter Nijhof (ed.), *De reis van Joris van Spilbergen naar Ceylon, Atjeh, en Bantam, 1601–04* ("WLV," XXXVIII; The Hague, 1933), *passim*. For an English translation of the section on Ceylon see Donald Ferguson (trans. and ed.), "The Visit of Spilbergen to Ceylon, Translated from Admiral Joris van Spilbergen's 'Relation,'" *JRAS, Ceylon Branch*, XXX (1927), 127–79, 361–409.

[65] *PP*, V, 208–9.

[66] *Ibid.*, pp. 213–16. The source for this account is in T. De Bry, *Petits voyages*, Vol. VIII (Frankfurt, 1607). See P. A. Tiele, *Mémoire bibliographique sur les journaux des navigateurs . . .* (reprint of 1867 ed., Amsterdam, 1960), pp. 167–69.

[67] *PP*, V, 216.

[68] See Abeyasinghe, *op. cit.* (n. 59), pp. 44–49.

continued to seek Dutch assistance, but without immediate success.[69] When Pyrard visits Ceylon in 1608 with the Portuguese fleet, he reports that the Portuguese have strong and well garrisoned forts at Colombo and Galle which are provisioned from abroad. He emphasizes the importance of the Cape of Galle to international navigation and trade, compares it to the Cape of Good Hope, and describes how the Dutch prey almost at will upon Portuguese shipping in its vicinity. The rulers of Ceylon prefer the other Europeans to the Portuguese, with whom they are constantly fighting a "cruel war." Little by little, it appears to Pyrard, the Portuguese have conquered the majority of these people and are "overcoming the rest."[70] Such must have seemed to be the case, for Senerat's succession was then being disputed militarily by Mayadunne of Uva. Taking advantage of this crisis, the Portuguese burned the city of Kandy in 1611.

At Goa meanwhile, Diogo do Couto (1542–1616), the Keeper of the Royal Archives, was completing his *Décadas*, a continuation of the work of Barros which covers the history of the Portuguese in the East from 1526 to 1600. Although the *Décadas* of Couto do not extend into the seventeenth century, they constitute the point of departure for many major accounts of Ceylon published in that century and later. Couto spent almost fifty years in the Portuguese East. In his *Décadas* V and VI, published respectively in 1612 and 1614 shortly before his death, he relates more authoritatively than any of his predecessors or contemporaries the early history of Ceylon.[71] He commences with the assertion, written in 1597, that Ceylon since its discovery in 1505 has "always been to the state of India another Carthage to Rome."[72] It alone has cost Portugal more in men, money, and munitions than all the other conquests in the East. From the Sinhalese princes residing in Goa, Couto learned about the native history. He was the first European, as he asserts, who knew anything about these traditions. He tried, but without notable success, to summarize the *Rājāvaliyas,* a chronicle in the Sinhalese language dating from the fourteenth and fifteenth centuries.[73] He relates the story about the solar origins of the kings of Ceylon as it was "chanted by a prince of Ceilão, in verses after their mode, which an interpreter went on interpreting to us."[74] Couto was interested in Buddhism and made sincere attempts to learn what he could about its Sinhalese and Burmese

---

[69] See K. W. Goonewardena, *The Foundation of Dutch Power in Ceylon, 1638–1658* (Amsterdam, 1958), p. 7.

[70] Gray and Bell (trans. and eds.), *op. cit.* (n. 8), II, 140–49.

[71] See *Da Asia de Diogo de Couto . . . Decada Quinta* (reprinted in Lisbon by the Livraria San Carlos, 1974), XII, 45–80; 163–80; 206–12; 454–61. For an English translation and explanatory notes see Donald W. Ferguson, "The History of Ceylon from the Earliest Times to 1600 A.D., as Related by João de Barros and Diogo do Couto," *JRAS, Ceylon Branch,* XX (1909).

[72] Ferguson (trans. and ed.), *loc. cit.* (n. 71), p. 62.

[73] *Ibid.,* pp. 62–71; also see G. E. Godahumba, "Historical Writing in Sinhalese," in C. H. Philips (ed.), *Historians of India, Pakistan, and Ceylon* (London, 1961), p. 75.

[74] Ferguson (trans. and ed.), *op. cit.* (n. 71), pp. 101–2.

forms from his observation post in Goa. From his Sinhalese informants he learned in detail about Adam's Peak and the belief that the footprint on its rock was left by the Buddha on his visit to the island.[75] He points out the similarities between the Buddha story and that of the Christian St. Barlaam.[76] He spent great time and effort in trying to prove from classical authors, from his more immediate predecessors, and from Roman artifacts that the Taprobane of antiquity was indeed Ceylon and not Sumatra.[77] Most of the later writers of the seventeenth century, as well as Valentijn in the eighteenth, accepted Couto's designation. Like most of the other commentators he praises the fertility of the island, enumerates its products, and notices that "it has many makers of arms, chiefly firelocks . . . the best in the whole of India."[78] Many of Couto's other assertions about the weakness, wiliness, and dishonesty of the Sinhalese were those of a patriot who shared the exasperation of his countrymen about their inability to control, pacify, and convert the island and its peoples.[79]

During the last years of Couto's life (1604 to 1616) the Portuguese and the Kandyans raided each other's territories without either being able to claim victory. While stalemate continued in Ceylon, the Portuguese supremacy in the Indian Ocean was being regularly challenged and steadily eroded by the Dutch and the English. When Dom Nuno Alvares Pereira became captain-general of Ceylon in 1616, the western flatlands were secure and the missions there expanding. Abruptly this enforced peace was shattered by the outbreak of rebellions in Kotte. Kandy immediately sought to take advantage of this crisis to drive the Portuguese into the sea. But Senerat soon faced revolt in his own mountainous domain and sought an accommodation with the Portuguese. Confronted by the rising tides of Dutch and English power at other points in the Estado da India, the viceroy in Goa decided to treat Senerat's peace overture seriously and to concentrate Portugal's dwindling resources upon the pacification of the western lowlands. The Luso-Kandyan peace treaty of 1617 enabled the Portuguese to turn from Kotte northward to complete the conquest of Jaffna, a feat accomplished by 1619. Dom Constantino de Sá, who became captain-general at this juncture, was never en-

[75] *Ibid.,* pp. 108–17. In the eighteenth century François Valentijn included a translation of Couto's description in his work, and Sá de Meneses (see below, p. 952) also quotes from it.
[76] *Ibid.,* pp. 113–14.
[77] While most modern scholars agree with Couto, this question still vexes some. As late as 1974, Professor Jean Filliozat presented a paper before the Sixth International Conference of Asian Historians at Jogjakarta in which he endeavored to identify Taprobane as Sumatra. See S. Arasaratnam (trans. and ed.), *Francois Valentijn's Description of Ceylon* ("HS," 2d ser., CXLIX; London, 1978), p. 99, n. 1.
[78] Ferguson (trans. and ed.), *loc. cit.* (n. 71), p. 117.
[79] The Portuguese priest and Jesuit authority Fernão de Queyroz makes extensive and critical use of Couto in his great work on Ceylon written between 1671 and 1686. It was first published in definitive form by S. G. Perera, S.J. (trans. and ed.), as *The Temporal and Spiritual Conquest of Ceylon* (6 books in 3 vols.; Colombo, 1930). Father Perera writes (I, 11*): "Queyroz has made large use of Couto's *Decada,* but his manuscript sources enabled him to elucidate, correct, criticise, and even reprehend Couto."

tirely convinced of the durability of the peace with Kandy. Nor were his contemporaries and successors; they never abandoned hope of making a more favorable peace arrangement or conquering Kandy totally. From 1620 to 1630, despite these tensions, a *modus vivendi* between the Portuguese and Kandy gradually evolved. The Portuguese controlled the coastal areas by the skillful use of Sinhalese forces in Tamil Jaffna and of Tamils in the Sinhalese territories. War between Kandy and the Portuguese erupted between 1630 and 1633. Thereafter Raja Sinha II (r. 1635–87), Senerat's successor in Kandy, turned to the Dutch for aid.[80]

Events in Ceylon were closely watched in a Portugal smarting from a series of reverses in the Estado da India and hoping for a complete victory in this island so vital to trade and empire. But contemporary publications recounting these events are notable by their absence. In Madrid, Faria y Sousa was collecting materials relating to Ceylon for his *Asia portuguesa* until the outbreak in 1640 of the Portuguese war of independence.[81] In Portugal those discontented with Spanish rule sought a scapegoat for their failures in Ceylon. Governor-General Constantino de Sá y Noronha, who ruled the Portuguese territories in Ceylon from 1623 to 1630 in the name of the Habsburg king, was held personally responsible by his Portuguese critics for the utter rout of the Portuguese force which invaded Kandy in 1630 and for his own death in this ill-fated campaign. To rehabilitate his father's reputation, João Rodriguez de Sá de Meneses collected materials and wrote before 1640 his *Rebelion de Ceylan*. Like Faria y Sousa's work, Sá de Meneses' book did not appear in print until long after its author's death.[82]

The *Asia portuguesa,* a distillation in Spanish of Faria y Sousa's manuscripts and papers prepared by his son, was finally published at Lisbon in 1675. A perusal of Volume III reveals that Faria y Sousa kept close track of events in Ceylon for the period from 1620 to 1633. Most of the references in this chronicle relate to military affairs and the barbarities of war. His account of the ill-fated invasion of Kandy in 1630 suggests that De Sá lost the battle and his own life because of his naive reliance on native informants by whom he was duped.[83] Occasionally Faria y Sousa inserts moral asides:

The Portuguese can recover what is lost, but know not how to preserve what they gain, which is the most glorious part, it being the Work of Fortune to gain, and that of Prudence to preserve.[84]

[80] Based on C. R. de Silva, *The Portuguese in Ceylon, 1617–1638* (London, 1968), chap. ii and pp. 247–51. For this period in the broader context of Portuguese imperial problems see G. D. Winius, *The Fatal History of Portuguese Ceylon: Transition to Dutch Rule* (Cambridge, Mass., 1971).

[81] For a discussion of this project see above, pp. 354–55.

[82] Many students of this period have claimed that Sá de Meneses wrote his book almost fifty years after his father's death. From internal evidence it now appears that he completed it before 1640. See C. R. de Silva, *op. cit.* (n. 80), p. 256.

[83] See the abridged English translation by John Stevens, *The Portuguese Asia . . .* (3 vols.; London, 1695), III, 375–76.

[84] *Ibid.,* p. 383.

He concludes his account of Ceylon on a more positive note by telling of the relief of the siege of Colombo and the peace overtures of Kandy in 1633. In the following year Kandy, probably unknown to Faria y Sousa, began its negotiations for an alliance with the Dutch.

The *Rebelion de Ceylan* of Sá de Meneses was finally published in Spanish at Lisbon in 1681.[85] As in most such apologias, the victories of the hero are exaggerated and his losses minimized.[86] Nonetheless this brief biography elevated its subject to a heroic *fidalgo* who lost his own life in a battle he was goaded into undertaking. The Viceroy Conde de Linhares, a zealous official new to Asia, had demanded the conquest of Kandy even though the Portuguese force was too small and weak and its commander reluctant to commit it to battle. Constantino's reputation for courage and honor was rehabilitated in Portugal, despite the strictures laid upon him by Faria y Sousa and others. He was also celebrated by many of his contemporaries and later writers for his humanitarian attitude towards the Sinhalese.[87] Accompanying the restoration of his reputation the tradition became ever stronger in Portugal that the Sinhalese were ungrateful and perfidious in their desertion of De Sá and the standard of Portugal. The Sinhalese explain their reaction against the Portuguese by recalling that paternalism and Christian charity are no substitutes for independence and internal peace.[88]

João Ribeiro (d. 1693), a Portuguese who fought in Ceylon in 1656–58 as Portuguese rule ended, admits that mistakes were made in the conquest of India. What had started out to be a Christian crusade was transformed by the avarice of particular individuals into an overextended empire of petty forts where commerce rather than religion was enthroned, and "where every friendly Prince was bled till in desperation he declared war." The wealth and potential of this empire stirred the envy of the other European powers and made competition and conflict inevitable in the East.[89] Whatever reasons may be adduced, Portugal's loss of Ceylon opened the road to Malabar for the Dutch and led to the destruction of the Estado da India.

News of the Dutch victories in Ceylon was relayed to Europe at large in

[85] Summarized in English in the *JRAS, Ceylon Branch*, XI (1890), by H. H. St. George, pp. 427–45.

[86] Queyroz, who thought highly of Sá de Meneses' little book, was led by following it to exaggerate vastly the number of Sinhalese killed by Constantin de Sá and his troops in the battle of Lellopitiya of 1618. See C. R. de Silva, *op. cit.* (n. 80), pp. 40–41.

[87] Antonio Alvares da Cunha, an editor of Camões, published a poem at Lisbon in 1689 called *Rebellão de Ceilão*.

[88] C. R. de Silva, *op. cit.* (n. 80), pp. 109–10.

[89] This work was not published in the seventeenth century. In 1701 the Abbé le Grand published at Paris an abridged version in French translation. See D. Ferguson (trans. and ed.), "Captain João Ribeiro: His Work on Ceylon and the French Translation Thereof by the Abbé (Joachim) le Grand," *JRAS, Ceylon Branch*, X (1887–88), 263. The original Portuguese version written in Lisbon between 1680 and 1685 was finally published by the Portuguese Academy of Science in 1836. Paul Pieris published an English translation of the Portuguese printed text in Colombo early in the twentieth century which has gone through four editions. The above is based on Pieris' second edition (1909) of Ribeiro's *History of Ceilão*, p. 393.

the writings of a number of Germans, some of whom had been employed by the VOC in various capacities. In 1639 Johann Albrecht von Mandelslo (1616–44), a German gentleman and traveler, was becalmed in his vessel off the coast of Ceylon for three weeks, during which time he gathered information on Ceylon and its environs.[90] Johann von der Behr (d. *ca*. 1692), who served as a soldier in Asia from 1644 to 1650, published the *Diarium* of his Ceylon experience at Jena in 1688.[91] On garrison duty at Negombo, whose fort had just been taken by the Dutch, Behr had time to keep a record of his movements about the island. He fleshed out his personal story with descriptions of the people, products, and customs of Ceylon mainly derived from other contemporary accounts. Since this was a period of truce (1642–50) between the Dutch and Portuguese, Behr saw only sporadic moments of violent action. In 1645–46 his unit advanced against Kandy, disputes having arisen between its ruler and the Dutch over certain of their previously concluded agreements. Behr traveled by sea to Galle and Colombo and made occasional forays inland from Negombo. His *Diarium* reveals especially aspects of everyday life in a Dutch garrison and of those products and practices of Ceylon which attracted or repelled him. He is particularly fascinated by drink and food, and even gives a few of his favorite recipes.

Albrecht Herport's *Reise* (Bern, 1669) includes accounts of his years in Ceylon from 1663 to 1666, a period when the Dutch were consolidating their hold on the island.[92] An amateur artist, Herport drew pictures on the spot, which were then engraved and added to his book in Bern.[93] His literary descriptions are fuller than those of Behr, possibly because he worked in Ceylon during a period of relative peace. The rupture between Kandy and the Dutch, which developed after the expulsion of the Portuguese, had not yet widened into war. He comments on the strict rule of the king of Kandy, lists the punishments he administers, and tries to present a rank ordering of administrators and castes. He indicates that the Dutch waited for eight years (1658 to 1666) before taking over the administration of the pearl fisheries and provides a full description of oyster fishing and the sale of pearls.

A more systematic account of Ceylon and of Dutch activities there in the mid-seventeenth century was contemporaneously being prepared in Nuremberg by Johann Jacob Saar (1625–72). A commander of the Dutch forces, Saar spent the years from 1647 to 1659 almost continuously in Ceylon and its

---

[90] A first short account of Mandelslo's voyage was issued in 1645 by Adam Olearius (d. 1671). After other printings of this abbreviated version Olearius published the entire account in German at Schleswig in 1658. The voyages of both Olearius and Mandelslo were published in English in 1662 as *The Voyages and Travels of the Ambassadors Sent by Frederick Duke of Holstein to the Great Duke of Muscovy, and the King of Persia* (2 vols. in 1, London). For Ceylon see pp. 111–16.

[91] Reprinted in 1689. A modern reprint is in NR, Vol. IV (1930). An English translation is included in Raven-Hart (trans. and ed.), *op. cit.* (n. 55), pp. 2–23.

[92] Original reprinted in NR, Vol. V (1930); English translation in Raven-Hart (trans. and ed.), *op. cit.* (n. 55), pp. 26–36. Also see above, pp. 532–33.

[93] For his depiction of Colombo see Raven-Hart (trans. and ed.), *op. cit.* (n. 55), facing p. 28.

environs, though he was sent on brief forays to Banda and Ormuz. He made his personal fortune by participating in the sack of Jaffnapatam in 1658. In the following year he left the Dutch service to return to Europe. He claims that a diary he kept was lost at sea on the homeward voyage. With the aid of Daniel Wülfer, a local Nuremberg pastor, he prepared an account of his voyage based on recall and published it in 1662.[94] Ten years later Wülfer published an amplified edition in which he cites in the notes the observations of Behr, Jürgen Andersen of Schleswig, Herport, and Johann Jacob Merklein in order to amend or expand his own account and to point up the differences in these various reports from one another and his own. He also considers the writings of Linschoten, Johann Nieuhof, and Olearius in the light of what he has observed and read.[95]

While Saar was revising in Nuremberg, the Reverend Philippus Baldaeus (1632–1672) in Holland was writing the story of his experiences in southern India and Ceylon from 1656 to 1665.[96] Part 2 of his *Naauwkeurige beschryvinge van Malabar en Choromandel, der zelver aangrenzende ryken, en het machtige eyland Ceylon . . .* (Amsterdam, 1672) relates mainly to the Tamil areas of north Ceylon where he spent most of his stay on the island.[97] For the materials on the period before 1656 Baldaeus depends on the descriptions and testimonies of others, especially the Portuguese writers and the records of the VOC. His description of the siege of Colombo in 1655–56 is based on the account of a Portuguese participant. The last thirty-two chapters, or about one-third of the description of Ceylon, derive mainly from his own experiences in northern Ceylon. Much of this material, as might be expected, is concerned with his missionary and ecclesiastical activities. Included also are engraved portraits of Baldaeus and General Gerald Hulft, views of Ceylon's principal cities and two Dutch fortresses, as well as quaint depictions of natives and their activities. The detailed map which introduces the Ceylon sec-

[94] J. J. Saar, *Ost-Indianische fünfzehen-jährige Kriegs-Dienste und wahrhafftige Beschreibung, was sich . . . von 1644 bis 1659 . . . begeben habe* (Nuremberg, 1662).

[95] The 1672 edition has the same title as the edition of a decade earlier. For Ceylon see especially pp. 53–100; 135–47. This edition is reproduced in NR, Vol. VI. In the foreword the editor discusses the differences between the two editions and notices that they are mainly in the notes and in the comments on other writers. Wülfer also includes a preface in which he ruminates on whether it is right or wrong for Christians to conquer and subjugate heathen nations. Later authors regularly plagiarized Saar's descriptions of Ceylon, especially Behr. His original version was published in Dutch translation in 1671.

[96] On Baldaeus see above, pp. 493–95, and Donald Ferguson, "The Reverend Phillipus Baldaeus and His Book on Ceylon," *Monthly Literary Register* (Colombo), III (1895), 144–48.

[97] The third part of Baldaeus' work is his *Afgoderye der Oost-Indische heydenen,* a discussion of Hindu beliefs and practices. The modern critical edition is by Albertus Johannes de Jong (ed.), published at The Hague in 1917. The whole work was immediately translated into German by the Dutch publisher and an abridged English translation based on the German translation first appeared in 1703 and was reprinted in 1732, 1745, and 1752. The portion of the *Beschryvinge* relating to Ceylon, in the nineteenth-century English translation of Pieter Brohier and with an introduction by S. D. Saparamadu (ed.), was published as Volume VIII (1958–59) of *The Ceylon Historical Journal.*

tion of the work shows very little advance over earlier European maps of the island.[98] In the eighteenth century Valentijn asserted that Baldaeus, his fellow countryman, had provided "the most detailed and the best" account of Ceylon.[99]

Wouter Schouten (1638–1704), a surgeon of Haarlem, published in 1676, the year of Baldaeus' first edition, a large volume divided into two parts, called *Oost-Indische voyagie* (Amsterdam). It includes forty-three copper engravings of Eastern scenes adapted from sketches by the author. Schouten left Europe in 1658, served in Ceylon and Malabar in 1661–62, became acquainted with Baldaeus, and returned to Amsterdam in 1665. His discussion of Ceylon which appears at the end of Part I is accurate, short, and not particularly new in substance. His book was extremely popular in northern Europe and was translated into German (1676) and French (1707 and 1725). The fourth and final edition appeared in Dutch printings as late as 1775 and 1780, and a French version was included in Prévost's *Histoire générale des voyages*, XVI (1758), 168–236.[100] As a physician, Schouten had a more than ordinary interest in flora and fauna and in hygiene and living conditions. He notes that Sinhalese medical men have very little understanding of anatomy and that "their principal knowledge rests upon experience" in concocting herbal medicines.[101]

Robert Knox (1640–1720), an English sailor in the service of the East India Company, put in to Katthia Bay late in 1659 on a crippled ship commanded by his father. After learning indirectly of their appearance, Raja Sinha II of Kandy took captive the captain and fifteen of his men. The prisoners were separated, each being quartered in a different village and at its expense. The English were well treated, as part of the ruler's numerous collection of European Christians. Many of these European captives were forced by economic necessity into various kinds of employment and settled down with Sinhalese women as mistresses or wives. The elder Knox soon died and young Knox stayed on in various villages where he earned his keep by knitting and trading. It was not long before he obtained a piece of property and a house. He planted his land, raised animals, and made profit by trading and by lending out grain at high rates of interest. While thus making the most of their lengthy captivity, Knox and an English companion repeatedly sought to escape. Finally they managed it in November, 1679. Through the good offices of the Dutch, Knox eventually got to the English factory at Bantam. He returned to London in September, 1680, after an absence of over twenty-three years.

[98] See Saparamadu (ed.), *op. cit.* (n. 97) p. xxxv.
[99] Arasaratnam (trans. and ed.), *op. cit.* (n. 77), p. 104.
[100] For an English translation of the materials on Ceylon from the first edition see Ph. Freudenberg (trans. and ed.), "Wouter Schouten's Account of Ceylon," *JRAS, Ceylon Branch*, XI (1889–90), 315–54.
[101] *Ibid.*, p. 346.

On the voyage home Knox wrote down his recollections of Kandy, evidently only for his personal satisfaction. At the urging of the East India Company and the Royal Society these reminiscences were put into book form by Knox in collaboration with his cousin, Reverend John Strype, and under the guiding hand of Dr. Robert Hooke, secretary of the Royal Society. The copyright was sold to Richard Chiswell, printer to the Royal Society, and the book was published on August 1, 1681. The imprimatur of the Company and the Royal Society testified to its "great truth and integrity." *An Historical Relation of the Island Ceylon in the East Indies* is divided into four parts, the first three being a description of Kandy and the fourth the story of Knox's personal capture and escape. German (1689), Dutch (1692), and French (1693) translations soon appeared; the original English version was evidently reprinted several times before Knox's death and an "improved" version was included in Volume II of J. Harris, *Navigantium atque itinerarium* (London, 1705).[102]

Knox's book is the least biased and best informed source for the study of seventeenth-century Ceylon. His experience of living almost twenty years in Kandy provided him with insights ordinarily not available to the passing traveler or to those who spend most of their time with fellow countrymen in seaport enclaves. The conditions of his captivity, and his youth, enabled him to adapt quickly, to learn rapidly the language and customs, and to fend for himself. His prison was large, for he was permitted after a time to travel from place to place within Kandy to carry on his business activities. Like the other foreigners there, he was thought to enjoy the royal protection. As a highly moral and successful individual he seems to have won the respect of people in all classes of society. He could not be the superior Christian or the swaggering colonial in his assessment of Kandy and its peoples, for he was far too long one of them himself. When he finally wrote down his reminiscences he did not have publication in mind; as much as anything else he wrote this account to teach himself how to write English again and not for the purpose of selling books or winning a reputation. His *Relation* is a genuine primary source because he did not have the writings of others available for consultation. In the preparation of his manuscripts for publication, he and Strype evidently limited their revisions to organizational and stylistic matters and were careful not to "improve" the substance of the text. In short, Knox's *Relation* is one of the most informative and reliable accounts of an Asian society published in the seventeenth century. In concentrating perforce on everyday activities, Knox has very little to say about the literary culture of Ceylon or about the seaport region. To modern students of Sinhalese so-

---

[102] A variety of reprintings and abridgments of Knox's work were issued in the nineteenth and twentieth centuries. The most recent of these, and the one on which this account is based, was introduced and edited by S. D. Saparamadu in *The Ceylon Historical Journal*, Vol. VI (1956–57). The bibliography at the end of this edition is especially useful.

ciety, it is a source of popular culture against which other materials, native and foreign, are regularly tested.

After the publication of Knox's *Relation* in 1681, very little that was original or new was added to Europe's store of information on Ceylon. In the following year Christoph Schweitzer of Württemberg, a soldier and bookkeeper employed by the VOC, published at Tübingen the *Journal- und Tage-Buch seiner sechs-jährigen Ost-Indianischen Reise.*[103] Recorded in Dutch but translated into German for publication, Schweitzer's *Journal* relates to his East Indian voyage of 1675 to 1682. Like Knox's *Relation*, this is an original account prepared without consultation of the writings of others. Since he traveled over all the coastal regions and into Kandy, his account is distinguished by the comparisons he draws between the Sinhalese and Tamil regions. In many ways he substantiates what Knox relates and provides descriptions of the Dutch enclaves which supplement those of Baldaeus. Schweitzer, who was also an amateur artist, provided the engraver with drawings from which to make the six prints included in the book. His is the last of the important relations published in the seventeenth century.[104]

The published Iberian authors—Couto, Guerreiro, Faria y Sousa, and Sá de Meneses—gave to their readers only brief and episodic glimpses into what was happening to the Portuguese in Ceylon during the first generation of the century. The best Iberian accounts—those of the Jesuit Queyroz and the soldier Ribeiro—were not published in the seventeenth century. Vennip's record of Spilbergen's embassy to Kandy was the only book published in the first half of the century to provide substantial fresh materials on Ceylon based on experience in the field. It was not until after the Dutch takeover of 1656 to 1658 that new works by firsthand observers began to appear in northern Europe. The books by Saar (1662; amended version of 1672), Baldaeus (1672), Knox (1681), and Schweitzer (1682) provided readers of German, Dutch, English, and French with a comprehensive overview of Ceylon. Baldaeus, who lived and worked mainly in Jaffna, is best on the Tamil country of the north. Knox, with his experience of almost twenty years in Kandy, is superb on the hill country. The German soldiers—Saar and Schweitzer—as employees of the VOC provide fascinating insights into its operations and make occasional independent observations about the maritime provinces which substantiate or call into question the assertions of the Dutch and English authors.

[103] Translated into Dutch in 1694 and into English in 1700. Reprinted in NR, Vol. XI. For a recent English translation see Raven-Hart (trans. and ed.), *op. cit.* (n. 55), pp. 37–82.

[104] Christoph Frick's *Ost-Indianische Räysen* (East Indian journeys) (Ulm, 1692) contains a few additional observations by a physician of what he observed in Ceylon during a visit of 1682 or 1683. See Raven-Hart, *op. cit.* (n. 55), pp. 84–85. It was followed just after the turn of the century by the abridgment of Ribeiro's previously unpublished account of Portuguese Ceylon in Abbé Le Grand's *Histoire de l'Isle de Ceylan . . .* (Paris-Amsterdam, 1701).

B. THE LAND AND ITS PRODUCTS

The placement, size, and natural features of Ceylon, along with its identification with the Taprobane of antiquity, had preoccupied the commentators
of the sixteenth century.[105] Baldaeus, who starts his discussion of Ceylon's
"situation" with references to Barros and Maffei, contents himself with a
few generalities about Dutch estimates of its size, "three hundred miles in
circumference," and with naming eight of its rivers. Some of these rivers
"empty into the sea, and the course of some is obstructed at the beach by the
sand but cleared and reopened at the termination of the monsoon."[106] Most
of the European commentators remain convinced that Ceylon is the most
important of the islands off the subcontinent, that it was once a part of India, and that it was constantly becoming smaller as its shores, particularly in
the north, were periodically being washed away. The Dutch commentators,
who were most familiar with the shoreline as it appeared on their charts and
maps, usually describe Ceylon as being like a ham in shape.[107] Baldaeus
notes that the indigenous people call their homeland not Ceylon but "Lan-
kawn."[108] Knox virtually ignores the maritime regions, for they may "be
seen in our ordinary Sea-Cards." To make clearer the inadequacy of previous descriptions of the interior, he procured a copy of the map prepared
for Baldaeus' work and revised it to show the areas of Dutch jurisdiction
and added detail to the interior in terms of its physical characteristics, place
names, and the sentry posts maintained by Kandy.[109]

In chapter i of his *Relation* Knox asserts that the proper name for Kandy is
"Conde Uda," words meaning "on top of the hills."[110] He itemizes its political divisions, "provinces and counties," which are separated by forests as
natural barriers of protection. These trees may not be felled, for they are
used as palisades and lookouts. The country is generally hilly and well watered by streams and rivers. Most of the numerous waterways are not navigable and are loaded with fish. The greatest of its rivers, the "Mavelagonga"
(Mahveli Ganga), arises in Adam's Peak and runs northward into the sea at

---

[105] See *Asia*, I, 342–45.

[106] Baldaeus, in Saparamadu (ed.), *op. cit.* (n. 97), p. 2. Most of the commentators of the
Dutch period estimate the size in terms of circuit, for it was only along the seacoast that the
VOC had forts and settlements. On the problem of siltation in modern times see B. H. Farmer,
Pioneer Peasant Colonization in Ceylon (London, 1957), pp. 191–94.

[107] See especially the remarks of Schouten in Freudenberg (trans. and ed.), *loc. cit.* (n. 100),
pp. 328–29. The language and religion of the Jaffna peninsula gave strong cultural support to
the belief in a close linkage to south India.

[108] Saparamadu (ed.), *op. cit.* (n. 97), p. 1. The name "Lanka" comes from the Indian epic
Ramayana. In 1972 Sri Lanka replaced Ceylon as the official name of the island. The "Sri" is an
honorific prefix.

[109] See *ibid.*, p. xxxv, and Knox's map in our pl. 176.

[110] Sinhalese, *Kanda Uda,* or "above the mountains."

Trincomalee. It runs within one mile of the city of Kandy and is not navigable, except by small canoes, for it is replete with rocks and falls (see pl. 179). This wide, swift, and deep river has no bridge across it because the king has no desire to encourage travel. Except for the "kingdome of Ouvah" (Uva), the country is heavily wooded and replete with deep valleys where they cultivate grain. Water is pure and plentiful everywhere except in a few northern places. The hills are covered with woods and huge rocks; Kandy can be entered only by narrow paths that are protected on either end by thorny gates and sentries. The climate varies greatly depending on the direction of the monsoon. When the winds blow from the west, it rains on the west side and is dry and fair on the east. When the monsoon reverses itself, it rains in the east and is dry in the west. While crops are being planted in the rainy season on one side, they are being harvested during the dry season on the other, "so that Harvest is here in one part or other all year long." This condition does not obtain in the lower hills at the northern end of the island where drought is common. In the coastal lowlands, when there is drought in Jaffna from May to October, the area from Colombo southward is subject to heavy rainfall.[111] In 1680 Schweitzer reports that he and his colleagues were frightened by an earthquake that shook the island and stirred up the sea.[112] Readers in Europe could readily adduce from these notices that the climate in Ceylon is not uniform, that certain zones are dry for most of the year, and that rainfall and land use are related to the vagaries of the monsoon.[113]

In this beleaguered land of Kandy stand five cities, all of them in rundown condition except for the place in which the king resides. The chief city, called Kandy by the Christians (probably from "Conde"), is correctly called "Hingodagul-neure" (Sengkadagala Nuvara), or "the city of the Sinhalese people." Because it is the metropole, it is also called "Mauneur" (Maha Nuvara) or Royal City. It stands in the middle of the island in "Tattanour" (Yati Nuvara) and, following custom, the king's palace is located in its easternmost corner. The city itself is triangular in shape, fortified only on its south side by an earthen rampart, and is surrounded by hills and protected by sentries who guard the paths. Since his royal city was often burned by the Portuguese, the king in 1661 removed his headquarters about twelve miles to the south to "Nellemby-neur" (Nilambe Nuvara) in "Oudipollat" (Uda Palata). Three years later a rebellion occurred here and the king moved his court eastward to "Digligy neur" (Diyatilaka Nuvara), a more defen-

---

[111] Baldaeus in Saparamadu (ed.), *op. cit.* (n. 97), pp. 295–96.

[112] Raven-Hart (trans. and ed.), *op. cit.* (n. 55), p. 71.

[113] The southwest monsoon is dominant from May to September and the northeast from November through February. Local thunderstorms in the afternoons and tropical cyclones also provide rainfall. The time of the southwest monsoon is the dry season in the dry zone of the north. See S. F. de Silva, *A Regional Geography of Ceylon* (Colombo, 1954), p. 63.

sible city. Kandy, in Knox's time, has access to the sea at "Leawava" (Lea-wawa), a port on the southeast side of the island in a remote coastal region not closely controlled by the Dutch, where they can obtain fish and sea salt; on the west side Kandy uses a port in the "Country of Portaloon" (Put-talam). Of their other towns and villages the best preserved and maintained are those which have temples. Located away from the highroads, their isolated villages of one hundred inhabitants or fewer are collections of indi-vidual houses, each enclosed by a hedge or ditch to keep out the cattle. In addition to the functioning cities and towns, Knox reports on ancient cities of which only ruins remain. In the north of Kandy stands the remains of "Anu-rodgburro" (Anuradhapura), a royal city of former times and a center of religion.[114]

Baldaeus, who is primarily interested in European activities in Ceylon, treats of its lowland regions and cities mainly in conjunction with his discus-sion of military activities and missionary progress. Although he provides engraved views of some cities and smaller communities, he is more inter-ested in depicting fortifications and churches than in showing native quar-ters. His best descriptions are those of the island of Mannar and the Jaffna peninsula, the northern places where he conducted his religious activities. In length Mannar "is about a good five hours walk, and two in breadth in-cluding the salt river" which runs through it. On the island there are seven villages, two of which are inhabited by pearl fishers. With the Dutch occu-pation oyster fishing was halted for a time and the island "with its stately building" was reduced from affluence to poverty.[115]

Between Mannar and the Jaffna peninsula lie the lands of the "Wannias" (Vanni), an extremely fertile territory where rice and elephants thrive.[116] The Jaffna peninsula is a twelve hours' walk in length and six in width. It is divided into four provinces, boasts 159 villages, and is densely inhabited. Its capital city of Jaffna (or Jaffnapatam), where the Portuguese originally built a fort, was badly damaged by the Dutch conquest. Near the ruins of an old temple of the city there is a remarkably large well hewn out of a huge rock.[117] While Baldaeus provides engravings of Galle and other coastal places, he confines his remarks to their forts and to the conquest by the Dutch. The other commentators likewise provide only terse descriptions of Colombo and the cities in its environs.[118] There is almost nothing about the east coast

[114] Saparamadu (ed.), *op. cit.* (n. 102), pp. 7–11.

[115] Saparamadu (trans. and ed.), *op. cit.* (n. 97), pp. 287–88.

[116] *Ibid.*, pp. 294–96. See map of Jaffna and the surrounding islands on p. 300. Vanni was an area of eighteen autonomous chiefdoms (*vanniyas*) who cooperated with the VOC to remain free of Kandy. See also Knox's map, our pl. 176.

[117] This is probably a reference to the well at Puttoor; Baldaeus in Saparamadu (trans. and ed.), *op. cit.* (n. 97), p. 316. On p. 324 see his map of the city.

[118] For example see Schouten's brief comments in Freudenberg (trans.), *loc. cit.* (n. 100), p. 330. For a more detailed description of Colombo under Dutch occupation in 1681 see Schweitzer in Raven-Hart (trans. and ed.), *op. cit.* (n. 55), pp. 77–78.

ports that adds anything to the descriptions given in Vennip's account of Spilbergen's embassy at the beginning of the century.

The staff of life in Kandy is grain, the most important being rice. "Of
Rice they have several different sorts, and called by several names according
to the different times of their ripening." Knox describes in some detail their
methods of paddy cultivation, irrigation, and terracing. Most kinds of rice,
a thirsty crop, must stand in water throughout most of the growing period.
Which type of rice they sow, early ripening or later ripening, is dependent
on their estimate of how long the supply of water will last. If possible they
sow that which matures slowly, for it produces a bigger crop than the early-
ripening varieties. In the northern dry zone of Kandy where there are not
sufficient streams, rainfall, or underground water for irrigation, they build
crescent-shaped reservoirs which hold enough water for the cultivation of
early-ripening rice. In other dry places where water cannot be stored they
grow yet another type of rice that will mature without standing in water
throughout its growth period. Ordinarily they sow in July or August, except in well-watered areas where the growing season is all year long. The
cultivation and harvesting of rice is usually performed by communes working together. Once the harvest is completed they open the fields to let their
oxen graze on the paddy stubble.

Oxen are used to pull their light plows, "a crooked piece of Wood, something like an Elbow" (see pl. 186). The plowman holds one end as a handle
while the other roots up the soil with an iron share that is affixed to it. Before plowing they soak the field with water. Their plows break the soil un-
evenly and do not turn the weeds and grass under. After plowing their small
field twice, they flood the land and the water rots the grass. After the first
plowing, they enclose the field with foot-high banks of packed mud which
contain the water and serve as footpaths. Once the banks are completed,
they flood the field and let the water soak in before they begin plowing the
second time. Once the fields are again flooded, they begin to prepare the
seedlings. They soak the seeds and cover a heap of them with leaves for five
or six days to let them sprout, and then this process is repeated. While the
seedlings grow, they flatten the field with a broad board drawn by a yoke of
oxen (see pl. 187). After eight days the seedlings are ready to plant. Then
they drain the field, smooth the soil, and make small furrows in it to keep
the field from becoming waterlogged in case of rain. They then sow the
field by strewing the paddy across it evenly. When the seedlings are three to
four inches high, they flood the field again. After another period of growth,
the women weed and thin the field and transplant the excess seedlings to
other fields. Once the rice is ripe they drain the field and let it dry out. Reaping, like tilling, is a communal activity; the men cut the paddy and the
women carry the sheaves to the threshing place. After the paddy dries, buffaloes and oxen trample out the grain while the cultivators perform certain

harvest rituals (see pl. 188). The husk is removed from the grain by beating it upon the ground or in a mortar.[119]

Despite the great time and attention paid to rice cultivation, Ceylon, then as now, did not produce enough for its own needs. According to Knox, they supplement rice with several other grains. "Coracan" (*kurakkan* in Tamil and Sinhalese; a coarse millet [*Eleusine coracana*] called *ragi* in India) is a small seed that produces good yields both in the hills and the plains.[120] They grind the seeds and from the meal they make cakes that are baked in a pot over a fire. Another grain called "tanna" (a millet [*Setaria italica*] called *Tana hāl* in Sinhalese) is cultivated and eaten mostly in the northern dry zone. This grain, which "gives the greatest increase of any one seed in the world," is boiled like rice for eating. Another dryland crop is "Moung" (Sinhalese, *mung; Phaseolus aureus*), a green grain which grows like a pea in a pod. "Omb" (Sinhalese, *amu; Paspalum scrobiculatum*), a small seed eaten as a rice substitute, acts as an intoxicant if it is consumed before it is mature. And there are other grains from which they make oil for cooking and for anointing themselves.[121]

The Kandyans supplement their diet of grain with the wild fruits that abound on the island, and cultivate only those which "satisfie their hunger when their Corn is spent." Some of these fruits they pick while unripe, cook them, and serve them as relishes with their "Carrees" (curries). The best fruits are reserved for the delectation of the king and his officials and are taken without compensation to the landowners. Consequently the cultivators are not eager to grow fruits that may be summarily confiscated. The areca nut trees which produce the coveted betel nuts are cultivated, but only on the south and west sides of the island to which they are native. The large leaves of this tree are used as dishes and as containers for liquids. Its hard and strong wood is made into laths and fence posts. The nuts not consumed at home are exported to the Coromandel Coast. Jackfruits are boiled and eaten as a vegetable and their kernels roasted as chestnuts are in Europe. Kandy has most of the edible fruits found in India: coconuts, plantains, bananas,

[119] Knox in Saparamadu (ed.), *op. cit.* (n. 102), pp. 11–18. Baldaeus has very little to report on rice cultivation in the Dutch-controlled lowlands. For the history of rice cultivation in Ceylon see D. H. Grist, *Rice* (3d ed., London, 1959), pp. 5–6; and for a modern exposition of the traditional cultivation and threshing techniques see *ibid.*, pp. 122–34. Knox, the young Englishman whose knowledge of Ceylon was greater than his knowledge of Europe, contends that the grains of Ceylon are "all different from ours." He was clearly unaware of the fact that rice had been grown in southern Europe, especially in Spain and Italy, since the fifteenth century and by similar methods.

[120] The very poor in South Asia, particularly in areas where rice is not cultivated, are often forced even yet to live on ragi. See Grist, *op. cit.* (n. 119), p. 348.

[121] Knox in Saparamadu (ed.), *op. cit.* (n. 102), pp. 18–19. This is a description of what is known as chena cultivation. A chena (anglicization of Sinhalese, *hēna*) is a patch in the jungle worked by villagers according to the method of shifting cultivation, that is, planting an area for a few years and then abandoning it. For full descriptions see S. F. de Silva, *op. cit.* (n. 113), pp. 202–5, and Farmer, *op. cit.* (n. 106), pp. 47–50.

sweet oranges, limes, mangoes, pineapples, watermelons, pomegranates, "grapes both black and white," and mirabelles.[122]

Three other trees which do not bear edible fruit are nonetheless valuable. The "tallipot" (Sinhalese, *talapata;* now generally called *talagaha*) stands as tall and straight as a ship's mast and bears nothing of use but huge leaves which can be opened and closed like a folding fan. When closed, the leaf is light and small enough to be carried under the arm. These leaves are used as sunshades, umbrellas, and tents. Knox was so impressed by this leaf that he carried one back to England.[123] The pith of the trunk is made into flour from which they make a bread to eat before the grain harvest. The "kettule" (Sinhalese, *kitul;* a palm, *Garyota urens*) yields a sap which is extracted from the tree two or three times daily. They boil the sap and make a sugar called "Jaggary" (jaggery). From the wiry veins of its leaves they make rope and from its black wood they make pestles to beat the rice. The cinnamon tree which they call "Corunda-gauhah" (Sinhalese, *Kurundu gas*) grows wild, and is as plentiful as hazel in England; it flourishes mainly to the west of the "Mavelagonga." The Kandyans, in contrast to the Europeans, esteem it but little; in addition to using the bark, they extract from its fruit an oil which they use as an ointment or burn in lamps. The fruits (myrobalans) of the "orula" (Sinhalese, *arulu; Terminalia chebula*) are sold in shops for use as a purge, a black dye, and a rust remover. A shrub called "Dounekaia gauhah" (Sinhalese, *dunukeyiya; Pandanas thwaitesü*) has leaves which they split and weave into mats, and roots that they split into thongs which are then woven into ropes. The "Capita gauhah" (Sinhalese, *keppitkya; Croton laccifer*) is a shrub, considered to be poisonous to cattle, from which they make brooms and which they use as fuel for gold-working. Rattans or canes grow everywhere, running on the ground like honeysuckle and even on the trees. Their fruit grows in bunches like grapes and is made into a "sour pottage to quench the thirst." The creeper that produces the betel leaf grows like ivy and twines about trees and poles that its cultivators plant. Finally there is the "Bo-gahah" (Sinhalese, *Bō gahah* or *Aswatha; Ficus religiosa*), called "the Godtree" by Europeans, a tree that is venerated and worshipped because in their tradition it is this kind of tree under which the Buddha sat when here on earth. These great and spreading trees, whose "Leaves always shake like an Asp," are planted everywhere but only by old men. They are tended assiduously, and images and sacrificial stone tables are set up under their boughs.[124]

[122] Knox in Saparamadu (ed.), *op. cit.* (n. 102), pp. 20–23. Some of these fruits were probably introduced by the Portuguese. Baldaeus (Saparamadu [trans. and ed.], *op. cit.* [n. 97], p. 386) writes about the Dutch: "we have now fortunately succeeded in raising cabbages and introduced the *pompelanoes* (pomelo or grapefruit) trees as also asparagus, root-crops, radish, and a variety of Dutch plants."
[123] Knox in Saparamadu (ed.), *op. cit.* (n. 102), pp. 24–25; see our pl. 195 in the present volume.
[124] Knox in Saparamadu (ed.), *op. cit.* (n. 102), pp. 24–29; the bo tree of Ceylon is called the pipul tree in India. It is venerated by both Hindus and Buddhists. At Anuradhapura a bo tree stands that is reputed to be the oldest tree on earth. A seedling was brought from India in

Nature is also bountiful in the roots, plants, herbs, and flowers it provides for food and medicine. Various varieties of aloes (*Aloe vera*) grow wild in the woods or are cultivated in gardens. One type climbs on trees or sticks and another runs on the ground. Both varieties produce enormous roots which serve as a basic food or as relishes for rice dishes. They boil many other wild herbs, which they butter so that they are "almost as good as asparagus."[125] Many English and European herbs and plants have been transplanted to Ceylon and Knox believes "all other European Plants would grow there." They also have ferns and Indian corn (maize). The "Woods are their Apothecaries Shop" for they make "all their Physics and Plaisters" with herbs, leaves, and the bark of trees. All their flowers are wild "for they plant them not." Roses and other sweet-scented flowers are worn in the hair by young persons. A flower called "Sindric-mal" (Sinhalese, *Sendrikka; Mirabilis jalapa*) is used as a timekeeper, for it opens at four in the afternoon and closes at four in the morning. People plant these four-o'clocks in their gardens "to serve them instead of a clock when it is cloudy that they cannot see the sun." A jasmine-like white flower which they call "Picha-mauls" (Sinhalese, *pieca; Jasminum sambac*) is the royal flower and is grown exclusively for the king by designated officials who bring a bunch to him each morning wrapped in a white cloth.[126]

Baldaeus makes a number of additions to Knox's list of plants and their uses. He notes the cultivation of sweet potatoes, papaws, sugarcane, ginger, pepper, cardamom, cotton, pumpkins, and tobacco. From the palm trees native to the island they obtain sugar and sweet toddy.[127] Mulberry plants, he observes, grow there "from which there is now annually a good collection of silk made."[128] Most of these, as well as the European vegetables grown in the Dutch gardens, were probably introduced by the Europeans from other parts of Asia and from their outposts in the Americas. Baldaeus is much more thorough than Knox in his discussion of the cinnamon tree. He observes that these trees do not grow profusely throughout the island but only in the wet low country along the west coast from the river of Chilaw (*Deduru oya*) southward to Galle (see pl. 184).[129] The natives extract

---

288 B.C. which grew into this sacred tree. See H. F. Macmillan, *Tropical Planting and Gardening with Special Reference to Ceylon* (5th ed., London, 1962), p. 441.

[125] For a list of the wild herbs still generally eaten by the poor of Ceylon see Macmillan, *op. cit.* (n. 124), p. 302.

[126] Knox in Saparamadu (ed.), *op. cit.* (n. 102), pp. 30–33. On the four-o'clocks of Malaya (*Wormia suffruticosa*) see E. A. Menninger, *Fantastic Trees* (New York, 1967), p. 216; for the jasmine, see our pl. 171.

[127] For a more detailed discussion of the coconut palms and their numerous products see Behr in Raven-Hart (trans. and ed.), *op. cit.* (n. 55), pp. 4–6.

[128] The worm of the omnivorous "Atlas moth" common to Ceylon produces a good second-rate silk. Repeated efforts to introduce sericulture have failed because of Buddhist objections to destroying the life of the silkworm. See Macmillan, *op. cit.* (n. 124), p. 413.

[129] Schouten concurs about locale and adds that they grow "wild by the thousand and in whole groves" (Freudenberg [trans. and ed.], *loc. cit.* [n. 100], p. 350).

a medicinal oil from its fruit, build houses of its wood, distill a water from its root, and construct little cabinets and boxes from its wood, one of which Baldaeus took back to Holland as a keepsake.[130] He notes that the cinnamon of commerce comes in three grades: fine from young and middle-aged trees, coarse from thicker and older trees, and jungle or wild cinnamon. "The Company is now (under God's blessing) the master of all this cinnamon . . . as well as all other spices, such as nutmegs, mace, and cloves."[131] Snakewood grows abundantly and is prepared as an ointment to cure external sores and itches and taken internally as a medicine for relief of colic, high fever, and snakebites.[132] A wonderful tree called *"Wortelboom"* ("root tree," or the banyan tree; *Ficus indica*) also deserves mention along with the stately tamarind trees whose fruits are edible and useful in the treatment of scurvy and dropsy. Baldaeus concludes that it is wise to be treated by local physicians with native medicines: "as every country has its own peculiar maladies so they have their own proper physicians and cures."[133]

The elephants of Ceylon beguile all the European commentators, for they are judged to be the best in the East; elephants native to other Asian places recognize them as superior beasts by kneeling in their presence.[134] The king of Kandy has the best specimens captured "onely for his recreation and pastime." Particularly prized are male elephants with tusks. Female elephants are used to lure the males into snares, traps, and corrals. The king uses certain bulls as executioners (see pl. 190) and others for exhibition. Roving elephants damage crops and homes, terrify travelers, and often kill those who hunt them. The elephants show a high regard for one another, the females being protected by the males. Young elephants may be nursed by females other than the mother. All members of the herd protect and aid the young. Captive females are bred to wild males; the period of gestation lasts for one year. Every so often the males go into rut and become uncontrollable, an event portended by an oil which exudes from their cheeks. Normally the captive elephant will obey its trainer willingly, even to the point of sucking up water in its trunk to squirt on command at a designated person.[135]

Baldaeus and the other commentators on the coastal regions complain about an excessive number of elephants and of the danger they pose to life

---

[130] Schouten (*ibid.*, p. 351) "was presented in Ceilon with a cinnamon stick which was very ingeniously inlaid with cinnamon."

[131] Baldaeus in Saparamadu (trans. and ed.), *op. cit.* (n. 97), p. 389. Frick notes (Raven-Hart [trans. and ed.], *op. cit.* [n. 55], p. 85): "None of the spices . . . may be carried away by any private person upon pain of death."

[132] Baldaeus repeats here (p. 389) a story still current in India and Ceylon to the effect that the mongoose chews this plant after fighting the cobra. See Macmillan, *op. cit.* (n. 124), p. 367.

[133] Baldaeus in Saparamadu (trans. and ed.), *op. cit.* (n. 97), pp. 386–90.

[134] In Asia today the elephants of Ceylon "are regarded as races distinct from that found in India" (S. H. Prater, *The Book of Indian Animals* [2d rev. ed., Bombay, 1965], p. 224).

[135] Knox in Saparamadu (ed.), *op. cit.* (n. 102), pp. 34–37.

and property. At Matara the newly captured elephants are tamed.[136] Once they learn obedience, they are sold to Moors of Bengal and of the Coromandel Coast.[137] Hoisting the elephants aboard ship for transport abroad is an onerous task.[138] While the elephants can swim for a long time in rivers and streams with their trunks above water, they seem to fear the ocean. The Dutch, like the native rulers, train elephants for their armies by teaching them not to panic at the sound of gunfire.[139] At Galle there is a stable of female elephants kept for breeding. Marauding wild elephants are driven away from settlements by lighted torches and by clamor and shooting. The merchants buy the tame elephants by height, for the largest and strongest are used to pull heavy artillery and to carry other burdens.[140] The Dutch keep elephants on their drilling grounds to teach soldiers how to fight against their charges on the battlefield. Elephants are sent regularly to the Dutch settlements as tribute from their Sinhalese vassals.[141] In their camps the Dutch soon learned that the elephant and the horse are natural enemies. By orders of the Dutch it is strictly forbidden to shoot elephants unless a man's life is in danger.[142]

In the interior there are many wild beasts but no lions, wolves, horses, asses, or sheep. Deer are numerous and range in size from a cow to a hare. The small "Meminna" (*Tragula meminna*, or mouse deer) is grey with white spots, has the features of a deer, and is good to eat.[143] They also have wild buffaloes, hares, dogs, jackals, tigers, bears, apes, and monkeys. The Kandyans hunt, snare, and trap deer and other wild animals to protect their crops. The hardest and most dangerous to catch are the elephants and the wild hogs. Six varieties of ants pester man and beast. The ones called "Vaeos" (Sinhalese, *veya*, pl. *veyo*) are particularly numerous and omnivorous. In uninhabited areas certain ants build hills four to six feet high, where they live and breed. With maturity they sprout wings and take flight. Birds and poultry feed on these and other ants. Three kinds of bees inhabit the woods. The Kandyans gather their honey and even boil and eat the bees themselves. Bloodsucking leeches that live on the land are a particular nuisance in wet areas.[144] Monkeys and apes of all kinds throng the woods. The smaller ones

---

[136] For a detailed description of elephant hunts see Herport in Raven-Hart (trans. and ed.), *op. cit.* (n. 55), p. 31.

[137] Baldaeus in Saparamadu (ed.), *op. cit.* (n. 97), pp. 391–92.

[138] See Behr in Raven-Hart (trans. and ed.), *op. cit.* (n. 55), p. 22.

[139] Schweitzer in *ibid.*, p. 41.

[140] *Ibid.*, pp. 49–51. In this rather lengthy account Schweitzer mixes traditional lore about elephants with personal observations of them.

[141] *Ibid.*, pp. 62–63.

[142] *Ibid.*, p. 72.

[143] See Prater, *op. cit.* (n. 134), pp. 296–97.

[144] *Haemadipsa zeylanica* do not occur near the sea. They are brown in color, about one inch in length, and readily able to attack human skin through light clothing. See Macmillan, *op. cit.* (n. 124), p. 464.

(probably the slender loris) do only a little mischief, but the apes prey upon garden and field. The Kandyans eat apes and squirrels when they kill them.[145]

Horses, first imported by the Portuguese, roam about the smaller islands in large, wild herds. Bands of wild buffaloes endanger those who travel inland. "Tigers" dangerous to man and especially to deer are hunted for their meat and skin; knapsacks and covers for boxes are made of their hide.[146] Bears are found in a number of places, including Jaffna and Mannar. Jackals (*Canis lanka*) prey upon smaller animals and are particularly fond of human carcasses. In the evenings they howl in packs outside Colombo and the other coastal settlements. A rare animal called "the Devil of Negombo" by the Dutch reputedly has a harness of thick, round, yellow shells around its body. When pursued it curls into a ball for protection.[147] The "laziest beast" looks like an ape and is readily captured (probably a reference to the "slow loris").[148] The common langur or Hanumant monkey (*Presbytis entellus*) called "Wandura" (Sinhalese, *vandura*) may be found everywhere in the woods gregariously jumping from tree to tree. Hedgehogs, porcupines, and wild cats complete this catalogue of beasts. In addition, the coastal settlements boast numerous domesticated animals: elephants, horses, cattle, buffalo, goats, pigs, big-tailed sheep from Persia, and big-horned hairy sheep from Africa.[149]

In Kandy there are birds just like those Knox remembered from England: crows, sparrows, tits, snipes, wood pigeons, partridges, and woodcocks. Among the birds of Ceylon new to him there are wild peacocks and small green parrots. A black bird called "Mal-cowda" (Sinhalese, *mal-kawadiya*, or the Ceylon grackle) learns to talk much more readily than the parrots, as does the "Can-cowda" (Sinhalese, *gon-kawadiya*, or the Ceylon common mynah bird).[150] Another bird called "Carlo" is black, swanlike in size, with a huge head and long bill; it travels in groups, never lights on the ground, and is never silent.[151] Knox also remarks on birds that dive and catch fish in ponds and marshes, probably a reference to pelicans and cormorants. While

---

[145] Knox in Saparamadu (ed.), *op. cit.* (n. 102), pp. 33–44.

[146] This may be a reference to any of the several great wild cats of Ceylon: panthers, leopards, and jungle cats (*kelaarti*). Schweitzer (Raven-Hart [trans. and ed.], *op. cit.* [n. 55], p. 51) describes his "tiger" as "spotted with yellowish and whitish spots" and as having "a scent of musk."

[147] The Indian pangolin (*Manis crassicaudata*) as described by Schweitzer in *ibid.*, p. 51. Modern description in Prater, *op. cit.* (n. 134), pp. 301–3.

[148] See Prater, *op. cit.* (n. 134), pp. 43–44.

[149] Baldaeus in Saparamadu (ed.), *op. cit.* (n. 97), pp. 392–93, and Schweitzer in Raven-Hart (trans. and ed.) *op. cit.* (n. 55), pp. 51–52.

[150] For these identifications see W. E. Wait, *Manual of the Birds of Ceylon* (2d ed., London, 1931), pp. 107, 111–12; and G. M. Henry, *A Guide to the Birds of Ceylon* (London, 1955), pp. 77–78, 81–82.

[151] Arasaratnam, *op. cit.* (n. 77), p. 181, n. 3, writes: "The word sounds like either *diya kāva* (Sinh.)- black diver, or *kurulla* (Sinh.)- woodpecker; but from the description it could be a Malabar Pied Hornbill."

the king has geese, ducks, turkeys, and pigeons, he keeps them merely for display and never eats them.[152]

In the maritime provinces the birds, like the animals, seem to be pests to humans rather than gifts of nature: crafty crows pilfer food and keep up an annoying cawing; thieving kites carry off pullets from the chicken pens. Certain birds build nests which are beautifully constructed and hang from the branches of trees.[153] Herons and parrots brighten the landscape while birds of prey and bats seem like threats from the sky. A nightbird, probably the Indian koel, reputedly cries "Navi, Navi" to announce the arrival of ships. Domesticated chickens and ducks produce enough eggs to keep them cheap. Pigeons from Holland are imported and bred.[154]

The rivers and streams of Kandy abound with fish, "nay every ditch and little plash of water but anckle deep hath fish in it." Fish are trapped in baskets (see pl. 193) or forced into fish pots placed between the rocks; in Kandy they seem to use no nets or the other fishing devices employed on the coast. While the common people eat ordinary fish with their rice, special fish collected for the king's pleasure are protected and become so tame that they will eat from the hands of those who feed them.[155] In the coastal settlements salt-water fish and seafood are everywhere abundant. Huge swordfish and sail-fish from the small shoals are important food sources. Vast catches of the "Jan-Egbertsen" (*Euthynnus katsuwonus palamis*) in February have the imme-diate effect of driving down all food prices in Colombo. Kingfish, skates, anchovies, sardines (salted and eaten like herring), mussels, and many other varieties of crustaceans contribute their share to the local diet. "Jacks" (bar-racudas), sharks, porpoises, and toadfish are also caught in fishing nets and sacks along with more desirable catches. Immense turtles are captured on the beaches when they come to lay their eggs. The shells of the smaller ones are made into boxes, combs, and other useful items. Alligators and crocodiles are common in all coastal localities, especially in Jaffna, as well as around tanks and wells. The Chinese residents feast on young crocodiles.[156]

Snakes, vipers, and lizards flourish in the jungles of Kandy. The "pim-berah" (Sinhalese, *pimbera*; *Python molurus*, or the Indian python) is a ser-pent of "prodigious bigness," slow and lethargic, that "will swallow a Roe Buck whole, horns and all."[157] A venomous snake called "Polonga" (proba-bly Sinhalese, *pala polonga*, or the Ceylon pit viper) attacks and kills cattle.[158]

---

[152] Knox in Saparamadu (ed.), *op. cit.* (n. 102), pp. 44–45.

[153] Probably Sinhalese, *kāhā-kurullā*; *Oriolus Xanthormis ceylonenis*, or the Ceylon black-headed oriole. See Henry, *op. cit.* (n. 150), p. 75.

[154] Baldaeus in Saparamadu (ed.), *op. cit.* (n. 97), pp. 393–94; and Schweitzer in Raven-Hart (trans. and ed.), *op. cit.* (n. 55), pp. 52–53.

[155] Knox in Saparamadu (ed.), *op. cit.* (n. 102), pp. 45–46.

[156] Baldaeus in Saparamadu (ed.), *op. cit.* (n. 97), pp. 394–98; especially see Schweitzer in Raven-Hart (trans. and ed.), *op. cit.* (n. 55), pp. 85–86, and the notes on p. 120.

[157] The omnivorous pythons seem to prefer large animals, especially deer. See Frank Wall, *Ophidia Taprobanica, or the Snakes of Ceylon* (Colombo, 1921), p. 57.

[158] *Ibid.*, pp. 560–64.

Another poisonous reptile is the "Noya" (Sinhalese, *naya; Naia tripudians,* or the cobra) which when aroused will "stand with half his body upright . . . , and spread his head broad open, where there appears like as it were a pair of spectacles painted on it."[159] The cobra and the pit viper are enemies who fight to the death whenever they meet. The Sinhalese have a fable to account for their enmity and a saying which compares two irreconcilable persons to these two snakes. The "Carowala," evidently a poisonous viper, lurks in the thatch of houses. The "Gerende" (Sinhalese, *garandiya; Zacocys mucosus,* or the *dhaman* [Sanskrit for rope], or the common ratsnake) is not poisonous and eats rabbits, birds, and other small animals.[160] The "Hickanella" (possibly of the genus *Callophis*) is a poisonous snake, "much like a Lizzard," which seldom attacks, and which hides in the thatch of houses.[161] A harmless watersnake is called "Duberria" (possibly one of the genus *Nerodia*).[162] A creature that looks like an alligator is the "Kobberaguion" (Sinhalese, *kabaragoyā; Varanus salvator,* a monitor lizard), which lives close to human habitations and eats carrion.[163] A smaller lizard called "Tolla guion" (Sinhalese, *talagoyā; Varanus dracoena*) feeds on leaves and plants and is itself edible.[164]

Baldaeus and Schweitzer concern themselves mainly with snakes and reptile-like creatures which make life dangerous or uncomfortable in the coastal settlements. Most feared are the cobras, pythons, and green tree snakes (Sinhalese, *esguela,* meaning "eye-plucker"; *Dryophis mycterizans,* or the common whipsnake), which reputedly attack the eyes of humans.[165] A so-called two-headed snake (Sinhalese, *depatanaya,* meaning "two-headed snake") is deemed to be the most poisonous of the tree serpents; it looks to the casual observer as if it has a head at each end.[166] Ratsnakes stay on the roofs of the houses and seldom if ever harm humans. Cobras and poisonous vipers enter the dwellings and are killed by the Christians and their converts. The non-Christians, especially the Hindus, dislike seeing them destroyed and win their friendship by feeding them; they even name their children and cattle after these snakes. They also know how to charm the cobras and make them dance to a tune. When administering an oath, they thrust the individual's hand into a pot holding the cobra; if the hand comes

[159] On the striking posture of the cobra see *ibid.,* pp. 463–66.
[160] *Ibid.,* pp. 172, 177.
[161] *Ibid.,* p. 496.
[162] *Ibid.,* p. 90.
[163] *Ibid.,* p. 478, and Schweitzer in Raven-Hart (trans. and ed.), *op. cit.* (n. 55), pp. 53, 119.
[164] Schweitzer in Raven-Hart (trans. and ed.), *op. cit.* (n. 55), p. 119. All the above discussion is from Knox in Saparamadu (ed.), *op. cit.* (n. 102), pp. 47–50, supplemented by materials from Schweitzer.
[165] This is a native belief still held about the green whipsnake. See Wall, *op. cit.* (n. 157), p. 294.
[166] But from the literary description it does not seem to be the *Typhlops braminus,* or blind snake, to which the Sinhalese name refers, but rather the *Bungarus ceylonlonicus,* or the Ceylon krait. See *ibid.,* pp. 9, 451–57.

out without being bitten, the truth has been told. The best cure for snake-bite is to lay the absorbent snakestone (also called adder stone) on the wound to draw the venom out, but there also are many other remedies used.[167] Other pests include scorpions, centipedes, biting and eating ants, fleas, and clouds of gnats. Between Colombo and Kandy bloodsucking leeches plague cattle and men. The Sinhalese claim that the sister of a former king of Kandy created these bloodsuckers to make life unbearable for the Portuguese.[168]

While the sea produces pearls, the land has its own riches to offer. Along the coast are found large pieces of costly amber, coral, and conch shells prized in Bengal. In the rivers and streams the Sinhalese search for the rubies and sapphires that are washed out of the hills by the heavy rains. Emeralds, topazes, moonstones, cat's-eyes, and dark garnets can be dug from the land or gathered from the streams. Crystals in various colors abound every-where, and walkers and horses often cut their feet by stepping on them. Euro-pean reports of diamonds being found in Ceylon are denied by Saar "no matter what Blaeu's *Atlas* says."[169] Iron and ebony come from the interior. The king of Kandy, who possesses a rich horde of gems, forbids his subjects to dig for precious stones and expects them to bring to him those found in rivers and streams.[170] Baldaeus reports on hearing rumors to the effect that gold and silver mines exist in the interior.[171]

C. GOVERNMENT AND SOCIETY

"Raja-Singa" (Raja Sinha II; r. 1635–87), which "signifies a Lyon-King," has a problem of descent that casts doubt on the legitimacy of his rule over Kandy. The son of "Dona Catharina," a Christianized princess, by Senerat, her second husband and a former Buddhist monk, Raja Sinha succeeded his father to the throne by forcefully eliminating his two older half-brothers whose claims were better. A heavy-set man of between seventy and eighty years of age, Raja Sinha in 1681 "bears his years well" and remains brisk in his actions and bold in his behavior. He designs costumes for himself which defy the fashions of his own and every other country.[172] His queen, "a Mal-abar [Tamil?] woman brought from the Coast," has been separated from him for twenty years; he left her behind in Kandy when he fled that city in 1661 to escape rebellion. At his new royal seat at "Digligy neur" (Diyatilaka Nuvara) his palace is located and designed "not so much for pleasure as se-

---

[167] For a modern listing of snakebite remedies thought in Ceylon to be effective see Mac-millan, *op. cit.* (n. 124), p. 317.

[168] The above discussion of coastal snakes and pests derives from Baldaeus in Saparamadu (ed.), *op. cit.* (n. 97), pp. 398–400; and Schweitzer in Raven-Hart (trans. and ed.), *op. cit.* (n. 55), pp. 53–54, 119–20.

[169] *Op. cit.* (n. 94), p. 55.

[170] Knox in Saparamadu (ed.), *op. cit.* (n. 102), p. 50.

[171] Baldaeus in Saparamadu (ed.), *op. cit.* (n. 97), p. 402. This was probably an untrue rumor.

[172] For a print of the king in the costume Knox describes see pl. 182.

curity."[173] Mandelslo notes that "he delights in the Portuguese manner of building and fortifies his hold after the modern way."[174]

Within the clay wall that encloses the courtyard stand houses which make the approach to the palace a maze of passages, turnings, and gates. Royal officials, soldiers, elephants, and trusted Negro slaves stand guard day and night. Spies are sent out at night to check the watchmen. The king's person is guarded by his Negroes and attended by boys and young men of good families. Many attractive young women are recruited from among the Sinhalese and Portuguese to prepare his meals and work in the kitchens. Those women who displease him are drowned in the river or sent into exile. Those who please him, whether married or single, he takes as concubines. Other female favorites live in nearby towns which enjoy special privileges for sheltering them. Knox concludes, however, that "he keepeth not many" concubines. Whenever Raja Sinha leaves the palace he is always accompanied by a protective guard. Usually he rides in a palanquin to a pleasure-house near a pond that stands no more than a musket shot away from the palace. He enjoys receiving foreign envoys, puts on fine displays to impress them with his grandeur, and discourses with them in a "very familiar manner."[175]

As a person the king is temperate. He eats but one meal each day, of herbs and fruits served by his noblemen. He does not lust after women and requires chastity of his servitors while they are at court. Prostitution, adultery, and sodomy are not tolerated. He himself once had an incestuous relationship with his daughter, but "only to beget a right Royal issue"; the daughter and her baby died in childbirth. From his subjects he demands all outward signs of submission. When appearing before him, they prostrate themselves three times and then sit upon their knees. When he bids them leave they walk backwards until they are out of his sight. Christians are privileged when in his presence, for they simply kneel and remove their hats. He is pleased when his people address him as if he were a god and delights in titles which glorify him. They even show respect to his personal laundry when it is taken out daily to be washed. His arrogance leads him to pretend that he does not care about defections by his officers or about the presents they bring him. Aware of his vanity, the Dutch send emissaries to acknowledge his overlordship and to flatter him into believing that they as loyal subjects build fortresses on the coasts simply to keep other foreigners from entering Ceylon.[176]

Raja Sinha is not a simple dupe of the Dutch. He retains all power in his hands, rarely consulting anyone for advice. Intelligent, cautious, and crafty, he controls his emotions and proceeds with great deliberation to win his ends. He conceals his objectives by lies and pretenses. Naturally inclined to

---

[173] Based on Knox in Saparamadu (ed.), *op. cit.* (n. 102), pp. 52–54.
[174] Olearius, *op. cit.* (n. 90), p. 115.
[175] Knox in Saparamadu (ed.), *op. cit.* (n. 102), pp. 54–58.
[176] *Ibid.*, pp. 59–62.

cruelty, he tortures and kills individuals without explanation. Whole families are often punished, even by death, for the offenses of one member. Public executions are common, and the dead, or parts of their bodies, are left in view as an example to others. Prisoners, of whom there are many, are chained in jail or committed to the custody of a nobleman. The streets about the palace are swept by prisoners in chains, some of whom are the king's former attendants. Most of those who serve the king eventually suffer from his wrath and are replaced by others. While most fear being called into the royal service, the family benefits during the period when their member enjoys the king's favor by being excused from taxes and other obligations. Once the member loses favor, as always happens sooner or later, he and his family are generally punished severely.[177]

At an artificial pond constructed near the palace the king takes his recreation by feeding fish or by watching his beasts sport on the nearby plain. In his menagerie he keeps twelve to fourteen horses, some presented by the Dutch and others taken in war. He likes to watch his hunters round up the wild elephants driven in from the surrounding forests. Occasionally he shoots at targets with his guns "which are excellently true, and rarely inlay'd with Silver, Gold, and Ivory." He also collects small iron cannons to fire on festive occasions. He is an expert swimmer and delights in it. Since he is not very religious personally, he tolerates all groups and seems to have great respect for Christian beliefs and practices.[178]

As a governor Raja Sinha is tyrannical and arbitrary in the extreme, "his own Head being his only Counsellor." The entire country literally belongs to him. He portions out the land and is paid rent in services by warriors, craftsmen, laborers, and farmers. These servants of the crown pay no other taxes, except for a gift to the king at certain celebrations. Many find the king's service too onerous, resign from it, and turn their houses and lands over to successors. At certain places there are royal towns whose inhabitants raise grain for the king's use. Often these towns and their revenues are bestowed upon the king's favorites among the nobility. Each town has a smith to make tools, a potter to craft earthenware, and a washerman to launder clothes. In return for their services to king or lord these laborers receive a piece of land; when they perform services for others they receive a wage. Under this system the king himself pays nothing directly for the maintenance of his court.[179]

The "tyrant" is concerned primarily about the security of his person and regime. He is ever vigilant and must constantly foil the plots of his rebellious subjects. For safety's sake he ordinarily conducts his business at night.

---

[177] *Ibid.*, pp. 62–65.

[178] *Ibid.*, pp. 65–68. His mother had been a Catholic, and his father a Buddhist monk.

[179] *Ibid.*, pp. 68–69. *Cf.* the system of Kandyan government vested in an absolute monarch as head of state and church as described in F. A. Hayley, *A Treatise on the Laws and Customs of the Sinhalese, Including the Portions Still Surviving under the Name Kandyan Law* (Colombo, 1923), Pt. I, chap. ii.

To limit access to the country Raja Sinha makes travel and movement as difficult as possible: the paths into the kingdom may not be widened, bridges are not built over rivers, and the forests between the provinces may not be felled. To keep his subjects occupied he undertakes vast public works, such as splitting a mountain to bring water to his palace. Many of these ill-conceived projects are abandoned before being finished. Forced to work on numerous unneeded undertakings, the people neglect the cultivation of their fields, sink into apathy, or plot his overthrow. To terrorize the people and to secure his own rule, Raja Sinha even poisoned his son and heir apparent to keep him from becoming a puppet for the opposition to manipulate.[180]

Three times each year they pay their rents to the king: at the new year called "Ourida cotamaul" (Sinhalese, *Avuruda Kāttimagula*), at "first fruits," called "Alleusal cotamaul" (Sinhalese, *Alutsāl Kāttimagula*), and at the annual sacrifice to the god called "Ilmoy Cotamaul" (Sinhalese, *Il Mahē Kāttimagula*). These rents are paid chiefly in grain, and extraordinary assessments in kind may be levied at any other time as well. The new year, which comes at the end of March, is celebrated lavishly.[181] On a day deemed auspicious by the astrologers, the king washes his head, "a very great Solemnity among them." For this occasion the gates of the palace have triumphal arches on tall poles placed before them. Flags fly from the tops of the poles and the poles themselves are encased in "painted Cloth with Images." Even taller individual poles display streamers of diverse colors with a bell at the end of each. Once the palace "is adorned beyond Heaven," the army parades into its courtyards. The king meanwhile goes to the washing houses to perform the ceremonial washing of his head. He then appears in public surrounded by his soldiers. After they fire the "great Guns," the highest officials and nobles present to the king the gifts customarily given by persons of their rank. The rich gifts laid at his feet are not accepted by this king and the giver is asked to carry them away. The gifts of inferior persons are likewise refused.[182]

Rents and taxes are paid in the form of grain, wine (palm-toddy?), oil, honey, wax, cloth, iron, ivory, tobacco, and money. These deliveries are made personally by the taxpayer, who must wait with his goods until the king is ready to accept them. In addition to these fixed dues, the king receives other taxes which are uncertain and periodic. Whenever a cattle owner dies, the king collects "Marral" (Sinhalese, *marála*), a death tax. At harvest every landowner pays a certain rent in grain relative to the size of the land he holds; in addition, the cultivators pay a tax in currency along with their grain. The lands of soldiers killed in battle are exempted from taxation, as are lands bequeathed to priests or temples. The king has lost all of his revenues from

---

[180] Knox in Saparamadu (ed.), *op. cit.* (n. 102), pp. 70–74.

[181] Dated by Knox according to the Julian calendar; it is actually celebrated in mid-April in the Gregorian calendar. See E. F. C. Ludowyk (ed.), *The Story of Ceylon* (London, 1962), p. 116, n. 2.

[182] Based on Knox in Saparamadu (ed.), *op. cit.* (n. 102), pp. 74–76.

customs since the Dutch have deprived him of access to and control over the ports. In his several treasure-houses the king keeps his collection of precious stones and the valuable gifts presented by other nations. He has his treasures closely guarded and shows no inclination to distribute this wealth to his subjects.[183]

Next to the king there are two chief judges called "Adigars" (Sinhalese, *adigār*) to whom all have the right to appeal the decisions of lower courts and administrators. The "Adigars" govern the cities and fill in as provincial governors when a vacancy occurs. Their numerous subordinate officers carry staves as badges of identification and authority and they act as tutors to newly appointed "Adigars." The next level in officialdom is occupied by the "Dissauvas" (Sinhalese, *dessaves*), an elite group selected from the governors of the provinces and counties; not all governors enjoy the distinction of being "Dissauvas." Provincial and other local officials are responsible for keeping order in their jurisdictions and for supervising the payment of the royal rents and taxes. They act as judges in their territories and may fine or imprison individuals who break the law. Under no condition may they pronounce the death sentence: that ultimate punishment may come only from the king. Local officials are sent on military expeditions and are often assigned to be attendants or guards at court.[184]

High government posts are given only to those of "good rank and gentile extraction." New appointees are treated especially well if they are Christians; they are provided with a handsome sword, a town (or towns) for maintenance, and gifts from the people under their authority. The governors must leave their wives and families to reside permanently at court. Since they cannot oversee their jurisdictions personally, they have subordinates to handle affairs in their districts. The chief of these local administrators is the "Courlividani" (Sinhalese, *kōralē vidana*) who squeezes and mulcts the people and is much hated. He is aided and abetted by a "Congconna" (Sinhalese, *kankāni*) or overseer, a "Courli-atchila" (Sinhalese, *kōralē arachchi*) or constable, a "Liannah" (Sinhalese, *liyannā*) or registrar and secretary, an "Undia" (Sinhalese, *undiyā*) or treasurer, and a "Monnannah" (Sinhalese, *manannā*) or measurer of grain. The size of the jurisdiction over which these officers rule is determined by what it is deemed they can manage well and is not strictly coextensive or coterminous with the provinces and counties. Even within these officers' established jurisdictions, temples, towns, and those assigned to royal servitors are independent of local authority and have their own officials. Collectors of the special royal taxes (such as "Marral") obtain their posts by bribery. All local officials hold their jobs only so long as they enjoy the governors' favor. If the people complain about a particular

---

[183] *Ibid.*, pp. 76–78.
[184] *Ibid.*, pp. 79–80.

official, the governor must replace him with another. Justice at all levels is purchased by bribes.[185]

Kandy, and particularly the site of the king's palace, is rendered secure by nature rather than by castles or forts. The thorn gates, the surrounding forests, and the guards make secret entry extremely difficult. Passports, a print of a seal in clay, are issued by the court. The seal depicts the occupation of the holder and indicates how many individuals belong to his party. Almost everyone who exits from the city is searched. The regular armed forces, headed by the 'Dissauvas" and "Mote-Ralla" (Sinhalese, *Mohoṭṭi rala,* or scribes), are organized into companies of 970 soldiers each. All high officers are required to be continually on guard duty at the court. The common soldiers, who belong to the army by inheritance rather than enlistment, are allotted lands rather than being paid wages. To prevent the soldiers from conspiring, the companies exclude as far as possible groupings of friends and neighbors and the various units are scattered widely throughout the realm. There is no single commander of the armed forces, for every major officer commands his own unit without reference to the others. Each reports to the king separately and directly, and commonly one informs on the other.[186]

When the armies are sent out to fight, "as he [the king] doth send them very often against the Dutch," the common soldiers have a difficult time of it. Besides their arms—swords, pikes, bows, arrows, and "good guns"— they carry their provisions, utensils, and "Tallipat" leaves for tents. Once in the field, they return home every so often to replenish their provisions so that after "a month or two a great part of the Army is always absent." Because the king is so secretive and so fearful of uprisings, neither the commanders nor the soldiers are informed of the campaign's objectives. They are instructed to lie in wait in the forest until ammunition or further instructions reach them. They avoid battle and direct confrontations, preferring to entrap their enemies and to follow the hit-and-run tactics of guerrillas. From long experience, and from the Portuguese who collaborate with them, the Kandyans have learned how the Europeans fight and how best to surprise and outmaneuver them.[187]

To illustrate the tyrannical character of Raja Sinha II, Knox relates whatever he remembered in 1681 about the rebellion of 1664. The object of the rebels was to dethrone the king and put the adolescent prince in his place. To the English in Kandy the leaders of the rebellion justified their attacks upon the king by explaining that his regime was irrational and destructive. Instead of negotiating with foreign emissaries, he keeps them prisoners. He cuts off his state from all intercourse with the outside world and brings trade

---

[185] *Ibid.,* pp. 80–84.
[186] *Ibid.,* pp. 86–89.
[187] *Ibid.,* pp. 89–91.

to a halt. He forces his subjects to leave their wives and families to serve him, and when anyone displeases him he arbitrarily executes the offender and often his entire family. The rebellion itself broke out on December 21, 1664, around midnight "about which time appeared a fearful Blazing-Star . . . right over our heads." Informed of the uprising, Raja Sinha fled from "Nillemby" (*Nilobe*), where he was holding court, to the mountain called "Gauluda" (Sinhalese, *Galauda*). Here he was joined by loyalists from the environs. In the meantime the rebels in the city of Kandy proclaimed the young prince as their king. At this juncture the king's sister fled with the prince to the king's side. The frustrated rebels began blaming and attacking one another and eventually the king restored his authority and imposed a repressive order upon the country. To prevent further rebellions the king executed, exiled, and imprisoned the rebels and ended by poisoning his own son. By the time another comet appeared in the sky during February, 1666, order had been firmly restored and so "no remarkable passages ensued upon it."[188]

Knox estimates, as of about the year 1680, that the Dutch control about one-fourth of Ceylon. The island's inhabitants include "Malabars" (Tamils) who live freely in the country but are not native to it; they own land and pay taxes just as if they were natives. The "Moors" of Ceylon own no land and live exclusively from trade, particularly at the seaports. Malabars, Moors, and blacks live in the coastal cities and some live under the Dutch, including Roman Catholics. The only "natural proper People of the Island" are the "Chingulays" (Sinhalese) to whom Knox confines his observations about history, religion, social customs, and language.

When queried about their origins, the Sinhalese "say their land was first inhabited by Devils, of which they have a long Fable." The Portuguese in Kandy told Knox that the Sinhalese are descended from an exiled Chinese prince and his attendants who sought refuge on the island.[189] But Knox considers this story to be highly improbable "because this people and the Chinese have no agreement nor similitude in their features nor language nor diet." He considers it more probable that they derive from the neighboring "Malabars," even "tho they do resemble them little or nothing." So he concludes, quite in harmony with his own experience, that the people of Europe more than any others resemble the "Chingulays."[190]

In the jungle of the "Bintana" (Bintenna) region of eastern Ceylon live wild people called "Vaddahs" (*Veddas*, *Weddas*, and even *Bedas*), aboriginals who

---

[188] *Ibid.*, pp. 92–96. On the comets of 1664–65 see G. W. Kronk, *Comets: A Descriptive Catalog* (Hillside, N.J.) pp. 10–11.

[189] This myth about the Chinese origins of the Sinhalese existed in one form or other in Ceylon before the Portuguese got there. Barros and other Portuguese writers sought to provide linguistic and historical underpinnings for this legend. See *Asia*, I, 342–43.

[190] Knox in Saparamadu (ed.), *op. cit.* (n. 102), pp. 97–98.

remain in total isolation.[191] They speak Sinhalese and eat dried deer meat. They never till the ground, for they are utterly carnivorous. They build no houses or villages, but live by a stream under the trees with a few boughs scattered about them.[192] They know by the rustling of the boughs that animals are approaching. Those few of the Veddas who live near other humans sometimes trade, pay taxes to the royal authorities, and are recruited for military expeditions. Rumor has it that if they need arrows they take meat during the night to a smithy and hang it there. Next to the meat they hang a leaf cut into the shape in which they wish to have their arrows made, for they are very particular about the shape of their arrows. If the smith ignores this silent request, they will shoot him.[193] Since they prey upon merchants, the king of Kandy has ordered that they be brought in dead or alive. They never cut their hair, but tie it into a bunch on top of their heads.[194] They wear a skimpy breechcloth and nothing else. In the forest they stake out their territories in each of which a certain person (or persons) has the exclusive right to hunt and to gather honey and fruit. They sacrifice to their own god under the trees. To preserve meat they line the hollow of a tree with honey, stuff the meat into it, and plaster it over with clay. A woman's dowry for marriage is given in the form of hunting dogs. The "tamer" of the Veddas are courteous and make friends with the Sinhalese; the "wilder," called "Ramba-Vaddahs," never show themselves.[195]

The civilized Sinhalese in general are "a people proper and very well favored beyond all people that I have seen in India." They dress well, ingeniously construct their own houses, and make every item they require except for ironwork. While smooth and courteous in conversation, they are crafty, treacherous, and customarily lie without conscience. Physically hardy, they are nimble, vigilant, satisfied with very little sleep, and conceited about their appearance. They are very conscious of caste ranking, but are mild tempered and gracious in their behavior, even towards inferiors. The lowlanders are kinder and more charitable to strangers than the false and ill-natured uplanders. Among the Sinhalese there are few robberies or thefts, for they particularly abhor larceny. While they extoll chastity, temperance, and truth, they are too weak to practice what they preach. Being highly superstitious they find omens everywhere: a sneeze portends evil; the

[191] Today remnant tribal groups of Veddas live in the most inhospitable and inaccessible parts of eastern and south central Ceylon. For their origins see N. Wijesekara, *Veddas in Transition* (Colombo, 1964), p. 23.

[192] When the Sinhalese refer to something that will never happen, they compare it to "Veddas talking about house construction." See *ibid.*, p. 68.

[193] This is one of the several mute exchanges recorded by the Europeans in Asia. This stock story appears in Ribeiro and Queyroz as well as in later writers on Ceylon. On the uses of the arrow by the Veddas see *ibid.*, pp. 85–86.

[194] For a woodcut of a "Vadda" see pl. 194. Notice that he is smoking a pipe.

[195] Wijesekara, *op. cit.* (n. 191), pp. 98–101. Modern anthropologists likewise distinguish two types of Veddas.

sound made by a certain lizard tells them whether they may expect success or failure in an enterprise; as in Malabar, whatever they see first thing in the morning on going out indicates whether the day will be good or bad; the sight of a white man or a big-bellied woman is taken as a sign of good luck, while that of a deformed or decrepit person signifies bad luck. They delight in deferring work and in taking their ease. In their carriage, deportment, and dress, both men and women seem to have learned much from the Portuguese, even though they refuse to admit it. [196]

The Sinhalese, like the south Indians, retain many caste divisions in their society. They do not eat, drink, or intermarry with any persons of inferior quality. A man of a higher caste may have sexual relations with a lower-caste woman but would never dare to eat or drink with her. A husband who catches his wife having intercourse with another man has the right to kill both partners, even if the man is of a higher caste. The "Hondrews" (Sinhalese, *hăñduru*), or noblemen, form the highest caste, and it is from this group that the king takes the royal governors and other high officials. [197] While they are socially at the top of the ladder, the "Hondrews" are not necessarily the wealthiest; their rank depends entirely upon birth rather than riches. They have special endings ("appow") on their names. Clothing, and caps of a particular design and length, distinguish them from others. There are two types of "Hondrews" and one is inferior to the other in matters pertaining to marriage arrangements. Most of the people of Kandy are "of the degree of Hondrews." [198] Christians, even though they eat beef and "wash not after they have been at Stool," are regarded highly and accepted as equals of the "Hondrews," and presumably belong to their own caste. Certain noblemen decorated by the king for distinguished service are called "Mundianna" (Sinhalese, *mudianse nama*). This title is rarely given to anyone and is not hereditary. [199]

Knox provides the names of fifteen of the occupational castes and subcastes, only a fraction of the number recorded in the next century by Valentijn, who adds many of the coastal and Tamil castes to Knox's list. [200] A caste of artisans—goldsmiths, blacksmiths, carpenters, and painters—"of one degree and quality" follows the "Hondrews" on the social scale. They dress like "Hondrews" and are also privileged to sit on stools. No "Hondrews," not even those of the inferior variety, will eat or marry with the artisans. The artisans who work for the king and live in royal towns enjoy a monopoly of the work in areas assigned to them. Usually they repair tools, for

[196] *Ibid.,* pp. 101–4.

[197] On this designation see Bryce Ryan, *Caste in Modern Ceylon* (New Brunswick, N.J., 1953), p. 78, n. 28.

[198] This was probably the *Radala,* a subcaste of the *Govigama* ("cultivator of the soil") caste that is dominant today and that constitutes at least one-half of Sinhalese society. On the Kandyan nobility see ibid., pp. 98–99.

[199] Knox in Saparamadu (ed.), *op. cit.* (n. 102), pp. 105–7.

[200] See Arasaratnam (trans. and ed.), *op. cit.* (n. 77), pp. 38, 66–82.

which they are paid a certain sum of grain at harvest time. To purchase new tools or to ask for anything else beyond simple repairs requires further payment. Elephant hunters and keepers are the social equals of the artisans. Barbers may dress like the upper castes, but may not sit on stools or eat with their social superiors. Potters may not dress like the upper castes, but they do enjoy the privilege, since they are potters, of pouring water into their mouths from a "Hondrews" pot. Great numbers of people belong to the caste of "washers" called "Ruddaughs" (Sinhalese, *Radau*) who launder the clothes of the castes superior to them. They scald the washing with lye water, and then take it to the riverside where they beat it against a rock to get it clean. The makers of jaggery sugar belong to the caste called "Hungrams" (Sinhalese, *Hangarammu*); the "Poddah" (Sinhalese, *Paduvō*) have no trade or craft, but function as farmers and soldiers. Then come the weavers, a caste that also practices astrology and serves in the temples as musicians and dancers. The two lowest castes are the basket-makers or "Kiddeas" (Sinhalese, *Kidiyō*) and the mat-makers or "Kinnerahs" (Sinhalese, *Kinnaru*).[201]

Foreigners are generally esteemed above people of the lower castes, probably meaning above those who rank below the artisans and elephant people. Slaves seem to be numerous and well treated, many of those in Kandy being Moors, Christians, and upper-class criminals. They are permitted to own land and cattle and are often provided with a wife. Slaves of "Hondrew" parents retain their name and other caste privileges except for the right to own slaves.[202] The lowest of all are the beggars, the descendants of the "Dodda Vaddahs" (the "tamer" group of Veddas?). The story is told that these Veddas were to furnish the king with venison but brought him human flesh instead. On learning about their deception, the king excluded them from society and ordained that they and their descendants should forever be forced to beg for their livelihood. They are untouchables who are not permitted to get water from wells but only from holes and streams. They travel about in bands carrying all their possessions with them. To obtain a handout they will dance, juggle, and perform tricks. They resort to any and all artifices to wheedle a gift. These beggars "live without labour," in mean hovels, and are free from all services and taxes. Their only task is to make cords for elephant snares from the hides of cows who have died natural deaths. Other beggars, called "Roudeahs" (Sinhalese, *Rodiyā*), compete with the weavers in carrying off and eating dead cows. Incest is common among beggars. The worst conceivable punishment for a woman of a higher caste is to be given to the beggars.[203]

---

[201] Knox in Saparamadu (ed.), *op. cit.* (n. 102), pp. 107–10.

[202] On the nature and generally mild character of Sinhalese slavery see Hayley, *op. cit.* (n. 179), pp. 133–45.

[203] Knox in Saparamadu (ed.), *op. cit.* (n. 102), pp. 111–14. Ryan (*op. cit.* [n. 197], pp. 133–34) quotes Knox's entire description of this caste and declares it to be "applicable to the present day." N. Yalman, *Under the Bo Tree* (Berkeley, 1967), p. 60, agrees in general with Knox in

D. RELIGION AND SOCIETY

One of the main concerns of people of all ranks and castes is the worship of gods and devils. In Kandy the supreme god is called "Ossa polla maupt Dio" (Sinhalese, *Ahasa polō mao Deyiyō*) or "creator of heaven and earth." He rules this earth through lesser deities and devils. Another great god is "Buddou" (Buddha) and to him "the Salvation of Souls belongs." They believe that he was once on this earth and that he usually sat under the bo tree; consequently, these trees are regarded as sacred and are the scene of religious ceremonies. Buddha departed this earth from Adam's Peak, where he left the footprint that may still be seen there. To the sun and moon they give names and titles which indicate that they seem to regard them as deities; they do not give similar titles to the stars.[204]

Their ancient temples are exquisite, innumerable, and "built of Hewn Stone, engraven with Images and Figures." Nobody is able to say who built these sumptuous structures. Knox concludes that their builders had to be "far more Ingenious Artificers" than his Sinhalese contemporaries, who were not even able to repair the old temples defaced and damaged by the Portuguese. In Bintenna stands a pyramid-like temple which has a square pinnacle on its peak (a reference to the Mahiyangana Hagaba at Alutnuwara). The lofty temple located between Galle and Batticaloa houses a huge statue of a man (Vishnu?) who holds a naked sword and is posed as if ready to strike.[205] Monasteries are numerous and contain religious images before which the yellow-clad monks keep lamps and wax tapers burning day and night. When they walk outdoors, these highly regarded monks are "constantly reading and slowly muttering." The chief abbot rides on an elephant when he leads their daily processions to the temple.[206]

Temples of recent construction are inferior wooden and clay structures. Buddhist temples are square, one or two stories in height, and crammed with images and idols of silver, brass, and other metals. These figures themselves are not gods, but represent the spirits of the departed holy men whom they honor and worship. While some temples house weapons and depictions of men-of-arms, the Buddhist temples do not permit warlike displays, since the Buddha stands for peace. Most of the Buddhist temples and their priests live from revenues derived from estates and towns assigned to their maintenance. Women and their male associates of the same house may not enter the temple during their menstrual periods. Many people build little

---

dividing the castes of the Kandyan highlands into three layers: the Goyigama and its subdivisions (on which Knox is not entirely clear), the service castes, and the lowest castes.

[204] Knox in Saparamadu (ed.), *op. cit.* (n. 102), pp. 114–15.

[205] For the temples at Bintenna and on the south coast see Baldaeus in Saparamadu (ed.), *op. cit.* (n. 97), p. 381.

[206] *Ibid.*, pp. 382–84. See the illustration of a religious procession facing p. 382.

personal shrines in which they place an image of Buddha before which they lay flowers and food each morning. Others make elephants' heads from stone or wood and place them alongside the roads or in trees or crevices.[207]

Their priests, like their religions, are of three sorts. The first are the Buddhists. Over the Buddhist temples called "Vehars" (Sinhalese, *vihara*) preside the most select order of priests, the "Tirinanxes" (Sinhalese, *terunansē*). At Diyatilaka Nuvara they have what is apparently a headquarters temple for the royally appointed "Tirinanxes," who live there in grand style. They manage their lands, collect the rents, and see that their temples and other properties are maintained. The ordinary Buddhist priests and monks are called "Gonnis" (Sinhalese, *gana*), dress like their superiors in yellow robes, shave their heads clean, and carry in their hands a round fan.[208] Buddhist priests and monks pay no taxes to the crown. They are reverenced everywhere they go and they have the privileges enjoyed only by the king of carrying the "Tallipot" with the broad end forward and of having a mat and a white cloth on their stools. They are not permitted to work for a living, cohabitate with or marry a woman, drink wine, or eat more than once each day. They will eat certain meats prepared for them, but they will not kill an animal or order it killed. When a person is religiously inspired, these priests come to his place to conduct ceremonies and give him gifts. The religiously moved individual "must sing Bonna" (Sinhalese, *bana*, meaning "sermon"), that is "matter concerning their religion out of a Book made of the leaves of Tallipot: and then he tells them the meaning of what he sings." A few of these Buddhist priests had cast aside their robes to participate in the revolt of 1664, and as a consequence they were killed by Raja Sinha, much to the consternation of the people who reverenced them as men of religion.[209]

The priests of their second religion (Hinduism) are called "Kappuhs" (Sinhalese, *kapurala*), and they belong to temples known as "Deivals" (Sinhalese, *dēvāle*). Unlike the Buddhist priests, these functionaries dress and behave in no special way and are not easy to distinguish from the rank and file of the population. They work the estates owned by the "Deival" and engage in other ordinary forms of employment. They generally wear clean clothes and wash themselves before religious services. Every morning and evening people bring boiled rice and other food to the priest and he presents it to the idol. After letting it stand before the god, he takes it away to be eaten by the retainers of the temple. To this god you can bring sacrifices of all food except meat.

[207] Knox in Saparamadu (ed.), *op. cit.* (n. 102), pp. 115–17. Women are always considered to be slightly "impure" because they menstruate. That is why their part in reaping and threshing paddy is limited to transporting it from the field to the threshing floor. See Yalman, *op. cit.* (n. 203), p. 107, n. 3, and above, p. 961.

[208] For an illustration of a chief priest in this garb, see Knox in Saparamadu (ed.), *op. cit.* (n. 102), facing p. 120.

[209] *Ibid.*, pp. 117–18.

The third type of priests are the "Jaddeses" (Sinhalese, *yak dessā*), and they are the guardians of the spirits called "Dayautaus" (Sinhalese, *dēvata*) and the temples called "Covels" (Sinhalese, *kovil*), which are dedicated to Hindu deities. These are inferior to other temples and have no estates from the king. Any man who is piously inclined builds a shrine at his own expense, and proclaims himself its priest. In the shrines are kept swords, shields, and arrows, as well as murals depicting fierce men. Usually the "Covels" are called the houses of "Jacco" (Sinhalese, *yakka*), or the Devil, and at certain festivals dedicated to "the Jacco" the priest shaves off his beard. The "Jaddeses" act as medicine men, exorcists, and intermediaries with the spirits. When a god enters one of them, he appears to go mad, a condition which the people call "Pissowetitch" (Sinhalese, *pissu veticca*). Everything he utters while in this possessed state is accepted as the word of God and he is revered as if he were God himself.[210]

Wednesdays and Saturdays are the chief days of worship when they pray for health and aid and appear before their gods to swear an oath. To regain health they perform complicated rites to locate and propitiate the god or devil responsible for their illness. The Sinhalese recognize nine deities or "Gerehah" (Sinhalese, *grahayo*) which are associated with the planets.[211] These supernatural beings, like the planets, influence men's lives, and, like devils, must be propitiated by rites and sacrifices. Deities, spirits, and devils of one locality are not known or worshipped elsewhere. All of Kandy appears to be plagued by evil spirits determined to make life miserable, though Christians seem not to be under their power. When possessed by a devil, men and women alike run amuck, quake, or become distracted. In Kandy, but not in the lowlands, the devil cries shrilly at night and frightens animals and humans. When the lesser devils fail to produce a cure, the Kandyans make offerings to the "Great Devil."[212]

Knox is well aware of the distinction between the popular religious practices of "ordinary and daily Worship" and the "solemn and annual Festivals" of Buddhism and Hinduism. He also distinguishes between festivals and processions relating to the earthly and secular concerns of this existence and those associated with spiritual affairs and the other life. At the time of the new moon in June or July they hold solemn feasts and assemblies throughout Kandy called "Perahar" (Sinhalese, *perahera*), the most popular of these ceremonials being held in the city of Kandy. Knox provides a de-

[210] *Ibid.*, pp. 119–21. Knox's "third religion" refers to practices associated with ancient, indigenous deities and rites, many of which have been merged over the centuries with Hindu gods and customs and to a lesser degree with Buddhism. See Ryan, *op. cit.* (n. 197), pp. 43–44. *Cf.* the description of their "False Worship" by Behr and Schweitzer in Raven-Hart (trans. and ed.), *op. cit.* (n. 55), pp. 8, 45.

[211] On planets and astral deities see J. Cartman, *Hinduism in Ceylon* (Colombo, 1957), pp. 82–83.

[212] Knox in Saparamadu (ed.), *op. cit.* (n. 102), pp. 121–25. Is this a reference to the cry of the "Devil Bird"?

scription of the annual temple procession in Kandy with its priests, elephants, "giants," drummers, pipers, and dancers. He notes that the temple's attendants march in caste order. The three deities who receive chief honor and attention are the gods "Alloutneur Dio" (Sinhalese, *Alutnuvara Deyiyō*) and "Cotteragoma Dio" (Sinhalese, *Kataragama Deyiyō*) and the goddess "Potting Dio" (Sinhalese, *Pattini Deyiyō*). The statues of these three and their attendants are followed by thousands of ladies walking three abreast, hand-in-hand. At the end come the king's officers and their soldiers, the overseers of the procession. "And in this manner they ride all round about the City once by day and once by night. This Festival lasts from the New Moon until the Full Moon."[213] At the full moon in November they hold another great and solemn festival called "Cawtha Poujah" (Sinhalese, *Karttika pūja*) that lasts for just one night. Poles are set up around the temple and the royal palace to hold up shelves on which they place oil lamps. This celebration consists in the ritual lighting of lamps in honor of those gods who aid them in this existence, a veritable feast of lights.[214]

The Buddha, who "must save their souls," is regularly remembered and honored by the small images placed everywhere in hollow rocks and small crevices as memorials. His great festival is celebrated in March, the beginning of the new year. On this occasion the faithful Kandyans either go south to "Hammalella" (Sinhalese, *Samanala Kanda,* or Adam's Peak), or north to "Annarodgburro" (Anuradhapura), the city where the ancient bo tree stands under which the Buddha sat. To worship the footprint of the Buddha the pilgrims have to pay fees to Moors who control access to the mountain. At the ancient city of Anuradhapura ninety kings in succession built temples and monuments in profusion to honor the Buddha. The pilgrims, who remain there for three or four nights, build small booths, tents, or houses around the bo tree. Those who are unable to make either of these pilgrimages celebrate the new year at a local temple. Men of substance and ladies of quality show a particular devotion to the Buddha; they even go begging for oil, rice, money, and cotton yarn for his use. The poorer people beg in his name for gifts for their own use and sustenance. When they make his image in metal, the figure becomes a god once the eyes are formed. Those who hire blacksmiths to make religious images receive contributions towards the cost from those who admire this form of devotion.[215]

The Kandyans tend to be indifferent about their gods, petitioning them only for relief from illness, the troubles of aging, and other problems caused by the evil spirits that swarm everywhere.[216] They talk to their god "as if he

---

[213] *Ibid.,* pp. 125–27. On the Kataragama god see Ryan, *op. cit.* (n. 197), p. 211, n. 6.

[214] Knox in Saparamadu (ed.), *op. cit.* (n. 102), p. 128.

[215] *Ibid.,* pp. 128–31. "Highly instructive for the state of [popular] religion in the 17th century is Robert Knox" (H. Kern, *Manual of Indian Buddhism* [Varanasi, 1968], pp. 132–33, n. 8).

[216] Here Knox seems to be trying to explain, as he also does elsewhere, the Sinhalese obsession with personal suffering (*duka*). See M. M. Ames, "Magical-animism and Buddhism: a

were there present in Person before them" and argue, expostulate, and curse him. If an individual's fortune or "Gerehah" (Sinhalese, *graha*) is predestined to be bad, they believe that appeals to the gods will avail nothing. Because they hold their gods in low esteem, they are tolerant of other gods. Their ceremonies are open to all, and no effort is made to molest worshippers of other gods or to force their religion upon others. The king has no interest in their idolatry and respects the Christians in his country. Beliefs of all kinds are tolerated, so long as they do not teach or lead to sedition.[217] The people and the king favor Christianity and in Knox's estimation they both "would be very easily drawn to the Christian or any other Religion."[218]

The Sinhalese believe in the resurrection of the body, the immortality of souls, and a future state of being. They believe their gods contain the spirits of their ancestors. Men who are good but poor in this world will become high and eminent in the other world, while wicked men will become beasts. Everyone's fortune is predetermined before birth, a belief expressed by the proverb "It is written in the head." Goodness includes giving sacrifices to the priests to offer to the gods in "Pudgiahs" (Sinhalese, *puja*), or temple ceremonies. They will not kill any creature, for they consider shedding of blood "Pau boi" (Sinhalese, *pao bohóyi*), "a great sin." Generally they abstain from eating meat, for they see herbs and plants as "more innocent food." It is a religious act to sweep under the bo tree to keep the sacred precincts clean. Charity is built into daily life, for they remove a handful of rice from every measure they boil and set it aside as "Mitta-haul" (Sinhalese, *mita hál* meaning handful) for distribution to the poor. Their charity extends to the Muslim beggars; landholders even contribute to the maintenance of the mosque in the city of Kandy. But they respect Christians more than any other foreigners and they probably learned from the Portuguese to carry prayer beads when they ritually place flowers every morning and evening before the images of their gods.[219]

Most Kandyans live in small, low, thatched cottages which every householder builds for himself from the timber and rattan so readily available. They are not allowed to build a house more than one story high, or to cover it with tiles, or to whiten the walls with lime. In their constructions they use no nails, but rather tie the timbers together with rattan. Most houses consist of one room in which they cook, eat, and sleep. They have no chimneys, so that the corner in which they build fires is blackened with smoke and soot. The upper classes have much more commodious homes, usually consisting

---

Structural Analysis of the Sinhalese Religious System," in E. B. Harper (ed.), *Religion in South Asia* (Seattle, 1964), p. 23.

[217] Baldaeus, the Calvinist missionary, confirms (Saparamadu [ed.], *op. cit.* [n. 97], p. 384) that "the nation is not bigoted" and that "there is no coercion on the part of the Emperor regarding any particular faith," and that many "have become converts to the Roman Catholic religion."

[218] Knox in Saparamadu (ed.), *op. cit.* (n. 102), pp. 132–33.

[219] *Ibid.*, pp. 135–37.

of two buildings joined on each side with a wall to make a square courtyard in between. Against the walls of these houses they build banks of clay to sit on, over which they daub soft cow dung to keep them smooth and clean. Their furnishings are few and small: several earthen pots hanging in rattan slings, one or two brass bowls, and a stool or two without backs. Only the king may sit on a stool with a back. Usually they have baskets to keep rice in, sleeping mats, pestles and mortars with which to prepare the rice, graters to shred the coconut, and flat stones between which they grind spices. They often keep their tools—axes, chisels, and hoes—in the house.[220]

They have no tables, but sit on the ground to eat. Their meager diet consists mainly of rice, a few greens, and condiments. Beef is never eaten, and other meats, including fish, are scarce; it is the foreigners who purchase and eat whatever meat there is. Even the upper classes, who always have five or six dishes in a meal, live mainly on rice and vegetables. The smaller animals—goats, poultry, and pigs—are regularly confiscated by the officials. In food preparation they are clean and their cooking, once you get accustomed to it, is "very savoury and good." An honored guest sits on one stool and his food is placed on another. Ordinarily they drink nothing but water with their meals, and they pour it into their mouths from spouted pots (see pl. 192). If they take arrack, they drink it before meals so that it will have more effect. Rice is served in china dishes, in brass bowls, or on leaves. The curries, or other foods served with the rice, are kept in the cooking pot until they are called for. While the husband eats, he is served by the wife; she eats whatever is left. They always wash their hands and mouths before and after meals. They do not converse while eating.[221]

Cooking and serving are female chores. No one must speak while she puts the rice into the pot; should someone talk the rice would not swell. When lemons are plentiful, they boil the juice until it becomes "thick and black like tar." Called "Annego" (Sinhalese, *anuga*) it keeps well in this form; a small dab of it flavors a sauce. They make sweet fritters of rice flour and jaggery, which they fry in coconut oil or butter; these are called "Caown" (Sinhalese, *kevuma*) and are esteemed to be superb delicacies. Another sweet is made of parched rice, jaggery, pepper, cardamom, and cinnamon. It is rolled into balls called "Oggulas" (Sinhalese, *aggalá*), which become hard. Travelers carry a bag of these balls for afternoon snacks. "Alloways" (Sinhalese, *aluvá*) are similar sweets, but flat and round in shape. They steam dumplings made of rice flour and the meat of jaggery and coconut to produce "Yacpetties" (Sinhalese, *yakpeti*), a sweet that tastes like "white bread, almonds, and sugar." To make "Pitu" (Sinhalese, *pittu*), they sprinkle "Corocan" (coarse millet or ragi) flour with water and crumble this paste into "corns like Gun-Powder." They steam this dough into a pudding

---

[220] *Ibid.*, pp. 137–38.
[221] *Ibid.*, pp. 138–40. On food in the relations between husband and wife see Yalman, *op. cit.* (n. 203), p. 108. See our pl. 192.

which they eat as a substitute for rice. Besides cooking the wife is obliged to pound the grain, to fetch both water and firewood, and to harvest and prepare the herbs and vegetables.[222]

Strangers are invited to sit down and are offered green betel leaves called "Bullat" (Sinhalese, *bulat*), which they eat raw with lime, betel nut, and tobacco. The man of the house after a while asks what is wanted, for they never "go one to visit the other, unless it be for their own ends, either to beg or borrow." When close relatives visit, they commonly stay more than one night and help the husband with his chores. When friends come to visit, they bring a gift of sweets and the host provides the best feast he can put together. When they meet outdoors, the men extend both hands palms upward and bow from the waist. To an inferior the superior extends but one hand, and to those of very low status they merely nod the head. As a greeting women "hold up both their hands edgways to their Foreheads." They ask "Ay" (Sinhalese, *áyu*), or "How do you," and the reply is "Hundoi" (Sinhalese, *hoñdayi*), or "well."[223]

When the nobles go outdoors, they wear jackets of white or blue calico and white underdrawers around their middle over which they wear a blue or other colored sarong. Around the waist they tie a blue or red sash in which they carry a knife with a carved handle. At their side they carry a short sword in a scabbard, both being carved and inlaid with brass or silver. In their hand they carry a painted cane and are followed by a bare-headed boy who acts as a "pocket" to carry betel leaves and areca nuts. Generally their hair is long and hangs down the back; when they work it is tied up behind the head. Formerly the Kandyans, like the "Malabars" (Tamils), had elongated ear lobes; this fashion has, however, almost died out for men, since Raja Sinha has not had his ears pierced and treated in this manner. The men wear rings on their fingers of brass, copper, silver, or gold, "but none may wear any silk" for ornament. A man's greatest pride is in the number of armed attendants who accompany him and in the elegance of his wife's costume.[224]

Women, when outside the home, wear a "short Frock" of fine white calico decorated with flowers and branches in blue and red needlework. On their arms they wear bracelets and on their fingers and toes, silver rings. Around their necks they hang strands of beads or silver chains. In their perforated and elongated ear lobes they hang "ornaments made of Silver set with Stones." Their oiled hair falls to the waist and to it they add a switch. Over their shoulders they casually throw a striped silk scarf as a bodice and around their waists they wear silver girdles. Much of the finery they wear is

---

[222] Knox in Saparamadu (ed.), op. cit. (n. 102), pp. 140–42. As an unmarried foreigner, Knox had to cook for himself (*ibid.*, p. 227). For the obligations of the wife see Yalman, *op. cit.* (n. 203), p. 109.

[223] Knox in Saparamadu (ed.), *op. cit.* (n. 102), p. 142.

[224] *Ibid.*, pp. 142–43. One of the five duties prescribed for husbands by Buddhism is to provide the wife with adornments. *Cf.* Knox's description of male costume to that given by Baldaeus in Saparamadu (ed.), *op. cit.* (n. 97), p. 385.

borrowed from others. No one may wear shoes or stockings, for they are apparel reserved to the king. Raja Sinha, as Knox has noted before, is idiosyncratic in his dress and appearance.[225]

In one-room houses the men sleep together at one end and the women at the other. The master of the house sleeps on a simple bedstead laced with canes or rattans; the king permits no canopy or curtains. Women and children sleep on mats thrown on the ground by the fire, which burns all night. For bedding and covers they use their clothing, the naked younger children sleeping under the mother's clothes. They arise many times during the night to eat betel or tobacco; when they again lie down they sing themselves to sleep and teach their children to do the same. Older children often sleep in the houses of neighbors to find bed companions. Public prostitution is strictly prohibited but sexual relations outside of marriage are not frowned upon when the partners are of equal status. They are also somewhat cavalier about sexual infidelity. Married persons commonly arrange clandestine meetings with their lovers. A husband will sometimes permit friends or important personages to enjoy his wife or daughter as an act of hospitality. Since no premium is placed on virginity, a mother will permit her daughter to accept a small reward from any equal who desires to initiate her. Women of high caste never co-habitate with lower-caste men.[226]

Parents commonly arrange marriages and provide either the bride with a dowry or the groom with the wedding clothes of the bride. There is no courtship or very elaborate wedding ceremony. Once the agreement is completed, the man sends the wedding clothes to the woman and the wedding date is set. On the evening of the agreed day, he and his friends appear at her house carrying sweetmeats for the wedding supper. The bride and groom eat from one dish as an indication of their equality in status. That night they sleep together. On the next day after dining he takes the bride to his home. The bride and her friends walk in front of the groom. Another feast is served in his house. A few days later her friends bring a present of food. On this occasion some couples perform a ceremony which involves pouring water over their heads and bodies as a testimony of their determination to live together as long as they are compatible.[227]

Many marriages are quickly severed, for the mates are free to leave each other at any time. If the separation is permanent, the bride's dowry is returned and she is ready for another marriage. Ordinarily both men and women marry four or five times before settling down permanently. Male children from a broken marriage go to the father, the daughters to the mother. No man may have more than one wife at a time; women often have

---

[225] Knox in Saparamadu (ed.), *op. cit.* (n. 102), pp. 143–44. For an illustration of "a Gentle-woman" in costume see *ibid.*, facing p. 152.

[226] *Ibid.*, pp. 145–48; on extra-marital sex relations see Ryan, *op. cit.* (n. 197), p. 156; on the ritual purity of high-caste women see Yalman, *op. cit.* (n. 203), p. 177.

[227] On the Kandyan concept of marriage and the ceremony of weddings in the twentieth century see Yalman, *op. cit.* (n. 203), pp. 159–80, and Ryan, *op. cit.* (n. 197), pp. 29–32.

two lawful husbands, usually two brothers. The children acknowledge both men as fathers.[228]

When a woman menstruates, both she and her house are polluted; everyone else avoids her place until she has performed a ritual ablution. No woman may sit on a stool in the presence of a man or accuse anyone of breaking the law. Women who inherit land are not required to pay "Marral" (Sinhalese, *marála,* death tax) and are not charged taxes on goods carried to seaports. Neighborhood women ordinarily perform midwife services for one another. If an astrologer decides that a child was born at an inauspicious moment, they either kill it or give it away in the belief that it will prove an intolerable burden to the family. They hardly ever dispose of the first child in this manner; astrology is otherwise used as an excuse to keep down the number of unwanted children. Infants are given names which are abandoned at maturity when they become known by the family title.[229]

Economically Kandy is essentially self-sufficient. A minimum of trade had been carried on with the Portuguese, but after the advent of the Dutch the king forbade all trade with the coastal regions despite the objections of his subjects. While a certain amount of necessary internal exchange takes place, most of the best men work as independent cultivators. No stigma is attached to any form of work, even for men of the highest castes, providing that they do not work for others and that it does not entail the slave-like occupation of carrying.[230] The farmers geld their cattle and make their own glue from boiled milk curds and lime; their wives churn butter (see pl. 185). Craftsmen make calicoes, earthenware, gold objects, paintings, and carvings. From native iron they produce steel, tools, and guns. Knox relates in considerable detail how they extract iron from stones smelted in a furnace fired by charcoal. Shops and markets exist in the towns, and Knox gives the prices of a few commodities. He discusses their measures and weights and observes that coinage being in short supply they accept grain as currency. Three kinds of coins are also mediums of exchange: Portuguese or Spanish reals, locally minted silver pieces shaped like a fish hook, and "the king's proper Coin" called a "Ponnam" (Sinhalese, *panama*).[231]

The Kandyans enjoy but few pastimes or diversions except at the New Year's festival. Their chief game is to bowl coconuts at one another to see which ones will crack first. To celebrate the goddess "Potting Dio" they set up a tug-of-war with crooked sticks that are hooked together and pulled in opposite directions by ropes until one of the sticks breaks. While they never bet on this contest, the victors put on a display that is so licentious and sordid that they are fined for engaging in it. At their festivals they put on ex-

---

[228] On marriage stability in modern times see Yalman, *op. cit.* (n. 203), pp. 185–88.
[229] Knox in Saparamadu (ed.), *op. cit.* (n. 102), pp. 148–51.
[230] On agriculture as a caste-free occupation see Ryan, *op. cit.* (n. 197), pp. 180–81.
[231] Knox in Saparamadu (ed.), *op. cit.* (n. 102), pp. 152–57.

hibitions of strength, balance, agility, and trickery. When otherwise at leisure, they most enjoy meeting at an inn or other public place to chew betel and to discuss the activities of the king and their own affairs. They abhor drunkenness and usually refrain from taking intoxicants. While tobacco is also considered to be a vice, both men and women chew it. Only a few smoke pipes. Betel they keep in their mouths at all times except when eating. Knox, who also became addicted to this habit, describes in detail the art of preparing the betel quid and of manufacturing the lime essential to it.[232]

Aside from the king's will, they observe as law certain established usages and customs. These traditions are recognized and upheld in their courts and government. Landholding is a hereditary right and properties pass on from parents to children. No right of primogeniture is enforced, so lands may be divided among all the children. Should the eldest son inherit the entire property, he is bound to provide for his mother and for the other children until they can take care of themselves. In the land of Uva where many cattle are bred, their owners must pay for any damage caused to another's grain fields by wandering cattle. They sometimes farm on equal shares, but the landowner usually comes off with only about one-third since he has to pay the tiller special customary fees in addition to his half-share. The owner is usually compelled to borrow grain to sustain his family; when the harvest comes in he pays a bushel and one-half for each bushel borrowed, "Which was the means," writes the entrepreneurial Knox, "that Almightly God prepared for my relief and maintenance." If a debt is not repaid in two years, it doubles; to protect long-term debtors, the king ordained that it should remain permanently at this level thereafter. A creditor may demand compensation for a substantial loss by taking the debtor's goods, cattle, or children, providing he has a legal warrant of seizure.

They follow many other laws and customs that seem odd to Knox. If a wife leaves without her husband's consent, she may not remarry until he does. If a slave has children by a freeman, the children are the slaves of her master; if a slave has children by a freewoman, the children are free. It is forbidden to cut down a coconut tree or to go back on one's word if a promise is made in the king's name. Anyone caught stealing must make restitution of seven to one; if he is unable to pay, he becomes a slave. A man in need may legally sell or pawn himself or his children. If a man builds a house on another's land and then decides to leave it, the house must be left standing for a successor. To resolve controversies the contenders take oaths in their temple, or by plunging their hands into hot oil when the issue is of great moment. When an individual is fined and delays payment, the officers place a large stone on his back and constantly add more until he complies.

---

[232] *Ibid.*, pp. 157–61.

To recover a debt a creditor will sometimes threaten to poison or otherwise dispose of himself. Should he actually kill himself, a heavy imposition is placed on the debtor for causing this loss of a life.[233]

Knox, with his twenty years' experience in the interior of Ceylon, returned to England with a genuine command of the Sinhalese spoken language. Robert Hooke of the Royal Academy wrote about Knox in his preface to the *Historical Relation:* "He could have given you a compleat Dictionary of their Language, understanding and speaking it as well as his Mother Tongue." Under prodding from Hooke, Knox actually wrote down a list of Sinhalese words, phrases, and expressions far more extensive than those printed in his book. This vocabulary, chiefly in Knox's hand, still exists in manuscript in the British Library (Sloane 1039, fols. 162–65). Most of the vocables which appear in both the manuscript vocabulary and the printed book are in a contrived romanization that is good enough to match them with their modern Sinhalese equivalents; the others are obsolete or vulgarisms of the time that have since fallen into disuse. To modern students of Sinhalese, Knox's vocabulary is still useful as a source for the pronunciation and the vocabulary current in the seventeenth century.[234]

Knox notes that the Sinhalese language is unique to the island of Ceylon and not in use elsewhere in Asia. The "Malabars" as speakers of Tamil cannot understand Sinhalese and the Sinhalese have equal difficulty with Tamil, even though each language includes loan words from the other.[235] Sinhalese is replete with titles which reflect the complex social system.[236] In speaking to women, they use twelve or more titles which accord to her rank and status. To compliment a woman one gives her a title higher than is her due. Titles for men are less numerous and are based on their occupations. Seven or eight different words mean "thou" or "you" and are used for addressing persons of diverse ranks. Everybody speaks elegantly, so no difference in speech separates courtier from cultivator; children as well as adults are courteous and adept in modes of address. The king is addressed by a name that places him above man and next to God. In addressing the king, they never use the first person with reference to themselves. They refer to themselves by title followed by a derogatory term. And when speaking to the king of their children they call them "Puppy-dogs." For each occasion there are certain forms and words of civility which must be mouthed for courtesy's sake.

[233] *Ibid.,* pp. 161–67. For an illustration of the stone method of "extorting their Fines" see plate facing p. 168.

[234] The vocabulary with meanings and modern Sinhalese equivalents is published in D. W. Ferguson, "Robert Knox's Sinhalese Vocabulary," *JRAS, Ceylon Branch,* XIV (1896), 155–99.

[235] Modern scholars classify Sinhalese as one of the Indo-Aryan vernaculars and quite different in grammar and style from Tamil, a Dravidian language. From linguistic evidence it appears that colonists from northern India first settled Ceylon, but opinion is divided as to whether they came from northwestern or northeastern India. See Wilhelm Geiger, *A Grammar of the Sinhalese Language* (Colombo, 1938), pp. vi–viii.

[236] On their modern interest in pedigrees, hereditary names, and titles see Yalman, *op. cit.* (n. 203), pp. 142–48.

Vulgarisms are frequently employed as words of reproach or jest. "The worst word they use to Whites and Christians, is to call them Beef-eating Slaves." The language is rich in proverbs, such as "'Pick your teeth to fill your Belly.' Spoken of stingy niggardly People." With respect to grammar, Knox gives examples of how nouns are made plural and how verbs are formed. He also gives specimens of their common words and a list of their numbers from one to fifty. Frequently, he asserts, they use numerals or adjectives after a noun rather than making it plural. He also believes that they borrowed from Portuguese their words for "God" ("Dio) and "Heaven" ("Dio loco").[237]

Knox, who apparently could not read Sinhalese, concludes that "their learning is but small." Ordinarily they can read and write, but they have no schools. Children learn to write with their finger on smooth sand in letters that are written from left to right. Their books deal only with religion and medicine and are in a language different from the vernacular and "like Latin to us."[238] Adults write by making impressions of their letters upon talipot leaves with an iron stylus. Books are made of talipot leaves cut into equal shapes and sizes that are fastened together with thongs and placed between wooden covers. Their priests write many books on religious subjects and sometimes offer them as a present to great men from whom they expect a reward. Orders from the king are written on leaves that are folded in a particular manner reserved for royal commands. Records that are to be preserved are also written on talipot leaves; ordinary letters are commonly written on "Taulcole" (Sinhalese, *tal-kola*), palm leaves that take a better impression but will not fold without breaking.

The high priests understand astronomy, but the ordinary astronomers are the weavers. They can predict eclipses of the sun and moon and make monthly almanacs. Written on a talipot leaf, the almanac gives the phases of the moon and the favorable times to plow, sow, travel, or undertake new tasks. From the astronomers they learn "when the old year ends to the very minute . . . and when to begin to wash their heads," a "Ceremony they observe very religiously." The astronomers, "or rather Astrologers" as Knox now adds, understand the movements of the stars and planets "of which they reckon nine." From their stellar and planetary calculations they claim the ability to foretell the future and to fix auspicious days for marriage by casting the horoscopes of the prospective bride and groom.

Their chronology begins with an ancient king called "Saccawarsi" (Sinhalese, *saka varsa,* or the Saka era). Their year of 365 days begins on either March 27, 28, or 29, possibly "to keep it equal to the course of the sun, as our Leap year doth." It is divided into twelve months or fifty-two weeks of seven days each. Sunday, the first day of the week, is regarded as an auspicious day for new undertakings. Days and nights are divided into thirty

[237] Knox in Saparamadu (ed.), *op. cit.* (n. 102), pp. 167–74.
[238] Pali in Brahmi script.

"Pays" (Sinhalese, *pä,* or hour) each, so that noon, halfway between sunrise and sunset, is the day's fifteenth "pay." The flower called "four o'clock" opens regularly at seven "pays" before nightfall, for the lengths of day and night vary little from season to season. Otherwise the people have no time-pieces; the king has a waterclock that measures the "pay" and an attendant to keep it going. He floats a copper dish that will hold one pint of liquid on top of water filling a clay pot. Water enters the copper dish through a hole in its bottom. For the dish to fill and sink to the pot's bottom takes one "pay." Knox also reports on seeing rocks at various places in Uva and the northern provinces which are deeply engraved with ancient writings. Upon inquiry he found that none of his contemporaries was able to read these inscriptions.

The Kandyans have no professional physicians or surgeons; each person treats himself with concoctions made from leaves, fruits, and barks found in the woods. Their most serious diseases are "Aques [malaria] and Fevours, and sometimes Bloody-fluxes [dysentery]," and occasional cases of small-pox. Knox tried some of their herbal remedies on himself and found them to be efficacious. While their remedies work well on external sores and bites, they must resort to religion, magic, and charms to cure internal ills. Death is greatly feared and they avoid for many days a house where death has struck. The upper classes burn the dead "because worms and maggots should not eat them" (see pl. 191). The corpse is washed and covered with a linen cloth before it is burned. The poor bury their dead without ceremony in a hole dug in the woods. The corpse is placed on its back with the head to the west and the feet to the east, "as we do." Several days after death a priest is invited to the house to pray and sing for the salvation of the soul. Women mourn the dead by loosening their hair, wailing, and extolling the virtues of the deceased; the men meanwhile "stand still and sigh." When a husband dies, the wife mourns "more for fashion than affection" and quickly begins to look for a replacement. Noblemen are embalmed, placed in a hollowed-out tree trunk, and then covered with pepper. The deceased remains in this state until the king commands that the corpse should be put on the funeral pyre. Burnings take place at a specific site and are carried out with great ceremony for people of high station. Should anyone die of smallpox, he is "Buried upon Thorns, without any further Ceremony."[239]

Baldaeus supplements Knox's full account of Kandy by the addition of material on the social and religious practices of the coastal region, especially the Jaffna peninsula. The "Malabars" of Jaffna are socially organized like the people of the Coromandel Coast of India.[240] The Brahmans are the highest

---

[239] Knox in Saparamadu (ed.), *op. cit.* (n. 102), pp. 175–87. On similar modern death prac-tices see Cartman, *op. cit.* (n. 211), pp. 157–61. For a detailed description and illustrations of the funeral and cremation of a prince of Kandy see Baldaeus in Saparamadu (ed.), *op. cit.* (n. 97), pp. 58–61.

[240] Although the caste system of the Tamil regions of south India and Ceylon show clear rela-tionships, the castes of Ceylon have developed distinctive features. See Cartman, *op. cit.* (n. 211), p. 132.

caste, closely followed in this Tamil country by the "Ballales" (Tamil, *Vellāla,* the caste of agriculturists). In Baldaeus' estimation those "Bellales" who convert to Christianity outrank the Brahmans, probably a bit of wishful thinking on his part. The "Bellales" are certainly the most numerous and richest caste and they live chiefly from agriculture. Ordinarily they reap their grain in January and February, but in some marshy areas they have two harvests annually. In November and December heavy rains flood the fields. During the dry season they water their fields twice a day; they must also water the young coconut trees until they reach their sixth year. In this rocky region, wells are difficult and expensive to sink, but they must dig them in order to survive the dry season.[241] Like the cultivators of Kandy, they thresh the grain by having oxen tread it out of the stalks.

The "Bellales" live in "good and neat dwellings" and they possess cows, oxen, sheep, goats, and buffaloes. When the grain begins to sprout, the animals are kept in corrals and fed on hay until after harvest; at other times they graze in the fields. These people make their own butter by whirling a stick in milk, but they have no interest in producing or eating cheese. They are very fond of liquid butter (ghee) as are the Muslims and the "Commety" (Tamil, *Sammati,* a high-level fisher caste). They drink thick sour milk as a cooling beverage and as a treatment for fevers and the smallpox "which is prevalent there." The men wear a dhoti which hangs from the waist and has a pocket in the front to carry their betel and areca nut as well as a slip or two of "ole" (Tamil, *olai,* a palm leaf) to write on. They also carry a sheathed knife and a steel for whetting it at the waist. From their elongated and pierced ears hang rings and on their feet they strap leather sandals. The "Bellales" always marry within their own caste and usually in the springtime. In their interpersonal relations they are quarrelsome and litigious.[242]

Baldaeus identifies a number of lesser castes in Jaffna. The "Chivias" (Tamil, *Koviyar?*) are water-carriers, woodcutters, and bearers of palanquins who formerly worked for the king of Jaffna and who now serve the Dutch governors and their associates. For lesser folks these tasks are performed by common "coelijs" (coolies). The "Parruas" (Tamil, *Parāva*) are seafarers who fish for pearls and for shells (chanks) used as ornaments and as musical instruments in Hindu processions. Many of the merchants belong to the "chittijs" (Tamil, *chetty*), "an arch and cunning set of people." The "Carreras" (Tamil, *Karaiyar*) live near the shore and fish with nets; another fisher caste of lower status is the "Mokkurs" (Tamil, *Muchavar*). A lower caste, the "Nallouas" (Tamil, *Nalava*) are blacker than the others and do menial work for the "Ballales" as toddy-drawers, farmers, and laborers. The most detested are the "Parreas" (Tamil, *Paraiyas*), or pariahs, who perform the most disagreeable tasks and "do not scruple to eat rats and mice." Caste members

[241] The limestone of the peninsula stores vast quantities of water that can be tapped by wells. See S. F. de Silva, *op. cit.* (n. 113), p. 241.
[242] Baldaeus in Saparamadu (ed.), *op. cit.* (n. 97), pp. 351–54.

always marry within the caste and follow the occupation of the caste. In a society extremely conscious of inferior and superior caste ranks, the husbands in every caste are treated like a special caste by their wives. Certain castes are principal groups from which others derive, or what scholars now call subcastes. Nobody in Jaffna will slaughter or eat beef except for the Dutch.[243]

Aside from persons of the lowest castes, the inhabitants of Jaffna are personally sober, neat, and clean. While most are not contentious, they are "great prattlers, and know well how to use their tongues." The greatest flaw in their moral character is sexual promiscuity, particularly among married men. Most disturbing to Baldaeus is their wrong-headed persistence in idolatry, devil worship, and faith in omens, signs, and witchcraft. Still, the locals are not so benighted as their superstitions and beliefs might indicate. Some understand local law and practice it; others even sit on the bench with Dutch judges. Physicians are numerous, and though they know no anatomy, they have a medical tradition preserved in books that they modify by experience. Skilled craftsmen weave fabrics that are dyed in fast colors. Many of the dyers brought their craft with them from Coromandel. Others work in ivory, ebony, gold, and silver, for which they have but few special implements.[244]

"Malabar" (Tamil) and Portuguese are the two languages most current in the northern provinces of Ceylon. Baldaeus, who spent most of eight years in Jaffna and its environs, learned to speak both of them.[245] Like the Jesuits, whom he acknowledges as masters of missionizing techniques and language study, Baldaeus preached in Tamil. Nobili himself had entered Jaffna in 1646 with two companions; the great missionary spent the next two years there writing Tamil instructional manuals for children.[246] Baldaeus had numerous of these Christian writings translated into that language, some of which were little more than the Jesuit translations revised along Reformed lines. In part 1 of his *Naauwkeurige beschryvinge* (1672) he included "an introduction to the Malabar language" in which he explains why and how he learned Tamil. For the instruction of his European audience he discusses the elements of Tamil grammar and reproduces specimen Tamil versions of the Lord's Prayer and the Creed with interlinear Latin translations and in romanized Tamil. On three double-page engravings he reproduces the Tamil alphabet in its entirety (*cf.* pl. 139).[247] He records that in the church of

---

[243] *Ibid.*, pp. 371–72. Recent writers on caste in Ceylon have not given Baldaeus the attention he deserves.

[244] *Ibid.*, pp. 372–77.

[245] De Jong (ed.), *op. cit.* (n. 97), p. xxiv, concludes that Baldaeus never learned to read Tamil or Sanskrit books.

[246] P. R. Bachmann, *Roberto Nobili, 1577–1656* (Rome, 1972), p. 253.

[247] Pp. 191–98 in the 1672 edition; these language materials have not been reproduced in the modern critical editions of Baldaeus' work. For an evaluation of them see Ph. S. van Ronkel, "De eerste europeesche Tamilspraakkunst en het eerste Malabaarsche Glossarium," *Mede-*

Jaffnapatam they have written on tables in large "Malabar" letters the Ten Commandments, the Lord's Prayer, and the Articles of the Christian Faith. Before Baldaeus left Ceylon, he had translated into Tamil from the Portuguese of Franciscus de Fonseca the Gospel of St. Matthew and various formularies and prayers for his converts as well as some of his own sermons.[248]

As a missionary of the Reformed faith, Baldaeus had but little interest in Hinduism while working in Ceylon and south India. He had read Abraham Roger's *De open-deure tot het verborgen heydendom* (Leyden, 1651) and cites it in his polemics against the Brahmans. He acknowledges that the Brahmans are "as modest in their deportment as could be wished . . . sober, alert, clean, civil, and friendly and very moderate in eating and drinking and never touch any strong drink." They wash twice daily and never eat "anything that was endowed with or can produce life." But, like the other natives, they persist in voluptuous and luxurious living. Even those who outwardly profess Christianity stubbornly hold to their traditional caste beliefs. They distinguish themselves from the lower castes by wearing their sacred triple threads over their shoulders and guardedly conclude marriages only with close members of their own families, generally with their nephews and nieces. They justify this marriage policy by their desire to keep intact their lineage which they trace back to Brahma. They possess strange ideas about the creation and age of the world and, like the Jews, they still hold to the erroneous Pythagorean doctrine of the transmigration of souls. Even professed Christians continue to follow the pagan custom by which the groom ties the *tali* around the bride's neck to make the marriage more binding. They arrange betrothals for their daughters before they are old enough to know their own minds and they are reluctant to marry mature women. Most commendable is their practice of never concluding a marriage without the consent of the parents.[249]

When Baldaeus returned to Europe, he was apparently asked to write a treatise on the Hinduism of Ceylon. He had read Roger and had evidently acquired other materials on Hinduism while in Ceylon and India. His *Afgoderye der Oost-Indische heydenen* (idolatry of the East Indian heathens) was published as the third part of the *Naauwkeurige beschryvinge*. This work, which has long been credited to Baldaeus, has very little in it that may be attributed directly to him. In essence it is a translation without attribution of the *Livro da seita dos Indios Orientais* (book of the sect of the East Indies), a

---

deelingen der Nederlandsche Akademie van Wetenschappen, n.s., V (1942), 543–45; for a translation into English, modern transliterations of the Tamil texts, and a note on the phonetic and other peculiarities of Baldaeus' Tamil see J. A. B. van Buitenen and P. C. Ganeshsundaram, "A Seventeenth Century Dutch Grammar of Tamil," *Bulletin of the Deccan College Research Institute* (Poona), XIV (1952–53), 168–82.

[248] Baldaeus in Saparamadu (ed.), *op. cit.* (n. 97), pp. 344–47.

[249] *Ibid.,* pp. 354–70. The Brahmans of Ceylon play a somewhat less dominant role than the Brahmans of south India and are generally attached to temples. See Cartman, *op. cit.* (n. 211), pp. 134–35.

manuscript prepared early in the seventeenth century at Calicut by the Jesuit father Giacomo Fenicio (ca. 1558–1632). Possibly this work was acquired by the Dutch and Baldaeus in 1663 at the conquest of Cochin, the city in which Fenicio spent his last years. To Fenicio's work Baldaeus added materials taken from a Dutch manuscript composed at Surat in the middle years of the century which deals with the ten avatars of Vishnu (see pls. 158–67), and this also without attribution. In summary, Baldaeus' *Afgoderye* brought to Europe a discussion of Hindu mythology which is a patchwork of translations from Fenicio and an anonymous author to which are added occasional quotations from Roger and others and a few observations based on his own experiences. In the process Baldaeus indiscriminately mixed stories, practices, and beliefs of southern and northern Hinduism without any apparent awareness of what he was doing.[250]

Pyrard's account of the Maldives and the Laccadives was the first and only European description based on personal experiences in these archipelagoes. Like Knox's book on Ceylon, Pyrard's is a work which stands by itself as an introduction to the physical features and social order then prevailing in insular South Asia. Modern scholars must rely upon Pyrard almost exclusively for their understanding of life in these archipelagoes during the seventeenth century.

The seventeenth-century European accounts of Ceylon divide, almost as Ceylon itself was partitioned, into materials on Kandy and those on the coastal areas, particularly the Jaffna peninsula, Colombo, and Galle. They all emphasize the outward features of life and make no inquiry in depth into the history and culture of the island. Physical features, flora, fauna, and natural resources emerge clearly and in most instances accurately. Knox, long recognized as a preeminent primary source for Sinhalese history as well as a major informant of Europe, is especially valuable for his discussion of caste and social customs in Kandy. Baldaeus and Schweitzer, while not quite as comprehensive as Knox, show clearly the relation of the Tamils of Ceylon to those of Coromandel and describe accurately the Hindu caste and social system of Jaffna and the western coast. All the writers are impressed by the temples of Ceylon and by the highly developed character of Buddhism and Hinduism. Knox, in particular, shows clearly how Buddhism was being penetrated by the gods and social customs of Hinduism. The Europeans were all appalled by the prevalence of devil worship and by the widespread belief in omens and astrology. The Sinhalese language was no mystery to Knox, and he provided a brief description for his European readers of the

[250] For the modern critical edition see De Jong (ed.), *op. cit.* (n. 97). The linkage between Baldaeus and his sources is established in two articles by Jarl Charpentier: "Preliminary Report on the 'Livro da seita dos Indios Orientais' (Brit. Mus. Ms. Sloane, 1820)," *Bulletin of the School of Oriental Studies* (London), II (1922–23), 731–54; and "The Brit. Mus. Ms. Sloane 3290, the Common Source of Baldaeus and Dapper," *ibid.*, III (1923–25), 413–20.

character of the spoken language. Baldaeus, who certainly knew enough of Tamil to talk and write it, provided Europe with the first printed samples of Tamil. While Knox had very little to say about Europeans in Ceylon (except for those few who were in Kandy), Baldaeus and Schweitzer provided rich materials on conditions of international trade and on the negotiations of the Dutch and the Danes with Kandy. Thus, by the end of the seventeenth century, Ceylon had emerged as an island civilization of importance in its own right and not just as an adjunct of India or as a trading center from which the valuable cinnamon and precious stones of commerce could be obtained.

Coromandel

The European accounts of the seventeenth century, like those of the sixteenth, do not always agree on what coastal areas and interior parts belong to "Coromandel."[1] Most writers and cartographers of the period indicate sketchily that Coromandel lies on the eastern side of India somewhere between the Godavari River and Cape Comorin and extends from the coast inland as far as the eastern Ghats. In 1616 Anton Schorer, an agent of the VOC who had resided at Masulipatam for seven years, claims that it "extends from Menar [Mannar] to the south of Narsapor [Narasapur at a southern mouth of the Godavari River] where the coast of Orissa begins," or in the region where the VOC had four factories.[2] Others run it northward of the Godavari to include the Gingelly or the Orissa coast. Since the Europeans became constantly more involved in the country south of the Godavari, in Golconda, and in Madura, and since Orissa meanwhile became politically more entangled with the Mughuls, Coromandel in our definition includes only the southeastern coastal plain of the peninsula as far north as the border of Orissa and inland to the eastern Ghats.[3]

Throughout most of the sixteenth century Coromandel had been subject to the Hindu empire of Vijayanagar. In 1564–65 a confederation of Muslim states—Ahmadnagar, Bijapur, Golconda, and Bidar—decisively defeated the forces of Vijayanagar at Talikota and laid waste its capital city. What was

[1] For the sixteenth-century definitions see *Asia,* I, 409–11.

[2] See B. Narain (trans.) and Sri Ram Sharma (ed.), "Schorer's Account of the Coromandel Coast," *The Indian Historical Quarterly,* XVI (1940), 827; and W. H. Moreland (ed.), *Relations of Golconda in the Early Seventeenth Century* ("HS," 2d ser., LXVI; London, 1931), pp. 51–52.

[3] In the map of the east coast included in P. Baldaeus, *Naauwkeurige beschryvinge van Malabar en Choromandel . . .* (Amsterdam, 1672), the cartographer divides the coast south of Point Palmyras (a promontory just north of Puri) into three regions: Coromandel northward to the

left of the Hindu empire, often referred to by contemporaries as "the Carnatic kingdom,"[4] survived this disastrous setback and continued to function
weakly, with occasional spurts of resurgence, for another century. Golconda
and Bijapur pressed strongly against its northern confines for a time, while
its enfeebled emperors tried to retain control over the region south of the
Krishna River. Here the imperial territories were subdivided into three viceroyalties according to the prevailing languages: Telugu in the north, Kanarese
in the west, and Tamil in the south and east. Each of the new viceroyalties
was entrusted to one of the sons of the Emperor Tirumala (r. *ca.* 1569–72).
The most powerful of these successors, Venkata II (r. 1586–1614), ruled by
1599 over the territory from Cape Comorin to the boundaries of the Muslim kingdoms of Bijapur and Golconda at the Penner River.

In or about 1592, Venkata had established his permanent imperial capital
at Chandragiri in hopes of keeping closer control over the nayaks (provincial
or district governors) and poligars (local chieftains) of the Tamil country.
The nayaks of Gingee, Tanjore, and Madura, whose territories occupied a
large part of south Coromandel, had resisted unsuccessfully the reimposi-
tion of imperial authority by Venkata. The nayak of Vellore, who allied
himself with Gingee, was the first of the restive nayaks to rebel against Venkata. In 1604 the emperor invaded and captured Vellore and two years later
made it into another imperial residence. From this vantage point Venkata
took action against the rebellious nayak of Gingee and captured his fortress
in 1608. Throughout most of Venkata's reign the nayak of Tanjore remained
loyal and helpful to the empire, particularly supporting Venkata in his actions against the Muslims and the Portuguese. Muttuvirappa, nayak of
Madura (r. *ca.* 1606 to *ca.* 1623), while not openly rebellious at first, ceased
paying tribute to the empire during the last few years of Venkata's reign.
With Venkata's death in 1614, a succession struggle ensued which brought
an open civil war to the Tamil country that flamed intermittently until 1630.
Thereafter the empire of Vijayanagar suffered a lingering illness until its
demise in 1672. Only two Hindu states, Mysore and Madura, survived its
collapse and remained outside Muslim control. The economic and moral disruptions that everywhere accompanied and followed the civil wars opened
Coromandel more than ever to external forces. Bijapur and Golconda extended their frontiers southward, and the Dutch and English established

---

Krishna River, Golconda between the Krishna and Godavari, and Orissa from the Godavari to
Point Palmyras. The names of many ports and coastal places appear on this map, a reflection of
Dutch preoccupation with maritime trade. Only a few names of cities of the hinterland are
noted, a serious deficiency, in that it fails to show the inland places where the Jesuits, the Dutch
merchants, and other European travelers were active during the seventeenth century. On
the eastern Ghats as a physical divide see Gopal Singh, *A Geography of India* (2d ed.; Delhi,
1976), p. 14.
    [4] On the vague boundaries of the Karnatak (Carnatic) country see H. Raychaudhuri, "Geog-
raphy of the Deccan," in G. Yazdani (ed.), *The Early History of the Deccan* (2 vols.; London,
1960), I, 40–42.

fortresses, as they began to dominate the Tamil coast both economically and politically.[5]

The Portuguese, who had a heavy investment in the trade of the Bay of Bengal, had established settlements at San Thomé in Mylapore (a part of modern Madras) and Negapatam (*Nagapaṭṭaṇam*) during the sixteenth century. Other groups of Portuguese merchants had been active at Pulicat, Masulipatam, and other Coromandel ports. At the beginning of the seventeenth century Mylapore was technically subject to the nayak of Gingee and Negapatam to the nayak of Tanjore. But both towns were dominated by their Portuguese settlers and merchants even though neither possessed a fortress. Relations between the local officials and the Portuguese were generally friendly; but the legal status of these towns within the Estado da India then remained vague and ambiguous. If anything, these towns were simply convenient outposts within the maritime trading area dominated by the Portuguese fleets based at Malacca and Colombo. Franciscans, Jesuits, and Dominicans served the Christians of these towns and nearby localities at the beginning of the century. After the defeat of the nayak of Gingee by Venkata in 1608, Mylapore was nominally placed under the administration of Tanjore. With the advent of the succession crisis in Vijayanagar, the Portuguese captains in both settlements assumed virtually full authority.

At the appearance of the Dutch on the Coromandel Coast in 1605, Lisbon, Goa, and the Jesuits began to take a more direct interest in these settlements and their protection. Still, it was not until 1642, after Portugal's declaration of independence from Spain and after the loss of Malacca to the Dutch, that the Portuguese of Negapatam were formally placed under the administration of Goa and given a permanent garrison and a fortress. At this time Mylapore and Negapatam each boasted around seven thousand inhabitants. It was not until 1658, in conjunction with the capture of Colombo, that Negapatam fell to the Dutch without a shot being fired. Mylapore, near which the English built a factory in 1640, was periodically under attack in the 1660's by the forces of Golconda. In 1674 the Dutch drove a French expeditionary force from the city and handed it over to the administration of Golconda.[6] While all vestiges of Portuguese political and military control

[5] This history has been painfully reconstructed from the Jesuit letters, the Persian histories, inscriptions on stone and copper, dynastic chronicles, and the notices of foreign travelers. Historians even disagree as to whether the Vijayanagar ruler mentioned here should be Venkata I or II. See K. A. Nilakanta Sastri (ed.), *Sources of Indian History with Special Reference to South India* (New York, 1964), pp. 91–99. For reconstructions see H. Heras, S.J., *The Aravidu Dynasty of Vijayanagara* (Madras, 1927), especially chaps. xiii–xv. For a more recent summary account see A. Krishnaswami, *The Tamil Country under Vijayanagar* (Annamalainagar, 1964), chaps. xii–xiv. Also see S. Krishnaswami Aiyangar, "Mysore and the Decline of the Vijayanagar Empire," *Quarterly Journal of the Mythic Society*, XIII (1922), 742–54.

[6] See T. Raychaudhuri, *Jan Company in Coromandel, 1605–1690* (The Hague, 1962), pp. 5–6; M. Abdul Rahim, "Nagapattinam Region and the Portuguese," *Journal of Indian History*, LIII (1975), 485–96; and on Mylapore and San Thomé see Jacques Dupuis, *Madras et le nord du Coromandel. Étude des conditions de la vie indienne dans un cadre géographique* (Paris, 1960), pp. 393–95, and S. Muthiah, *Madras Discovered* (New Delhi, 1987), chaps. i–iv.

were hereafter eliminated, the Portuguese language and the Catholic faith continued to exert a profound influence on everyday affairs in these two towns and all along the coast.

I

THE JESUIT ENTERPRISES

Notices of the early Portuguese and Jesuit activities on the Coromandel Coast had appeared in the writings of Linschoten that circulated in Europe at the turn of the century. From what he had learned in Goa, Linschoten reports that "it is a very rich and plentiful country in all things" and that the Portuguese and other Europeans fare better there than on India's west coast. From Mylapore, Negapatam, and Masulipatam the Portuguese obtain cotton textiles which they trade in Bengal, Pegu, Siam, and Malacca for other eastern products. The colored Coromandel cottons are "much worne in India, and better esteemed then silke . . . because of the fineness and cunning workmanship." Dyed and figured cottons called "Rechatas" (or "Regatas")[7] and "Cheyias" ("chelas" from Tamil, *seelai*) are commonly exported to the further east or made into clothes for both Europeans and Indians. Women garb themselves in skirts of rich materials called clothes of "Sarassa" (Hindi, *sarasa*, meaning "superior") "which are sometimes stitched with threads of silver and gold."[8] On the coast they "growe the great and thick reeds [*Bambusa arundinacea*, bamboo]" that are used as palanquin poles.[9]

The Jesuit letterbooks and mission histories published in Europe during the first two decades of the century include substantial detail on Christian progress and secular affairs in Coromandel. The Jesuits, who had been active at Mylapore, on the Fishery Coast, and in Travancore since Xavier preached there, launched a new initiative in Jaffna, Mannar, and Coromandel at the turn of the sixteenth century.[10] The Jesuit Visitor, Nicolas Pimenta (1546–1614), who inaugurated this new enterprise in 1597, reported to General Acquaviva at Rome in a letter of January, 1599, on the general condition of the southern mission stations. Later information was relayed to Pimenta in Goa by Simão de Sá, the rector of Mylapore, and by Manoel da Veiga of Aveiro (1549–1605), previously rector of the House of the Professed in Goa, from the imperial city of Chandragiri. In 1601 these letters, along with similar reports on Bengal and Malacca were published in

[7] Derived from Sanskrit, *raktaka*, colored cloth. On this term see S. R. Dalgado, *Glossário Luso-Asiático* (2 vols.; Coimbra, 1919, 1921), II, 252.

[8] For discussion see John Irwin, "Indian Textile Trade in the Seventeenth Century, II: Coromandel Coast," *Journal of Indian Textile History,* II (1956), 24–42.

[9] See A. C. Burnell and P. A. Tiele (eds.), *The Voyage of John Huyghen van Linschoten to the East Indies* (2 vols.; "H.S.," o.s., LXX–LXXI; London, 1884), I, 82, 90–92.

[10] See *Asia,* I, 269–71; 274–75.

Latin at Rome. This substantial book of 160 pages was quickly reprinted and by 1602 had been issued in Italian, French, German, and Portuguese translations.[11] In essence this book announced to the Christian world that the empire of Vijayanagar, like Akbar's northern realm, was officially open, and that the Jesuits enjoyed the favor of Venkata II. This publication was followed in 1602 by an Italian collection of letters in which Father Veiga, acting on behalf of Pimenta, reports on his visitation in 1599–1600 of the mission stations from Negapatam to "Bisnaga" (Chandragiri).[12] In 1625 Samuel Purchas published extracts in English from the earlier of these two collections. Because he presents a convenient summary in English, what follows comes in large measure from the Purchas translation even though he omits certain portions of the letters.[13]

It was learned in Europe that Travancore was at war with Madura in 1597. In Punical, Pimenta met Henrique Henriques, who had been left on the Fishery Coast fifty-two years earlier by Xavier; Henriques, who was to die in 1600, was at the time of Pimenta's visit "of able bodie, and daily writing in the Malabar language [Tamil]" of Christian matters.[14] At "Periapatan" (Periapatam, or *Periyapaṭṭaṇam*), the chief city of the "Paravelines" (Paravas), two priests are left behind to start a mission in the Ramnad country. At Negapatam, where the late Father Francisco Peres (d. 1583) is revered as a saint, the Portuguese congregate from all over the East, especially during the winter months. Pimenta reports on his overland trip of twelve days from Negapatam to Mylapore through a pleasant and fertile land marred only by a prodigious number of native temples and idols. These huge idols are transported from place to place "in Chariots as high as steeples, by thousands of men setting their shoulders to the Wheeles."[15]

"Cidambaran" (Chidambaram in South Arcot) is "the mother of their superstitions and furnished with gorgeous Temples." There the Jesuits were

---

[11] The original edition was called simply *Epistola Patris Nicolai Pimentae . . . ad R. P. Claudium Aquavivam*. For its contents and a list of the translations see Streit, V, 8–9.

[12] Entitled *Copia d'una de P. Nicolo Pimenta . . . al molto Reverendo P. Claudio Acquaviva . . . del primo di Decembre 1600* (Rome). Reprinted at Venice in 1602, and translated into Latin (1602), German (1602), Portuguese (1602), and French (1603). See Streit, V, 12–16.

[13] Purchas (*PP*, X, 205–21) summarized and extracted materials from one of the versions of the *Epistola* published at Rome in 1601. We have compared the Purchas translations to the Italian rendition of the *Epistola* published at Milan in 1602 as *Lettera del P. Nicolo Pimenta . . . di Goa, li 25 Decembre, 1598*. This rare edition, not mentioned by Streit, is probably related to the Venice edition of 1602 listed in Streit (V, 12). Comparing the Milan edition held by the Newberry Library with Purchas' translation, we found that he presents the letters in exactly the same order in which they appear in the *Lettera*. Most of his extracts are taken from the materials on Pimenta's visitation (pp. 17–34, 49–67 in the *Lettera*), and from the 1598 letter from Pegu (pp. 34–49). The extracts from the other letters mentioned in the Purchas text are much briefer, often not more than a quick summary of one or two points made in the original letter. In general, Purchas omits materials relating to conversions and other Catholic and Portuguese successes.

[14] Cf. J. Wicki, S.J., "Ein vorbildlicher Missionar Indiens, P. Henriques (1520–1600)," *Studia missionalia*, XIII (1963), 113–68.

[15] *PP*, X, 206–7. This is an obvious reference to "car" festivals.

received by Krishnappa Nayaka, the ruler of Gingee, within whose territories the city then lay. The nayak, who was then superintending the reconstruction of the Chidambaram temple, received the Jesuits courteously and was surprised when they refused the betel he hospitably offered them. The ruler requested a priest for the "new city" he was then building.[16] Pimenta mentions the "Perimal" (*Perumāḷ* [Tamil, "distinguished"], an epithet of Vishnu) temple where they worship an ape called "Hanimant" (Hanumant). This ape-god, it is said, leaped over the water to Ceylon and each time he lighted an island was created; it was reputedly the tooth of this ape that the Portuguese had captured and burned a half century before. The name "Cidambaram," which means "A Golden Chaine," derives from a fable in which it is recounted that God, in dancing there before a holy man, dropped from his foot a chain of gold.[17] Pimenta reports on the great controversy which was then going on as to whether "the signe of Perimal (which is nothing but a Mast or Pole gilded, with an Ape at the foot)" could be admitted to the temple as the nayak decreed it should be. Despite bitter resistance, suicides, and threats, Krishnappa Nayaka nonetheless erected "the Mast with the Ape" inside the confines of the temple.[18]

The Jesuits, by the favor of the nayak and his retainers, travel overland from Chidambaram to Mylapore. This port, "sometime chiefe Citie of the Kingdome of Coromandel," is at that time subject to "the Ragiv or King of Vissanagor [Vijayanagar]." This ruler, who boasts a long and elaborate title that the Jesuits give in translation, resides in "Chandegrin" (Chandragiri).[19] Previously he had "raigned farre and wide, from Cape Cori to the Kingdomes adjoyning to Goa, on the coasts of both Seas." Now some of his former governors have "shooke off his yoke" and he is embroiled in war with Madura. While in Mylapore, Pimenta appointed Simão de Sá (1560–1614) to be rector of the Jesuit college of San Thomé and gave orders to begin an inland mission as soon as possible. A seminary, financed by local Christians, exists there for "the chiefe children of the Badagades [the "northerners," from Tamil, *vaṭakkar*]" who dominate the Vijayanagar officialdom. Adjoining the seminary there is "a Schoole of the Malabars [in this instance

---

[16] Krishnapatam on the banks of the Vellore River near Porto Novo.

[17] A reference, vague as it is, to Nataraja, Lord of the Eternal Dance and a common name for Siva. The translation of Chidambaram as "chain of gold" appears to be incorrect; the name derives from Sanskrit and means "the atmosphere of wisdom." For a discussion of Chidambaram at this period see B. Natarajan, *The City of the Cosmic Dance. Chidambaram* (New Delhi, 1974), chap. v.

[18] *PP*, X, 207–9. Krishnappa Nayaka, a loyal follower of Venkata II, was a zealot of Vaishnavism like his imperial master. The Chidambaram temple of Siva was not prepared to accept quietly the introduction to its innermost enclosure of this symbol of Vishnu. See C. S. Srinivasachari, *A History of Gingee and Its Rulers* (Annamalainagar, 1943), pp. 120–25. On the sectarian disputes of the local worshippers of Siva (Nataraja) and of Vishnu (Govindaraja) see T. B. Balusubramanyan, "Chidambaram in Vijayanagara Days," *Journal of the Bombay Historical Society*, IV (1931), 40–53; and Heras, *op. cit.* (n. 5), pp. 553–54.

[19] The titles given here "are fairly good equivalents of those which are found in the inscriptions of Venkata I" (Krishnaswami, *op. cit.* [n. 5], p. 281).

meaning the Tamils] in which is taught the Tongue of Tamil (or vulgar) and the Badagan [Telugu] used by the Courtiers." The town of San Thomé itself is "famous by the Cathedrall Church, the Apostles Sepulchre, his house in the little Hill, his martyrdome in the great Hill, and the miracle of the Cross."[20]

From here the Jesuits journeyed to Gingee, "the greatest Citie we have seene in India, and bigger than any in Portugall, Lisbon excepted." Pimenta, who wished to thank Krishnappa Nayaka for his good treatment of the Jesuits who had earlier visited these territories, describes in some detail the old walled city of Gingee in the days of its splendor.[21] The ruler shows his golden treasures to the visitors. They are intrigued by "two great Pots" in which water from the Ganges was carried by yogis to Gingee. In the inner part of the castle they see an exercise yard, an armory, and a "store of Jewels." They are shown the "new city" (Krishnapatam) near the mouth of the Vellore River, asked "to fixe a residence and erect a church" there, and granted letters patent in Tamil and Telugu, as well as a stipend of two hundred pieces of gold for the priest to be assigned there. The Jesuits go southward to "the River Colocam" (Coleroon) where they are kindly received by "Cholgana" (Solaga), an "old and severe" vassal of Krishnappa Nayaka.

Going by way of Tranquebar, the Jesuits travel to "Tanjoor" (Tanjore) "the walls whereof are built of hewen stone." Its ruler, Achyutappa Nayaka (r. 1560–1614), "had lately renounced the world and prepared himselfe for death." His seventy wives "were to be burned in the same fire with his carkasse."[22] Krishnappa Nayaka II (r. 1595–1601) of Madura is, according to Pimenta, "very superstitious and resigned his Palace to his Idol Chochanada [*Cokkanāta*, or Siva]."[23] The ruler sits in judgment daily, a Brahman beside him, who "whineth out the name of the Idoll Aranganassa [*Aranganata*, or Vishnu at Srirangam]."[24]

In a letter (November 19, 1598) from Mylapore, Simão de Sá writes of a hostel for three hundred Brahmans who make pilgrimages to "Tripiti [Tirupati, close to Chandragiri] where a famous Idoll" is located. Here they worship Perumal "in many figures, of a Man, an Oxe, Horse, Lion, Hog, Ducke, Cocke." The monkeys which cavort in this fertile valley are tame

---

[20] *PP*, X, 209–10, 217. See our pl. 51.

[21] For an analysis of this account in relation to the site itself see H. Heras, S.J., "The City of Jinji at the End of the Sixteenth Century," *Indian Antiquary*, LIV (1925), 41–43.

[22] This is a vague reference to the "retirement" of Achyutappa in favor of Raghunatha, his heir apparent and associate administrator. In this case the Jesuits seem to be ill informed, for Achyutappa, according to indigenous sources, continued to reign at Tanjore until 1614. See V. Vriddhagirisan, *The Nayaks of Tanjore* (Annamalainagar, 1942), chap. iv.

[23] At Madura, Siva is called "The Handsome Man" (*Cokkan* or *Cōmacuntaran*). See C. G. Diehl, *Instrument and Purpose. Studies on Rites and Rituals in South India* (Lund, 1956), p. 129, n. 2.

[24] *PP*, X, 217–19. On Madura at this period see R. Sathyanatha Aiyar, *History of the Nayaks of Madura* (Madras, 1924), chap. v. The nayaks of both Madura and Tanjore were patrons of the temple at Srirangam, the *koil* or the supreme temple of Vaisnavism. For its history in this period see V. N. Hari Rav, *History of the Srirangam Temple* (Tirupati, 1976), pp. 174–77.

and "the people take them for a nation of gods which hold familiaritie with Perimal."[25] In September, 1599, Manoel da Veiga writes of his journey from Mylapore to Chandragiri. At a stopover at Trivalur (*Tiruvaḷḷur*, near San Thomé) they see a "solemne Procession by night" led by an elephant and accompanied by "30 Women [*devadāsī*] dancers which have devoted themselves to the Idols perpetual service, which may not marrie but prostitute themselves for the most part." The idol, with its carriers and priests "living on the revenues of the Temple," is followed by common people carrying lights. The idol is lodged in the temple where four Brahmans feed it and perform various rituals and services. Once arrived in Chandragiri, the Jesuits are granted permission to build a church and residence, to erect crosses, and to make converts. "Mélchior Cotignas" (Melchior Coutinho [1571–1610]) describes in a letter of 1600 the Hindu belief that an eclipse occurs when "the Dragon (one of their constellations) biteth" either the sun or the moon. "At the feast of Perimal's marriage" at Tirupati the emperor and his court are present to observe the triumphal car; one month earlier the "Feast of Kowes" had been celebrated, "for they hold Perimal to have beene the sonne of a Kow."[26] At this time rumor had it that the emperor would "warre upon the Naichus of Tangoor [Tanjore] called Astapanaicus [Achyutappa Nayaka] had he not died before this could happen."[27] In Chandragiri the principal inhabitants are "Bramenes [Brahmans], Rajus [Rajas or Kshatriyas], and Cietius [Vaisyas?]." Perumal, it is said, "brought forth the first out of his head, the second out of his breast, the third out of his bellie, the rest as baser vulgar from his feet."[28] Veiga also transmitted to Pimenta a letter from Venkata thanking the Jesuits for sending the missionaries.

A more systematic treatment of the Jesuit missions in south India appears in the histories of Fernão Guerreiro, the Portuguese Jesuit, and of Pierre Du Jarric, his French colleague of Bordeaux.[29] In five biennial relations based on the Jesuit letters, Guerreiro reports on the religious situation in south India (as well as elsewhere in the *padroado*) from 1600 to 1609. Du Jarric, in Part III of his trilogy, deals with the period from 1600 to 1610. Much of his material on south India is drawn from the Jesuit letterbooks and especially from Guerreiro's relations. What follows is a summary, region by region, of Guerreiro's account supplemented by materials from Du Jarric's work.

[25] *PP*, X, 219. This refers to the Thiruvengadam temple on the Terumala hill at Tirupati. Vishnu is worshipped there in five forms. See Heras, *op. cit.* (n. 5), p. 315. For a description of the temple and its history see T. K. T. Viraraghavacharya, *History of Tirupati* (3 vols.; 2d ed., Tirupati, 1977), Vol. I.

[26] *Perumāḷ* (Vishnu) has three wives: *Lakṣmī* (Sri), *Bhūmi* (Pusti), and *Nīladevi*. The marriage festival at Tirupati occurs in September or October. The association of Vishnu with the cow is rare, even though he was brought up by a cowherd. See Jan Gonda, *Aspects of Early Visnuism* (Utrecht, 1954), pp. 153, 226. On cow worship and the *Māṭṭup-Pongal* festival see P. V. Jagadisa Ayyar, *South Indian Festivities* (Madras, 1921), chap. iii.

[27] Probably misinformation; see above, n. 22.

[28] *PP*, X, 220–22. *Cf.* our pl. 133.

[29] On their works see above, pp. 315–18, 396.

Guerreiro reports in some detail on the Fishery Coast, the oldest of the Jesuit missions in south India and a region in which the Portuguese were particularly well established. From the college at Tuticorin the Jesuits in 1601 administer twenty-two parishes, sixteen coastal and six inland, manned by twenty Jesuits, seventeen secular priests, and three lay brothers. Over the course of the mission's history the Europeans had Christianized the entire caste of Paravas, numbering around ninety thousand at this time. The Paravas, the most pious community of Christians in India, are especially devoted to the shrine and tomb of Henriques (d. 1600) in Tuticorin. Although Christian in religion, they are legally the vassals of the nayak of Madura. Until 1600 the nayaks had tolerated foreign enterprise along this coast, the Portuguese being welcomed as a counterweight to the Arabs. Muttu Krishnappa Nayaka (r. 1601–9) resolved at the beginning of the seventeenth century to reassert his authority in this region and to end the anarchy prevailing among the Maravas, a "barbarous and ferocious" forest people of the Ramnad country who live by robbery. Heavier taxes are levied upon the Christian Paravas as part of this new policy. Ariya Perumal, the Palaiyarakan of "Vigiabodi" (Vijayapati, near Ramnad) and enemy of the Christians and their priests, begins in 1602 the systematic oppression of the Christians inhabiting the tract between Cape Comorin and "Manapadu" (Manappatu) on the Fishery Coast. A contingent of three hundred Christians attacks Vijayapati, invests the town, and kills Ariya. Undiscouraged by these events, the Jesuits seek now to establish new missions in the territory of the Maravas.[30]

To punish the Christians for their revolt, new and heavier taxes are levied and an army is sent by Madura to restore order. Many of the Christian Paravas thereupon flee from the region of Tuticorin to an uninhabited island off the coast. Both the "king" of Tuticorin (Udaiyan Sethupati?) and the nayak of Madura pay tribute to the Portuguese annually to protect this coast from Moor and heathen alike. Nevertheless they exact an unjust tribute from the Christians through their "patangatins" (Tamil, *pattankaṭṭi*, headmen) who are judges that enforce both civil and criminal law. These officials also consider themselves to be in charge of ecclesiastical government and make life miserable for the Christians. Many Christians emigrate from Tuticorin and its environs to a nearby island called "Of the Kings." With the permission of the viceroy, De Saldanha, the Parava refugees have begun to fortify the island and to build shipyards and warehouses at its harbor. Here the Paravas are protected by the Portuguese and are no longer subject to the tyranny of Moors, Hindus, or Dutch. When a ship is wrecked off their island, the Paravas keep whatever they salvage, instead of turning it over to the nayak

---

[30]Guerreiro in A. Viegas (ed.), *Relação anual* . . . (3 vols.; Coimbra, 1930, 1931, 1941), I, 31–40. Also see Heras, *op. cit.* (n. 5), pp. 352–53. For a modern confirmation of Guerreiro's description of the Maravas see K. P. K. Pillay, *The Caste System in Tamil Nadu* (Madras, 1977), pp. 28–29. Also see S. Krishnaswami Aiyangar, *Sources of Vijayanagar History* (Madras, 1919), pp. 89–92.

who, like other Indian rulers, customarily confiscates for himself the booty from shipwrecks. Although the nayak has a considerable army in the nearby Marava country, the Paravas are protected by the Portuguese, with whom they share their loot. Pacification of this area is essential, since the roads must be kept safe for pilgrims to "Ramanacor" (Ramesvaram) "where there is the most famous temple in the whole Orient."[31]

While the Jesuits and Portuguese suffer on the Fishery Coast from Madura's efforts to reassert authority, their compatriots enjoy a better time in the port towns north of Point Calimere. None of these ports is as favorable for shipping as Tuticorin, but the political conditions there are better for foreigners. San Thomé (Mylapore) had become during the sixteenth century the most important Portuguese settlement and Christian center on India's east coast. The Franciscans, the first of the Europeans to work there, had established a friary and a church. Beginning around 1550, the Jesuits had begun to carry the mission to the native population. Their successes in making conversions were immediate and steady, even though they lacked the military support which the Portuguese provided on the Fishery Coast and on India's west coast to the Christian enterprise. In the early seventeenth century the Portuguese settlement continues to prosper and the Franciscan Madre de Deus province of San Thomé boasts more than five thousand European and indigenous Christians.[32]

Until Pimenta's visitation in 1597, Christian missionizing activities had been generally confined to San Thomé and its immediate vicinity. The six or so Jesuits who served in the college there were not numerous enough, according to contemporaries, to undertake missions inland. The European priests, as well as the Portuguese captain who administered the foreign settlement, had all they could do to keep peace among the Portuguese of San Thomé. The natives of the city of Mylapore were governed by an *adigar* (governor) appointed by the nayak of Tanjore on behalf of the emperor of Vijayanagar. This official also collected levies and duties imposed by the nayak and the emperor.

Disputes occur regularly between the Europeans and the natives which produce riots and fights. The Hindus sometimes charge, quite wrongly, according to Guerreiro, that the Jesuits are using undue influence and force in effecting conversions. Neither the *adigar* nor the Portuguese has enough authority or police power to control the frequent disorders plaguing the city. In 1606 an unusually severe riot between the Portuguese of San Thomé and the Hindus of Mylapore ends in an orgy of burning and pillaging. The *adigar,* who had been forced to flee from the city, dispatches a report to Venkata II blaming the Portuguese for the affair. Outraged by their temerity, Venkata temporarily turns against the Portuguese and threatens to destroy

---

[31] See Viegas (ed.), *op. cit.* (n. 30), I, 322–24; II, 323–27; III, 102–3.

[32] See A. Meersman, O.F.M., *The Franciscans in Tamilnad.* Supplement XII of *NZM* (1962), pp. 6–18. For this figure on the number of Christians see Viegas (ed.), *op. cit.* (n. 30), II, 21.

their settlement. Nicolau Levanto, the rector of the Jesuit college, manages by explanations and gifts to placate the emperor.

In an effort to make the east coast clerics more responsible, Pope Paul V published a bull on January 9, 1606, separating Mylapore from the jurisdiction of Cochin. The newly created bishopric of Mylapore was to possess jurisdiction over the Coromandel Coast, Orissa, Bengal, and Pegu. Sebastião de São Pedro, an Augustinian Eremite, was named its first bishop; he arrived at his see late in 1608.[33]

In Coromandel the new bishop of Mylapore governs Christian activities in the coastal cities stretching from Negapatam northward to Masulipatam. The Jesuit college of San Thomé retains jurisdiction over Jesuit activities at the court of Venkata II. At Negapatam, as elsewhere on the coast, the Franciscans had been first on the scene.[34] The Jesuits had begun only after 1597 to build a residence and chapel at Negapatam. Later, they carried their ministry to neighboring Tranquebar, "a gentile city where some Christian Paravas live." From San Thomé individual Jesuits visit Christians in 1607–8 northward to Pulicat and "Arimagão" (Armagon), and southward to Seven Pagodas and Porto Novo. Everywhere they are startled by the great number of idols and temples and aghast at the devotion of the natives to their gods and shrines. At the ports northward from San Thomé to Masulipatam they confront Moors and learn that Portuguese trade and shipping are suffering more and more from the competition and depredations of the Dutch. The Jesuits even use their influence at the imperial court to force the nayak of Gingee to rescind his permission granting the Dutch the right to build a fort at Devanapatam. Father Levanto, engaged as an emissary by Venkata, even convinces Krishnappa Nayaka of Gingee to expel the Dutch in 1610. Their partially completed fort is then turned over to the Portuguese.[35]

About Vijayanagar, Chandragiri, and the court of Venkata II, Du Jarric is more comprehensive and descriptive than Guerreiro. Du Jarric defines in some detail the extent of Vijayanagar, or the kingdom of "Bisnaga" as it is called by the Portuguese who trade there, or "Narasinga" as it is ordinarily named by writers.[36] Both sketch the history of the Jesuits at Venkata's court on the basis of the published and unpublished reports of the missionaries in the field. After Visitor Pimenta had urged the Jesuits of San Thomé to establish a mission at Chandragiri, Rector Simão de Sá quickly gets in touch with a Christian merchant from Chandragiri who was then living in San Thomé.

[33] Guerreiro in Viegas (ed.), *op. cit.* (n. 30), I, 317–21; II, 32; also Heras, *op. cit.* (n. 5), pp. 437–38.

[34] Meersman, *op. cit.* (n. 32), p. 57.

[35] Viegas (ed.), *op. cit.* (n. 30), III, 76–77; Heras, *op. cit.* (n. 5), pp. 443–44.

[36] In 1630 Mandelslo, probably in the additions of Olearius (see above, pp. 667–68), seems to believe that "Bisnaga" refers to Chandragiri and "Narasinga" to Vellore, the two imperial residences. See B. A. Saletore, *Social and Political Life in the Vijayanagara Empire (A.D. 1346–A.D. 1646)* (2 vols.; Madras, 1934), I, 141–42. This is patently incorrect since these two names were current long before Vellore became an imperial residence in 1604. See *Asia,* I, 371, nn. 233–34.

Through his good offices the Jesuits obtain an introduction to "Oboragiu" (Obo Raya or Prince Obo), the father-in-law of Venkata. On this prince's invitation, Fathers De Sá and Francesco Ricci (*ca.* 1545–1606) went in October, 1598, to Chandragiri. Soon they are received in audience by the emperor himself and by Ranga, the heir to the throne. Venkata, dressed in yellow, is seated with a pillow at his back on a high tribunal covered with a mat, and next to him, off the mat, sits the heir apparent. Obo and his brother sit facing the imperial pair, on another mat. The two priests and the courtiers stand close to the imperial dais to extend and receive greetings. After affably questioning the priests about their calling, Venkata pronounces them to be like *sannyasis* and even *gurupis* (learned priests). The emperor assigns the proceeds of two villages for their maintenance and for the construction of a church. He also gives them a golden palanquin of the sort reserved to the use of *gurupis* and nobles. The two priests return to San Thomé to inform Pimenta of their success and to request the dispatch of new priests to open a mission in Chandragiri.[37]

In August, 1599, Father Manoel da Veiga, who was to be the superior of the new mission, went to Chandragiri in the company of Ricci, its secretary. Some months later they were joined by Melchior Coutinho, and these three immediately began the construction of a church and a residence on land donated by Obo. In 1600 Brother Alexander Frey, an Englishman and a painter, appeared at the court for a short while. When the Jesuits failed to receive the revenues from the two villages assigned to them, Venkata endowed them with an annual stipend that was paid regularly until 1603. While they enjoyed Venkata's personal support and interest, conversions were few and the Brahmans hostile. After the conquest of Vellore in 1604, the Jesuits decided that some of them at least had to follow Venkata to his new residence. On the death of Ricci in 1606 he was replaced at Chandragiri by two other Italians: Father Antonio Rubino (1578–1643), a mathematician and astronomer, and Brother Bartolomeo Fontebona, an artist. It was at this juncture that the riot in San Thomé occurred, an event that temporarily brought Venkata's wrath down upon the Jesuits and forced them to leave his court at Chandragiri and return to San Thomé.[38]

During this first era of friendly relations, the Jesuits have a splendid opportunity to observe the court life of Vijayanagar. Venkata, a devotee of Vishnu, listens tolerantly to the Jesuits as they proclaim Christian doctrine and talk of his personal salvation. He consults the fathers on secular matters, especially war-making, commerce, science, and painting—and occasionally uses them as emissaries. When Tatacharya, his personal Brahman adviser, asks how the priests could be sannyasis since they eat meat, Venkata replies

[37] Pierre du Iarric (Jarric), S.J., *Histoire des choses plus memorables advenues tant ez Indes Orientales . . .* (3 vols.; Bordeaux, 1608, 1610, 1614), I, 567–71. For further details on this first audience see Heras, *op. cit.* (n. 5), pp. 465–67.

[38] See Heras, *op. cit.* (n. 5), pp. 468–75.

that they are chaste and have no wives. The emperor is particularly interested in the paintings they show him of Christian subjects and the portraits
of Xavier, Loyola, and the kings of Portugal. Once the Jesuits are allowed to
return to Chandragiri in 1607, Fontebona paints the emperor's portrait. On
his return from exile in San Thomé, Rubino presents to Venkata a map of
the world with a Telugu inscription describing the principal kingdoms, the
four elements, and the "eleven heavens." His favorite queen when the Jesuits
first arrived was Oboyama, the daughter of Prince Obo; she was the ruler of
Pulicat by a bequest of the emperor. Like her father and husband she favors
the Jesuits and offers at this time to aid them in building a residence at
Pulicat, a port that the Dutch covet. The fathers, according to Guerreiro,
must look to the future and continue to learn local languages and customs
and to cultivate people in high places.[39]

The Jesuits are especially intrigued by the ceremonies, festivals, and processions of the Hindus. They visit "Tripeti" (Tirupati), a very large and
beautiful city not far from Chandragiri that is "the Rome of these gentiles,"
to whose temple of Vishnu pilgrims flock from all over the Orient with
offerings.[40] The pilgrims, especially the Brahmans, are provided shelter and
hospitality by the chieftains of the surrounding area. As they walk to the
shrine, the pilgrims continually repeat the name of the idol they call "Goya"
(Govinda?).[41] Before entering the temple, they are told by the Brahmans to
purge themselves of their sins by shaving their beards and heads and by
washing their bodies in water.[42] During the Jesuits' first stay in Chandragiri
in 1598, Venkata entertained his queens at a feast in a pleasure-house located
outside the city. The procession from the palace to the suburb was beautiful
in its pomp and magnificence:

At its head came one of the principal royal captains, a Muslim, who was followed by
a cavalry detachment and four or five elephants, gayly rigged out in silken ensigns
and standards of diverse colors. After this there came the flutes, drums, and oboes
making very melodious sounds. The players were mounted on camels, guided by
many foot soldiers. Then came the "Delevays" [*dalavays*], or chief captains of
the armies, followed by an innumerable number of foot soldiers carrying pikes,
arquebuses, and other kinds of arms. Behind them walked one of the royal elephants
bearing the royal standard and surrounded by court nobles. Next came a huge iron
gong . . . which was carried by four porters and struck continuously by four soldiers. . . . The king himself followed in a golden sedan chair accompanied by a

---

[39] Guerreiro in Viegas (ed.), *op. cit.* (n. 30), I, 42; II, 321–23.

[40] *Ibid.*, p. 41. Venkata Tarava, one of the five forms of Vishnu worshipped at Tirupati, was
the god to whom Venkata was most devoted. See Heras, *op. cit.* (n. 5), pp. 314–15.

[41] Govinda is an epithet of Krishna and also an aspect of Vishnu. In Tamilnadu this name is
very often used as a call in village temples, at funerals, and possibly in pilgrimages. When used
as a call it has no apparent connection to Krishna. See Diehl, *op. cit.* (n. 23), p. 260, n. 2. According to the Abbé Du Bois, the *harismarana*, or recital of the names of Vishnu, begins with
"Hail Govinda" (H. K. Beauchamp [trans. and ed.], *Hindu Manners, Customs, and Ceremonies*
[3d ed.; Oxford, 1959], pp. 237, n. 1; 279).

[42] Du Jarric, *op. cit.* (n. 37), I, 571.

number of gentlemen servants and other courtiers. Four of the gentlemen bore handsome umbrellas. One of them carried behind him other emblems: the hairy tails of wild cows, white as snow, which are greatly esteemed by all Eastern peoples. Finally came another standard, a big representation of a very large fish and another of a lion. All these were carried on long poles, and after them another standard was carried in front of the chief "Delevay" or Constable of the Kingdom; then came the prince [Ranga] and heir-apparent. After him came the wives of the king accompanied by a large number of ladies who were carried in silver and gold sedan chairs with great pomp. The queens themselves were carried in shiny golden litters covered with rich brocades adorned with an infinity of pearls and precious stones. Next to every litter two silken canopies were carried to keep off the glare of the sun. . . . There were besides many handmaidens who walked next to their mistresses to fan them with the golden and silver fans they held in their hands. In such an order they proceeded to their pleasure house and returned later in the day with the same pomp. Since it was after sunset so many torches illuminated the return procession that it seemed as if the daylight had come back.[43]

On January 27, 1607, King Philip addressed a letter to Venkata thanking him for his hospitality to the Jesuits and assuring him that "I shall be pleased, for the sake of all this, to oblige you in all your things."[44] In his reply Venkata promised to treat the Jesuits well and to aid the viceroy of Goa "with the whole of my army and power" against the Moors, "our old common enemies," and to stop the Dutch from completing their fortress at Devanapatam .[45] While construction of the fortress was halted, the friendly relations portended by this exchange of letters evaporated over the next several years. During 1608–9 Venkata retained his good will towards the Jesuits in spite of the attacks launched against them by the Brahmans and courtiers. Philip III meanwhile began to listen to those in Europe who were criticizing the Jesuits in south India for failing to make converts and for accommodating too readily to the practices and beliefs of the Hindus. In March, 1610, the king ordered the viceroy to request the Jesuit superior to withdraw the missionaries from Chandragiri and Vellore. By the end of 1611 the king's order to the Jesuits had been obeyed to the letter and no more missionaries remained at Venkata's court. The emperor himself responded by turning against the Portuguese. He permitted the Dutch to take over the fort at Pulicat and besieged the city of San Thomé for the next nine months. In staving off the army of the old and ailing emperor, the Portuguese were aided by the nayak of Tanjore, their immediate overlord. After Venkata's death in 1614, the Portuguese took advantage of the succession crises which followed to fortify San Thomé and to attack the Dutch at Pulicat.[46]

[43] *Ibid.,* pp. 586–87.

[44] For the text of this lettter in English translation see Heras, *op. cit.* (n. 5), p. 445.

[45] Text of this letter in *ibid.,* pp. 445–46. A summary of Venkata's letter by Guerreiro is in Viegas (ed.), *op. cit.* (n. 30), III, 76.

[46] Heras, *op. cit.* (n. 5), pp. 447–50, 477–85. Rubino was the last of the Jesuits to leave Chandragiri. See the Jesuit letterbook *Raguagli d'alcune missioni fatte dalli padri della Compagnia di Giesu . . . nell' Indie Orientale* (Rome, 1615), pp. 51–52 for events of 1611.

Contemporary Jesuit writers turned their attention to the mission at Madura once news reached Europe of Nobili's activities there.[47] They recall that Father Gonçalo Fernandes had been sent to Madura, perhaps as early as 1595, to minister to the Paravas and to negotiate on their behalf with the nayak of Madura, their secular overlord.[48] They candidly admit that the locals then paid no attention to Christianity, for they esteemed it to be the faith of the low-caste and casteless Paravas and Portuguese. The Hindus disdain the Christians because they drink wine, eat meat, and consort with pariahs, palanquin bearers, and other mean people. A Brahman would rather die of hunger than to eat anything prepared by a lower-caste individual and will avoid being touched by or caught in the shadow of a pariah. Because of these attitudes, Fernandes made very few converts in Madura. Old and weary, Fernandes in 1606 was sent a companion and associate in the person of Roberto de Nobili, an Italian Jesuit and nephew of the famous Cardinal Sforza.

Guerreiro describes in detail how Nobili dissociated himself from Fernandes and the Portuguese in his efforts to win the respect of the Hindus. As "new wine" he proclaims that he came of a high caste comparable to Brahmans or Rajas. To persuade them of his sincerity he sustains himself with rice, milk, and herbs, refuses to touch meat, fish, eggs, or wine, and retains a Brahman to cook for him. Like the fathers in China he dons the garments of the literati; he wins his early successes in the robes of the holy and lettered "saneasses" (*sannyasis*). He moves from Fernandes' residence to a simple abode of his own where he lives as a recluse occupying himself with study and contemplation, and in conversations with visitors.

His first teacher, a high-caste schoolmaster hired by Fernandes, showed very little deference for Fernandes and no interest in Christianity, even though he had translated into Telugu the Tamil version of the Credo prepared by Fernandes.[49] After an eclipse of the sun occurred on February 25, 1606,[50] Nobili begins to question the teacher about Hindu beliefs. They talk for twenty days, four or five hours each day until the schoolteacher becomes convinced of the error of believing in a plurality of gods and in the trans-

---

[47] See especially Guerreiro's account in Viegas (ed.), *op. cit.* (n. 30), II, 327–33; III, 89–113. The excellent modern biographies of Nobili (see above, p. 149, n. 74) are based much more upon materials not published at the time. They especially depend upon the unpublished biography of Father A. Saulière and upon a multitude of only recently available manuscripts, some of which were printed in the nineteenth-century collections of Joseph Bertrand, S.J.

[48] Du Jarric, *op. cit.* (n. 37), III, 750, asserts that Fernandes first went to Madura in 1595, whereas others, such as Heras, *op. cit.* (n. 5), p. 313, give 1596 as the date. Fernandes, according to Du Jarric, built a house, church, and school at Madura and hired a Brahman to teach the Parava children the Tamil and Telugu languages.

[49] The schoolteacher was a high-level Sudra according to V. Cronin, *A Pearl to India* (London, 1959), p. 46.

[50] Guerreiro (Viegas [ed.], *op. cit.* [n. 30], II, 329) gives this incorrect date. It should be 1607. Nobili did not arrive in Madura until November, 1606. See P. R. Bachmann, *Roberto Nobili 1577–1656* (Rome, 1972), p. 63, and Cronin, *op. cit.* (n. 49), p. 61, both of whom give 1607. Heras, *op. cit.* (n. 5), p. 398, gives 1608 as the date.

migration of souls.[51] Nobili secretly baptises the teacher and gives him the Christian name "Alberto." A number of other Hindus of high station follow Alberto's lead and become disciples of Nobili.

Their secret is soon exposed. Sivadharma, a *pandara* (Tamil, *pandāram,* a mendicant of the Sudra caste), Alberto's former teacher and an influential figure at court, claims that Alberto has dishonored his caste and family by accepting Christianity. The *pandara* and some of his followers visit Nobili to discuss with him their belief in "Chocanada" (*Cokkanāta*), the Hindu god most revered in Madura.[52] Convinced by the Jesuit of the errors of his faith, Sivadharma leaves the house praising the converts and promising to help Nobili in his mission. He advises Nobili to adopt the dress of the gurus who profess the law of God. When Nobili objects that this dress is too ostentatious for one who has taken a vow of poverty, the *pandara* replies: "Father, if you alone want to attain salvation you may dress as you like; but if you want to teach others the way to salvation . . . , you must adopt the customs of the country . . . as much as you can."[53]

In following this advice Nobili, according to Guerreiro, adopts the practices of the local "sandassas" insofar as they do not compromise Christian beliefs. He lives now as a chaste recluse clothed from the shoulders to the feet in a pale yellow tunic. Over this he wears a short surplice of the same color topped with a scarf of vermilion or of pale yellow that is thrown across the shoulders; around his head he winds a cloth in the form of a "biretta" (*i.e.,* a turban). Over his shoulder he wears a cord of five threads, three gold and two white, from which a cross is suspended. The three gold threads signify the Trinity and the other two the body and spirit of Christ.

Nobili and a new European companion are instructed by a young Brahman in the language, literature, and sciences of the Brahmans. The father's command of spoken and written Tamil is perfect. He reads their books of history, memorizes passages of their laws, and recites verses by their most esteemed poets. He sings their hymns to the great admiration of his listeners. Now he is beginning to study "Gueredão," the Latin of the Brahmans (Grantha, the Tamil script of Sanskrit). Already he knows how to read and speak Sanskrit moderately well. He uses passages from their writings to confound them and to prove that traditionally they do not believe in a plurality of gods, but in just one incorporeal god. His disciples spread the evangel to other places: "Daraporão" (Dharapuram) and "Manamaduré" (Manamaturai).[54] In the autumn of 1608 he baptizes thirteen prominent men, some of whom are "totias" (Tamil, *toṭṭi*), an honorable caste of great num-

---

[51] For details of their disputation see Heras, *op. cit.* (n. 5), pp. 378–81, and Cronin, *op. cit.* (n. 49), p. 62.

[52] The temple of Madura is dedicated to Siva in the form of *Cokkanāta* and to his wife *Mīnāksi,* the "fish-eyed." See Cronin, *op. cit.* (n. 49), p. 60).

[53] Guerreiro in Viegas (ed.), *op. cit.* (n. 30), II, 331; also Heras, *op. cit.* (n. 5), pp. 381–83.

[54] Dharapuram was three days' journey from Madura towards the interior. Manamaturai is southeast of Madura and on the same river, the Vaigai.

bers, whose members are scattered throughout all the cities and habitations of the "Conquam" (Konkan, low country) from "Bembar" (Bempara, or Bempiaer, just north of Tuticorin) northward to "Bisnaga" (Chandragiri).[55]

What helps Nobili in the conversion of these people, especially the Brahmans, is his deep knowledge of their laws (Vedas). He discovers that in ancient times they had four Vedas, only three of which—those of Vishnu, Brahma, and Siva—the Brahmans still teach. The fourth Veda, which presents a wholly spiritual approach to salvation, has been lost, so they claim, and no person is wise or good enough to recover it. In their most secret books it is affirmed that it is impossible to attain true salvation through any of the three Vedas being taught. Consequently many think there is no salvation and nothing beyond this life. Since they perform penances, give alms, and go regularly to their temples, clearly they are most anxious to save their own souls. Nobili, using passages from their own sacred writings, does his best to convince them that they live in sin and that good works will avail nothing without the true faith. Nobili, following the examples of St. Paul in dealing with the Athenians and their "unknown God," tells the Hindus that he has come from a distant land to teach the true way to salvation that their Brahmans say is lost. To recover the lost law and to learn its meaning they become Nobili's disciples and adopt the "dixi" (Tamil, *tītcai,* meaning initiation) from him—the act by which they become Christian converts.[56]

Nobili's successes of 1608 bring forth a reaction from the local gurus. They complain to the nayak that his followers no longer worship at the temples of "Chocanada" or any other Hindu god. They identify Nobili as a new "Mori," or spiritual ascetic and teacher who has come to Madura to destroy their sects by denying the efficacy of their insignia and rites. The priests of "Chocanada" appeal to the nayak to suppress Nobili and his doctrine as a threat to church and state. Charges against the Jesuit are summarized in seven points: he teaches that the Hindu gods are false; he mocks the trinity (*trimurti*) and invents his own, while describing Brahma, Vishnu, and Siva as monsters; he denies that "Chocanada" is lord of the fourteen worlds and sees him as nothing; he promises a deluge that will destroy "Chocanada's" temple and its "lingão" (*lingam*);[57] he makes disciples of leading Brahmans; he dishonors the whole Brahman caste by hiring a Brahman as a servant, since he is a Turk or subject of some other inferior nation; and

---

[55] The *totti* are Sudras who usually work as laborers in the villages.

[56] Guerreiro in Viegas (ed.), *op. cit.* (n. 30), III, 97–98. *Cf.* the technique used by Ricci in China of recovering the "true faith" of the primitive Chinese from the ancient Confucian texts (above, pp. 183–84). Also see Cronin, *op. cit.* (n. 49), pp. 90–91.

[57] Guerreiro explains (Viegas [ed.], *op. cit.* [n. 30], III, 100) that the lingam is a tall stone which stands in the middle of the temple. The Hindus believe that they receive a great blessing by touching this stone; they also wear a small lingam around the neck as a protective talisman. In fact, the Siva Lingam was kept in the *sanctum sanctorum* of the Madura temple since its origins around 1200 A.D. See Sri K. Palaniappan, *The Great Temple of Madurai* (Madura, 1963; reprint 1970), p. 64.

finally he offends by learning the sacred letters of the Brahmans and by using their own writings against them.

The Brahmans condemn Nobili and Sivadharma, his pundit, to the other Brahmans of the city. Finally a date is set for a trial, an event which draws an audience of eight hundred Brahmans. One of Nobili's visitors acts as prosecutor, and Sivadharma presents the defense. Nobili's accuser commences:

Be it known to you, O Brahmans, that one is among us who calls himself a Saniassa [*sannyasi*] even though he is lower than the lowest frangue [Frank]. "Saniassa" is the name given to chaste and spiritual men who live religiously. "Frangue" is the name given to Portuguese and other Europeans. Even a child can see that he is of white color like the frangues, but let us leave color aside and consider the blasphemies he made before me in the presence of another Brahman and his pundit who is present here. He asserted that the teachings of the Brahmans are false and deceptive and that giving alms to them is not meritorious. He avowed that bathing in the sea at Ramanancor [Rameshvaram] or in the Ganges will not bring salvation;[58] he asserts that the Rajas are higher in nobility than the Brahmans and that none of us has knowledge of the true God and that the people of this land can never attain salvation.

Ponder then, O Brahmans, the stupidities mouthed by this man. Only he knows God; where then are those more learned men—Nhanis [Tamil, *ñāni*, an individual learned in spiritual matters] and Saniasses—whom we hold in such great honor . . . ? Has this man alone a monopoly on salvation?

He even tried to pervert some of my friends, but I persuaded them not to follow him, for they would have fallen into hell. To prove the truth of all I have said, I call on his teacher [Sivadharma] to be my witness. . . .

The young Sivadharma bows to the assembly and apologizes for his immaturity and for his inexperience in talking before a distinguished audience. He continues:

This Brahman accuses me of serving a frangue and proves it by saying that my Aier [Tamil, *aiyar*, meaning master] is white. This proves nothing, for by the same token I could show that he is the lowest of pariahs since in this country men of high and low birth are of the same color. Is it therefore not possible that men living in other countries can be of the same color even though they are of different classes by birth?

Even the prosecutor agrees to this argument, but adds that the others are his fundamental points. Sivadharma then goes on:

The plaintiff and his friend asked my Aier, the father, whether a man living their way of life would achieve eternal glory. He responded that there are two kinds of life, one which consists only in ceremonies . . . and this way of life is no help in winning salvation; the other consists in knowing, loving, and serving God, and this is the only path to glory. The accuser then asked what would happen to a person

---

[58] Guerreiro explains (Viegas [ed.], *op. cit.* [n. 30], III, 101) that, according to their superstitious beliefs, whoever bathes at the famous temple of "Ramanancor" on the Fishery Coast receives a plenary indulgence. Those who bathe in the Ganges, a river that courses through Bengal, are purged of all guilt of sin.

who, without knowing God, made pilgrimages to the Ganges and Ramanancor. My Aier replied that he will not win glory. The Brahman asserted that it follows there-fore that he believes our religion is false. It is a law of the plaintiff's own invention of which our books make no mention, that by merely bathing in the Ganges a person can thereby obtain salvation.

At this point the presiding Brahman, turning towards the accuser, says:

It is obvious that you are a great ignoramus and that you failed to understand the words of this Saniasse. You are in error if you think you can win salvation merely by taking baths and rubbing your body with ashes. When this Saniasse spoke as he did, he showed that he was learned and well versed in our doctrine.

Sivadharma continues:

As to the second part of the charge concerning almsgiving, my Aier answered in the same way, that without knowing God they are of no use in salvation and that the same applies to baths taken at Ramanancor or in the Ganges. As to the point that the Rajas are higher in nobility than the Brahmans, the Father simply said that the human race, like the body, has many members, the head of which is the Rajas, not by reason of greater nobility, but because they govern us who are members of the body politic, for even the Brahmans live under their protection and are subject to their government. Finally, the Aier said that in this land few, if any, might attain salvation, for very few know God, but he did not say that nobody knew God, or that he alone knew him and would be saved.[59]

Although Nobili wins his case with the Brahmans, his trials in Madura are not over. In 1609, as his congregation grows, Nobili decides to build a larger and more beautiful church. To this end he obtains a convenient site from "Heremechiti Naique" (Erumaikatti), lord (*poligar*) of the quarter where he resides.[60] Once the building begins, the Brahmans can see, from the height of the walls and the general dimensions of the church, that this is to be a grand edifice. Their jealousy is reawakened and rumors are circulated which greatly exaggerate the number of Nobili's Christian converts. The chief Brahman of "Chocanada" asserts that the site assigned belongs to the temple and that nobody has the right to dispose of it. He denounces Nobili as a base man, a "frangue," who had lived and eaten with Fernandes. To punish him for his audacity, the chief Brahman declares, he will obtain an order from the "Great Nayak" expelling the Jesuit from the land. The Brahman and his entourage visit Nobili and question him in detail about his background and his intentions. Dissatisfied by the modest responses of the priest, the haughty Brahman leaves vowing to take all sorts of reprisals. He

---

[59] Translated from Guerreiro's account of the trial which he summarized from the letters of Nobili and other Jesuits. See Viegas (ed.), *op. cit.* (n. 30), III, 101–3. Also see Du Jarric, *op. cit.* (n. 37), III, 751–90. For a rationale as to how Nobili's beliefs were understood by the learned members of the Madura school of Hinduism see Cronin, *op. cit.* (n. 49), pp. 102–3.

[60] For this identification see Sathyanatha Aiyar, *op. cit.* (n. 24) p. 95.

quickly changes his tune, however, when Nobili offers to pay for the site. Once a deal has been struck, the Brahman offers his friendship and promises his protection to the priest.[61]

Guerreiro concludes his summary of Nobili's successes by commenting on the increasing number of high-caste persons both male and female who have become converts, including even a principal member of "Heremechiti's" household. The Portuguese author attributes Nobili's success to the favor of God and to the adaptation policy being followed in Madura. He notes with approval Nobili's willingness to permit his converts to boil rice with milk at the beginning of the new year. Since it is a great dishonor not to boil rice on this occasion, the Christians may boil it in honor of Jesus.[62] He praises Nobili for his study of Hindu writings and for his ability to use them in disputations. Guerreiro then goes on to tell about the dispatch of two native Christians to the college of Cochin and of their welcome there. His entire account of the Madura mission, which ends with 1609, is a homily based on letters from the field, in which Guerreiro celebrates the successes won in Madura and foresees even greater future victories for the faith.[63]

2

THE ADVENT OF THE DUTCH AND ENGLISH

While the Portuguese and Jesuits were reinforcing their positions in Coromandel, the Dutch were carving out places for themselves in a number of its port cities. In 1605 they received the right to trade at Masulipatam, the chief port of Muslim Golconda. During the following year they investigated Pulicat and concluded an agreement to trade at Petapoli (Nizampatam), another port of Golconda. They received a *farman* in August, 1606, fixing export and import duties for trade in Golconda, and thereafter they set up factories at Petapoli and Masulipatam. In 1608 the VOC elevated Masulipatam to the position of governing factory for their trade on the Coromandel Coast.

While consolidating their position in Golconda, the Dutch contempo-

---

[61] Guerreiro's account of this incident is directly based on a letter (November 20, 1609) sent by Father Manuel Leitão to the Jesuit provincial A. Laerzio. For its text see J. Bertrand (ed.), *La mission du Maduré, d'après des documents inédits* (4 vols.; Paris, 1847–54), II, 59–63.

[62] This is a reference to the feast of *Pongal* (Tamil for boiling over, one way of cooking rice).

[63] See Viegas (ed.), *op. cit.* (n. 30), III, 103–13; for the subsequent history of the Madura mission see above, pp. 159–62. A summary account of the state of the Madura mission as of 1612 is to be found in the Jesuit *Raguagli* (1615) (see n. 46, above), pp. 107–59. It adds little of substantive value to what is found in Guerreiro and Du Jarric. It is noted that the catechism of the bishop of Braga was printed in Tamil translation by 1612, and there are remarks on the three principal gods ("Rudren, Vesnur, Brama") and the ceremony of hook-swinging. The relative silence of the sources printed in Europe may possibly be attributed to the conflicts within the Society about Nobili's methods, which began to surface in 1612. See above, pp. 151–57.

raneously sought to establish trading posts in the Hindu-controlled territory of south Coromandel to compete with the Portuguese based at San Thomé and Negapatam. Direct access to the cloths of Pulicat, so essential to the trade in the Spice Islands, spurred them in this enterprise. They were also attracted by Pulicat's central location, just to the north of Mylapore, and by the opportunity to lessen their dependence upon the good will of Golconda and its Muslim rulers. Pulicat itself being closed to them, the Dutch worked out a series of agreements between 1608 and 1610 with the nayak of Gingee to establish a trading-factory at "Tierepopelier" (Tirupapuliyur) to the south of Portuguese San Thomé. By 1610 Gingee agreed to exclude all other European traders from its territory.

Venkata II received Dutch emissaries at Vellore in 1610, who worked out with him an agreement for the opening of Pulicat despite the machinations of the Portuguese and the Jesuits. Pulicat became by the end of 1610 the official headquarters of the VOC on the Coromandel Coast. The Portuguese, who had not yet broken with Venkata, still continued to harass the Dutch and, in 1612, sacked the Pulicat factory. The withdrawal of the Jesuits from the imperial court brought an end to Portuguese influence.[64] With the cooperation of Queen Oboyama, the designated regent of Pulicat, the Dutch completed their Fort Geldria in 1613. The civil wars which followed the death of Venkata in 1614 brought trade to a virtual halt in south Coromandel for the next two years. By 1616, despite continuing problems in both south Coromandel and Golconda, the VOC began to administer all the Coromandel factories through their "Government" centered at Pulicat.[65]

In Europe the Dutch activities in Coromandel received most of their publicity in writings by servitors of the English East India Company. Its directors had been alerted by 1607 to the vital importance of the cloth trade of the Bay of Bengal to the commercial exploitation of the spice regions further to the east. But they were not able until 1611 to send out a voyage to reconnoiter the Bay of Bengal and to initiate efforts to break into the trade of the Coromandel Coast. Two Dutch merchants, Pieter Floris and Lucas Antheunis, were employed by the English to open the Coromandel trade for them. They initiated the four-year (1611–15) voyages of the "Globe" to investigate trading conditions in the Bay of Bengal, especially on the Coromandel Coast. Floris, who had served the VOC as a junior factor at Masulipatam from 1605 to 1608, kept a journal in Dutch of the voyages of the "Globe." Shortly after he returned to England in 1615, Floris died. An unidentified Dutchman translated his journal into English, and this manuscript translation remained unpublished in the India Office until it was edited and put into print in 1934. Excerpts and summaries from the translation were published by Purchas in 1625 along with the ship's log kept by Nathaniel Martin, the ship's master's mate. All the subsequent versions of

---

[64] See above, p. 1011.
[65] Based on Raychaudhuri, *op. cit.* (n. 6), pp. 15–27.

Floris' *Journal* published between 1625 and 1934 were either reprintings, condensations, or translations of the Purchas version.[66]

Floris visited the ports of Coromandel on the voyage out from August, 1611, to April, 1612, and on the return from December, 1613, to December, 1614. On his first visit Floris learned that the Dutch had factories at Tegnapatam, Pulicat, Petapoli, and Masulipatam. At Pulicat he was shown by the Dutch a patent from Venkata which excluded all Europeans, except subjects of Prince Maurice, from trading there. Governess Kondamma, the appointee of the queen, and the captain of the port (the *shahbandar*) confirmed this understanding and advised the English to appeal directly to Venkata. Not wishing to spend the time required for a trip to the imperial court, the English went on to Petapoli and Masulipatam. From Masulipatam they sent a gift to "Mir Sumula" (Mir Jumla, the chief minister of Golconda) at "Condapoli" (Kondapalle) from which town he "farmeth out his [the king's] revenues." On January 20, 1612, "Cotobara" (Muhammad Quli Qutb Shah, r. 1580–1612), the ruler of Golconda, died, and it was feared that "great tumults" would occur in Masulipatam since the king was childless and without a direct heir. Through the wisdom of "Mir Masunim" (*Mir Mu min*) a succession crisis was averted by the selection of the deceased king's nephew as ruler. "Mahamud Unim Cotobara" (Muhammad Qutb Shah, r. 1612–26), the new king, did not favor, as had his predecessor, the Persians and "Mir Sumela" (Mir Jumla) "the fountaine of Tyrannie." Since the English did not profit from these political changes, Floris left Masulipatam after a tiff with its Muslim governor over customs charges.[67]

On their return to Masulipatam (December 19, 1613) the English met the "James" in the harbor, a ship "sent expressly to second us in our Voyage," as well as two Dutch vessels. Floris and his colleagues were well received by the new governors of the city and landed goods on which they had to pay only the normal duty. In February, 1614, Floris went to "Narsapur Peca" (Narasapur on a southern mouth of the Godavari River), the principal shipbuilding center on the Coromandel Coast, to superintend repair of the ship. In April, Governor Atmachan went to Golconda to give his annual accounting to the "Great Treasurer, his friend Malick Tusar." In May letters arrived in Masulipatam from Vijayanagar promising Floris "that if I would come thither they would grant me a place right over against the Fort of Paleacatte [Pulicat], with all such Priviledges as we should desire." Floris sent a messenger to Vijayanagar to request a safe conduct. On July 29, emissaries from Vellore arrived with the "Gaul" (safe-conduct pass) and Venkata's own "Abestiam" (*abhayahastam*?), "which is a white cloth where his owne hand is printed in Sandall and Saffron." They also brought letters from the queen

---

[66] The accounts of Martin and Floris appear in *PP*, III, 304–42. The modern critical edition of the complete contemporary translation of Floris' *Journal* is in W. H. Moreland (ed.), *Peter Floris, His Voyage to the Indies in the Globe, 1611–15* ("H.S.," 2d ser., LXXIV; London, 1934).

[67] For the identifications see Moreland (ed.), *op. cit.* (n. 66), pp. 10–20.

and the governors of Pulicat, as well as a letter from the emperor "written upon a leafe of Gold . . . desiring that now we would come into his Countrey and chuse a place to our best liking." The emperor, despite the objections of the Dutch, offered the English the right to build a fortress and assigned them revenues from a town "with promise to doe more at my coming thither." Floris believes that Venkata is responding to the people of Pulicat who grieve "to see every yeare English ships passe by without any profit to them." Before the English could take advantage of this offer, news arrived at Masulipatam in October of the death of Venkata and his three wives. "Great troubles," Floris writes, "are feared."

While these negotiations went on, Floris experienced a great flood at "Narsapur" and its vicinity, and at Golconda, the capital city, where houses and stone bridges, "as artificially [artistically] made as the like may scarsly bee seene in Europe," were washed away by the swirling waters of the overflowing rivers. He also notes that on November 21 a Hindu festival took place "which Solemnitie happens thrice a yeare, when the New Moon commeth on a Monday." Men and women, including Brahmans and "Cometis" (*Kōmaṭi,* a Telugu trading caste) bathe in the sea "esteeming thereby to have great indulgence."[68] To obtain payment for the goods he had delivered, Floris kidnapped the governor's son and imprisoned him on board the "Globe." The youth being a Brahman would neither eat nor drink anything "but what he hath dressed himselfe." Once he exacted payment by this means, Floris sent letters of complaint to the ruler of Golconda. He dispatched the emissaries back to Vellore with letters to be delivered to the first English ships to arrive at Pulicat. On December 7, 1614, he put to sea still at odds with the authorities of Masulipatam.[69]

The indefatigable Samuel Purchas, who had published in 1625 the Floris account in his *Pilgrimes,* had hoped to include in it also the *Relations of Golconda* by William Methwold (1590–1652). To this end Purchas had requested Methwold to write up his experiences; consequently the *Relations* is directed to Purchas and is expressly designed to augment materials on the Coromandel Coast published in the *Pilgrimes.* Although Methwold's *Relations* arrived too late for inclusion in the *Pilgrimes,* Purchas printed it in 1626 at the end of the fourth enlarged edition of his general survey of the world called *Pilgrimage.* Methwold, who was English factor at Masulipatam from 1618 to 1622, reputedly was "perfect in accounts, and hath the Dutch and French languages." From perusal of his *Relations,* it can readily be asserted that Methwold possessed a good education, a talent for observation, and a genuine curiosity about Indian life, beliefs, and practices. His *Relations* in-

[68] This festival is generally called *Somwati Amawas.*
[69] For identifications see Moreland (ed.), *op. cit.* (n. 66), pp. 111–39. For a contemporary Dutch account (1616) of trading conditions on the Coromandel Coast see the report of Anton Schorer to the VOC in Narain (trans.) and Sharma (ed.), *loc. cit.* (n. 2), and in Moreland (ed.), *op. cit.* (n. 2), pp. 51–65.

cludes comments about matters that piqued his personal interest and that would presumably help to satisfy the curiosity of Purchas' audience, the general reader. As a consequence he tends to ignore mundane and ordinary matters and to embellish the eccentric and bizarre. He is nonetheless honest and accurate in his reporting and scrupulous in informing the reader when his information derives from others rather than from personal observation or inquiry.[70]

While Methwold surveys generally the entire trading region of the Bay of Bengal, his focus is on those places he knew best: the Coromandel Coast, the city of Masulipatam, and the kingdom of Golconda.[71] He reports on the disruptions arising from the civil war which followed Venkata's death. Suffering from famine and war, "parents have brought thousands of their children to the sea side" to sell them into slavery for rice. He observes that the Portuguese at San Thomé are not entirely independent of native authority, and are forced to "buy their peace" by contributions to the nayaks. They are in no position to resist attacks from inland since San Thomé "is onely fortified towards the sea." The Portuguese have "a badde neighbour" at Pulicat, for severe trading losses at the hands of the Dutch are impoverishing the inhabitants of San Thomé. For their part, the Dutch at Pulicat recovered from the Portuguese assault of 1612, built Fort Geldria with the emperor's help, and have since 1619 permitted the English to keep a garrison and to trade at Pulicat.[72] The local Portuguese, who have helplessly watched these developments, receive no aid from Goa and fruitlessly seek to turn the nayaks against the Dutch. To avoid conflict with the feuding nayaks, the Dutch limit their activities to trade and make no exactions from the natives.[73]

Most of what Methwold recounts of native affairs is based upon his experiences at Masulipatam "from almost five yeares residence in that place." Although it is the chief port of Golconda, the town of Masulipatam was little more than a fishing village until the Europeans began trading there. It is still "a small towne, but populous, unwalled, ill built, and worse situated." Regular floods from the sea make its spring water brackish. Still, it is a convenient harbor and its healthful climate makes the town a satisfactory residence for merchants. In the hot season from March to June many natives and even Europeans suffocate to death. Relief comes in the rainy months of July to October when floods from inland inundate the land so that it "becomes the better enabled to endure an eight moneths abstinence." The weather in the cooler months is "as hote as it is here in England in May."[74]

[70] Based on Moreland (ed.), *op. cit.* (n. 2), pp. xxv–xxxvii.

[71] The full title is *Relations of the Kingdome of Golchonda, and Other Neighbouring Nations within the Gulfe of Bengala, Arreccan, Pegu, Tannassery, etc., and the English Trade in Those Parts.*

[72] On the treaties between the Dutch and English regarding the division of eastern trade see above, pp. 50–51. After the massacre of Amboina, the English withdrew from Pulicat in 1623.

[73] Moreland (ed.), *op. cit.* (n. 2), pp. 2–6. As time went on the Dutch gradually assumed a greater political jurisdiction at Pulicat.

[74] *Ibid.*, pp. 6–7.

The perpetual heat keeps the trees constantly green, so they produce fruits "in their severall seasons." In a few places, two and occasionally three crops of rice are produced, but in most places just one crop is harvested annually. They cultivate certain pulses "different from ours" and produce a small quantity of "good wheat" in the interior. Root crops, including potatoes, are common, but they grow but few herbs or flowers. In this fruitful country, food is plentiful and cheap. Meat is especially inexpensive since many of the natives refuse to eat "any thing that hath life."

The kingdom of Golconda, "as most others in India," receives its name from the royal city which the natives call "Golchonda" and the Moors and Persians "Hidaband" (Hyderabad).[75] This city, ten days' journey inland from Masulipatam, is well situated in a fertile region blessed with an adequate water supply and "sweetness of ayre." Its royal palace "for bignesse and sumptuousnesse . . . exceedeth all belonging to the Mogull or any other Prince." A stone edifice garnished with golden trimmings befits a ruler "who in elephants and jewels is accounted one of the richest Princes of India." Descended from Persian ancestors, this prince is a Shiite Muslim and like his co-religionists he hates the Turks or Sunni Muslims most vehemently. He retains the title "Cotubsha" (Qutb Shah) assumed by his predecessors. During Methwold's tenure in Masulipatam, this prince married the daughter of "Adelsha" ('Adil Shah), the king of "Viziapore" (Bijapur, the Muslim kingdom adjoining Golconda on the west). He has three other wives and at least one thousand concubines. In league with Bijapur and the "Negaim Sha" (Nizam Shah) of Ahmadnagar, this prince and his allies annually pay tribute to the Mughul emperor.[76]

The sultan of Golconda "as all others in India" is the only freeholder, and his subjects are his tenants. For administrative purposes the country is divided into "great governments," lesser subdivisions, and villages. The ruler himself farms out the governments to "eminent men," who sublease sections to others, who then rent them "to the country people" at excessive rates. Lessors of all levels who default in payment of their dues suffer corporeal punishment. Should they flee, their families must pay the debt or suffer punishment on their behalf. Annually, in July, the leaseholds are put up for sale to the highest bidder. As a consequence, exactions of every sort are extorted from "the poorer inhabitants" to the profit of the great and independent leaseholders who "raigne as petty kings."[77]

[75] Golconda was the original seat of government. Hyderabad, a new city five miles to the east, was founded in 1589. See *ibid.*, p. 8, n. 4. Most European maps of the time show only the city of Golconda.

[76] On the reign (1612–26) of Sultan Muhammad Qutb Shah see H. K. Sherwani, *History of the Qutb Shāhī Dynasty* (New Delhi, 1974), chap. v.

[77] For a comparison of this account to certain seventeenth-century Dutch reports see W. H. Moreland, *From Akbar to Aurangzeb. A Study in Indian Economic History* (1972 reprint of the original English edition of 1923, New Delhi), pp. 239–45. For confirmation of the general accuracy of this description see J. F. Richards, "The Seventeenth Century Concentration of Power at Hyderabad," *Journal of the Pakistan Historical Society*, XXIII (1975), 33–34.

Golconda boasts sixty-six fortresses commanded by "Naicks" (nayaks, in this sense "captains") garrisoned by "Gentile" (non-Muslim) soldiers native to the country. These fortresses sit on high rocks or hills and usually are accessible by but one route. Methwold himelf saw the fortresses of "Cundapoly" (Kondapalle), "Cundavera" (Kondavidu), and "Bellum Cunda" (Bellamkonda), and correctly notes that "Cunda" (*konda*) "in that language [Telugu]" means hill. At "Cundapoly" he saw a series of forts located on a steep mountainside and surrounded by a stone wall. At this virtually impregnable retreat, around twelve thousand soldiers are regularly stationed. Within its walls are large rice fields, orchards, and great ponds of water to help the garrison sustain itself during a siege. Nightly the soldiers at "Cundapoly" communicate with "Cundavera" by raising torches "according to the order contrived betwixt them."[78]

Religious freedom for all prevails in Golconda. The followers of the "king's religion" (Shiite Islam) constitute a predominant minority. They are the only Muslims permitted to have their own "Mesgits" (mosques) and to practice their religion publicly. The "ancient naturals of the countrey" are Hindus and they are far more numerous than the Muslims. The Hindus follow faithfully and unquestioningly the tenets taught by their Brahmans as well as the religious customs of their ancestors. According to their doctrine God was originally one. God recruited "divers that have sometimes lived upon earth" to assist Him. The Hindus build temples to honor these "demigods or saints" and worship those "of them as they stand most particularly affected unto." They believe in the immortality of the soul and in its transmigration "from whence followeth much abstinence from killing or eating anything that had life." Their religious practices and morality derive from family tradition rather than doctrine. Murder and serious thievery are uncommon, but cheating in trade and business is universal. Polygamy is permitted but is generally not practiced unless the first wife is barren. Adultery is uncommon, since women are punished for transgressing.[79]

The Hindus are divided into castes, "they say fortie four," which are based on lineage and have no necessary relation to economic wealth. Every Hindu in a community knows the caste of his neighbor. The Brahmans are not only their high priests but also "very good and ready accountants." They are consequently employed by their Muslim overlords to keep written records. They keep alive—and to themselves—the literary content of Hinduism; the other castes rely solely on oral traditions. Among all groups the Brahmans are highly regarded as astronomers and astrologers, and are sought out even by high officials for their prognostications. Similar to the

[78] Moreland (ed.), *op. cit.* (n. 2), pp. 11–12. Kondavidu, the chief of the cities south of the Krishna River, appears to have been the main fortress of the region. See Sherwani, *op. cit.* (n. 76), pp. 18–19. The ruins of the celebrated fortress of Kondapalle, whose construction began in 1360, may still be seen. See L. F. R. Williams, *A Handbook for Travellers in India, Pakistan, Burma, and Ceylon* (20th ed., London, 1965), p. 378.

[79] Methwold in Moreland (ed.), *op. cit.* (n. 2), pp. 13–14. *Cf.* Sherwani, *op. cit.* (n. 76), p. 522.

Brahmans, and also highly regarded, is the "Fangam" (*Jangam*) caste.[80] They follow identical dietary practices but wear "sanctified stones [*lingam*] tyed up in their haire" rather than the threads of the Brahmans. Those "Fangam" who work are limited to the craft of tailor. Since there is not enough tailoring to occupy them all, many become beggars.[81]

The highest of the nonpriestly castes is the "Committy" (*Kōmaṭi*) who are the chief merchants of the region. Some are travelers who deal in textiles, and others are money changers; the poorest are shopkeepers who sell foods. A caste called "Campo Waro" (*Kāpu*) are farmers, urban servants, and soldiers.[82] This most numerous caste kills and eats all meat except beef; its members show unusual reverence for the cow as the animal from which "their countrey receives its greatest sustenance." The "Boga" (*Bogam* is the Telugu name for the *Devadāsi*) caste, "in English the Whoores Tribe," are of two types: "one that will prostitute themselves to any better tribe then themselves, but to none worse, the other meeteth none bad enough to refuse."[83] As children they are taught to dance and tumble and in these activities they display remarkable skill and agility. Once a year they are required to perform at the court of Golconda. They dance free for the governor on public occasions, but charge for performing at private rituals or functions. Many are wealthy and most dress elegantly. Craftsmen of several sorts belong to a single caste and they consequently intermarry.[84] Other crafts and occupations are constituted as separate castes. The lowest are the "Piriawes" (pariahs) who live in isolation outside the towns and are "avoyded of al but their own fraternity." They eat dead cows and tan their hides. They act as public executioners and palanquin bearers.[85]

Though socially divided, the Hindus "are in religion one body" and their temples open to all. Many of their temples are "worth the gazing upon, and may well bee (as they report) the ancient works of great kings." In these unlighted temples a Brahman keeps the idols in a special room. Annually they hold a festival attended by many thousands of people. Some come for devotions, others for conviviality, and others for profit. Dancers, tumblers, snake charmers, fakirs, and beggars make money at the festival before the formal ceremony starts. At midnight the idol procession comes forth from the temple accompanied by musicians and lighted by fireworks. After circling the city, the idol is returned to the temple and left there "without guard or regard" until another year rolls around. Four times annually they perform their ablutions in the sea where they receive the blessings of their Brahmans.

[80] Priests of the Lingayat sect.

[81] Methwold in Moreland (ed.), *op. cit.* (n. 2), pp. 15–16.

[82] "Waro" (*wāru*) is the Telugu word for group or caste. See *ibid.*, p. 17, n. 1.

[83] Probably a reference to the "right-hand" group, which will have nothing to do with artisans, and the "left-hand" group, which is not so particular. See *ibid.*, n. 3.

[84] A reference to the Kammalan caste with its occupational septs. See *ibid.*, p. 19, n. 1.

[85] Based on *ibid.*, pp. 16–20.

Certain gods, temples, and rituals appeal to some believers and not to others. Some gods are thought to possess miraculous powers, while others must be propitiated to keep away disease or other misfortunes. To appease a particular god, some sick persons promise the god that they will be "hanged" in his honor. Methwold and two other Englishmen observed a ritual "hanging" or hook-swinging ceremony, in which the penitent is hanged from a beam by two hooks, one thrust through each shoulder. The beam is hung between two wheels and the dangling person is pulled "at least a quarter of a mile." All Hindus revere household gods and annually hold a feast in their honor at the home of the head of the family.[86]

Marriages are arranged by the parents. The children readily accept the mate chosen without ever seeing the selected individual. A spouse must be of the same caste and closely related, "no degree of consanguinity hindering but brother and sister." A bride brings no dowry; she and her parents receive gifts of jewels and clothing from the bridegroom's family and often the marriage has to be postponed until the heavy wedding expenses can be met. Parents of substance often marry their children at a very early age (husband at five and wife at three years of age), but they do not live together before reaching puberty. The wedding ceremony, whatever the age of the couple, is a public affair. They are carried in the same palanquin to "the most publike places of the towne." On this tour they are accompanied by friends, dancers, and musicians. They halt before the homes of relatives and friends, from whom the bridal couple receives gifts. When they return to the bridegroom's home, a Brahman performs the wedding ceremony. He hangs a cloth between the bride and groom, "mutters (none heares what) orisons," and instructs the couple "to tread upon one another bare feet, so mingling legges, and making these first short steps an introduction to their future better acquaintance." After three days of feasting the relatives leave. If the bride is a child she returns to her parents until she is old enough to reside with her husband. A mature married couple always lives in the husband's household. Should the husband die, a widow may not remarry, irrespective of her age. She ordinarily remains as "the drudge for the whole family," for she is an embarrassment to everyone. Those widows who cannot endure these constraints flee to a distance, become prostitutes, and always live in fear that their relatives will poison them for the disgrace they have brought upon the family.[87]

While young Hindu children are not baptized or circumcised, they are named in infancy after their gods; other appellations are added relating to the family's occupation, caste, or "some defect or quality most eminent

---

[86] *Ibid.*, pp. 20–24. For hook-hanging see our pls. 130, 131, 199.

[87] This is a composite picture, probably based on Methwold's experiences at Masulipatam, which does not reflect the differing marriage ceremonies followed by the various castes. Otherwise it specifies accurately a number of common practices. See *ibid.*, pp. 24–26. *Cf.* Roger's account, below, pp. 1038–40.

about them." Until the age of seven or eight they run about "starke naked" and receive very little attention from their elders. Women cover their bodies with a "fine calico or silken cloth" which they bind about them (a sari) and cover with a "thinne wastcoat [bodice or *choli*] their breasts and arms unto the elbowes." On their lower arms they wear bracelets, on their necks chains of pearl and coral, and in their ears and right nostril they set jewels; in addition, they often wear rings on their fingers and toes and decorative girdles about the waist. They do not wear ornaments on the head, but simply comb their hair back and tie it into a knot. The men wear a waist-cloth (dhoti) and a white calico jacket. They bind up their hair and cover it with a turban. In their ears they wear rings of gold, and on their necks chains of silver. In their complexion these people "are not black but tawny, or rather a wainscot [oaken] colour." [88]

Like most European observers, Methwold discourses on *satī* (suttee) (Sanskrit, "a woman who is pure") or widow suicide at the death of the husband. Unlike most of the other witnesses, Methwold made a serious effort to understand this form of behavior without sensationalizing it. [89] He reports that the Indian tradition holds that wives were so immoral in the past that they poisoned their husbands to be more freely with their lovers. To prevent this from occurring, it was decreed that wives should burn in the fire that consumed the husband's corpse. While this practice continues in Bali, the custom of ceremonial suicide was abandoned in India and replaced by "perpetuall widowhood, as it is at this day." Still, despite the efforts of the Muslim authorities to prevent suttee, some widows persist in following their husbands into death. Methwold witnessed at Masulipatam the voluntary burial of a weaver's widow with her husband's body. He also saw the self-immolation of a widow of the *Kāpu* caste on the funeral pyre of her husband. He stresses the voluntary character of these suicides and includes reports from other Europeans which confirm his personal observations. While recognizing that the widows die "in pure love to their deceased husbands," he denounces "these cruel and heathenish customs." [90]

Methwold announces that diamonds were "lately discovered" in Golconda. He and another English merchant, accompanied by the Dutch gov-

---

[88] See *ibid.*, pp. 18–19, 26–27.

[89] For a sensational account of suttee by Sir Thomas Herbert (1606–82), a contemporary of Methwold, see his *Some yeares travels into divers parts of Asia and Afrique . . .* (London, 1638), pp. 309–10. This lurid description comes under his discussion of Negapatam. We doubt if Herbert himself ever traveled east of Ceylon. Certainly his description of Coromandel is neither fresh nor accurate. In many instances, here as elsewhere, his learning and biases obscure his observations. Nonetheless his book was reprinted three times in the seventeenth century and translated into Dutch (1658) and French (1663).

[90] See Moreland (ed.), *op. cit.* (n. 2), pp. 28–30. The theory of poisoning as the reason for suttee goes back to the Greeks. Suttee may still be practiced occasionally in Bali. Ordinarily suttee took the form of burning, but in the Telugu country the weaver caste in particular followed the practice of live burials. See Edward Thompson, *Suttee. A Historical and Philosophical Enquiry into the Hindu Rite of Widow-Burning* (Boston and New York, 1928), pp. 39, 128. Meth-

ernor of Pulicat, quickly "resolved to make a voyage" to the site on the Krishna River "to see at least the place and order of it." After a journey of four days through "desolate mountaynous country," they arrived at the diamond field now called Kollur. There they presented themselves to its Brahman governor who administered justice "to the rabblement of different nations that frequented this place" and who collected the sultan's revenues. They were told that thirty thousand people work the fields located two miles outside this new town of one hundred thousand souls. Instead of tunneling, the workers dig large square pits, from which they carry the earth in baskets to a level spot to dry in the sun. Once it has dried, they break up the earth and sift it as they search for diamonds. Methwold oberves critically that they employ no mechanical devices and rely entirely on human labor at every stage of mining. The sultan in this case follows his usual practice of farming and taxing. The diamond fields are rented by a goldsmith who sublets plots to other speculators. All diamonds weighing more than ten carats belong to the sultan and the remainder to the private investors. Despite stiff penalties, large diamonds escape the detection of the royal officials and wind up in the hands of smugglers. Living in the ramshackle town is expensive because the imported necessities of life are subject to excessive transit duties. In 1622 the mine was temporarily closed, possibly because the market was glutted or because of the demands for diamonds being made by the Mughul emperor. Methwold reports "since I came from thence, I heare it was opened againe but almost exhausted, and very few found."[91]

Aside from diamonds, Golconda produces crystals, garnets, amethysts, topazes, and agates. While it has no precious metals, tin, or copper, it possesses "great stores of iron and steele, [which are] transported into many places of India." Bezoar stones, concretions in the stomachs of goats found in "one onely part of this country," are sold as antidotes against poison. Calicoes, or plain cotton cloths, are as cheap in Golconda "as in any other part of India," and its *pintados* (patterned and painted cloths) "are indeed the most exquisite that are seene."[92] Their superiority over other Indian textiles

---

wold's description is not mentioned by Thompson or by Arvind Sharma in his essay "Suttee: A Study in Western Reaction" in his *Thresholds in Hindu-Buddhist Studies* (Calcutta, 1979), pp. 83–111. Sharma holds (p. 96) that the Western reaction from the fourth century B.C. to 1787 was "a mix of admiration and criticism," a description which succinctly describes Methwold's attitude. Suttee was formally outlawed by the British in 1829; thereafter it became a controversial issue in British-Hindu relations.

[91] Moreland (ed.), *op. cit.* (n. 2), pp. 30–33. Diamonds have been found since antiquity in the alluvial deposits near the Krishna. Here, in contrast to Europe, diamonds are found close to the surface in clay and sandy soils which had merely to be washed or sifted to find diamonds. See Moreland, *op. cit.* (n. 77), pp. 151–53, for a synopsis of Tavernier's later account of diamond mining. For Tavernier's account, see below, p. 1077. Methwold may be correct about the exhaustion of these fields, for in recent times "only stones of very small size were found, the gangue have been worked out by the old miners" (*Imperial Gazetteer of India. Provincial Series*, *Hyderābād State* [Calcutta, 1909], p. 40).

[92] On the superiority of Golconda chintz see Irwin, *loc. cit.* (n. 8), p. 30, n. 2.

derives from their fast red and blue colors. The red dye (madder) is made from the chay root, "a plant which groweth only in this country."[93] The Dutch purchase the indigo of Golconda in preference to the indigo of Lahore. Tobacco, introduced but recently, is raised and exported to Mocha and Arakan. Most of Golconda's exports, while "dispersed in some measure through the world," are marketed in India. Even so, "they still build great ships and good ones too" for their overseas trade.[94]

Very little new material on Coromandel appeared in print in Europe from the publication of Methwold's description in 1626 until the middle of the century.[95] Until 1630 the Dutch merchants traded under difficult conditions at Masulipatam as is attested by David Pieterszoon de Vries (b. 1593) in his journal first published in 1655. He arrived in its vicinity during September, 1628. The appointee of Governor-General Coen as deputy in charge of the VOC's Coromandel enterprise, De Vries was sent from Batavia to reconnoiter the coast, study English activities there, and establish friendly relations with the Islamic rulers of Golconda. After arrival he sent his ship northward from Masulipatam along the coast to search for a cargo of rice (Batavia was then experiencing food shortages). The envoy himself traveled overland with a guard of fifty armed men from Masulipatam to Vizegapatam, a port town north of the Godavari River on the Gingelly Coast where the Dutch also had a factory. De Vries explored the country around Vizegapatam for four months while rice was being loaded on his vessel. He was most impressed, and perhaps depressed, to find that the secular authori-

---

[93] Chay is from Tamil, *cāyam*. This is the *Hedyotis umbellata* which grows wild in many sandy places along the Coromandel Coast. For its economic uses see Hebert Drury, *The Useful Plants of India* (2d ed., London, 1873), pp. 240–41.

[94] Methwold in Moreland (ed.), *op. cit.* (n. 2), pp. 33–36. For a retrospective description of Golconda see the "Anonymous Relation" in *ibid.*, pp. 67–86. It relates to the period 1608 to 1614 when Pieter Gierliszoon van Ravesteyn, a Dutch factor and the probable author, lived in Nizampatam. This account was inserted into the 1645 and subsequent editions of Commelin's *Begin ende voortgangh . . .* (Amsterdam), IIa, 77–86. For the identification of the author see Moreland (ed.), *op. cit.* (n. 2), pp. xl–xliii.

[95] The reports of the Dutch and English factors were not printed. The *Morgenländische Reyse-Beschreibung* of Johann Albrecht von Mandelslo (1616–44), first published at Schleswig by Adam Olearius in 1645, includes an interesting description of San Thomé and Mylapore (in the 1662 English translation on pp. 116–17), as of 1639 and little else on Coromandel. *Les voyages fameux du sieur Vincent Le Blanc, marseillois . . .* (Paris, 1648), compiled and rewritten by the editors Pierre Bergeron and Louis Coulon, deals with the last quarter of the sixteenth century. Similarly the work of Faria y Sousa (see above, pp. 354–55) is retrospective; it is concerned almost entirely with conditions in the Portuguese ports rather than with native life. The *Relatione delle missioni . . . scritta del P. Francisco Barreto* (Rome, 1645) provides some additional information (pp. 75–87) on the Madura mission and on Jesuit activities in Coromandel and Bengal (pp. 110–32). For a translation of Barreto's unpublished account of the political situation in south India from 1644 to 1646 see A. Saulière, S.J., "The Revolt of the Southern Nayaks," *Journal of Indian History*, XLII (1964), 89–105; and for Antony de Proença's continuation, which carries the story to 1665, see *ibid.*, XLIV (1966), 163–79. After Nobili's time the Jesuits more generally treat of the Madura mission in connection with their activities in Malabar. For example, see below for the activities of Giacinto de Magistris, pp. 1057–63.

ties in this region were all Muslims.[96] On a second voyage in the spring and summer of 1629 he hurriedly surveyed the Dutch factories south of Masulipatam and was more encouraged by conditions there. He visited Tranquebar, the Danish outpost then being offered for sale to the Dutch, and held inconclusive conversations with Roelant Crape.[97] He returned to Batavia in the autumn only to learn of Coen's death, an event which ended his personal career in the East.[98]

The Dutch position in Coromandel, in both the Hindu and Muslim areas, was regularized around 1629 concurrent with De Vries' final departure. During a lull in the civil war in Vijayanagar, the emperor, Rama Deva (d. 1630), awarded a contract to the Dutch at Pulicat which legalized their position there and enabled them to expand their commercial activities in south Coromandel. The Dutch in Golconda, like everyone else, suffered severely from the famine of the early 1630's which swept central India from Gujarat to the north Coromandel Coast. In the south, where they increasingly concentrated their activities, the Dutch managed to establish closer commercial ties between Pulicat and their trading outposts around the Bay of Bengal despite the recrudescence of civil war. In Pulicat itself, the Dutch factors and merchants lived in relative safety around Fort Geldria. And because the VOC permitted and encouraged marriages between the Dutch soldiers and Indian women, Pulicat in the 1630's began to look more and more like a Dutch colony.[99]

3

HINDUISM AT PULICAT (TAMILNADU)

To minister to the Christians of Pulicat, the Amsterdam *Classis* sent Reverend Abraham Roger (Rogerius; d. 1649) to the Coromandel Coast in 1632. A product of the *Seminarium* of Waleus, Roger preached and taught there for the next ten years. His sermons were generally delivered in Tamil, Portuguese, and Dutch, the languages then most current in Pulicat. To inform

[96] Much of southern Orissa was subject to Golconda from 1575 to the middle of the eighteenth century. See Sherwani, *op. cit.* (n. 76), pp. 237–38.

[97] For the Danish East India Company see above, pp. 88–93.

[98] The journals of De Vries' voyages were first published at Hoorn in 1655 and remained in obscurity during the remainder of the seventeenth century. The modern critical edition appeared as No. III of the publications of the Linschoten Society: H. T. Colenbrander (ed.), *Korte historiael end journaels aenteyckeninge van verscheyden voyagiens in de vier deelen des wereldtsronde . . . door D. David Piertersz. de Vries* (The Hague, 1911). For his experiences on the Coromandel Coast see pp. 118–31. For commentary see Charles McKew Parr, *The Voyages of David de Vries, Navigator and Adventurer* (New York, 1969), pp. 96–101.

[99] See Raychaudhuri, *op. cit.* (n. 6), pp. 37–42, 203–4. For a description of the present-day desolated village of Pulicat see Dupuis, *op. cit.* (n. 6), p. 337.

himself about the Hindu customs and beliefs then prevailing in northern Tamilnadu, Roger enlisted the aid of the Brahman "Padmanaba" (Sanskrit, *Padmanābāh*) and at least one other, named "Damersa." Padmanaba, who had gotten into trouble with the Portuguese authorities, had fled for refuge to the Dutch at Pulicat. He was possibly also a renegade of his caste, although this conjecture is dubious since he brought other local Brahmans to converse with Roger and to explain or translate for him those materials in which they were more expert than Padmanaba. Generally their conversations seem to have been in Portuguese, the *lingua franca* of trade on the Coromandel Coast. Even though Brahmans were not supposed to reveal their mysteries to others, these educated Brahmans nonetheless instructed him in the Sanskrit classics while he took notes. In several cases Sanskrit texts were even translated verbatim so that he could paraphrase them in Dutch. In 1642 he was sent to Batavia where he remained for the next five years. He returned to the Netherlands in 1647 and two years later died at Gouda.[100] His materials were put together by his widow, possibly with the help of Jacobus Scerperus (d. 1678), a noted preacher of Gouda and the author of the dedicatory epistle in the book. The publisher, F. Hackes of Leyden, possibly with the aid of a professor (the "A. W. JCtus" at the end of the preface) of the city's university, issued Roger's book in 1651 under the title *De open-deure tot het verborgen heydendom.*[101]

The published version appeared in two parts: the first deals with the life and customs of the Coromandel Brahmans, and the second with their religion, beliefs, and rites. This division of life into secular and religious spheres, so natural to Western ways of thinking, does violence to the unity of Hinduism and imposes upon it a separation foreign to its doctrine and practices. This organization also produces repetitions, particularly of Indian terms and names, which tend to confuse and irritate the reader. Even with these drawbacks, Roger's *Open-deure* is still one of the most complete and objective accounts of South Indian Hinduism produced by a foreigner. With the help of his several Brahman friends, particularly Padmanaba, Roger made a sincere effort to understand the fundamental ideas of Hinduism and

---

[100] See H. Terpstra, *De Nederlanders in Voor-Indië* (Amsterdam, 1947), pp. 183–87.

[101] It was translated into German (1663) and French (1670) during the seventeenth century. The German version was published at Nuremberg by Christoph Arnold. The French translation by Sieur Thomas La Grue appears to be true to the original, even though notes comparing Hindu to Jewish and Christian customs and beliefs have been added as well as two appendices (see below, p. 1055). The French version was translated into English and published in London by William Jackson in the collection, originally in French, by Bernard Picart (comp. and ed.), *The Ceremonies and Religious Customs of the Various Nations of the Known World . . .* (7 vols. in 6, 1733–36), III, 344–405. The modern critical edition is W. Caland (ed.), *De open-deure tot het verborgen heydendom door, Abraham Rogerius* ("WLV," X; The Hague, 1915). A detailed comparison of the English edition published by Jackson with the critical edition of Caland reveals that Picart, the French collector, omitted, rearranged, and elaborated on the original work. For some unknown reason Picart omitted most of Roger's references to Padmanaba, the Brahman informant, and many of Roger's personal observations.

of the beliefs that lay behind the practices that the Europeans often denounced as "superstitious" and "abhorrent."[102]

Because he received answers to his questions from Brahmans, Roger's book centers on the Brahmans and reflects their views. No Hindu doubts that of the four main castes, the Brahman caste is the most worthy and pleasing to God of all human groups, just as the cow is, in the family of animals. The *Vēdam,* or their book of law, ordains that it is one of the five great sins to kill a Brahman, a deed that can be expiated only if the offender makes a twelve-year pilgrimage and builds a temple to "Eswara" (Hindi, *Īśvara,* or Tamil, *Īcuvarar,* an epithet of Siva).[103] No Hindu doubts that the second caste in rank is that called "Settreas" (Kshatriyas) comprising the nobles of the country. They are also called "Rājas," and the king, their head, is called "Rāja of the Rājas," or "God of the Rājas." In the past there were two subcastes of Rajas, one named for the sun and the other for the moon. Some members of the "Settreas" have debased themselves by intermarrying with those of lesser nobility. Sons of some impoverished nobles even serve as soldiers to the more elevated members of this caste. The Rajas are obliged to defend and govern the country, administer justice, and tend to the needs of Brahmans.[104] The third caste in order is the "Weinsjas" (Vaisyas), who are divided into "Comitias" (Telugu, *Kōmaṭi*) and "Sitti Weapari" (Tamil, *ceṭṭi viyāpāri;* Malayalam, *chetty*). Each subcaste claims to be the true Vaisyas and each lives from commerce. According to Padmanaba they must trade honestly and without cheating or excessive profit. Like the Brahmans they are vegetarians.

The rest of the people are "Soudraes" (*Sūdra*s), and included within this caste are many subcastes of different names and occupations. The highest of these subgroups is the "Wellala" (Tamil, *Veḷḷāḷā*), who are administrators and cultivators.[105] The "Ambria" (?) are next in rank order; most of its members are cultivators and servants, and in Pulicat a few work as bricklayers. Of the other subcastes no particular rank order is discernible, since each claims to outrank the other and all frequently clash over customs of burial and marriage. The "Cauwreas" (*Kavarai*) are numerous and they call themselves the "family of 300." They admit members of other castes into their community so readily that this subcaste may be compared to a sea with many rivers flowing into it. Some of them govern, others paint cloths or are soldiers.

---

[102] For similar evaluations see A. C. Burnell in *Indian Antiquary,* VIII (1898), 98; Caland (ed.), *op. cit.* (n. 101), p. xxii, points out that it is virtually free of the sort of zealous Christian bias that runs through the nineteenth-century work on *Hindu Manners, Customs, and Ceremonies* by the Abbé Du Bois (see n. 41); Holden Furber characterizes it as "a work of outstanding importance for the history of Hinduism" (*Rival Empires of Trade in the Orient, 1600–1800* [Minneapolis, 1976], p. 327).

[103] *Vēdam* is the Tamil form of the Sanskrit *Veda.* Probably refers at this period to the *Mānava Dharmaśāstra,* or law-book of Manu, perhaps the last offshoot of the Vedas.

[104] Caland (ed.), *op. cit.* (n. 101), pp. 1–3. The existence in earlier times of two subcastes named for the sun and moon is a tradition derived from the Vishnu Purana.

[105] For further detail on the important role of this group see Pillay, *op. cit.* (n. 30), pp. 22–24.

The "Pali" (*Paḷḷi* or *Vanniyan*) are poulterers and pork merchants, as well as cultivators, painters, and soldiers.[106] The "Ienen" (Jains) are weavers, one-twentieth of whom become soldiers.[107] The "Cottewannias" (*Kotta vanniyan*), the "Pisang" (*Pāsi?*), the "Sittijs" (*Ceṭṭi*, merchant/traders' caste), and the "Illewanion" (*Illavan* or *Izhavas*) sell fruits, such as bananas and coconuts, as well as jaggery.[108] The "Kaikulle" (*Kaikkolar*) women are often "whores, a calling not shameful to them;" the men are dancers, weavers, sowers, and soldiers.[109] The "Sitticaram" (*Chitrakara?*) are merchants who differ from the "Sittiis" traders by the greater diversity of their wares.[110] The "Caltaja" (*Kaltaṭṭān*) are occupationally a composite caste of goldsmiths, blacksmiths, stonecutters, carpenters, and masons.[111] Fisher castes include the "Carrean" (*Karaiyān*), the "Patnouwa" (*Paṭṭaṇavan*), the "Maccova" (*Mucua* or *Mukkuvan*), and the "Callia" (?); they are distinguished by the size of the nets they use. The "Conacupule" (*Kaṇakkuppiḷḷai*) are scribes; the "Gurrea" (Telugu, *golla*, cowherd) and the "Bargerrea" (from *bargura*, cattle) or "Bergas" (from *gorrel akaapari*, shepherd) are shepherds. The "Reddi" (*Reddi*) are cultivators, and many are soldiers.[112] The "Camawaer" (*Kārālar?*) are likewise cultivators and soldiers. Most of the "Bergawillala" (probably a subdivision of the *Veḷḷāḷā*) are cultivators, while most of the "Innadi" (Telugu, *Eenaadi*, one of the untouchable castes) and "Mouttrea" (?) are soldiers. The "Palla" (*Paḷḷan*) are the lowliest of the Sudras and the closest in rank to the pariahs.[113] The "Correvaes" (*Kuravan*) are Sudra nomads who live in little huts outside the towns and survive by making baskets and telling fortunes. They transport their own possessions on little asses, as well as salt, which they carry inland from the seashore. They pay no transit taxes and are never bothered since they are so poor.[114]

"Perreaes" (*Paraiyan*s or pariahs) are generally considered to be outside the established caste system. "Perreaes" applies only to males; females are called "Perresijs."[115] The *Paraiyan*s do not ordinarily live in towns with the castes, but if they do they hole up in an obscure corner. In the countryside they have their own villages. They may not draw water from caste wells,

[106] On their diverse occupations of more recent times see *ibid.*, pp. 16–17.

[107] This description fits the occupations followed by the Kaikkolar (*ibid.*), who are mentioned below as "Kaikulle."

[108] On the Izhavas see E. Thurston, *Castes and Tribes of Southern India* (7 vols; Madras, 1909). These four castes seem all to be toddy-drawers.

[109] Cf. *ibid.*, III, 37–40.

[110] In *ibid.*, p. 102, the Chitrakaras are described as being painters and makers of images.

[111] In the eighteenth century, the missionary Ziegenbalg talks of "Kaltáttscher, who are masons." See W. Caland (ed.), *Ziegenbalg's Malabarisches Heidenthum herausgegeben mit Indices versehen* in *Verhandelingen der Koninklijke Akademie van Wetenschappen*, Letterkunde, n.s., vol. XXV, No. 3 (Amsterdam, 1926), p. 196.

[112] *Reddi* is the title used by the Kapu caste of cultivators, a numerous group of south India.

[113] See Thurston, *op. cit.* (n. 108), V, 472–86.

[114] Caland (ed.), *op. cit.* (n. 101), pp. 4–6.

[115] *Paṭaiyacci* in Tamil.

but must dig their own. Around their wells they scatter the bones of dead animals to warn off those who might be polluted by drinking therefrom. They are not permitted to go near places where there are Brahmans or into caste temples. To eke out an existence they work in the earth; they do all dirty chores voluntarily because it is their vocation. They eat the unclean flesh of dead and putrifying animals. Even more lowly than the "Perreaes" are the "Siriperen" (*Ciru-pataiyan,* possibly lesser pariahs), who work as tanners and sometimes as soldiers. The "Perreaes" will not eat with "Siriperen"; the latter respect the "Perreaes" and salute them by raising their hands. The "Siriperen" prepare the dead and follow the corpse to the burial ground or funeral pyre. For this service they are paid. When they marry, the "Siriperen" are not permitted to erect a "Pandael" of more than three poles.[116]

According to Padmanaba, the Brahmans are named for "Bramma," the god from whom all the castes descend. They have his name because they came from his head. The "Settreas" are from his arms, the "Weinsjas" from his thighs, and the "Soudraes" from his feet.[117] The Brahmans themselves are differentiated by their beliefs and their ways of life. Six groups differ on matters of belief: "Weistnouva" (Vaishnavites), "Seiva" (orthodox followers of Siva), "Smaerta" (*Smārta*), "Schaerwaecka" (*Chárvaka*), "Pasenda" (*Pāsanda*), and "Tschectea" (*Śākta*).[118] The followers of Vishnu claim that he is sovereign lord and beyond comparison. Sudras who revere Vishnu are called "Daetseri" (*Dasari*) and are honored servants of Vaishnava Brahmans.[119] Should a Sudra die in defense of a Brahman they both go to "Dewendre" (*Devendra*).[120] Vaishnavites are divided into "Tadwadi" (*Tattvandin*) and "Madeva" (*Madhva*) groups. Some are called "Tadwadi" because they are great disputers who discourse profoundly of God and divine matters. In Sanskrit "Tadwa" (*tattva*) means "knowledge of God." The "Madwa" sect derives its name from "Madwa Atraria" (*Mahdvāchārya*), its founder.[121] There is also another group of Vaishnavites called "Ramanouja" from a certain "Ramanouwa Atsgaria" (*Rāmānujāchārya*), its founder and poet.[122] Each of these Vishnu sects is known by its own distinctive markings. The "Tadwadi" every day paint a white line from the nose to the forehead and also to

[116]Caland (ed.), *op. cit.* (n. 101), pp. 7–9. "Pandael" is Tamil *pandal,* meaning canopy. Usually it is suspended on twelve poles.

[117]A tradition derived from the Rigveda. See pl. 133.

[118]Du Bois (Beauchamp [trans. and ed.], *op. cit.* [n. 41], p. 109) writes: "The four principal sects of Brahmins south of the Kistna are: the Vishnavites, the Smarthas, the Tatuvadis, and the Utrassas." *Smārta* is an offshoot of orthodox Sivaism. *Pāsanda* is a general term meaning "heretics," a special sect. *Śāktas* are worshippers of *Śākti,* God as woman.

[119]*Cf.* Thurston, *op. cit.* (n. 108), II, 116.

[120]In the *Indro-loka,* the Valhalla of the Ksatriyas. See Caland (ed.), *op. cit.* (n. 101), p. 10, n. 3.

[121]A movement inaugurated by him in the fourteenth century. See J. N. Farquhar, *A Primer of Hinduism* (2d ed.: London, 1912), p. 138.

[122]A twelfth-century commentator on the *Vedānta-sūtras* who became immensely popular in south India. See *ibid.,* p. 120.

the temples. Where the arms are joined to the shoulder blade and on both breasts they paint a round mark called the mark of Vishnu. It protects them, they say, against the devil and "Iamma" (*Yama*), the judge of hell. The "Tadwadi" believe that Vishnu is the only god and they promise to live a virtuous life for him. The chief of the "Tadwadi" lives at a place inland from Pulicat called "Combeconne" (Kumbakonam in Tanjore) which is well known there. He does not wear cords and is celibate. Ordinarily he carries a bamboo stick in his hands.[123]

The "Ramanouja" mark themselves on the forehead with a sign that looks like the Greek "Upselon" (upsilon or Y). They do it with a "Namon," a substance similar to white chalk.[124] They burn a permanent mark into the flesh where the arms join the shoulder blade. Their god is merciful and will not abandon them even if they sin, not anymore than a father would kill a bad child. These Brahmans do not wear a turban, leave their heads bare, and cut their hair short except for a tuft on the top of the head which hangs to the back in a knot. The superior of this group resides in "Cansjewaram" (Conjeevaram or *Kānehīpuram*) in the Carnatic (Karnatak). Unlike his followers, he wears a small piece of cloth on his head whenever he speaks to anyone. The "Ramanouja" say they are better than the "Tadwadi," since they never engage in trade or visit brothels. Neither sect is permitted to visit brothels, but the punishment for doing so is far more severe for the "Ramanouja."[125]

The second major sect, "Seiva" or the Saivites, are often called "Aradhiha" as well.[126] They revere "Eswara" (*Īśvara*, or the lord Siva) as the reigning god and consider all other gods, including Vishnu, to be inferior to him. Sudra believers in Siva are called "Sjangam" (*Jangama*). Members of this sect smear three or four lines on the forehead with the ashes of cow dung and some carry around the neck or in the hair a certain stone, or idol, that they call *lingam*. Children of eight to ten years of age carry it on a waxed cord around the arm. Sudras of the Lingayat sect, like its Brahmans, never eat anything which has had life, neither meat nor fish.

The third major sect, the "Smaerta" (*Smārta*), is the one to which Padmanaba belongs. Its founder, "Sancra Atsjaria" (*Sankara Āchārya*), taught that Vishnu and Siva are one even though they are served and adored in di-

---

[123] Caland (ed.), *op. cit.* (n. 101), pp. 10–12. In Du Bois' day the *simhasana* of the *Tattvandin* was located in Sravenur (Beauchamp [trans. and ed.], *op. cit.* [n. 41], p. 109).

[124] Roger is apparently referring here to the Tamil *nāmam*, the general name for these marks. Du Bois (Beauchamp [trans. and ed.], *op. cit.* [n. 41], p. 112) confirms that the clay is called *nāmam*, "hence the name given to this emblem." The white clay used is generally called *Gopichandana*. See H. H. Wilson, *Sketch of the Religious Sects of the Hindus* (2 vols. in 1; London, 1861), I, 41.

[125] Caland (ed.), *op. cit.* (n. 101), pp. 12–13.

[126] In south India the *Ārādhya* are priests of the Lingayats. See Wilson, *op. cit.* (n. 124), I, 225. For Siva's portrait see our pl. 150.

verse forms.[127] The thought of this sect is profound and beyond the frail understanding of the common people. Its Brahmans therefore keep its teachings to themselves as a mystery.[128]

Members of the fourth major sect, "Schaerwaecka" (*Chárvaka*), are like Epicureans, for they believe that this life is all there is. They deny what all the others say about transmigration and future lives. Nonetheless they are well behaved and lead exemplary lives. The fifth sect, "Pasenda" (*Pāsanda*, the general name for heretics), deny all the Hindu doctrines and concern themselves only with their personal, immediate welfare. The sixth sect, "Tschectea" (*Śākta*), believe that all the other gods exist only through *Śakti*, the female source of existence. They repeat the Vedas but are otherwise concerned only with the sensual. These last three sects are all considered to be heretical by the others.[129]

Those who are set apart by their manner of living, that is, their asceticism, are called "Iagijs" (Yagins?) when Brahmans and "Iogijs" (Yogis) when Sudras. They come in three varieties: "Wanaprastas" (*Vānaprasthas*), "San-jasis" (*Sannyāsīs*), and "Avadoutas" (*Avadhūtas*). The *Vānaprasthas* live in the forest with their wives and children and sustain themselves only on such herbs and fruits as they can obtain without the work of cultivation. Some are so strict in their asceticism that they will not pull up a root for fear of separating the soul of the plant from its body. Most Hindus respect these people for the holy way of life they lead.[130] Sannyasis are Brahmans who abstain from marriage, betel-chewing, and all worldly pleasures. They take but one simple meal daily and live on alms. All their utensils must be of earthenware, their clothes are dyed in red clay, and they carry a bamboo cane. They must not touch gold or silver or live in a fixed residence unless they find a proper abode in a holy place. According to Padmanaba, the sannyasis must vanquish six foes: lust, anger, avarice, pride, love for worldly things, and revenge. They combat these enemies full-time by meditating upon divine matters. When ascetics are of the next two castes below the Brahmans, they are called "Perma-ampha" (*Paramahamsa*). Sudra ascetics are simply called yogis and are freer in their way of life than sannyasis. Other Brahmans who follow a special way of life are the "Avadoutas." They not only give up wife and children, but also try to be holier than sannyasis by renouncing more. They observe all the rules of the sannyasis but wear

---

[127] Sankara (A.D. 788–ca. 850) is the supreme *Āchārya* (teacher) of the Vedanta school. He held that nothing is real except Brahma and taught an unqualified monism. See Farquhar, *op. cit.* (n. 121), p. 118.

[128] Du Bois writes: "The Vedanta school . . . is distinguished from the rest by its metaphysics, and, we may add, by the obscurity of its dogmas" (Beauchamp [trans. and ed.], *op. cit.* [n. 41], p. 407).

[129] Caland (ed.), *op. cit.* (n. 101), pp. 13–15. The Śāktas are also worshippers of Kali, the wife or the dual aspect of Siva.

[130] See Farquhar, *op. cit.* (n. 121), pp. 167–68.

only meager garb, and some even go about nude. Others rub their bodies with ashes. When they are hungry, they go mutely into a house to await an offering of food. Certain ones simply go to a holy place and wait for others to feed them in order to win merit. The Hindus esteem these ascetics as saints, particularly those who are nude.[131]

The *Vēdam* accords five privileges to Brahmans.[132] They may sacrifice a beast at the festival called "Iagam" (*Yajña*). Since they cannot spill blood, they choke the animal, cut it into pieces, cook it, and eat a portion of the heart. The person who requests the sacrifice must pay the expenses of the Brahmans in attendance. The purpose of the sacrifice is to win a place after death in "Dewendre-locon," the heaven over which "Dewendre" presides.[133] Second, the Brahmans may teach the Rajas how to perform *Yajña*, but no other caste. Third, Brahmans may read the *Vēdam*. This Sanskrit classic contains all the secrets of the pagans, and the Brahmans memorize it. It is divided into four books: "Roggouevedam" (*Rigveda*), "Issourevedam" (*Yajurveda*), "Samavedam" (*Sāmaveda*), and "Adderawanavedam" (*Atharvaveda*). The first of these treats of the first cause, primal matter, angels, the soul, punishments and rewards, the generation and corruption of creatures, and what constitutes sin. The second deals with governors and how to rule. The third contains moral preachments, and the fourth, now lost, treats of temple ceremonies, sacrifices, and festivals. Disputes over interpretation of the *Vēdam* are resolved in the "Iastra" (*Śāstra*), a work of explanation and a commentary. The fourth privilege of the Brahmans is to teach the *Vēdam* to other members of their caste and certain Rajas. Finally, Brahmans have the right to ask for alms, since the giver obtains merit thereby. Gifts to Brahmans are regularly given at "Samcramanam" (*Samkramana*) in memory of deceased friends. Yogis also look for alms. Brahmans talk a great deal about charity and compassion but practice it little. Perhaps this is why Roger suppresses that aspect of the privileges which grants the Brahmans the right to give alms.[134]

Since the Brahmans are privileged to teach others, they instruct in reading, writing, and calculating, to help inculcate the faith into their pupils. If they are poor, the Brahman teachers receive maintenance from their students, the villages, and the king. The Brahmans are so numerous that the king cannot maintain them all. Even though people say that one-third of the country's revenues go to maintain Brahmans, still many of them are poor. By necessity, some Brahmans become merchants or practice medicine. Under no conditions, however, may they perform menial services such as

[131] Caland (ed.), *op. cit.* (n. 101), pp. 15–19.

[132] Ordinarily six privileges are cited. Roger here combines the fifth and sixth privileges into his fifth.

[133] For a more detailed description of the character and meaning of this sacrifice see Beauchamp (trans. and ed.), *op. cit.* (n. 41), pp. 510–13. "Locon" (*Loka*) means place, or locus.

[134] Caland (ed.), *op. cit.* (n. 101), pp. 19–23.

washing feet. They are permitted to act as secretaries, legates, and councillors. Often the kings assign particular villages (*agrahāras*) to the Brahmans
for their maintenance. To prevent the king from taxing or confiscating their
villages, the Brahmans obtain royal grants written on copper plates allowing them to keep their properties intact for their descendants.[135]

Brahmans believe children are polluted for the first ten days of life. Nobody may touch the child except for those who care for it. The house of
birth is likewise unclean and nobody will enter it during these ten days.
After the tenth day they begin to purify the house by washing the linen used
at birth, by throwing out earthen pots, and by cleaning copper vessels. On
the twelfth day they make a holy fire called "Homam" (*Homa*) into which
they throw incense and over which they say prayers.[136] When the fire burns
out, they give the child a name. Once the child has received its name, they
pierce its ears, not just to put jewels into them, but as a sign of devotion to
the gods.[137]

Roger then discourses on the cord or thread called "Dsandhem" (Telugu,
jandemu?) which the Brahmans wear around the neck. It hangs like a golden
chain from the left shoulder under the right arm and down the back to the
right hip. Children of Brahmans are invested with it between the ages of
five and ten. Delay sometimes occurs because of the expense involved in
keeping the holy fire burning for four days. They burn "Rawasettou" (?), a
holy wood, on which they throw paddy, butter, "Zingeli" (Gingeli, the
commercial name for the seed and oil of *Sesamum indicum*), wheat, rice gruel,
and incense. The parents must also maintain the attending Brahmans and
give them costly presents. Once children receive the cord, they are called
"Bramasariis" (*Brahmācharis*), a name they retain until married. During this
period they may not sleep with a woman or chew betel; they may eat only
once each day and must beg for their food. While this is the rule, Padmanaba
reports that they do not observe it strictly except for refraining from betel.
The cord itself, as fine as sail thread, consists of three cotton strands, each of
which is composed of nine threads. The cords must be made by hand and
exclusively by Brahmans. Annually the cords are renewed during August at
the festival of "Transwana-la-poudewa" (*Sravanapurnima*) at the time when
the first cord is also given. Other castes are permitted to wear cords, but
they must buy them from Brahman makers.[138]

Brahmans teach their own, and one another's, children. Those who are
not teachers send their children to other Brahmans or bring a teacher into
the home. They never engage teachers of a lower caste. All parents except

---

[135] *Ibid.*, pp. 23–25.

[136] Not quite exact. *Homa* is the sacrifice, and the fire is *aupāsanāgni*. Du Bois (Beauchamp
[trans. and ed.], *op. cit.* [n. 41], p. 156) makes the same error.

[137] The ceremony of ear-piercing does not take place until the seventh or eighth month of the
child's life at a separate occasion known as *karṇavedhana*.

[138] Roger in Caland (ed.), *op. cit.* (n. 101), pp. 27–30. For a much more detailed description
see Du Bois in Beauchamp (trans. and ed.), *op. cit.* (n. 41), pp. 160–72.

pariahs encourage their children to learn to read and write, but many families do not have the means to pay for education. Brahman children are also taught the elements of religion. But most of the Brahmans themselves are very ignorant in philosophy and astrology. Only a few are able to calculate eclipses and the conjunctions of the planets. They do not understand the true reasons for eclipses and laugh at Roger's explanations. Instead, they persist in believing their books which recount myths attributing natural phenomena to their gods. Roger then goes on to summarize stories from the *Mahābhārata* and other classical writings as examples of their ignorance.[139]

The rich and powerful marry earlier than the poor and weak. As soon as a Brahman boy has his sacred cord, his father begins to look for a wife so the boy can be married by the age of eight. The girl chosen must be younger. Brahmans may not marry girls who have attained puberty. If a Brahman daughter is not married before puberty, nobody will want to marry her; consequently they keep secret the first menstruation of an unwed girl. But Kshatriyas marry girls of their caste who have reached puberty. When a Brahman begins looking for a bride for his son, he studies the omens closely. After encountering bad omens three times, he no longer pursues this match. Once the omens are propitious, the girl's father asks to see the prospective bridegroom. If father, daughter, and family friends are content with the male, the marriage is arranged. Among the Sudras, the bride's father will not concur until he has received a certain amount of money as a gift.

Once the marriage is arranged, a propitious day is selected for the arrangement ceremony, at which the bride's father certifies before an assembly of the friends of the two families that he has given his daughter to the son of the other family. Since the Hindus do not marry at all times of the year, the marriage date must fall in February, May, June, October, or the beginning of November, on the precise day and hour deemed most propitious. At the marriage ceremony itself they have a fire of holy wood, before which a Brahman prays. The groom then puts three handfuls of rice on the bride's head; the bride then does the same to the groom. The bride's father gives clothes and jewels, according to his wealth, to both the bride and groom. After that he washes the feet of the groom, and the bride's mother throws water on the groom. Finally, the bride's father puts water and money into his daughter's hand and in the name of God vows to place her in the hands of the groom and his family.

When the girl is turned over to the groom, she has in her hand a small ribbon on which there is the golden head of an idol. This is called the *tāli* and it is displayed to the assembly. After well-wishes and prayers, the groom ties the *tāli* around his bride's neck as the bond of matrimony. Until the *tāli* is tied the marriage is not firm and assured. If the tying of the *tāli* is postponed for a long time, it sometimes happens that the bride's father will

[139] Caland (ed.), *op. cit.* (n. 101), pp. 29–33.

demand money before permitting completion of the ceremony. When a husband dies, the *tāli* is burned with him whether or not the bride elects suttee. Public announcement of the wedding is made by erecting a "Pandael" (*pandal*), or canopy, in front of the bride's house several days before the ceremony. After the ceremony the bride's father gives a banquet for the wedding party and feeds the poor. For five days the fire burns and they eat. On the seventh day the bride and groom leave at night for the groom's house. They are carried in a palanquin through the principal streets accompanied by torchlights and music. A pre-puberty bride stays in her husband's house for only three or four days, and then returns to her father's house. The husband is no longer called "Bramasari," but is now a "Grahasta" (*Grahatha*) who has received a second cord, and ordinarily even a third. Every decade thereafter another cord is added, and also at the birth of each child. As usual, Padmanaba reminds Roger that these are traditional rules not always precisely followed in practice.[140]

Brahmans as a rule marry only within their own caste, but they will sometimes marry lower-caste women. Other castes ordinarily do not intermarry, but they will sometimes offer their daughters to higher-caste men. A husband who tires of the wife chosen by his father will take wives or mistresses of a lower caste. It is a great sin for a Brahman to marry a Sudra woman and to have children by her. He will be barred from heaven so long as such children and their descendants remain on earth.[141] In the "Poranen" (*Purāṇa*) it is recorded that a prominent Brahman grieved because "Barthrouherri" (Bhartrihari, mid-seventh century A.D.), his son by a Sudra, had three hundred wives, whose numerous offspring would keep him out of heaven for a long time indeed. Brahmans abhor incest and designate it as one of the five great sins.[142] The *Vēdam* prescribes the excision of the shameful parts and a languishing death for the offender with them in his hands; the woman is not punished for incest. Generally the Hindus differ very little from Christians in the degrees of consanguinity permitted for marriage. A husband may marry the sister or sisters of his wife, but it is not permitted for two brothers to marry two sisters. An uncle may marry his niece who is the daughter of a sister, but in no case may he marry the daughter of a brother. Sudras are not bound by these rules of consanguinity. For example, the Governor "Sinama" of Pulicat, a Sudra, married the daughter of his brother.[143]

Polygamy is more common to the Sudras than to the Brahmans, even though it is legally permissible for all men to have more than one wife, an

---

[140] *Ibid.*, pp. 33–8. *Cf.* the accounts by Du Bois in Beauchamp (trans. and ed.), *op. cit.* (n. 41), pp. 212–30, and by Methwold, above, p. 1025.

[141] "A Brahman who takes a Sudra wife to his bed, will (after death) sink into hell; if he begets a child by her, he will lose the rank of a Brahmana" (G. Bühler [trans.], *Laws of Manu*, III, 17, in *The Sacred Books of the East*, Vol. XXV, p. 78.

[142] See *Laws of Manu*, XI, 59, in *ibid.*, pp. 441–42. On Bhartrihari see below, p. 1055.

[143] Caland (ed.), *op. cit.* (n. 101), pp. 38–40; *cf.* Du Bois in Beauchamp (trans. and ed.), *op. cit.* (n. 41), pp. 20–21.

ancient tradition recorded in their Puranas. Those who can afford it in all castes have more wives than Roger dares to say for fear of not being believed. Padmanaba considers it better to have just one wife, even though it is not sinful to have more. He thinks it lecherous to maintain a concubine if a man has one or more wives, and feels that adultery is a mortal sin. Although Brahmans do not easily leave their wives, both concubinage and adultery go unpunished. Wives who are convinced of their husband's infidelity go into seclusion or commit adultery themselves. If it becomes generally known that the wife is an adulteress, the house is considered to be polluted. To purify his home the husband holds a feast for the Brahmans at which the adulteress waits upon the guests. Once they accept food from her the house is again pure.[144]

The Brahmans, and all other Hindus, make and alter their plans according to auspicious days and omens. They will even miss sailing with the monsoons if the signs are not right. To determine good and bad days they consult the "Panjangam" (*Pañcānga*), a work similar to our almanacs. There are two kinds of "Panjangam." The one prepared by "Brahaspeti" (*Bṛhaspati*), teacher of the "Dewetaes" (*Devatās*), indicates which days and hours are good or half good. It is drawn up annually like our almanacs and is widely followed in the low country.[145] The other "Panjangam," produced by "Succra" (*Sukra*), teacher of the "Raetsjajaes" (*Rākṣasas*), or evil genii, is much more precise, in that it records each of the sixty hours into which they divide the day and night and indicates which are good and bad. They say this one never fails.[146] "Damersa," another of Roger's Brahman informants, orally translated this second book to the Dutch cleric.

According to this almanac, the year begins on the new moon in April when they celebrate the festival called "Samwat-tsaradi panduga." "Panduga" (*Pandugā*) means festival, "Samwattsaram" (*Samkranti?*) a year, and "adi" (*adi*) the first day of the month. The year is divided into twelve months, and Roger gives correctly their Tamil names in his own transliteration.[147] Every third year is divided into thirteen months to make the calendar accord with planetary movements. Their week is divided into seven days, and he gives the Sanskrit names, which are taken from the planets, as are our Latin names. They divide time into sixty-year cycles; he lists all sixty of their Sanskrit names. Official letters are all dated by the name of the year, month, and such and such a day after the full or the new moon. Their salutations, like our "Looft Godt," invoke the names of their gods. As Christians start

[144] Caland (ed.), *op. cit.* (n. 101), pp. 40–42. Du Bois, by contrast, concludes that polygamy is unusual and tolerated mainly in persons of high rank and great power. See Beauchamp (trans. and ed.), *op. cit.* (n. 41), p. 207.

[145] See A. Daniélou, *Hindu Polytheism* (New York, 1964), pp. 324–25.

[146] This is based on traditional and widely accepted lore. On *Sukra* and the *Rākṣasa* see *ibid.*, pp. 309–10, 325–26.

[147] *Cf.* the table of the solar months given in R. Sewell and S. B. Dikshit, *The Indian Calendar* (London, 1896), p. 10.

their era with the birth of Christ, the Hindus reckon theirs from the birth of the great king "Salawgena" (*Sālivāhana*).[148] This king was born in the last years of "Wicramaarca" (*Vikramārka*), a person about whom they tell many tales.[149] Roger then goes on to relate one of the stories, based possibly on an episode from the *Vikrama-charita,* a collection of stories about Vikramarka's adventures as he traveled about the world with his brother.[150] To offer his reader a sample of the "Panjangam" as an almanac for daily use, Roger gives the sixty hourly indications for the thirty divisions of day and the thirty divisions of night of a selected Sunday. For example, "Beginning with sunrise the first hour is good for every sort of discourse and discussion." With this translation he concludes his discourse on Hindu ideas about astrology, calendars, eras, and time.[151]

According to the *Vēdam* the Brahmans may not divulge their mysteries and secrets to others, even to the non–Brahmans of their own nation. Roger, nevertheless, learned from Padmanaba how the Brahmans spend the day in their private quarters. They usually arise at least one hour before sunrise and, once awake, begin to repeat the names of the gods. If they have no need to get out of bed, they remain there for one-half hour, but with all their thoughts on the gods. After completing their toilet, they sit down on a plank or a rug—never on the bare ground. They turn the face toward either the east or north and never to the west or south. They face the east because the sun rises there and the north because many of their holy places and sacred mountains are there. While seated thus they begin to chant the history of "Gasjendre Mootsjam" (Tamil, *Gajendramōtcam*).[152] Thereafter they wash the mouth and teeth and bathe in a holy river or tank, if one is nearby, and if not, they bathe at home and put on clean clothes.

To Brahmans, clothes are clean when they have not been worn or touched by others since being washed.[153] All silken garments are considered to be clean, even after being worn or touched, because of silk's pure nature. Before eating they remove their silken garments to keep them pure. After dining, they get fresh water from the well and sit down where they had sat on rising. With this water they mix the material with which they mark the face. Then they throw three handfuls of water into the mouth being careful in the process not to touch the mouth with the hands. Then they repeat the

---

[148] The Saka era, which begins in A.D. 78.

[149] Vikramaditya or *Vikramārka,* the name or title of an unidentified king of Ujjain (?98 B.C.–A.D. 78?), is celebrated in Hindu literature as the patron of the "nine gems," or nine leading figures in learning. The other major Hindu era, called *Vikrama Samvat,* traditionally begins with his reign. On the connection of Vikrama with the Vikrama era see Franklin Edgerton (trans. and ed.), *Vikrama's Adventures* (2 vols.; Cambridge, Mass., 1926), I, lviii–xi.

[150] *Cf.* above, p. 900.

[151] Caland (ed.), *op. cit.* (n. 101), pp. 42–57. On the temporal division of the day in India see above, p. 811, n. 487.

[152] From the Bhagavata Purana (VIII, 2–4). Roger summarizes this story in Caland (ed.), *op. cit.* (n. 101), pp. 63–4, following his discussion of the daily practices of the Brahmans.

[153] Sanskrit, *Ahataṃ vāsaḥ,* or the ritual of wearing clean clothes.

twenty-four names of god in the "Iapon" (Tamil, *japam,* or the repetition of mantras) while they touch the twenty-four parts of the body. Once the sun rises they throw three handfuls of water on the earth in honor of the sun. This follows an old belief that the sun lives in the mountains, where devils hide who try to stop the sunrise. When someone long ago threw water to the sun a great clamor was produced which made the devils flee. Now they perform this rite in remembrance of this earlier act and to show their own devotion to the sun.

After they worship the sun, the Brahmans of Vishnu put on a small belt on which little wooden bells hang, and some attach "Toleje" (*tulasi,* or sacred basil) flowers to it or, as in Pulicat, wild "Masilicam" (another variety of *basilicum,* or basil?). The Brahmans of Siva put on a belt to which they attach coral beads. Some throw this belt around the neck; others hold it in the hands or secrete it under their clothes or in a little pouch, or ball, or sack made expressly for it. Each time they say a prayer they let the pouch fall. Those who are busy customarily pray twenty-eight times daily, or one time for each of the beads in their belts. Those who have less to do repeat the same prayer one hundred and twenty-eight times, and those without other occupations pray many more times. After saying their customary prayers, the Brahmans take an idol from the belt and wash it with pure water. This image is a stone of a particular kind with a hole in the middle, and it is called "Salagramma" (*sālagrāma*).[154] They preserve the water with which they wash the idol and it is called "Tiertum" (Tamil, *tīrttam*). They give the idol a new covering and perfume it with sandalwood and sweet-smelling *tulasi* flowers. Then they turn to a copper image of this same god and treat it similarly. Thereafter they burn tapers on each side of the copper idol and place in front of it offerings of cooked meat, milk, and fruits. After throwing flowers on the image, they make three turns around it to the right, bow down with hands extended, prostrate themselves, and pour the "Tiertum," or sacred water, onto their heads and into their mouths. They drink the water with the *tulasi* and put a bit of the *tulasi* in their ears. They rub their foreheads with "Angaram," or benzoin, which has been offered to the idol to protect themselves against sin. They put the *tulasi* in their ears to offset pollution in case they should happen to touch a Sudra or anything dead. The sacred water purifies them from all sin. They pass the sacred water around and then begin to eat. They pray before and after meals. As evening approaches, and before sunset, they again wash, mark themselves, chant a "Iapon" (Tamil, *japam*), and give water to the sun as before. If they usually eat at this time, they now begin to dine. Young Brahmans and sannyassis eat but once each day. Married Brahmans, or "Grahastas," eat twice. When they say the "Iapon," they also read from the Puranas and wash their ears to

---

[154] An ammonite stone thought to resemble the discus of Vishnu. It is revered by Brahmans as a sacred symbol of Vishnu. See Farquhar, *op. cit.* (n. 121), p. 183.

be better able to hear and understand. These rules for Brahmans, while the law, are not strictly observed by all of them. The temple Brahmans generally follow them more faithfully than others.[155]

While Brahmans and Vaisyas will never eat anything that once had life and breath, Kshatriyas and Sudras will eat fish, flesh, and anything but cow. Killing either a man or beast separates the soul from the body. That is a sin, for such a soul is thereafter required to enter another and inferior body. The souls of cow always go to lesser beasts. Men, beasts, and plants all have souls; only the bodies differ. The Hindus eat vegetables, nonetheless, because they must eat something and because the souls of trees and plants have nowhere to go but up. This problem torments many Hindus and some actually refrain from eating the leaves of certain trees or plants. Brahmans eat moderately and are not particularly delicate in their tastes. Ordinarily they drink plain water and will sometimes take cow's milk with their meals. On a diet of rice, fruits, roots, and vegetables they easily live a perfectly sober life. The five great sins of the Brahman are to sleep with his mother, to kill a Brahman, to steal gold, to become intoxicated, and to associate with sinners who do these things.

In December the Brahmans prepare a soup which they eat for the entire month. According to Padmanaba this practice relates to the month when Krishna was in this world; the soup contains the foods eaten by the god and his companions. Although Brahmans will not eat or drink in the house of non-Brahmans, they will take with the lower castes the "Tayer" (*tayir*), or curd, deemed to be of the same nature as the "Amortam" (*Amṛta*) or nectar of the gods. A Brahman may not eat with a Brahman of another sect or with his wife.[156] Nobody is permitted to see a Brahman eat except his equals. Brahmans are obliged to fast regularly. They observe all the ordinary fast days and keep them strictly. They also fast on the eleventh day after the full moon and again after the new moon for forty-eight hours. They abstain from betel at these times and spend their time in praying and reading.[157]

When ill, the Brahmans prefer fasting to bleeding as a remedy. A Brahman prays with a dying person and his friends distribute alms to the poor. The sick individual keeps repeating the names of the gods, and when he can no longer do so his friends repeat them for him. If married, the dying man asks his wife if she will be burned or buried with him. If the answer is yes, she is obliged to live up to her vow. While self-immolation is voluntary, the general feeling prevails that no virtuous woman will refuse to sacrifice herself. If she has children she may live with them after her husband's death. According to the *Vēdam*, a wife has three duties. First she must acquiesce at all times to the desires and wishes of her husband. Roger cites at some length

---

[155] Caland (ed.), *op. cit.* (n. 101), pp. 57–62.

[156] Roger does not explain that a Brahman could not eat with his wife because she is considered to be a Sudra religiously.

[157] Caland (ed.), *op. cit.* (n. 101), pp. 65–70.

the example of "Draupeti" (*Draupadī*), the heroine of the *Mahābhāratā* and the Hindu exemplar of wifely duty. Second, a wife must exhibit modesty and simplicity in dress and decorum and never leave the house in her husband's absence. Finally, she is to die when her husband dies. The Brahmans are less demanding than the Kshatriyas about suttee.

When a sick person is about to die, two "Jamma-douta" (*Yama-dūta*), or servants of the judge of hell, make an appearance to terrify him. But then a "Wistriou douta" (*Vishnu-dūta*), or messenger of Vishnu, likewise appears.[158] The latter carries away the souls of the virtuous; the former take the souls of the wicked to "Jamma-locon" (*Yamaloka*), or the place where Yama presides. While a judgment is being made, the doomed soul returns to earth for ten days until sentence is pronounced. The corpse is shaved, washed, and clothed in a clean garment. The mouth is rubbed with lime and betel, and the women rub it also with raw rice. The burial is attended by friends, who put a little rice in the corpse's mouth and participate in the "Beteani" (?), a procession led by a pariah that walks three times around the corpse. This rite is followed by a sermon on death. Not all Brahmans are burned; some are buried. Vaishnavite and Smarta Brahmans are always inclined to obliterate acquired impurities by fire. Followers of Siva and sannyasis are buried, for they see no need for such purification. The former believe in divine justice and the latter in divine mercy.[159]

Like most of the other European commentators, Roger wrestles with the problem of trying to understand suttee. In general, he strives to point up caste differences in the practices followed. Brahmans and Vaisyas are strict in maintaining that the widow must be burned on the same day and in the same fire with the husband. Kshatriyas allow suttee at different times and places, since husbands sometimes die in foreign parts or expire many years before the wife is ready to follow. Slave girls often join their mistresses voluntarily on the pyre. A widow who refuses to die with her husband has her hair cut off, is not permitted to touch betel or wear precious stones, may not marry again, and is constantly exposed to insults. She inherits nothing and lives at the mercy of the eldest son, or the husband's brother if she has no son. Roger reports that near the end of his residence in Pulicat the sixty wives of a Kshatriya were burned with their husband.

With respect to mourning and prayers for the dead, Roger again stresses that practices differ according to caste. Generally, the mourner who is younger than the deceased will shave his beard, abstain from betel, and eat but one meal daily during the ten-day period the soul may be in this world. No formal mourning or penance is required if the deceased is younger, or a wife, or a child. Sudras mourn for both young and old by shaving their beards and head (though they leave a tuft on the head) and by abstaining

---

[158] On this point *cf.* B. Ziegenbalg, *Genealogie der malabarischen Götter* (Madras, 1867), p. 238.
[159] *Cf.* description in A. L. Basham, *The Wonder That Was India* (3d rev. ed.; London, 1967), p. 178.

from betel for three or four days. When any member of a household dies, all bearded slaves shave themselves. If the deceased is of the Sudras or of other low castes, Roger lists twelve types of people who pay last respects. Once the funeral pyre burns out, they gather up the bones and ashes and throw them in a sacred river, preferably the Ganges. Often they will build "Tampandaels" (?) or memorial huts along the roads as rest stations for travelers. Shrines are sometimes built over graves, but since they are impure, they cannot be used as places of worship. Tanks, or great pools of water, are also constructed as memorials.[160]

Part II of Roger's book deals with the religious tenets of the Brahmans of Coromandel and its environs as he learned about them from Padmanaba. Whatever sect they belong to, the Hindus unanimously believe that there is but one God and that Brahma created the world and everything in it. Brahma himelf issued from the water with a blossom of the "Tamara" (*tāmaraai*) in his navel. With respect to the traditions of the gods, Roger begins to cite here materials from the *sataka*s of Bhartrihari (mid-seventh century A.D.), a compiler of three collections of Sanskrit verses of one hundred stanzas each, two of which Roger publishes later on in his book.[161] He identifies "Dewendre" (*Devendra*) as commander over all the chiefs of the eight worlds of the sphere we inhabit, which is named "Bou-locon" (*Bhūloka*). "Brammalocon" (*Brahmaloka*) is the place where Brahma resides. Between it and our world lie the eight worlds: (1) "Indre-locon" (*Indraloka*), where "Dewendre" resides who is also called "Indre"; (2) "Achni-locon" (*Agniloka*); (3) "Iammalocon" (*Yamaloka*), or hell; (4) "Niruti-locon" (*Nirṛtiloka*); (5) "Warounalocon" (*Varunaloka*); (6) "Cubera-locon" (*Kuberaloka*); (7) "Waiouvia-locon" (*Vāyuloka*); (8) "Isangja-locon" (*Iśānaloka*). Each of these places has a governor who is under "Dewendre," the subordinate of Brahma. These governors are believed to have special jurisdictions: Agni over fire, Varuna over water, Vayu over the wind, and Kubera over wealth.[162]

The Brahmans think of the gods as people, so that what is agreeable to human kind is also agreeable to divinities, especially wives. Vishnu, according to Brahman tradition, was given a beautiful Venus-like wife named "Laetsemi" (Lakshmi) and Siva was given "Parvati" (Parvati). Both wives are divinities and are known under many other names. Roger gives in detail Parvati's descent from the son of Brahma as related by Padmanaba.[163] In a Siva temple of Pulicat, Roger noticed an image of Parvati engaged in a sex act with her husband. Padmanaba was at first reluctant to explain the mean-

---

[160] Caland (ed.), *op. cit.* (n. 101), pp. 70–83.

[161] See below, p. 1055.

[162] Caland (ed.), *op. cit.* (n. 101), pp. 164–67. This is a cursory and somewhat confused account of the gods of the Vedas and the eight spheres of existence (*Vasus*), the most immediate of the numerous aspects of divinity in Hinduism. See Daniélou, *op. cit.* (n. 145), pp. 85–88; also *cf.* Du Bois in Beauchamp (trans. and ed.), *op. cit.* (n. 41), pp. 632–33.

[163] The stories told here relating to Daksha, the father of Parvati, appear to be drawn from the Skandha Purana.

ing of this sculpture, but finally related the story of how Siva shamelessly continued to have intercourse with his wife while unexpected and divine guests looked on.[164] The lingam of the temple and the lingam worn by persons are reminders of this bold act.[165]

Vishnu entered the world at Brahma's behest in ten different corporeal forms. In these incarnations (avatars) Vishnu appeared as "Matja" (*Matsya*), a fish; as "Courma" (*Kūrma*), a tortoise; as "Warraha" (*Varāha*), a boar; as "Narasimha" (*Nṛ-simha*), half man, half lion; as "Wamana" (*Vamana*), a dwarf priest; under the name of "Parasje Rama" (*Paraśu-Rāma*), a "Settrea" (Kshatriya); under the name of "Dajerratha Rama" (*Dāsaratha Rāma*) of "Ayot-ja" (*Ayodhyā*); under the name of "Kristna" (Krishna), the brother of "Bella Rama" (*Balla-Rāma*), a "Settrea" (Kshatriya); under the name of "Bouddha" (Buddha); and in the form of "Kelki" (*Kalki*), a horse.[166] Roger then goes on to relate, usually from the stanzas of Bhartrihari, some of the stories and meanings traditionally attached to these incarnations of Vishnu and confesses that in a number of instances he knows little more about them than their names. He does not associate Buddha with Gautama, and fails to understand that *Kalki* is an incarnation still to come. Minor deities associated with Vishnu are the bird "Garrouda" (*Garuḍa*) and the wind "Annemonta" (*Hanumant*),[167] who serves Vishnu on earth as "Garrouda" does in heaven. Roger then relates, probably on the basis of the *Mahābhārata* and the *Ramayana,* some of the stories told about the lineages and activities of these two servants of Vishnu. The followers of Siva also revere minor deities: four of his sons, as well as "Nandi" (*Nandi*), the bull, "Suria" (*Sūrya*), the sun, and "Schendra" (*Candra*), the moon.[168]

In their chronology the Hindus conceive of four ages for the world: "Critaigom" (*Kṛta Yuga,* or Tamil, *yukam*), "Treitagom" (*Trēta Yuga*), "Dwapaugom" (*Dvāpara Yuga*), and "Kaligom" (*Kali Yuga*). The first three are already ended; in the last, in which we are now living, the Christian year 1639 corresponds to their year 4739.[169] Their first age lasted for 1,728,000 human years, their second for 1,296,000, and their third for 864,000.[170] The state of humankind degenerates in virtue from gold to silver, brass, and iron during the four ages: the world is constantly becoming, from stage to stage,

---

[164] The story told here is similar to that related in the Linga Purana. For an abridgment of it see Du Bois in Beauchamp (trans. and ed.), *op. cit.* (n. 41), p. 629.

[165] Caland (ed.), *op. cit.* (n. 101), pp. 85–93.

[166] *Cf.* the modern and more comprehensive list in Daniélou, *op. cit.* (n. 145), chap. xiii; for the list for Malabar, see above, pp. 914–17. *Cf.* pls. 152–67.

[167] Vayu, god of the wind, is the father of Hanumant. See Daniélou, *op. cit.* (n. 145), p. 92.

[168] Caland (ed.), *op. cit.* (n. 101), pp. 93–104. The "four sons" listed here are *Vigneshwara, Virabadha, Bhairava,* and *Kumāra.*

[169] *Cf.* above, pp. 646–50.

[170] Correct, except for the third age, which possibly lasted for only 834,000 human years. See Daniélou, *op. cit.* (n. 145), p. 249. But Du Bois (Beauchamp [trans. and ed.], *op. cit.* [n. 41], p. 415) also gives 864,000.

less and less good. As previously mentioned, the Hindus believe that in the beginning the world was an egg which split into heaven, earth, and abyss. Brahma resides in this heaven, which acquired the name "Surgam" (*Svarga*), while humankind resides in "Bou-locon" (*Bhūloka*). In the middle of this world stands a beautiful and fruitful mountain called "Merouwa" (*Meru*). Around this mountain the sun, moon, and stars revolve, so that when it is night the sun hides behind this mountain. It is so high that it is above the eight worlds which stand above "Bou-locon." Mount Meru, being the home of the gods, is never visited by people. "Bou-locon" itself is divided into seven worlds, each of which is surrounded by a sea. At the end of the *Kali Yuga* all these worlds will be consumed by fire and destroyed by flood.[171]

Angels are called "Dewetaes" (*Devatās*) and devils "Raetjasjaes" (*Rākṣasas*). "Kassiopa" (*Kaśyapa*), the father of both angels and devils, had two wives. The mother of the "Dewetaes" is "Diti" (*Diti*) and "Aditi" (*Aditi*) is the mother of the "Raetsjasjaes."[172] These devils assume the forms of men and swarm over the world as unhappy and poisonous intelligences who have harmful powers. Oppressed by hunger and thirst, some of these devils become cannibals like those who reside in the "island of Andaman" that lies between Pulicat and Pegu. The "Dewetaes," on the other hand, are happy and beneficent intelligences and include in their number the sun, moon, and stars. The Hindus agree that man is the best of all created creatures. But the excellence of man is more in his body than in his soul, for they believe that the best bodies have the most highly developed souls. Souls are eternal, but the Brahman informants of Roger disagree, at least in his view, on their nature. Finally they reassure him that the souls of true believers in Siva or Vishnu will be saved. In short, the Dutch preacher, like many of his Christian successors, has difficulty in understanding Hindu ideas about souls and the doctrines associated with this conception.[173]

Roger is much more at home in handling Hindu worship in both its inward and outward aspects. From his Brahman friends he learned that the true believer never worships with a proud heart but gives his soul and heart to God, remains a servant of God, knows God always as a great friend, and thinks constantly about God's grandeur and majesty. To be further blessed, he is required to worship outwardly as well. He must speak of God's majesty, repeat his names and attributes, and do obeisance before his images. "Pagodes" (temples) of Vishnu and Siva, as well as those dedicated to lesser gods, exist in most cities of the "Carnatica," since devotees of each major sect live in the same towns. Not all temples are equally sacred, and so Roger lists the most famous temples of the "Carnatica." At Madura a very lofty

---

[171] Caland (ed.), *op. cit.* (n. 101), pp. 104–8.
[172] Actually Roger is here reversing the tradition, for Diti is the mother of the devils or antigods.
[173] Caland (ed.), *op. cit.* (n. 101), pp. 108–11.

and beautiful temple honors Vishnu under the name of "Iockenata" (*Cok-kanāta*).[174] There is a Vaishnavite temple at "Trismápoli" (Trichinopoly, or Tiruchirapalli) called "Sriringam" (*Śriraṅgam*), one at "Wistnou Canje" (*Viṣṇukāñcī*, Kanchi as sacred to Vishnu) called "Warderásou" (*Varsdarāja*),[175] and one in "Trivelour" (Trivellore) called "Wire Ragna" (*Srivīrarāghava*). The temples of Siva are dedicated to the five elements: at "Seve-Canj" (*Śivakāñcī*, Kanchi as sacred to Siva) the temple called "Ekaubraňata" (*Ekāmbaranātha*)[176] for "Prettevi" (*Prithivi*), the earth; at "Triwanakawere" (*Tiruvanaikkavu*) the temple called "Iembounateswara" (*Jambunātheśvara*) for "Apou" (*Appu*), water;[177] at "Trinamula" (*Tiruvaṇṇāmalai*) the temple called "Aranajaleswara" (*Arunāchaleswara*) for "Tseijem" (*Tejas*), fire;[178] at "Kalist" (*Kālahasti*) the temple called "Kalest Eswara" (*Kālahasteśwara*) for "Waijou" (*Vāyu*), the wind; at "Settamberam (Chidambaram) the temple called "Settamberam Eswara" (*Chitāmbareśwara*) for "Akasjem" (Sanskrit, *ākāśa*), the air.[179] At "Tripeti" (Tirupati) there is another temple and it is called "Winket Eswara" (*Venkateśvara*).[180]

The image (*Ranganatha*) which Brahma himself worshipped is housed at Srirangam. The creator, according to the Puranas, gave it to the ancestors of Rama who passed it down from generation to generation. Finally it fell into the hands of "Wisphisena" (Vibhishana), the brother of the evil Ravana. Vibhishana started to carry it off to Lanka (Ceylon), and on the way stopped at the "Cawari" (Kaveri) River to worship. He handed the image over to a young Brahman with instructions not to place it on the ground. Since Vibhishana took longer than expected, the youth tired of waiting and put

[174] Actually a smallish temple where Cokkanata is worshipped as Siva.

[175] Kanchi is today, along with Srirangam and Tirupati, among the most important Vaishnavite centers. The foremost of its several temples dedicated to Vishnu is called *Varadarajaparumal*. See S. Padmanabhan, *Temples of South India* (Nagercoil, 1977), pp. 59–60.

[176] An epithet of Siva which means "Lord of the unique mango tree." See *ibid.*, p. 57. As Roger indicates, Kanchi is a city sacred both to Vishnu and Siva. Siva is still worshipped there in the form of the Earth Linga.

[177] For a description as of today see V. Meena, *The Temples of South India* (Kanyakumari, n.d.), p. 14.

[178] See Padmanabhan, *op. cit.* (n. 175), pp. 51–55.

[179] The Abbé Du Bois writes (Beauchamp [ed.], *op. cit.* [n. 41], p. 551): "As far as one can see, in ancient times the elements had temples specially dedicated to their worship; but I confess that I have not been able to discover any vestiges of such buildings still remaining. Nevertheless, if we may believe the evidence of a Brahman who was consulted on the subject by Abraham Roger, there was when this traveller visited India in a district not far from the Coromandel Coast, a temple dedicated to *the five elements*. Be this as it may, however, one may not unfrequently see upon the door or in the interior of the temples existing at present day the symbols of these elements represented either by five *lingams* arranged in a line, or by only three which are symbols of the material *Trimurti*—earth, water and fire." This is the only specific reference to Roger's work in the memoir by Du Bois; clearly the good Abbé did not fully understand Roger's text or know much about the Dutch preacher's career in India. Also see B. V. Subbarayappa, "The Indian Doctrine of Five Elements," *Indian Journal of the History of Science*, I (1966), 60–67.

[180] At this period *Venkateśvara* temples were also built in many villages around Tirupati. See Viraraghavacharya, *op. cit.* (n. 25), p. 380. The main temple at Tirupati is the most sacred Vaishnavite temple of south India.

the idol down. When Vibhishana returned, he found the idol rooted to the spot. In anger Vibhishana hit the youth and chased him to the summit of a rock. The image thus remained at Srirangam, whose temple is dedicated to Sri Ranganatha. This is essentially a local legend.

Roger mentions several other temples about which he has heard strange stories, and he remarks on the offerings daily put before, and on, their idols. He observes that the temples dedicated to Vishnu and Siva are higher and more spacious than those honoring minor deities, even though none can be compared to the churches in "our cities." The Hindu temples are not very lofty, but rather long and flat. Many of their gates are of great height, especially those before the temple of Tegnapatnam which is called the "white temple." All the light comes into these temples through the entrances, for they never have windows. Many temples are divided into three parts: a vaulted roof under which all may come to worship; a second area open by day but closed at night, in which only Brahmans may worship; and an inner sanctuary which houses either a statue of Vishnu in the form of a man with four arms, or that of Siva in the form of a man with three eyes who stands beneath a lingam. Day and night many lamps burn in honor of these gods.[181]

The great temples usually stand in the center of a courtyard which is enclosed by a wall. Around the main temples, but within the wall, are smaller temples to the minor deities. Near Vishnu's temple are those of Lakshmi, his wife, of the bird Garuda, and of Hanumant. Near the small temple of Garuda stands a tall mast-like tree to which a number of sticks are nailed; Garuda himself is represented as a human with wings on each side which make him look like a red sparrow hawk. Hanumant, who was born as an ape, is represented by an ape's head. In the square there is a stone tub in which the "Tulege" (*tulasi*) plant is cultivated. The arrangements around Siva's temple are similar. There are small temples honoring Parvati, his wife; *Sūrya*, the sun; "Schindica" (*Siṁhikā*), the lioness; "Comaraswari" (*Kumāreśvara*), the son of Siva; and *Nandi,* the bull. "Schendra" (*Candra*), the moon, has no particular temple of her own, but she is always over Siva's head.[182] In addition to these temples the statue of "Vicgneswara" (*Vighneśvara*), the son of Siva who is also called "Pullari" (*Piḷḷaiyār*) and "Winnaike" (*Vināyaka*), is worshipped everywhere. He is represented as a man with a very large belly, and often as an elephant with one tusk.[183]

The Brahmans show their respect for the temples by the ceremonies they observe. When Roger accompanied Padmanaba to a temple of Siva, he learned that Brahmans always keep the temple to their right, leave their sandals at the door, and throw a garment over their shoulders before entering. Temples are maintained by taxes on trade and by a kind of poll tax

---

[181] Cf. Du Bois' description in Beauchamp (trans. and ed.), *op. cit.* (n. 41), pp. 572–82. For Siva *cf. our* pl. 150.
[182] Candra is usually masculine.
[183] Caland (ed.), *op. cit.* (n. 101), pp. 111–18. These names of deities relate to the cult of

levied annually on the various castes. Roger lists in detail the percentages collected for the temple on various commodities in trade as well as the amounts expected from each caste in Pulicat. Revenues are also derived from the offerings of pilgrims at the most sacred temples. For example at "Tripeti" (Tirupati), just a few days' journey from Pulicat, three festivals are held annually to which pilgrims throng. In September, Sudras and other inferior classes make pilgrimages to Tirupati, and in December the Brahmans go there; Roger does not know the date of the third festival.[184] Tirupati had received endowments from many former kings, and would be even richer now except for the following circumstances. The Vijayanagar ruler "Weincatapeti" (Venkata II, d. 1614), greatly in need of money, took Tirupati's endowment in return for a promissory note. His successor, "Rama Deuvello" (Rama Deva, or Rama IV), wanted to seize all its treasures, but he and his council died at the foot of the mountain where the temple stands.[185]

In Pulicat, on a number of occasions, Roger visited the local temples honoring Vishnu and Siva. He was struck by the fact that Hindus, unlike Christians, have no regular public assemblies at which to pray, sing, or hear sermons. Their divine worship consists of processions and offerings to the idols. Siva's monthly procession falls on "Amavvasi" (*Amāvāsya*), the first day of the new moon; Vishnu's is on the day of "Ieccadesi" (*Ekādaci*) or the ninth day after the new moon. On these occasions the idol is paraded through the streets and then returned to its sanctuary. The procession includes torchbearing musicians, singers, and temple dancers.

Roger finds it strange that these female dancers and temple prostitutes (*devadāsi*) are highly regarded and permitted to dance in temples and before idols held to be so sacred that they would be polluted by the mere touch of a Sudra. Padmanaba explains that the *devadāsi* themselves are esteemed in this world and may even enjoy the felicities of the next life, especially if they remain true to the man to whom they sacrificed their virginity. To illustrate his point the Brahman tells the story of how "Dewendre" (*Devendra*), assuming a human shape, went to a courtesan to determine whether or not she would be faithful to him. After striking a bargain, she indulged him in his every wish. Then "Dewendre" feigned illness and death. His mistress, despite the protests of friends and relations, resolved to burn herself with his body. Once the funeral pyre was prepared, and when it became clear she would throw herself upon it, "Dewendre" returned to his living human

---

Ganapati or Ganesha. Ganapati has just one tusk; he lost the other while wrestling with Parasurama. See our pl. 151. On the sons of Siva see Daniélou, *op. cit.* (n. 145), pp. 291–300.

[184] "Among the several festivals conducted in the temple Niyotsavam which starts on the Telugu New Year day (Ugadi) and Brahmatsavam which falls during the Tamil month of Puratsi and Vaikunta Ekadesi during the month of Markali are most important" (Padmanabhan, *op. cit.* [n. 175], p. 74).

[185] As a result of the civil wars and Vijayanagar's struggle with Golconda, the finances of Tirupati began to be plundered openly around 1638. See Viraraghavacharya, *op. cit.* (n. 25), II, 832–33.

form and declared that he would reward her fidelity and promised her a place in the heaven where he reigns.[186]

In worshipping, they bedeck the statues of Vishnu with flowers, rich clothes, and precious stones. Siva delights in having his statues washed with water, essences, and perfumes. Twice each day worshippers light lamps and offer food to these idols. In addition to regular monthly processions, they celebrate a solemn festival every year at which the idol is carried about in a high tower which runs on wheels and is drawn by members of the "Maccoas" (Mucuas), a caste of fishermen. Other processions for the two gods are held at Pulicat in January and June when the idols are taken into the countryside. Aside from the celebrations honoring the sun, their festivals divide into three kinds: "Trenala" (*tirunal,* or "holy day") are those dedicated to Vishnu and Siva; "Panduga" (*Panduga*) are those of the lesser gods and the wives of Vishnu and Siva; and "Iataro" (*yāttirai,* or "festival"), those of the "Ganga" (*Gaṅgā*), or the devil. On January 18, married women of the Brahman caste celebrate for nine days the festival of "Gauwri Dewo" in honor of Parvati to obtain a long life for their husbands.[187] They make an image of the goddess from rice meal and red grain. They clothe it, adorn it with flowers, and generally attend to it. On the tenth day they carry it out of the city and throw it into one of their sacred pools.[188]

On February 8 the Saivites and Smartas celebrate the festival of "Tseweratre" (*Śivarātri*), an event not observed by the Vaishnavites. They fast for one day and night in memory of "Kalecote wissiam" (*Kālakūṭa viṣam*), that deadly poison from which Siva delivered the world by drinking it himself.[189] On the fourteenth day after the new moon of August, the Brahmans and Sudras of both sexes celebrate on a river bank the festival called *Anantā Padmanābha Vratâm.* Only the Brahmans officiate before the idol. The celebrants tie bands of fourteen threads around their right arms. Believers are obliged to participate in this annual festival for fourteen times after first celebrating it.[190] At every full moon in August the Brahmans celebrate "Traswanalu pondema" (*Sravana purnimā*) when the children receive the sacred cord of the caste and the married Brahmans take new ones. On the eighth day after the full moon of August the Brahmans and Sudras celebrate the festival of "Gokoulástemi" (*Gokulāṣṭamī* or *Kṛṣṇāṣṭami*) honoring the

---

[186]Possibly a story from one of the Puranas? It is very probable, according to Caland (ed.), *op. cit.* (n. 101), p. 125, n. 2, that this story gave Goethe his material for the ballad *Der Gott und die Bajadere* (1797). Also see H. H. Schaeder, *Goethes Erlebnis des Ostens* (Leipzig, 1938), pp. 146–47.

[187] *Kauriviratam* honors Parvati in the month of *Aippaci* (Oct.–Nov.).

[188] *Cf.* description of "Gowry" in Jagadisa Ayyar, *op. cit.* (n. 26), p. 200.

[189]This is the high point of the religious year for the devotees of Siva. For a detailed study of its history, meaning, and contemporary status see J. Bruce Long, "Mahāśwarāti: The Saiva Festival of Repentance," in G. R. Welbon and G. E. Yocum (eds.), *Religious Festivals in South India and Sri Lanka* (New Delhi, 1982), pp. 189–217.

[190]An important Vaishnavite festival honoring Narayana, an avatar of Vishnu. See Jagadisa Ayyar, *op. cit.* (n. 26), pp. 118–23.

birthday of Vishnu under the name of Krishna. According to their legend this marvelous child was brought up by a certain cowherder named "Nanda" (*Nanda*). On this day the Brahmans dress themselves in their finest, treat one another, and exchange "Teyer," or curd, coconuts, and other kinds of refreshments usually associated with herdsmen. At this annual festival the streets are adorned with native greens and leaves.[191] To explain the meaning of this festival Roger relates the story behind it as told to him by Padmanaba.[192] At the first new moon of September the wives of the Brahmans celebrate "Maharna haumi" (*Mahānavami*) in honor of Lakshmi, the wife of Vishnu. For nine days the women pray for long lives and riches for their husbands. On the ninth day the Brahmans themselves worship Vishnu. At the same time the Sudras, especially the soldiers, celebrate a festival of the arms used in battle.[193] One week after the new moon of October comes the festival of "Dipáwali" (*Dīpāvalī*), at which they honor Vishnu as Krishna. Before sunrise they wash their heads and put on their finest garb; they invite friends into the home, and at night they illuminate their houses and temples and send the children into the streets with lighted candles.[194] The "Malabars" (*i.e.,* Tamils) hold a festival in July called "Ati Panduga" (*Aṭi pandugā*) and another in November named "Cartica Panduga" (*Kārttikai pandugā*).[195] Besides festivals, they observe holy days when great merit may be won for the donor by almsgiving.[196]

Aside from the festivals dedicated to Vishnu and Siva, the Hindus celebrate the lesser deities as well. On January 9 they honor the sun at the festival called "Pongol" (*Poṅkal*). The first act of the feast is to boil rice and milk in the sunshine. When the sun sets, they shout "Pongol" four times. Tradition has it that "Raetsjasje Beelli" (*Rākṣasi, makara raasi,* or Capricorn?) descends on that day from "Patalan" (*Pātāla*), the abyss, to survey the state of things on earth.[197] On the second day, cows, buffaloes, and wild oxen are adorned with garlands and allowed to roam in the countryside. Prayers and offerings are made regularly to Garuda, "Annemonta" (Hanumant), "Vicgneswara" (*Vighneśvara*), and "Virrepadri" (*Virabhadra*). Strictly speaking, these are not deities, but only the dispensers of health and other temporal blessings. Vighnesvara, who is looked upon as a kind of tutelary deity, is the most esteemed, especially by women who desire to have children. They also honor "Dewendre" (Devendra or Indra) and invoke "Achni"

[191] See *ibid.,* pp. 113–15.

[192] The Brahman gave him an account derived mainly from the Bhagavata Purana of the upbringing of Krishna by Nanda at the city of "Gocalam" (Gokulam).

[193] On these two aspects of the *Dasara* festival see Du Bois' description in Beauchamp (trans. and ed.), *op. cit.* (n. 41), pp. 569–70.

[194] On this "festival of lights" see Jagadisa Ayyar, *op. cit.* (n. 26), pp. 151–54. Roger follows the description with a story from the *Harivaṃśa,* a biography of Krishna, telling of Krishna's defeat of Narakasura, a devil, as the occasion for the festival.

[195] For descriptions of these two events see *ibid.,* pp. 79–84; 155–58.

[196] Caland (ed.), *op. cit.* (n. 101), pp. 120–37.

[197] *Poṅkal* really celebrates the day when the sun enters Capricorn and turns northward.

(Agni) for good reputation, "Warouna" (Varuna) for water, "Waiouvia" (Vayu) for vigor, "Cubera" (Kubera) for riches, and "Isangja" (*Īśāna*, or Siva), for rule or dominion. But with all these idols and temples, Brahma, the creator and universal governor, has no temple erected in his honor and is not worshipped publicly.[198]

The Hindus worship many devils, of whom the two most famous are "Ganga" (*Gaṅgā*) and "Gournatha" *Gauri-nātha*, lord of Gauri, or Siva).[199] "Ganga" (better identified as Kali) is depicted as a female with one head and four arms. She holds a small bowl in the left hand and a trident in the right. There are a few temples in her honor, one being at "Carmellon" (Kodungal-lur?), a place not far from Pulicat.[200] At certain places they have festivals in her honor, but the Brahmans are not supposed to participate in them. Zealots on these occasions throw themselves under the wheels of the car carrying the idol. At other times those who are ill or frenzied swing from a hook in her honor. Others sacrifice goats and buffaloes in a bloody exhibition. Many Brahmans condemn these practices, but they fear to oppose them openly since other Brahmans participate in them. "Gournatha" (Siva) is thought to have even more extensive powers of destruction. There are no temples in his honor and only a few images in the fields. People worship him under a tree where they claim to have seen him in person. Roger, like most contemporary European observers, is professedly repelled by these sacrifices while dwelling at length on their enormities.[201]

When Roger attempts to deal with Hindu theology, he relies on the proverbs in the first book of "Barthrouherri" (Bhartrihari) and on the answers of his Brahman informants. While they make no distinctions between the souls of humans and animals, the Hindus contend that the body and spirit of man give his soul a greater freedom to display itself. Beasts would be able to function as humans if they had similar bodies. While man's soul remains the same throughout life, its capacities are limited by a body that is too young or too old to function fully. The Brahmans do not agree on the origin of the soul; some say it exists solely by the will of God and others argue that it is eternal. They believe in rewards and punishments; the wicked receive various punishments. The soul transmigrates from man to beast and even to plants, as well as in the reverse direction. The most desirable migration, next to that of the human body, is to an ox or cow. Evil souls sometimes become devils, or are sent (temporarily or permanently) to hell, where Yama lives. Good souls may go to any one of seven different heavens and all become angels or "Devetas" (*devatās*).

---

[198] *Cf.* Du Bois on the position of Brahma in Hinduism (Beauchamp [trans. and ed.], *op. cit.* [n. 41], pp. 613–15).

[199] These names do not seem to correspond to the description which follows. As used here, *Gaṅgā* is not "the fair one," but is rather another name for Kali, the power of destruction. Roger himself seems to be confused about the identification.

[200] Kodungallur (Cranganore) has a popular shrine dedicated to Kali.

[201] Caland (ed.), *op. cit.* (n. 101), pp. 137–46.

A doctrine of rewards and punishments implies a belief in good works. Since divine justice is exercised only in the life to come, most obtain merit through practicing spiritual exercises and austerities in this world. Roger then cites a number of the austerities he observed: for example, standing on one's head while praying. Pilgrimages to holy places to obtain forgiveness of sin and purification of the soul is one of the most popular ways of receiving grace. The most famous holy places are "Ayot-ja" (Ayodhya), "Matura" (Mathura), "Casi" (Kasi), "Canje" (Kanchi), "Awentacápouri" (Avanti-kapuri), and "Devaraweti" (Dvaravati). In all there are seven places that the Brahmans consider most holy. Ayodhya, north of Kasi, is holy because Vishnu was born there under the name of Rama. Mathura, not far from the Mughul court at Agra, is holy because Vishnu was born there under the name of Krishna. Kasi, also called "Waránasi" (Benares), is in Bengal on the banks of the Ganges. When a Hindu dies there, Siva blows in his right ear to purify him and he never returns to earth. "Cansjewaram" (Conjeevaram) is a great Carnatic city with many temples. "Aventecapouri" or "Awenteutica" (Avantika), north of Agra, is another city renowned for its sacred centers. "Dwaraca" (Dwaraka) or "Dwareweti," near Surat, is the place where Krishna died; it has been swallowed up by the sea. Krishna's body was rescued from the sea and taken to "Sjangernata" (Jaganata, or Jagannath) or "Prousótamai" (Purusottama in Orissa). At "Preyaga" (Prayaga), up the Ganges from Kasi, the waters will wash away all sins, even suicide. Believers everywhere receive merit from simply repeating the names of these shrines, especially at morning prayers, and by thinking about them. Ablutions with waters from these shrines, especially salt water, give Hindus merit. Salt water is especially efficacious because "Agastea" (Agastya, the Mover-of-Mountains, *i.e.,* teacher) swallowed the sea and urinated it— hence the sea is salty.[202] At all seasons the sea at "Ramaneswara" (Ramesvaram) is pure.

The fresh water of the Ganges is especially sacred, for it washes away all sins. Hindus strive throughout their lives to make a pilgrimage to the Ganges to drink and bathe in its most purifying water. Those who bathe with fresh water from another source may gain equal merit by praying "Ganga Sjanam" (*Ganges snānam*), that is, "Ganges, wash me."[203] Bottles of water from the Ganges are carried to other parts as waters are from the spas of Europe. To account for the Hindu belief in the absolute purity of the water of the Ganges, Roger recounts legends from the Vedas, Puranas, and the *Mahābhāratā* which tell of the mythical origin of the Ganges in heaven. Brahmans who bathe in the Ganges are not immediately admitted to heaven but are certain of not being excluded from heaven. Pilgrims also go to "Gaya" (Gaya), a holy city where a rock is shown in which God left his

---

[202] *Mahābhārata*, III, 105, 106.
[203] Correctly translated as "Ganges bath."

footprint. On their way to Gaya the pilgrims first go to "Preyaga" (Prayaga) for one month to bathe in the Ganges. Then they journey to "Casi" (Kasi) where they again bathe in the sacred river. Arrived in Gaya, the pilgrim prepares dough pieces (*pindas*) which are placed on the sacred rock in memory of the deceased. To explain this custom Roger recounts the story of the footprint of God as it appears in the Vayu Purana.[204]

Roger's book ends with a brief biography, based on Hindu tradition, of Bhartrihari, the seventh-century collector of epigrams. The father of Bhartrihari was reputedly a Brahman who had married a woman of the lowest caste. Bhartrihari himelf had three hundred wives. Famous for his wisdom, Bhartrihari became a sannyasi and traveled widely. When he refused to let his wives accompany him, he freed them from their marital ties and encouraged them to marry again. He himself, feeling that mankind was overburdened by the vast amount of available knowledge, decided to digest all of it into three hundred proverbs divided into three books. Each book is divided into ten chapters with ten proverbs in each. The first book is entitled "Of the Way which Leads to Heaven," the second "Of the Conduct of a Rational Creature," and the third "Of Love."[205] Padmanaba paraphrased the first two into Portuguese but scrupled to do the same for the erotic stanzas of the third book. Roger himself translated them from Portuguese into Dutch prose and used them as sources for his understanding of Hindu life and religion. For the first time in history, Roger and his Brahman friend brought directly over into several European languages, and published, an adaptation of a substantial work from Sanskrit.[206]

Added to the French edition of Roger's book is a summary of the religion of the Hindus of the Coromandel Coast prepared by a Brahman who worked as an interpreter for Governor Arnould Heussan and other members of the VOC. In a measure it confirms some of the points made by Roger but adds nothing substantial to his pioneering account of Hinduism.[207] Roger's work,

---

[204] Caland (ed.), *op. cit.* (n. 101), pp. 146–64. A temple at Gaya is built over the *Vishnupada,* the rock on which the sacred footprint of Vishnu may still be seen. See K. Lal, *Holy Cities of India* (Delhi, 1961), pp. 199–204.

[205] These are the titles in the order given in the English translation of Picart's collection (see n. 101), p. 405. Picart does not include a translation of the two śatakas, even though they are in the French translation of Thomas la Grue, the version of Roger's work which Picart used in the preparation of his original collection in French. Ordinarily the śatakas are said to include three topics in the following order: love, wise conduct, and indifference to worldly enjoyment. See R. C. Majumdar (ed.), *The History and Culture of the Indian People. The Classical Age* (Bombay, 1954), pp. 312–13.

[206] Caland (ed.), *op. cit.* (n. 101), pp. 168–73; translated from Dutch into French in La Grue (trans.), *op. cit.* (n. 101), pp. 293–341, and into German in Christoph Arnold (ed.), *op. cit.* (n. 101), pp. 469–536. For a modern English translation of the *Śatakatrayam* see Barbara S. Miller (trans.), *Bhartrihari: Poems* (New York, 1967). Stories from other Indian writings had filtered indirectly into European literature many centuries earlier. See *Asia,* Vol. II, Bk. 2, chap. ii.

[207] The French edition of Roger's work also includes an extract from A. Kircher's *China illustrata* (Antwerp, 1667) relating to Hinduism. Kircher depended on the letters of Father Heinrich

based on Vedic and Puranic literature and on the almanacs (*Pañcāngas*), as well as on stories from the *Mahābhāratā, Ramayana,* and the proverbs of Bhartrihari, provided Europe with a summary of the substance of Hinduism. It contains a wealth of information on the names, usually identifiable, of the castes, gods, temples, sacred centers, and festivals then important in south India. Like any foreign observer, Roger concentrates on those social and religious customs which differ from his own: caste rules; marriage customs; death, funeral, and mourning rites; suttee; fasting; austerities; and omens. Nor is he satisfied merely to summarize his personal observations. He regularly queried his Brahman informants about the traditions and principles which lay behind the practices. He learned that Hindus of all sects believe in one God and in Brahma as the creator of the world. Like a good European and Protestant scholar of his age, he is concerned about the creation, time and the calendar, the works of God, afterlife, and the apocalypse. It is not surprising, therefore, that he investigated Hindu ideas about these subjects. He was perhaps most surprised to learn that the Hindus have no public religious services and no temple honoring Brahma, and that the gods are expected to be like men, with wives, mistresses, and children. He is impressed by Hindu dedication to private worship and prayer, by the public processions and numerous festivals, and by the conception of anti-gods or evil deities. He distinguishes correctly, though perhaps naively, between the beliefs, idols, and temples of the followers of Vishnu and Siva. He knows of some of the epithets and attributes of the two major gods and seeks to relate them to the minor deities whose shrines appear within the confines of the temples dedicated to the great gods. He lists the avatars of Vishnu and tries to explain, albeit somewhat reluctantly, the character and meaning of the lingam. Throughout the work he is conscious of the omnipresent belief in transmigration of souls and in man's position as the highest of created beings. Most of the time he refrains from making value judgments, but he is clearly astonished by the respect accorded the *devadāsi* and by the general recognition given to the special position of the Brahmans in religion and society. Perhaps most surprising is his willingness to study Hinduism as a living religion which must be understood in its own terms.

As the first comprehensive and objective account of Hinduism available in Europe, Roger's *Open-deure* did not belie its title. Aside from the translations which shortly appeared in French and German, Roger's work opened the door to Hinduism for his successors. Its text was pilfered by Baldaeus and Olfert Dapper. Bernier and Melchior Valentin knew and appreciated its worth. Its illustrations, probably of Indian inspiration, presumably brought an end to the monster stereotype of Indian gods which had previously pre-

---

Roth, his fellow Jesuit and the individual who first supplied European scholars with the Sanskrit alphabet (see pl. 129). This appendix deals primarily with the avatars of Vishnu.

vailed in European engravings.[208] Eminent literati, such as Goethe and Herder, later used it as a source book. Students of comparative religions made use of it, especially Bernard Picart, who reprinted Roger's book in French in his *Cérémonies et coutumes religieuses des tous les peuples du monde* (1723). Bartholomaeus Ziegenbalg, the eighteenth-century Danish missionary at Tranquebar, used Roger as a source for his famous *Genealogie der malabarischen Götter,* which remained unpublished until 1867. Max Müller, the great Indologist of the nineteenth century, compares the *Open-deure* favorably to Ziegenbalg's more detailed geneaology. The Abbé Du Bois, the nineteenth-century Catholic student of Hinduism, knew of Roger's work and certainly drew from it, even though he was apparently uncertain about its reliability. For modern students of Hindu society and religion, this book is indispensable for the detail that Roger gives about conditions on the Coromandel Coast in the mid-seventeenth century with respect to caste, to social practices, and to the religious beliefs and rites then prevailing.[209]

4

THE DOWNFALL OF TWO EMPIRES: VIJAYANAGAR AND GOLCONDA

The European commentators of the generation following the publication (1651) of Roger's work are not in any way as well informed on Hinduism and southeastern India. They were much more concerned with the civil wars and disruptions attending the demise of the old empire and the Muslim expansion southward. Giacinto de Magistris (1605–68), an Italian Jesuit, worked in India for twenty years before returning to Rome in 1660. From 1644 to 1659 he acted as secretary and companion to Archbishop Francisco Garcia (r. 1641–59) of Cranganore. He returned to Europe as procurator of the Malabar mission and as an apologist for Archbishop Garcia's policies toward the St. Thomas Christians and the Carmelites.[210] In 1661 Magistris published at Rome his *Relatione della Christianità de Maduré* as a call to his confreres to enlist for service in Madura, Tanjore, and other places in southern and eastern India.[211] In this region the climate for Jesuit missionaries was

---

[208] See P. Mitter, *Much Maligned Monsters* (Oxford, 1977), p. 60. See our pl. 152.

[209] Cf. Raymond Schwab, *La Renaissance orientale* (Paris, 1950), pp. 149–53; and A. L. Willson, *A Mythical Image: The Ideal of India in German Romanticism* (Durham, N.C., 1964), pp. 8–10.

[210] See Streit, V, 156. On Magistris' rôle as an apologist for Garcia see Joseph Thekedathu, S.D.B., *The Troubled Days of Francis Garcia, S.J., Archbishop of Cranganore, 1641–59,* (Rome, 1972), p. 149 *et passim*.

[211] Translated into French in 1663 as *Relation dernière de ce qui s'est passé dans les royaumes de Maduré, de Tangeor, et autres lieux voisins du Malabar aux Indes Orientales* (Paris). The references which follow are to the French translation.

far more favorable than on the Malabar coast, where the St. Thomas Christians were still openly hostile to the Jesuits.[212]

Magistris' *Relatione* deals with events in Madura and its neighboring states from 1656 to 1659, the last four years of Garcia's tempestuous term of office. In brief, he recounts what happened to the Madura mission after Nobili's death in 1656.[213] This account is based on Magistris' own experiences in this region, as well as on information obtained from fellow Jesuits in charge of the various residences and dependencies maintained by the Society. Magistris, since he was looking for recruits and financial aid in Europe, stresses Christian successes and failures and provides many edifying stories about the fortitude and staunchness in the faith of both the missionaries and their converts. Unlike Roger, he pounces at every opportunity upon the "errors" of the Indians and upon their superstitious practices. While he had only a superficial partisan interest in Hinduism, he is sometimes surprisingly full and precise on political, military, and broadly cultural matters—or what he calls "temporal conditions." He justifies his attention to secular life by claiming that it is his purpose to show that "men everywhere are men" and that Europeans need to know and understand more about the interior of India if it is "to become and remain a part of the Kingdom of Christ."[214]

Madura is presently ruled by "Tirumala" (Tirumala Nayaka, r. *ca.* 1623–59), a wise and generous prince held in high esteem by his subjects. His country is of vast extent, broad and fertile, and is larger and more powerful than the neighboring states of Tanjore and Gingee. The entire country is traversed from west to east by the "Collara" (Coleroon) River.[215] In earlier times Madura paid tribute to "Narsinga" (Vijayanagar) but now Tirumala is an absolute ruler and his office hereditary. He commands an army of eighty thousand men and concludes alliances with his neighbors to remain free of Vijayanagar and the growing threats coming from Bijapur and Golconda. The soldiers of Madura are vigilant and commonly fight with bows and arrows, swords, and firearms. They employ large cannons, the most powerful of which are called "Basilesques," after the name of a dangerous snake; however, they are not really experts in using cannons. After having reigned for more than thirty years through troublous times, Tirumala died at seventy-five years of age. More than two hundred of his most beautiful wives accompanied him to the funeral pyre.

The capital city of Madura, from which the state takes its name, is vast and densely populated. Its inhabitants are lovers of learning, and they support several celebrated universities as well as diverse schools which specialize in the liberal arts, medicine, and theology. The city is resplendent

[212] On the troubles which swept the Serra in 1653 and thereafter see above, pp. 162–65.
[213] On Nobili at Madura see above, pp. 149–58, 1012–17.
[214] Magistris, *op. cit.* (n. 211), pp. 22–23.
[215] The Coleroon is a branch of the Cauvery River, the so-called Ganges of the south.

with colorful and magnificent temples dedicated to their four principal gods and to some of their lesser deities. Painting is an art they hold in high esteem, and native painters are often employed by the Portuguese to decorate churches. While they have artisans of all kinds, their workers in wood and their alchemists who make false gold are the most famous. The urbane residents of the capital enjoy discussing learned subjects with the missionaries, including disputations about immortality, divine justice, heaven, and hell. Upper-class women study music and learn to play the lute; but they rarely leave their houses. At the new moon of September they hold a festival for fifteen days, which is strictly kept by the "king" and court as well as by the general populace.[216] At this time the "king" grants audiences in person, on a particular day. To those whom he favors, the ruler gives a gift of cloth and the permission to ride around the city on one of the royal horses or elephants.

Aside from the capital Madura's important cities are "Tricierapelli" (Tiruchirapalli or Trichinopoly) and "Satiamangalou" (Satyamangalam). Everywhere the caste system makes conversion difficult. The Brahman caste of Madura includes the members of the royal house, priests, teachers called "Sanjas" (Sannyasis), and those who preside at funerals or make prognostications. People of the second level are called "Pandari Raggi" (*Paṇḍāram?*) or "Chintri" (*Chetty?*) and are occupationally soldiers, merchants, or important townsmen. The third level belongs to the "Pareas" (*Paṟaiyan*) or "Poleas" (*Pulayan*), who are artisans, cultivators, and villagers. Although their beliefs are ridiculous fictions, the Brahman priests are exemplars of virtuous living, and they subject themselves to various austerities. Certain Brahmans shave the head completely, while others wind a cloth around it. They purify themselves by bathing in the temple tanks. Some of the penances the priests demand of others are preposterous. Many of the people believe in evil spirits; others worship snakes, especially one called "Cheneven," who is Vishnu.[217]

In the early years of his reign, Tirumala of Madura continued to pay tribute to Vijayanagar as his predecessors had. Because these payments drained the lifeblood of his subjects, he delayed the payments to his overlord. Emperor Venkata III (r. 1630–41) overlooked these postponements and continued to accept the formal homage of Tirumala. Venkata's successor (Śriranga III, r. 1641–72) altered this policy and determined to collect Madura's unpaid tribute by force. The nayak promised, as an artifice, to pay his debts immediately, but again delayed until he could fortify his outposts and

[216] The festival called Pitra Paksha is specially set apart to honor departed ancestors, and strict rules obtain regarding the rites to be followed. See C. H. Buck, *Faiths, Fairs, and Festivals of India* (reprint of 1917 edition, New Delhi, 1977), pp. 98–99.

[217] Magistris, *op. cit.* (n. 211), pp. 2–29, 182. A reference to Sesha, the snake on which Vishnu rests. See Daniélou, *op. cit.* (n. 145), pp. 162–63.

arrange an offensive and defensive alliance with Tanjore and Gingee. He also appealed for help to the "Turks"[218] of Golconda, who attacked the empire from the north and forced Śriranga to desist in his southward attacks on Madura. Then, growing fearful of the spreading power of the "Turks," the three Hindu nayaks concluded peace with the empire and sent military aid to Śriranga. But this belated effort proved ineffective and the forces of Golconda overran "Bisnaga" (Vellore) and Śriranga himself was forced to take refuge in "Messur" (Mysore). Golconda in association with Bijapur then besieged and took the strategic fortress of Gingee. This accomplished, they turned their armies loose in Tanjore and Madura and demanded tribute. Mysore with the aid of forces from "Marava" (Marava, or the Ramnad country) tried fruitlessly for a time to punish Tirumala for his betrayal of the dying Hindu empire. Thereafter a shaky peace was restored just before Tirumala's death in 1659.[219]

During these wars the Christian missionaries and their converts were forced to flee in all directions and only gradually were they able thereafter to return to their permanent residences. Nonetheless, from 1655 to 1659 the missionaries claimed 9,231 new converts, a figure Magistris adds to the 100,000 made since the beginning of the Madura mission. Most of the new converts accepted Christianity at Tiruchirapalli, "the frontier town where the wars started," at Satyamangalam, at Tanjore city, at "Parcur" (?) in Tanjore, and in the lands of the "Larrons" (French, robbers).[220] Aside from war and disruption, the mission is hampered by the many languages: "Malabar" (vernacular Tamil), the "most common tongue," Tamil, "Chaldean" (?), and Syriac. Other obstacles are the vast distances, epidemics, and the entrenched caste system. Finally, there are the open enemies of the faith: Muslims and "Ioques" (Yogis) called "Pareas" (*Paṟaiyars*).[221] During and after the wars these "Ioques" fomented civil disruptions in which the Christians were charged by their "Great Prophet" with turning the Hindus away from their gods and as acting as agents of the Portuguese. Despite the letters patent the Jesuits possessed to preach and convert freely in Madura, the "Ioques" combined with local officials to harass the Jesuits and their converts.[222]

The invasion of Madura by the "Turks" of Golconda began with the capture of the Tiruchirapalli fortress, a success which opened the whole country to them. The "Turks" ruthlessly destroyed Christian churches and residences but left the Hindu temples untouched. Christian children were carried off and sold as slaves to the heathen merchants who follow the ar-

---

[218] Magistris applies the word "Turks" to the Islamic forces of both Bijapur and Golconda.

[219] Magistris, *op. cit.* (n. 211), pp. 29–38. This account of "Tirumala's" wars corresponds roughly to what modern historians recount about this turbulent era. See Sathyanatha Aiyar, *op. cit.* (n. 24), chap. viii.

[220] On these thieves (*Koḷḷars* or *tēvars*) see below, pp. 1062–63.

[221] Magistris, *op. cit.* (n. 211), pp. 39–43. Those referred to as "Ioques" by Magistris are probably Vaḷḷuvar, the "Brahmans of the Pariahs." See Thurston, *op. cit.* (n. 108), VII, 303–10.

[222] Magistris, *op. cit.* (n. 211), pp. 51–87.

mies of the "Turks" for this purpose. The "Turks" cruelly tear off the earrings of the Christians whom they capture. At first the "Turks" seek to exterminate the "Larrons," but these thieves easily escape into the forests and hinterlands they know so well. The "Larrons" rob the Christian refugees as they flee, but never harm their priests. The Muslims are not the only ones to practice cruelties; when Mysore invaded Madura, its soldiers overran Satyamangalam and ruthlessly cut off the noses of their captives.[223]

"Tangeor" (Tanjore), so far as Magistris can determine, is not known to European geographers and map-makers and so he endeavors to fill this void. The nayakdom receives its name from its capital and lies east of Madura on the Bay of Bengal. Tanjore city stands in a rich region and rivals in grandeur the great cities of Europe—and is perhaps superior to most of them in strength because of its well-designed fortifications, the walls of which are mounted by artillery of bronze and iron. Had its nayak supplied Tanjore with enough good soldiers, especially those called "Rager" (Rajputs?), its citadel could easily have withstood the onslaughts of the "Turks." The armies of the "Turks" had no cannons to batter its walls, or even firearms. Fighting with bows, arrows, swords, and lances, the "Turks" overwhelmed Tanjore by sheer numbers.[224]

The second city of Tanjore is "Manaracoil" (*Mannārkovil* or Mannargudi) situated just east of the capital on another plain. The nayak makes his residence here to be near the celebrated idol called "Mannar" (*Mannāru*, or Vishnu) from which the city gets its name.[225] The nayak believes that this god is his father and is consequently devoted to this cult. At one time he had magnificent palaces in this city, but the Brahmans induced him to demolish them and to build others at great expense to himself and the people. His new palace is of a fine design but its ornamentation remains unfinished. It was here that he received the Portuguese emissaries from Negapatam to whom he promised aid in their coming struggle with the Dutch. Negapatam, however, fell to the Dutch in 1658 before his army arrived there. And in a short while the "Turks" took absolute mastery of this opulent state. His subjects believe that the cause for his ruin was his betrayal of the Portuguese who had helped by their trade to enrich the country. Christianity, in its Catholic form, consequently lost out in Negapatam and throughout Tanjore.

The third city of Tanjore is "Vallancotte" (*Vallan Kōttai*, or "the mighty fortress") and it is situated on a huge rock just to the west of the capital. As the citadel and frontier fortress of the nayakdom, it is heavily fortified and has but a single gate of entry. When the "Turks" came, the nayak sent his

---

[223] *Ibid.*, pp. 87–139. A reference to the "War of the Noses" of 1656–57 in which Kanthirava Narasa Raja of Mysore sought to punish Madura for its betrayal of the empire. See Sathyanatha Aiyar, *op. cit.* (n. 24), pp. 135–36. Also see above, p. 873.

[224] The "Turks," in this case, were the forces of Bijapur.

[225] The ruler was Vijayaraghava Nayaka (r. 1633–73) who was better known as Mannarudasa. For his reign see Vriddhagirisan, *op. cit.* (n. 22), chap. viii. *Mannāru* was the nayak's family god. See *ibid.*, p. 26, n. 9.

treasure and his favorite wives to what he believed to be his impregnable fortress. But when the "Turks" took "Manaracōil" quickly, he fled into an almost inaccessible forest called "Palvacades" (*kādu* means "forest" in Tamil). The "Turks" chose not to follow him but to proceed directly to "Vallancotte." Its defenders, discouraged by their nayak's flight, left the fortress themselves and took the nayak's treasure with them. On their desertion, the "Larrons" plundered the city and then the "Turks" occupied it without trouble, capturing only the prisoners sequestered there. While the "Turks" are now masters of this rich and fertile land, they do not want to occupy it permanently, but are content simply to extort tribute.[226]

The Jesuit residence at Tanjore had before it a large stone inscribed with the nayak's permission to preach Christianity in his land. This inscription served to keep the "Ioques" quiet and to let the Hindus generally know that it was legal to become a convert. However, the nayak himself, a man of vacillating character, would occasionally turn against the Jesuits because of the baneful influence of the Brahmans and a certain eunuch adviser at his court. The nayak, a follower of "Perumal" (Vishnu), determined to make a pilgrimage to "Ramanacor" (Ramesvaram) to bathe in the waters where "Perumal" had once bathed. As part of their preparation the nayak and his entourage shaved themselves from head to toe. Even though pilgrimages are expensive affairs, the nayak felt compelled to give rich gifts also to the local deity to keep it from becoming jealous and vindictive. Despite his devotion to "Perumal," the nayak shows a certain curiosity about Christianity. He questions a young convert who is Grand Master of the Royal Wardrobe about his beliefs. On another occasion he employs a native painter, who had worked in the churches of Negapatam, to make a painting showing the principal Christian mysteries and to explain to him their meanings. The painter, whose understanding was probably vague at best, explains the story of Christ by associating its mysteries with Indian traditions that "we read about in our books."[227]

Finally, Magistris digresses to the subject of the "Larrons," a people who live for the most part by theft. They inhabit the forest south of "Tricierapelli" (Tiruchirapalli) and along the coast. Some are wild and widely scattered but Magistris' comments refer only to those who "form an entity in a Republic divided into Cantons," which is subject to the nayak of Madura. These "Larrons" number thousands, and they support an army of six thousand good soldiers. While they live by pillage, they are unbelievably hospitable to strangers. Christians from other parts are free to go there and to build their own houses and churches. Some "Larrons" are themselves Christians converted by the Jesuits. Since they are of one caste, the "Larrons" are easier to convert and they are all free to attend the same church. Their forests are so

[226] Magistris, *op. cit.* (n. 211), pp. 237–49.
[227] *Ibid.*, pp. 250–317 *passim*.

deep and impenetrable that they need no forts for protection. The governors appointed by Madura levy heavy taxes on them and will often punish them by burning their villages and churches. One of the "Larron" captains, a famous brigand called "Maicondono," was converted to Christianity and thereafter became a protector of Christian refugees.[228]

Much of what Magistris reports on Madura and Tanjore can be found in the letters of his Jesuit contemporaries; indeed, certain passages seem to have been reproduced almost verbatim from their informative letters.[229] The Jesuit residence in Madura, the largest in the nayakdom, is run by Balthasar da Costa (d. 1673), who first arrived there in 1639, with the help of Jean Fereira. Father Joseph Francis Arcolino, who dresses as a sannyasi, studies Tamil and Sanskrit at Madura. At Tiruchirapalli, Emanuel Alvarez is imprisoned by "Cupejando," the governor, on the insistence of the "Ioques." Emanuel Martinz (1597–1656), superior of the residence at Tiruchirapalli, dies while fleeing the city during an attack by Mysore. Leonardo Cinamo (1609–76), a Neapolitan, is transferred along with Fortunat Senataccio of Lucca from their posts in Mysore to the mountain refuges of these displaced Christians.[230] At Tanjore the mission is headed by Antão Proenza (1625–66), a Portuguese Jesuit who compiled an important Tamil vocabulary; he is aided by Estienne (Stefano) de Arez. Magistris concludes his work with eulogies to and biographical sketches of the Jesuits who had died in the Madura and Tanjore missions.[231]

Philippus Baldaeus (1632–72), a Dutch clergyman who was in the East from 1655 to 1666, traveled much more in south India and Ceylon than Roger and other sedentary preachers. On his return home Baldaeus prepared for publication his *Naauwkeurige beschryvinge van Malabar en Choromandel, der zelver aangrenzende ryken, en het machtige eyland Ceylon* . . . (1672).[232] This book, like that of Roger, is based on a thorough examination and adaptation of the works of earlier European authors and on letters from the files of the VOC. He sometimes acknowledges his debt to others and sometimes he unabashedly plagiarizes them. Generally, although not always, he credits his

---

[228] *Ibid.*, pp. 317–73 *passim*. By the "Larrons" Magistris is referring to the *Koḷḷars*, a term used for thieves in general and, in particular, for the inhabitants of certain regions of Madura headed by local chieftains technically required to pay tribute to Madura. The *Koḷḷars* who live in the vicinity of Madura city are related to the Maravas of the Fishery Coast to whom Magistris refers here. See Thurston, *op. cit.* (n. 108), III, 53–91.

[229] For example, see Bertrand, *op. cit.* (n. 61), II, 317–400.

[230] Cinamo founded the Jesuit mission in Mysore in 1648. For its history see D. Ferroli, S.J., *The Jesuits in Mysore* (Kozhikode, 1955).

[231] *Op cit.* (n. 211), pp. 372–432. He gives sketches of the careers of "Nobili, Roman" (pp. 375–406), "Simon Morato, Portuguese" (pp. 410–17), "Estienne Daresi [de Arez], Portuguese" (pp. 417–21), "Gabriel Lentecoskhi, of Lithuania near Orsa [Warsaw]" (pp. 412–32). Biographies of "Daresi" and "Lentecoskhi" do not appear in the standard Jesuit reference works.

[232] In what follows our references are to the English version published in A. and J. Churchill, *CV* (3d ed.; London, 1774–76), III, 509–793.

non-Portuguese sources, such as Roger, Twist, and Kircher. Part III, his *Afgoderye der Oost-Indische heydenen,*[233] is his attempt to deal with Hinduism. Since this section of his work applies mainly to west coast Hinduism, we have dealt with it in our discussion of Malabar. Baldaeus' materials on the inland and coastal regions of Ceylon are taken up in chapter 12.[234]

In his description of the Coromandel Coast, Baldaeus is best, perhaps because of his personal experiences, on its physical features, political alignments, products, and trade. The "kingdom" of Karnatak, he asserts, extends 210 Dutch miles (or 630 English miles) from south to north and 120 Dutch miles (or 360 miles) from Pulicat to the Malabar coast. Its coast extends from Tuticorin in the south to Masulipatam in the north. Tuticorin and the Fishery Coast are swept by furious winds from October to December and in the winter the land is deluged with sudden and heavy rains. From January to March the days are terribly hot, but the nights are kept cool by heavy fogs. Even though Tuticorin and "Comoryn" (*Kumarī,* or Cape Comorin) are close to each other, they have quite different seasons. From April to September those south of the cape mountains enjoy summer's calm; those on the north side suffer from the tempestuous winds of winter. Baldaeus accounts for this difference by reference to the mountains of the cape, like those at the Cape of Good Hope, which act as a partition between summer and winter.[235]

Three great nayaks rule the Karnatak empire as vassals of the emperor at Vellore to whom they pay annual tribute and perform personal services. The "Vitapanaike" (Virappa Nayaka, who ruled for only three or four months in 1659)[236] of Madura is the emperor's basin-bearer; the "Christapanaike" (Krishnappa Nayaka) of "Chengier" (Gingee) is the emperor's betel-box-bearer, and the nayak of Tanjore is his umbrella-bearer. They are all obliged to attend personally the emperor's coronation. Payment of annual tribute insures their hereditary rights to power.[237]

Tuticorin is "properly no more than a large village, without walls, ditches or gates." It boasts three large churches and numerous houses built of stone; in this region the best lime in India is found. The Dutch have installed their factory in one of the churches, and several times have tried unsuccessfully to obtain permission from the local nayak to build a fort. The Paravas, despite

[233] See above, pp. 493–94, 911–12.

[234] See above, pp. 910–18, 946–47.

[235] Excessively heavy rainfall occurs in summer when a main westerly current of air from over the Bay of Bengal meets the Western Ghats at nearly right angles and flows across peninsular India. See Glenn T. Trewartha, *An Introduction to Climate* (New York, 1954), p. 98.

[236] See D. Devakunjari, *Madurai through the Ages* (Madras, 1957), p. 189.

[237] This may be a thumbnail sketch of the traditional relations previously obtaining between the nayaks and the emperor. Baldaeus, after all, probably learned of these relationships from informants who were not certain themselves as to who would emerge victorious from the series of wars that went on in south India from 1656 to 1660. For the above geographical and political descriptions see *CV* (1774–76 ed.), III, 585–86, 590.

Baldaeus' efforts to reform them, remain stubborn in their devotion to Catholicism and look upon the Dutch as iconoclasts and the enemies of their religion who drove out the Portuguese in 1658. Pearls from the Mannar fishery are marketed at Tuticorin. These pearls are not comparable in color or brightness to those obtained from Ormuz. But pearl dust is shipped from here to Europe, where it is used in making "cordial medicines." Tuticorin is "much regarded" by the VOC, since it produces good textiles and provides "plenty of eatables," such as rice and sugar.[238]

Between Tuticorin and the island of "Rammanakoyel" (temple of Rama) live the Paravas to whom Xavier taught Christianity. Here may still be seen a number of their churches, especially at "Baipaar" (Vaipar) and "Manapaar" (*Maṇappārai*). The island itself abounds with cattle and is dominated by a "Teuver" (*tēvar*, a deity), or the temple of the lord of the island, situated on the shore. This temple is said to contain "an incredible treasure." The lord of the island has built a strong fort facing the Coromandel Coast, where Baldaeus and a friend were held captive for a short while in 1662. Its cannons command the narrow strait separating the island from the mainland, through which ships pass when traveling between Negapatam and northern Ceylon. The passage is so narrow and shallow that it can readily be blocked by dropping a few stones into its channel.[239]

The southern parts of Coromandel are subject for the most part to the nayaks of Madura and Tanjore. From the mainland port of "Tondy" (Tondi) large numbers of cattle are exported to Jaffnapatam in Ceylon. Near Tondi on the road to Negapatam stands a lofty temple called "Kailiemeer" (Calimere). Negapatam, or "city of serpents," is so named because its region abounds in poisonous snakes called "Cobres Capellos" (hooded cobras), which are revered by the natives. In 1658 this city was captured by the Dutch "without striking a stroke." The Portuguese residents there were permitted to depart with their goods in ships provided by the VOC. While the city is situated on the shore, its harbor, like most of those on the Coromandel Coast, is not adequate. Baldaeus visited Negapatam in 1660 to preach the Reformed faith. He found the city in confusion because of the sieges it had recently experienced at the hands of the nayak of Tanjore and the "king" of Bijapur. Overrun by these invading armies, the people of the countryside fled to Negapatam for rice and security. Many sold themselves into slavery; five thousand of the slaves bought by the Dutch were sent to Jaffnapatam, an equal number to Colombo, and several thousand to Batavia. On the north

---

[238] *Ibid.*, pp. 584–85.
[239] *Ibid.*, p. 581. At this time the island was technically under the jurisdiction of Chokkanatha, the nayak of Madura from 1659 to 1682. The "lord of the island" was Raghunatha Setupati, a vassal of Madura who was not then cooperating with his overlord in fighting the southward advance of the Muslims. See K. Rajayyan, *Rise and Fall of the Poligars of Tamilnadu* (Madras, 1974), pp. 8–9.

side of the city stands a temple called "China" (China).²⁴⁰ Near it there is the former summer residence of Francisco d'Almeyda, a rich Portuguese who now lives in Tranquebar. The Dutch at Negapatam, under occasional pressure from Tanjore, successfully repelled an attack in 1659.²⁴¹

North of Negapatam a number of coastal towns are worth mentioning. "Carcol" (Karikal) produces "rambotyns" (*rambutins*), white cotton textiles much in demand by the Japanese. A bit further north is the Danish fort at Tranquebar. It has four bulwarks and a garrison, mainly of Negroes and "Topasses" (Luso-Asians), under the command of Erkel Andres. Its variegated population of Hindus, Moors, and Portuguese live mainly from the loot they gain from piracy and from raids on the neighboring Muslim territories.²⁴² At Porto Novo (Newhaven) a few Portuguese merchants still do business, and the Dutch now have a factory at Tegnapatam. Next to this town lies "Tirepaplier" (Tirupapuliyur in Cudalore) with its fortress in which the Dutch factory was formerly housed. It also boasts a large temple with a lofty stone tower that is flat on top; this tower, like the old fortress formerly held by the Portuguese, serves as a guide to mariners. This town is under the jurisdiction of "Christappaneyk" (Krishnappa Nayaka), the ruler of Gingee.

The nayak of Gingee has his residence at "Chengier" (Gingee), about two days' journey inland north of Tirupapuliyur. This is a very populous city three times the size of Rotterdam. It is located in a pleasant valley that has a delightful river to its south. The city of Gingee is enclosed within double stone walls and has fortresses perched on three of the great rocks that surround it, and a temple on the fourth. The rocks are enclosed at their bases with strong stone walls whose gates are guarded by a considerable number of soldiers. Steps are cut into the steep, straight sides of the rocks, but even by this route, their crowns are virtually inaccessible. On the tops of these huge rocks there are springs, ponds, and gardens. Outside the city, another fortress stands upon a rock which commands the city's main entrance. The nayak's fortified palace is snugly and pleasantly situated between two of the four great rocks within the city. They have only a few large cannons and those are primitively made of long, broad bars of iron held together with iron hoops. From these guns they shoot stone balls, like those which fell on Negapatam in the siege of 1658–59. The countryside of Gingee abounds in rice, salt, fruits, and other edibles. Still, because of the vast numbers living in the city, provisions must be imported from abroad. Exports are mainly cotton and woolen textiles. The commodities imported and marketed in-

---

²⁴⁰ This was a four-sided brick tower that was destroyed in 1867. See *Manual of the Administration of Madras Presidency* (Madras, 1893), III, 581; also Sir Walter Elliot, "The Edifice Formerly Known as the Chinese or Jaina Pagoda at Negapatam," *Indian Antiquary,* VII (1878), 224–27.
²⁴¹ *CV* (1774–76 ed.), III, 587–88. See the engraved map of the city between pp. 586 and 587.
²⁴² On the Danes at Tranquebar see above, pp. 88–93.

clude the fine spices, pepper, sandalwood, Chinese silks, velvets, satins, carpets, raw silk, *Patana* (silk of Patan, a weaving center northwest of Ahmadabad) girdles, musk, cinnabar, quicksilver, tin, lead, and copper. But they import no porcelain or Chinese camphor.[243]

Resuming his coastal itinerary northward, Baldaeus briefly mentions the towns between Tirupapuliyur and Pulicat. San Thomé was seized from the Portuguese by the Moors "about eight or nine years ago."[244] At nearby St. George the English maintain a fortress garrisoned by Luso-Asians and mestizos. Pulicat, "the old fort" in Tamil, is protected by the VOC's new Fort Geldria with its garrison of eighty to ninety men. Pulicat has a good harbor that is a haven during the south monsoon. A nearby forest supplies Pulicat with wood for fuel and construction. The land in this region is so nitrous and sandy that it is unable to produce anything nutritious in quantity. It dries out almost totally during the south monsoon and floods during the north monsoon.[245] North of Pulicat lie "Penna" (Penner) and "Caleture" (Kal-turai); between these two towns are found the "essaye-roots" (chay or dye root) used by dyers.[246] The safest harbor on the coast during the north monsoon is "Petapouli" (Petapoli or Peetapolee), a small coastal town inhabited by Moors, Persians, and native Indians. It is subject politically to Golconda. In the vicinity of Petapoli grow the best "essaye roots," called "Tambrevelle" (Tamil, *tamirai-valayam*, a lotus root used for dyeing). Consequently, the painted and dyed cloths of Petapoli are even finer than those of Masulipatam. Its governor monopolizes textile production, for which he pays to Golconda an annual tribute, mostly in the cloths themselves. The governor employs the weavers himself and strictly controls the town's textile trade. Most of the local cloths are exported to Persia.

Masulipatam is a great trading center located near a large river. Its resident governor pays an annual tribute to Golconda which he squeezes out of the city's inhabitants, especially the Hindus. He and the local Persians and Moors together control the textile industry and trade. To conduct profitable trade in textiles is difficult, because monopolies of both production and distribution are farmed out to the highest bidder. It is essential to have royal patents for successful trading, but they are difficult to obtain, for the gover-

---

[243] *CV* (1774–76 ed.), III, 589. On the city of Gingee in earlier seventeenth-century literature see above, p. 1004; for a modern description of the ruined city see Srinivasachari, *op. cit.* (n. 18), chap. i. Baldaeus probably visited Gingee before it was taken by Bijapur in 1660; possibly he was there in 1659 or 1660.

[244] In 1662 Golconda drove the Portuguese out of San Thomé. For further detail on San Thomé, an engraved ground plan, and a map of south India as of *ca.* 1662 see the book of Johann Nieuhof (1618–72), who was in this region at about the same time as Baldaeus, entitled: . . . *Zee- en lant-reize door verscheide gewesten van Oostindien* . . . (Amsterdam, 1682), pp. 106–7.

[245] For further description and a ground plan of Pulicat see *ibid.*, pp. 112–13.

[246] "Chay" is spelled in various ways, including "saia," "shaii," and "shaya root," in the seventeenth-century sources. These spellings are all derived from Tamil *cāyam*.

nors oppose their issuance and the court is too far away to make simple a direct approach to the king or to bribe an influential courtier. The biggest trade is in gems and diamonds.[247]

Baldaeus then launches into a discourse, lengthy for him, on precious stones and the trade in them. Diamonds are called "Jutan" (?) by the Tamils;[248] Baldaeus describes how they are valued and cut in India. The rubies sold in Masulipatam are bigger and brighter than German rubies. Emeralds, called "Jasche" (Hindi, *yashm*) by the Indians, are so valuable that glass imitations are made at Pulicat and Chandragiri. Sapphires are found on both coasts of south India and in Ceylon, but those found in Siam and Pegu are superior and bring higher prices. The amethysts of the East Indies are preferred to all others. Amber from Königsberg and other places in East Prussia is held "in great esteem among the Japoneses and the Indians in general." Possibly they are beguiled by the shapes and light which can be seen in it and by its ability to attract "straw, paper, and such light matters."[249] This is followed by lengthy discussions of the bezoar stone and indigo. The Dutch in the Eastern ports have come "of late years" to prefer China tea to their ordinary drink made of water and sugar boiled together.[250]

Here follows his short introduction to the "Malabar language" (Tamil) with alphabet, grammatical rules, examples, transliterations, and translations of the Lord's Prayer and the Creed.[251] In his preface to this first printed Tamil grammar, Baldaeus acknowledges that the Portuguese Jesuits had preceded him in analyzing the Tamil language according to European (*i.e.,* Latin) grammatical principles. Father Gasper d'Aquilar, a Portuguese Jesuit about whom nothing else appears to be known, "excelled in the uncovering of the Malabaric language." While in Jaffnapatam for three and one-half years, Baldaeus had as an interpreter a native speaker of Tamil who was also well versed in Portuguese. This convert, named François, translated the Portuguese versions of the Lord's Prayer and the Creed into Tamil, as well as Baldaeus' own analysis of these prayers. He also wrote, in excellent Tamil script, the alphabet and the grammatical examples. Baldaeus admits that he himself had to struggle valiantly to master the Tamil letters "first learning with the children to write in the sand." After a while he began to use a stylus and to write letters on palm leaves.[252] But, he concludes, "I consider myself, not an accomplished man, but hardly yet a youth in the knowledge of that

[247] *CV* (1774–76 ed.), III, 590–91. *Cf.* earlier accounts above, pp. 1019–22.
[248] Tamil *vairame* means "diamond."
[249] Amber was one of a very few European natural products that could readily be marketed in the East. At the end of the seventeenth century, Leibniz hoped to use the amber of Brandenburg-Prussia to help finance some of his projects designed to encourage German religious and intellectual relations with China.
[250] *CV* (1774–76 ed.), III, 591–95.
[251] For other early examples of printed Tamil, see pls. 139–44, 147.
[252] See pl. 173.

language." In his brief grammar Baldaeus remarks that he possesses a more complete grammar, which might one day appear in print.[253]

The fabled diamond mines of Golconda regularly attracted European as well as Asian merchants, jewelers, and adventurers. In England, the word "Golconda" would quickly become a synonym for a "mine of wealth."

Jean Baptiste Tavernier (1605–89), French Huguenot adventurer and merchant, began making a series of trips to India, five in all from 1638 to 1667. Tavernier was in Golconda, or the Qutb Shahi sultanate, in 1641–42, 1645, 1651, 1653, and 1659–60. On his return to France in 1668, Tavernier was interviewed by King Louis XIV, who conferred upon him the title of Baron d'Aubonne for his services to France. Once settled on his estate near Geneva, Tavernier began to organize his voluminous notes and to prepare a text for publication. In this enterprise he was aided by Samuel Chappuzeau (*ca.* 1625–1701), a writer of modest distinction and a fellow Huguenot. They amplified Tavernier's materials with data obtained from other travelers and their publications, sometimes with, and sometimes without, due acknowledgment. At Paris in 1676–77 Tavernier published in two volumes *Les six voyages . . . qu'il fait en Turquie, en Perse, et aux Indes*. This work, with its engravings, was published by Chez Gervais Clouzier et Claude Barbin.[254] The original almost immediately became popular, for it sparked controversies with respect to its veracity. No doubt lingers in our day about the essential truthfulness of this work or of its value for the study of India in the mid-seventeenth century, though admittedly it needs to be used with care and constantly checked.[255]

[253] For a modern English translation of the introduction and the grammar, as well as new transliterations following modern Tamil pronunciation, see J. A. B. van Buitenen and P. C. Ganeshsundaram, "A Seventeenth-Century Dutch Grammar of Tamil," *Bulletin of the Deccan College Research Institute* (Poona), XIV (1952–53), 168–82. One cannot help but wonder whether Baldaeus' "more complete grammar," so far not known, might not have been, in fact, the work of the mysterious Father Gasper d'Aquilar. It was Baldaeus, after all, who "liberated" Fenicio's work on Hinduism and published it without acknowledgment (see above, p. 911). Tamil dictionaries were compiled and circulated by the Jesuits in south India, particularly by those who worked at Jaffnapatam and Madura. One of those manuscripts most widely circulated was prepared, primarily at Jaffnapatam, by the Italian Jesuit Ignacio Bruno (1576–1659). See Xavier S. Thani Nayagam, "Antão de Proença's Tamil-Portuguese Dictionary, 1679. An Introduction," *Tamil Culture*, XI (1964), pp. 117–19. Proença's dictionary was printed by the Jesuit press in Ambalacat, Malabar. European scholars generally knew it only by report until Thani Nayagam in 1954 found a copy at the Vatican Library (Borg. Ind. 12) which had belonged originally to the library of the Sacred Congregation of the Propaganda. In 1966 he published *Antão de Proença's Tamil-Portuguese Dictionary, A.D. 1679* (Kuala Lumpur), a photocopy of the original.

[254] V. Ball's *Travels in India by Jean Baptiste Tavernier, Baron of Aubonne* was reprinted as recently as 1977 in Pakistan. A second edition of Ball's translation, edited by William Crooke (2 vols; London, 1925), is the best critical edition available.

[255] Before the end of the century it appeared in at least seven further French reprints and was translated into English (1677, 1678, 1680, 1684, 1688), German (1681), Dutch (1682), and Italian (1682). See above, pp. 416–18.

Jean de Thévenot (1633–67), fellow countryman of Tavernier and also an ardent traveler, was in India in 1666. He, too, spent a portion of his time at Golconda in the course of traversing the subcontinent. Like Tavernier, he was conversant in several Middle Eastern languages, including Persian, and was in a good position to understand much of what he saw and heard from the ruling Muslims of Golconda. His *Relations* were published in successive parts between 1664 and 1684, with the *Relation de l'Indoustan* (Paris) appearing only in 1684 for the first time.²⁵⁶ In 1670 Friar Domingo Navarrete (1618–86), the Spanish Dominican spokesman in the Chinese rites controversy, landed at Mylapore (Madras) on his way back to Europe from China. From here he traveled overland to Golconda and Masulipatam, from whose port he sailed for Surat. His tracts for the times, the *Tratados historicos,* were published at Madrid in 1676.²⁵⁷

Since the capital of Golconda was located well into the interior, these three European travelers provide rich materials on the routes, stages, and conditions of travel around and after mid-century. The two Frenchmen provide itineraries for the journey from Surat to Golconda; all three authors give itineraries for the route commonly followed from Golconda to Masulipatam. They all give, in greater or lesser detail, something about the conditions of overland travel from Masulipatam to Madras, the region then being invaded by Golconda. Throughout these parts of India, they observe, goods are ordinarily carried on the backs of oxen and in carts drawn by ten or twelve oxen. For safety, individuals and goods usually travel in caravans, the people riding in small, light carriages (*tongas*) pulled by two oxen. Horses, elephants, and camels are used primarily in the rainy season. Those persons who can afford it buy or hire palanquins, the most comfortable form of overland journeying; teams of twelve men take turns in carrying the litter. Since the route from Golconda to Masulipatam is so rough, wheeled vehicles are generally replaced by palanquins and pack animals. Distances are measured in "gos" (*coss*), a variable unit that equaled around eight English miles in south India at this time.

Many of the larger rivers are without bridges or ferries; consequently they are crossed in coracles, small basketlike boats covered on the outside with ox hides and on the inside with carpets. The coracles are propelled by four men who stand in their corners and row with paddles. In the lowlands the roads are lined with trees and whitened stones to make travel easier by

---

²⁵⁶His first three travel books were published under one title in 1689 as *Voyages de M. de Thévenot tant en Europe qu'en Asie et en Afrique* (5 vols.; Paris). This version was reissued repeatedly in French during the eighteenth century and translated into Dutch (1681), English (1687), and German (1693). The English edition of the Indian portion is reproduced in Surendranath Sen (ed.), *Indian Travels of Thevenot and Careri* (New Delhi, 1949). For bibliographic details see above, p. 411.

²⁵⁷For his brief tour in India see J. S. Cummins (ed.), *The Travels and Controversies of Friar Domingo Navarrete, 1618–86* (2 vols.; "H.S.," 2d ser., CXVIII, CXIX; Cambridge, 1962). The materials relating to his Coromandel tour are in Vol. II, pp. 297–326.

night, the preferred time, particularly for foreigners unaccustomed to the sweltering heat of daytime. The roads near the cities are crowded with animals and men, and frequently by processions of pilgrims. Food and lodgings are readily available on the main routes and not overly difficult to find elsewhere. The inns in both villages and towns called "Chauril" (*choultry*) are shelters without doors, in which the traveler is perfectly safe despite the fact that they are wide open to all the world. Leather bottles made in Golconda keep milk and other liquids cool and fresh for the traveler. Frequent tolls and corrupt, overbearing collectors are constant irritants. The toll collectors of Golconda are much worse extortioners than similar officials of the Mughul Empire, for they are Brahman agents of Islamic private tax farmers rather than royal appointees; they consequently exact as much as the traffic will bear for themselves and their employers over and above the stipulated tax. Official letters are almost always carried by relays of runners, the fastest and best organized means of communication in Golconda.[258]

The "kingdom of Golconda," one of the most powerful states of the Deccan, is bordered on the east by the Bay of Bengal, on the north by the mountains of Orissa, on the south by the several remnants of Vijayanagar, and on the west by the province of "Balagate" (Balaghat) belonging to the Mughul Empire and by Bijapur, the domain of the 'Adil Shah.[259] The frontier between the Mughul Empire and Golconda is marked by plantings of trees on either side of a rivulet near Calvar: "mahouas" (Hindi, *muhovas*) on the Mughul bank and "cadjours" (*khajurs*), or wild palms, on the Golconda bank.[260] From this frontier to Bhagnagar,[261] the common Hindu name for the capital city of Hyderabad, it is a journey of six days by caravan through a countryside dotted with villages and small towns, resplendent with green fields of rice and wheat, and replete with reservoirs. Hyderabad stands on a high plateau and is hemmed in by little hills. The approach to the city itself runs through a lengthy suburb of mud-and-straw huts in which brokers, artisans, and merchants dwell. The road terminates at a bridge over the "Nerva" River, evidently a stream which ran into the Musi River.[262]

Bhagnagar, or Hyderabad, is often called Golconda from the name of the

---

[258] Based on Tavernier with additions from Thévenot and Navarrete. See Ball and Crooke (eds.), *op. cit.* (n. 254), I, 9, 34–39, 119–20, 141–42, 232–34, 235–36, 239; Sen (ed.), *op. cit.* (n. 256), pp. 130–32, 146, 150; Cummins (ed.), *op. cit.* (n. 257), II, 306, 310, 313. For a modern discussion of the trunk roads, based in part on Tavernier and Thévenot, see Sherwani, *op. cit.* (n. 76), pp. 493–502.

[259] For a map of the Qutb Shahi dominions as of about 1670 (including roads and highways) see Sherwani, *op. cit.* (n. 76), facing p. 493.

[260] The Mahwah-tree (*Bassia latifolia*) and the wild date palm (*Phoenix sylvestris*) are both common trees which grow to a height of about forty feet. See Drury, *op. cit.* (n. 93), pp. 69–70, 340–41.

[261] Bhagnagar means "Place of Gardens." Hyderabad is the Persian or Islamic name of the city.

[262] Thévenot in Sen (ed.), *op. cit.* (n. 256), pp. 130–32; and Tavernier in Ball and Crooke (eds.), *op. cit.* (n. 254), I, 121–23.

old fortress nearby, where the king resides and holds court. This new capital was built by the great-grandfather of the present ruler at the request of one of his wives.[263] It was built a few miles east of Golconda city and across the Musi River; at the end of the bridge are surrounding walls that are little more than barriers.[264] According to Thévenot, "the Town makes a kind of Cross, much longer than broad, and extends in a straight line from the Bridge to the four Towers [*Chārminār*]."[265] Almost the size of Orleans in France, this new city was especially designed to accommodate the sultan, his nobles, and his bureaus. The bridge over the Musi, an edifice "scarcely less beautiful than the Pont Neuf at Paris," runs into a straight, wide road flanked on either side by inns and the houses of nobles. It leads directly to the great square where the sultan gives public audiences and administers justice. The royal palace stands on one side of the square and abuts on the "Four Towers."[266] Its heavy stone walls are topped at intervals with "half-Towers," and pierced with many windows; from its balconies, elevated gardens, terraced roofs, and open galleries, the courtiers can watch the activities in the square: musical performances, processions, and even elephant fights. The palace is served by a special water system. Water brought from a distant reservoir is stored on the top of the square "Four Towers" monument. From here it is conveyed by pipes to the royal palace and even into its highest apartments. Admission to the royal palace is almost never granted to outsiders with no specific business there. While the "Four Towers" is the city's most impressive structure, its external appearance is spoiled by the ugly wood-and-straw fruit shops which surround it.[267]

Like any early Islamic city, Hyderabad boasts mosques and gardens. Thrust into the Telingana plateau, this Muslim capital preserves a Hindu tradition in its two great tanks, or artificial lakes. These were constructed as part of the city's irrigation system and as a boating resort for the sultan.[268] About fifty years before Tavernier's visit, the construction of a mosque was undertaken which "will be the grandest in India if it should be completed." The French traveler expresses "special astonishment" at the huge size of the

---

[263] Muhammad Quli (1580–1612) built this magnificent new Islamic city on a grid pattern. Begun in 1589, it was mostly completed by 1600. See Sherwani, *op. cit.* (n. 76), facing p. 543 for a plan of the city's layout at this time.

[264] Evidently the planners felt that the defense of Hyderabad could be assumed by the Golconda fort. See Richards, *loc. cit.* (n. 77), p. 2.

[265] Sen (ed.), *op. cit.* (n. 256), p. 132. The four major roads intersect at the precise center of the grid, which was marked by a towering central monument called the *Chārminār*, or "Four Towers." For a photograph of the "Four Towers," as it stands today, see Sherwani, *op. cit.* (n. 76), facing p. 544.

[266] Thévenot is evidently mistaken in placing the palace immediately adjacent to the "Four Towers." See Sherwani, *op. cit.* (n. 76), p. 305.

[267] Based on Tavernier in Ball and Crooke (eds.), *op. cit.* (n. 254), I, 122–24; and Thévenot in Sen (ed.), *op. cit.* (n. 256), pp. 132–33. On the water system see Sherwani, *op. cit.* (n. 76), p. 304.

[268] The tanks still exist. See Richards, *loc. cit.* (n. 77), p. 2.

stones that were laboriously quarried and transported for its construction.[269] But perhaps even more impressive than the city's buildings are its gardens. Thévenot waxes eloquent over their beauty, symmetry, and waterworks. He describes in some detail the internal plan of what seems to be the *Bāgh Lingampalli,* a garden then on the city's outskirts.[270] Tavernier comments on the tombs of the sultans located near the fort of Golconda and exclaims: "When you wish to see something beautiful, you should go to see these tombs on the day of a festival, for then, from morning to evening, they are covered with rich carpets."[271] Every one of the six mausoleums is set in the middle of a garden, according to Thévenot, who was permitted, although a stranger, to enter these sacred precincts.[272]

In Thévenot's day, the fort of Golconda, situated around five miles west of Hyderabad city, was the actual seat of government and the regal residence.[273] This fortress town was founded by "Cotup-Cha" (Quli Qutb Shah, r. 1512–43), who called it Golconda from the Telugu "Golcar" (*gulleru* or shepherd), after the shepherd who guided him to its site.[274] The fort is "of a large compass" and surrounded by stone walls and deep water-filled ditches. Cannons are mounted on five round towers and on the wall; the two gates which are kept open lead to a great inner gate guarded by armed Indians. To reach the sultan's quarters it is necessary to pass through twelve gates. Aside from the royal palace, Golconda includes little else but the houses of the nobles and a few bazaars. Most of the upper-level officials have houses within the fortress as well as at Hyderabad. The sultan, who keeps his treasure at Golconda, maintains jewelers and stonecutters in its palace at his own expense.[275]

The reigning sultan, Abdullah Qutb Shah (r. 1626–72), is a Shiite in religion and the seventh ruler of his dynasty.[276] Early in his reign he was overcome by the Mughuls and forced to pay them tribute.[277] He now maintains a

[269] Reference here is to the Jami Masjid, or principal mosque, started by Muhammad Quli (d. 1612). Actually this was the first mosque completed after the mosque on the top of the "Four Towers." For a description see Sherwani, *op. cit.* (n. 76), pp. 312–13.

[270] Sen (ed.), *op. cit.* (n. 256), pp. 133–35. Also see Sherwani, *op. cit.* (n. 76), pp. 310–11.

[271] Ball and Crooke (eds.), *op. cit.* (n. 254), I, 125. This is the great necropolis called the *Dā'irā Mīr Mu'min.* See Sherwani, *op. cit.* (n. 76), pp. 318–19. See our pl. 201.

[272] See his detailed description of the tombs in Sen, *op. cit.* (n. 256), pp. 139–40.

[273] After 1639, when it had become clear that Hyderabad could not be adequately protected, the sultan and the chief officers of the realm began again to be housed at Golconda. See Richards, *loc. cit.* (n. 77), p. 5.

[274] This is apparently the tradition accepted in Thévenot's day. Actually the founding sultan called it Muhammadnagar. He built it on the highest hill in the region, on the site of an older fort. See Sherwani, *op. cit.* (n. 76), p. 47.

[275] Sen (ed.), *op. cit.* (n. 256), pp. 137–38. For the plan of the fortress and its entryway see S. Toy, *The Strongholds of India* (London, 1957), pp. 54, 56. Also see below, p. 1090.

[276] Actually he was the sixth ruler in the Qutb Shah line. He was the son of his predecessor and of *Hayāt Bakhshī Bēgum,* daughter of the founder of Hyderabad. Thévenot is wrong in his assertion that the mother was "a Bramen lady." See Sen (ed.), *op cit.* (n. 256), p. 140.

[277] For the terms of the "Deed of Submission" (1636) see Sherwani, *op. cit.* (n. 76), pp. 436–37.

large army of five hundred thousand mercenary soldiers, or at least he pays wages for that number. In fact, the number of effectives is but half of what he pays for, since the "Omras" (*umarā*), or noble retainers, skim a great deal of the money intended for the soldiers. Native Indian levies are paid much less than the mercenary Mughuls and Persians; foreign cavalrymen are paid twice as much as infantrymen. Despite such precautions, the sultan was unable to keep Aurangzib from invading and pillaging Hyderabad. The sultan escaped the Mughul forces and took refuge at Golconda. Although he occasionally appeared thereafter at Hyderabad, "he hath not been there this eight years [before 1666]." [278]

In his forced retirement at the fortress of Golconda, Sultan Abdullah is "apprehensive of everything." He trusts nobody but the queen mother, his favorite "Sidy Mezafer" (Sayyid Muzaffar), and his Brahman advisers. In his isolation the sultan depends utterly on his advisers for information. In his weakness he does not dare to discipline his nobles even when they deserve it. His son-in-law usurps his place in the court and openly pretends to be his legitimate successor. To forget his woes the sultan "lives in worldly pleasures and pastimes, without the least regard to the Government." [279] He is attracted to learned men and artisans of all nationalities and is generous in patronizing them. [280] As the proprietor of all the lands in Golconda, the sultan derives vast revenues from farming them out to the highest bidder. His treasury is also replenished from port taxes, internal transit duties, and the monopoly of mining and the commerce in diamonds and precious stones. In fact, he derives a considerable revenue from practically every type of activity pursued in his territories. [281]

The "Omras" (*umarā*), or leading nobles of the kingdom, are for the most part Persians or their sons. They are extremely rich because of the pensions and tax farms they hold from the crown; they add to this wealth by the deceptions they practice and by the extraordinary exactions they demand from the Brahmans who are their tax farmers. In public they cut a very fine figure in the towns and display their riches in lavish processions in which

---

[278] Sen (ed.), *op. cit.* (n. 256), pp. 140–41. Hyderabad was taken early in 1656 and an armistice was granted Abdullah when the queen mother agreed to pay an indemnity, to give Abdullah's second daughter in marriage to Prince Muhammad Sultan, and to promise that this new son-in-law would succeed to the throne of Golconda. See Sherwani, *op. cit.* (n. 76), pp. 443–44. By 1667, when François Bernier was in Golconda, the ambassador of Aurangzib in Hyderabad "speaks and acts with the uncontrolled authority of an absolute sovereign." Although the sultan was clearly presiding over a state in decay, Bernier was assured that his weakness, indecision, and seeming indifference was "assumed for the purpose of deceiving his enemies." See A. Constable (trans. and ed.), *Travels in the Mogul Empire, A.D. 1656–1668, by François Bernier* (New Delhi, 1968), pp. 195–96.

[279] According to Navarrete in Cummins (ed.), *op. cit.* (n. 257), II, 315.

[280] Tavernier in Ball and Crooke (eds.), *op. cit.* (n. 254), I, 132, 138–39. He also encouraged portrait painting, especially of himself and his courtiers. See Sherwani, *op. cit.* (n. 76), pp. 540–43.

[281] Thévenot in Sen (ed.), *op. cit.* (n. 256), p. 142. See Sherwani, *op. cit.* (n. 76), pp. 485–86.

they are surrounded by retainers and servants. They mount guard around the towns with their horses, elephants, and camels from Monday to Monday. The changing of the guard in Hyderabad provided Tavernier with a weekly spectacle of pomp.[282] In addition to these great lords there are lesser "Omras" of little wealth or quality. The title has been adopted so freely and commonly that even low-paid Hindu officials "must needs be called Omras also."[283]

The people of Golconda, both men and women, are "well proportioned, of good stature, and of fair countenances, and it is only the peasantry who are somewhat dark in complexion." Soldiers cover the middle of their bodies with a breechcloth and knot their long hair on top of the head. From a belt they suspend "a broadsword like the Swiss." The muskets they carry are made of a better grade of iron and are superior to European firearms in that they are not so likely to burst. In the towns there are many public women who are officially registered and permitted legally to ply their trade. In the evening, when the shops selling *tārī* open their doors, these women put lighted lamps or candles in their doorways to attract customers.[284] It is possibly because the sultan derives substantial revenues from the tax on *tārī* that he legalizes prostitution. Public women also put on dancing and acrobatic performances for the king and his nobles.[285] While unregistered women are not permitted to prostitute themselves, commoners give their wives great freedom to appear in public places.[286]

Thévenot, on the return from his trip to Masulipatam, arrived at Hyderabad in time to witness the Muslim festival of "Hussein, the son of Aly."[287] In Golconda it is celebrated with more glitter and display than in Persia. For ten days they parade around the streets with their bodies and their costumes covered with sifted ashes. Soldiers dance in a circle and clap their extended swords together while crying "Hussein." In their numerous processions they carry a silver plate that represents Husain's hand. Everyone dresses extravagantly, and the public women take part in the festival as dancers. For their part, the local Hindus participate in this rite and make it into a holiday for themselves. The Sunnis mock the celebrants, and fights often break out

---

[282] Ball and Crooke (eds.), *op. cit.* (n. 254), I, 126–27.

[283] Thévenot in Sen (ed.), *op. cit.* (n. 256), pp. 143–44.

[284] *Tārī* (Hindi) is a popular liquor made from the fermented sap of the *tār* or palmyra. English "toddy" is a corruption of this word. See H. Yule and A. C. Burnell, *Hobson-Jobson* (London, 1968), p. 927. Also see Sherwani, *op. cit.* (n. 76), p. 487.

[285] See Tavernier in Ball and Crooke (eds.), *op. cit.* (n. 254), I, 127–28. *Cf.* the *devadāsis* of Hindu temples.

[286] Thévenot in Sen (ed.), *op. cit.* (n. 256), p. 136. See Sherwani, *op. cit.* (n. 76), pp. 520–21.

[287] The anniversary of the martyrdom of Isnam Husain, the second son of Ali and grandson of the Prophet. Known as the Ashura of Muharram, this festival is described on the basis of indigenous sources in I. A. Ghauri, "Kingship in the Sultanates of Bijapur and Golconda," *Islamic Culture*, XLVI (1972), 144–45. On these celebrations elsewhere in India, see above, pp. 790–91. Also pl. 132.

between the coreligionists. On the day following the festival "they make other processions, sing doleful ditties, and carry about coffins . . . with a Turban on each coffin to represent the interment of Hussein and his Men who were killed at the Battel of Kerbela by the forces of Calif Yezid."[288]

Many foreigners live and work in Hyderabad: Persians, Armenians, Mughuls, Portuguese, Luso-Asians, Africans, Dutch, French, English, and Spanish.[289] Most are employed as soldiers or engage in commerce. Navarrete held religious services for the Portuguese soldiers and visited the Dutch factory where he was given the "Cha [tea] of China" to drink.[290] He also visited the French envoys, whose leader spoke Spanish. The Frenchmen offered Navarrete passage on a French ship from Masulipatam to Surat, a favor which the Spanish friar readily accepted.[291] The English likewise have merchants in Hyderabad, but they are evidently no competition to the Dutch, who purchase textiles there for sale in the East Indies.[292] The most important foreigners are without doubt the Persians, who are involved in every form of activity and at the highest levels.

Hyderabad attracts foreign merchants because of its strategic location on internal trade routes, its tolerance for outsiders, and its special products. The painted cotton cloths of the coast, always in short supply, are supplemented by cloths of bright colors produced around Hyderabad. Plain spun cottons and local indigo are also available and cheap.[293] The Dutch exchange pepper at Hyderabad for opium and the tobacco which grows so abundantly in its region. Diamonds and other precious stones, particularly those of small size, abound in most of Golconda's marts. Many of the Indians, Muslims and Hindus alike, conclude their deals by silent barter carried on by means of hidden signs to prevent others from learning the prevailing prices.[294] New gold coins (*pagodes*) are made for the sultan of Golconda by the Dutch and English at their factories; these are the only coins accepted in exchange for

---

[288] Sen (ed.), *op. cit.* (n. 256), pp. 148–50. In A.D. 680 Husain, on the way from Mecca to Iraq to make good his claim to the caliphate, was massacred by the troops of al-Kufa on the plain of Karbela. The place where the decapitated bodies were buried soon became, and still is, a pilgrimage site for Shiites.

[289] For example, a Madrid apothecary was employed there as physician and surgeon to the royal army. See Navarrete in Cummins (ed.), *op. cit.* (n. 257), II, 313–14.

[290] *Ibid.*, p. 316. The Dutch factory, founded in 1661, is described in some detail by Daniel Havart. See below, pp. 1088–89.

[291] *Ibid.*, p. 317. A French delegation of 1669–70 to Golconda received the sultan's permission to carry on trade in his territories and to establish a factory at Masulipatam. See S. P. Sen, *The French in India. First Establishment and Struggle* (Calcutta, 1947), p. 68. François Martin, the founder of Pondicherry, was one of the envoys.

[292] See Thévenot in Sen (ed.), *op. cit.* (n. 256), pp. 135–36. On European trade rivalries in Golconda at this time see Raychaudhuri, *op. cit.* (n. 6), pp. 59–60.

[293] For a detailed discussion of the planting of *Indigofera tinctoria* and of its preparation as a dye see Tavernier in Ball and Crooke (eds.), *op. cit.* (n. 254), II, 7–9. Also see below, p. 1082.

[294] *Ibid.*, pp. 53–54. A common practice described by many other European writers, but not in so much detail.

the diamonds of Kollur.[295] The Dutch supply copper to the mint of Hydera-bad, which produces "Pechas" (Hindi, *paisā*) or common cash.[296]

All these European authors traveled the route from Hyderabad to Masuli-patam and they all found it difficult. Tavernier, the jewel merchant, was the only one to leave the direct route: he went to inspect the diamond mines on the Krishna River, seven days' journey east of the city of Golconda. The diamond deposits at Kallur, discovered about a century before Tavernier's first visit, employed by the mid-seventeenth century almost sixty thousand workers. The French merchant describes in detail how the men excavate the earth, which is then carried to previously selected washing and drying sites by the women and children. Once the earth is dried they winnow off the fine part and then pound the remaining clods until they are completely broken. It is in this pulverized clay that they search for diamonds. At Kallur they find an unusually large number of big stones which, unfortunately, are not as clear and bright as they should be.[297]

From Kallur, Tavernier followed the valley of the Krishna River to its out-let in the Bay of Bengal near Masulipatam. Thévenot stayed at Masulipatam with one of the French envoys just long enough to inform himself about the other trading ports along the Coromandel Coast. In the summer of 1652 Tavernier traveled southward from Masulipatam in search of "Mir Jumla" (Muhammad Sa'īd, the *Mīr Jumlā*),[298] the first minister of Golconda and the commander of its armies then operating in the Carnatic (Karnatak) king-dom. Mir Jumla was at Gandikota, a strategic fortress perched on a hill overlooking the Penner River in the Cuddapah district of Madras. From this fortress Mir Jumla commanded the inland region from Masulipatam to San Thomé in the name of the sultan of Golconda. Tavernier, informed by the Dutch about Mir Jumla's influence at court, hopes to obtain his permission to sell certain jewels to the sultan. On his way to the fortress Tavernier stops at Bezevada on the northern bank of the Krishna River. Here he visits a number of Hindu temples, which he describes in some detail, and he ob-serves that pilgrims visit them especially in October. At this point he crosses the Krishna and proceeds overland across Nellore to Pulicat, the site of the Dutch factory.

Received hospitably by the Dutch, Tavernier observes that there are gen-

---

[295] *Ibid.*, pp. 69–71.

[296] Thévenot in Sen (ed.), *op. cit.* (n. 256), p. 136. On the minting of copper coins see H. K. Sherwani, "The Reign of Abdu'l-lah Qutb Shah (1626–1672), Economic Aspects," *Journal of Indian History*, XLII (1964), 443–44.

[297] Ball and Crooke (eds.), *op. cit.* (n. 254), II, 56–62. Also see above, pp. 1026–27. *Cf.* Tavernier's account of the diamond mines he visited in Bijapur and Bengal. On the prices and weights of diamonds see Thévenot in Sen (ed.), *op. cit.* (n. 256), pp. 136–37.

[298] "Mir Jumla" is an office roughly equivalent at this time to Prime Minister. See Sherwani, *op. cit.* (n. 76), pp. 196–97. The European writers often use this title as if it were the personal name of the holder.

erally about two hundred soldiers at Pulicat's fort and many merchants and retirees of the VOC who live permanently in the town. He notices that the inhabitants of Pulicat obtain fresh water from holes that they dig into the coastal sand when the tide is out.[299] From Pulicat, Tavernier goes on to "Madras, otherwise called Fort St. George, which belongs to the English." Here he stays at the convent of the Capuchins with Fathers Ephrem de Nevers and Zeno de Bauge.[300] At San Thomé he visits the churches of the Augustinians and the Jesuits. He meets Portuguese and native Catholics who are employed by the Protestant English as soldiers and laborers.[301] After ten days in Madras and its environs, Tavernier strikes out northwest- ward towards Gandikota. On the way he is amused to see troops of monkeys fighting over baskets of rice and is so curious about the captive elephants he sees that at this point in his account he launches into a lengthy discussion and history of the elephant.[302]

After a number of other adventures on the road, Tavernier finally arrives at Gandikota, the fortress on the Penner, which had been weakly held by Mir Jumla and his forces since 1650. He describes its setting, its fortifi- cations, and its artillery. He notices the Europeans who are employed as gunners and gun-founders, especially Claude Maillé of Bourges, a French gunner whom he had first met in Batavia. Early in September, he is ad- mitted to see Mir Jumla and to show off the jewels he is hoping to sell to the sultan. While he awaits Mir Jumla's decision, Tavernier learns that the Euro- pean gunners are threatening to leave Gandikota if they are not paid wages owed them. He notes that Maillé had built a foundry in the fort so that the heavy guns for its protection would not have to be dragged up its steep hill. But Maillé was never able to cast a single gun for want of enough metal. Tavernier notices that the Muslims do not keep accused criminals in prison, but bring them immediately to trial. If deemed innocent, the prisoner is re- leased at once, and if guilty, is immediately punished. In his final interview with Mir Jumla, Tavernier observes, the military leader sits like a Turk on the floor while dictating answers to his correspondence. Between his fingers and toes he holds the letters to be answered. Some replies he dictates to his secretaries and others he writes himself. Finally, Mir Jumla turns to Taver- nier to give him permission to proceed to Golconda with an official escort. From this discussion it becomes clear that Mir Jumla operated at Gandikota as a viceroy or even as the head of a state within the rapidly declining sultanate of Golconda. It also becomes clear, in following the peregrinations of Tavernier, that Mir Jumla's authority was generally shaky and that both

---

[299] A method of obtaining fresh water from springs still followed in certain places along the coasts of India and the Persian Gulf. Ball and Crooke (eds.), *op. cit.* (n. 254), I, 214, n. 2.

[300] On their careers see above, pp. 257–58.

[301] *Cf.* the description of the relations between Catholics and Protestants at Madras some eighteen years later as recounted by Navarrete in Cummins (ed.), *op. cit.* (n. 257), II, 207–304.

[302] Ball and Crooke (eds.), *op. cit.* (n. 254), I, 206–27.

Pulicat and Madras—and perhaps other seaports as well—were beyond his control.[303]

Daniel Havart (*ca.* 1650–1724) was in the service of the VOC on the Coromandel Coast from 1674 to 1686. A young man of education, Havart spent most of his twelve-year stint in north Coromandel and within the confines of Golconda. On his return to the Low Countries in 1686, Havart resumed his academic career and in 1691 received his doctorate in medicine from the University of Utrecht. Two years later he published at Amsterdam his *Op- en ondergang van Cormandel*.[304] This lengthy book is divided into three separately paginated parts totaling 568 quarto pages. The first part deals with the major coastal factories of the VOC from Negapatam to Masulipatam; the second with the inland factories, especially Hyderabad-Golconda; and the third with the less important factories and exchange places on the coast. He put together this work from his personal experiences, correspondence, and records; from VOC documents and reports; and from the writings of Roger, Baldaeus, Schorer, Tavernier, and Thévenot. Since he was personally most familiar with north Coromandel and Golconda, he generally depended on the reports of others about the places south of Pulicat. He was especially indebted to an unpublished manuscript of Herbert de Jager (d. 1689), a physician and naturalist in the employment of the VOC who had spent time in both Golconda and Persia and who was an adept in the Persian language.

An ardent student of foreign languages himself, Havart was proficient enough in Persian to translate and publish two books of Persian poetry in 1688–89. In the text of his book on Coromandel he translates into Dutch most of the Persian titles used in Golconda. He was certainly well enough versed in Telugu to do business in that language. Since he was mainly involved in the textile trade, he gives his attention to everything connected with it, including its place in the general economic system. Even though his work focuses on trade and the European establishments in Coromandel, he also discourses at length on local conditions and on the political decline of Golconda. The "rise and fall" of his title refers to the declining fortunes of the VOC in this region, as brought on in part by the unstable political conditions obtaining in the 1670's, and 1680's.[305]

Part I of *Op- en ondergang* concentrates on the Dutch coastal factories and their fortifications (if any), warehouses, personnel, and principal commodities in trade. In chapter vi he provides a detailed ground plan of Masulipatam,

---

[303] *Ibid.*, pp. 227–35.

[304] The title continues: . . . *als mede de handel der Hollanders op Cormandel, met een beschrijving aller logien van de E. Compagnie op die landstreek; ook op- en ondergang der koningen, die zedert weynige jaren in Galconda. . . geregeerd hebben . . . met kopere platen.*

[305] For Havart's biography and a more detailed analysis of his works see H. Terpstra, "Daniel Havart en zijn 'Op- en ondergang van Cormandel,'" *Tijdschrift voor geschiedenis*, LXVII (1954), 165–89. There appear to be no other editions, printings, or translations of Havart's book. In Havart's work there are produced a number of engravings, including a ground plan of the for-

lists the tolls on trade, and itemizes the types of textiles for sale there. From old documents he puts together a chronology of the hardships suffered by the Dutch in Masulipatam: Muslim attacks of 1619 and 1629 and a bad fire which burned one-half the city in 1666. Coming down to his own day, he reports battles of 1673 with the French and English for control of the sea. He translates three orders from the sultan of Golconda granting free trade to the Dutch, the last being dated 1674. These concessions were followed by a visit to Masulipatam by young Sultan Abu'l Hasan (r. 1672–87) during which the Dutch presented the ruler and his entourage with a great many rich gifts. The Dutch were amply rewarded by nine *farmans* issued by the sultan. The most important concession granted an exemption from tolls at Sadraspatam and Bimlipatam, thus legally guaranteeing the Dutch toll-free access to all the ports of Golconda in which they were then doing business. Since the local authorities resisted these royal concessions, the VOC decided on a policy of retrenchment in Coromandel and began a withdrawal of funds, goods, and money from Masulipatam in 1678. In December of that same year the sultan, much beleaguered by advancing Mughul armies, paid a second visit to Masulipatam. Havart's description of the sultan's visit to a Dutch church on Christmas day is hilarious and revealing. The royal visitor, seated on a throne and smoking a water pipe, first listened to a sermon.[306] Once the Christmas message ended, the sultan asked questions about Dutch religious books and beliefs. Most of these were answered with somewhat more tact than orthodoxy. In response to a question about the Seventh Commandment, the sultan was assured that it prohibited taking another man's wife rather than having multiple wives. Although the sultan was evidently satisfied with these answers, he was apparently not impressed by the gifts of gems he received at this Christmastide. He refused most of the Dutch petitions addressed to him, including one requesting the cession of Pulicat.[307] Hereafter the decline of the Dutch position in Masulipatam became precipitous. In 1679 they suffered from a great flood and later from a series of attacks by the marauding enemies of Golconda and from renewed mercantile activity on the part of the English.[308]

Part II deals with the two inland Dutch factories west of Masulipatam at "Nagelwanze" (Nagalvancha)[309] and at Golconda-Hyderabad. Havart, who

---

tress of Golconda and portraits of its last sultans and other prominent persons. The portraits of Golconda princes and officials are based on miniature paintings brought from Golconda to Holland in 1686 by Laurens Pit. See Herman Goetz, "Notes on a Collection of Historical Portraits from Golconda," *Indian Art and Letters*, X (1936), 12–13; in the same author's *The Indian and Persian Miniature Paintings in the Rijksprentenkabinet (Rijksmuseum)* (Amsterdam, 1958), illustration no. 1, there is a reproduction of the portrait of Muhammad Quli Qutb Shah, ruler of Golconda from 1580 to 1612. See pls. 202–6.

[306] See pl. 207.

[307] See Raychaudhuri, *op. cit.* (n. 6), p. 67.

[308] Havart, *op. cit.* (n. 304), I, 141–225.

[309] Nagalvancha (see map 7) is about twelve miles southeast from Khammam-mett. See Irfan Habib, *An Atlas of the Mughal Empire* (Delhi, 1982), plates 15 A–B and p. 60.

made seven trips to Golconda from Masulipatam (in 1673, 1675, 1677, 1679, 1680, 1681, and 1682), gives a detailed description of the route usually followed by the Dutch.[310] On leaving Masulipatam the traveler crosses a swamp over a renowned wooden bridge built in 1638 by Sultan Abdullah.[311] Havart gives its dimensions and characteristics and complains about the inaccuracy of Baldaeus' description. The bridge was washed out by a flood in November, 1679, but was quickly restored by royal order. After crossing the bridge, the traveler passes by a number of delta villages whose names, locations, and products he specifies. He describes in some detail the village and way station of "Ourier" (Wuyyur) in the region of "Condepilly" (Kondapalle) on the Krishna River with its canal, walled mosque, Hindu temple, and fruit orchards. He reports on the mountain called "Soerna Gieri Perwatam" (Telugu, *suvarna giri parvatam*, golden-topped mountain) where gold was reputedly mined in earlier times. Nearby there is a low-built Siva temple dedicated to "Malisparam" (Mallikayuna?) which stands on a hill named "Indrakiladri." In its vicinity there are several other temples of both Siva and Vishnu. Havart notes the town and fortress of "Condepilly," its great stone inn, and the semi-precious stones produced in its region. The Krishna River, named in honor of the god, floods so much in the rainy season that the houses near its banks have to be protected by stone dikes. Upstream from the village of "Kiezera" a river runs into the Krishna.[312] At the town of "Pennegentspoel" (Penuganchiprolu) on the Manuru River there is a popular caravanserai where merchants assemble who come there to buy its high-grade textiles.

"Nagelwanze," the fifth way station on the route to Hyderabad, includes four market streets and three small villages. In the villages live two hundred households of textile merchants, one hundred fifty of weavers, one hundred of cultivators, twenty of copper workers, fifteen of smiths, twenty of goldsmiths, twenty of dyers, one hundred fifty of Brahmans, twenty of accountants, fifteen of ox-drivers, and a fair number of metal workers, leather dressers, and pariahs. The town also includes twenty plantations of mango trees, ten tanks, and ten Hindu temples (five dedicated to Vishnu and five to Siva). In the middle of the town stands the compound of the VOC. Its construction was begun in 1670 by Nicolas Faber, its first chief. Havart includes

---

[310] This is different from the routes supplied by Tavernier and Thévenot, since the Dutch went to Nagalvancha, a site not visited or mentioned by the Frenchmen. In brief, they went from the Krishna-Godavari delta to Wuyyur (also *Vayyūru* or *Ūyur*), Penuganchiprolu, Nagalvancha, Mangali, Anantagiri, Amangal, Pangal, Walganda, Almasguda, Hayatnagar, and through the Sundar Nagar (or Sultan Nagar) gate into Golconda. Havart gives the names of many additional places on the route, some of which are not readily identifiable.

[311] In more recent times a causeway two miles in length ran through this wasteland, a swamp during the rainy season, connecting the fort and the native town. See "Masulipatam" in *Imperial Gazeteer*.

[312] The Manuru River, on which Nagalvancha is located, combines with the smaller Wyra River near Nandigama before emptying into the Krishna. See the map at the end of Moreland (ed.), *op. cit.* (n. 2).

a ground plan of the compound as well as a written description of each of its parts as of 1686. All the textiles, stones, saltpeter, and indigo of north Coromandel are sold here, and Havart lists the names of the textiles and stones. He discusses the development of the indigo trade in north Coromandel and provides a lengthy description of its cultivation in this region and of the methods followed in preparing the dye.[313]

After treating of VOC personnel and activities at Nagalvancha, Havart traces in minute detail the route from this rural factory to the royal capital of Golconda. Going westward for about nine hours, the traveler arrives at the way station called "Monigale" or "Moregale" (Mangala). The road then passes through a series of villages, all identified by name, before ending in "Anantagier" (Anantagiri), a large town near the Musi River. Anantagiri boasts two mosques, five Hindu temples, and a tank surrounded by tamarind and mango trees.[314] East of the town an old walled fortress is perched on a hill which Havart describes. In the days of Sultan Quli Qutbu'l Mulk (d. 1543), the founder of the Golconda sultanate, it was heavily garrisoned, but it has since fallen into desuetude. In the vicinity much rice, tobacco, and a limited amount of saltpeter are produced; throughout the entire area the "Nely-velden" (paddy fields) are luxuriant.

The second stage or resting place is at "Madekoer" (?). The way to it runs along a road lined with shrubs that leads to a village named for Sayyid Muzaffar, the Mir Jumla who brought Abu'l Hasan to power and who fortified this place in 1662. Rice fields and palm plantations in this neighborhood are irrigated with water from a great tank. In another village there stands a decorative stone mosque; this village quickly paid tribute to Muhammad Sayyid, the Mir Jumla, when his armies invaded it. Just outside this village runs the "Moezie" (Musi) River, a waterway which rises in Hindustan, passes by Hyderabad, and joins another stream near the town of "Amenagel" (Amangal). In "Madekoer" itself they make "Sury" (palm toddy) and sell copper.

The third stage is at "Apasia-peente" (Telugu, *peeta,* means "hamlet"), eight hours further on, named for "Apazia," a Brahman who founded it. On the way to it the traveler passes through a fertile countryside which has historical associations with "Muhammed Resa" (Muhammad Riza) for whom one of its villages is named. Nearby is a plantation of the thorn trees on whose leaves the "Arabian Gom" grows.[315] The road then leads through a countryside dotted with tanks, some of which bear inscriptions to Gol-

[313] Havart, *op. cit.* (n. 304), II, 4–26. For the career of Nicolas Faber see pp. 27–32. Havart's dissertation on indigo was possibly indebted to a paper published on that subject by Herbert de Jager in the *Actis der Leopold.-Carolinischen Akademie der Naturforscher* (Bonn) for 1683.

[314] On the old Vishnu temple at Anantagiri see Sherwani, *op. cit.* (n. 76), p. 619.

[315] "Arabian gum," or gum arabic, is a water-soluble gum obtained from several types of acacia trees. It is used in the manufacture of inks and adhesives, in textile finishing, and in pharmaceuticals.

conda's heroes of the past. The gate to the ruined city of "Panigaal" (Pangal), the next major town, has no door or guardian for its protection. Still standing, though a few are half-ruined, are a number of mosques and Hindu temples. The city was destroyed at the time (1656) when Aurangzib besieged the Golconda fort, and numerous gravestones mark the spots where its inhabitants fell victim to war. On a nearby hill stands the famous fortress of "Nelgonda" (Nalgoda) which gives its name to the surrounding countryside. In this lush region, where "Martesa-Aly" (Murtaza Ali) had been active, there are many plantations of tamarind and mango trees. In "Apasiapeente" itself is to be found the best "Nely" (*nel,* rice in the husk), most of which is reserved for the sultan and his nobles. In addition to a rest house, "Apasia-peente" boasts a mosque originally built by a certain "Chojalakraja" (Hoysala king).

The fourth stage is "Almaas-peente" (Almasguda), nine hours further on, a place named for "Bara Almaas" (the great Almaas) who had helped Sultan Abdullah gain power in 1626. Along this road there are many "Devotaris" (*devoltari,* guardians of the property of the gods), who are fed by the local people and who sell food and drink to the wayfarer. Much of the best palm toddy is produced in this region and from its sale the sultan derives great revenues in taxes. At the village of "Oepul" (?) there is a house of prayer founded by Sultan Muhammad (r. 1612–26). From this point onwards there are placed stone pillars, like milestones, at regular intervals along the road which indicate the distance to Golconda.[316] A bit further on the road crosses the highway which runs to "Carnatica" and Pulicat. "Almaaspeente" is quite large and is built around a stone house of prayer. It boasts a deep well from which water is drawn by oxen.

The fifth and last stage is at Golconda fort, one hour's journey from the city of Hyderabad, or "Baagnagar" (Bhagnagar) where the VOC has its main factory. The nine-hour journey from "Almaas-peente" to Golconda is over a stony and sandy road lined with pipul trees and is mostly uphill. Along the way there are numerous canals, wells, and plantations of mango and other trees. Many of the biggest elephants graze in this region and are sold from here. It is also in these environs that the deeds of "Martesa Aly" are still remembered by good Muslims.

The most impressive sight on this route is the town of "Heyaat-nagar" (Hayatnagar), the "city of life." It was founded by the grandmother of Abu'l Hasan Qutb Shah (r. 1672–87) who named it for herself.[317] Here there are five principal sights to be seen. First comes the great square, or extended quadrangle, called the "Merdaan Dadimahel" (that is, the square where shelter will be given to whoever requires it). On its east side there is the

---

[316] These round mile posts are called *Kos-minārs.* See Sherwani, *op. cit.* (n. 76), p. 545.

[317] Hayatnagar was founded in 1625–26 by Hayat Bakhshi Begam, the virtual ruler of Golconda during her son Abdullah's minority. See Sherwani, *op. cit.* (n. 76), p. 544.

exalted "Sjauwery Koetewaal chana" (Persian, *Sarài-Kotwāl Khāna*), a hostel for officials who hold trials and collect taxes on certain agricultural products. In the middle of the south side stands a large high gate without doors, above which there is an open veranda called "Nagarch chana" (*Naggāra Khāna*), a place where at certain times they play kettledrums, trombones, and trumpets. On the west side, right across from the "Sjauwery Koetewaal chana" is another hostel, named "Sjauwery thanee" (that is, a hostel for guild masters) reserved to those who oversee shops or guilds. The whole quadrangle is superintended by a judge so that it has the order of a city. The entrance to the square is on the north side, and on the west stands a palace called "Asjoerchana" (*A'za Khāna*), a house for commemorating the ten days of mourning for "Hosseyns" (Husain) which they decorate for the various Muslim festivals.

The second showplace is the royal palace located north of the great square and separated from it by a fairly wide and deep moat that is dry except when the sultan is in residence. The walls of the castle are of solid stone, and Havart goes on to give details of their construction. On all sides the walls are pierced with windows covered with doors, through which the sultan can view the quadrangle. Through these windows he can also hear the blare of horns announcing the arrival of his great ministers, and that is why this tower is named "Daadmahal" (the Place of Rule). Beyond the south wall of the palace to the west and on the right-hand side there is an entrance which leads to the square of the caravanserai. Over this entry gate there is a small door of egress from the palace which leads to a broad avenue well planted with trees native to Europe as well as India. On the left-hand side, one sees the apartment for the sultaness and the other wives in a flat, square stone building which is elevated four feet above ground level. A stone stair leads into an inner courtyard in the middle of which there is a tank fully equipped with a fountain that sprays the flowers. The sultan's quarters in this same building are entered through a reception hall, which opens into a round apartment that looks out onto the square. A second room is like a theater or audience chamber. From the front room, one sees from east to west a row of high, thick pillars made of "Kiaten" (Telugu, *khadira, Acacia catechu*) wood. At the end of the row is a high portal which opens into the royal audience chamber. A similar covered entryway is on the other side of the audience hall. On top of these passageways are verandas and galleries. In general the palace is of simple construction and without paintings or much ornament.

The third showplace is the caravanserai (that is, a hostel for travelers), which was built in 1664 by "Bibiheyaat" (*Bibi Hayat*) who, as above mentioned, specialized in building lodgings for travelers. It is a building of cut natural stone, brick, and mortar, oval in shape, longer east by west than north by south. In the middle of each of its four sides there are great doors. When the west and north doors are closed, the east is open; the general entrance is the south door, which is closed and locked only at night. The rooms are built around an open quadrangle topped with pillared galleries. Underneath is a passage ten feet deep where baggage is kept dry and animals stabled. Doors open from the rooms directly into this underground chamber. From the northeast corner along the north side there are seventeen sleeping rooms. Along the northwest side there are twenty, on the west fourteen, on the south twenty, on the southeast twenty-two, on the east thirteen, and on the northeast twelve: a total of 118 rooms. So this building provides a great amount of comfort for travelers.

The fourth showpiece is the "Madjed" (*Masjid*, or house of prayer) which stands within the aforementioned quadrangle. It is a great and elevated four-sided structure topped by a minaret to which a "Molla" (Mullah) climbs three times daily to call the people to prayer. Its stairs are of the same sort of stone as the rest. The "Madjed" occupies most of a square in which there is also a four-sided tank. The mosque is open on the east, and the three other sides have walls with decorated ceilings. Within these walls there are seven entrances to the interior of the mosque. Pillars decorate its facade; otherwise one sees nothing but white walls. In every corner stands a tower, but not all the towers are of the same height. Havart goes on to give many more details.

The fifth and last showplace is the great well just outside the northwest corner of the caravanserai. It is dug into rocks and its sides are strewn with stones. It supplies much water for people and the royal gardens. From the seven arches in the building hang pulleys over which the ropes for the buckets pass. In between the top and the bottom of the well, there is a small tank for storing water. On the north side there is a descending walkway on which the oxen trudge as they raise the buckets. Nearby, at the top of twenty-three stone steps, are three storage tanks to which the water is brought. The water is raised from these tanks to a higher tank in the king's palace, from which it supplies water to the fountains.[318]

From Hayatnagar one road leads to the gate to Golconda called "Meti Mali Faraaschan" and another to the one called "Meti Sultaan Nager."[319] The second route is the one generally followed and it passes nearby the fortress and town of Sultan Nagar. The construction of this new place was started by Sultan Muhammad (r. 1612—26), but since it was not completed

---

[318] Havart, *op. cit.* (n. 304), II, 82–91. Most of Hayatnagar has been destroyed, only the mosque and a few other remains exist today. Neither Tavernier nor Thévenot supplies more than a few casual observations on this city. Indeed a question remains as to whether or not they actually visited there, since neither gives the place its correct name. Havart certainly supplies the fullest description of Hayatnagar prepared by any author to visit there in its heyday. Modern scholars appear to be totally unaware of Havart's full description of this once famous spa. For a description of the remains as of today and for a somewhat dubious reconstruction based on personal observations see Sherwani, *op. cit.* (n. 76), pp. 544–45.

[319] For the gates to the fortress see below, p. 1090.

during his lifetime this ambitious project has been abandoned.[320] A short distance within the Sultan Nagar gate, Havart finds the merchants of the VOC lodged in a good house. Once at his destination Havart denounces Tavernier for providing Europeans with misleading and incorrect information on the route, and asserts that the Frenchman's placenames are so distorted that they cannot be recognized in India by persons who have traveled many times from Masulipatam to Golconda.[321]

Havart lists the employees of the VOC who have worked in Golconda, describes its Dutch graveyard, and notes the names of those buried there. He follows this with a history of the VOC's negotiations with the government over the fixing and stabilizing of tolls on trade. To this account is added the story of the earlier Dutch embassies to Golconda, with detailed personal information on the participants and with lists of the gifts they brought with them.[322] Particularly instructive are Havart's accounts of Pieter Smith's embassy of 1671–72 and that of Laurens Pit, Jr., of 1686, which was the last Dutch embassy to the independent sultanate of Golconda.

Pieter Smith, a senior merchant, was delegated by his VOC superiors in Batavia and Coromandel to undertake a mission to Golconda to obtain a toll-free status for the Dutch, of the sort the English already enjoyed, and to work out a clearer status for the VOC's stations at "Policol" (Palakollu) and Bimlipatam. The emissary, accompanied by Indian servants, three junior merchants, and a Dutch diamond expert, left Pulicat on November 17, 1671, to undertake the twelve-day overland journey to Masulipatam. Since it was customary for the Dutch to make this journey by sea, the record of Smith's overland trek provides reliable information on inland conditions evidently derived by Havart from the diaries of the participants. Of special interest are notes on the towns, villages, and temples lying in the delta of the "Penna" (Penner) River and along the banks of its tributaries.

After a week in Masulipatam, the Smith embassy left on December 5 for the Dutch outpost at Nagalvancha, its first major stopover. The original embassy was strengthened by the addition of twenty-three native soldiers and many bearers. Herbert de Jager, a junior merchant who was well informed on the region, also joined the expedition. Included among the gifts taken along were eight elephants, fourteen Persian horses, seven mirrors, a golden chain, various Asian and Dutch textiles, and a wide variety of fine spices. On the ten-day journey to Nagalvancha they took the same route previously described by Havart. Nine days later, or nineteen traveling days in all from Masulipatam, they arrived at the VOC lodge in Golconda. Here

[320] Sultan Nagar was designed to be the country seat of the Golconda rulers. Most of what was completed has since been eroded by time and ravished by vandals. See Sherwani, *op. cit.* (n. 76), pp. 407–9.

[321] Havart, *op. cit.* (n. 304), II, 91–92. For a ground plan of the VOC lodge see plate between pp. 92 and 93.

[322] *Ibid.*, pp. 92–118.

they negotiated with "Seeyidmusaffer" (Sayyid Muzaffar) and his aides. On January 21, 1672, they were officially received by Sultan Abdullah, an event which Havart describes in detail. The old sultan remained generally cool to the Dutch proposals until his death on May 2. Havart reports on the succession crisis which surprisingly resulted in the immediate elevation of Abu'l Hasan and in his quick marriage to the third daughter of the former sultan through the machinations of Sayyid Muzaffar. In their negotiations with the new government the Dutch began to work through "Sjarasoe" (Sarasu?), who is described as the father-confessor of the sultan. Another new figure on the scene is "Madoena" (Madanna), the secretary of Sayyid Muzaffar. On September 26 the Dutch emissaries were received by the new sultan and noticed that Madanna stood next to Sayyid Muzaffar during the ceremony.[323] Despite the gifts and petitions, the Smith mission ended fruitlessly. On October 9 they left Golconda for Masulipatam. Their overland journey brought them back to Pulicat on November 9, or almost one year after their departure. From the Golconda-Masulipatam leg of their journey, Havart was able to skim off many more details about the east Deccan region through which they passed.[324]

The Smith mission occurred before Havart's arrival in Coromandel; before he left for Europe in 1685, Havart was married to Smith's daughter. In the following year, Laurens Pit led the final Dutch embassy to Golconda. The occasion for this mission was provided by Madanna, the Brahman Mir Jumla, and Akkana, his brother and governor of the Karnatak region. The Telugu Brahmans, who were rapidly taking over the administration from the native and foreign Muslims, had begun systematically to challenge the position of the VOC. In 1685 Akkana took direct action against the Dutch by seizing their store of copper, by forbidding the local weavers to sell them cloths, and by seizing their ships.[325] To obtain an indemnity for their losses and to seek removal of the new obstacles to trade, the VOC sent Laurens Pit, Jr., their new governor of Coromandel, to Golconda at the head of an impressive negotiating commission. Pit sailed from Pulicat on February 16, 1686, with six of his countrymen. Arrived at Masulipatam eight days later, Pit began to put together the delegation which arrived at Golconda on March 26. His grand entry to the capital was led by one hundred troopers on horseback followed by two elephants carrying the banners of the VOC, by Golconda officials, by the palanquins of the ambassador and his aides, and by camels with the baggage.[326] The following day a messenger was sent to

---

[323] This was a harbinger of things to come, for Madanna soon thereafter became Mir Jumla. See Sherwani, *op. cit.* (n. 76), p. 626.

[324] Havart, *op. cit.* (n. 304), II, 119–52. It was not until 1676, on the occasion of the sultan's visit to Masulipatam, that the Dutch obtained a toll-free status. See above, p. 1080.

[325] See Raychaudhuri, *op. cit.* (n. 6), pp. 68–69. For a portrait of Akkana see our pl. 206.

[326] For an engraving depicting this grand entry see Havart, *op. cit.* (n. 304), II, between pp. 154 and 155.

"Piespat Wenkaty" (Pasupati Venkati?), the Brahman minister of foreign affairs, asking for an audience with the sultan. On April 3, an audience was held in which Pit presented his credentials, explained the purpose of his visit, and formally offered his gifts to the sultan.[327] After discussions with the Golconda officials, Pit and his aides, on April 16, again met with the sultan at his new residence across the river. Several more meetings in the same place were held and again there were no positive results or indemnity for the Dutch. This is hardly surprising, since Golconda was then being hard pressed by the Mughuls, and its political and economic life was steadily ebbing away. In 1687, just about one year after Pit returned to Masulipatam, the Mughuls occupied the fortress of Golconda and brought an end to the Qutb Shahi dynasty.[328]

In Holland the events connected with the demise of independent Golconda were being closely watched by Havart. A few representatives of the VOC, as well as other Europeans, had remained at Hyderabad and the fortress of Golconda during the Mughul takeover.[329] From their reports Havart learned about the chaos sweeping the Karnatak as a result of war, famine, and pestilence. Naturally, under these adverse conditions, the trade of the VOC suffered, and many of its factories, including Nagalvancha and Masulipatam, were plundered while others were abandoned. Only the factory at Bimlipatam, the northernmost of the Dutch outposts in Orissa, continued to function normally.[330] Rice from the Bimlipatam region and iron ore and steel products from "Samtomannum" (?) were the only commodities still obtainable.[331]

From his own experiences and his informants' Havart produces a brief description of Hyderabad. Its twelve gates are named for the founders of the city or for the outside place or direction to which they lead.[332] The city boasts twelve mosques or houses of prayer, one of which is modeled on the mosque at Mecca.[333] Another temple is called "Nimass-gah" (*Namāzgāh*, or the Place of Prayer); in all the mosques the entrance faces west towards Mecca, with the pulpit in the east, even though they do not preach sermons, and with fine mats lining the floor. They close the mosques when the Mughul ambassador comes with his army to collect the annual tribute. In the great square there are three famous inns which are festooned and ornamented on festive occasions.

[327] For an engraving of the audience see pl. 208.
[328] Havart, *op. cit.* (n. 304), II, 154–65.
[329] For names and details see *ibid.*, pp. 165–96.
[330] See Raychaudhuri, *op. cit.* (n. 6), pp. 70–71.
[331] Havart, *op. cit.* (n. 304), II, 196–203. Both came through Bimlipatam. Havart here describes how the Indians make iron and steel.
[332] The city wall, built after the Mughul conquest, had thirteen gates and thirteen doors. The gates are mostly named for the city they lead to: *e.g.*, Delhi gate. See S. A. Asgar Bilgrami, *The Landmarks of the Deccan* (Hyderabad, 1927), pp. 94–95.
[333] Probably a reference to Mecca Masjid, one of the largest and most impressive mosques of the Deccan. See *ibid.*, pp. 40–41.

Directly opposite the royal palace is an arch on which there is a display telling how many hours of the day have elapsed. The Muslims, who have no striking clocks, divide the day into four parts of three hours each. Morning and evening each begin at seven o'clock. Every part of the day is divided further into eight "gerrijs" (*gharis*). The length of each "gerry" is deter- mined by a cup that has a hole in its bottom. The cup is put into water and the time that it takes to sink constitutes one "gerry." At this point they strike a copper beaker to announce the time. At 10:30, for example, they strike the beaker four times followed by a short pause and then another strike, to let it be known that one-fourth of the day is gone. Then they make four marks on the red plank above the gate so everyone can readily see how late it is. At night they use hour glasses instead of cups and do not announce the quarters as they do by daylight.[334]

The "Sjaarmonaar" (*Chārminār* or "Four Towers") is named for its four minarets which rise high above the four corners of this square structure. Be- low is a bath, a great tank, and many inns. The nobles and officials all have striking and costly houses and vie with one another to have the most impres- sive establishment. More than fifty gardens grace the city and its suburbs, all of which are orderly and full of trees, water tanks, sprinkling fountains, and lovely pleasure houses. When the sultan visits certain gardens, they gild and silver the leaves of the trees. The Dutchmen and their families are permitted to roam about freely in many of the gardens. It would take a whole book to describe all these gardens and pleasure places. Four of them are particularly important: the "Barre Sultaan Sjahie" (*Bār-i Sultān Shāhī*), or the great royal garden; the "Nanne Sultān Sjahie" (*Nauna Sultān Shāhī*), or the small royal garden; the "Amber-peente" (*peęta*, hamlet; *Amar,* a name?), or the hamlet of "amber"; and the "Lingam pilly" (*Lingampalli*), or the place of the lingam.[335]

About one hour outside the city stand the tombs of the Qutb Shahi rulers. They are tended by "Devotaris" (guardians) who will give the curious visitor a flower from one of the graves for a bit of money. The grave of the first Qutb Shahi ruler, Sultan Quli (r. to 1543), who was popularly known as "Barra Melk" (*Baṛā Malik*), or the great ruler, is not very distinguished in construc-

---

[334] This timekeeper was probably on the eastern arch, now called the *Kālī Kamān* of the *Chārkāman*, or the great place of four arches. See Sherwani, *op. cit.* (n. 76), pp. 306–7. For similar descriptions of timekeeping elsewhere in India and in Kandy, see above, pp. 675, 811, 991–92. In traditional India the day and the night were divided into four quarters (*pahr*) each. Eventually the *pahr* came to be divided into *gharis* of twenty-four minutes each, thus dividing a full day into sixty units of twenty-four minutes each. This is precisely the reverse of the West- ern system which divides a full day into twenty-four units of sixty minutes each. The system here described for Hyderabad is certainly one variation on the system in general use in India. See A. J. Qaisar, *The Indian Response to European Technology and Culture A.D. 1498–1707* (Delhi, 1982), p. 68.

[335] Cf. Sherwani, *op. cit.* (n. 76), pp. 309–11. Thévenot describes the *Lingampalli*, built in 1609, in some detail. See above, p. 1073. For the garden's history see Bilgrami, *op. cit.* (n. 332), pp. 30–31.

tion when compared to the tombs of the other sultans.[336] These tombs are held in such veneration that criminals, even murderers, are granted amnesty if they take refuge in the grounds. Havart cites the example of an Englishman who took refuge therein in 1676 after killing his wife. Despite the objections of the Christians, he was permitted to escape. In speaking of Christians, Havart notes that there are two Christian churches, one within the city and the other in its outskirts. Both are attended by the European Catholics in the service of the sultan and by occasional travelers. The sultan provides an annual sum for the maintenance of the priests and the churches; Goa provides the rest. The church of "Maget Maria" within the city is a very proper and clean building and is served by "Frei Antonio de St. Josepho." The other is old, small, and in disrepair.[337]

The fortress at Golconda, a good hour's journey from the Dutch lodge at Hyderabad, is large in area and has within its walls what amounts to a little city. Nobody may enter it except for those who live or work there. Havart gives a rough ground plan of the fortress, locates the seven gates in its walls and gives their names, and shows the placement of three tanks outside the walls. He also portrays the new fort which is really the residence used by the sultan.[338] He goes on to list the sultans of the Qutb Shahi dynasty. He derived the lives of the five early sultans from several different Persian chronicles, and those of the last two from his personal experiences and those of his European contemporaries.

Abdullah Qutb Shah (r. 1626–72), according to Havart, was given his title by the "Great Mogol" on condition that he pay a handsome annual tribute. The sultan's failure to keep his promises satisfactorily led to more Mughul demands, including a marriage alliance with the "Provincie Rammagier" (Ramgir province) as the wedding gift. Although this sultan ruled for more than fifty years, he was a melancholy person who occupied himself with the collection of precious stones and metals.[339] While the sultan enjoys large annual revenues from his provinces, Havart is not able to provide statistics on the monies and soldiers each sends annually to the sultan. Among the best-known favorites of this sultan is "Miersa Ahmed" (*Mīrzā Ahmad*), the husband of his eldest daughter named "Barre-Sahbini Sahib" (*Barī Ṣāhibni,* "the greatest princess of all princesses"). "Miersa Ahmed" enjoys great revenues and has twelve hundred troops in his entourage; he is also reputed to

---

[336] Sultan Quli, the founder, had his dome erected during his own lifetime. For a description see Bilgrami, *op. cit.* (n. 332), pp. 112–16.

[337] Havart, *op. cit.* (n. 304), II, 204–8.

[338] *Ibid.,* facing p. 208. *Cf.* the plan in Toy, *op. cit.* (n. 275), p. 54. Toy claims that the "new-fortress" or the extension was built only in 1724. From Havart's description and sketch, it seems that it was certainly built before his book was published in 1693; since it was used as the sultan's residence, it probably should be dated from before the Mughul takeover in 1687.

[339] For an engraving of Abdullah see pl. 203. Havart, who collected and wrote gravestone inscriptions, provides little dedicatory verses to this and to most of the other portraits in his book.

have fifty-two children by a variety of women and not a single child by his wife. His wife, on the other hand, is a wise and well-loved person with her own following at court. Another favorite is "Miersa Aboe-il-Hassan" (Mirza Abu'l Hasan), the husband of the sultan's youngest daughter.[340]

Sayyid Muzaffar, chancellor and keeper of the great seal, was the most powerful minister and favorite of the sultan; he acted almost as if he were sultan himself. "Sjah-Miersa" (*Shāh Mīrzā*), nephew of Sayyid Muzaffar, was a young man of the greatest promise, who unfortunately died in 1672, or at about the same time as the old sultan. Another favorite was "Nikona-amchan" (*Nēknām Khān*), a great general of the army and faithful old servant of the sultan who also died in 1672. Sayyid Muzaffar, "Mosachan" (*Mūsā Khān*), and the members of their party at court were responsible for the coup which brought about the rise to power of the last sultan, Abu'l Hasan.[341] As a reward for their deeds, Sayyid Muzaffar was named "Miersjumla" (Mir Jumla) and secret adviser, while his bosom friend Musa Khan was named "Chan-chanaan" (*Khān-Khānān*) and Supreme Field Marshall. The sultan, who is compared to Croesus, squandered money that his advisers felt might better be spent on the army. Consequently both nobles shortly fell from favor and power.

Once Abu'l Hasan had failed in all his efforts to halt the Mughul advance, he paid Aurangzib a constantly mounting tribute and began searching for allies. As early as 1676 he negotiated a treaty witth "Sieqagie" (Sivaji), by which Golconda subsidized the rapidly rising Mahratta state in its raids upon Mughul territories. Once embarked upon this dangerous game, Abu'l Hasan sought to mollify Aurangzib with rare gifts, including a huge diamond in the rough which he sent in 1684. Throughout his entire reign, the sultan's favorites and advisers were numerous and dominant in the making of policy. The ruler himself continued to squander both his wealth and time in a selfish pursuit of personal pleasures. His most intimate favorite was "Sjarasoe," his "confessor" and a kind of demigod on earth to the Muslims at court. His favorite physician and brother-in-law, "Miersa Mehdi" (*Mīrzā* the Physician) was learned in the fundamentals of medicine, astrology, and history; he was granted the honorary title of "Serief-il Molk" (Sharif-ul Mulk) even though he was overly inclined to drink. While these Muslim favorites participated in the personal life of the sultan, state power gravitated steadily into the hands of "Madoena" (Madanna), the Mir Jumla who was granted the honorary title of "Sure Perkass Rouw" (*Sūrya Prakaas Rao*).[342]

---

[340] For the complications attending these marriages see Sherwani, *op. cit.* (n. 76), pp. 601–2. Havart's account appears to be mistaken, even though he claims to have known these favorites personally.

[341] For portraits of the last sultan see pls. 204–5 and Goetz, *op. cit.* (n. 305), p. 41.

[342] Madanna ruled as first minister from 1673 to his death in 1686. He was a Telugu Brahman who filled the government posts with high-caste Hindus. For Madanna's portrait see Havart, *op. cit.* (n. 304), II, facing p. 219, and Havart's pl. 1.

Madanna ruled both the sultan and the state and drove most of the Persians out of high office. He appointed Akkana, his brother, as generalissimo, despite his obvious lack of training for the job.[343] "Muhammed Ibrahim" (Muhammad Ibrahim), a capable military leader and a friend of the Dutch, was made "Cancelier" and commander of the army fighting Aurangzib.[344] Besides these royal favorites, Madanna brought into Golconda's service many other lesser lights, mostly Hindus and members of his family. Much of this material on the court, Havart admits, was obtained from an unpublished manuscript by Herbert de Jager who was then in Persia receiving reports on Golconda.[345]

From several letters received from Coromandel, Havart describes the last days of the Qutb Shahi dynasty. On October 26, 1685, the sultan was informed that the Mughul army was approaching. On the following day an uprising occurred against the Brahmans, in which many were murdered. On October 28–29 the Mughuls entered Hyderabad and began the sack of the city, including the destruction of its gardens and temples. Muhammad Ibrahim and two other field commanders, "Mohammed Takki" (Muhammad Taqi) and "Miersa Momien" (Mirza Momein), deserted to the enemy, as did "Serief-il-Molk" and his family. The sultan and the court took refuge in the fortress of Golconda, as the Mughuls began to set up an administration for the rest of the country. Shortly thereafter, Madanna and Akkana and many other Brahmans were murdered and dragged through the streets of Golconda by its outraged inhabitants.[346] Havart sees Muhammad Ibrahim as an ungrateful traitor who deserted his sovereign in the hour of his greatest need.[347]

After the elimination of Madanna and the Hindu party, it looked for a time as if the Golconda dynasty might be spared. While his agents plundered Golconda and extracted double tribute from its sultan, Aurangzib began to occupy Bijapur in the spring of 1685. Bribes of jewels and diamonds were meanwhile prepared in Golconda to keep Aurangzib from completing the destruction of the fortress and the dynasty. Madanna's role was contem-

---

[343] For his portrait see pl. 206.

[344] Eventually Muhammad Ibrahim, a Persian nobleman, was granted a title on Madanna's recommendation and for a financial consideration. In the Muslim sources he is described as a "time server" and a "hypocrite." See J. F. Richards, *Mughal Administration in Golconda* (Oxford, 1975), p. 39; also see Sherwani, *op. cit.* (n. 76), p. 628. For his portrait see Havart, *op. cit.* (n. 304), II, facing p. 226.

[345] Havart, *op. cit.* (n. 304), II, pp. 216–20. Also see above, p. 1086. Herbert de Jager was with a Dutch embassy in Persia from 1684 to 1688. After his earlier ten-year tour of duty in Golconda, he evidently sought to keep in touch with the events transpiring there no matter where he happened to be. The Persians, of course, were vitally interested in the fate of the Golconda state where so many of their nationals worked and lived.

[346] See the engraving in Havart, *op. cit.* (n. 304), II, facing p. 224, and on p. 225 the two verses on Madanna and Akkana written by Havart for publication under these portraits. Havart claims to have known and to have spoken with the brothers. They were killed by Muslim members of the royal bodyguard in March, 1686. See Richards, *op. cit.* (n. 344), p. 47.

[347] See the verse under his portrait in Havart, *op. cit.* (n. 304), II, facing p. 226.

poraneously taken over by the Brahman called "Piespatwenkaty" (Pasupati Venkati?). Despite all efforts to appease Aurangzib, the Mughul army began the siege of Golconda on February 2, 1687, and overran the fortress thought to be impregnable on October 2. The sultan was taken prisoner and his treasury plundered.[348]

Havart concludes his discussion of Golconda with general remarks, not made by other writers, about the officialdom and its people. The education of the prince takes place in the harem. Here he is taught reading, writing, and Islamic religion and traditions by a tutor. Brought up otherwise by women, he tends to be frivolous even after succeeding to the throne. He is more interested generally in diversion than in statecraft. In spite of the injunctions of religion, he drinks wine, indulges himself in loose living, and sets a bad example for his officials. While this was the life followed by some recent sultans, certain earlier rulers lived more modestly. Abdullah Qutb Shah, the father-in-law of the last ruler, was obsessed by a passion for curiosities, especially jewels and jewelry. He entrusted all matters of state to secretaries, especially to a Brahman who was called an "Aitemaadrauw," or "the support of the state" (Urdu, *Itmad Rao,* "the glory of the realm"). This man read aloud all the letters to the sultan, including official commands or orders from the Mughul emperor, as well as sensitive matters relating to tribute. This practice led to breaches of security and secrecy so serious that on one occasion the sultan had his traitorous secretary beaten to death in his own presence.[349] The "Koetewaal" (*kōtwāl*), or commissioner of law and order, is directly responsible to the sultan and the governors of the provinces; he is the most important of the local officials in the larger cities and towns. An official called the "Kazie" (*qāzī*, kazi) is a judge who settles spiritual as well as secular differences and draws up and authenticates official papers. Another official of importance is the "Mudstehid" (*mujtāhīd*), a legal scholar, who settles differences over religion between Muslims and Hindus in Golconda and acts as an interpreter of the Koran and the "Haddies."[350] Although the number of these officials has declined, their moral influence continues to be great with all levels of society. Havart concludes that the people of Golconda, while they exhibit the weaknesses of people everywhere, possess

---

[348] *Ibid.,* pp. 220–35. At the end of the seventeenth century there was published in English "The History of a Late Revolution in the kingdom of Golconda." This somewhat garbled story was included as an appendix to John Ovington, *A Voyage to Surat in the Year 1689* (London, 1696), pp. 525–45. It is omitted, since it "has no direct bearing on the narrative," from the critical edition (Oxford, 1929) of Ovington's book edited by H. G. Rawlinson. See above, pp. 579–80.

[349] For an engraving of this act see Havart, *op. cit.* (n. 304), II, facing p. 238. Possibly Havart is here talking about the *dabīr* or secretariat in charge of drafting and analyzing documents in Persian and Telugu. See Sherwani, *op. cit.* (n. 76), pp. 508–9.

[350] From Arabic, *hadīth,* a written collection of oral reports about what the prophet Muhammad or a member of the early Muslim community said or did. In the ninth century all *hadīth* were gathered and put into a written collection which became second only in authority to the Koran as Muslim legal theory developed.

definite virtues. Many of those he knew were upright, pious, true-hearted, polite, grateful, helpful, friendly, and beneficent; in these regards they compare favorably to Christians.[351]

In Part III, Havart describes the smaller ports along the coast and discusses their major industries, arts, and other economic activities. For example, he provides a brief but vivid description of how the cotton painters work at "Palicol" (Palakollu) in the delta of the Godavari River. Here there are four sets of painters, each with its own family name. These poor people, including children, barely eke out an existence by their painting. Most of the profits they earn go to the monopolists and the sultan. Havart describes how they laboriously prepare the cloth and mix their paints. The "Parecalas" (the calicoes woven in this region best suited for chintz) are then painted according to musters given to the painters. Work proceeds at a snail's pace and Havart remarks: "Yes, he who would wish to depict patience would need no other object than such a painter."[352] Havart also describes in some detail how grey saltpeter (potassium nitrate) earth is scooped from the surface and dug from the superficial layers of the soil, how the saltpeter is leached by a water process from the accumulated soil, and how this liquid is boiled and the salt crystallized for commerce.[353]

Havart's *Op- en ondergang van Coromandel* is still an indispensable source for the study of Coromandel and Golconda in the latter half of the seventeenth century. While it is sometimes mentioned in modern bibliographical and historiographical lists and essays, scholars of the twentieth century have generally ignored it or have used it only superficially.[354] Not only does Havart add considerably to general knowledge of the region, as for example by his excellent description of Hayatnagar, but he also provides a corrective to the usual, and overly heavy, reliance of modern scholars on the writings of Tavernier and Thévenot. Havart's Dutch contemporaries were better informed. Pieter van Dam, the great chronicler of the Dutch East India Company (1701), relied heavily on Havart for his discussion of the Dutch trade and factories on the Coromandel Coast.[355] Two decades later François Valentijn depended almost exclusively on Havart's book for the description of Coromandel which appears in Volume V, Pt. 2 of his *Oud en Nieuw Oost-Indien*

---

[351] Havart, *op. cit.* (n. 304), II, 235–41.

[352] *Ibid.*, III, 13–14. Also see Irwin, *loc. cit.* (n. 8), pp. 30–31.

[353] Havart, *op. cit.* (n. 304), III, 51–54. This discussion occurs in the chapter relating to the Dutch stations at "Daatzerom" (?) near "Thuny" (?).

[354] For example, one summary paragraph relates to it in K. W. Goonewardena, "Dutch Historical Writing on South Asia," in C. H. Philips (ed.), *Historians of India, Pakistan, and Ceylon* (London, 1961), p. 171. J. F. Richards is perhaps justified in making only slight use of Havart, since Richard's book (*op. cit.* [n. 344]) deals mainly with Golconda after the Mughul conquest. H. K. Sherwani, the leading Indian historian of the Qutb Shahi dynasty, seems to be ignorant of it and other Dutch sources. In his excellent *Atlas of the Mughal Empire*, Irfan Habib might have improved his maps of the Eastern Deccan through consultation of Havart.

[355] See above p. 44 n.

(1723).[356] In Holland, Havart continues in the twentieth century to be highly regarded as a source of inspiration by Dutch writers of historical novels and romances.[357] It is to be hoped that a competent Dutch historian will one day soon undertake the preparation of a critical edition of this major source.

European materials on Coromandel published during the seventeenth century divide into two groups unequal in size and different in emphasis: the Jesuit and the northern European sources. Jesuit publicists of the century's first decade concentrated on the successes won by the Catholics in south Coromandel, the Fishery Coast, and Madura. Individual members of the Society penetrated from San Thomé to Vijayanagar to found missions in the interior of the empire. Paralleling the policy then being followed in China, the Jesuits of Vijayanagar tried to win esteem and converts by making powerful friends at the imperial court. In their pursuit of friendship they presented the ruler and his courtiers with gifts and made strenuous efforts to learn local languages and to avoid violating Hindu customs and sensitivities. The policy of accommodation followed at Vijayanagar was transformed by Nobili at Madura into a policy of personal adaptation to and imitation of Hindu practices. While the Jesuit writers in Europe, particularly Guerreiro and Du Jarric, hailed these activities as innovative triumphs, members of the other orders, as well as seculars and some other Jesuits, evidently raised questions at Madrid and Rome which brought a quick end to the mission in Vijayanagar and hushed the friends of Nobili in Europe. At any rate, very little was published in Europe for a long time after 1615 dealing directly with Madura, whose mission nonetheless continued to grow steadily.[358]

European readers of these early Jesuit reports learned that the declining empire of Vijayanagar and the Iberians had a common enemy in the "Moors." The Muslims threatened European trade as well as Vijayanagar's continued existence. Also apparent was the fact that the emperor had only a loose hold upon his own vassals and could never be entirely sure of their loyalty. The Jesuits, ever on the lookout for allies, visited several of these nayaks in their fortress cities and reported vaguely on the political and religious affiliations of these local rulers. Among other things, they showed clearly that Hinduism, like Christianity, suffered from internal divisions and bitter rivalries which carried over into political life. Officialdom in the empire was dominated by Telugu retainers often at odds with the Tamil nayaks of the south, who were, in turn, competing one with the other. While the Jesuits evidently got along well enough with Venkata II, the influential Brahmans of the court remained unimpressed by these priests from afar. When the Jesuits did make converts—and there were admittedly few at Vijayanagar in these

---

[356] See S. Arasaratnam, "François Valentijn's Description of Coromandel," in *Professor K. A. Nilakantra Sastri Felicitation Volume* (Madras, 1971), pp. 1–8.

[357] See Terpstra, *loc. cit.* (n. 305), p. 183.

[358] On the possible reasons for this turn of events see above, p. 1017n.63.

years—the new Christians were low in caste or possessed more than a passing interest in commerce.

Madura, as it appeared in the Jesuit reports, ruled the eastern tip of the subcontinent to an indefinite frontier well to the north of the Vaigai River. Muttu Krishnappa Nayaka (r. 1601–9) was determined to keep Travancore at arm's length, to reassert his authority over the Paravas, and to pacify the Marava country. The Paravas, who remained staunch in their Christianity, looked to the Portuguese for protection. But the Portuguese, who were themselves beginning to feel heavy pressure from the Dutch, could only provide succor for those Paravas who lived close to Tuticorin and other Portuguese bases. To escape the new impositions being placed upon them by Madura, many of the Paravas fled the Fishery Coast for more hospitable port cities to which Madura's authority did not extend. In the city of Madura itself the nayak tolerated the Paravas and tacitly permitted Nobili to carry on his adaptive mission. The opposition to Nobili came from the Tamil Brahmans who dominated the religious and intellectual life of the city, one of the greatest centers of south Indian Hinduism. Even they were willing to tolerate Nobili and his followers once they understood that his teachings did not endanger their position.

In the European literature the scene shifted abruptly at this point to the activities of the Dutch and English at Masulipatam, the major port of Golconda in north Coromandel. Caught up in the civil wars sweeping Vijayanagar after 1614, and faced by the unrelenting hostility of the Portuguese, the northern Europeans concentrated upon working out satisfactory trading relations with the Muslim governors and port authorities of Golconda. Floris and Methwold, both of whose reports first appeared in English, were the earliest to provide systematic accounts on conditions of trade at Masulipatam. What they had to say applied to the years from 1611 to 1623, a period during the latter part of which the Dutch and English in India were trying to maintain a united front against the Portuguese. The northern European traders, unlike the Portuguese and Jesuits, were not involved in a worldwide struggle against Islam and were willing for the sake of trade to ignore their religious differences with the Muslims. And from their vantage point at Masulipatam, the northern Europeans continued to negotiate with Vijayanagar and the nayaks of the south in an effort to retain and expand their precarious foothold at Pulicat and elsewhere in Tamilnadu.

Methwold made clear that the Dutch and English in the south continued to war against the Portuguese from their major station at Pulicat. But his main interest was in Masulipatam and Golconda. He told Europe for the first time of the extent of this Islamic state and described a number of its hilltop fortresses. The sultan and his officials had close connections with Persia, and indeed most of his nobles were Persians. The official religion was the Shiite type of Islam, but all other religions were tolerated. Although they were not allowed to have their own mosques, Sunnis from Arabia and

Turkey lived in Golconda. The Hindus, the religious majority and the group of greatest interest to Methwold, continued to maintain intact their religious and social customs. He described in detail the castes of Masulipatam as well as Hindu rites and marriage ceremonies. While the authorities ordinarily did not interfere with Hindu practices, the Muslims endeavored to stamp out suttee and widow burial. The sultan, as monopolist of land, industries, and tolls, farmed out to the highest bidder, usually Brahmans, the right to control agriculture, the textile industry, and taxes. Even the diamond mine at Kollur was treated as a royal monopoly and its administration sold annually to the highest bidder. Methwold also noted that tobacco cultivation had but recently been introduced into Golconda.

Again the scene shifts abruptly in the European literature; this time to Pulicat and to the work of Abraham Roger. At Pulicat from 1632 to 1642, Roger had remarkably little to say about life or trade at the chief Dutch factory on the Coromandel Coast. This Reformed preacher, while he ministered to his Christian flock in Dutch, Portuguese, and Tamil, reported to Europe primarily about his understanding of Hinduism. Certainly Nobili was better informed than Roger on Indian languages and Hindu texts, but the Jesuit never wrote about Hinduism in systematic fashion for the general public of Europe. Informed by his Brahman friends, Roger pieced together a comprehensive account of the practices of south Indian Hinduism in the seventeenth century. He distinguished clearly between the practices associated with Siva or Vishnu and listed the various types of Brahmans and ascetics. He even gave the daily religious routine followed by the Brahmans. Like Methwold, he observed that though the gods are many, the Hindus believe in a single supreme God. Roger described in detail Hindu weddings, funerals, and mourning ceremonies and customs. He identified by name the castes of Pulicat and noted that polygamy was legal and widely practiced. From his study of the almanacs Roger was led to discuss the Indian calendar with its sixty-year cycles and its four ages. He gave the names of the months in Tamil and the designations of the eras in Sanskrit. He depicted in words the ground plan of the Hindu temple. He listed the holy places and leading temples of India and tried to give the routes followed and the temples ordinarily visited by pilgrims to these shrines. He was also indirectly responsible for bringing into European languages most of two important Sanskrit works. As a result, Europeans had at hand by 1651 a serious and objective account of Hinduism which remains to this day one of the best Western works on the subject, as well as a primary source for the history of Hinduism.

Magistris, the Jesuit, generally was unsympathetic to Hindu beliefs and practices in his survey of the missions in Madura and Tanjore between 1656 and 1660. His *Relatione* (1661), however, provided Europe with an update of events in Madura and presented for the first time a sketch of Tanjore and the conditions obtaining there. In connection with his effort to portray the difficulties faced by the mission, Magistris provided a brief but essentially accurate history of the wars of Tirumala Nayak of Madura with Vijayanagar, Bijapur-Golconda, and Mysore. In the process he also described for the first time a number of the lesser cities of Madura and Tanjore. He portrayed vividly the disruptions brought on by those wars and by the civil disturbances inspired by the organized bands of *Valluvars*, the so-called Brahmans of the Pariahs. Finally, he depicted the role played in these troubled years by the *Kollars* of Madura and their close relations, the Maravas of the Fishery Coast. Much of what Magistris wrote on "temporal conditions" had to be extracted by his readers from a lengthy book of edification in which long sections recorded examples of the staunch faith of the missionaries and their converts.

Baldaeus, a preacher involved in the Dutch takeover in south India, was on the Coromandel Coast from 1658 to 1662. His account, more than any of the others, supplemented and extended the Jesuit and other earlier materials on Vijayanagar in its years of decline. He was good on cities and especially on Gingee just before its surrender to Bijapur. He reported on Tuticorin and on the intransigence of the Paravas, who stubbornly resisted Dutch efforts to shake them loose from their Catholicism. He provided maps for a number of the port cities and commented on their individual commercial importance to the general economy of the region. With respect to Hinduism, he deferred to Roger on many points, while adding observations of his own on gods and temples. Acutely aware of the importance of the Tamil language to work in south Coromandel and Ceylon, he studied the language himself and assembled materials in that language as a basis for the abbreviated grammar and the texts he had published. While Baldaeus was not always careful about citing his sources or about giving due acknowledgment to others, his book remains a fundamental collection of materials for the study of Coromandel at the time of the Dutch expansion.

For Golconda and its Karnatak empire the works of Tavernier, Thévenot, and Havart provided firsthand materials covering the period from mid-century to the end of the Qutb Shahi dynasty in 1687. Direct relations between the Europeans and the sultanate of Golconda became more regular at this time. The sultans of Golconda encouraged foreign trade, particularly at Masulipatam and Hyderabad-Golconda, by providing protection and offering concessions to the European merchants. English, Dutch, and French traders safely traversed the interior routes of the Karnatak and Golconda despite the disruptions attending the fall of Vijayanagar and the constant strife between Golconda and the Mughuls. As a by-product they provided materials on routes and traveling conditions not readily found in indigenous sources. They observed with some astonishment that messages and other communications were sent over interior routes by relays of runners. Operating far inland from the ports, these traders were forced to learn something of the Asian languages. All three knew Persian, the language of government, and probably enough of "bazaar" Telugu and Portuguese to carry on business and travel, for it was not always possible to have an interpreter on hand who knew a European language.

Because the sultanate tolerated all religions and nationalities, these European businessmen were generally left alone and allowed to move about freely. They all kept full records of their activities and observations. Tavernier traveled much more widely and over a longer period of time than the other two. Thévenot, who was in Golconda for the shortest time, was especially good in his descriptions of nature and gardens, for which he clearly had a special feeling. Havart spent a much longer continuous period on the soil of Golconda than the other two; he also had the advantage of using the other two as sources as well as the materials derived from fellow VOC agents. He provided portraits of the last sultans and ground plans of the Dutch factories and of the fortress of Golconda. As a consequence, Havart's work, while it suffers from a surfeit of repetitive detail, is more informative than either of the other two. The Dutchman was in Golconda long enough to understand in depth the internal workings of the sultanate and to have a genuine feeling for its people and their problems. His continuing interest and involvement are best attested by the great pains he took after returning to Holland to keep himself informed about the fate of Golconda.

All three of the European writers on Golconda, like the Jesuit observers of Vijayanagar, commented in detail on architecture: palaces, fortresses, temples, mosques, inns, bridges, and gardens. They were obviously impressed by the new and planned city of Hyderabad, its extent, monuments, and magnificent gardens. They were intrigued by the wells and water systems which supplied fountains, watered gardens, and irrigated fields. Havart, who traveled in this particular part of India much more than the others, was almost ludicrous in the attention he paid to resting places and inns, information that obviously might be of interest to future VOC agents and others traveling in Golconda. Havart described the royal spa of Hayatnagar, now mostly destroyed. He must have remained there for an extended period, since he actually gives measurements and other minor points that required time and patience to collect and record. All three discussed the fortress of Golconda with its massive walls and gates. They were all moved to comment admiringly on the royal tombs near the fortress, and Havart correctly noted that criminals could find sanctuary in their grounds.

Golconda's agriculture and industry likewise caught the eye of these businessmen-travelers. They were naturally attracted most by commodities related to trade: indigo, diamonds and other stones, textiles, saltpeter, iron, and metalworks. Rather abashedly, they acknowledged the superiority of the swords and muskets manufactured in Golconda. They were intrigued by its intricate textiles, especially by the painted cloths. On the other hand, they sometimes showed impatience with the unwillingness of the textile workers to change their patterns or to experiment with new or different techniques. The monopoly system, since it inhibits free trade by controlling production and distribution, also aroused their ire from time to time. But they admired the lush paddy fields and the control of water by tanks and artificial lakes. They noticed that the cultivation of tobacco, but recently introduced, had spread to many parts of the country. Near Hyderabad, elephants, a valuable item in the intra-Asian trade, were raised for sale. And in this same region opium was cultivated for the Hyderabad market.

About social and religious conditions they were less inclined to comment on specifics. They noticed, however, that polygamy and prostitution were legal. They observed that the monopoly system placed a heavy burden on the native workers, especially on the lower-caste Hindus. The sultans and the nobles, on the other hand, were rich, and many wasted their lives and fortunes in an aimless search for pleasure. Nobles of all levels lived in pretentious houses. The Persian nobles and their entourages paraded about ostentatiously as they performed their nominal duties. The education of the prince was conducted in the harem, a background which produced effeminacy and dissolute living in the mature sultan. Among the best officials were the Kotwals, who were in charge of police work. Certain legal authorities also provided stability by mediating differences between Hindus and Muslims. Officially the Islamic authorities discouraged widow burial and suttee. Hindus participated in Shiite festivals, even if only to have a holiday. All religious groups, except Sunnis, seemed to have great freedom. Christians had two churches of their own in Hyderabad which were state-supported, but Sunnis were not allowed to have their own mosques.

Like most travelers, they commented on strange sights, customs, and devices. Where no bridges existed, rivers and streams were crossed in coracles. At Pulicat they obtained water at low tide from coastal springs. Oxen and elephants were used to draw water from the country's numerous wells. In the main square of Hyderabad a strange device let the public see how much of the day had elapsed; Havart discussed daily timekeeping practices. Stone mileposts lined the roads to let the traveler know how far he was from the capital. Just outside Golconda stood Sultan Nagar, the unfinished summer residence of the sultans. Merchants in Hyderabad, as elsewhere in the East, engaged in silent barter to keep prices from being known. Tavernier told how the Mir Jumla he visited answered correspondence by dictating letters to his secretaries. Justice and punishment were quick and harsh under Islamic law.

The European sources reflected the shift in the center of gravity from south to north and depicted clearly the disruption attending the decline of both Vijayanagar and Golconda. They noticed the development of the Hindu reaction in Golconda and the efforts of its leaders to find allies against the Mughuls in Bijapur and in Sivaji's movement. Most of the writers were much more fascinated by Hinduism than by Islam. While the Protestants did not let religious differences interfere with business, the Jesuits and the Portuguese officialdom remained uncompromising in their attitude towards the "Moors" of India and its surrounding seas. The English and Dutch writers, especially Roger, made serious efforts to understand Hinduism and its social practices for their own sake and in their own terms. The Protestants, even a preacher like Roger, were more interested in business than in conversions. As a consequence, their observations on Hinduism, unlike those of the Jesuits, were about as objective and perspicacious as might reasonably be expected from seventeenth-century viewers of an utterly foreign religion whose social practices often shocked sensibilities and reinforced beliefs in the superiority of Christianity and the European way of life.

APPENDIX

The Castes of South Asia
in the Seventeenth Century
(According to European Authors)

Caste is a system of social stratification that has been most highly developed over time in South Asia and its adjacent regions. Modern students of caste estimate that Indian society alone includes around three thousand castes. Westerners, especially the Portuguese and their European successors in South Asia, concentrated their attention upon caste as a social system peculiar to India and nearby areas. The preoccupation of Western scholars and laymen with theories about the origin, nature, relationships, and attributes of caste has often puzzled South Asians. Nonetheless, Westerners persist in their efforts to understand and explain this social system in their own terms. While most observers have been aware that castes and their relationships to other castes have changed over the past two thousand years, there have been few systematic efforts to study the evolution of castes before the British period, or the eighteenth century. The following caste names and attributes have been gathered from European writings of the seventeenth century to illuminate in a slight way what the caste system looked like before the British period in the Mughul Empire, Malabar, Coromandel, and Ceylon. The names of Malabar castes were checked by Dr. Cyriac Pullapilly, a native of Cochin, and those of Tamil Nadu by Dr. Rani Fedson, a native of Madura and a Tamil specialist. With regard to Ceylon, Knox and Baldaeus are disappointingly thin on caste names. There are much fuller listings in François Valentijn's *Oud en nieuw Oost-Indien* (1724–27). See S. Arasaratnam (trans. and ed.), *François Valentijn's Description of Ceylon* ("HS," 2d ser., CXLIX; London, 1978), pp. 38–40, 67–81.

TABLE 1: Castes and Tribes of Mughul India

Name in European Texts	Standard Name[1]	European Authors	Occupations, characteristics, etc., according to Europeans
Backeires (see also Dravizes)	*Fakīr*	Bruton (English)	Muslim mendicants, beggars, rogues
Baloches and Boloohes	*Balūchs*	De Laet (Flemish)	Tribesmen who have "courage"
Bandarines	Mahratta, *Bhandāri*	Fryer (English)	Militia
Banians, Banyans, Benjanen	*Vāniya*	Lord (English); Van Twist (Dutch)	Merchants
Baraguy	*Bairagi*	Thévenot (French)	Mendicants, recluses. They like the color white, dislike yellow.
Bengiara	*Banjaras*	Thévenot	Bearers, painters, artisans
Billewani	*Bahlwani*	De Laet	Those in charge of carts, carriages
Bisnouw	*Vishnu*	De Laet	Merchants, realtors, interpreters
Bogowaro	related to Telugu, *bogam?*	Van Twist	Whores of Gujarat
Brahmans, Brammon, Bramen, etc.	Brahmans	Lord, Thévenot, *et al.*	Teachers, lawgivers
Butts	*Bhat*	Fryer	Mendicants, learned physicians, teachers of law. They are Brahmans.
Canarins	Konkani or Luso-Asians of Kanara	Careri (Italian)	Lawyers
Cataris; Kataris	*Khatri*	Manrique (Portuguese)	Tradesmen, merchants
Colis; Collees; Covillis	*Kōlī*	Thévenot, De Laet	Cotton-dressers, tribal insurgents, palanquin-carriers
Columbeens	*Kunbi*	Fryer, Thévenot	Cultivators of fields, salt-makers
Courmy (see also Souders)	*Kurmi*	Thévenot	Tillers of the soil
Curawaeks	*Srāvaka*	Van Twist	Jain laymen
Cuttery	*Kshatriya*	Lord	Rulers, those who maintain order, soldiers

(continued)

[1] Caste names listed are of Sanskrit or Hindi-Urdu derivation, unless otherwise indicated.

TABLE I (*continued*)

Name in European Texts	Standard Name[1]	European Authors	Occupations, charac- teristics, etc., according to Europeans
Der (or Halalcours)	*Dher* or *Dhēd;* Persian, *Halālkhor* (*Bhangi*)	Della Valle (Italian); Thévenot	Field laborers, private ser- vants, sweepers, town scavengers
Dodagors	*Saudagar*	Manrique	Merchants
Dravizes (see also Backeires)	Persian, *Darwesh*	Manrique	Religious mendicants
Frasses; Frassi	*Farrāsh, Farrashi*	Fryer, De Laet	Porters, tent raisers
D'Goegy; Jaugis	Yogis	Van Twist; Ber- nier (French)	Holy men
Gratiates	*Garasias*	Thévenot	Toll collectors, guardians of travelers (?), highwaymen
Gujars	*Gujar*	Thévenot	Shepherds
Halalcours: see Der			
"Hammer-men"	?	Thévenot	Armorers, smiths, masons
Herbood	Persian, *Hirbad*	T. Herbert (English)	Parsi priests
Jaugis: see D'Goegy			
Kataris (see also Cuttery)	*Khatri; Khsatriya;* or Rajputs (see Rasboots)	Manrique, Thévenot	Soldiers, weavers, merchants
Kenchens	*Kanchani*	Bernier	Dancing/singing girls
Mahauti	*Mahouti*	De Laet	Tenders of elephants
Merdi-Couras	Persian, *Maracklhor*	Thévenot	Cannibals
Meteranis	*Miḥtrani*	Manrique	Female servants
Metres	*Miḥtar*	Manrique	Male servants
Naites	Naites, *Nawayits* or newcomers	Mandelslo (German)	Muslim traders, mariners, seafarers
"Nautch-Girls" (see also Quenchenies)	*Kanchani*	Fryer	Dancing girls
Necesselars	*Nasāsālār*	T. Herbert	Bearers
Pattamars	Konkani, *Patamar*	Ovington (English)	Foot messengers
Piriaves	*Pariyan*	Thévenot	Leatherworkers

(*continued*)

TABLE 1 (*continued*)

Name in European Texts	Standard Name[1]	European Authors	Occupations, characteristics, etc., according to Europeans
Quenchenies (see also "Nautch-Girls")	*Kanchani*	Thévenot, Ovington	Dancing girls
Radias	*Rāh-dāri*	De Laet	Road guardians
Rasboots (see also Kataris)	Rajputs	De Laet	Brigands, murderers
Samareths	*Smārta*	Van Twist	Tradesmen
Santones	Gujarati, *Santa*	Ovington	Ascetics
Seluidares	*Silahdari*	De Laet	Tenders of horses
Serriwani	*Sarbani*	De Laet	Tenders of camels
Shuddery	*Sudra*	Lord	Merchants
Sinais	Mahratta, *chhianave*	Fryer	"All other Brahmans" except Bhats: civil servants, physicians, accountants, secretaries, interpreters
Sodagores	Persian, *Saudagar*	Manrique	Merchants
Souders (see also Courmy)	*Sudra*	Thévenot	Tillers of the soil
Tchoguis	*Chauki*	Thévenot	Guards
Tehrons	*Charan*	Thévenot	Traveler escorts
Tuppaes	*Tapā*	Lord	?
Vaish	*Vaish*	Lord	Carpenters
Verteas	*'Svetāmbara*	Lord	Ascetic monks (Jain)
Wyse	*Vaisya*	Lord	Farmers, merchants, artisans
Zantelis	*Jellabdar*	De Laet	Runners
Zattersus	*Sharbatdar*	De Laet	Butlers

[1] Caste names listed are of Sanskrit or Hindi-Urdu derivation, unless otherwise indicated.

Name in European Texts	Standard Name[1]	European Authors	Occupations, characteristics, etc., according to Europeans
Ambuteres	*Ampaṭṭaiyan*	Vincenzo (Italian)	Barbers
Bati (or Canacas)	*Cāṇar*	Vincenzo	Makers of jaggery
Belles	*Vēlan*	Vincenzo	Washers, beaters of drums at festivals
Boroas	*Parayan*	Vincenzo	Riceworkers (type of *Pulayan* or serfs)
Boyes	Konkani, *Bhūi*	Pyrard (French)	Carriers
Butts	*Bhat*	Fryer (English)	Brahmans (purest, most rigorous type)
Cacoreas	*Kakkalam* (?)	Vincenzo	Clowns, quack doctors
Cagners	*Kanian* (?)	Vincenzo	Magicians, enchanters
Caramucuaras	*Mukkuvan*	Vincenzo	Those who fish at sea
Cegos, Bandarines	*Chegos, Pandaran*	Vincenzo	Palm cultivators
Charados	*Kárádás*	Careri (Italian)	Cultivators, fishers, rowers, bearers
Ciatada namburi	*Nambūdiri* (?)	Vincenzo	Malayali Brahman subcaste: philosophers, religious teachers
Colloni	*Kollan*	Vincenzo	Blacksmiths
Corombinis	*Kuṙumbar* (?)	Vincenzo	Cultivators of vegetables (type of *Pulayan*)
Coulombins	*Kurava* (?), *Kuricchan* (?)	Pyrard	Cultivators
Cregianens	*Kalamkoṭṭi* (?)	Vincenzo	Potters
Doladas	*Ulladan*	Vincenzo	Honey-gatherers
Dowlys	*Devalī*	Fryer	Dancers
Eledas	*Ilayatu*	Vincenzo	Brahman subcaste: performers of death rites, traders
Embrandeci	*Emprantiṇi*	Vincenzo	Brahman subcaste: custodians of temple treasury, traders
Eulunambi	*Elaytus* (?)	Vincenzo	Brahman subcaste: Idol-carriers, traders
Faras, Pareas	*Parayan*	Vincenzo	Those who eat cows
Garippis	*Tōle Kuruys*	Vincenzo	Makers of leather shields
Giangamis	*Jangami*	Della Valle (Italian)	Priests (lingayats)

(continued)

TABLE 2 (*continued*)

Name in European Texts	Standard Name[1]	European Authors	Occupations, characteristics, etc., according to Europeans
Giaris	*Āsāri* (?)	Vincenzo	Carpenters
Gregianen	*Kalamkotti* (?)	Vincenzo	Potters
Jangay	*Gangada*	Pyrard	Guides, soldiers
Maleas	*Malayar*	De Brito (Portuguese)	Hill tribes
Maruas	*Marava*	Vincenzo	Soldiers who live like gypsies
Moucois	*Mukkuvan*	Pyrard	Fishers
Mucuas	*Mucuar*	Vincenzo	Fishers
Muggiaci	*Muchi* (?)	Vincenzo	Sawyers
Nairi	*Nayār*	Vincenzo	Soldiers
Namburi	*Nambūdiri* (?)	Vincenzo	Brahman subcaste: helpers, traders
Othigalas	*Ōdattu*	Vincenzo	Bricklayers
Paellacumareres	*Palla-Kumārar*	Vincenzo	Chego subcaste: palm cultivators and nut-gatherers
Pateres	*Pattar*	Vincenzo	Brahman subcaste (foreign Brahmans): performers of certain ceremonies, traders
Patodesi Namburi	*Āḍhyan* (?)	Vincenzo	Brahman subcaste: royal advisers
Patysulias	*Pasa Pulayan*	Vincenzo	Foresters, type of *Pulayan*
Pecilla Pateres	*Piccha Paṭṭars* (?)	Vincenzo	Brahman subcaste: attendants of idol's palanquin, traders
Pulias	*Pulayan*	Vincenzo	Diggers and peasants
Quetris (title of the king)	*Kṣatrya*	Vincenzo	Soldiers
Tacciares	*Thayyalkar*	Vincenzo	Shoemakers
Tirinamburi	*Tampurākkal* (?)	Vincenzo	Brahman subcaste: guardians of idols
Tivas	*Tiyan*	Pyrard	Prostitutes, toddy-drawers, sometimes artisans
Tiveris	*Tiuuers, Tiyan*	Vincenzo	Toddy-drawers
Totas	*Taṭṭan*	Vincenzo	Goldsmiths and jewelers
Tottias	*Tōṭṭi*	Vincenzo	Unarmed nomads

[1] All standard names in Malayalam or Tamil, unless otherwise indicated.

TABLE 3: Castes and Tribes of Coromandel

Name in European Texts	Standard Name[1]	European Authors	Occupations, characteristics, etc., according to Europeans
Ambria	?	Roger (Dutch)	Sudra subcaste: cultivators and servants
Bergas	*Gorrel skaapari*	Roger	Shepherds
Bergawillalas	?	Roger	Cultivators (probably *Vellala* subcaste)
Bogas	Telugu, *Bogam*	Methwold (English)	Whores
Callias	?	Roger	Fishers
Caltaja	*Kal-taṭṭān*	Roger	Stonecutters
Camawaer	*Kārālar* (?)	Roger	Cultivators and hunters
Campo Waros	*Kāppiliyar*	Methwold	Cultivators
Carreans	*Karaiyān*	Roger	Fishers living near the seacoast
Cauwreas	*Kavarai*	Roger	Sudra subcaste: many occupations
Comitias, Committy	*Komatī*	Roger, Methwold	Vaisya subcaste: merchants
Conacupules	*Kaṇakkuppiḷḷai*	Roger	Scribes
Correvaes	*Kuṟavan*	Roger	Sudra nomads, snake-catchers, basket-makers, fortune-tellers
Cottewannias	*Kotta vaṇṇiyar*	Roger	Sellers of fruit
Fangams	*Jangam*	Methwold	Tailors, beggars
Gurreas	Telugu, *Golla*	Roger	Cowherds
Ienen	Jains	Roger	Weavers
Illewanion	*Ilavan, Izhava*	Roger	Sellers of fruit
Innadi	Telugu, *Eenaadi*	Roger	Soldiers (untouchables)
Kaikulle	*Kaikkolar*	Roger	Women are whores; men are dancers, weavers, sowers, soldiers.
Maccova	*Mucua, Mukkuvan*	Roger	Fishers
Mouttrea	?	Roger	Soldiers
Palis	*Palli*	Roger	Poulterers, pork merchants, cultivators, painters, soldiers
Palla	*Paḷḷan*	Roger	Lowest of the Sudras
Pandaras	*Paṇḍāram*	Viegas (Portuguese)	Sudras, religious mendicants, and non-Brahman Saivites
Pandari Raggi	*Paṇḍāram* (?)	Magistris (Italian)	Soldiers, merchants
Pareas, Poleas	*Paṟaiyan, Pulayan*	Magistris	Artisans, cultivators, villagers

(*continued*)

TABLE 3 (*continued*)

Name in European Texts	Standard Name[1]	European Authors	Occupations, characteristics, etc., according to Europeans
Patnouwas	*Paṭṭaṇavan*	Roger	Fishers
Perreas	*Paṟaiyan*	Roger	Outside the caste system, do dirty chores[2]
Pirawes	Pariahs	Methwold	Public executioners, palanquin-bearers, eaters of dead cows
Pisangs	*Pāci* (?)	Roger	Sellers of fruits and fish
Reddi	*Reddi* (title of the *Kāpu* caste)	Roger	Cultivators, soldiers
Sanjas	*Canniyāci*	Magistris	Religious mendicants
Settreas	*Kshatriya*	Roger	Nobles, also rajas
Siriperen	*Ciru paṭaiyan*	Roger	Tanners, soldiers. Lower than pariahs; they prepare the dead for burial.
Sittiis	*Ceṭṭi*	Roger	Merchants
Sittijs	*Ceṭṭi*	Roger	Fruitsellers
Sitti Weapari	*Ceṭṭi viyāpāri*	Roger	Vaisya subcaste: traders
Soudraes	*Sūdras*	Roger	Many subcastes and occupations
Totias	*Tōṭṭi*	Viegas	Laborers, honorable Sudras
Weinsjas	*Vaisya*	Roger	Traders
Wellala	*Vēḷāḷa*	Roger	Sudra or Vaisya subcaste: administrators and cultivators

[1] Caste names are Tamil, unless otherwise indicated.
[2] The *Paṟaiyan* are drummers (*paṟai* = drum). Considered unclean because drumheads are made of leather.

TABLE 4: SINHALESE CASTES OF CEYLON

Name in Knox	Name in Sinhalese	Remarks of Knox
Hondrews	*Hãñduru*	Noblemen from whom the king chooses royal governors and high officials
Christians		Highly respected, equal to "Hondrews"
Lesser nobles	*Radala*	Inferior subcaste of "Hondrews"
Castes of artisans	*Navandannō*	Goldsmiths, blacksmiths, carpenters, and painters

(*continued*)

[1109]

TABLE 4 (*continued*)

Name in Knox	Name in Sinhalese	Remarks of Knox
Elephant-hunters and -keepers	*Couratto* (?)	Social equals of the artisans
Barbers	*Ambattayō*	Dress like social superiors, but may not sit on a stool
Potters	*Kumballu*	May not dress like superiors; may drink from "Hondrew" pot
Ruddaughs	*Radau*	Launder clothes of superiors
Hungrams	*Hangarammu*	Jaggery sugar-makers
Poddahs	*Pāduvō*	Farmers and soldiers without trade or craft
Weavers	*Hīna Jāti* (?)	Practice astrology, serve as temple musicians and dancers, carry off and eat dead cows
Kiddeas	*Kidiyō*	Basket-makers
Kinnerahs	*Kinnaru*	Mat-makers
Dodda Vaddahs	?	Untouchables who dance, juggle, and perform tricks; they make cords for elephant snares from hides of dead cows
Roudeahs	*Rodiyā*	Compete with weavers in carrying off and eating cows; incest common among beggars.

TABLE 5: TAMIL CASTES OF CEYLON

Name in Baldaeus	Name in Tamil	Remarks of Baldaeus
Bramines	*Brahman*	Highest caste
Bellales	*Vellāla*	Agriculturists
Chivias	*Koviyar* (?)	Water-carriers, woodcutters, bearers of palanquins for Dutch governors
Coelijs	*Kūli* (coolies in English)	Water-carriers, *etc.*, for lesser folk
Commety	*Sammati*	Fishers of high status
Parruas	*Parāva*	Seafarers who fish for pearls and shells
Chittijs	*Chetty*	Merchants
Carreas	*Karayyar*	Fishermen who fish from the shore with nets
Mokkuas	*Muchavar, Mukkuvā*	Fishermen of a lower status
Nallouas	*Nalavar*	Blacker than others and do menial work for "Bellales"
Parreas	*Parayar* (Pariahs in English)	Perform the most disagreeable tasks and eat rats and mice

Index